LORD JOHN RUSSELL

Lord John Russell, by Sir Francis Grant

Lord John is holding a copy of the Reform Bill of 1854, and
the portrait was exhibited at the Royal Academy in 1854, but
the general impression is of Lord John as he might have
appeared ten or even fifteen years earlier.

LORD JOHN RUSSELL

John Prest

UNIVERSITY OF SOUTH CAROLINA PRESS
COLUMBIA, S. C.

First published 1972 in Great Britain by
THE MACMILLAN PRESS LTD
London and Basingstoke

and in the United States of America by the
UNIVERSITY OF SOUTH CAROLINA PRESS
Columbia, South Carolina

International Standard Book Number: 0-87249-269-9
Library of Congress Catalog Card Number: 72-5340

Suggested Library of Congress classification furnished by
McKissick Memorial Library
of the University of South Carolina: DA536.R9P

Manufactured in the United States of America

To J. R. B. Moulsdale

Contents

List of Illustrations

The author and publishers acknowledge with thanks permission to repro-
duce the plates and figures: National Portrait Gallery for the frontispiece,
plates 1, 3; Bodleian Library for plate 2 and figures 1–7; the estate of
Bertrand Russell for plate 4; Ashmolean Museum for plates 5–7; National
Library of Scotland for plate 8; and British Museum for plate 9 and
figure 8

Preface

First, I wish to thank Her Majesty the Queen for her gracious permission to use the Royal Archives, and to thank the Assistant Keeper of the Queen's Archives, Mr R. C. Mackworth-Young, the Registrar, Miss Jane Langton, and the Assistant Registrars, Miss Julia Gandy and Miss Sheila Russell, for their help and hospitality through the long vacation of 1967.

I also wish to thank the Most Hon. the Marquess of Lansdowne and the Marquess of Normanby, the Right Hon. the Earl of Derby, the Earl Spencer and the Earl of Clarendon, Mr George Howard of Castle Howard, and Mr Russell Ellice of Aberchalder for leave to use the papers in their possession; the staffs of the Bodleian Library, the National Library of Scotland, the British Museum, the Public Record Office, the Library of University College London, the National Register of Archives, and the Department of Palaeography and Diplomatic in the University of Durham, and in particular Mr G. R. Porter, Mr A. S. Bell, Mr E. K. Timings, Mr M. J. Franklin, Mr G. H. Ashby, Miss M. Skerl, Miss Christine Ranger and Mr J. M. Fewster for their assistance with the records in their keeping; the Trustees of the Broadlands Archives for permission to quote from the Palmerston Papers; Dr F. A. Dreyer and the University of St Andrews and Mr R. Job and the University of Durham for permission to read and refer to their theses; His Grace the Duke of Bedford, the Right Hon. the Lord Blake, Mr H. N. Blakiston, Mr T. J. Burchell, Professor S. G. Checkland, Mr D. M. Davin, Mr A. P. Donajgrodski, Professor M. R. D. Foot, Professor J. A. Gallagher, Professor N. Gash, Dr A. H. Graham, Dr J. E. C. Hill, Dr R. W. Hunt, Mr P. A. Kennedy, Dr R. B. McDowell, Dr A. F. Madden, Dr J. F. A. Mason, Dr L. G. Mitchell, the Right Hon. the Viscount Morpeth, Mrs Rosemary Morris, Sir Roger Mynors, Major P. Peel, Mr E. V.

Quinn, Mr C. W. Ringrose, Dr P. H. Scherer, Miss Gladys Scott-Thomson, Rev. R. M. V. Stapleton, Mr J. M. Sweeney, Mr A. J. P. Taylor, Dr W. E. S. Thomas, Professor H. R. Trevor-Roper and Mr P. Walne, all of whom have answered queries or sent me information; the General Board of the Faculties of Oxford University for the grant which enabled me to carry out my research; Miss Margaret Bamford and Miss Caroline Tucker, who made extracts from the Russell Papers for me; Mrs R. H. Parry, who had me to stay; the Leverhulme Trustees, who made it possible for me to settle down for a whole year at a time to write the book; my wife for her encouragement and our children for their forbearance; Miss Aud-Sissel Eide for placing a cup of hot chocolate at my hand every morning at 10.40: Mrs Budge, Mrs Jayakar, Miss Joy Langham, Miss Pat Lloyd and Mrs Christine Windsor-Lewis, who copied and typed and re-typed my drafts; Macmillan's reader for his criticisms of the second draft; Mr M. G. Brock and Mr E. T. Williams for their criticisms of the third draft; Mrs Angela Aitchison, who has given up all her spare time for eighteen months to check the references, select illustrations, and compile the index; and my sister Jean and Mr T. M. Bannister, who have read the proofs.

Introduction

LORD JOHN RUSSELL was born in 1792, and he was elected
to the house of commons for the first time in 1813, while still
under age. He sat in the lower house for forty-eight years until
1861, when he went to the house of lords as Earl Russell. He
entered the cabinet in 1831, and for twenty years, from 1835
to 1855, he was the leader of the Whig or Liberal party in the
house of commons. For fourteen of those twenty years he was
also the leader of the house, and between 1830 and 1866 there
were only seven years in which he did not hold office. He retired from active politics early in 1868, after a career of fifty-
five years in which, except in the case of the secret ballot and
the reform of the civil service, he had consistently taken the reforming side.

Why, then, have historians not accorded him much honour?
The answer is, on account of his personal defects. As Jowett
said, 'No one who is so deficient in social and external qualities
can ever have justice done him.'[1] He was shy, and his manners
were stiff. He neglected and, if pressed, he scorned the arts by
which a leader wins the affections of a party; and unlike Peel,
who also scorned them, he lacked the authority to dominate a
cabinet. In time his situation told upon his temper, and from
about 1850 he began to find himself – and even to set himself –
at a distance from his friends. In the Aberdeen coalition it
grieved him to take second place, and he gave vent to complaints, and pelted colleagues and former colleagues with unworthy accusations. For a year or two after he brought the
coalition down it was impossible not to wish he would retire.
Although he returned to high office in 1859, and regained his
good humour, he never recovered from that disastrous period of
nearly ten years in which his life was a lesson in how to lose
friends and to antagonise people.

Contemporaries were inclined to attribute his extraordinary downfall to the second Lady Russell. It was obviously difficult for Lord John's biographer, Spencer Walpole, to say either that he agreed or that he disagreed with this interpretation. The formidable Lady John had invited him to write the life, and had expressed her desire not to appear in it. But in private letters Spencer Walpole referred to 'the Influence', and suggested that it had been not only Lady Russell, but her father, Lord Minto.[2] Bertrand Russell, in his turn, blamed Lady Russell for the disasters that overtook Lord John, saying that 'a meticulous conscientiousness . . . was preached to him at home', which 'made him vacillating, with unfortunate political results'.[3] This tells us what Bertrand Russell disliked about his grandmother, but it is ungallant and inadequate. Lady Russell did her husband harm, but the deficiencies in Lord John's personality and character (deficiencies which left him open to the influence of such a nonentity as Lord Minto) were of earlier origin. It is to Lord John's own family, the Russells, as much as to the Elliots that we must look for our answers. For after all, as Lady John's sister was once stung to remark, the Russells 'are very odd people themselves'.[4]

Part One, 1792–1834

CHAPTER I

Family

MODERN research traces the Russells back to John Russell
(1486–1555), a wine importer at Weymouth, who was at home
one day in 1506 when the Habsburg Archduke Philip was shipwrecked on the Dorset coast.[1] Russell hurried the Archduke up
to London to present him at court, and never looked back. In a
career of scarcely paralleled opportunism he became a courtier,
a captain, a diplomat, a baron and an earl, and was favoured
with grants of land at Chenies (where he and many of his descendants are buried), at Tavistock, at Woburn Abbey and in
Covent Garden.

The second earl (1527–85) became a protestant, and the
fourth (1593–1641) a parliamentarian. Then, in 1683, William,
Lord Russell (born 1639), the heir to the fifth earl, was executed
for his part in the plot to exclude James II from the throne.
After the Revolution the Whig party kept alive the legend of
his having been martyred by a tyrant, and the fifth earl (1613–
1700) was made a duke.

The fifth duke, Lord John Russell's uncle Francis (1765–
1802), was only six years old when he inherited the title. By the
time he came of age, the coalition of Fox and North had been
outwitted by the King, and Pitt was in power. The fifth duke
did not attempt to play an independent role in politics,[2] and
unambitiously attached himself to Charles James Fox. In the
long years of opposition which followed the Whigs took renewed inspiration from their ancestors who had made the revolution of 1688. They opposed the war against France in 1793,
protested against the suspension of *habeas corpus* in 1794 and
denounced the methods used to suppress the rebellion in Ireland in 1798. Into this political atmosphere Lord John Russell
was born.

Lord John's father, whose name was also Lord John Russell,

was born in 1766. In 1786 he married Georgiana, the daughter
of the fourth Lord Torrington. They had three sons: Francis,
later Marquis of Tavistock, born in 1788, who became the
seventh duke; William, born in 1790, who became a soldier and
a diplomat; and John, who was born on 18 August 1792, and
became prime minister. Georgiana revered her husband,[3] and
saw in him some of the features which can be recognised in any
character sketch of Lord John:

> I am sure if *he* is not a patriot there never was one . . . I never
> heard *one* thought expressed by him that showed either a want of
> candour and Liberality or which publicly told would not have
> shewn the Uprightness of his Mind . . .[4]

She was not the only one to notice a resemblance, for in 1810
Lord John's schoolfellow, Lord Clare, after meeting Lord John's
father for the first time, said, 'I really could have fancied it was
you I was speaking to, with a few more years on your back.'[5]

Lord John Russell was a seven-months child,[6] and his small
size was a handicap from which he never recovered. Spencer
Walpole began his *Life* with the first entry from Lord John
Russell's first diary: '*Woburn, August 18, 1803*. This is my birthday. I am eleven years old, 4 feet 2 inches high, and 3 stone 12
lbs weight.'[7] Fully grown he stood 5 feet 4¾ inches,[8] and
weighed about eight stone. He was also very frail,[9] though it is
not easy to say exactly what he suffered from. There is no
record of dangerous illness in his whole life, and he survived to
an old age in which the most noticeable things about him were
his 'bright, clear, and honest' blue eyes, his fine hands and his
skin, which was 'remarkably clear, almost like a child's'.[10] But
we do know that he suffered all his life from coughs and colds,
and from hay fever,[11] that he was subject to fainting and that he
was affected by 'hot rooms, late hours, and bad air'.[12]

His mother bore no more children, and was never in perfect
health again. Her youngest, under-sized and delicate child was
her favourite, and as Lord John recorded in 1871, 'I was very
fond of her. I used to call her in the morning, and from that
hour during the whole of the day she showed me the utmost
affection.'[13] From her he learned to recite the months of the
year: Snowy, Flowy, Blowy, Showery, Flowery, Bowery, Beauty,
Fruity, Shooty, Breezy, Sneezy, Freezy.[14] Lord John had just

gone to his first school, and received her letter addressed 'To the best of all good little boys J. R., I miss your dear voice when I wake, and I regret you every moment of the day',[15] when she died on 11 October 1801. Lord John was then nine years old.

Less than a year later, in 1802, Lord John's uncle Francis died, and his father became the sixth Duke of Bedford. The new duke was a bad manager, and in due course he left the estate encumbered with over half a million of debt.[16] But he had many of the instincts of an improving landowner, and he employed Telford and the Rennies to reconstruct the drains of the Bedford level, and rebuilt Covent Garden. He attended the annual sheepshearing, and experimented with the nutritive effects of different grasses. He did not actually write, but caused to be written, the *Hortus Gramineus Woburnensis* (1816), the *Hortus Ericaeus Woburnensis* (1825), the *Salictum Woburnense* (1829) and the *Pinetum Woburnense* (1839), and he urged his son to impress upon the young Queen Victoria 'the vast importance . . . of converting the Kew Gardens, into a Royal Botanical Garden . . . similar to the *Jardin des Plantes* at Paris'.[17]

In 1803 Lord John's father married again – another Georgiana, the daughter of the Duke of Gordon. She wished to be a good step-mother to Lord John. But she produced a family of seven sons and three daughters of her own, and she cannot have had much time to spare. The duke, on the other hand, still managed to take an interest in the welfare of his third son by his first wife. To Lord John he wrote letters that were bluff, to the point and full of good sense. In 1805, when Lord John, who was thirteen, was away on a visit, he wrote: 'I enclose you £5 . . . You will give a guinea to the man who takes care of your pony; half a guinea to the person who cleans your clothes; and five shillings to the housemaid; and pay your washing bills.'[18] In 1812, when Lord John was twenty, he suggested that an excursion to the Mediterranean might 'be of service to your health and to your mental improvement'.[19] In 1819, when Lord John was twenty-seven, he wrote that he had had a good deal of conversation with the Whig leader in the house of commons, Mr Tierney, because 'I felt anxious to know in what way he thought you would be most useful in your senatorial capacity'.[20] Eleven years later, when Lord John was thirty-eight, and had been invited to join Grey's government, the duke wrote that he

need not wait the result of his election: 'after having called
upon every freeholder, and given each a friendly shake of the
hand, you may make an excuse of *urgent publick business*, and
come away'.[21] The duke never noticed that his son was growing
up, and he was apt to write sharply when he felt warmly.[22] But
his language was straightforward, and his meaning was plain.
There were strains between father and son, but in 1830,
when the duke turned Lord John's horse out of Woburn, Lord
John remarked good-humouredly that his father was 'quite
Joseph Humeing it',[23] and when the duke died in 1839 Lord
John was able to look back upon 'most affectionate intercourse
for so many years between father and son'.[24]

There was a decade and more between the sixth duke's two
families, and after their father married again the three sons of
the first marriage were much in each other's company. Lord
John stood close to both his brothers, but on different terms with
each. Lord William, like Lord John, was not marked out to become a duke, and in time he would have to earn his living. He
was simple, direct, and hot tempered. He chose to be a soldier,
and Lord John went to see him in the Peninsula. In 1830 when
Lord John came into office for the first time he offered Lord and
Lady William three-quarters of his official residence to live
in.[25] In return William offered Lord John loyalty and encouragement that meant much to him. 'So you are turned
Radical,' he wrote in 1822, 'never mind, I will follow you. Whatever you propose, I will vote for . . .'[26] In 1830 he assured Lord
John that he was 'much improved in speaking', and 'gaining on
the public confidence'.[27] In 1835 he declared that of all leading
English statesmen 'you alone are intelligible'.[28] In 1841, when
Melbourne's government was coming to an end, and Lord John
had made a particularly spirited speech, he congratulated him
on the way in which 'When one thinks you beat to a mummy,
you are on your legs again knocking about you with renewed
vigour.'[29]

Tavistock on the other hand was every inch the elder
brother. We should not read much into the fact that when the
two boys were out riding together, Tavistock 'made me leap
some places I was afraid of'.[30] But in 1803, when Lord John
arrived at Westminster School, he was set to fag for his brother,
and when the boys acted a play Tavistock was the King and

Lord John Tom Thumb.[31] The relationship thus begun was to continue through life. Lord John did not resent this, and the two brothers held a common line in politics. But the nearer the Whigs came to office, the more apparent it became that Tavistock lacked both the ambition and the appetite to take a lead in public affairs. From the age of fourteen he had been heir to a dukedom, and that was the career which suited him best. It would have been better had he frankly abandoned the political stage to his brother. Unfortunately he continued to guide Lord John's footsteps, and although he is not the villain of this story, he did unwittingly contribute much to the troubles of its hero.

CHAPTER II

Education

LORD JOHN's small size and his weak health were not at first allowed to affect his schooling. When he was eight his mother was induced to part with him to 'a very bad private school at Sunbury'.[1] Next, he was sent to Westminster School, where he stayed for less than a year from 1803 to 1804 before his stepmother interposed with the duke to have him taken away. He was brought home and handed over to the domestic chaplain, Dr Cartwright, the inventor of the power loom and the brother of Major Cartwright the reformer, for his lessons. From him, Lord John acquired 'a taste for Latin poetry'.[2] The wonder is that he acquired anything, for – clockwork boats apart – Dr Cartwright was not an inspiring tutor. The inventor of the power loom had, as he said, completed his 'grand climacterical year':[3] he had no interest in the industrial revolution, and the volume of letters and sonnets which he addressed to Lord John is pedantic.

After a few months working at Dr Johnson's lives of the poets,[4] Lord John was sent to Mr Smith, the vicar of Woodnesboro' near Sandwich, where he stayed from the spring of 1805 to the autumn of 1808. Mrs Smith lodged about half a dozen boys at a time, and was 'truly formed to be a schoolmistress',[5] carrying her economy so far as to save the drops of gravy which fell upon the tablecloth.[6] The Smiths had three daughters and one son: the first girl, Lord John thought, was modest and pleasing, the second affected and unbearable, the third plain; the son made it his delight 'to contradict every thing that is said'.[7] These were jaundiced words. It was not too bad a school, and after lessons the boys spent their afternoons with their dogs and their guns, and their evenings playing cards with Mr Smith by the fire.[8] Among Lord John's companions were Lord Hartington, the Duke of Leinster, and Lord Clare, who was also short and small. In 1810, after they had been separated for a while, Lord Clare wrote: 'I am very much grown, so I dare say are you, don't be frightened I am not as yet a Giant, *entre nous*, I am only 5f. 6in. and ½ . . . in your next letter tell me all about you but don't forget your height.'[9]

While Lord John was at Mr Smith's, Pitt died and was succeeded by the ministry of all the talents, and Mr Smith gave the boys a holiday to celebrate Fox's return to power.[10] Lord John had already drunk deeply at the fountain of family and party history, and the Russell family treasure a story of his being told to creep across the floor of the Long Gallery at Woburn until he reached Mr Fox's chair, and to 'tickle the silk-clad legs until the sleeper woke up and stopped snoring'.[11] How much inspiration there was in this it is impossible to say, but a Frenchman once said of the first Lord Holland, when he fell asleep after dinner, 'Le voilà qui pense',[12] and throughout his life, whenever he had to look for an authority upon the constitution, or for enlarged principles, Lord John referred to 'the precepts, and the maxims of Mr Fox'.[13]

When the Whigs came back into office, Lord John's father went to Ireland as lord lieutenant, where, in one year, he ran up a debt of £40,000.[14] In the summer of 1806 Lord John and his brothers went to stay at the viceregal lodge in Dublin. They passed the time riding, shooting, playing cricket, and going to the theatre.[15] We cannot tell whether the duke expounded, and Lord John listened to the principles upon which his government of Ireland was conducted, but five years later he put them into a letter which Lord John noted was one of the best he had ever read.

> I think I am not mistaken . . . when I say that I . . . conciliated the affections and obtained the confidence of the Irish people, that throughout the whole of my administration I . . . proceeded upon the broad Principle that all governments are made for the happiness of the many, and not for the benefit of the few; that I consequently set my face resolutely against a system of exclusion . . . and endeavoured to dispense the blessings of a mild and conciliatory Government to all sects.[16]

It was to no avail. Fox died, George III rejected the Duke of Bedford's plea for roman catholics to be allowed to hold commissions in the army, and within the year the Whigs were out

again. Nearly seventy years later, Lord John recalled that the
no-Popery cry which followed at the general election of 1807
was 'the proceeding most discreditable to the English people of
any that has occurred in my time'.[17]

Fox had not been dead long before Lord John began to see
much more of Lord and Lady Holland. Did they already see in
Lord John a young man serious minded enough to achieve
what the incomparable Fox had only talked about? At that age,
it is not likely. They took Lord John up because he was a
motherless boy to whom they could offer a second home at
Holland House, where they 'kept a knife and fork for him'.[18]
For many years thereafter Lord John was as a son to them, and
in 1820 he wrote to Lady Holland of his bill to disfranchise
Grampound as his child, 'your grandchild'.[19]

In 1807 the Spanish people revolted against the French occupation, and in 1808 a British army under Sir John Moore was
landed at Corunna to assist the insurgents. A majority of the
Whig leaders, led by Grey and Grenville, disapproved of the
new campaign. But Lord and Lady Holland, who knew the
Peninsula well, thought that in Spain, France and Britain were
fighting 'for the soul of Europe, the French representing extreme democracy and military despotism, and the British
moderate parliamentary institutions and temperate liberty.
There was talk of a new *cortes*: Lord and Lady Holland decided
to go to Spain to help their friends, and they invited Lord John
to come with them. The Whigs might be a beaten party with a
barren future at home, but southward, look, the land was bright.

Lord John was now sixteen, and he must have been delighted
to escape from school. The Hollands' party reached Corunna in
November 1808. Before they could make their way to Madrid,
the French advanced, and the Hollands retired by way of
Lisbon, which they reached on 3 January 1809, to Cadiz,
where they passed the remainder of the winter. Lord John was
supposed to be having lessons in latin and Euclid[20] from Lord
Holland's librarian, Mr Allen, but what he was really absorb-
ing was a gigantic lesson in constitutional history. Allen's
thoughts stemmed from Burke: it was not necessary to a free
government that it should have been formally constituted by
the people; systematic uniformity should be avoided; every
interest should be represented, but there should be no artificial

striving to represent them equally. These were the general maxims which Lord Holland and his librarian now taught the Spaniards and Lord John. While the Spaniards deliberated end-lessly upon the constitution of the new *cortes*, Allen urged them to retain the separate representation of the clergy and the nobility, to have two houses rather than one or three, to elect representative peers from among the lesser nobles, and to en-courage the growth of a class of independent country gentlemen. Everything was seen in English terms. The English constitution was still worth a panegyric, and you would not know from any-thing Lord Holland and Mr Allen told the Spaniards that the Whigs were the party of Fox's martyrs, the party that was always out of office because its opponents had perverted the British constitution.[21]

While Lord John was away in the Peninsula, his father dis-covered that 'nothing was learned in the English universities',[22] and determined to send his son to Edinburgh. The plan was opened to Lord John, and his immediate reaction was that he did not want to go: 'the thing I should most dislike . . . would be an endeavour to acquire Scotch knowledge in a Scotch town. Political economy may surely be studied in England. As for metaphysics I cannot even understand the word.'[23] Lord and Lady Holland and Mr Allen, however, persuaded him to change his mind, and in October, after their return to England, Lord John wrote to Lady Holland to say that he was not sure when he would be allowed to go to Edinburgh, as he was being 'blister'd, bled, and physick'd' for a cough.[24] He soon recovered, and in November he took up residence in the house of Professor Playfair, whom he found 'quite delightful in every way'.[25] Playfair was a man of profound mind and unaffected habits and there is little or nothing dated about a letter of his which sur-vives in the Russell papers:

> you say very truly that out of 500 Philosophers each gives a differ-ent opinion . . . Suppose for example that the subject is the sub-lime . . . Let us take some particular instance for example the sound of Thunder which all admit to call forth such emotions as the word sublime is usually employed to denote . . .[26]

Lord John liked Edinburgh. In December he told Lady Holland that 'instead of intercepting convoys and despatches I

hear of nothing but intercepting straight lines'.[27] Two months
later he was full of Dugald Stewart's lectures: 'like causes produce like effects', ergo, you who wrote me a very good letter
before, will write me a very good letter again.[28] Then there was
Jeffrey, the editor of the *Edinburgh Review*, 'quite a God – when
people talk of a pleasant party they mean Jeffrey was there'.[29]
Greatest wonder of all, was 'an Infant Davy, a boy of fifteen
who gives lectures on Chemistry'.[30]

The duke wanted his son to stay at Edinburgh over Christmas
and Lord John thus missed seeing his brother William, who was
home on leave from the Peninsula.[31] William went back to
Portugal, and when Lord John proposed to visit him in the long
vacation of 1810, the duke forbade the journey.[32] It was in no
good humour, then, that Lord John commented to Lord
Holland in the first political letter of his that survives, upon a
speech by Lord Grey, who still disapproved of the war in the
Peninsula, and was for postponing Reform indefinitely.

> He still seems to think himself a Whig, and I am afraid the Tory
> Opinions which he wears under that cloak will bring the name
> into great discredit . . . it is clear a man's consistency depends not
> only on his constancy in opinion, but on his zeal in supporting it,
> and here Lord Grey is as cold as the North wind – all the violence
> and heat for which he is distinguished flies against the Reform-
> ers.[33]

Lord Holland answered patiently, and point by point,[34] and
then a few days later prevailed upon Lord John's father to let
his son pay a flying visit to William.

Lord John left England on 30 August, carrying raspberry
vinegar and pickles for the Hollands' son Charles.[35] He reached
Gibraltar on 12 September, and went on to Cadiz, which was
besieged by the French. There he saw both William, and the
Spanish *cortes*, which had assembled at last. On 25 September
he wrote to Lord Holland:

> After all your anxiety to see Cortes in Spain, you have missed the
> opportunity . . . and I . . . have been a witness of this great event
> . . . It is true there was much confusion, many speaking together,
> no respect to the President, and rather too much cavilling; but
> they showed a very proper sense of their own Power and Authority,
> a great eagerness to speak and propose plans which they think for
> the advantage of the country, and no intrigue . . . the guerillas

seem to be in all parts of the country and plague the French much. The Cortes, having the confidence of the people, will raise a new spirit, and I hope give the people a prospect worth fighting for . . . in short there seems a better chance for Spain than at any time since the battle of Baylen – but even if they should drive the French out, the work will require four, five or ten years.[36]

On his way back Lord John stopped at Lisbon, and was conducted along the lines of Torres Vedras by General Hill.[37] He returned to England at the beginning of October, was detained for a few days by a cough, and reached Edinburgh in the middle of November.[38] In the next few weeks he was busy preparing a paper on the *cortes*, which he read to the Speculative Society. Lord John now thought that the want of a sufficient number of nobility among the representatives elected to the *cortes* weakened 'the stamp of universal consent'. But, he went on,

the Nobility of Spain may be said to have drawn this stigma upon themselves and they are indeed an admirable lesson to every hereditary Nobility. In the time of Charles 5th they deserted the people, and they have in their turn been deserted by the Monarch whom they served, and the people whom they abandoned.[39]

Next, Lord John composed an article on parliamentary reform for *The Whig Register*, a magazine which never saw the light of day.[40] George III had gone mad, the Regent had disappointed the Whigs and shown no inclination to change his ministers, and Lord John argued that the time had come to 'add cautiously and gradually to the power of the people' until it could 'make head against the power of the Crown'.[41] The rest of the academic year passed uneventfully, and in the long vacation of 1811 Lord John's father again intervened, and in order to prevent his son heading straight for the Peninsula arranged for Professor Playfair to take him on a tour through the manufacturing districts. The professor took him to Birmingham, Liverpool, Manchester, Sheffield and Leeds, and Lord John reflected in an orthodox way upon the quality of British manufactures, the folly of the continental system, and the superior intelligence and inferior morals of an industrial as opposed to an agricultural population.[42]

At the end of three years Lord John left the university, in the summer of 1812, without taking a degree.[43] His health was better – which he attributed to Sir H. Halford's medicine, 'not that I always take it, but it keeps me in terror for fear I should get ill' – and he now spent a week with the Bedfordshire militia, which 'instead of killing me, has only made me fit for service'.[44] There could be little doubt where he would go next, and on his twentieth birthday he was on board ship. He stayed away for over a year. In 1812 he went, like a tourist, to examine the field of Salamanca, and watched a French column advance upon the British positions at Burgos. In 1813 he examined the fields of Barrosa, where William had been in action, and of Talavera, where William had been wounded. Finally he joined William upon the last hill in Spain, whence the brothers gazed down upon the fair land of France.[45]

In the meantime things were not going well for the friends of constitutional liberty in Spain. Lord John found that the guerillas terrorised their countrymen with their demands for rations, and in the midst of these troubles 'the commonalty' did not enjoy 'the dignity of freedom which the Cortes have given them'.[46] In July 1813 Lord John reported to Lord Holland from Madrid, which had just been liberated, on the prospects for the *cortes*.

> I never saw so fine a people as this. They are anxious for the Cortes to come here, and I hope to God they may, for the spirit of this town is the only thing that can check the folly of the liberales. These people have now gained a complete victory over the serviles and they want to put in practice all their foolish notions of a Republick. Their folly and ignorance have turned the whole country against the Cortes. The clergy and the army are against them from . . . professional feelings . . . I have heard it held forth that the unity of Religion, which you know the Spaniards consider their happiness, can exist no longer, and that sects will arise and bring on a religious war.[47]

A few years later, in an essay on national character, Lord John made his representative Spaniard, who was 'by no means a Liberal', argue in favour of the inquisition, and go on to say that liberty was 'a poor substitute for a fine climate'.[48] The vision of Spain soon faded, but for Lord John, at least, something remained. In Spain he first learned by experience how a Whig could stand in the middle between the Tories and the Radicals, and by becoming an ardent peninsularian Lord John

both gained credit for his patriotism, and made sure that future
controversy with the Duke of Wellington would be tempered by
respect.

In 1813 Lord John came back from the Peninsula in order to
present himself to the electors of the family borough of Tavistock. The next year he spoke in the house of commons against
the enforced union of Norway with Sweden.[49] But his health
was still bad, and he decided upon another trip abroad. The
war seemed to be over, and after two doctors had signed a chit
for his 'transportation',[50] he set sail for Italy. He landed at
Leghorn, where he was quarantined in the Lazzaretto for a few
days with 'two old and dirty Capuchins',[51] and by the beginning of December he was in Florence. The opportunity then
arose for his well-known interview with Napoleon on Elba,
which took place on Christmas eve 1814.

There are several accounts of their conversation, which was
in French. The family tradition is that Lord John did all the
talking, that he talked about the Russell family, and that when
he stopped, Napoleon got up, and without a word, went over
to the corner of the room and relieved himself against the wall.
Lord John's version was that after he had elicited from Napoleon the view that the superiority of England to France was to
be attributed to her aristocracy, Napoleon explained how he
would have regenerated Spain by plans of philosophy and improvement. 'I told him that the Spaniards were not at all prepared for the confiscation of great estates and the abolition of
the wealth and privileges of the clergy.' Napoleon then asked
about the *cortes*. Lord John told him they made good speeches
on abstract questions, but failed in any practical debate on war
or finance.[52] Napoleon then said he was convinced the Duke of
Wellington aimed at the throne of England for himself:[53] Lord
John, we may be sure, knew better. It is easy to make fun of
Lord John's behaviour upon this occasion, and it is only fair,
therefore, to give the estimate of Napoleon which he published
ten years later. Napoleon's life, he said, would stand in history
'like an isthmus between two great ages, and not less memorable
than either of them.'[54]

After this interview Lord John spent the first few months of
1815 travelling round Italy. Everywhere he went he found that
there was a party for and a party against Napoleon, and that

the first was the stronger of the two. Lord John closed his
Italian diary with the comment that French government,
though not good, was 'very useful to prepare the people for a
better'.[55] By that time Napoleon had escaped and the war had
started again, and Lord John was obliged to return home
through Austria and Germany. He reached England in time to
denounce the new war, and its unjust object of compelling the
French to submit to the Bourbons.[56] But his words were uttered
only thirteen days before the battle of Waterloo, and he was
probably happy to have them forgotten in the pages of the
parliamentary debates.

Lord John was now twenty-three. At this point Spencer
Walpole summed up his early life in a passage of almost lyrical
beauty, in which he contrasted Lord John's lack of formal education with the advantages he had derived from travel: 'the
deficiency had been amply repaired. He had graduated in the
University of the World'.[57] But in fact the world was in many
ways a university in which Lord John never did graduate. It
would be absurd to speak of his having had a deprived up-
bringing: he had been in contact with some of the finest minds
of the day, and he had acquired some rational methods of
thought to lay on top of his family prejudices. But there was very
little system about his work. He had not gone unsupervised, but
both at Mr Smith's and at Professor Playfair's his frail health
may have won him some indulgence. Above all, his education
had taken place in homes in which his father bought him a
place. Nowhere had he been able, or required, to mix outside a
small company of friends, and this was a defect his travels had
done nothing to remedy.

CHAPTER III

Author and Ideologue, 1815–30

IN THE next few years after the return of peace Lord John's health was worse than at any other period of his life. In 1816 he voted in only three of the thirty-two divisions in the house of commons. In 1817 nothing but the need to protest against the suspension of *habeas corpus* made him drop his resolve to quit 'the fatiguing business of this House altogether'.[1] In January 1818 Althorp advised him that Tierney and Mackintosh were such instances 'of the wonder performed on unintelligible complaints by Dr Scott's baths, that they are most anxious you should become one of his patients'.[2] A month later Lord John told Lord Holland that he hoped to re-enter parliament next year 'like a dwarf refresh'd',[3] and he was re-elected for Tavistock at the general election of 1818. But towards the end of that year his health was still held against him when his name was being canvassed as a possible candidate for the Westminster by-election.[4]

In 1819 Lord John attended parliament more regularly, but at all times between 1819 and 1830 his health was a problem. In April 1822 ill-health prevented his presiding over a reform dinner in London.[5] In 1825 Hobhouse recorded that Lord John 'fell down in a sort of fit; his face was a little distorted, but he recovered immediately. His brother did not show any great anxiety, and he told us that Lord John did not like to have these attacks noticed.'[6] In 1828 Lord John wrote to Brougham that hard work suited neither his health nor his disposition,[7] and that he wondered whether it was worth his while to waste his 'small portion of strength on midnight debates'.[8] It was all very puzzling, because, as he told Lady Holland, 'I am not really ill, but only weakened, and worried, and made ill by London and the house of commons.'[9]

In as far as Lord John could find a remedy for his condition he found it in travelling abroad. Hitherto he had gazed into France from Spain; he had circled France in 1814–15, and he had spoken to Napoleon; but he had never yet set foot in France itself. As soon as the war was over Lord John made good the deficiency, and went to Paris where 'The English and the French, after an absence of twenty years, have again met . . . and are exchanging bows, ideas, and sentiments.'[10] Lord John was struck by the way in which a nobleman would submit to live in a garret in order to show great apartments for receiving company, by the common staircase where you might find an old woman frying eggs in the entrance, and by the difference in the British and French attitudes to nature.[11] These were commonplace observations, but he was an appreciative traveller, as he showed in an essay on *An Agreeable Man*:

> France, perhaps, affords the best models of an agreeable man. In them we see the most refined politeness towards others, mixed with a most perfect confidence in themselves . . . a skill in placing every topic in the situation which alone can make it amusing in conversation – a grace in treating the most frivolous matters, a lightness in touching the most serious, and a quickness in passing from one to the other, which to all other Europeans must seem quite unattainable.[12]

In 1816 Lord John was in Brussels, and in 1817–18 he undertook a long journey. In May he was at Antwerp, preparing for a tour through Holland. 'I am going to read hard on butter and cream, and study all that has been written on ditches of every kind.'[13] In June he was in Amsterdam, and he travelled on through Germany to Frankfurt and Dresden. After a week in Vienna, he set off before the snows came to winter in Italy. From Bologna he sent Lady Holland an account of Lord Byron, and of the origin of his relationship with Marianna Segati, which is an early example of his power to tell a story:

> Ld. Byron is living . . . near Venice with a lady whom he has taken under his protection. You have probably heard the story – she was and is the wife of a merchant who being ruined was forced to let his house. Ld. B. going to take it saw her playing at the pianoforte, and was suddenly smitten – he offered a ring – no – a diamond of great value – no – at last he one day found her in tears and forced her to confess that her husband was going to prison for £500 – he

paid the money, restored the merchant, and has been six months constant to his wife.[14]

Lord John came back to England in the spring of 1818, but in July he set off again for Paris. In 1819 he went via Paris to Geneva, where his uncle William had a villa, and on to Milan and Genoa, before coming home for the Peterloo parliament. Towards the end of 1820 he was again in Paris, whence he wrote to Lady Holland, 'my father has no right to be *grieved* with my coming here, nor you to mention it. He must have given me the moving mania he has himself, and you put the faculty in action by taking me to Spain.'[15] Thereafter he went to France almost every year, and as often as he could to Italy as well. It was an axis to which he was to remain faithful all his life.

All this time Lord John was able to consider what to do with himself. He was already marked out for politics, but the Whigs were out of office, and for a time he was equally attracted to writing. In 1820 he published *Essays and Sketches of Life and Character by a Gentleman who has left his lodgings*. The essays have charm, but are slight. Then in 1822, drawing upon his knowledge of Spain, he published both a little novel, the *Nun of Arrouca*, and a five-act play, *Don Carlos*, which was dedicated to Lord Holland, and ran into five editions in a year, but was never put on the stage. In 1836 a jealous Disraeli described the *Nun* as 'the feeblest romance in our literature', and *Don Carlos* as the 'feeblest tragedy in our language'.[16] Without accepting so harsh a judgement, it may be well to pass over these two works without comment.

Don Carlos was written in blank verse, and at this period of his life it was Lord John's ambition to be a poet.[17] He took up with Thomas Moore, and when the Irish poet fell into debt, conveyed him to Paris. In Moore's company Lord John soon realised that poetry was not for him: 'to use the language of Mark Lane, "the supply is abundant, but the trade heavy, and there are few fine samples" '.[18] But he never gave up the poet: he offered Moore the profits from his first successful history,[19] and one of his first actions on becoming leader of the Whig party in the house of commons was to secure Moore a pension.[20] When Moore died in 1852, Lord John edited his papers with despatch, and handed the proceeds to the widow.[21]

It remains to speak of the histories which Lord John wrote between 1819 and 1832. His first work was a life of his ancestor, William Lord Russell, the martyr of 1683, which was published in 1819 with a dedication to Lord John's father. Lord John was refused access to Barillon's letters by the French authorities (who relented after the book was published),[22] but Sidmouth allowed him to search in the state paper office, and he had access to the letters of Lady Russell in the possession of the Duke of Devonshire.[23] It is a spirited book, for nobody could describe William's last hours without imagining himself in the same situation, and the interest of the book is that Lord John obviously thought the story still relevant in his own day. This does not mean that he thought liberty might yet have to be preserved upon a scaffold erected by Lord Liverpool, and that his own head might fall to an executioner chosen by the holy alliance and paid by Castlereagh. The point of the book was that William had not called the people out on to the streets, or led a revolution. William was a decided enemy 'not only to regal encroachment, but to turbulent innovation',[24] and the reason Lord John thought Lord William still had a message for the nineteenth century was that

> in these times, when love of liberty is too generally supposed to be allied with rash innovation, impiety, and anarchy, it seems to me desirable to exhibit to the world . . . the portrait of a man who, heir to wealth and title, was foremost in defending the privileges of the people.[25]

The people of England had no need to rebel against Lord Liverpool's administration so long as they had an aristocratic Whig party to air their grievances for them.

The book brought Lord John £200,[26] and the congratulations of General Fox, who said he had almost forgotten 'the rational and true principles' of the party.[27] Even so, it is probably fortunate that Lord John did not follow the advice of one flatterer, who wished he would go on to 'favour the public with a history of the house of Russell from the earliest period'.[28] His next work was *An Essay on the History of the English Government and Constitution, from the reign of Henry VIII to the present time.* This was composed in 1820 and published in 1821. A second enlarged edition was published in 1823, and new and revised editions

were issued in 1865 and 1873. It was translated into French in
1821 and 1865, and into German in 1872.

The essay starts with an important preface. The author's
original idea was to prove first, that

> the monarchies of the continent of Europe have been, generally
> speaking, so ill adapted to make their subjects virtuous and happy,
> that they require, or required, complete regeneration

and secondly, that

> the government of England ought not to be included in this class;
> that it is calculated to produce liberty, worth, and content . . .
> whilst its abuses easily admit of reforms consistent with its spirit.

Lord John apologised for having had time to write only the
second half. But he went on to publish the first volume of the
Memoirs of the Affairs of Europe from the Peace of Utrecht in 1824, the
Establishment of the Turks in Europe in 1828, the second volume of
the *Memoirs of the Affairs of Europe* in 1829, and *The Causes of the
French Revolution* in 1832, and when these works are put together they go a long way to filling in the outline of the grand
design he entertained in 1820–1.

Lord John's histories are difficult to evaluate because he
found it hard to keep a standard, but what they amount to is
that in the 1820s the world was divided into outer' darkness,
darkness, pale daylight, and enlightened day.

The inhabitants of outer darkness were of two kinds. There
were primitive peoples, and decayed civilisations like those of
India and China. The two were very different, but they could
be bracketed together because, in each case, when they came
into contact with European civilisation they collapsed. When
they collapsed, we had no right to turn primitive peoples into
slaves, or to exploit the weakness of the effete, but there was
nothing we could learn from them. These peoples were fit
objects of curiosity, like the oriental pines planted by the fourth
duke at Woburn, but in morals, manners, and politics, it was
for them to imitate us. Consequently Lord John never did
travel outside Europe, and he specifically rebuked Montes-
quieu for writing at unnecessary length about the Japanese.[29]

The inhabitants of darkness were the Arabs and the Turks.
both of whom had stood up to the Europeans in their time,

There must, therefore, have been some good in them, and in his
Establishment of the Turks in Europe Lord John set out to discover
what it was. The Turks were men of simple passions, who went
straight to their objectives, and destroyed the Greeks 'as men
crush insects, with little effort and no sympathy'.[30] But the
integrity upon which political development depends is the
virtue either of extreme simplicity or of extreme refinement, and
'the Turks soon passed the one point, and never reached the
other'.[31] The arrival of scientific warfare now placed the Turks
in an insoluble quandary, for if they went on refusing to learn
from other peoples they would be defeated, and if they opened
the door to knowledge they would have to accept reforms at
home.

The great mass of European roman catholic states lived in
pale daylight. At the bottom of the league table of European
liberty came Spain. The vivid hopes of youth had faded, and
Lord John now found it hard to distinguish Spain from Turkey.
Having successfully excluded the progress of knowledge, the
Spaniards now sat on a lower rung among the nations of
Europe.[32] The Austrians still lived in civil and religious slavery,
and Austrian policy after the Vienna settlement was to be compared with that of Spain in the sixteenth century, and would be
attended by the same result.[33] The Italians were not, at the
moment, much better off, but having recently enjoyed equal
laws and prompt justice at the hands of the French, they had
the capacity to be.[34]

Both catholic France and protestant Britain had reached the
haven of enlightened day. For the French it had been a stormy
passage. Five hundred years ago their aristocracy had begun to
diverge from that of England, by admitting a double doctrine,
which allowed luxury, profligacy, and power to themselves,
while it recommended religion, morality, and submission to
the people.[35] In England, on the other hand, no law was passed
to prevent additions to the peerage, the son of a peer could sit
in the house of commons, and gentlemen were not exempt from
taxation or screened from punishment.[36]

The history of France took a new turn in the seventeenth
century when the King excluded the aristocracy from the
government. In the eighteenth century, in what in Lord John's
eyes was both a sociological and a theological judgement, 'The

vengeance of the people followed close upon the vices of the court.'[37] The people were set in motion, and the government overthrown by the progress of knowledge. But, unfortunately, obsessed by the evils around them, Voltaire and Rousseau 'tore up the tares and the wheat together' and made 'purity of manners as ridiculous as prejudice'.[38] Voltaire scoffed at the English revolution of 1688 as the criminal enterprise of a son against his father-in-law,[39] and Rousseau exhorted men to recover a natural liberty they had never possessed. The revolution took its colour from the regime, and that was the explanation of the paradox of French history, the occurrence of deeds so cruel in a nation so polished.[40]

The lesson of history, as Lord John told the house of commons in 1831, was this, 'that it is upon law and government, that the prosperity and morality, the power and intelligence, of every nation depend'.[41] Lord John was anti-Pope. Governments did determine what ills their peoples had to endure, and it did matter who held the government. Monarchy and a 'pure' democracy were equally bad forms of government. A monarch was surrounded by sycophants,[42] and a successful popular movement would always fall into the hands of men who were ready to beggar millions in an attempt to tear up society by the roots.[43]

And so, with youthful certitude and ideological conviction, Lord John stood forth as the champion of the aristocratic middle. All history taught us that

> if great changes accomplished by the people are dangerous, although sometimes salutary, great changes accomplished by an aristocracy, at the desire of the people, are at once salutary and safe.[44]

It is fashionable to dismiss this as an untenable position, or as a pose for a conservatism more damaging than the real thing, and there may be something in this when we look at Lord John's elders like Grey and Melbourne. But it was not Lord John's case, because, if you compelled the Whigs to jump off the middle, while Grey and Melbourne would jump to the right, Lord John would generally jump to the left.

This was to be the fundamental point about Lord John's political career, and it was already to be seen in his histories.

In the *Memoirs of the Affairs of Europe* he began by condemning
the national assembly in France, but went on to turn even more
fiercely upon the statesmen responsible for the treaty of Vienna.
After observing that the monarchical principle now appeared
as 'an expedient for closing all bright prospects of improvement
to the human race', he ended with a passage in which he delivered the most deeply felt articles of his political creed.

> We are perpetually asked if the nations at present declaring their
> independence . . . are fit to be free . . . It would indeed be a hope-
> less case for mankind if despotism were thus allowed to take ad-
> vantage of its own wrong, and to bring the evidence of its crimes
> as the title-deeds of its right. It would be indeed a strange per-
> version of justice if absolute governments might say, 'Look how
> ignorant, base, false, and cruel, our people have become under
> our sway; therefore we have a right to retain them in eternal
> subjection . . . '. But no. When I am asked if such or such a nation
> is fit to be free, I ask in return, Is any man fit to be a despot?[45]

> Again, we are told that it is desirable indeed to reform the abso-
> lute monarchies of Europe, but that revolutions are accompanied
> by acts of violence and outrage. To be sure they are; but on whom
> lies the blame of their excesses? . . . On those who have long and
> patiently borne what no man ought to inflict; or on those who have
> inflicted what no man ought to suffer? On those who desire the
> improvement and happiness of mankind, or on those who set up
> the image of insolent rapacity, and call it a government?[46]

Gladstone thought this passage rose to a level of excellence not
exceeded by Burke.[47] It was also eloquence in a better cause.
Blame the revolutionaries by all means, but blame the Bourbons more. Lord John grew up with an exaggerated notion of
his family's role in English history, and of England's standing
in the world, but his instincts were in the right place, and for
that reason he was able, for a time at least, to reinvigorate an
old-fashioned party and to restore its popular image.

CHAPTER IV

Politics, 1815–30

i. 1815–26

IN everything Lord John wrote, politics kept breaking through. In *Essays and Sketches* Lord John made his farmer of good sense impute the ancient quarrels of England and France to their governments,[1] and in 1823 when he was composing the *Memoirs of the Affairs of Europe* he told Grey that he wanted to throw a good book at the holy alliance.[2] The more he wrote the more he wanted to be a politician. Travelling abroad, and writing history, he was impressed with the superiority of British institutions, but when he turned his attention to affairs at home, he found much amiss.

After 1815 it was common form among the Whigs to talk as though the country were falling under a despotism. Lord John professed to see no distinction between the policy of the British government and that of the holy alliance, with its object 'of enslaving mankind'.[3] Alarmed at every sign of popular discontent, Liverpool and Castlereagh no sooner heard of snow in Russia than they said 'that is our snow'.[4] Ministers were keeping up a standing army 'unexampled in magnitude'.[5] In 1816 this army was in France, suppressing the liberties of the French people, but who could avoid seeing how it might be employed upon its return, to enact 'the same disgusting scenes in England'.[6] When Lord John asked ministers why they kept 210,000 troops under arms, the only answer they could give was to point to the growth of the manufacturing towns and to the danger of tumults.[7]

However much the Tories might dismiss all dread of a standing army as 'superstitious panic',[8] an army of this size evoked many fears, and any growth in the influence of the crown evoked still more. The term 'the crown' was used extremely loosely at

the time. Nobody could suppose that either the imbecile
George III or the indulgent Regent wished to model himself
upon James II and Louis XIV. But the scope of government,
and the influence of ministers, had grown with the wars. Every
pound increase in the debt and in the taxes to service the debt,
Lord John argued, was so much weight taken away from the
people and given to the government. Every fundholder was
tied by interest to the government, every colony seized from the
French required an establishment, and in order to keep the
whole indebted empire running an ever increasing army of
officials was necessary.[9]

These thoughts were common to every Radical of the day.
The difference was that where Paine and Bentham saw an aristocracy deliberately engineering wars in order to raise taxes in
order to make more jobs for their children, Lord John and other
Whigs who rallied to the cry of peace, retrenchment and reform, merely thought that Pitt had blundered into war because
'he did not know how any longer to remain at peace'.[10] Ministers' wickedness consisted not in their having intended to establish a system of influence based upon the national debt, but in
the satisfaction with which they regarded it once it was there.

Lord John identified the keystone of the whole system as the
280 M.P.s sitting for small boroughs of fewer than 5000 inhabitants,[11] who prevented that 'vigilant stewardship of the public
revenue' upon which liberty depended.[12] Members sitting for
small boroughs consistently voted for the government and
against the interests of the nation. Who, after all, as Lord John
said, would buy a borough in order to vote in minorities?[13]
Taking it for granted that proposals to reduce government expenditure were popular, Lord John analysed the votes cast in
the house of commons. He found that in one session (which he
did not identify), there had voted upon proposals to reduce
government expenditure:

Population of Borough	In favour	Against
under 500 inhabitants	1	19
with 500 to 1000	12	33
1000 to 2000	17	44
2000 to 3000	19	46
3000 to 5000	25	44
over 5000	66	47[14]

Making the further assumption that county members were 'popular', Lord John then proceeded to examine two votes taken in 1822. The proposal to reduce the salt tax had been lost by 169 votes to 165. Among the 169 he could find but 14 county M.P.s and no fewer than 61 placemen. Among the 165 he could find 42 county M.P.s and 55 members for large towns. He concluded that the salt tax ought to have been reduced. The proposal to reorganise the postmaster's office had been defeated by 184 votes to 159. Among the 184 he could find 11 M.P.s for the counties of England and Wales, and 23 members for large towns. Among the 159 he could find 29 members for English and Welsh counties, and 40 for the large towns. He concluded that the postmaster's office ought to have been reorganised by 69 votes to 34.[15]

Two hundred and eighty M.P.s for the small boroughs were returned by an electorate of under 8000, and that was why on every question which involved the issue of whether Britain was to have 'a large, expensive military government' or a 'cheap, economical, civil government', the wrong decisions were taken.[16] Curwen's act of 1809 was inefficacious,[17] and 'The produce of the taxes descends in fertilising showers upon the proprietors, the agents, and the members of boroughs. For them there is a state lottery which is all prizes.'[18] Even if the country's liberties survived the threat posed by a standing army, there would still be another army waiting to destroy the freedom of England, an army of corrupt senators and civil servants.[19]

Now things were not so bad as this, and there was not much, except a reputation for exaggeration, to be gained by pretending that they were. But Lord John can be pardoned for having over-stated the case, for in the period after Waterloo ministers were rapidly showing by their actions that they were out of touch. The pattern of popular disturbance after 1815 followed the state of trade, and when, less than two years and one bad harvest after the peace, the government suspended *habeas corpus*, Lord John sensibly objected that this was no remedy for the discontent of thousands of unemployed manufacturers,[20] and warned the house that the time was coming when it would have to consider the whole question of parliamentary reform.[21] The government was precipitating the kind of chain reaction which Lord John believed to have occurred in eighteenth-

century France. The opposition out of doors became more
extreme, and in 1819 Lord John actually spoke against Bur-
dett's motion for a general inquiry into the state of the representation.[22] The Radicals attributed his action to his supposing
he had an exclusive property in motions for parliamentary reform, and to pique,[23] and four days later Lord John moved
moderate resolutions of his own, pledging the house, in its next
session, to consider the case of the borough of Grampound. Lord
John's resolutions were carried *nem. con.*, but then, in the
autumn, the magistrates allowed the yeomanry to charge the
crowd at Peterloo, and the whole issue was thus thrown open
again. Parliament was recalled, and Mackintosh wrote to Lord
John, who was in Italy, to come back, saying that 'reform must
be immediately brought forward, if possible, as the act of the
party, but at all events as the creed of all Whig reformers'.[24]

The country stood in danger of a deadlock between a democratic movement which made demands without limit, and a
government which met all demands by 'total and peremptory
denial'.[25] In these circumstances there was a golden opportunity to prove to the people that the Whigs were not just Tories
out of power, and to exhibit to the propertied classes that there
was something more to popular discontent than the fact that
unpatriotic Whigs encouraged it. When parliament met, Lord
John began by observing that if there had been elections at
Manchester, the house would not have had to hold an inquest
on Peterloo, and then went on to propose that all boroughs
where gross bribery was proved should cease to return members, and that the seats should be transferred to towns with
over 15,000 inhabitants.[26]

Castlereagh congratulated Lord John upon his moderation,
and offered, if Lord John would withdraw his general proposition, to support a bill to disfranchise Grampound. The
subsequent history of the disfranchisement of Grampound is
complicated. Early in 1820 George III died. Before parliament
was dissolved Lord John moved to suspend the issue of writs to
Grampound (and to Penryn and Camelford). His proposal was
accepted by the commons and rejected by the lords. When the
new parliament met, Lord John, who now sat for Huntingdonshire, duly brought in a bill to disfranchise Grampound, and to
transfer the seats to Leeds with a £5 rental suffrage. Castle-

reagh then declared himself in favour of the disfranchisement, for which there were precedents, and against the transfer, which was a novelty. Lord John politely accused Castlereagh of deception, but before the two men could get into a wrangle Queen Caroline returned to England, and Grampound was left to the next session. In 1821 Lord John reintroduced his bill, and as a concession agreed to make the franchise in Leeds £10 instead of £5. But he refused to accept the transfer of the seats to the hundred of Powder and Pyder, and when the house of commons, becoming more timid with every week, raised the franchise to £20, he gave up the charge of the bill. But he continued to support it, as a change for the better, even when the lords finally voted to transfer the seat to the freeholders of Yorkshire.

In recent years the struggles over the Reform Bill of 1831–2 have distracted attention from the earlier struggles of the 1820s. But the first steps were the hardest, and Grampound was the first success gained by the reformers since the war. In the debates upon this one convicted borough, the enemy had revealed how stubborn he was, and as soon as the victory was won, Lord John stated his conviction that there were fifty to sixty such cases of gross corruption at every general election, and moved resolutions in favour of setting up improved machinery to investigate it, and to stamp it out by confiscation and redistribution.[27] He was defeated, but the small majority of 155 votes to 124 encouraged him to bring on a new and much more carefully thought out motion for the reform of parliament in 1822.

On 25 April 1822 Lord John made his first major speech. It was the most important case he ever argued in favour of reform, and it has deservedly found its way into the annals of English oratory. Lord John raised his bid. In 1819 he had disclaimed any intention of introducing 'reform upon a principle',[28] and in 1821 he had said that we ought to have as good reasons for disfranchising Old Sarum as we had for expelling James II.[29] Now, he boldly proposed to strip one member from each of 100 small boroughs, and to transfer 60 seats to the counties and 40 to the large towns. He defended himself from the charge of inconsistency by saying that things had not stood still. By refusing to make even the smallest changes in the representation, and to take account of the enormous increase in the

numbers of the middle classes, the government was bringing the
country nearer to the convulsion that had already overtaken
France.

> I think the people judge wisely, because . . . the abuses they en-
> dure, though flagrant, do not amount to a justifiable ground for
> actual resistance. But let not any thing be inferred from their
> obedience, even if pushed still farther.[30]

Lord John now stood nearer to 1831 than to 1819, and
familiar as it is, one passage deserves to be quoted at length.

> At the present period, the ministers of the Crown possess the con-
> fidence of the House of Commons, but the House of Commons
> does not possess the esteem and reverence of the people . . . We
> have seen discontent breaking into outrage . . . we have seen alarm
> universally prevailing among the upper classes, and disaffection
> among the lower – we have seen the ministers of the Crown seek a
> remedy . . . in a system of severe coercion – in restrictive laws – in
> large standing armies – in enormous barracks, and in every other
> ersource which is not founded on the hearts of its subjects. . . . It
> is my persuasion, that the liberties of Englishmen, being founded
> upon the general consent of all, must remain upon that basis, or
> must altogether cease . . . We cannot confine liberty in this country
> to one class of men . . . If we ask the causes, why a system of
> government, so contrary to the spirit of our laws, so obnoxious to
> the feelings of our people, so ominous to the future prospects of the
> country, has been adopted, we shall find the root of the evil to lie
> in the defective state of our representation. The votes of the House
> of Commons no longer imply the general assent of the realm . . .
> The ministers of the Crown, after obtaining triumphant majorities
> in this House, are obliged to have recourse to other means than
> those of persuasion, reverence for authority, and voluntary respect,
> to procure the adherence of the country. They are obliged to en-
> force, by arms, obedience to acts of this House – which, according
> to every just theory, are supposed to emanate from the people
> themselves.[31]

Lord John's motion was lost by 269 votes to 164. But the 164
were the largest number to have voted in favour of reform since
1785. The result showed that Lord John's policy of moderate,
but substantial reform was the one most likely to consolidate
opinion in the party, and Dr Mitchell says that the high vote
marked both a movement in the counties, which hoped to gain

by reform, and among the Radicals, who were being weaned from their own more visionary proposals.[32]

In 1823 Lord John did not repeat his great effort of the year before. Instead he asked for a plain arithmetical statement of the number of voters who returned members for the various cities and boroughs.[33] Even this was refused him. The episode passed almost without notice at the time, but in retrospect it seems a master stroke, for the suspicion was, as Lord John said, that while there were a million independent men who had no vote, 8000 people returned a majority of the house of commons.[34] In 1824 and 1825 Lord John brought forward no further motion in favour of reform. In 1826, however, as the old parliament approached its end in the middle of a depression, he again brought forward a general motion, which was defeated by 247 votes to 123.[35] His support had fallen away since 1822; he had exhausted the arguments, there was no sign of a popular movement, and he concluded that he must wait for times to change.

Lord John had made two miscalculations, both of which he was to make again. First he had underestimated the skill of the Tory party in moving just enough to keep him at a distance. Second, and more serious, he had been over-sanguine as to the unity of his own party. In 1819 Althorp, Fitzwilliam, and the Grenvilles were still against reform altogether,[36] and, in 1822 Tierney refused Lord John the notes usually allowed to members (the whip).[37] Although Grey once said that if the Whigs came into office they should insist on something not far short of Lord John's plan of 1822,[38] that was not a view he held for long. Grey was morose, and out of love with Westminster; year after year he gave no lead, and the violent laughed at the moderate, while the moderate looked grave at the violent.[39] As Lord William said in his down-to-earth way in 1826, the opposition in the commons was like a pack of hounds, ready to follow the huntsman's call, but there was 'no one fit to lay them on the right scent'.[40]

This lack of organisation was not, however, an unmixed handicap to Lord John, for in that army, in which there were no generals, there were no subalterns either. Correspondence was conducted in terms of outspoken equality. Young or old, you simply wrote what you thought, and took up what issues you chose. If, like Lord John, you made a good choice, there was no reason why you should not become an acknowledged authority even as a young man, and after all that Lord John had done between 1819 and 1826, it was certain that when the reform issue did come to life again, somebody would send for him.

ii. 1826–30

At the general election of 1826 Lord John lost his seat in Huntingdonshire, and promptly left England for a tour through France to Italy. While he was away, his old schoolfellow Lord Hartington, who was now the Duke of Devonshire, offered him the borough of Bandon, in Ireland, and added that as

> It may be necessary to name the member before your answer can have arrived . . . I hope you will not be dissatisfied at finding yourself *elected*.[41]

Soon after the new parliament met in 1827 everything was changed when Liverpool suffered a stroke, and was succeeded by Canning. Canning was an enlightened Tory, with the talent to dissolve parties. Wellington, Eldon, and Peel refused to serve with him, and left him with no alternative but to offer places to the Whigs. Grey and the Duke of Bedford would have none of them, but Lansdowne was interested, and led three Whigs into the cabinet, and in May a majority of the Whig party left the opposition benches and crossed the floor of the house. Althorp, Tavistock, and Lord John were not among them.[42] Lord John condemned Lansdowne's 'negligent and unnecessary sacrifice of our importance as a party',[43] and he preferred Althorp's policy of 'watching' – of judging and voting on each issue as it came up. But he was too happy to find Canning at the head of the government to moot against him any general project of parliamentary reform,[44] and he intervened only in one small instance. Two cases of notorious bribery had occurred at the general election of 1826, at East Retford and Penryn. Bills were introduced for transferring the franchise of East Retford to Birmingham, and that of Penryn to the neighbouring hundred. Lord John proposed that, if Penryn were disfranchised, the seats should be transferred to Manchester, and he carried his proposal by 124 votes to 69.

In August 1827 Canning died, and everything was changed

again. Goderich was, as the Duke of Bedford put it, 'a good-natured and good-humoured man, but totally unfit for a Prime Minister'.[45] Lansdowne was too weak to keep the Whigs' end up, and the only hope lay in Lord Holland's coming in to inspire him with 'timely resolution'.[46] The next session, Lord John thought, might then 'do much for the objects we have been contending for'.[47] But the King refused to have Lord Holland, and early in 1828 Goderich's government fell, and Wellington and Peel came back into office. Parliament appeared to be back where it was in Lord Liverpool's day, but the strength of parties was not easily measured, and no sooner had the new government taken over than Lord John succeeded in wringing from them the largest concession to the spirit of the age since he had entered parliament.

For many years the Whig party had been in favour of relieving both dissenters and roman catholics of their disabilities. Dissenters were excluded from office, and roman catholics from parliament as well. But the party was in a quandary as to the order in which to relieve the two communities. The Whigs' relations with the dissenters were close, but a dissenter who broke the law was protected by an indemnity act, and although many dissenters would not take office on such terms, the dissenters suffered a grievance rather than an injury. Ever since the act of union with Ireland, however, the exclusion of the catholics had been both a breach of faith and a great practical evil. The Whigs were understandably reluctant, therefore, to relieve the dissenters first, lest the dissenters then take sides against the catholics, and it has always been something of a mystery how things happened in the order they did.

It is a mystery upon which Lord John's papers throw no light at all.[48] The dissenters' elder statesmen, the united deputies, were familiar guests at Holland House; Lord John was a member of, and even took the chair at meetings of the Protestant Society; and Whigs and dissenters were associated with the utilitarian Radicals in the foundation of London university. There were plenty of contacts, but the details of what happened in 1827–8 still await elucidation.

The dissenters were stirred by the retirement of Liverpool. In February 1827 the committee of deputies decided in favour of a new campaign to secure relief from the test and corporation

acts, and within a few days the crucial meeting was held with
Lord Holland, Lord John, and a number of other Whig M.P.s,
at which the dissenters gave assurances that, if relieved first,
they would support the catholics' claim to relief. The dissenters
then set to work to secure the support of other interested parties
like the Scottish presbyterian church and the Wesleyan conference, and Lord John gave notice of a motion in parliament.
But at the end of May 1827 the campaign was called off – the
new united committee had come into being too late to prosecute
its campaign in the present session.

The preparations that preceded Lord John's motion in 1828
belong rather to the history of the dissenters than to the life of
Lord John. The united committee arranged for petitions to be
sent from all parts of the country, and thousands of copies of
their case were distributed with the *Quarterly* and *Edinburgh*
magazines. Well before Lord John rose on 26 February 1828 to
move the repeal of the test and corporation acts, the deputies
furnished him with all the facts he needed.

It was Lord John's second major speech, and he moved the
repeal in the exact words used by Fox in 1790. His language was
temperate, he did no more than hint at the danger to the church
if the dissenters ever came to feel that the road to civil liberties
lay over the property of the establishment, and his best point
came from the contrast with other countries:

> The English Protestant Dissenter, if he were to leave his country,
> might be admitted to all the employments of Catholic Austria,
> might go from exclusion at Bath or Huntingdon, to sit in the muni-
> cipality of Prague or of Milan, might even be admitted to the
> council of state of Vienna, and yet here he still stands a suppliant,
> imploring tardy justice from the parliament of Protestant
> England.[49]

Lord John himself was surprised when fifteen Tory ultras
changed sides and his motion was carried by 237 votes to 193.
Lady Spencer thought the result 'the greatest demonstration of
the increasing good sense of the country' that she had witnessed
in her long life.[50] Peel swept out of the house in anger, but he
was already, as Lord John said, 'a very pretty hand at hauling
down his colours',[51] and he accepted the verdict – though not
without meanly substituting for the existing test a declaration

'on the true faith of a christian', which survived for forty years. Russell, of course, deplored the declaration, but he accepted the irritation rather than lose the substance of the reform, and persuaded the deputies to do the same.

A few days after the acts had been repealed Lord Holland and Lord John were the guests of honour at a dinner given by the dissenting deputies. Lord John's own feeling at the time was that while it was 'a gratifying thing to force the enemy to give up his first line, that none but Churchmen are worthy to serve the state', he hoped it would not be long before they could make him give up his second, that none but Protestants were.[52]

Catholic emancipation, however, stemmed from a different chain of events. When Wellington and Peel came back into office they decided to accept Lord John's resolution for transferring seats from Penryn to Manchester, but not to support Tennyson's bill for enfranchising Birmingham out of East Retford. Lord John then brought in a bill which passed the commons, but was amended by the lords, who cut out Manchester and merged Penryn into the neighbouring hundred. All the Huskissonites, Dudley, Grant, Huskisson, Lamb and Palmerston, thereupon resigned from a divided cabinet. They were not all equally committed to a reform of parliament, and Palmerston, for instance, voted for the transfer of seats precisely because it was the only way to forestall reform,[53] but henceforth they sided with the Whigs rather than the Tories. It was a decisive shift in the balance of power.

The resignation of the Huskissonites led through unexpected consequences to O'Connell's candidature at the Clare election. Lord John gave notice of a motion for emancipating the catholics, but his colleagues thought he was going too fast, and made him withdraw it.[54] He did not stay quiet for long. In October 1828 he wrote to Grey to propose the formation of a society to exploit 'the machinery of correspondence, petitions &c' which the dissenters had used, 'for the purpose of obtaining the complete establishment of religious liberty'.[55] Grey refused to join,[56] and Althorp feared a backlash from the Brunswicker clubs.[57] Lord John consoled himself with the thought that petitions could be solicited 'as well by private correspondence'.[58] He need not have worried. Politics had entered that strange period in which Wellington and Peel appeared to be willing to concede anything so long as they could keep their places. When parliament met early in 1829, Wellington and Peel announced their conversion to catholic emancipation. Lord John was glad they preferred the obloquy of changing their opinions to putting the country in peril,[59] but he disapproved of the countervailing disfranchisement of the Irish 40s freeholders, who 'had as good a right to their franchise as the owners or voters of . . . Gatton',[60] and he felt that there was no need for him to speak either for or against the ministers' bill.

Catholic emancipation was a second great gain for the reformers, and not least because the Tory ultras now concluded that a protestant country had been sold by an unprincipled pack of borough owners. But it was not at first apparent that it would give an impetus to the reform question, and in 1829 Tennyson's latest proposal to transfer seats from East Retford to Birmingham was defeated by 197 votes to 111. But three years in which the transference of seats to Manchester and Birmingham had been proposed, discussed, apparently agreed to, cavilled over, and then refused, had not passed without making an impression. In Manchester and Birmingham hopes had been raised, and things were already beginning to stir before the new session opened in 1830.

In 1830 Lord John was still for supporting what measures the Whigs believed in, without regard to ministers 'or whether we may hurt them or help them'. At the same time he looked forward to co-operating ever more closely with the Huskissonites: 'They have what we want men of official experience, and we have what they want, numbers.'[61] Three men in succession then tried their luck with the reform question. First the Marquis of Blandford proposed a permanent apparatus to disfranchise decayed towns and to enfranchise rising ones. Lord John voted for this, though he did not give it his blessing. Then Lord John introduced a bill to enfranchise Birmingham, Leeds and Manchester, and argued that the claims of these large towns were now so urgent 'as to call on us to go up to the House of Lords, not with a mixed Bill of penalty and investiture, but with one in which we shall make our stand on the broad principles of . . . Representation'.[62] He was defeated by 188 votes to 140. Finally, O'Connell brought in a much more radical plan for triennial parliaments, universal suffrage, and vote by secret ballot.

Althorp was in favour of the ballot, Lord John was not averse from triennial parliaments, and the Whigs concocted an amendment along the lines of Lord John's scheme of 1822, for taking 100 seats from the smallest boroughs. They were defeated by 213 votes to 117, but Huskisson presciently remarked that before long something of that kind would be carried.

There was still a majority against reform, but in order to maintain his position, and partly no doubt because it was his nature to act openly, Wellington had made much more widespread use of influence than any government had done for decades. The effect was, from his point of view, disastrous. The old system was tolerable only so long as its operations were invisible. Wellington and Peel had the power to kill every specific proposal of reform, but they could not kill the issue itself. When the King died in June, and the country prepared for a general election, reform was in the air, even before the revolution in Paris. The elections had an anti-aristocratic ring. There were many changes, and the Reformers gained ground, though Lord John himself had a hard contest at Bedford. His opponent republished some passages from the second volume of the *Memoirs of the Affairs of Europe*, in which Lord John accused Wesley's followers of fanaticism and self-deception.[63] Lord John was beaten by one vote. He then went off to Paris, where we may leave him pleading with Louis Philippe and Lafayette to spare the life of the fallen Polignac.[64]

CHAPTER V

The Reform Bill, 1830–2

Lᴏʀᴅ Jᴏʜɴ lost his seat in parliament just as the reform issue on which he was the expert came to the fore. The result was to let in Brougham, who was not slow to see the chance his celebrated victory in the popular constituency of Yorkshire gave him. On 28 September Brougham declared that he would leave the cause of parliamentary reform in no other man's hands.[1] It was a dangerous moment for Lord John. But he appreciated Brougham's talents, and found his vices so transparent that he was less upset by them than were most of Brougham's colleagues. As soon as he came back from Paris in October, he wrote to Lord Holland that he had thought of publishing something about reform, 'But I believe it is better to wait, and let Brougham run riot as he pleases.'[2]

When the new parliament met in November there was a meeting of Whig supporters at Althorp's. Lord John was apparently still canvassing his plan to enfranchise Birmingham, Leeds and Manchester, and was out of touch with the changing mood of the party, which wanted something larger.[3] Brougham then jumped in with a scheme of his own. It was bold as to the franchise, but vague as to the disfranchisement of rotten boroughs. 'He, Ld. B., was asked whether he intended to disfranchise any boroughs, but his answer was so confused it cd not be made out whether he did or not.'[4] The meeting agreed to let Brougham bring in a motion on 16 November, but many Whig M.P.s would have preferred to see the motion entrusted to Lord John and regretted that this was impossible,[5] and Brougham was already removing himself from the list of possible fathers of a Reform Bill.

The Whigs busily sought Huskissonite support, but Brougham's motion never came up for debate. On 16 November, a few days after his notorious encomium on the constitution,

Wellington resigned, and Grey was invited to form an administration. One of his first problems was what was to be done with
Brougham. Brougham held out for the mastership of the rolls,
which was a permanent appointment worth £7,000 p.a., and
was compatible with a place in the house of commons. Nobody
grudged Brougham the salary, but many jibbed at the prospect
of his holding an irremovable office with a seat in the lower
house. Althorp then set the pattern for the next four years by
speaking decisively. He would not belong to an administration over which Brougham held such a stranglehold, and so
Brougham's bluff was called, and faced with the alternatives of
going to the upper house as lord chancellor or of not being in
the government at all, Brougham gave way. This was a piece of
good fortune both for the Whig party and for Lord John.

In the meantime Lord John was out of town. Ebrington had
been returned both for Devonshire and for Tavistock. He chose
to sit for the county, and the Russell family's pocket borough
became available for Lord John. It was hardly the ideal place
from which to launch a Reform Bill, but time pressed, and Lord
John was already canvassing the electors when he received
Grey's invitation to join the administration.[6] The offer came
through Althorp, who had already agreed to take the lead in
the commons. Up in London Tavistock heard that what they
had in mind for Lord John was the post of under-secretary at
the foreign office. He wrote hurriedly, 'I hope you will come to
no decision in your own mind till I see you'.[7] The plan was for
either Holland or Lansdowne to take the foreign office, and it
fell through when each in turn refused, and the office was accepted by Palmerston, who could answer for himself in the
house of commons. Finally Grey offered, and Lord John accepted, a place as paymaster of the forces. People have wondered
ever since why Grey offered Lord John this particular post. The
most likely explanation is that Lord John was frail, and the work
was not onerous, but it may be that we are wrong to look for any
deliberate motive. In making a government the order in which
the pieces are put in helps to determine what places the remaining pieces occupy. Lord John was still young, and so he ended
up with the paymaster's office when older men had been satisfied.
It brought him £2000 p.a. and a house, where he installed a
bath, and became one of the first Englishmen to bathe every day.[8]

There is a more serious question. The Whigs came in agreed
to a reform that would satisfy all but extreme Radicals. Even if
it was not yet clear that Grey would turn to Lord John to introduce the bill in the commons, his omission from the cabinet was
bound to cast doubt upon Grey's seriousness of purpose. Lord
John had never held office, and Grey had no need, therefore, to
consider whether personal feelings prompted keeping him out.
But Lord John interpreted his omission as a slight, and the
point his anxious mind fixed on was that Graham, with even
less experience and smaller claims, had been taken in. Grievances are not pleasant things to write about, but it is clear from
Lord John's letters to Ellice and to Howick that this one went
deep, and that as late as 1839 it was still an open wound. [9]

In the 1790s Grey knew all about reform, but by 1830 he was
too old to undertake the detailed preparation of a great measure.
Rather carelessly, one day early in December, as they were
walking down the steps of the house of lords, he asked his son-in-
law, Lord Durham, to form a committee and to take the chair.
He went on: 'You can have no objection to consult Ld. J.
Russell?' 'Certainly not', Durham replied, 'but the reverse.' [10]
Durham invited Lord John to call on him, and proposed the
Duke of Richmond for a third. Lord John objected that the
duke had never been a reformer, and they agreed instead to invite Graham and Duncannon. [11] Graham lived in the north of
England, and may have been supposed to know something
about the constituencies in Scotland; Duncannon lived in and
knew Ireland, and had been the party whip for a decade.
Durham was the most Radical man on the committee, Lord
John and Duncannon occupied the middle, and Graham, who
was alleged to be Durham's puppet, soon proved to be the most
alarmist.

Grey recognised that the time for palliatives was past, and the
committee did not even consider the two easy solutions, of
simply adding new members, and of piecemeal disfranchisement
consequent upon proof of corruption. They began with a rough
sketch submitted by Althorp for taking 100 seats away from the
smallest boroughs. [12] Althorp himself put this forward as a minimum, and the committee rejected it as inadequate. They then
passed on to the more extensive and more detailed plan drawn
up by Lord John. Many years later the *Daily News* alleged that

Lord John drafted the Reform Bill 'in one day . . . upon a half sheet of notepaper'.[13] The document runs to two folios only,[14] and Lord John himself said that he drew it up 'in a short time'.[15] But that does not mean there was anything wrong with it. Lord John had served a long apprenticeship to this subject, which engaged both his convictions and his appetite for work. His papers do not tell us much, but they do tell us that in the early 1820s he kept in touch with the state of affairs in Grampound after it was disfranchised,[16] and that he was in communication with the reformers of Manchester during the parliament of 1826–30.[17] There was, in fact, only one man in parliament who could match his knowledge, and that was Croker, who sat on the other side of the house.

Lord John himself said that the plan contained hardly anything that was new,[18] and it would have been absurd to have denied an element of continuity going back to the reform movement of the eighteenth century. But Lord John's plan was upon a larger scale. It provided for fifty of the smallest boroughs to be stripped of both seats, and for fifty of the next smallest to lose one member each, making a total of 150 seats disfranchised. Holding that the house was already too large, and presumably realising even at this stage that it would be as well to be able to make concessions in the course of the debates, Lord John proposed to enfranchise only eighteen large towns, to allot six additional members to London, and to give the twenty most populous counties two more seats each, making a total of eighty-two. In the counties Lord John proposed to enfranchise copyholders and leaseholders with an interest of more than twenty-one years. In existing boroughs the franchise was to be conferred upon persons qualified to serve on juries, provided that (except in London, Westminster and Southwark) they were householders rated at £10 a year. In the new boroughs Lord John proposed a £15 householder franchise. The original plan, then, did not contain what was ultimately the most revolutionary feature of the Reform Act, the uniform borough suffrage.

What followed is best described in Lord John's letter to Durham:

> We had many and anxious discussions. Sir James Graham proposed a plan of registration, which we adopted, with some alterations. Plans of reforms for Scotland and Ireland were discussed

and adopted. At my suggestion it was proposed to limit the duration of Parliament to five years. In the course of our discussions
you very much pressed the mode of voting by ballot. I was very
reluctant . . . but finding the other members of the committee
against me, I consented, on condition that the franchise in towns
should be raised to twenty pounds. [19]

The committee's report, together with three draft bills for
England and Wales, Scotland, and Ireland, was delivered to
the cabinet in January 1831. In their covering letter the committee said they had tried neither to evade nor to stifle 'the
general demand for a complete alteration of the existing
system', but to effect a permanent settlement that would put a
stop to the restless spirit of innovation.[20] Prime minister,
cabinet and committee all wished their measure to be 'final'.
Sydney Smith said that this meant they expected it to last for
forty years.[21] Lord John's definition was that Britain should escape the course of events in France after 1789. If, when the
reformed parliament met, its first act was to introduce another
schedule A, and to lower the franchise, then the Whigs would
have failed. That was why the plan to take 100 seats, one from
each of the smallest boroughs, was no longer sufficient. 'If, upon
my former [1822] plan of Reform, Gatton and Sarum preserved one Member each, would not the first motion in the reformed Parliament have been to do away with the remaining
Representatives of those places?'[22]

The next few weeks must have been anxious ones for Lord
John. Durham and Graham were in the cabinet, and he and
Duncannon were not. Lord John relied mainly upon Lord
Holland for his information,[23] but it was Grey himself who told
Lord John that one of the members of the cabinet had objected
to the extent of the disfranchisement. Grey asked him who he
thought it could have been. Lord John 'said he cd not tell, there
were several Ld. Holland, Ld. Melbourne, Ld. Palmerston who
were not much in favour of Reform and it might be any of
them'.[24] But it was Brougham, still smarting at the way the issue
had been taken out of his hands. Nobody supported him, and
the cabinet actually made the disfranchisement more stringent.
And when they came to the ballot, Durham was ill and unable
to attend the meeting of the cabinet, Althorp, for once, was not
persuasive, and to Lord John's relief Grey got it thrown out.[25]

This left the £20 franchise as a target for Radical attack. Lord John was at all times busy doing his sums, and he now found that in Helston there were only 20 £20 householders, in Thirsk 15, in Wilton 14, in Great Marlow 11, in Amersham 7, in Wenlock 6, in Westbury 3 and in St Germains 1. He passed this information to the cabinet, and recommended coming down to a £10 franchise.[26] Later, he added various suggestions for avoiding an uniform franchise,[27] but the cabinet disregarded these, and adopted the uniform £10 householder franchise. Here indeed was 'reform upon a principle', and a leaf taken out of the Radieals' book, which Lord John had always tried to avoid. He reflected that it need never have come to this had the Tories agreed to piecemeal reforms in time. If Grampound had been transferred to Leeds in 1821, and if Penryn had been transferred to Manchester in 1828, you could have had as varied franchises as you pleased, and you could even have defended the different franchises upon Radical principles, for the value of property varied from town to town.

Finally, it is worth noticing that neither Lord John nor the cabinet tried to sweeten their proposals by offering compensation. Parliament was not niggardly in these matters, as was shown in 1833 when the reformed parliament voted £20m to the slave owners. In 1821 Lord John had referred to the provision in the act of union with Ireland for compensating boroughs which ceased to return members,[28] and in his *History of the English Government and Constitution* he had optimistically asserted that 'many a corporation and little borough would be glad to make their escape over a bridge of gold'.[29] In May 1830 the Whigs still spoke of compensation, but by 1831 the time was past, and when Peel objected to 'confiscation', Lord John replied that had there been none the present want of confidence in public men would have been perpetuated.[30]

On 31 January 1831 Lord Holland wrote to Lord John from Brighton that the child 'in the begetting of which you took so active a part' had been royally and '*almost affectionately*' adopted.[31] The next question was, who was to introduce the bill in the house of commons? There were only four members of the cabinet in the lower house. First came Althorp, beloved and trusted, but, as Greville put it, Althorp 'cannot speak at all'.[32] In order of seniority the other three were Palmerston, Grant and

Graham. Palmerston and Grant were Huskissonites, and it
would have upset the Whigs had the honour gone to either of
them. Palmerston in any case was too busy at the foreign office,
and Grant was below the work. Graham had the merit that he
had been a member of the committee of four, but Greville
thought him 'inconsiderable',[33] and he, too, was at that time
no speaker. The process of elimination brought the cabinet
back to Lord John. Brougham did all he could to prevent the
honour falling to his rival,[34] but his intervention was counter-
productive, and on 3 February Althorp announced that the
Reform Bill would be introduced on 1 March by Lord John
Russell.

The bill's unveiling was a moment of great drama. Lord
Holland had managed to tell Lady Holland nothing about it,
nobody believed the one backbencher who did get wind of what
was intended,[35] and the surprise was complete. When the hour
came, Althorp walked over from Downing Street to the house
with Lord John: 'the general interest was in Lord Althorp, Lord
John being then so little known that few persons noticed him . . .
Lord John looked very pale and subdued . . .' After casting
occasional glances at the immense array of the opposition in
front of him, Lord John rose at five o'clock and spoke for two
hours.[36] He began by doing away with the notion 'that this
question, not being brought forward by a member of the Cabinet, is not a measure of the King's Ministers'.[37] To this end he
suppressed his own part in the framing of the bill, and went
almost so far as to imply that Gray had drafted it himself.[38]

He then placed himself and the government on the ground
they were to occupy for over fifteen months until the bill
passed, in the middle between the two hostile parties, the bigots
who would concede nothing, and the fanatics who wanted universal suffrage.[39] He disdained to argue with either. In old age
he recalled that

> I . . . purposely omitted, or passed slightly over, those arguments
> in favour of reform which in 1822 I had developed at length . . . It
> seemed to me . . . that the great novelty of my speech must consist
> in a clear and intelligible statement of the nature of the proposition
> I had to make.[40]

In fact, he treated the house to a few minutes of prosy history which aroused 'a slight degree of languour and impatience',[41] and then got down to the real business of the day.

The people complained of nomination by individuals, elections by close corporations, and the expense and corruption of elections. For remedy, the government proposed that all boroughs with fewer than 2000 inhabitants were to lose both members and all boroughs with more than 2000 but fewer than 4000 inhabitants were to lose one member. The census of 1821 showed that there were 60 in the first category and 47 in the second. After allowing for a special case or two there would be 168 vacancies. Believing that the house was at present much too large, the government proposed to allot 97 of these seats, 42 to the metropolis and large towns and 55 to the counties, and after adding 5 members to Scotland and 3 to Ireland to extinguish the rest. At this point Lord John was interrupted by requests for lists of the boroughs to be disfranchised. He obliged, and began to take the house through schedule A. 'As each venerable name was read, a long shout of ironical laughter rang from the benches opposite. "More yet", smiled Russell unperturbed, at the end of the fateful roll, and turned to the second schedule of forty-seven boroughs.'[42] The jeers of the opposition were answered, and a conflict developed which lasted through the enumeration of the boroughs in the two schedules.[43] 'It was a ludicrous spectacle to see members lying back in disgust, not knowing whether to be amused or enraged, while "a little fellow, not weighing above eight stone" solemnly pronounced the doom of the ancient boroughs for which they sat.'[44]

When the noise died down, Lord John was able to explain that the new borough franchise was to be £10. Altogether he expected the electorate to be increased by between 400,000 and 500,000, which he said was very modest. He ended by making two points about what was not in the bill. There was nothing about the duration of parliaments, and the house might take that up if it wished. There was nothing about the ballot – that, in his opinion, would afford a cover to much fraud and falsehood. Le Marchant says he sat down in a profound silence, and Butler thinks Le Marchant left the house before the cheering began.[45]

Althorp noticed that while Russell was speaking Peel turned black in the face.[46] Perhaps he was too angry to move the

rejection of the bill right away. It is often said that had he done
so he would have succeeded. That may be true, but it is a silly
thing to dwell on, because it takes no account of where Peel
would have found himself thereafter. The second reading was
carried on 22 March by a majority of one (302–301) amidst
mounting excitement. Taking his old measure of the 1822 debate, Lord John noticed that thirty-nine out of the forty-five
members for the metropolis and largest towns had voted for the
bill and only six against, and that in the fifteen largest counties
twenty-seven members had voted for the bill and only nine
against.[47] Thus encouraged the government met their defeat on
19 April, when General Gascoyne's motion not to reduce the
number of members for England and Wales was carried by 299
votes to 291, by deciding to appeal to the country.

Lord John now had the chance to escape from his pocket
borough at Tavistock. He was in demand all over the country
from Southwark to Lancashire, and Lord Holland advised him
to run for Buckinghamshire,[48] which was one of the greatest
Tory strongholds of the age. This would have broken all the
rules of etiquette among county families, and Lord John simply
stepped sideways into the county of Devonshire. At this or the
next election was born the most famous story about Lord John's
size. Sydney Smith came down to visit Lord John. He found the
rustics were surprised that the principal agent in bringing forward the Reform Bill was a very small man:

> My dear friends [Sydney Smith said], before this Reform agita-
> tion commenced Lord John was over six feet high. But, engaged in
> looking after your interests, fighting the peers, the landlords, and
> the rest of your natural enemies, he has been so constantly kept in
> hot water that he is boiled down to the proportions in which you
> now behold him.[49]

Backed by this advocacy Lord John displaced Acland, who had
voted for Gascoyne's motion. All over the country the story was
the same, and the Reformers returned with a majority of about
140. As Lord John's brother William wrote, with a backward
glance at the brave days of the Spanish *cortes*: 'you have raised a
noble spirit in the country . . . I know no sight so grand as a
People roused from their Apathy . . .'[50] It was now clear that
there would be no insurmountable obstacles to the bill in the

house of commons, and that if there was to be a fight to the
death it must be with the lords.

Before the new parliament met, Lord John wrote to Lord
Holland to say that 'When on the formation of the ministry I
found I was not to be in the Cabinet, I concluded . . . that my
vanity had led me to esteem myself too highly.' Now he could
only conclude that his continued exclusion was personal.[51] Lord
Holland had known Lord John long enough not to be surprised
by a letter of this kind, and his answer, which was presumbly
written after speaking to Grey, was masterly.

> Whatever were the causes, now too long and complicated to ex-
> plain, which prevented a better arrangement of [the] House of
> Commons last November, they certainly did not proceed from
> any disposition to undervalue you or your powers or your influ-
> ence there – nor did much time elapse before Grey reverted to
> what I suspect was part of his original design (disturbed by acci-
> dents, refusals and exchanges of others during your absence and
> the formation of the Ministry), viz., your introduction into the
> Cabinet.[52]

The Duke of Bedford thereupon wrote to Grey that Lord John's
being in the cabinet ought to be a *sine qua non*: 'I have written
my opinion . . . strongly and decidedly, and shall say no more –
liberavi animam meam.'[53] Grey gave way. But when he took Lord
John into the cabinet he took Stanley in at the same time, with
consequences that were ultimately to affect him as much as Lord
John and Stanley.

Parliament met on 14 June, and on 24 June Lord John rose,
as a cabinet minister, to introduce the second edition of the
Reform Bill. The bill was almost identical with the one before –
why at this stage should it have been anything else? There is
nothing more difficult than to speak a second time to a measure,
and it is only necessary to pick out two points about Lord John's
speech before passing on to his contribution to the committee
stage of the bill, which was more important. In the first place, it
is significant that with such a secure majority behind him, he
felt able to dwell in a more friendly way upon the abuses they
were attacking.

> In the Representation, as we propose to leave it, there will still be
> a class which some may think a blot on our system, but the exist-
> ence I think, will add to the permanence of Parliament . . . I mean

that there will be a hundred or more Members from places of
three, four, five, or six thousand inhabitants, who will not perhaps
immediately represent any particular interest, and who may,
therefore, be better qualified to speak and inform the House on
great questions of general interest to the community.[54]

Had he said this any earlier, there would have been no case for
a bill. Now, steering down the middle, it was time to give a rebuff to reform upon a principle. His speech is also noteworthy
for his facing up to the specific problem of Tavistock, which
would be left intact by the bill. He candidly admitted that in
the course of the eighteenth century the number of electors at
Tavistock had fallen, at the instance of his own family which
had bought up the freeholds, from 110 in 1716 to between 27
and 35. But if every borough the size of Tavistock had been
disfranchised the number of seats abolished would have risen
from over 160 to over 260 and, if it was the influence of the
Duke of Bedford that was being spoken of, it was only fair to
recall that in Bedfordshire there would now be the largest
population of any county left with only two members.[55]

The second bill passed its second reading by a majority of
136. It then went into committee where it was fought night
after night for two hot and weary months from July to September. At the end of it all, Hardinge's verdict was that Althorp had
carried the bill. It would be fairer to say with Althorp's biographer that Althorp and Lord John did it together.[56] Althorp
was in charge of the house, and Lord John was in charge of the
bill. It was a situation which might have led to difficulties. But
Althorp knew no envy, and he seems to have been delighted to
let Lord John take an equal part. They were a strange pair, for
Althorp stood over six feet tall and had a huge frame. He loved
boxing, and he possessed the wholesome control over his own
temper that boxing is supposed to induce. In debate the two
men were as oil and vinegar; Althorp could soothe and Johnny
sting. In fact Althorp was at least as Radical as Lord John, but
in public Althorp appeared to conciliate the Conservatives,
while Lord John was the Radicals' guarantee against any back-
sliding.

Lord John knew the bill and Althorp knew the house, and
together they saved the ministry from being shown up as bad
draughtsmen. The in-fighting began on 4 July, when an attempt

was made to allow counsel to be heard against the disfranchisement of Appleby – the first test-case on Schedule A. Had this
succeeded, the work would have gone on for years. But it was
successfully resisted. Thereafter Lord John and Althorp were up
night after night, doing the dull but all-important work of
listening to objections, answering questions, and making statements. In all this Lord John showed a flair for distinguishing a
fair point from a spoiling one, and sufficient discretion in giving
a reasoned answer in the one case and a snub in the other. He
patiently explained the ministers' preference for the results of
the 1821 census even after the results of the 1831 census were
available. This was because, by the time the census of 1831 was
taken, the details of the Reform Bill were public property, and
boroughs on the borderline had been under the temptation to
cheat, and to push their population up over the magic figure of
2000 for census night.[57] The very next day, he scornfully announced his willingness to allow members to make any funeral
orations they chose for the boroughs in which they were interested.[58]

But it was not all plain sailing, and the two men got into a
number of what Althorp called 'scrapes'. They underestimated
the difficulty of distinguishing between the parish boundaries
used by the census enumerators, and the actual boundaries of
boroughs; and their attempt to restrict the £10 franchise to
those who paid their rents at intervals of half a year or more
collapsed under the revelation of the sheer number of £10
householders who paid their rents quarterly. In Althorp's and
Lord John's defence it is only fair to say that all subsequent
Reform Bills struck the same rocks and many were wrecked on
them. In 1831 there was a will to bring the bill through, and
two of the principal factors in creating this will were the cabinet's willingness to concede as to numbers, and Althorp's manner
of making concessions. As early as 12 April the government had
announced that if the house preferred to have 658 members,
they would not think it necessary to reduce the number.[59] Even
before Gascoyne's motion put an end to the first bill 31 seats
had been reprieved, bringing the house up from 596 to 627, and
by the time the committee stage of the second bill was over the
house was back to 635, and schedules A and B had been pro-
portionately reduced.[60]

Lord John felt the strain of these continual sittings in committee. He was fed with arrowroot by a benevolent lady,[61] but
on 10 August he was obliged to place the conduct of the bill in
Althorp's hands.[62] Shortly afterwards the government were defeated, when members of the Whig aristocracy joined the Tories
to pass the Chandos clause, which enfranchised the £50 tenant
at will in the counties, and in the absence of ballot increased the
dependent vote. It was a bitter pill, but the cabinet had already
made up its mind to swallow it. Recovering his health very
quickly, Lord John continued to attend the house, and on 30
August, when Althorp himself was indisposed, Lord John again
took charge for the Freemen's abolition clause.[63] He felt strongly
that no more freemen's votes should be created, and that after
the expiry of existing interests, they should become extinct. He
carried the house with him, but in due course the house of
lords differed, and the freemen survived the act. Lord John's
reaction to this setback is not without interest. To Lord Lansdowne he wrote, that the freemen had their votes for life by
agreement '& after that!'[64] 'After that!' seemed to have come
in 1835, when Lord John unforgivingly tried to disfranchise
them by the municipal corporations reform act. But on that
occasion too he was defeated by the house of lords, and the freemen lasted until 1867.

At last the labours of the house of commons came to an end.
The committee stage was finished on 7 September. The bill
passed through all its stages by 21 September, and on the very
next day Althorp and Lord John, accompanied by an unusually large number of M.P.s, carried the bill up to the house of
lords. On 24 September the Reform party gave a great dinner
at the Thatched House Tavern to the two heroes, Lord Althorp
and Lord John.

For ten months Lord John had lived at a gallop. The bill was
now in the hands of the lords, and there was nothing for him to
do but wait. On 7 October the lords rejected the bill by 199
votes to 158, and within a few days the Duke of Wellington's
windows were broken, Nottingham castle was burned, and
Bristol sacked. Everything that happened justified the stand
taken by Lord John since 1819. Reaction and popular outrage
had now begun to feed upon each other as the gospel according
to C. J. Fox had always said they would. As Lord John said on

12 October, the house of lords were not going to prevent the bill passing, they were only going to ensure that at its passing there would be excitement.[65]

Lord John had very little direct contact with the reformers out of doors, and in general there is no reason to doubt the accuracy of his statement that he never acknowledged votes of thanks from the political unions.[66] But there could be no doubt where his sympathies lay. He had already been in trouble in December 1830 for taking the part of a London trades' procession which carried a tricolor flag, and he now jumped into much hotter water. The Birmingham political union called a meeting (supposed to have been attended by 150,000 people), which asked the King to create peers, and addressed votes of thanks to Althorp and Lord John. Althorp's reply aroused little comment, but Lord John's contained the phrase that he believed it to be 'impossible that the whisper of a faction should prevail against the voice of a nation'. This embarrassed Grey and angered the King, who dashed off a remonstrance. Lord John assured the King that he did not wish to justify 'a phrase which, had he not written in the first moments of disappointment at the rejection [of the bill] . . . he would not have used'.[67] In the house of commons, however, he dwelt much more upon the distinction between the house of lords as a whole, to whom he did not wish the expression to apply, and the party in it to which he did wish it to apply.

> He had undoubtedly said, and he now repeated the assertion, that 'it was impossible that the whisper of faction should prevail against the voice of a nation' . . . The Reformers did constitute the nation, and . . . the greater part of the opponents to the Bill did belong to, and might justly be denominated, a faction.[68]

Lord John was unrepentant, and the incident confirmed the King's suspicion that he was a dangerous Radical.

Grey's government did not resign (thus making constitutional history), but met their defeat in the lords by a vote of confidence in the commons moved by Lord Ebrington. Then they decided to reintroduce the bill in December. For weeks beforehand Grey and Althorp negotiated with the waverers in the house of lords, while Althorp and Lord John resourcefully drew up scheme after scheme for modifying the bill to satisfy

another impressible peer or pliable bishop. With every month
that passed Lord John became more and more the 'ideas' man
of the cabinet, while his only possible rival, Durham, overcome
by grief for his dead son, dropped out of the running. Durham's
colleagues resented his wayward conduct at cabinet, where the
expression of his countenance 'spoke volumes', while his voice
'uttered no arguments for their consideration'.[69] Now, early in
December, Durham complained that he had not been consulted: but, as Althorp said, 'I doubt whether he knows anything about the alterations, as he will not allow anybody to tell
him what they are.'[70]

Had Durham been willing to listen, he would have learned
first that the ministry had finally given up their attempt to
make the house of commons smaller, with the effect of reducing
schedule B, and secondly that they had abandoned the population tables in the census of 1821 as a means of arriving at their
schedules. Instead, they adopted from the census of 1831 a new
criterion of the number of houses in each borough (as being less
liable to fraud than the number of the inhabitants), and coupled
it with the amount paid in assessed taxes. The new statistics
were collected in a hurry, and Lord John was due to introduce
the third bill on 12 December. Nine of the reports needed for
compiling the schedules were not to hand until the morning of
the twelfth, and at five o'clock Lord John was still working on
them. The speaker looked for him to open the debate, 'but he
was absent, and half an hour passed away before he made his
appearance, looking very pale, and . . . feeling very ill.'[71] His
reception was cool, but he carried on as if nothing had happened, and when he began none of his colleagues knew exactly
which boroughs had been reprieved and which condemned.

The bill had been reconstructed to conciliate the house of lords,
but it still contained schedule A and the £10 householder
franchise and it passed its second reading in the commons in
December. The main interest of the months that followed lay in
its passage through the lords. Grey's position was not an easy
one; he dare not risk another failure after a refusal to create
peers, and the waverers threatened that if he created peers they,
in turn, would vote against the bill. In the cabinet the decisive
voice was Althorp's, and there is no need to do more than summarise Lord John's part. His voice was given, as we would

expect, for haste and for decision. In February he urged Grey
to try out the ground with resolutions, before bringing in the
bill: 'If they are hostile or tricky you must play your honours
forthwith'.[72] In March he pointed out that if there had to be a
creation, Tavistock, who was already heir to a title, would be as
unexceptionable as any.[73] Finally, in a letter which is not dated
he suggested that until the lords passed the bill the commons
should vote the mutiny act for one month at a time.[74] In the
end it was not necessary to create peers. Moral pressure persuaded many to abstain and a few to change sides. Members of
the cabinet wrote to individual peers. Lord John himself wrote
to three: one voted for the bill, one abstained, and one voted
against it.[75] This time the lords passed the second reading on
14 April by 184 votes to 175.

But this was not quite the end of the story. In committee on
7 May Lord Lyndhurst moved for the disfranchising clauses to
be postponed until the enfranchising clauses had been considered. Grey then asked the King to create peers. The King
refused, and sent for Wellington instead. In old age Lord John
said that this was the only moment of real peril to the country
that he could recall in his whole life.[76] Ellice and Parkes set up
a 'committee of public safety' in Richmond Terrace,[77] and
Place coined the phrase 'to stop the duke go for gold'. But the
danger was soon over, for Peel having 'ratted'[78] once on the
catholic question dare not rat again, and Lord John sarcastic-
ally congratulated him on his refusal to serve in an administration 'into which honour could not enter'.[79] Wellington gave
way, and the King agreed to create peers. They were not needed.
The bill went through unaltered and became law on 7 June 1832.
Many years later Lord John thought it very doubtful

whether the manner in which the vote of the House of Lords was
nullified by the compulsory absence of a great many of the majority was not more perilous for their authority than the creation of
peers . . . a House of Lords sympathising with the people at large,
and acting in concurrence with the enlightened state of the prevailing wish, represents far better the dignity of the House . . . than
a majority got together by the long supremacy of one party in the
State, eager to show its ill-will by rejecting Bills of small importance, but afraid to appear . . . in face of a measure which has
attracted the ardent sympathy of public opinion.[80]

He had cause to know: the Reform Act of 1832 did nothing to solve the problem of the relations between the houses, and the chief victim of the continuing ill-will of the Tory majority in the lords was Lord John himself.

After the bill became law on 7 June 1832 there was still much to do. Jeffrey took charge of the Reform Bill for Scotland, Stanley took charge of the Reform Bill for Ireland, and Lord John took charge of the boundaries bill. In addition there was a bill for curtailing bribery at elections. It was humdrum work, but it was also a summer of triumph. In an article on Grey and Spencer, written in 1845, Lord John said that the Tories had been wrong in thinking that the bill could be rejected, the Whigs had been wrong in foreboding failure for so large a measure, and the Radicals had been wrong in thinking that 'so large a ruin must lead to a more uniform construction. The authors of the plan were alone justified by the event.'[81] Allow him his moment of self-congratulation. The passage of four more Reform Acts in 1867, 1884, 1918 and 1928 has emphasised the status of the act of 1832 as the Great Reform Act.

CHAPTER VI

The Condition of Ireland Question, 1832–4

AFTER the Reform Bill became law, the eager spirits in the cabinet met to discuss what was to be done next.[1] 'There was a feeling that everything was to be reformed',[2] and Lord John confessed to Palmerston that he found it difficult to play the part of a cautious minister.[3] But what was Lord John himself to reform? From his own office he could do no more than provide allotment gardens for seventy Chelsea pensioners,[4] and he began to look about him for something more to do.

The question which was worthy of a reformed parliament was Ireland, with its huge catholic population and its tiny minority of protestant landlords. Devotion to Ireland was something Lord John had grown up with. In 1824 he applauded when one of Moore's poems gave 'all the Orangemen the jaundice with spleen'.[5] In 1826 his brother William called his attention to

a noble field of ambition and utility opened to a Statesman. It is Ireland, suffering, ill-used Ireland, the gratitude of millions, the applause of the world would attend the Man who would rescue this poor Country . . .[6]

In June 1831 Lord John himself said, 'When I am told, that the government of a country does not affect the condition of its people, I say, look to Ireland.'[7] It was a hint for the future.

The chief cause of complaint in Ireland was the church. There were three churches, the roman catholic, the presbyterian, and the Church of (England in) Ireland. Four-fifths of the population were roman catholic, one-tenth were presbyterian, and one-tenth belonged to the established church. Yet the Church of Ireland was both richly endowed, and in law entitled to tithe from the entire population. It is the chief stain upon the reputation of Sir Robert Peel that, in the 1820s, he did all he could to maintain both the established church and the orange ascendancy, and it is the glory of Lord John Russell's career that, in the 1830s, he tried to give the Irish what they had been promised at the union, and what, even without any promise, might have been called natural justice.

In the context of the Reform Bill Grey's Irish appointments may have been wise, but to the Irish they came as a challenge. Anglesey had been lord lieutenant under Wellington, and Stanley, the new chief secretary, had talents enough for any post, but a careless imperiousness that ought to have disqualified him from an Irish one. Stanley's measures tended 'to exasperate and inflame'.[8] In 1831 the government resorted to the use of troops and police to collect the tithes, and brought in an Irish arms act. In 1832 Stanley introduced a tithe composition act, which did not, as he claimed, abolish tithes for ever, but converted the tithe from a payment in kind to a payment in money, and the government undertook the large and open-ended commitment of advancing tithe monies to the incumbents, and recovering them if it could. Grey's government had brought Ireland to its worst state since the union. Even the Irish Reform Bill, the first draft of which was made by Duncannon with the object of securing an electorate proportioned to the new electorate in England,[9] was taken over by Stanley and modified until it left Ireland with only one person in 115 enfranchised compared with one in 24 in England.[10] The one measure of Stanley's which Lord John approved of was the Irish education act of 1831, which, if it did not altogether succeed in creating a system of undenominational schools supported by the state, did provide schools within which an increasing number of children (107,000 in 1833 and 355,000 ten years later)[11] learned to read and write.

The tension between Lord John and Stanley must have been apparent from the moment Grey brought the two men into the cabinet in May 1831. There was no point in risking a break-up until the Reform Bill was passed, but within a few days of its reaching the statute book Lord John told the house that he thought the established church in Ireland too large both for the work it had to do and for its own safety.[12] Thereafter his behaviour goes through two periods. Until May 1834 he and Stanley were still in the same cabinet, and in this period his public utterances must be compared with what he said in private.

After May 1834 he was unmuzzled and could say what he thought.

Everyone knew that something must be done about the Irish church, and the decisive question was, as Althorp said, 'whether the whole present revenues of the Church in Ireland are to be kept sacred for the Protestant Church or whether any part shall be in future diverted to other purposes'.[13] In the autumn of 1832 the cabinet met to consider Stanley's Irish church bill. Stanley proposed to reduce the number of sees from twenty-two to twelve, to abolish church cess, and in order to supply the deficiency to introduce a graduated tax on all clerical incomes over £200. In what became known later as clause 147 he provided that upon the renewal of the leases of the bishops' lands, the increment from rising land values should be creamed off and put into a fund. It was around the uses to which this fund should be put that argument took place first in the cabinet, and then in parliament. Following the principle that nothing was to be 'alienated' from the church Stanley proposed to apply this fund to the augmentation of small livings and the establishment of new ones.

Lord John, on the other hand, did not believe that any amount of extra money would enable an anglican clergyman to convert an Irish peasant, and both he and Althorp wanted to see the surplus revenues of the established church put to useful purposes like the schools set up under Stanley's act of 1831. But Grey took the view that however much the Whigs might think the Church of England and the Church of Ireland were two, they would have to deal with the matter in an united parliament,[14] and he threw his weight behind Stanley. The next day Lord John wrote angrily to Grey:

I set out on the principle that a clergy ought to teach religion. It follows that when there neither are nor will be any, or more than an infinitely small fraction of, Protestants of the Established Church, it is not necessary or useful to have a clergyman of that Church.

This seems no very extravagant proposition, but I should be content not to insist upon it were it not that the disorders of Ireland, at the present moment, hinge upon this very question; and you have to govern by military law in order to maintain the reverse of my proposition, viz. that the incomes of the Church should be devoted exclusively to the use of one-tenth of the population.[15]

He ended with an offer of resignation.

What followed illustrates both Lord John's uncertainty and his openness. Before sending his letter to Grey, he showed it to Althorp. Althorp sent Lord John away to think it over, and warned Grey what was in the offing.[16] Five days later Lord John forwarded his original letter to Grey, enclosed in a second in which he explained what had happened since. He left it to Grey to decide whether he ought to resign or not.[17]

Grey answered that any attempt to apply Lord John's principles would lead to the 'complete overthrow' of the government, and knowing his man, advised him to have a word with Lord Holland.[18] Holland went calmly into the whole case, and soothed Lord John by an appeal to his vanity.

> The resignation of the mover of the Reform Bill just at the moment when the manner in which that great experiment would work was about to be tried would . . . quite dishearten those . . . who relied on its wisdom and good consequences because proposed by you, and likely to be carried into effect under your auspices and superintendence.[19]

He urged Lord John to stand by Althorp, and Tavistock appealed to Lord John 'to continue in the same Boat with Althorp, and to sink or swim with him'.[20]

Lord John remained in the cabinet, feeling that he had been overpersuaded. Four years later he told Howick, with aggressive tactlessness, that he had never found the cabinet gained much in Grey's day by meeting early: 'we never settled any thing that way except Stanley's Church bill, and a precious bad bill it was'.[21] In the meantime Althorp repeated in November 1832 what he had already told Grey in August, that he thought Stanley ought to be moved to another office.[22] But Grey would not give way to pressure, and when Durham made a second and more personal challenge to Stanley, Grey made it clear that anyone who did not like Stanley's bill could go.

At this point Lord John took pains to avoid any misunderstanding. On 30 December he wrote to Stanley that in Stanley's notes on the Irish church bill he found it more than once stated that the Cabinet agreed upon a principle in respect to the Irish church and that principle was non-alienation. I lose not a moment in declaring to you that I never heard such a principle mooted and am no party to its adoption . . . What I understood was that the plan went upon the practical expediency of establishing protestant clergymen throughout the country. Of that expediency I was not convinced, but gave my reluctant assent to the plan, *as an experiment*, but with very faint hopes of its success.[23]

Stanley met him in the same spirit, and twelve days later Lord John wrote again:

You describe our position thus: 'No member of the government is committed upon the abstract right of Parliament to alienate the church property: . . . but the Govt as a whole, and each individual member of it stands committed to a plan (in the main) which does not propose to alienate, and which limits the appropriation to church purposes: and we are pledged to resist any amendment which may be proposed by others, and which may proceed upon the principle of alienation'. Now these are not exactly the terms I should have used, but I do not wish to cavil, and I agree that the statement is in substance correct.[24]

In December 1832, while the cabinet was being forced into line behind Stanley, the enlarged electorate was returning a house of commons sympathetic to the views of Lord John. Lord John himself was returned for South Devonshire, and the Whigs came back about 300 strong. Together with about 100 Radicals, and 70 or more out of the 105 Irish, they made a body of reformers so large that Althorp told Grey that unless the government took a firm lead in popular measures reform would lead to revolution,[25] and confided to his father that Ireland was the rock they would split on.[26] Lord John did not take much part in the session of 1833, but he was bound to support both Stanley's Irish church bill and the new coercion bill. With a kind of courage he would have been better without, he spoke more freely than he need in favour of the coercion bill, and contrasted the inspired resistance of the American patriots with the cowardly atrocities of the Irish.[27] When the church bill came on the Radicals wanted to amend clause 147 in order to appropriate the surplus revenues of the Irish church for useful purposes. The government took alarm and dropped the clause, and Lord John defended their action on the ground that the country could not stand a revolution every year. If the house was to enter into a contest with the lords, 'they should do it for something worth contesting. The present was but the shadow of a claim, to prosecute which would be risking the peace and tranquillity of the country, for the sake of an abstract principle.'[28] These were words that Lord John would later have preferred to forget, and it is not surprising that at this point O'Connell, who had started the session by saying that he had lost all patience with the base, brutal, and bloody Whigs, accused the King's ministers of having sold their principles to keep their places.

Could O'Connell have seen Lord John's private correspondence he might have spoken differently. When clause 147 was given up Lord John wrote to Grey to say that he would agree to abandon that part of the bill which carried the imputation of spoliation, provided Grey did all he could to carry the remainder and to create sixteen or eighteen peers.[29] Grey did not create the peers, but he did at last make changes in the Irish administration. Anglesey was succeeded by Wellesley, and Stanley, who went to the colonial office, was replaced by Littleton – according to Greville, at Lord John's suggestion.[30] But this re-arrangement was a failure, for Stanley continued somehow to dominate the cabinet's debates on Ireland. When this became apparent, Lord John wrote to Althorp, at the end of the session, that he was more than ever convinced

> how unfit you and I are to act with the present Cabinet. But I wish to do nothing rashly, so I will wait till the 1st Nov., when my mind will be made up – for I hate pottering. But I believe you will think with me, whatever you may think right to do.[31]

Lord John had now become immersed in the Irish problem, and at the end of the session in 1833 he went to Ireland for the first time since 1806. He landed on 5 September, and stayed until 18 October at least. He kept a journal of the first ten days of his tour, from which we learn that, in addition to conferring with the officials in Dublin Castle, he dined with the officers of the guards, met two officers attached to the police and two gentlemen from the Bank of Ireland, saw the college at Maynooth, met one other catholic priest, and inspected one model farm and four cottages.[32] It does not sound much, but was there one other English statesman, not connected with Ireland by office, who had seen as much? After those first ten days Lord John stayed with Duncannon at Bessborough and with Ebrington near Waterford, visited Cork, and ended up at Belfast, where the author of the Reform Act was entertained at a public dinner, at which he was alarmed to find many Repealers.[33]

From Ireland Lord John wrote to Lord Holland of what he had seen, and to Althorp and Grey of what he thought ought to be done next. He found, to his surprise, that the coercion act 'worked very well',[34] and that no unpopularity attached to the Irish M.P.s who had voted for it.[35] He attributed this to the fact that it 'has this merit over other bills of the sort, that it is not left to the execution of Magistrates. The Court Martial has terrified very much.'[36] Even so, with true liberality, he told Grey that Ireland 'resembles nothing so much as Spain in 1810, in the occupation of the French'.[37] His main recommendations were: first, to promote the formation of a party favourable to the government by even-handedly repressing the orange magistracy of the North and the repeal agitation of the South; second, to put an end to the present system under which exorbitant rents were exacted 'by the distress of the landlord and from the distress of the tenant', by a scheme for enabling the crown to purchase land on a large scale; and third, to provide for all three religions from state funds. This third proposal became known as concurrent endowment, and in dealing with it, he trod warily, in his memorandum to his colleagues, upon the subject of appropriation:

> Future inquiry may lead to some diminution of the revenues of the Established Church after all its proper uses have been provided for. But this subject requires long and patient investigation before any decision is made.[38]

But these two sentences of studied moderation mis-stated Lord John's real thoughts, which were set down in his diary on his third day in Ireland – 'after all it must come to this – the Catholic Clergy must be paid, and paid out of the revenues of the P. church, which are ample for that purpose.'[39] We have here the outline of the policies Lord John was to follow in what he once called 'the great and holy cause' of Ireland[40] between

1835 and 1852. Only one thing was missing from the letters he wrote to his colleagues, and that was the abolition of the lord lieutenancy. But he had already noted in his journal that 'A Chief Secretary in the cabinet, without a Lord Lieutenant would be much better.'[41]

Lord John had also hit upon what was to remain his favourite method of approaching these objects, which were to be accomplished under a reform of the tax system. He sent Althorp the plan of a budget 'which will immortalize you'. Ten million pounds were to be raised in England and £2m in Ireland by a tax on property and income. Althorp could then do away with the house tax and with half the poor rate in England, abolish church tithes, church rates and grand jury cess in Ireland, and still have £½m left over for the support of the catholic clergy and the relief of the Irish poor. The plan involved switching resources from England to Ireland, and as Lord John light-heartedly said, it did away with fifty difficult questions, and there were only three objections, Scotland, the church, and the fundlords.[42]

The wonder is that another eight months passed before Lord John came to an open breach with Stanley. The main measures of the session of 1834 were a dissenters' marriage bill drafted by Althorp and introduced by Lord John, a church rates bill introduced by Althorp, the reconstruction of the English poor law, and a tithe bill and a new coercion bill for Ireland. The marriage bill would have allowed dissenters to celebrate marriages in their own chapels, and retained the calling of banns and the keeping of registers in the parish churches. It was badly received by the dissenters themselves, one of whom said, 'that the name of Lord John Russell was for ever disgraced',[43] and it was dropped. Althorp's church rates bill, which provided for church rates to be abolished and for an equivalent sum to be advanced to the church out of taxation, fared no better. Lord John argued that the whole community benefited from the order preached by an established church,[44] but the dissenters would have none of that, and the session ended with relations between the Whigs and the dissenters at their lowest point for many years.

Lord John had little to do with the conception of the poor law amendment act. In his *Recollections* he made the extraordinarily insipid remark that 'A commission had been appointed on this subject, and their labours had for result a valuable report',[45] and he spoke to the bill only as a matter of form. That being so, it is interesting that subsequently, when the main burden of carrying the act into effect, and beating down the opposition to it, fell upon Lord John, he defended the act with conviction, even when it became clear, in 1837 and 1841, that it was electorally disadvantageous. Lord John accepted the wages-fund theory of the classical economists, and in 1846 he spelled it out in what were perhaps the most rigorous terms ever used by a nineteenth-century politician. He began with a judgement upon the Speenhamland system.

> By this system, society was placed in the greatest peril. According to the natural distribution of wages and labour, a young man earning the value of his work, is obliged to calculate, before he marries, whether those earnings will enable him to support a wife, and bring up a family of children . . . This forethought marks him for a reasonable being . . . But when his wages are measured by the lowest amount of money on which he can live, and the provision for a married couple is made by the parish, all motive for provident forethought is taken away . . . It is obvious that such a system must produce more labourers than could find profitable employment . . . Forty or fifty labourers were to be found in a parish, whom no employer wished to hire; who lowered the general value of labour, . . . and by absorbing a large sum in poor-rates, diminished the whole fund applicable to the commodity which the employer wishes to buy.[46]

As home secretary, Lord John administered the system with humanity, and winked at outdoor relief in the North. But he met all appeals for a change in the 1834 system with a firmness of refusal that does not accord with his reputation for open-minded impressibility. Lord John really did think there was a danger of hungry mouths eating up the nation's capital, and in this at least he had a majority of each successive house of commons with him.

Stanley's Irish tithe act of 1832 had settled nothing. The Irish still refused to pay, and threw the burden on to the British taxpayer. In 1834–5 there was a wide measure of agreement among the leaders of the Whig and Tory parties that the best thing to do would be to ask the Irish to pay a percentage only of

the composition under the act of 1832, and to interest the landlords in collecting the reduced amount along with the rent.
Only O'Connell pointed out that though this new 'rent-charge'
might mitigate the church problem, it would be bound to aggra-
vate the landlord problem, and the point of difference between
Grey and Peel could have been kept to the negotiable one of the
exact percentage the rent charge should bear to the composition. But the mass of Grey's supporters in the house of commons,
having failed to secure appropriation of the endowed revenues
in 1833, were now determined to force the issue on tithes.
Littleton's tithe bill of 1834 asked the Irish to pay 80 per cent,
and said nothing about appropriation. That is to say it went
upon Stanley's principles, and when it came before the cabinet
in February Lord John was up in arms.

Lord John circulated a memorandum on the wretchedness
and ignorance of the people of Ireland, and said that there was
no part of Europe outside Russia so barbarous.[47] But it was not
at all clear at some points what Lord John was getting at – a
sure sign that he was feeling helpless, and that he feared he was
being outmanoeuvred by Stanley. Lord John asked the cabinet
to appoint a commission with power to recommend the appropriation of surplus tithe revenues to the educational needs of
the inhabitants of Ireland, and said that he would not agree to
the tithe bill unless the commission were appointed. Stanley
replied that he would go if it were. The cabinet separated, and
pressure was put upon Lord John, who let fly at Lord Holland:

> I have read your long lecture and will only say in reply, Why not
> preach to Stanley? . . . I will tell you. Because Stanley is deter-
> mined – because he says that if such a measure is passed, the
> sooner the ministry breaks up the better – and you none of you
> *dare* to urge him to change his opinion.

But in the end Lord John gave way, because, as he told Stanley
five months later, driving you out was 'an extremity I wished to
avoid, if possible, till the commencement of next session'.[49]

Ever since October 1832 Grey's cabinet had been balanced
on a knife's edge, between Stanley who would not allow them to
commit themselves to what he called alienation and Lord John
called appropriation, and Lord John who would not allow them
to commit themselves against it. But a majority of their col-

leagues took Stanley's threats to resign more seriously than they took Lord John's. Nothing tells upon a frail man more than this, and on 6 May Lord John thought, and as he was later to admit mistakenly,[50] that Stanley in his speech on the second reading of the tithe bill had crossed the cease-fire line and committed the government against appropriation. Lord John at once rose to announce that in his opinion

> the revenues of the Church of Ireland were larger than necessary for the religious and moral instruction of the persons belonging to that Church . . . [and that] when Parliament had vindicated the property to tithes, he should then be prepared to assert his opinion with regard to their appropriation

even if it led to a separation from his colleagues.[51] It was little more than he had said in July 1832, but it was said to a much more militant house of commons which had known for a long time that this was an issue upon which ministers were at odds. Lord John's speech was loudly cheered by the government's supporters, and Stanley passed his famous, and very good-humoured note along the bench to Ellice that John Russell had upset the coach. A few days later, Ward, a backbencher, gave notice of a motion to reduce the temporal possessions of the Church of Ireland. An attempt was made to patch the cabinet up by the appointment of a commission of inquiry to discover what the revenues were and whether they were too large. But Stanley thought this would commit him to the principle of appropriation, and at the end of May he, Graham, Richmond and Ripon resigned, as Althorp had feared ever since December 1832 that they would do.[52]

No more important event occurred in Lord John's career, for Stanley's resignation opened up to Lord John the road to the top. It is a striking fact that even after the part Lord John played in 1831–2 nobody supposed he could lead a party. It is an even more striking fact that after Stanley's policies had kept Grey's cabinet in hot water for two years after the Reform Bill, nobody supposed that he could not lead one. Nothing shook his colleagues' faith in him, and early in 1834, when Disraeli confided to Melbourne that it was his ambition to become prime minister, he received the reply that there was no chance of that in their time: 'It is all arranged and settled. Nobody can compete with Stanley . . . Stanley will be the next Prime Minister, you will see.'[53]

It has often been suggested that when Lord John upset the coach he did it in order to drive his rival out, and to secure the lead of the Whig party in the house of commons whenever it should please God to make Lord Spencer die and to make Lord Althorp Lord Spencer. Grey was furious, and came close to an accusation when he wrote that Lord John's declaration was 'very unkind to me. A stronger objection to it I am unwilling to state.'[54] Deliberate ambitious calculation formed no large part in Lord John's make-up, and was certainly not such a large one as spontaneous combustion, but in 1834 Lord John was tense and it would be absurd to suppose that there was nothing unpremeditated in his outburst. He cannot have been unaware that the great majority of the party thought with him and not with Stanley. It was common knowledge that Grey wanted to retire at the end of the session, and Liberals, Radicals, and O'Connellites were all afraid of a break-up, and were anxious to pass a resolution on the Irish church which would make it impossible for the Tories to come back. Lord John may well have foreseen Ward's motion coming, and in his letter of 28 May to Stanley, expressing admiration of his conduct in resigning, he said:

> My inclinations would have led me some time ago to retire . . . but having the greater number of our friends with me in opinion, I could not do so without a total dissolution of the government and the party . . . I feel quite sure that if this vexatious question should be once settled, it will be the anxious desire of our party that you should be in a position to take the lead when it shall fall vacant.[55]

Althorp, who, like Grey, was very angry with Lord John, also knew that he was in the right. As he told his father, the property of the Irish church was too great, and 'the House of Commons and a great majority of the people are convinced of it'.[56]

After Stanley's departure, Lord John was left unmuzzled, and on 2 June he asked and answered an oratorical question. 'Gentlemen asked what was the Government? He said the Government was the Government of Earl Grey, and of his noble friend the Chancellor of the Exchequer [Althorp], framed on the principle that reform was necessary in the Church of Ireland.'[57] Grey must have been horrified. This little-regarded paymaster of the forces appeared to have taken over the ministry, and on 23 June Lord John made his first deservedly celebrated speech on Ireland. Rising to the stirring and noble strain which the house was to hear again and again in the next seven years, he said that it was the duty of ministers to look deeper into the causes of the long-standing and permanent evils of that country.

> I am not prepared to continue the Government of Ireland without fully probing her condition. I am not prepared to propose Bills for coercion and the maintenance of a large force of military and police, without endeavouring to improve, as far as lies in my power, the condition of the people . . .[58]

Moore said that he recognised in this speech all that he had ever admired and loved in Lord John. Lord John himself said that 'there are occasions on which one must express one's feelings or sink into contempt'.[59] Here at last was the real Lord John, who a few days later was challenging Peel to say whether, if he were in office, he would have his own religion instilled into the Irish 'by troops of dragoons and heaps of Exchequer processes'.[60]

Lord John's coup was a factor in making Grey decide to quit. But nobody has ever suggested that Lord John had anything to do with the intrigue that actually led to Grey's going. Brougham began conspiring for the succession, and for this he was to be sentenced to a lifetime in the political wilderness. At his instance Littleton approached O'Connell with a promise to tone down the new coercion bill. But when the matter came before the cabinet the conspirators failed to get their way, and when ministers went on with the original bill, O'Connell told the house what had happened, and Grey resigned. The King sent for Melbourne, who as home secretary from 1830 to 1834 ought to have played a decisive part in settling the eternal disputes about Ireland in Grey's cabinet, and never did, and Lord John, seeing there was nothing more to be done that night, went off to the opera.[61]

Melbourne refused the King's request to form a Whig–Tory ministry, and went on with a wholly Whig one which lasted just

over three months. The chief importance of the period was that
it saw a change in the relations of the government with
O'Connell. It would be going too far to speak of an accommoda-
tion, but there was a willingness to abandon entrenched positions. Hitherto, Lord John himself had kept at a distance from
the Irish party, but when he went to Ireland in 1833 he noted
how by a mixture of good sense and good feeling O'Connell had
'conciliated the people who by religion and politics were most
opposed to him'.[62] Now, the proposed tithe rent charge was
lowered, at O'Connell's suggestion, from 80 per cent to 60 per
cent of the composition, and the clauses prohibiting political
meetings were, after all, omitted from the coercion bill. But this
was too much for Wellington and the Irish interest in the house
of lords, who passed the coercion bill, but threw out the tithe
bill. Politics were becoming a battle between the Irish and the
house of lords, with the hapless Whig party in the middle.

The beginning of the recess found ministers in a fever of
deliberation about Ireland. Lord John was all for 'a decided
course of policy' in place of the 'wretched, wavering, blunder-
ing course of policy which was adopted last session'.[63] But, like
other people, he found some difficulty in propounding one. In
August he was for making O'Connell an Irish judge, or even
attorney general. The first proposal might have been meant to
buy O'Connell off, but the second envisaged co-operation, and
it is clear that we are beginning to move towards the Lichfield
House compact. And yet, only a few days later, after hearing
Melbourne's reply, that O'Connell would not sink into being a
mere judge, and that if you made him attorney general he
would be your master,[64] Lord John was writing to Grey stig-
matising O'Connell's proposal for a central Liberal club as
'disgusting',[65] and telling Melbourne that he hoped no member
of the government would seek any intercourse with him.[66] It is
difficult to know what to make of all this, but Lord John seems
to have been in danger of allowing his opinions to take their
colour from the prejudices of the person he was addressing.
Fortunately it hardly mattered, for Melbourne's administration was quickly overtaken by events.

Early in November Spencer died, and Althorp went up to the
lords. Howick's first reaction was that Abercromby must be
leader, but he soon heard that both Ellice and Wood were in

favour of Lord John.[67] In fact, as Brougham said, the house 'may transfer as much or as little as they chuse, of their love and confidence to J. Russell, and I am clear they will give him quite enough to carry on the Govt.'[68] Melbourne agreed, and the only doubt concerned the King. The King recalled the 'whisper of a faction' speech, and feared Lord John would ally with O'Connell to attack the church. He had already told Melbourne in September that Lord John lacked both the abilities and the influence to lead, and that he would cut a wretched figure when opposed by both Peel and Stanley.[69] Now he heard Melbourne out, and then dismissed his ministers and sent for Wellington, who in turn sent for Peel from Italy. Melbourne had only just got the reins into his hands when his first riding lesson was over. Nobody has ever explained why he, who clung so tenaciously to office after 1837, quitted it so acquiescently in 1834.

CHAPTER VII

Lord John Russell

Next cool, and all unconscious of reproach,
Comes the calm 'Johnny who upset the coach'.
How formed to lead, if not too proud to please, –
His fame would fire you, but his manners freeze.[1]

THERE were marks of boyish gallantry in Lord John's letters
to Lady Anna Maria Stanhope just before she married Tavistock in 1808. Nine years later Lord John actually proposed to
Elizabeth Rawdon, and was refused, a couple of hours after his
brother William had proposed to her, and been accepted.[2] For
a long time thereafter Lord John remained single and lonely.
But when we ask what his private life was like, all is surmise.
There is a story that there were bastards, and that they were
shipped off to America. If this is true, then the secret has been
well kept. In one place only have I come across what might be
regarded as evidence. It occurs in a correspondence between
Joseph Parkes and Edward Ellice, both of whom knew Lord
John well. On 21 November 1853, when Lord John was busy
preparing another Reform Bill, Parkes, who was in practice as
a solicitor, wrote, can you believe it

> We had at our office on Saturday a case in which an old Country
> Gentleman left *103* Living *Bastards* and a Legacy to each! . . . No
> doubt Johnnie would bestow the Franchise on *all* the males (if he
> knew of the Monstrosity and being such a sure Fraegetter him-
> self) had he his will.[3]

Fraegetter is not a recognised word, but the meaning would
seem to be clear, and if there is any truth in all this, then it
seems unlikely that Lord John's liaisons took place very high up
the social scale. Mrs Clara Bolton, who enjoyed adultery for the
money, boasted of receiving franked letters from Johnny. But

there is nothing to suggest that she meant anything more than that he was keeping her up to date politically, and in any case, as Robert Blake says, there is something about her boast that 'does not quite ring true'.[4] At this level of society a lady might not have consented to have her bastards shipped off to the States. A servant girl, on the other hand, might have consented to this, and an affair with a servant might much more easily have escaped notice.

We know that Lord John admired Madame Durazzo and attended her in Milan, that he fancied Lady Holland's daughter Mary, and that in 1829 he wanted to marry Lady Emily Cowper. Lady Emily was just out and was the leading favourite of the town, very natural, lively and goodnatured.[5] Hearing he was bent on marriage, William wrote to Lord John warning him to

> remember when once in, you can't get out, and if it don't suit it is 'Hell upon Earth'. You are a man of settled pursuits and habits and must have a wife that will take an interest in them – a gadding, flirting, dressing, ball-going Wife would be the Devil.[6]

Madame Durazzo regretted 'that the *nice girl* should be so much younger than yourself',[7] and Spencer Walpole says that Lord John steeled his heart, and resisted the nice girl's fascinations.[8] It seems much more likely that Lord John proposed in 1829, and that Lady Emily turned him down. She preferred Lord Ashley, to whom she became engaged early in 1830. On 20 April 1830 Lord John wrote to Lady Holland that he had seen them:

> Lord Ashley and Ly Emily were much loving as might have been expected – he is the most so of the two, but she seems very well pleased with his devotion. I believe him to be an excellent and amiable man, and I hope it may all turn out right.[9]

If this last phrase sounds ungenerous, it is as well to remember that Lord John was not the only one to doubt whether a marriage which cut right across political connections would work. Lord Ashley and Lady Emily were married on 10 June 1830. Lord John's attachment had almost certainly gone deep, and anyone who wonders why he never took a lead on the factory question must bear this in mind. Shaftesbury, who had been preferred, could condescend a little to Lord John, and treat his lack of commitment to the factory cause more leniently than he did Peel's.

As Lord John tried to forget that Lady Emily now lay in the arms of a taller man, he threw himself into the Reform Bill. In the course of its passing he was a good deal in the company of the three daughters of Sir Thomas Hardy (Nelson's captain) and Lady Hardy. All three came to the first dinner party he gave in his official residence on 11 June 1831.[10] The acquaintance ripened into what Spencer Walpole referred to privately as a romance with 'Miss Hardy, or rather with two of the Miss Hardys'.[11] Lord John preferred Emily, and when she refused him turned to Louisa. Fearful of a second rebuff he allowed William to propose for him. William was not tactful, Louisa was not flattered, and Lord John was still a single man when Melbourne asked him to take the lead in the house of commons.

At that time the King was not alone in his doubts about Lord John. When Lord John wrote to Grey that he was 'rash enough' to try and lead the house of commons,[12] Grey doubted whether he would be able 'to support the fatigue . . . of duties, to which Althorp with his immoveable temper and strong constitution was hardly equal',[13] and warned Ellice that Lord John must learn 'a little discretion, both in speaking and writing'.[14] After William IV had dismissed his ministers, and Melbourne had told the retiring cabinet that he thought Lord John ought to lead the opposition, Lord John's father wrote:

> I conclude that your decision is made to take what is called the *Lead* of the opposition in the House of Commons. I most sincerely regret it, for I am quite convinced that neither your health nor strength of constitution are equal to this irksome and laborious task.[15]

Tavistock, too, trembled for his brother's health,[16] while Lord Holland raised more serious considerations:

> John . . . is and must be leader, and he has many of the best qualifications of one; but yet there are certain requisites . . . in which he is lamentably deficient . . . He takes no pains, nor, if he did, has the knack, to collect the opinions of others or to enlist their vanity, their ambition, their interests, and their affections in giving effect to them.[17]

It was not an auspicious beginning. Everyone agreed that

Lord John must lead, and yet those who knew him best doubted his capacity the most. In order to understand why, we must consider in more detail what Lord John was like. In 1835 he was forty-three, and his life was, as it turned out, exactly half over.

The first thing about Lord John was his high birth. Without it he could never have become prominent. As Parkes put it: 'Johnny in a U.S. county meeting would not be a second rate speaker; but he is a Russell – a Lord . . .'[18] To be a Russell was to be identified with English history, and as Lord John put it to his brother (then the duke) in 1841:

> In all times of popular movement the Russells have been on the 'forward' side. At the Reformation the first Earl of Bedford, in Charles the First's days Francis the great Earl, in Charles the Second's William, Lord Russell, in later times Francis Duke of Bedford – my father – you – and lastly myself.[19]

This devotion to the family ideal was one of the things that kept Lord John going, but it was also a handicap. To be both a Russell and a Lord was to have a position in society, certainly, but an exclusive one. It meant being a Russell among lords and a lord among the people. The result was that everyone from Bulwer in the 1830s to the *Spectator* in the 1870s was struck by the fact that Lord John was proud.[20] As the present Duke of Bedford has said, 'My family have always thought themselves slightly grander than God'.[21] Time and again Lord John conveyed the impression that he thought he had a divine right both to lecture the aristocracy and to rule the people. Neither the aristocracy nor the people were impressed, and then, feeling himself held at a distance by both parties, Lord John was tempted to make a virtue out of standing in the middle and being known to have nothing to do with either. This is what Jowett meant when he said in 1861 that high rank had the opposite effect with Lord John from what it did with most people – it 'prevented his being a man of the world'.[22]

Pride separated Lord John from other men but not to the extent that shyness did. If it was not genetic, his shyness presumably originated in his physique, which led to his being taken away from school. It was perpetuated by his aversion to late hours and hot rooms, which shut him off from society. By the time the Whigs came into office, it was incurable. Being both proud and shy, he had become self-centred, and 'a little careless of the personal feelings of others'.[23] Stories of the want even of an ordinary polish to his manners are legion. To give but one example:

> Once, at a concert at Buckingham Palace, he was seen to get up suddenly, turn his back on the Duchess of Sutherland, by whom he had been sitting, walk to the remotest part of the room, and sit down by the Duchess of Inverness. When questioned afterwards . . . he said, 'I could not have sate any longer by that great fire; I should have fainted.' 'Oh, that was a very good reason for moving; but I hope you told the Duchess of Sutherland why you left her.' 'Well no. I don't think I did that. But I told the Duchess of Inverness why I came and sate by her!'[24]

It is not unusual for a shy man to present an appearance of equanimity and self-possession. Lady William found Lord John sanguine, and chaffed him on his habit of saying '*I suppose it is all right*' whenever things went wrong.[25] Le Marchant referred to Lord John's usual coolness and self-possession.[26] Sydney Smith, who knew Lord John well enough to have known better, found classic words to express the impression Lord John made. He said that Lord John

> would perform the operation for the stone, build St. Peter's, or assume . . . the command of the Channel Fleet; and no one would discover by his manner that the patient had died, the church tumbled down, and the Channel Fleet been knocked to atoms.[27]

But in fact Lord John was desperately unsure of himself, and it is a measure of his insecurity that forty years later he defended himself from this charge of Sydney Smith's, which, he said, had been made in a witty mood but with 'an angry temper'.[28]

All his life Lord John seemed to be demanding from his colleagues the unmixed praise and approbation that only a mother can give. In no way was this more evident than in his concern to get the credit – not for what he had not done, he was far too scrupulous for that – but for what he had done. It is not an endearing quality. At the very moment we have now reached, Lord John was unable to resist challenging Durham's claim to have fathered the Reform Bill.[29] Brougham's indiscretions in the *Edinburgh Review*, and Durham's north-country speeches did not

upset Althorp, nor need they have upset a man half as steady as
he. Durham had left the cabinet by the front door, slamming it
behind him, and was now trying to force his way in again at the
back, by making a bid for Radical support. But Lord John had
nothing to fear: men would recognise Durham as the unstable
opportunist that he was, and history would do justice both to
him and to Lord John. But Lord John could not let it alone, and
the incident is revealing. Grey thought it was a controversy that
ought never to have been started, and asked him not to answer
Durham in public.[30] Lord John had loyalty enough to respond
to this appeal. But he complained to Lord Holland at having
had to let Durham have the merit of a plan 'nine-tenths of
which was mine',[31] and when he had received an answer, wrote
again:

> I do not think you have much ground for accusing me of im-
> patience or vanity. Had you been the author of a great measure of
> this kind, I doubt whether you would have borne patiently that
> another should . . . have the credit of it . . .[32]

Lord John could keep his feelings in check for a time but he
could never conquer them, and thrèe years later he published
his side of the story. In a letter to Lord Lansdowne justifying his
action he said that

> the King and Ministry having ceased to live, and the Bill being
> continually quoted agst me as Lord Durham's bill, on which my
> opinion was of no weight or authority, I thought it time at last
> to tell my Constituents the real facts.[33]

Being so unsure of himself, Lord John rose to anything which
reflected either upon his honour or upon his sagacity. It says
something for his strange lack of understanding of other people
that he was stung equally easily to defend either, for there were
few occasions when his honour was in doubt, and many when
his sagacity was. He was equally easily led, therefore, into defending what needed no defence, and what was indefensible.
Melbourne, a shrewd judge, told William IV in 1834 that Lord
John was 'utterly incapable of anything of an underhand or
clandestine character'.[34] Much later, the *Daily News* said Lord
John was so open that 'If he had been engaged in the Gun-
powder Treason, he would have walked down to the Houses of

Parliament with the matches in his hand and the barrel of gun-powder under his arm.'[35] It is a pity, therefore, that Lord John was so sensitive. He was for ever drafting angry letters of self-vindication, most of which, to do him justice, on reflection, he did not send. But many of his speeches are spoilt by his having thought fit to rebut some insignificant charge of inconsistency. At all times what entirely escaped him was Althorp's easy assurance that men would have confidence in him.

As for a man's sagacity, that is to be defended by his showing that he had grounds for his decisions. Lord John sometimes found the way, but not often. Depending upon his humour, he justified a course of action which he already knew to have been a mistake (like his resignation in January 1855), or confessed his mistake too readily, and asked to be allowed to carry on as before. As he put it in his *Recollections*, 'I have committed many errors, some of them very gross blunders'.[36] The people of England no doubt are, as he said, forbearing and forgiving, but Lord John's light-hearted confessions of error did not earn him all the forgiveness he hoped, because they seemed to assume that however many mistakes he had made he ought still to be allowed to govern the country.

It follows that Lord John was not the easiest of colleagues. He was like the boy who always wanted to play with the others, and he could not bear being left out in the cold. His mind would then busy itself with some fancied slight, and rush on to threats of resignation. Then would come the outburst, and the release of other trivial, hoarded and irrelevant complaints. After Lord John had been soothed, grateful at being back in favour again, he would become too warm, and accommodate himself to opinions with which he did not wholly agree. Then, as he ceased to oscillate between excessive mistrust and over-eager bonhomie, he would return to his own opinion, and a little bit of the original bitterness would remain. Between each cause of tension he would become himself again – good-humoured on top.

To vagaries of behaviour caused by temper, Lord John added those caused by intellect. He possessed a very quick mind: be-yond all other men, said Lecky, 'he had the gift of seizing rapidly in every question the central argument, the essential fact or distinction . . .'[37] and nobody could make a more masterly summary of a problem. But all too often his quickness also prevented him understanding other people's opinions, in the same way that shyness prevented him understanding their feelings. As befitted a man educated at Edinburgh, Lord John believed in rational discussion. But paradoxically, as an ideologically committed Whig, he also believed that on any fundamental issue there was only one conclusion to which rational men could come. More than any other Whig, Lord John believed Whig beliefs. He brought a touch of Woburn dogma to the discussions of Holland House, and the consequence was that sometimes Lord John was quick because he had a quick mind, and at other times because he had a rigid one.

The results have puzzled people ever since. There were practical issues, both in the house and in the cabinet, to which Lord John brought an open mind. This is one reason why colleagues found him so impressible. Because he might easily be struck by the arguments first of one speaker and then of another, they also found him wavering. And further, because he went on thinking after a meeting was over, they occasionally found him vacillating. But every so often Lord John did not need to listen to a debate at all, and had very little sympathy with slower fellows who did. His colleagues were then confronted, not with the pliability but with the impatience of his mind. He behaved as though he expected the mere statement of his opinions to convert the opposition. When it did not, he became cross.

The combination of Lord John's personality with Lord John's intellect could lead to results which were not always easy to interpret. Either ill temper or intellectual conviction might lead him to lay down a dead body one day, and either excess of warmth at being received back into the fold, or conversion as the result of discussion might lead him to change his mind the next. But on some occasions personality and intellect told the same way. Consider, for example, the brevity of his letters. This was early remarked upon. In 1819 Playfair wrote that: 'I was glad once more to see your handwriting, tho I had the mortification to find there was nearly as much of it on the outside of the letter as on the inside.'[38] Having once been noticed by friends, who were amused by it, this became a habit, and Palmerston realised that it was a thing Lord John was not above being flattered on. Your letter 'contains in a few words the Pith

of the Whole Matter, Past present and future', he wrote when
he wanted to humour Lord John.[39] But the truth is that both
the selfishness of a shy man and the quickness of a dogmatic intellect inclined Lord John to write short letters. The *Spectator*
saw this when it referred to 'that crispness which comes equally
of sense and pride, which is at once pithy from the former
quality and curt from the latter'.[40] There is no need to follow
the fourth Lord Holland so far as to condemn Lord John's
letters as flippant, epigrammatic and offensive,[41] but it is clear
that Lord John sometimes wrote a short letter because he was
being careless of another man's feelings, and at other times because he was being heedless of another man's opinions. His
friends, like his enemies, often felt they had been snubbed.

It is better to be brief than long-winded, but what was missing
in Lord John was the judgement as to when it was in place. The
consequences were not confined to wounded feelings. Lord
John's abrupt manner made it difficult for others to distinguish
a considered opinion from a judgement off the cuff. On the
Reform Bill his opinion deserved respect. On Ireland in 1832–4,
his colleagues may perhaps already have suspected that he spoke
from good feelings rather than from extensive knowledge. Thereafter, the longer he stayed in office, the more difficult it became
for his colleagues to tell whether he was being serious or not.
His brevity prevented his being understood, and ultimately contributed much to his loss of weight in his own cabinet.

When Grey said that Lord John must learn a little discretion, he was thinking not so much of the effect Lord John had
upon his colleagues, as the effect he had upon people at large,
including of course the opposition. Mixing so little among men,
Lord John still carried about with him, in addition to the rashness of inexperience, the certitude of the closet. He was for freedom and against slavery, he was for knowledge and against
ignorance, and he was for humanity and against torture and
cruelty. So far so good. But in exactly the same way he was for
Whigs and against Tories, for protestantism and against roman
catholicism. Consequently he was not a reconciler, and he was
always in danger, as Normanby put it, of 'raising great prejudices for an inadequate result'.[42] He could rouse the Whigs, but
only at the expense of dividing the nation, by rousing the Tories
too. Grey thought this too high a price to pay.

Nowhere was Lord John's courageous impetuosity of speech likely to do more harm than in matters involving the relations of church and state. In fact Lord John was neither an atheist nor a scoffer. He was a believer, though in almost the narrowest possible creed, and in religion as in politics he was a party man. In religion he was in favour of reason, and against superstition. In the spectrum of religion in England reason stood in the middle between the ceremonial and priestly superstitions of Rome and the literalist superstitions of the dissenting churches. In religion as in politics the middle was the best place to be. And although we may be sure that, had he been forced to abandon it, he would have preferred to move to the 'left' to dissent, rather than to the 'right' to Rome, it was to old-fashioned eighteenth-century dissent that he would have moved. Like Sydney Smith he felt that it was almost as dangerous to society and to morals to teach a man to expect God to speak to him directly as it was to teach him to think that priests had been entrusted with the keys of heaven.

As a young man Lord John praised the English divines of the eighteenth century who sought to show that scripture was rational.[43] As an old man he rested in the faith of Jeremy Taylor, Barrow, Tillotson, Hoadly, Samuel Clarke, Middleton, Warburton and Arnold, and he used to call Dean Stanley his Pope 'though not an infallible one'.[44] His outlook was broad-church. He believed in the divinity of Christ, the inspiration of the commands given in the Sermon on the Mount, and in judgement, reward and punishment after death. He accepted the view that if you take away religion

> you take away the obligation to restrain . . . passions – to speak truth – to respect the rights and feelings of others. It is not enough to say that you leave the obligations of natural morality and the penalties of the law: these have never yet been found sufficient.[45]

But he did not believe in the 39 articles or in the authority of the church. For the time being he agreed with the bishop of Durham who, speaking of bishops, said that of course men could be saved without them, but that it was the system adopted by the apostles and that it suited Englishmen,[46] but he looked forward to the day when faith would be defined, not as

> an exact conformity with the doctrines of the Church of Rome, or

the Church of Antioch, or the Church of England, or the Church of Scotland, but a pious, steadfast, humble belief in God, and in Christ the son of God . . . producing a fervent desire to have the soul saved alive, and a confiding trust that through Christ : . . that mercy may be vouchsafed.[47]

It is little wonder then that when the author of the repeal of the test and corporation acts upset the coach, his motive was misunderstood, and he was taken for an enemy of the church. In fact, the church never had a more well-meaning friend in the nineteenth century than Lord John, or a more utilitarian one. Religion being necessary to morals and morals to the health of society, there ought to be an established church, and that church should be established which happened to be the largest. In 1836 Lord John said that

the duty of a State is, not to choose and select that doctrine which the Legislature . . . may consider to be founded in truth, but to endeavour to secure the means by which they can inculcate religion and morality among the great body of the people.[48]

In England that meant supporting the church at the risk of offending the voluntaryists; in Ireland it meant establishing the Roman Catholic Church at the expense of the Church of Ireland. Lord John's views were consistent, but they were not likely to make him any friends, and were certain to make him many enemies.

The upshot of all this was that although politics were Lord John's life blood he was almost totally unpolitical. And the reason why he had come through the period of the Reform Bill with such flying colours (over and above the reason that he knew what he was talking about) was that on that occasion he did not have to be political. His fertile mind supplied expedients. The cabinet weighed them, and sorted them. Nor was Lord John required to enlist support for them. There was a tide in favour of reform, and Lord John had neither to persuade minds nor to reconcile men. There were others to do that. Grey could conciliate the King and the house of lords, Althorp the house of commons, and Ellice could handle the political unions. All three were, in their own ways, very persuasive men. Lord John could just be himself, very active, not a little aloof, and not quite belonging anywhere.

PLATE 1   Posthumous terra-cotta bust of Lord John Russell,
by Sir J. E. Boehm

This little bust, two and a half inches high, was a preliminary study
for the full-length statue in Westminster Abbey, and was executed
c. 1880.

PLATE 2   Lady Ribblesdale, the first Lady John Russell

This drawing by A. E. Chalon was commissioned for Findens'
Portraits of the Female Aristocracy of the Court of Queen Victoria. Lady
John died, at the age of thirty-one, before the book was published.

PLATE 3   Lord John Russell, by G. F. Watts

This portrait was painted *c.* 1851, and shows how the cares of office weighed upon the Prime Minister. In 1892 Watts himself wrote 'I think it was like'.

PLATE 4   The second Lady John Russell and her eldest son John,
by R. Thorburn.

PLATE 5   Robin Hood and Friar Tuck, HB 14 April 1835
(O'Connell   Lord John)

At the time Doyle drew this cartoon he probably meant no more than that having carried the Whigs into power, O'Connell would ask to be paid. In that case the analogy was even more apt than he supposed. The Whigs and the Irish gave each other several good cudgellings and an upset or two, but their alliance endured, and between 1835 and 1841 the two parties took it in turn to ferry each other across the river.

PLATE 6   A Day after the Wedding

Lord John: You don't appear in the best of spirits my love this morning, I hope if I have the misfortune to displease you, you will consider the weight of my public and not be too exacting in my domestic duties.

Lord John and Lady Ribblesdale were married on 11 April 1835, and the next day Lord John was sent for to help Melbourne form an administration.

PLATE 7   Swell's Out of Luck
(Morpeth Melbourne Lord John Russell Normanby)

To mark the end of the Melbourne administration the artist has picked out the four men most closely identified with the policy of justice to Ireland.

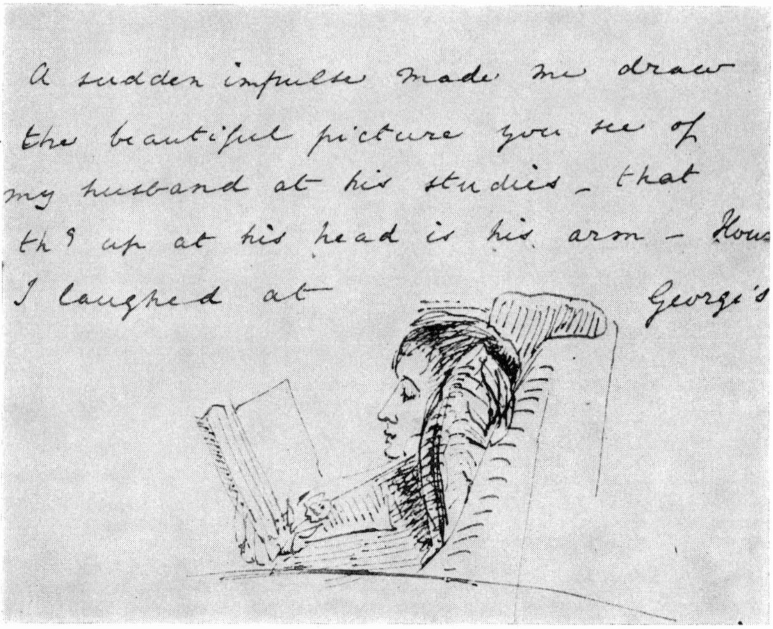

A sudden impulse made me draw the beautiful picture you see of my husband at his studies — that th⁹ up at his head is his arm — How I laughed at — George's

PLATE 8   Sketch of Lord John by Lady John contained in
a letter to her brother Viscount Melgund, 30 September 1841

That was why nobody warmed to the idea of his becoming leader of the party. He so obviously lacked winning ways, temperate common sense and good judgement. His defects were visible to all, and the dazzling success of the Reform Bill blinded him to the fact that he was still a political apprentice. The repeal of the test and corporation acts, the emancipation of the catholics, and the reform of parliament all appeared to him as the triumph of reason over prejudice. He made the mistake of supposing that there had been enlightenment and progress. He would have been astonished to hear Gladstone mutter that there was an element of anti-Christ about the Reform Act, and to learn that Disraeli was meditating turning Whig ideology upside down by reinvigorating the concept of the monarchy as the ally of the people. He was taken aback when a moderate reform of the church in Ireland gave rise to the Oxford Movement. Had the Whigs really passed the Reform Act only in order to see England revert to the middle ages? Lord John could not believe it. To him, the deliberate abandonment of the practices of the reformed church in favour of others which had been condemned at the time of the reformation as superstitious was simply unintelligible. In 1835 he still believed that 'gross and notorious abuses, which could not be reconciled with reason . . . could not withstand the scrutiny and examination of a Reformed Parliament'.[49] That is why he was ready to make the appropriation issue the battleground between the parties. He had as yet a very insufficient idea of the prejudices he was to encounter.

Part Two, 1835–41

CHAPTER VIII

Glorious John, 1835–7

i. Opposition, 1835

WHEN Peel took over, he dissolved parliament, and unwittingly did Lord John the best turn of his life. Lord John went off to
his constituency in Devonshire, and while he was staying at
Torquay he met Lady Ribblesdale, who was, like himself, both
tiny and frail. Adelaide Lister came from a Staffordshire family.
In 1826 at the age of nineteen she married Lord Ribblesdale,
who was only moderately addicted 'to the manly pleasures of an
English country gentleman', and was an artist of merit. In
December 1832 Ribblesdale died from the 'rupture of a blood-
vessel on the lungs', and left his widow with four children. Now,
at the age of twenty-seven, Lady Ribblesdale's 'miniature loveli-
ness' was at its peak. She had a brilliant complexion, shining
eyes, fine and delicate features like porcelain, animation even
in composure, and a sense of fun spiced with femininity. Her
portrait resembles that of Lord John's mother, and Lord John
fell in love with her. He courted her up and down the zigzag
path that led from his lodgings to her hotel, and even before
the results of the elections were known, there were rumours of
an engagement.[1]

The overall results of this, as of every other general election
in the period, are easy to summarise and hard to quantify. The
Tories recovered ground in the counties, the Radicals more than
held their own in the boroughs, and the Whigs suffered heavy
losses. It began to look as though politics would polarise into a
struggle between extremes. Spencer thought the next government would be Radical.[2] Howick expected the large Radical
vote to stampede the middle-of-the-road men back into the Tory
camp.[3] Peel now had reason to hope that one more dissolution
would give him a majority, and both Lord John and Ellice

feared this.[4] The Whigs were in the same danger as Fox in 1784, and the parallel was much in Lord John's mind.[5] The King had snatched the government away, and as Wellesley said, if Peel were allowed to stand for three weeks, his power would be secure.[6] How was England to be saved from another forty-six years of almost uninterrupted Tory rule?[7]

Grey, who still counted for much, was against even making the attempt. He would not come to London himself, but ran a mail-order advice service from Northumberland, whence he wrote to Melbourne urging him 'to bring forward no direct question', and to trust to Peel's bringing in measures of moderate reform.[8] Melbourne himself had no doubt that the Whigs ought to vindicate themselves, but was worried whether they were 'justified in declaring a decided opposition to the present Government' unless they saw a reasonable prospect of being able to form another in its place.[9] Ellice, too, confessed that he did not see how the Whigs were to get on in a house of commons in which they were the smallest of three minorities.[10]

It was a situation in which a more subtle politician than Lord John might easily have been less successful than he. But Lord John was inspired by his new attachment to Lady Ribblesdale, and both his courage and his readiness to sharpen party conflict came to his aid. The King had slighted Lord John, and outraged his sense of constitutional propriety. Lord John saw himself, like his ancestor, upon a seventeenth-century stage, and on the day parliament met he declared that 'if the sword of prerogative were drawn, it was time to be prepared with the shield and buckler of popular privileges'.[11] Fair trial was for the Old Bailey, not for Peel's government,[12] and Grey's advice was given in ignorance of the temper of the party.[13] Holland thought there would be no stopping the Radicals,[14] and Melbourne soon realised that if the majority were determined on a vote against Peel 'nothing will restrain them from coming to it'.[15]

In the ordinary way an opposition moves an amendment to the speech from the throne. But in this crisis Lord John was already meditating an exceptional move. Manners Sutton had been speaker since 1817. In May 1832 he had offered to help Wellington form an administration. Grey forgave him for this, and in 1833 he was re-elected speaker in the first reformed house of commons. But in November 1834 he attended the meetings of the privy council giving effect to the change of ministry, and the Whigs now decided to punish him and to run another candidate. Grey asked 'How the devil' Lord John could 'make out the question of the Speakership to be one of principle?'[16] But Melbourne replied that 'upon principle' it was right 'to oppose his re-election',[17] Spencer did not think it improper,[18] and Palmerston, who had lost his seat, made no doubt of success, provided 'we put up a good candidate'.[19]

Lord John's first thought was to run Abercromby, but Abercromby refused, and Lord John next approached Rice, who was eager to stand.[20] It then turned out that many of the Radicals and Irish would not vote for him, and at the risk of hurting Rice's feelings, the Whigs had to come back to Abercromby. He was a good candidate, but there was one important group in the new parliament whose votes he would not obtain. When Stanley resigned in 1834 he took about ten members with him. He now claimed the support of thirty-eight – the Derby dilly.[21] They had not yet joined the Conservatives, and Grey still looked forward to their return to the Whigs. Stanley made it clear that he would not vote for Abercromby, and that he would have to hear a much stronger case than he believed could be made before voting against Sutton.[22] Lord John answered:

> The case against Manners Sutton is that he appeared in open day to further the penal dissolution of the house of commons which appointed him. And if appointed again, he will no doubt do the same by the present. For the Tory party, whose tool he is, never can or will be satisfied with a house so full of reformers as the new house.[23]

His letter hardly reads as though it were intended to win, and in due course Lord John told first Brougham,[24] and then Grey,[25] that he would not rejoin Stanley until the Irish church question was settled. It was a rival eliminated.

Towards the end of January the Whig leaders, Melbourne, Lord John, Duncannon and Hobhouse met at Woburn.[26] In order to make their opposition effective they must secure the support of the Radicals and the Irish. It was a prospect to which Melbourne looked forward with distaste, Lord John with a mixture of excitement and alarm, and Duncannon, who was in

communication with O'Connell, with enthusiasm. Melbourne
had already made up his mind that there were three men with
whom he would have 'nothing to do', Brougham, Durham, and
O'Connell.[27] But as Lord John said, 'I cannot avoid communicating' with both Durham and O'Connell, 'if they wish it, on
the subject of the course we propose to take in the House of
Commons.'[28] Melbourne then agreed to let the whips 'send out
letters for an attendance to oppose Sutton'.[29] But when Lord
John raised the point that co-operation on the speaker must lead
'either to actual coalition or to reproaches hereafter',[30] and
asked how far he could go, Melbourne refused to sanction any
regular contact with the Irish, and Lansdowne wrote to protest
'against being involved in . . . such communications, should
they in any degree assume the character of party concert and
alliance'.[31]

At Woburn Lord John seems to have thought that, not being
sent by him, the notes committed him to nothing. Incredi-
bly enough neither he nor Melbourne seems to have realised
that the notes sent to O'Connell and his supporters would take
the form of an invitation to attend a meeting of all Lord John's
supporters at Lichfield House on 18 February. To this day nobody knows whether Duncannon was leading his masters by the
nose,[32] or whether there was a misunderstanding. At any rate
the notes went out about 3 February,[33] and two days later a
worried Melbourne wrote to Lord John that it was impossible
to tell what communications might have taken place between
'some of our friends' and O'Connell – 'They worship him as the
Savages do the Evil Demon'.[34]

As the truth began to dawn on Lord John he added a postscript to his letter of 11 February to Melbourne:

> There is a question of having a meeting on the 18th, to which
> Whigs, Radicals, and Repealers should be invited. I feel doubtful
> about it, for although it would concern only the Speaker, a
> marked union or disunion between the parties might be expected
> to follow. What say you?[35]

These are the lame words of a man who, having failed to ask to
see one of the notes before they were sent, now realised he had
made a blunder. Melbourne replied that it would be most in-
advisable to have a meeting until after the eighteenth. The

speaker was a question they could all agree on, and after that
they would know whether a meeting was likely to be useful.[36]
This was better than Lord John had feared, and he wrote back
straight away to say that he could not pretend to lead any
party, unless he could bring them together and see if they were
disposed to act with him.[37]

The next day Lord John received a letter from O'Connell,
accepting the invitation to the meeting, and offering to co-
operate beyond the immediate issue:

> the Irish members of the popular party will avoid all topics on
> which they may differ with you and your friends, *until the Tories
> are routed* . . . you will find us perfectly ready to co-operate in any
> plan which your friends may deem most advisable to effect that
> purpose. In short, we *will be* steady allies without any mutiny in
> your camp.[38]

Lord John took fright: his immediate reaction was to pen a
frigid answer to O'Connell. His second thought was to show it
to Duncannon. Duncannon told him to do two things, both of
which were sensible, not to rebuff O'Connell, and to see Melbourne.[39] There was nothing left for Melbourne to do but to let
the meeting take place on 18 February, for the Whigs had already had experience of the consequences of repudiating
arrangements with O'Connell the previous summer.

And so the famous meeting of Whigs, Radicals, and Irish took
place at Lichfield House. How much of a compact was there?
Formally, the three parties agreed to combine to vote against
Manners Sutton and in favour of Abercromby. That was all.
Of the Radicals, Lord John said that he was disposed to resist
them when they were violent, but that he saw no policy 'in
refusing to act with them where our opinions agree'.[40] To
O'Connell he laid it down that he would neither renounce his
opinions nor ask O'Connell to renounce his.[41] Lord John told
Grey that he stood by his former principles, 'Let those who like
them come to us'.[42] None of the three parties gave up its indi-
viduality, and the Radicals actually held a separate meeting of
their own to 'brigade' the opposition.[43] But everyone who came
to the meeting at Lichfield House must have known that it was
pointless to agree to vote together on this one issue, unless they
were prepared to continue.

On 19 February parliament assembled, and after a 'very pretty race'[44] the confederates defeated Manners Sutton by 316 votes to 306. Lord John told the house that by choosing Abercromby 'they would give the country an earnest that they meant to set zealously about real Reform, and that they were not going to cheat the people by any unsubstantiated and mock Reform'.[45] It was a good start, but Peel did not resign, and the allies then had no alternative but to move an amendment to the address. In a scathing attack on Peel, Lord John in effect asked the house to express confidence in the ministry which William had dismissed in November.[46] He carried his amendment, but by 294 votes to 287, and Peel at once dismissed the vote as a retrospective gesture, and challenged Lord John to propose a motion of no confidence. This put Lord John in a quandary. There was a strong feeling that Peel ought to be allowed to bring his measures in,[47] and so Peel's Irish tithe bill became the *experimentum crucis.*

Peel's bill was similar to the Whig bill of 1834 which the lords had rejected. Even so, it was still not good enough for the Reformers, and H. G. Ward at once wrote to warn Lord John that if he did not move the appropriation question against the government it would be moved for him from the back benches.[48] There were two more meetings at Lichfield House, on 12 and 23 March, and then on 28 March Lord John presided over an opposition dinner. Two hundred and sixty-four members of the Whig, Radical, and Irish parties drank a toast together, and O'Connell called it the most enjoyable evening of his life. On 30 March, in the debate on the tithe bill, Lord John declared

> there has been no time in the history of Ireland since this country obtained footing and dominion there, in which there was not some dreadful contest, something amounting to a civil war, and a state of law which induced the people to consider themselves rather as the victims of tyranny, than the subjects of just Government.[49]

At the end of the debate, on 3 April, Peel was defeated by 322 votes to 289. On 6 April, on the motion that the surplus revenues of the Church of Ireland ought to be applied to the education of all classes of christians, Peel was defeated again by 262 to 237. The next day, when Lord John moved a resolution that no settlement of the Irish tithe question which did not embody the principle of the resolution of the day before would satisfy the house, Peel was again defeated by 285 to 258. 1835 was not, after all, to be like 1784. On 8 April Peel resigned; on 9 April O'Connell proclaimed that 'a new era opens for Ireland – an administration is formed, pledged . . . to . . . justice for Ireland';[50] and on 11 April Lord John and Lady Ribblesdale were married, and set up house in Wilton Crescent, and Lord John became the stepfather of Adelaide, Thomas, Isabel, and Elizabeth.[51]

No British monarch has since dismissed a ministry on his own initiative, and Peel's resignation was a famous victory for Lord John. Peel was no novice, and his own performance in the first three months of 1835 was much admired, but in his first campaign as leader Lord John rose to Peel's level and perhaps surpassed it. Before the session opened Holland had cast about for some way of inspiring Lord John and giving 'authority to all he says and does'.[52] He need not have worried. Stung by the King, 'languid Johnny' glowed to 'glorious John'.[53] Lord John consulted Melbourne and Lansdowne, wrote conciliatory letters to Grey, and delighted his supporters. Even Ellice grudgingly admitted that 'Johnny must have some sense in his head on which he . . . succeeds in prevailing on such discordant materials to act together.'[54]

Not the least surprising thing about Lord John in this period was his moderation. Molesworth records that at the first meeting in Lichfield House Lord John 'told us not to abuse Sutton, and not to cheer if we gained the victory'.[55] When it came to the amendment, Lord John told Melbourne that the more cautiously worded it was the better, and that he had sent it off to Lansdowne, who would 'infuse a few more drops of wisdom into it'.[56] Lord John's father praised 'the equanimity of temper which distinguished you . . . and by which you gained *golden opinions*'.[57] It was no wonder, then, that when it was done, and Peel was out, Wellesley said that Lord John 'possesses all the temper and tact of Lord Althorp, with ten thousand times his eloquence and power'.[58] It was probably the first three months of 1835 that Parkes was referring to, when he said years later that Lord John's garden of Eden was the lead of the opposition.[59]

ii. Office, 1835

The King turned first to Grey, who refused to lead another government, and then on 11 April to Melbourne. The very next day 'the widow's mite' was sent for from his bride. Ellice wanted Lord John to take the foreign office,[60] and Melbourne toyed with this solution to what was already known as the Palmerston problem. But the home office, which Lord John took, handled Irish affairs, and was much more compatible with the lead in the commons, and Palmerston, who was still without a seat, returned to his old post. Melbourne consulted Lord John about the apportionment of offices between the two houses, but his appointments were his own, and so were his exclusions. In the lords were Lansdowne, lord president of the council; Holland, chancellor of the duchy of Lancaster; Duncannon, the lord privy seal; Grant, who was created Glenelg, and took the colonies; and Auckland who accepted the admiralty, but went out to India later in the year, and was succeeded by Minto. In the commons, in addition to Lord John, were Rice, the chancellor of the exchequer; Poulett Thomson, president of the board of trade; Hobhouse, president of the board of control; and Howick, secretary at war.

Melbourne formed a purely Whig government. The ministry depended upon the votes of the Radicals and the Irish, but both Durham and O'Connell were excluded. Durham's commitment to household suffrage, vote by ballot, and triennial parliaments was incompatible with Lord John's views on the finality of the Reform Act. But the exclusion of O'Connell was a different matter. Some kind of promise had been made to him, and when the King objected, Lord John was obliged to send an envoy to tell the Liberator that he was to be disappointed. It was the kind of thing Ellice did very well; and he went into the room with Lord John's offer to join O'Connell in the political wilderness, and emerged with O'Connell's anxious wish that Lord John should take a leading part in the administration.[61] The third man excluded was Brougham. Lord John thought Brougham's merits 'great and conspicuous; his demerits vexatious but not vital'.[62] But Melbourne would not have him back – though for the time being he preferred not to drive him into open opposition by appointing anyone else as lord chancellor, and the great seal was put into commission.'

Melbourne had purged the party at the expense of weakening the team, and it was difficult to know whether the new ministry was more likely to be upset by its avowed enemies or by its alleged supporters. Men less pessimistic than Grey agreed that the Whigs were too weak to survive with the forces that would operate on either flank.[63] Nor did the ministry start well, for when Lord John sought re-election on accepting an office of profit under the crown, his opponent accused him of having congratulated Lord Londonderry in person upon his appointment as ambassador to St Petersburg, and of having subsequently attacked the appointment in the house of commons.[64] Lord John was defeated, and William IV was delighted at this setback,[65] which was overcome when the Hollands' son, Colonel Fox, vacated his seat at Stroud in favour of Lord John, who rejoined the house towards the end of May.

Lord John's defeat drew from Hobhouse the sober reflection that

> we are in a position anything but encouraging. Our leader and our other Secretary of State are out of Parliament, the King is against us, the Court also, a majority of nearly a hundred Peers also. The Army, the Navy, the Church, the law, the squires, the magistracy, against us . . . To balance this we have a precarious majority of about 30 in the House of Commons.[66]

But this ministry, whose life already seemed to hang in the balance, lasted for over six years, and one of the reasons why it went on so long must lie in the harmony established in 1835 between Melbourne and Lord John. Melbourne had been schooled by his disastrous marriage not to exhibit his feelings, and was a man of indolent temper and cynical outlook, whose chief enthusiasm in the whole period was an old man's gallant affection for Queen Victoria. But there was more to him than this: he had an acute grasp of political realities, and he was, if not an ardent Whig, at any rate an ardent anti-Tory.

Three things cemented the relationship between Melbourne and Lord John. In the first place Melbourne had need of Lord John almost as much as Lord John had of him. Where Lord John saw political issues in black and white, Melbourne saw political behaviour in those colours, and no prime minister has ever been more ferocious in his bans. Lord John softened Melbourne's unforgivingness. He did not, for instance, share Melbourne's abhorrence of Brougham's 'whole character and his whole conduct'.[67] He thought Brougham 'had never entertained any deliberate design of injuring the ministry the party or individuals',[68] and in December 1835, when Melbourne decided that the great seal could not remain in commission any longer, Lord John wrote that in Melbourne's place he would still feel able to recommend Brougham to the King.[69]

In the second place it turned out that Melbourne sympathised with Lord John's policy of justice to Ireland. As home secretary Melbourne had actually made a dent in the system by which clergymen called on the police for aid in collecting tithes,[70] but so reticent had he been about Irish matters in general that in February 1835 Lord John still feared he might prefer to form another ministry in which the revenues of the Irish church would remain an open question. Lord John must have been delighted to receive Melbourne's encouragement

> to be explicit about the Irish Church. You know, that in general nobody is so much for shuffling over differences of opinion and getting over matters as well as one can, as I am. I was always exhorting the different sections of Grey's Government to this course, which was very often followed. But this is really an important moment, and a fresh start, and it is nonsense now not to understand one another at least upon matters so important and so urgent.[71]

It was the decisive moment in their relations. Melbourne was committed to Peel's government being turned out and his own substituted for it on the basis of the appropriation clause. And when the government was formed Melbourne told the King that he could not be allowed to refer his scruples to fifteen judges, and that it must be understood from the start that he would sign an appropriation bill when it had passed both houses.[72]

In the third place Melbourne was a big man. Almost everything Lord John did at the home office between 1835 and 1839, in England as in Ireland, implied criticism of his predecessor. Take the case of the Dorchester labourers: Lord John had not been in office long before he became convinced that it had taken two acts of parliament put together to convict them.[73] But how was he to do justice to the Lovelesses without offending Melbourne, who had had them transported? Had Lord John's chief been a lesser man, he could not, within six months of taking office, have persuaded him to agree to the Lovelesses being joined by their families, and he could not, within twelve months, have secured them a free pardon.

When the government set to work, the Radicals and the Irish both expected their reward, and the Whigs decided to oblige them with one bill to reform the municipal corporations in England and Wales, and another to regulate the Irish church and tithes.

The reform of the municipal corporations has only recently received the attention it deserves.[74] The measure has often been dismissed as a postscript to the Reform Act. But it was not so regarded at the time, and even before the report of the royal commission appointed in July 1833 was published in April 1835, tempers were rising. From the Tory side there were many complaints about the partisan behaviour of the commissioners. The Reformers, on the other hand, felt that with the Tories now only thirty seats away from a return to power, something must be done quickly to make the boroughs safe for representative government. Many of the old corporations still had influence over the return of candidates to parliament and used it in the Tory interest. At all costs, the Reformers must open the corporations in order to consolidate their majority in the house of commons.

In their report, the commissioners advocated household suffrage and ballot. Lord John was not in favour of the ballot, and according to Parkes, who drafted the bill, it was Melbourne who induced the cabinet to agree to household suffrage.[75] However that may be, when Lord John introduced the bill on 5 June, it provided for what he called bold interference after cautious inquiry[76] and Parkes called clearing 'the roost from top to bottom'.[77] Two hundred old corporations were to be abolished, and in their places 183 new town councils were to rule over a population of two millions. Councillors were to be elected by inhabitant ratepayers of three years' standing. Peel, who knew very well what was at stake, attacked this simple household franchise as an abandonment of the finality of the Reform Act.

Lord John replied that the government had considered adopting the £10 householder franchise used in parliamentary elections, but that it would lead to jealousy if those who had the
parliamentary vote possessed an exclusive right to the municipal
one too.[78] It was not a very effective argument, for Grey's
government had entertained no such fears when they adopted
the £10 franchise for the Scottish municipalities reformed in
1833. Nor did it conceal the fact that the government had sold
out to the Radicals, who gained another plank in their platform
with the election of councillors for a term of three years. One-
third of the council were to retire, and there was to be an
election, every year.

Almost as important as the machinery of elections was the
question of what the new councils were to do. Charities were to
be taken away from them, and in return they were to be given
responsibility for the police, for the appointment of magistrates,
and for licensing alehouses. Finally, in contrast to the Reform
Act, which set up no machinery for the continuous redistribution of seats, the bill included provisions for the establishment
of new councils in the future.

The bill was too cleverly drafted to be opposed on principle
by Peel, who knew that if he tried to stop the Whigs and Radicals taking his municipal corporations, there would be a popular outcry, in which he might lose his house of lords instead.
When the bill reached the lords, Melbourne showed resolution,
and Brougham fought hard by his side. But the lords were
determined to spoil what they could not stop. They put a brake
upon what they regarded as the naked democracy of the new
councils, by providing for the appointment of aldermen for life
– thus saddling every one of the new town councils with a little
house of lords of its own. Next they inserted a property qualification for councillors, and insisted on the towns being divided
into wards. Finally they took the right of appointing the magistrates away from the councils and returned it to the crown,
handed the right of licensing alehouses back to the magistrates,
and ended up by disqualifying dissenters from voting on matters
of church patronage.

When the bill came back from the lords towards the end of
August, Hume was for stern – O'Connell for moderate courses.[79]
Lord John told his supporters that he preferred to settle for

what he could get so late in the year. Aldermen were totally opposed to the spirit of the bill, but Lord John made them less objectionable by having them elected out of the councils, and by compelling them to retire after six years, half of them going out every three years. In place of the property qualification inserted by the lords, Peel suggested a rating qualification, which Lord John adopted. Division into wards was accepted. On magistrates, Lord John announced that he would agree to appointment by the crown, but gave a pledge that so long as he held power he would appoint magistrates from lists of names submitted by the town councils.[80] He then accepted the amendment as to licensing, and trumped the disqualification of dissenters by arranging for all the livings in the possession of the corporations to be sold. Anyone who regards these concessions as an abject surrender should recall Parkes' satisfaction when the bill passed that '*it is done*. Certainly no Conservative majority can ever be got in a British House of Commons'.[81]

In 1835 Melbourne chose as lord lieutenant, Mulgrave, who was moved by two things, genuinely liberal sentiments, and vanity. His approach to his work was revealed in his first action, which was to go to his tailor and order a fancy, *green* uniform.[82] Thereafter he continued to embarrass his colleagues by his style; by his pardons and progresses;[83] by his indignation at the governor of Canada being put on a level with the lord lieutenant of Ireland;[84] and by his habit, whenever he was not importuning the government for leave to confer titles on other people, of asking them to confer titles on him.[85] But they put up with him because nothing could be 'on a more agreeable footing' than his communications with Lord John,[86] whose policies he executed loyally.

For chief secretary, Melbourne gave him Morpeth, and for his under-secretary Thomas Drummond. Morpeth was mother-dominated, devout, inclined like Lord John to take Whig sentiments seriously, helpful, busy, and not outstanding. Drummond, on the other hand, has been celebrated from that day to this as the success of the Irish administration. He was discovered by Althorp, who found he had the proverbial head for strategy and nose for detail of the born administrator. In Ireland, Drummond became committed to governing in the interests of the majority of the people, and he brought the threads into his own office, not in order to tie everything up in red tape, but to cut it. He sometimes treated subordinates with what Morpeth called a want of considerateness,[87] but he, Morpeth, Mulgrave, Lord John and Melbourne all worked well together, and in complete contrast to the previous Whig governments of Ireland between 1830 and 1834.

The first task of this new Irish administration was to prepare a church and tithe bill embodying the principle of the appropriation resolution of 7 April 1835. The bill was hastily drawn up after the commission of inquiry appointed in May 1834 had published its report. The rent charge was to be fixed at £68 5s, and in parishes where there were fewer than fifty members of the established church, the government proposed to suspend the presentation to livings. As Morpeth said, 'If we will not do this, we do nothing at all.'[88] By this measure the government expected in time to derive a surplus of nearly £60,000 p.a. In addition, whenever a living worth more than £300 became vacant, an inquiry was to be held, and if the income was considered excessive for the needs of the parish, it was to be reduced. Further sums would thus become available for 'the religious and moral instruction of all classes of christians'. The bill passed the house of commons by 319 votes to 282. But Lord John made a mistake if he thought that he could pass appropriation through the house of lords under cover of the English municipal corporations bill. The lords had no difficulty in distinguishing a ball which they could hit to the boundary from one which they must keep out of their stumps. They bisected the bill, passed the rent charge, and threw out the appropriation clause by a majority of 138 to 41. The whole bill was therefore lost.

Even before the fate of the Irish church and tithe bill was known, Lord John allowed Perrin, the Irish attorney general, to bring in a bill to reform the municipal corporations in Ireland. There was no time for it to pass that session, and the move was interpreted as a promise to the Irish and a threat to the house of lords. But the more likely explanation is that Lord John already wanted to draw attention away from the appropriation clause. Appropriation could only be shown to be consistent with a policy of equality under the union by a train of reasoning too long for most people to follow. But here was a much better issue for presentation to public opinion. Why should not Ireland have the same new town councils as England and Wales?

At any rate, from this moment Lord John began to ground his Irish crusade much more specifically upon the broad principle of equality between the kingdoms. He developed the argument in a letter to the King, who answered that he could not admit there was the slightest ground for the notion that Ireland did not already receive equal treatment in parliament.[89] In 1836 Lord John made the King eat his own words by inserting the new policy into the speech from the throne, and thereafter he made it the theme of all his great speeches on Ireland. In 1837 he rounded upon the opposition: 'Scotland is inhabited by Scotchmen, and England by Englishmen, yet, because Ireland is inhabited by Irishmen you will refuse them the same measure of relief that you have applied to Scotland and to England.'[90] In 1838 he said that he wanted the Irish treated as if they lived in England, Wales or Scotland,[91] and in 1839 he put his case in the words which between twenty and thirty years later ultimately converted Gladstone to the Irish cause:

> Sir, I know not why, if we conduct the Government of England according to the wishes of the people of England and if we conduct the government of Scotland according to the wishes of the people of Scotland – I know not why in Ireland the opinions and wishes of a small minority only should be consulted.[92]

Before the session of 1835 came to an end, it was clear that by bringing the wretched wavering course pursued by Lord Grey to an end, Lord John had put new heart into the Reformers, and into the Conservatives too. Henceforth there would be fewer neutrals and fewer moderates. Stanley's men had started the session on the Whig benches, voted with Peel on the speaker, and split upon the appropriation clause. But on 1 July Stanley and Graham crossed the floor of the house, and joined Peel. Disraeli was still outside the house, but the events of 1835 were the decisive formative influence in his career. He now saw in the Whigs the anti-national party, which had seized power in order to hand out pieces of the country's institutions as booty to the country's foes – the dissenters, the Radicals, and the Irish.

Disraeli dedicated his *Vindication of the British Constitution* to

Lord Lyndhurst. It was symbolic. Just as the Reformers gathered round their majority in the lower house, so the Conservatives rallied round theirs in the upper one. Conservatives thought the Whigs were going at a railroad pace to a republic, and the immediate issue being Ireland, the lords began to take their tone from the Irish interest. In the eighteenth century, when there were about 200 peers, one in eight had an interest in Ireland. By 1833 105 out of 423 peers had Irish interests, and only 34 of the 105 were even nominally Whig. The rest were ready to be marshalled by Lyndhurst – a born wrecker with an outside chance of becoming prime minister upon the ruins of Melbourne's administration.[93]

As the two houses of parliament drew apart, there were rumours of something much more serious. Ireland was bedevilled by orange societies. Recent research suggests that the danger of a coup d'état was exaggerated,[94] but in the frenzied atmosphere of the time there was a sensation when Hume called attention to the existence of orange lodges in the army. Confronted by an intransigent upper house, and by an orange 'conspiracy', it would not have been surprising had the three parties supporting the government drawn closer together. But this did not happen. The Radicals and O'Connell both preferred to hold their distance from the Whigs the better to bring pressure to bear on them. The Whigs stood aloof, in order to be able to resist it. The Radicals' response to the new developments was to contemplate resurrecting the political unions: O'Connell's was to tour Britain addressing mass meetings on the need to abolish the peers. From the home office Lord John passed a strange autumn keeping watch over his allies of the parliamentary session.

The Lichfield House compact could not be turned into an alliance, but then it would not break down either, because, as Lord John said, O'Connell knows that if he has not us, he has worse.[95] And among that vast army which was rushing to arms in defence of the ancient constitution there were many weaknesses. Lyndhurst was out in front of Wellington, and Wellington was out in front of Peel. That being so, it made sense for Lord John to go on professing to believe that the house of lords was a rational body which could be persuaded by argument to pass an appropriation act. He reassured the King that he was against any remodelling of the lords upon a popular basis,[96] wrote to Melbourne that he was against any large creation of peers, and told an audience in Plymouth that he would rather trust to 'the effect of public opinion . . . than to organic changes' for a way out of the impasse.[97]

iii. Office, 1835–6

Lord John was tired at the end of the session, and he went down to Endsleigh with his family to recover in the fresh air.[98] It was not long before his spirit was on the march again. There was to be an inquiry into charitable bequests for education. Would Brougham head the inquiry?[99] When Brougham accepted, the King objected. If William IV persisted, it would mean, as Lord John told Melbourne, 'Mr. Brougham's Monarchy Abolition Bill read a first time'.[100] Melbourne talked the King round, and having found Brougham something to do, gave the great seal to Cottenham.

Next, Lord John turned to the new commissions of the peace for the towns affected by the municipal corporations reform act. The remodelling offered a unique opportunity for the revolutionary exercise of patronage. The temptation was strong for a party that had only recently returned to power, but Lord John decided to issue the new commission before the first elections took place under the act. The magistrates were thus appointed from lists of names supplied by the old corporations, not by the new town councils. In this way Lord John avoided a proscription of Tories. But in order to please the Reformers he made up his mind to broaden the magistracy. Melbourne had always admitted a man's being in trade as an objection to his becoming a magistrate, and thought that 'Country Gentlemen have held, and still do hold, a higher character than Master Manufacturers'.[101] Lord John agreed that the landed gentry were humane, but thought they were also the 'most ignorant, prejudiced, and narrow minded' class in the country, and that the uneducated labourers beat them hollow in intelligence.[102] Words like these would not have been persuasive with Grey, but Melbourne was never put out by Lord John, and he agreed that some manufacturers and persons in business should be admitted. It would be interesting to know how many changes Lord John made: in

due course the Tories complained about the appointment of
Frost, the chartist, in Monmouthshire, and of Fryer and Muntz,
the Radicals, in Wolverhampton and Birmingham. But had
Lord John done much more, we would have heard more, and
it seems likely that he only made a beginning.

When ministers returned to London, there were the bills to
be prepared for the next session. In 1836 the dissenters were to
be given priority, and Lord John took the chair at the committee of cabinet appointed to consider their grievances. Melbourne asked Hobhouse, Howick, Rice and Thomson to join
him, and by mistake omitted Lord Holland. With a deft allu-
sion to North's famous letter to Fox in 1783, Lord John wrote
to Holland to say that looking at the commission he did not per-
ceive his name, which he ventured to add.[103]

The committee gave priority to a solution of the marriage
problem. In the 1820s the dissenters had suggested a national
system of registration. Under the new poor law of 1834 it was
now possible, for the small sum of £80,000 p.a., to turn every
union into a registration district.[104] The dissenters could then
be allowed to marry in their own chapels. In order to facilitate
the passage of this reform, the committee decided against a
frontal assault upon the universities of Oxford and Cambridge,
and the practical grievance that a dissenter could not get a
degree was to be overcome by giving a charter to London university. The problem of church rates was left to the future.

The year 1836 was also to see a start upon the reform of the
church, which, like the unreformed parliament, was strong in
the agricultural south, and weak in the industrial midlands
and north. The church had her sinecures, and her extreme
inequalities of income between one bishop and another and
between the bishops and the parochial clergy. Grey had approached this topic, as he approached most things, with caution,
by appointing a commission of inquiry. Peel, who had already
made up his mind what he would sacrifice, what he would
reform, and what he would die in the last ditch for, seized the
opportunity presented by his short tenure of office in 1834–5 to
re-model the commission by putting in safe, conservative
ecclesiastics.[105]

When Melbourne came back into office, the ministerial
members of Peel's commission retired, and were replaced by

Melbourne, Lord John, Cottenham, Lansdowne and Rice. Melbourne appointed his own bishops, but on this general question of church reform, he consulted Lord John at every step, even as to the exact wording of the letters which passed between him and the archbishop of Canterbury. Fearing Lord John as he would the unclean beast, the archbishop attempted to bargain with the prime minister over the terms on which the church leaders would continue to sit on the commission. At first he asked the government to resist all motions on ecclesiastical matters in the house of commons.[106] Melbourne and Lord John refused to commit themselves to resist motions for the appropriation of the surplus revenues of the church in Ireland, and for the abolition of church rates. The first point was clearly not negotiable, and the archbishop held out only for no part of the property of the church being taken to make good any deficiency caused by the abolition of church rates.[107]

A bargain was struck according to which the Whigs would defend the church from the Radicals, so long as the church was willing to set its own house in order. Compared with the rotten boroughs and the municipal corporations, the church was handled very tenderly, and Lord John understood that in going on with Peel's commission, no extreme reforms could be attempted.[108] When the commission began its meetings in earnest, the Whigs rarely attended, and the proceedings fell more and more into the hands of bishop Blomfield, who knew where he was going, while his fellow dignitaries only knew that they would have to go somewhere.[109] Some time in 1836 the commissioners would be ready to lay their first batch of proposals before parliament.

There was, however, one matter relating to the church on which the Whigs were determined to take direct action. Tithes were an irritant setting even churchmen against the clergy. The ancient claim of the church to one-tenth of the produce of the land had long ceased to be enforceable, but it depended upon local circumstances how far a clergyman could secure his rights, or a farmer resist them. Melbourne's cabinet decided upon a compulsory commutation, carried out by three commissioners (two appointed by the crown and one by the archbishop of Canterbury), 'empowered, after examination, to proceed by certain fixed rules to a final adjudication'.[110]

The registration bill, the dissenters' marriage bill, and the English tithe bill were comprehensive but conciliatory measures, and the Whigs hoped that, together with the concordat reached with the church, they would allay the fears raised in 1835, and create the mood in which the parties could escape from their deadlock over Ireland.[111] During the recess Lord John contemplated trying to get himself and his enemies on to new ground on the Irish church and tithes question by dropping the rent charge in favour of a straight land tax. But Morpeth advised against this: it would have to be fought as a new measure, 'and we have the recorded assent of both Houses to the other mode',[112] and Lord John decided not to draft the Irish tithe bill until parliament had had time to consider the Irish municipal bill, which was believed to be less controversial.

Before the new session began in 1836, *The Times* joined the opposition with an attack upon O'Connell. But the Reformers came up in good heart because they had just swept the country at the first elections for the new town councils. Ebrington thought the results showed that 'though the House of Lords with the Hierarchy and Squirearchy' might make it difficult for the Whigs to govern the country, the opposition of the towns would make it impossible for the Tories to.[113] Thus encouraged Hume started the session by asking the crown to remove every orangeman from both civil and military office. Lord John's own view was that there was no distinction between the oaths taken by the Tolpuddle martyrs and by the Duke of Cumberland and Lord Wynford except that the latter were acting 'with more cunning, and *deserve* at least a more severe punishment'.[114] But he was still trying to placate the opposition by conspicuous moderation, and he moved an amendment inviting the King to take such measures as he thought fit to discourage orange societies. Greville praised Lord John's speech as 'far surpassing his usual form, dignified, temperate, and judicious', and added that it drew 'tears from the Orangemen, enthusiastic approbation from Stanley, a colder approval from Peel, and the universal assent of the House'.[115] Not even the Duke of Cumberland could resist a united house of commons, and on 26 February Lord John was able to announce the dissolution of the orange lodges.

Next Lord John indicated the lines along which the church was to be reorganised, and introduced the English tithe bill.

The bill soon became law, and within seven years all claims had been weighed, all payments adjusted, and the tithe in England had ceased to be a political problem.[116] Then he brought on the two related bills for the establishment of a system of national registration and for allowing dissenters' marriages. There was little difficulty over the registration, and only one minor point of controversy arose over the marriage bill. The lords were determined to preserve some distinction between marriage in church and marriage in chapel. Lord John had proposed that in each case the same notice should be given to the registrar. The lords hit upon the distinction according to which at a church wedding no registrar need be present, while at a wedding in chapel one must be. It was annoying, but the dissenters accepted it, and the registration act and marriage act have continued in operation to this day. In one year Lord John had settled questions that had been vexatious for decades, and for which neither Althorp nor Peel had been able to find an answer.

Unfortunately the settlement of these problems did not put the opposition in the right mood to discuss Irish legislation. Exact conformity to the English ratepaying franchise being impossible, the Irish municipal bill provided for a £10 householder franchise in the seven largest towns and for a £5 householder franchise in forty-seven smaller ones. This was moderate enough, but it was too much for Wellington and Peel, who grasped at a phrase of Stanley's about total extinction, and then took the line that the ancient corporations were indeed corrupt and ought to be abolished, but that there was no need to put new elected town councils in their place.[117] It was a disreputable argument, and in the commons it did them very little good, for the bill was carried by a majority of 61. But what use was a majority even of that order when the bill came before the upper house? Lyndhurst recalled that the English in Ireland were in danger of being driven into the sea by the natives, and while Lord John was speaking up for O'Connell in the Carlow election inquiry, the lords were busy turning a bill to reform the corporations into a bill to extinguish them.

This was the main bill of the session, and it embodied 'the principle of *equal justice to Ireland*'.[118] But surprisingly enough the Irish themselves thought 'the destruction of the old abominations' was 'the great point gained'.[119] Lord John, therefore, agreed to allow the Whig peers to support a compromise suggested by the neutral Duke of Richmond, for giving elective councils to the seven largest cities only. But government and neutrals together were outvoted by the recalcitrants. Even Peel then thought the lords had gone too far, and when the mutilated bill came back to the commons Lord John secured all-party support for a new proposal to set up councils in the eleven largest towns only. But the lords threw that out too, and the bill was abandoned.[120]

While Lord John was holding the Irish tithe bill back, Mulgrave reported that the main interest of the Irish in the appropriation clause was that, if it could be carried, 'they would consider it as an instalment of triumph over the other party'.[121] There was no point in encouraging that, and at the beginning of June, when the fate of the ministry's compromise plan for the Irish municipalities still hung in the balance, Lord John unveiled a church and tithe bill which was designed, not to raise cheers from his supporters, but to elicit a sober sense of compromise among his enemies. As it was the most carefully thought out of all the plans produced for the Irish church in this period, it is worth following Lord John into its details.[122]

The proposals he made were, as he said, even more generous than those Peel had intimated the government should adopt if it wanted to settle the question. The rent-charge was set at 70 per cent, and there was to be no suspension of the presentation to livings. At the bottom of the scale, in the parishes with fewer than 50 protestants, the clergy were to receive £100 p.a. and 30 acres of glebe. At the top, in the 51 parishes with 3000 protestants or more, they were to have £500 p.a. and 30 acres of glebe. At every point the clergy in Ireland were to be left better off than those in England. The income of the church was £683,737, and when Lord John had finished with the church there would be:

		Cost
2	archbishops	£ 17,780
10	bishops	49,587
	dignitaries and prebends	11,042
	minor canons and vicars choral	14,824
1251	parochial clergy	368,350
241	curates	18,075

which, together with various sums for the repair of old churches and the building of new ones, would come to £618,288 for a church with 805,000 members.[123]

There would then be a surplus of £65,439, and this was the amount to be appropriated. But Lord John now promised that the first use to which the surplus would be put would be to repay the annual grant of £50,000 out of the consolidated fund to the schools set up under the act of 1831. There would remain only £15,439 for new purposes.[124] Lord John could scarcely have conceded more, or claimed less. In committee he ended his speech by saying that he had been entreated

> not to insist upon a mere abstract principle, but I must ask the right hon. Gentleman and others, not for the sake of the people of Ireland, who are groaning under the weight of the Established Church – not for the sake of religion, for that too is suffering – not for the sake of the State, for that is also paralysed by the existing state of things – but for the sake of an abstract principle, not to continue a struggle against the wishes of the people, and to refuse to remedy that grievance which is a just cause of complaint.[125]

It was a good point, and better than any made by the professed friends of the church, who turned down the settlement he offered them in 1836 and ended up in 1869 with Gladstone's scheme of disestablishment and disendowment.

The bill passed the commons, with one vote of 300 to 261 and another of 290 to 264, but when it came back from the lords, the rent-charge had been raised to 75 per cent, no benefice was to be left with less than £300, and any surplus was to be transferred to parishes with over 1000 protestants. As Lord John said 'this seems introduced for the purpose . . . of preventing the accumulation of any surplus'.[126] The principle of appropriation had been voted on in the commons four times in 1835 and twice in 1836, and he could not agree to give it up. So this bill, too, was abandoned.

Only one thing relieved the gloom in which the session ended. In July Lord John brought in three bills prepared by the ecclesiastical commission, to regulate and equalise the bishops' incomes, to adjust capitular revenues, and to restrain pluralities, and a fourth bill to make the ecclesiastical commission permanent. The Radicals were not pleased either by the proposals,

or by their being introduced so late in the session, and the
chapters and pluralities had to be left to another year. But the
bishops were all put on a flat rate of £4,000 p.a., except Canterbury, York, London, Durham and Winchester, which remained
objects of translation for ambitious ecclesiastics. A first step had
at last been taken in the reform of the church, and as Lord John
said, 'as soon as you bring the question to one of degree, from
that moment you free the institution itself from danger'.[127] It
was a fair claim, but it was really the bill converting the ecclesiastical commission from an inquiring to an executive body
which put the church out of danger. Henceforth the commissioners would be empowered to make orders, and although the
orders would still be laid before the house, the reform of the
church of England had, in effect, been put outside politics. The
Whigs had saved the church from the Radicals, and the Radicals knew it.

In 1836 it seemed as though the upper house was determined to
bring on a constitutional crisis, and Lord John began to consider the remedies. When the lords murdered the Irish municipal bill Mulgrave suggested a dissolution,[128] but Melbourne
dismissed this as 'being . . . no remedy for the evil',[129] and Mulgrave and Lord John themselves concluded that the policy of
such a step must depend 'upon the degree of maturity which
sympathy in Irish Affairs has already attained in England'.[130]
The alternative was a creation of peers, and at the beginning
of June Lord John wrote to Melbourne that it was evident a
majority in the lords

> are combined, not to stop or alter a particular measure, but to
> stop or alter all measures which may not be agreeable to the most
> powerful, or, in other words, the most violent, among their own
> body. Both the Tories and the Radicals have the advantage of a
> definite course with respect to this state of things. The Tories
> praise the wisdom of the Lords, and wish to maintain their power
> undiminished. The Radicals complain of a mischievous obstacle
> to good government, and propose an elective House of Lords. The
> Ministers stand in the position of confessing the evil and not con-
> senting to the remedy.

The best thing to do would be to embark upon a 'steady and
gradual' creation of peers, starting at once, and to couple it

with a warning that the ministry would be prepared 'to advise a similar creation whenever it is *provoked*'.[131]

With this memorandum, which he intended for the cabinet, Lord John sent a letter which was much too weak for the occasion. 'If you are not of the opinion stated in the paper I send you, it will be better not to send it round. One day or other we shall all come to one mind upon it, and, till we do, it is well not to have my propositions debated.' Lord John was being considerate. Melbourne had passed a wretched session being dragged through the courts by the Hon. George Norton, who maliciously accused him of having fathered an 'heir' by his wife Caroline. The charge gave rise to vicious political satires, which made more impression upon the public than Melbourne's acquittal did. Melbourne's reputation had sunk, he was in no position to embark upon a new conflict of any kind, and he replied to Lord John that an attempt to create peers would be a very serious step, and that it would lead to the resignation of the government and to attempts to form another.[132] The decisive moment of the Melbourne administration had come and passed.

At the end of the session Lyndhurst taunted the government with his call for 'a return of the public bills which had been introduced into Parliament during the present Session, with the dates of their being rejected, or abandoned, or receiving the royal assent'. Lyndhurst sneered that 'in this House they are utterly powerless – they can effect nothing'.[133] In the lower house Hume put a different point of view. Arguing that a contest was going on whether aristocracy or democracy should prevail, he said that 'The Municipal Corporations and the rotten boroughs were as old as the Peerage. These had been swept away, and why might not the Peerage be swept away?'[134]

As O'Connell had forecast two years earlier, the Whigs must displace the peers, or the peers would displace them.[135] Lord John finished the session, and joined his family, which now included his first child Georgiana Adelaide, at Tunbridge Wells,[136] with his head revolving perpetually between schemes of creation and of dissolution. In August he again pressed Melbourne to create peers, and alleged that Grey had given him a pledge to create them in 1834.[137] To Brougham, he wrote that after the last session one of four results must ensue:

1. the Lords must pay more deference to the Commons, or
2. the Tories must get a majority in the Commons, or
3. the House of Lords must be increased by creation, or
4. Public opinion will run high for a change in the construction of the Lords.

My opinion is that the first will not happen; the second can not happen; the fourth is dangerous beyond measure; and the third will, one day, take place.[138]

At the same time Lord John consulted Parkes about the likely consequences of a dissolution. Parkes expected a gain of fifty seats, but went on: 'how any gain of the limited degree here calculated is to *force the Lords* I can't discern!'[139] Parkes thought the answer lay in a new Reform Bill, but that was something for which Lord John was not yet ready, and he preferred to go a little deeper into one of the specific problems involved in an immediate dissolution. The King could not live long, and when he died there would have to be an election. How could one dissolve now, knowing that the new parliament might not see the year out? Lord John's answer was to suggest a parliament bill, which would put an end to the dissolution of parliament upon the demise of the crown, do away with the law requiring ministers to seek re-election on taking office, and limit the duration of parliament to five years.[140] That, Lord John hoped, not altogether logically, would bring the lords to heel, and keep the Radicals at a distance for many years yet. But Melbourne was not enthusiastic, and no more was heard of it.[141]

iv. Office, 1836–7

The Whigs could not legislate for Ireland, but it was not true, as Roebuck alleged, that their continuing in office resulted in nothing for the public.[142] Ireland was governed through the judges, the magistrates, and the police, and for the first time since 1806–7 there were Reformers in Dublin Castle.

What could the new regime do? In the first place it could make symbolic gestures. In June 1835 Lord John gave orders that no flag was to be flown at the castle 'on occasion of any Victory gained in Civil War'.[143] Then, in October 1835, when O'Connell came to leave his card at the Castle, Mulgrave asked him to dinner. The King was furious, but Lord John stood up for the lord lieutenant.[144]

In the second place the administration brought a fresh approach to the collection of tithes, and for legislative failure it exacted an executive revenge. When the lords threw out the appropriation clause in 1835, Ellice heard that 'the Govt will say nothing, . . . and allow the Bishops, Lords and Church to settle their own affairs, and collect their own rents and tithes'.[145] No more public money was advanced to the Irish clergy, and Lord John prohibited the use of troops and police for the collection of tithes. If the attempt to collect tithes led to a riot, then troops and police might be called in to keep the peace.[146] But why should there be a riot, when there was no chance that a clergyman could collect his tithe unless he came supported by troops and police? The house of lords did not hold all the trumps, and the longer they held up a settlement, the harder it would become to collect any tithe at all.

In the third place the Irish executive pursued a policy of even-handed justice. The orange ascendancy had stimulated the growth of rival catholic riband societies in the south, and there were frequent fights between the different catholic groups, which helped to keep alive the notion of a disaffected population unfit to take any part in affairs of state. The administration knew where to break that vicious circle, and without actually proscribing the orangemen, they began to 'discourage and damp' them.[147] In December 1835 Lord John explained to Grey that a policeman was dismissed if he attended an orange lodge, and that a magistrate was not dismissed but that no new magistrate was appointed who had attended one.[148] Stipendiary magistrates were appointed to stiffen the bench in orange areas, orange processions were discouraged, and after an unusually violent procession on 12 July 1836, there were 400 prosecutions. Fewer precautions were needed in 1837 and 1838, and as the policy began to show results, the Irish executive was able to drop a hint to the catholics about the ribband societies and faction fights. The result was that after two or three years of Mulgrave's government Ireland was being transformed into a law-abiding country.[149]

In the fourth place, the exclusion which had been sanctioned by law until 1829 was no longer maintained by the executive.[150]

As vacancies arose, the judiciary was remodelled, the crown stopped challenging jurors on the ground that they were catholics,[151] and catholic solicitors were employed to conduct crown cases.[152] Above all, catholics were recruited into the police. The police act of 1836 merged the four provincial forces into a single body, and transferred the responsibility for appointing the constables from the lord lieutenants of counties to a new inspector general appointed by the executive. When the house of lords woke up to what was happening they found that the inspector general was taking on 1000 men a year, in the proportion of two catholics to every protestant. With the normal rates of wastage and recruitment the Whigs would not have to stay in office long before the police ceased to be identified with the ascendancy.[153]

Lord John's aim was to detach 'from the former partizans of Separation', and to recruit to 'the ranks of Order and British Connexion',[154] and on 29 December 1836 O'Connell wrote that the ministry was 'for the first time in History conquering the "Anti-Saxon" spirit of Ireland and adding eight millions to the King's subjects'.[155] There is no evidence that the King was grateful. Even without his approbation, however, the government had a strong incentive to stay in office, for as Mulgrave said, even 'the shortest interregnum here would be most mischievous'. It would allow the Tories to pour in a fresh supply of partisan judges 'and the old story would then be continued for another generation'.[156]

In preparing the government's legislation for 1837, Lord John had in mind Mulgrave's advice to devise something 'to satisfy the Dissenters (if possible!) and to interest the English Liberals at the very beginning of the Session, because if we are to go to the Country . . . it will not do to hang exclusively upon Irish questions'.[157] The one thing that could satisfy these criteria was the abolition of church rates, and a committee of cabinet was appointed which recommended that church leases should be 'nationalised' and the increment arising from proper management used to keep the churches in repair. Spencer Walpole thought this plan was adopted against Lord John's advice,[158] but Lord John referred to it as his own, and defended it as 'our only escape from the support of Church Rates on the one hand, or the adoption of the voluntary principle'.[159]

Melbourne agreed there was no other way, and was 'not against entering upon another desperate battle with the Church', but thought 'they will very likely effectively beat us this time'.[160]

When it came to Ireland, Lord John was in two minds whether to be conciliatory or not. He contemplated letting the Irish church retain its property, if the opposition would agree to support the roman catholic church and the presbyterians out of the consolidated fund, and to apply the proceeds of a land tax to education.[161] Nothing came of this, and Lord John finally decided, once again, to hold the tithe bill back. Tavistock had heard that many Tories were disgusted with the attitude their party had taken to the municipal corporations bill in 1836,[162] and Lord John now hoped to be able to establish elective councils in forty-eight towns.

There was also to be an addition to the session's fare. The introduction of an Irish poor law had been under consideration for some time. Grey had appointed a commission of inquiry headed by the archbishop of Dublin, of whom Melbourne said that it was impossible to be with him for ten minutes 'without perceiving not only that he can do no business, but that no business can be done where he is'.[163] When the report arrived it was found that the archbishop had been unable to resist playing to the gallery, and that he had, in the words of one of the commissioners, recommended 'some very strong measures with a view to improving the condition of the able bodied poor, by giving them employment and bringing into cultivation the waste and unimproved lands'.[164] This was not at all what was wanted. Lord John was not in a position to sponsor a raid on the British exchequer for the cultivation of marginal land, even had it been economic, and he courageously put the archbishop's report on the shelf.

But Lord John then determined to impose on Ireland the new English workhouse system which the report had rejected as 'totally inapplicable to the circumstances of this country'.[165] He chose one of the assistant commissioners of the English poor law, and sent him to Ireland. The archbishop scoffed at Mr Nicholls being sent 'to get one bottle of water out of the Liffey and one out of the Shannon',[166] and 'pho pho'd him unmercifully'.[167] After three months Nicholls, who had never been in

Ireland before, reported that he had no doubt as to the applica-
bility of the English poor law to Irish conditions.[168] Fortified by
what in this case was his dogmatic determination to treat
England, Scotland, and Ireland alike, Lord John prepared to
legislate in 1837.

His bill would not establish a right to relief, but it would provide for the division of the country into unions, the election of
boards of guardians, the levying of a local rate, and the construction of workhouses. It would thus begin to place the burden
of the Irish poor upon the Irish landowners. The English and
Scottish landowners already supported their poor, and they
were not likely to assist the Irish landowners evade a similar
responsibility, for far too many of the Irish poor at present
found their way over to England and Scotland. Lord John
hoped, therefore, that the bill would lead to a break in the parliamentary stalemate, and when he ventured to write to Stanley
about it, Stanley replied that he thought Lord John was on the
right track.[169]

Lord John's hopes were not fulfilled. O'Connell reacted to
the lords' behaviour in 1836 by starting a 'General Association'.
The protestants of Ireland replied, just before the new session
began, by calling a meeting in Dublin at which, behind locked
doors, they passed resolutions condemning the policies of the
Irish executive. The consequence was that when Lord John rose
on 7 February to ask for leave to bring in the Irish municipal
bill, he was, as Melbourne put it, 'teeming with some impru-
dence'.[170] He went far beyond the matter in hand to an outspoken defence of the government's whole Irish policy. First he
vindicated Mulgrave: then he turned upon the lords of the
protestant ascendancy:

> Sir, however much I disliked . . . this miserable monopolising
> minority, however much my mind revolted against the virulence
> of its exclusive spirit . . . I will confess, that in former days I had
> given them credit for candour and frankness.[171]

Roused to the defence of a friend, Lord John was like a scourge.
It was magnificent, and in due course when the bill was going
into committee the government defeated an amendment by 322
votes to 242, but it was not likely to lead to an adjustment between the two houses.

After this the session of 1837 was not productive. The Irish poor law bill passed the commons with little more opposition than was provided by the Irish themselves, but the church rates bill brought the government into unexpected difficulty. The bill violated the 'Lambeth Palace compact' of May 1835, and the archbishop of Canterbury refused to go on with the work of the ecclesiastical commission.[172] Melbourne excused himself by saying he had forgotten, and coaxed the archbishop back into harness with some asperity.[173] But in order to avoid a charge of dishonour against Lord John, the conduct of the bill in the commons was handed to Rice. The dissenters and Radicals malevolently objected to any scheme for improving the management of the church estates. The government majority sank to twenty-three on the second reading, and to five in committee, and it became clear that the bill would not pass. The problem was too intractable, and remained so until 1868.

Spencer thought the lords had been disposed to pass the Irish municipal bill until they were provoked by the church rates bill;[174] and the Stanleyites now moved in to take their revenge for 1834, by giving a decisive shift to the tactics of the opposition with regard to Ireland. The Tories announced that through their majority in the lords they would suffer no municipal bill, no poor law bill, and no remedial bill of any kind to pass, until the Whigs brought in a tithe bill without an appropriation clause. As Lord John said, this course 'has not been followed with a view to come to an adjustment'.[175] In 1837 the conduct of the opposition was even more outrageous than it had been in 1836. But this time there was no need for Lord John to press upon a reluctant Melbourne the creation of peers. The King fell ill in May, and when he died in June, the ministry were glad to abandon all those measures which they could not pass, and to dissolve.

So ended the appropriation parliament, in which the Whigs pursued what some men thought a noble principle and others a will o' the wisp. Both points of view were well put in a correspondence between Lord John and Palmerston in 1843. Lord John wrote that what he had always dreaded was

being responsible for the government of Ireland without having any thing just or kind to offer. The appropriation clause saved us from this dreadful position and when we gave it up [in 1838], we had established such a character for good administration in Ireland, that we could still govern.[176]

To this Palmerston replied that the appropriation clause had been most just and rational, but that it had not been well chosen as an issue on which to turn out one government and substitute another.[177]

CHAPTER IX

Finality Jack, 1837–9

i. *Office, 1837–8*

THE death of William IV removed one obstacle from the Whigs' path, and they lost no time in publishing a letter from the young queen to her lord lieutenant, expressing her desire to see her Irish subjects 'in the full enjoyment of that civil and political Equality to which by recent statutes they are fully entitled'.[1] With her approval Mulgrave now switched his attention from the police to the magistrates, and in issuing the new commission of the peace took the opportunity of 'rather purifying' the bench:

> The neglectful non-attendance of some . . . will furnish a very good reason in several cases. We have got also several instances of persons . . . proclaiming themselves Orangemen in a manner which would have justified perhaps their immediate expulsion but certainly their omission upon a new occasion.[2]

In particular, Mulgrave was anxious to exclude the protestant clergy, if it could be done without giving the Tories 'additional proof of our determination to persecute Protestantism'.[3]

Not even royal favour, however, could now do the Whigs much good at a general election, and in July Lord John asked Melbourne to reconsider taking Durham into the cabinet. Melbourne refused,[4] but Lord John still expected a net gain of twenty-five to thirty seats.[5] That was wildly optimistic: the Tories made progress in the counties, and the Radicals – despite the municipal corporations reform act – lost ground in the towns. Lord John himself was returned for Stroud, and on 13 August he sent Melbourne a detailed statement of the results.[6]

	Ministry	Opposition	Doubtful
English counties	46	109	4
English boroughs	190	151	
Scotch counties	11	19	
Scotch boroughs	22	1	
Irish counties	40	24	
Irish boroughs	29	12	
	338	318 [316]	4

In subsequent estimates Lord John put the majority at twenty-six to thirty.[7] This was on general issues: on an appropriation clause it would fall to between five and twelve, compared to the majority of twenty-seven in 1836.[8]

The Whigs' losses were in the counties. In the 1820s Lord John had taken it for granted that county elections were popular, but Grey's government had accepted the Chandos clause and the consequences were now apparent. The counties had become the new pocket boroughs. Lansdowne found that in Wiltshire 'the farmers are completely in the dependence of the squires who are nineteen out of twenty against us, and at present in close alliance with the church, so that every country parish is organized against us'.[9] Mulgrave wrote that the parsonry and squirearchy had 'knocked about our English counties in the most unexpected manner',[10] and Ellice thought that the squires were now ready to arrest 'the experiment now fairly going on for the first time, of rational and benevolent government'.[11]

As Mulgrave said, 'this is very different from what we had flattered ourselves would have been the result'.[12] What had gone wrong? Melbourne quoted his steward, a dissenter, who said it was 'the cry against O'Connell, and the notion of England being governed by Irishmen and Roman Catholics'.[13] But there were other factors, and Melbourne himself regretted stirring the church rates question.[14] Lord John did not think church rates had contributed much either way. The only election he heard of where they turned the scale was at Lichfield, where the question worked in the Whigs' favour.[15] He could find no reason for the Whigs' great overthrow in Bedfordshire 'except it be the Poor Laws . . . O'Connell is not now mention'd'.[16] In the country as a whole, he thought the way the opposition exploited the cry against the poor law exceeded 'any thing in Tory profligacy before known',[17] and by the middle of August Lord John and Melbourne agreed that the poor law was to blame.[18]

Melbourne and Lord John responded to the results in different ways. It did not take the equable Melbourne long to conclude that 'we have lost ground' as the representatives of liberal opinions, 'and that our adversaries have in some degree gained'.[19] When Lord John had himself under control, he agreed with this, and was glad 'the Peel profession of faith' was 'very liberal compared to the Tory creed of former days'.[20] But in a more sorrowful moment he wrote to the Queen that the Tory party had gained 'the appearance of a change of opinion which has not in fact taken place'.[21] This was a delusion, and Melbourne was right to remind Lord John that it was vain to argue and analyse: 'all elections by plurality of votes have been and will be subject to the objection that votes have been improperly obtained. We cannot help that. We must go by the result.'[22]

Melbourne thought that in Peel's place he would not be put off making a bid for power by the necessity to govern Ireland,[23] and Lord John admitted that it was impossible for the Whigs, 'as honest men, or even as party men', to remain in office unless they could carry good measures. But in Ireland, which was the field of battle, every act of administration was a measure in itself, and one which tended 'to consolidate a good system so thoroughly, that future tories must govern justly however much they dislike it'.[24] Furthermore, as Mulgrave pointed out, 'no Government of an opposite character could stand',[25] and Lord John concluded that a Tory ministry with three-fourths of Ireland, more than half Scotland, and not fewer than 300 members of the house of commons against them, would be far more weak and inefficient 'than our own'.[26]

The Whigs must carry on, but it was not going to be an easy parliament to manage. The old parliament had been pledged to them from the first day to the last.[27] Melbourne expected the new house of commons to contain more decided party men,[28] and Lord John doubted whether the parties to the Lichfield House compact would now pull so well together.[29] The Irish would still be staunch, but the Radical remainder would be impatient. Lord John made a new effort to persuade Melbourne to take Durham into the cabinet. Melbourne admitted the cabinet was too narrow, but

> Durham I am clear for having nothing to do with. His temper is his least fault. He is dishonest and unprincipled. There is no opinion nor person he will not sacrifice to further his immediate end . . . People have been always afraid of him and have dealt with him as if they were afraid.[30]

That being so, the Whigs, as Lady Holland joked, now had nothing to rely on but the Queen and Paddy. Lord John good humouredly rebuked Morpeth for saying he could see his way through all difficulties except the Irish tithe bill: 'Did you ever hear of the gentleman who read thro' Euclid with great success, only he had not attended to the figures?'[31] Privately, he admitted that he dreaded the coming session: 'I feel that any slight mistake of mine, or even an untoward and inevitable accident may expose me to the blame of ruining the concern.'[32] There could have been no surer way of bringing on the evil he anticipated.

In a speech at Stroud Lord John once again spelled out the traditional position of Whig in the middle. He denounced the fifty years of Tory rule, proclaimed his wish if the Tories now called themselves Conservatives, to call himself a Reformer, and then turned on the Radicals and announced that he could not follow them to ballot, triennial parliaments, household suffrage and an elective house of lords. Instead he looked forward to a new reign that would be glorious for the reduction of crime, and for the spread of education.[33] His speech was well received, but the government was still faced with that old difficulty of a Whig administration: 'if they attempt little their friends grow slack, and if they attempt much their enemies grow strong'.[34] There was a danger that they would lose the initiative and find themselves at the mercy of events. Lord John, therefore, wanted to bring parliament 'to an issue on some large intelligible question of policy', before the administration's force was gradually 'frittered away by personal matters and general weariness'.[35]

But first the ministry must disentangle itself from church rates and the appropriation clause. Lord John took the view that having proposed one church rates bill in 1834 which was objected to by the dissenters, and another in 1837 which was objected to by the church, the government was not bound to try again.[36] As for the appropriation clause, the new house was not bound by the resolution of 1835. O'Connell had already assured Lord John that he did not wish to see the ministry put in jeopardy,[37] and Mulgrave now repeated that the Irish would make no difficulty about putting the Irish tithe bill in any shape in which 'it shall be considered safest and least embarrassing for the Government'.[38] Melbourne suggested taking the Irish measures in the order in which the house of lords wished to have them,[39] but both he and Mulgrave realised that the exact manner in which appropriation was given up must be a matter for Lord John.[40]

The death of the King had, however, opened a door to two reforms in which Lord John was interested. These were a solution to the house of lords problem through the creation of life peers, and the reform of the army. Melbourne replied shortly that Lord John's recommendation of life peers was not likely to make them either acceptable or popular.[41] Every proposal Lord John made for the reform of the lords thus fell to Melbourne's determination never to be regarded as a blackguard in his own club, and all Lord John could do was to repeat that there was much to be said for life peers, which he reserved for another opportunity.[42]

Army reform, on the other hand, was something that Melbourne was prepared to discuss. Lord John told Melbourne that the majority of the Radicals did not seek grounds of difference. That being so 'we should do well to unite such people with us as much as possible'. The question they most cared about was removing 'the Tories from the political command of the Army', which was now by far the most obviously unreformed institution in the state.[43]

The government already had a committee considering the question. Everyone agreed that the administration of the army ought to be placed either under a secretary of state or under a board, and Lord John himself was in favour of a secretary of state.[44] But the longer Melbourne pondered the problem, the more he felt he had no wish to offend the Horse Guards, and no wish to please the Radicals either. Lord John returned to the topic early in 1838,[45] and again in 1839, and Howick even contemplated making the necessary changes by order in council.

But this brought Melbourne out in the colours of the constitu-
tionalist,[46] and nothing was done. Ten years later Lord John,
then prime minister, told Howick, then the third Earl Grey,
that he could not enforce a measure which Wellington said
would destroy the army. The results were seen in the Crimea.[47]

Searching desperately for some means of satisfying the Radicals, Lord John now found himself for the first time flirting with
the idea of the ballot. Hitherto he and Melbourne had agreed
to resist it, on the ground that it would be followed by demands
for household suffrage and an elective house of lords.[48] But he
realised that the issue was an exception to the general decline
of Radical politics: he consulted Brougham on the propriety of
making it an open question,[49] and he prophesied that 'it will
be a very awkward affair if nearly all our supporters out of
office vote for ballot'.[50]

At this point Lord John was getting onto dangerous ground,
because the ballot was one of the few issues upon which, in his
heart of hearts, he utterly disagreed with the Radicals. First, he
shared the common feeling that it was a 'bad, secret, shabby
way of voting'.[51] Secondly he used the argument that M.P.s
cast their votes in public – so therefore should the voters who
returned them.[52] Thirdly he took the line that those who did
not have votes ought to be able to influence those who did, and
that to concede the ballot would shut the masses out of politics
altogether, and drive them into an irresistible demand for an
extension of the suffrage.[53] Deeper than any argument, however, Lord John feared ballot as the beginning of an attack upon
his order and its property.

Nevertheless, if there was a chance of agitation being successful, it was Lord John's duty, as a Whig, to take control of
innovation out of the hands of dangerous men. That is why he
now asked Melbourne to consider making ballot an open
question.[54] Melbourne replied that it was something the cabinet
ought to consider in due course,[55] but quickly recovered his
nerve, came out firmly against making it an open question,[56]
and finally convinced himself that the ministry had been formed
upon the principle of resisting it.[57] Lord John was left with no
alternative, but to meet parliament empty-handed.

The new parliament was called up early under the six months
after the demise of the crown rule. Lord John asked Peel

whether he intended to oppose Abercromby's nomination as speaker. Peel did not: but he answered in the third person that he had not received notice of the intention to oppose Manners Sutton in 1835.[58] Melbourne muttered that he had thought Lord John would get 'a roughish kick from Peel'.[59] 'Peel's answer is cross and sarcastic, but I take that to be the real nature of the man, and it is only prudence and calculation that ever makes him otherwise.'[60]

When parliament met, the Radicals, led by Wakley, at once accused the Whigs of going into coalition with the Conservatives, announced that they wished to remind the government that it had some Radical supporters, and moved amendments pledging the new parliament to consider extending the franchise, shortening the duration of parliaments, and introducing the ballot. Lord John had come up edgy and felt it was impossible to let himself 'be carried away in the flood of Wakley and Hume'.[61] When stung he spoke out far too bravely for his own good, and that is how he came to earn the title of Finality Jack. Instead of just saying that in the present parliament further reform was obviously out of the question, Lord John turned on the Radicals, and then went out of his way to commit himself against a further extension of the franchise.[62]

Lord John's speech embarrassed both his colleagues, who found themselves publicly committed against the ballot, and his supporters, who thought it could not have been worse had it been intended to raise a cheer among the Tories. Lord John had lost his character without any proportional gain. Charles Buller at once charged him with having repeated the blunder of the Duke of Wellington in 1830,[63] Spencer doubted whether the ministry would swim or drown,[64] Tavistock wrote that John's declaration had raised 'great alarm for the stability of the administration',[65] and Lord John himself immediately realised that he had gone too far. The very next night he began to try and extricate himself, and made something more like the speech he ought to have made in the first place. Greville thought it a complete vindication.[66] But it was not that, and Melbourne's ministry never recovered from the manner in which the new parliament began.

Lord John was not to be allowed to forget that he had made a bad start. In 1835 his first triumph over Peel had been to secure the election of Abercromby as speaker. Now, at the end of 1837, Abercromby complained that he received no support from the leader of the house.[67] Lord John reacted sharply to this, and while Abercromby's resignation still hung in the balance, Spencer and Tavistock tried to draw a helpful distinction between Lord John who was now committed against the ballot, and the rest of his colleagues, who, they thought it might still be argued, were not,[68] and Mulgrave chipped in with the Radical argument that the ballot was peculiarly a question upon which a member 'might fairly consider first not those with whom he was acting but those by whom he was sent'.[69] Melbourne spent Christmas talking Abercromby round, and trying to prevent his government from falling as a result of 'embarrassments arising within itself in a manner unintelligible and unsatisfactory to the great body of its supporters'.[70]

When parliament reassembled in February 1838, the Radicals, marshalled by Grote, led off with a debate on the ballot. Their motion was disposed of by 315 votes to 198. But the debate and the vote showed the government in the new and unenviable position of relying upon their Conservative enemies to save them from their Radical friends. Barely one-sixth of the Whig party voted in the majority,[71] and embarrassment followed embarrassment. Some ministers wanted to concede the ballot in municipal elections;[72] Sir Hussey Vivian offered his resignation from the ordnance;[73] and Sheil, a roman catholic whom Lord John was particularly anxious to promote, was so deeply committed to the ballot that he had to be content with a post at Greenwich hospital instead.[74] As Tavistock said, how are you to go on with 200 of your supporters shut out of office?[75] For once, Tavistock was gloomy with good reason.

In the meantime Lord John himself was busy making up his mind how to bring the long struggle between the two houses over Ireland to an end. One good thing happened straight away. Alarmed at the prospect of the imminent dissolution of the ministry, O'Connell agreed to disband the General Association.[76] It was not the last time that O'Connell was more faithful than the Radicals, and his conciliatory action encouraged Lord John, once again, to bring before parliament a new and wider scheme intended to satisfy both parties.

The Tories were to get secure incomes for the clergy paid out of the consolidated fund. But the Liberals – as they were now beginning to be called – were to get appropriation, for the rent-charge (or if Lord John could manage it, a land tax in its place) was to be used to pay the Irish constabulary.[77] O'Connell seems to have agreed to this on the understanding that as the Irish became more peaceable the cost of the constabulary would be reduced, and the Irish would gradually free themselves from the burden of this substitute for tithe.[78] Lord John, on the other hand, had no intention of letting the rent-charges fade away with the good behaviour of the Irish (though he did play with the notion of redemption). His plan was that the money that was not wanted for the police would be paid into the consolidated fund. The Irish would not, he thought, object, because he was busy with a new plan for the concurrent endowment of the three religions.

The new scheme pleased nobody. The Irish primate, Dr Murray, agreed that endowment 'would present itself in a very different aspect . . . coming from this Government than it would from any which had preceded it', but ventured to suggest that it was premature.[79] Drummond did not like the plan because he wanted to lay his hands on the surplus rent-charges for the construction of railways,[80] and Mulgrave did not like it because he wanted to take them to pay for the Irish poor law.[81] Poulett Thomson witheringly pointed out that the scheme would offend everybody,[82] and Lord John finally decided, as in 1836 and 1837, to keep his church and tithe plan in cold storage until he had been able to observe the fate of his other Irish measures.

Drummond pointed out that the poor law bill was not popular with the Irish M.P.s,[83] but Lord John decided to go on both with that and with the municipal corporations bill in much the same form that he had introduced them the year before. The poor law bill passed its second reading in the commons in February 1838. It was opposed by O'Connell, and the debate underlined the increased dependence of the ministry upon Peel. The municipal corporations bill also passed its second reading, and Lord John then demanded to know whether Peel and Stanley now conceded that there should be corporations in Ireland, in which case the two parties could discuss how many there were to be and upon what franchise? Peel refused to say until he knew what Lord John proposed to do about the church.

Lord John replied that it was time to bring this fruitless contest
to an end, and indicated the lines along which his new tithe
measure was drafted. Peel then told him that the preservation
of the Irish church in its present form was the condition of a
municipal corporations settlement.[84] Once again, Lord John
had offered to make generous provision for the Irish church,
within the framework of a wider settlement of Irish problems.
Once again he was snubbed by a short-sighted foe.

There was nothing for Lord John to do but to put Peel's terms
to Mulgrave, whose answer was that tithe was

> a subject on which all sides have been so long accustomed syste-
> matically to *lie* . . . The Parson has been accustomed to exaggerate
> his receipts and his scruples, the Farmer to exaggerate his sense of
> grievance. But whatever they may say I am sure that they are all
> heartily sick of the Question. It had for the time a fictitious im-
> portance in the eyes of the Irish people, being then considered by
> them as the link in their chains which rattled most. But they are
> now very ready to believe that those chains are dropping off, and
> if Corporate Enfranc] isement was to accompany any settlement
> of the Tithe Question I do not believe they would be very punc-
> tilious as to what the terms of that settlement were.[85]

Fortified by this letter, Lord John was all set to give up appropriation when Acland introduced into the debate a motion to
expunge the famous resolution of 1835 from the Journals of the
house.

It was one thing to abandon a policy – it was another to be
asked to recant. Lord John turned at bay, and in one of his most
rousing speeches poured scorn on those who, professing attachment to the church, raised this angry debate. He had agreed to
bring forward the tithe plan before going into committee on the
municipal corporations. Now he was met by this motion to res-
cind the resolution of 1835. 'The only advantage I have, is the
advantage I shall derive for my future guidance from the past
conduct of my opponents, which is, that whenever they make
professions I shall consider those professions as snares.'[86] He
warned the Tories that they had already gone too far for their
own objects. The plan produced by the government in 1835
would have been accepted as final. A new plan without appropriation could not now be final, and even a new plan with it

might not be.[87] At the division sixteen Liberals were absent un-
paired. Molesworth was ill, Cowper was 'in bed', Gore Langton
was 'sulking and ill', Leader's mother had just died, and T.
Martin was in Galway jail.[88] Nevertheless, the ministry won by
317 votes to 298, and the majority of nineteen was encouraging.

Lord John could now afford to concede what he could not
carry. On 29 May he committed himself publicly to abandon
appropriation provided the municipal corporations bill was
allowed to pass.[89] He had some reason to hope that he had escaped from his dilemma with credit. But the rest of the story
was exactly what might have been feared. The Whigs made
their concession, and did not obtain an equal one in return. The
tithe bill was modified to suit Peel. The rent charge was fixed
at 75 per cent of the composition and there was to be no appropriation for any 'useful' purpose. The only concession the Tories
made was that arrears of tithe were to be cancelled. Turning to
the Radicals, Lord John agreed this was unfair on those who
had paid their tithes, but there was nothing he could do about
it.[90] The time had come to take what tithe bill he could get,[91]
and at the end the bill looked remarkably like that of 1834: Peel,
Stanley, O'Connell and Lord John all voted for it, and its
passage through the lords was then a formality. The act relieved Mulgrave from 'the fear of a fatal collision with the
people',[92] and Lord John later boasted that no measure had
tended more to the peaceful progress of Ireland than the tithe
act of 1838.[93] It is true that in many places the Irish forgot to
pay and the English forgot to prosecute, but where the rent
charge was collected it had the effect of taking the clergy out of
the firing line, and putting the landlords in their place.

Once they knew that the church was safe, the lords allowed
the poor law bill to pass. In committee a sharp attack was made
by the Irish interest on the clause allowing the guardians to give
relief to the able-bodied,[94] but this was beaten off, and the bill
received the royal assent. The impetuous Nicholls then showed
that whatever he lacked in sympathy he made up in drive. In
June 1839 Ebrington wrote that the unions were going up
rapidly,[95] and by the time the Whigs left office in 1841, workhouses had sprung up all over Ireland: in 1842 over 15,000
people were being relieved, and in 1845 over 40,000.[96]

When the coronation took place in June, Melbourne missed a

golden opportunity to create peers. He made no political creations, and only eight new peers. But he promoted Mulgrave,
who became the Marquis of Normanby. The lords did not like
that, and when the Irish municipal corporations bill came back
to the commons, twenty-six clauses had been left out and ninety-
two new ones had been added. The number of towns in schedule
A to be given free institutions had been cut to twelve, and the
£5 rating franchise had been changed to £10.[97] It was difficult
to know what to do. The lords had at last agreed that there
should be municipal corporations in Ireland, and they had also
agreed to a schedule B of places which might, under conditions,
apply to the lord lieutenant for incorporation. These were
great points gained, and at first Melbourne and Lord John were
inclined to accept the amendments.[98] But Tavistock warned
Lord John that this would lead to a revolt in the party,[99] and
Normanby took the view that they were bound to be able to get
as good a bill next year.[100] Lord John therefore attempted to
drive a bargain. He would accept the restriction to twelve
towns if the lords would accept an £8 franchise.[101] There was a
conference between the houses, but the lords would not give
way, and the bill was dropped.

It is time to turn, as the Whig ministry did, late, to the affairs
of Canada. Canada was governed under the Quebec Act of 1774,
which left the French their ancient laws and land tenures, and
Pitt's Canada Act of 1791, under which the two provinces of
upper (English) and lower (French) Canada were ruled separ-
ately. In each province there was a council, nominated by the
governor, which was in no way responsible to the elected assembly. When the Whigs took office in 1830, the Canadians
hoped for constitutional advance, and the English, who were
now settling in lower as well as upper Canada, also hoped to see
English laws and customs promoted at the expense of French
ones. All they received from Grey's government was Ripon's
act of 1831, which turned over crown revenues of £38,000 to the
colonists, out of which they were expected to vote a civil list.
The Canadians became restive, and Melbourne and Glenelg
appointed a commission of inquiry under Lord Gosford. The
commission worked methodically, and in 1836 Lord John asked
the house of commons in Westminster to be patient.[102]

In 1837 Lord John had no Canadian policy of his own.[103] His approach to Canada was that it was another problem like Ireland, the burden of debt, the bad poor laws, and the composition of the house of lords, which the Whigs had inherited from Pitt and from the fifty years of Tory rule.[104] But Canadian affairs brought out in him an unusually doctrinaire constitutionalism, unrelieved by the fine sentiments with which he approached the problems of Ireland. If the cry for responsible government came from lower Canada, he dismissed it as a request by the French for leave to oppress the British – the assembly in lower Canada was using 'the weapons of Hampden, in support of the principles of Wentworth'.[105] If the demand came from upper Canada, he met it by the argument that responsible government was incompatible with the relations between a colony and the mother country. The governor of a colony was responsible to the imperial parliament. He, and the executive he chose, could not at the same time be responsible to the elected assembly, and if the colonies did not like the present arrangements it would be better for them to separate from the United Kingdom altogether.[106] Lord John could see no half-way house between British dominion and Canadian independence, and before the session of 1837 was wound up, he secured the assent of the commons to ten resolutions vindicating imperial supremacy. The assembly in lower Canada promptly rejected the resolutions, and Canada was in a state of crisis.

At this point Canadian and British history began to revolve round each other in the person of Durham. This man, with whom Melbourne would not work himself, now occurred to him as a suitable person to settle the affairs of Canada. An approach was made to Durham, but nothing had been settled before Papineau took up arms against the administration in lower Canada in October. The news reached England on 22 December, and on 26 December Lord John urged Melbourne to remove Glenelg from the colonial office, and suggested that, if it would soften the blow, he and Glenelg should change places.[107] Melbourne refused to make a scapegoat of Glenelg, but on 31 December he agreed that the ministry ought either to take such measures as the crisis required, or to resign and to allow others to do so.[108] In the meantime, in Canada, Sir John Colborne easily suppressed the rebellion.

The classic solution was to assume special powers, and to send out a new man to make a fresh start. But special powers troubled Whig consciences, and Howick said that, unless he was satisfied by the proposals for a fresh start, he would resign rather than agree to them. In these circumstances the cabinet decided to make another approach to Durham, and Howick withdrew his threat.[109] For him, and for the more Radical members of the cabinet, Durham's name was a guarantee that something would be done for Canada that was Liberal. For others, like Melbourne, and perhaps also Lord John, there was a second advantage in getting Durham out of the way, for after Lord John's speech at the opening of parliament, Durham was the one man who might have given an effective lead to the campaign for the ballot.

While Durham was making up his mind whether to go to Canada, Lord John was trying to bring the cabinet to one mind about the special powers. They could either suspend the *habeas corpus* act, or they could suspend the constitution of 1791. Lord John set out the difference with dramatic clarity, and concluded that if Colborne were to remain in charge the first course would be better, but that if Durham would agree to go the cabinet ought to choose the second.[110] On 15 January Durham met the cabinet and accepted their invitation, and the next day Lord John introduced a bill to suspend the constitution of Canada for four years, and to give Durham and a special council power to pass any necessary legislation in the meantime. In 1833 Lord John had defended the Irish coercion act with the curious argument that ordinary times ought not to be confounded with extraordinary ones, and that therefore the more completely the constitution was suspended the better.[111] Now, in the case of Canada, he was proposing one of the most draconian measures ever to come before parliament.

Lord John consulted Stanley, who thought Peel's party were not likely to oppose the suspension bill.[112] But the Irish newspapers and the Irish M.P.s saw in Canada a case like their own, and there was still a danger that the Tories would be tempted to do a deal with O'Connell over Canada and throw the government out – for they could at least offer the Irish a municipal corporations bill in the certainty that it would pass. Lord John was particularly gratified, therefore, to find that by his policy of

justice to Ireland he had earned enough credit to be able to secure O'Connell's silence. When Mulgrave asked Drummond to
'endeavour to put some check upon the absurdities the Press
have been perpetrating', he had some success;[113] and when
Mulgrave himself saw O'Connell he persuaded him not to
attend the house at the beginning of the session, and extracted
from him the promise that when he did he would say that

> he did and does disapprove of the Policy of the Government to-
> wards Canada . . . but that Papineau having . . . resorted to civil
> war, it would be contrary to the whole tenour of his [O'Connell's]
> public life to approve . . . these recent proceedings.[114]

Six months later, when O'Connell spoke, this was exactly the
line he took.[115]

The government passed its bill and Durham went out with
his special powers. Molesworth's premature assault on Glenelg
on 7 March, and Peel's fair amendment, were defeated by 316
votes to 287, and Spencer supposed that Lord John would
then get smoothly over the rest of the session.[116] But anyone who
had considered what sort of man Durham was, and with what
motives ministers had chosen him, might have known that his
appointment would raise more problems than it solved. In Durham the Prince was as strong as the Democrat, and to Mulgrave's love of posturing he added Duncannon's love of wine.
Even before he sailed, there was trouble about his expenses, and
about his choice of Wakefield and Turton for his staff. Wakefield
was an expert on colonial affairs, but had been sent to prison
for abducting an heiress, while Turton had shown a wayward
sexual appetite for his wife's sister. Lord John thought Melbourne had better say to Durham, 'You cannot expect us to
approve' these appointments, 'but seeing the difficulties you are
under in other respects we shall say no more about it.'[117] But
Melbourne promised the lords that no public appointment
would be offered to Turton, and Durham was obliged to pay
him out of his own pocket.

When he arrived in Canada, Durham had to decide how to
deal with the prisoners taken in the rebellion of 1837. He released most of them on the day of the Queen's coronation. But
he spared the lives of the remainder on condition they sign
confessions of guilt. He then banished eight of them to Bermuda,

and these eight and seven other rebels who had fled were put on pain of death if they returned. In a Roman emperor this proceeding would have been clement, and both Melbourne and Glenelg incautiously expressed their approval. But in the nineteenth century there were strong objections in law, and in the house of lords there was a strong lawyer waiting to take advantage of them. Brougham had been moving steadily into opposition ever since Melbourne gave Cottenham the great seal. Campbell is probably exaggerating when he says that by 1837 Lyndhurst acquired an ascendancy over Brougham's mind, and that when Campbell asked him what he proposed to do about the Irish municipal bill, Lyndhurst replied, 'Me! . . . What I mean to do! I never open my mouth now, and I oppose nothing. Ask Brougham there, what he means to do. He is the man now.'[118] But Brougham was the man in the summer of 1838, and right at the end of the session, in August, posing as the innocent champion of the constitution, he introduced a bill to indemnify Durham from the illegality of his actions.

It was equally difficult for the government to oppose this bill and to amend it. But in the ordinary way men pull together to help a colleague out of trouble, and even an opposition party hesitates to press home an advantage against a newly appointed governor faced with a crisis. But Melbourne made no effort, became rattled, and drove the Duke of Wellington into Brougham's arms. The bill passed the lords and was sent down to the commons. It was the most delicate situation Lord John ever encountered. Everyone realised that Durham had got himself into an impossible position: 'His appointments universally condemned, and almost cancelled, and his proclamation declared illegal! His advisers without character, and now, it seems, without legal knowledge!'[119] But, somehow, Lord John must defend him, and do so without saying that Melbourne had been feeble. To this task he rose: he accepted the bill, but he put himself at Durham's side.

> I know that in spite of illegality, in spite of informality, in spite of the violation of principle . . . he has taken a course which . . . has reconciled the ways of mercy with that which was due to the safety of the province, and to the interests of her Majesty's faithful subjects there . . . looking at the conduct of the Earl of Durham as a whole . . . I shall be ready to take part with him.[120]

Then, for the first time in his life, he turned on Brougham: 'no bitterness of sarcasm, accompanied by professions of friendship . . . will in the least degree affect the noble Earl against whom they have been levelled.'[121] The thrust went home and the speaker, who had begun the session by complaining about Lord John, now made the *amende honorable,* and congratulated him upon having done

> more than I thought possible to extricate Lord Melbourne from a difficulty of the most painful and serious character; for I never could see how he could reconcile himself to remain in office when he could not defend or protect a person in so very arduous a situation as Lord Durham.[122]

Before they separated for the vacation, the cabinet hastily drafted Durham new instructions on how to deal with the prisoners.

A session which had begun disastrously thus ended in a personal triumph for Lord John. But there was not much else to show for his year's work. He had defeated an attempt by the Radicals to shorten the term of negro apprenticeship under the emancipation act of 1833, and he had carried a bill to restrict pluralities. But this was not enough to erase from the public mind the impression that the ministry had been almost equally humiliated by the several steps forward which it took in Ireland, and by the several steps back which it took in Canada. Normanby wrote that with the exception of Melbourne and Lord John there was not a single man in the government for whom the country cared a straw.[123] Ellice thought the whole concern was déconsidéré,[124] and Lord John's father concluded that with the exception of Lord John, and perhaps Melbourne and Howick, 'there is not a man among them fit to be called a minister'.[125]

Worst of all, the Reformers were beginning to complain about their leader. Lord John's private secretary noticed that when M.P.s came out of Lord John's room, they appeared 'much dissatisfied with their reception. His manner was cold and shy, and even when he intended to comply with the request made, in his answer he rather implied no than yes.'[126] The Irish felt no notice was taken of them,[127] Spencer tactfully suggested that 'a leader sometimes takes the sanction of his Colleagues a little too much for granted',[128] and the Duke of Bedford told Lord John bluntly:

> you give great offence to your followers . . . in the H. of Commons by not being *courteous* to them, by treating them superciliously or *de haut en bas*, by not listening with sufficient patience to their solicitations, remonstrances, or whatever it may be . . .[129]

A man in office can spare but little time for his supporters, and in Lord John's case there was now doubt as to the inclination.

> Like or dislike, he does not care a jot;
> He wants your vote, but your affection not.[130]

ii. Office, 1838–9

In August 1838 Lord John went to Ryde with Lady John who was expecting his second child. Next he paid a visit to Ireland,[131] where he had not been since 1833. Then, at the beginning of September Melbourne received a despatch from Durham in which he reported that the British party in lower Canada would throw themselves into the arms of the Americans rather than endure the restoration of political power to the French Canadians, and recommended that 'any settlement to be successful must be founded upon the subjugation of the French people and the destruction of their peculiar laws and institutions'.[132] While Melbourne and Lord John were digesting this ferocious communication, they were still waiting anxiously to find out how Durham would react to the indemnity act. Lord John told Durham that if he (Lord John) had been in the lords he could have done no better than his colleagues there,[133] and assured Melbourne that Durham could not fairly say Melbourne had given him up.[134] But Melbourne thought Durham would 'concoct a general arrangement by the end of October', send it home, follow it himself, and boast of the effect he had produced,[135] and Lord John, too, feared that Durham would 'come home not a little bitter against us'.[136]

Durham had been badly done by: and he now did worse back. In private he made a distinction between Lord John, whom he thanked for his advocacy, and Melbourne and Glenelg, who had betrayed him.[137] In public he pretended that he had been reduced in status to a clerk, and threw up his post in

time to leave Canada before the winter. Disdaining his new instructions for dealing with the prisoners, his last act was to
stress that since the ordinances had been disallowed, there was
nothing to prevent the eight ringleaders from returning to
Canada. As Lord John said, Durham was virtually encouraging
a second rebellion (which duly took place) 'against an abdicat-
ing Governor, and a shaken authority'.[138] To Palmerston, Lord
John wrote, in words remarkably like those which Palmerston
later applied to him, 'One may be dragged thro' the dirt once
or twice and wash oneself clean, but it will not do to wear a coat
of mud permanently.'[139] Palmerston joined in the condemna-
tion of Durham, and from Ireland both Normanby and Morpeth wrote hoping there would be no truckling to him when he
got back.[140]

In October Lord John pressed Melbourne to recall parliament, and to redefine the special powers granted to the government of Canada.[141] Granted that the Whigs had a bad case, it
was the kind of bad case Lord John had simplicity and courage
enough to speak well to. But Palmerston argued that it was the
executive government which had got itself into this mess, and
must get itself out again.[142] Consequently Lord John renewed
his pressure upon Melbourne to remove Glenelg from the
colonial office. On 25 October he wrote that he had received
Glenelg's latest despatch, which was *mere verbiage*, proposing
nothing, asking nothing, deciding nothing'.[143]

> I never felt in such embarrassment as when last year I had to de-
> fend the Canada papers. What Peel said of them was in many
> instances indisputably true; and one had only to revert to the bad
> plea that preceding Tory Governments had done much worse.[144]

At this point, on 21 October, Lord John's second child was
born, a little girl, who was named Victoria. For a day or two
afterwards, all went well. But then Lady John caught a fever,
and on 1 November she died.[145] Very little is known about Lord
and Lady John's three and a half years together. Lord William
condemned his brother's *mésalliance*, and Lady Holland quarrelled with Lady John: both were jealous. Tom Moore thought it
would not be easy to find 'a nicer little pair',[146] but then Moore's
memoirs were edited by Lord John, and must be treated with
caution. Nor is it easy to discover the truth from letters of

condolence. But there is no reason to doubt the sincerity of Elizabeth Villiers, who wrote that 'nothing could be more complete than your poor Adelaide's happiness during the few joyful years she spent with you . . . you restored her from a state of solitary suffering to even more than her former happiness'.[147] And Queen Victoria, who claimed to have known Lady John '*very* well and liked her', did not believe 'two people ever were happier together'.[148]

Lord John was quite overcome, shut himself off, and told Tavistock that he did not know when he would be able to attend a cabinet again. He was unable to concentrate on business, Howick took charge of some of his papers, and an unkind newspaper hinted at retirement.[149] In the meantime Durham returned to England, and he too, though for very different reasons, refused to communicate with his colleagues. It was a bizarre spectacle. Canada must be legislated for, and both the leader of the house of commons and the abdicated governor were incommunicado. Lord John, of course, came round faster than Durham. Tavistock came to see him, which pleased him, for 'There is no one in the world I love better',[150] and Tavistock, like his father and Lord Spencer, urged Lord John to go back to work as the best cure for sorrow.[151]

Lord John had every incentive to come back, for the cabinet was discussing his new education bill. All Russells are interested in education. Lord John's father was convinced that it could not be the intention 'of the divine Founder of our Religion' that little children should have the curse of ignorance put upon them,[152] and he consistently took the view that 'the Cause of Education is still higher than Politicks'.[153] It is not surprising, therefore, that from the moment Lord John came into office he wanted to take the matter up. But Brougham was also interested, and Brougham having been forced to yield to Lord John on the Reform Bill, delicacy suggested letting Brougham take the lead on this issue.

Once the question was in Brougham's hands it was difficult to get it out again, for he was, as Lord John said, a dog in the manger on that subject.[154] But after the general election of 1837 Lord John wrote to him, pointing out that education was becoming a matter of urgency, and stressing the importance of relying upon the agency of the state to make it general.[155] Two weeks later he and Brougham were contemplating erecting education boards all over the country, and the true depth of Lord John's liberality, and of his belief in education then became apparent. 'I have no doubt', he wrote, that 'much jealousy will be felt of the Tories seizing hold of the Education boards, as they do of all other machinery.'

> But unless we could take the whole matter into the hands of Govt., which would be both wrong and impracticable, I do not see any means of preventing those who have great local property from having local influence. And as education in the end must have a liberal tendency this evil ought to be submitted to, rather than leave such multitudes in ignorance and debasement.[156]

Lord John was ahead of his time, and the cabinet preferred to go on working through the voluntary societies. The year 1838 was spent in extended negotiations with the National Society and the British and Foreign School Society. Lord John's own sympathies were known to lie with the B. and F.S.S. He had been a vice-president of the Society since 1824,[157] and he preferred the B. and F.S.S.'s Bible instruction, which excluded formularies. But by October 1838 he was willing not to ban the catechism from church schools in receipt of government aid, and to insist only on nonconformist parents having the right to withdraw their children from it.[158] For their part the dissenters were willing to withdraw their objection to state inspection, being convinced that 'there was no living Statesman to whom they could so fully confide the doing of it, as Your Lordship'.[159]

When the scheme came before the cabinet in November, it provided for local taxation in addition to a government grant.[160] Lord John was not present, and Melbourne confessed that he was against the thing altogether, on which Howick said 'Thank God there are some things which even you cannot stop, and that is one of them.' Melbourne only smiled,[161] and at the end of the meeting wrote to Lord John that the general opinion was that the question could not be escaped or deferred. He went on: 'Upon the question itself, I differ. I am against it. I think education at present stands in England upon a better ground than any new one upon which you will place it.'[162] Had he chosen his words to that end, Melbourne could not have said anything more likely to rouse Lord John from sorrow, and the very next

day, Lord John promised to resume responsibility for the education plan.[163]

Lord John did not return to London until the middle of
January, and in the meantime the ministry tried to approach
Durham through Ellice. But, as Lord John told Melbourne, it
was no use sending an ambassador to Durham to ask him to
hush things up,[164] and in fact it was no use sending an ambassador to Durham at all. Durham brushed aside even Lord John's
assurance that there was no wish to press hard on him or to
make a quarrel.[165] He was busy writing his report, and no
member of the government was going to hear from him until
his report was ready to be published. Ministers were left with
no more idea of what he was going to recommend than they
could derive from the despatch they had received at the beginning of September. All they knew, or thought they knew, was
that Ellice was helping him with it: and Ellice was 'fond of
change and scheming, and when he has done his best, is discontented with his own work'.[166] Durham finally put his report
into the hands of the cabinet a few days before the session
opened on 5 February. Simultaneously he, or someone else on
his staff, leaked the contents to *The Times*.

Durham painted a highly coloured picture 'of the animosities
existing between the two races' in lower Canada.[167] If anything approaching self-government were granted to the existing
province, the French majority would drive the British minority
into the arms of the United States. To forestall this disaster,
Durham advocated a union of the two provinces of upper and
lower Canada. The French would then be subordinated to the
British, and in the united province constitutional development
could go on apace. Durham strongly recommended granting
the united province the 'responsible' government for which the
Canadians were asking. Having published his report he was impatient to see his recommendations carried out. But serious
problems are not solved with the stroke even of an intelligent
and Liberal pen, and Durham did not suggest how either of his
two main proposals was to be implemented. For once, ministers
pleaded with reason that they needed time to consider the problem. The Whigs did not always rush their fences.

When Lord John was bereaved, he stopped writing to Melbourne about the need to make a change at the colonial office.

But early in 1839 it became clear that as the time approached for the emancipation of the slaves throughout the British empire, there would be a constitutional crisis in Jamaica. The thought of having Glenelg even nominally in charge of two crises rather than one was too much for Howick, who sent a threat of resignation to Melbourne via Lord John.[168] Lord John did not think the ministry would be totally disabled by the loss of Howick's services (as he tactlessly put it to Howick himself),[169] and in order to make the threat effective he told Melbourne that if Howick went, he must go too. In a style that Aberdeen would later have recognised, Lord John wrote that unless Glenelg were moved, 'I shall give in my resignation next week, and state that I thought that the destinies of our Colonial empire could no longer be continued in their present hands without imminent peril . . .'[170] It was some years since anyone had talked Lord John out of a threat to resign, and Melbourne took him seriously and at last plucked up courage to remove Glenelg.

Soon after he received his coronation marquisate Normanby indicated that he was ready for a change.[171] He had already been in Ireland over three years, and in October 1838 it was in Melbourne's mind that when Glenelg went, Normanby might take his place. But, now, in February 1839, Normanby himself thought his Irish experience would come in more useful if Lord John moved to the colonies, and surrendered the home office to him.[172] Melbourne's first reaction to this was that it was not a bad scheme:[173] Lord John's is not known, but he had already suggested changing places with Glenelg, and he probably wanted, as Palmerston thought, to settle the Canada problem himself.[174] But in February 1839 he was still at work upon his education plan, and he wanted to deal with the chartists in his own way. The upshot was that Lord John stayed where he was for the time being, while Normanby took the colonies. Lord John never spoke to Melbourne or Normanby in terms of a compact. But it looks as though Lord John's interpretation was that Normanby had gone to the colonial office to keep the seat warm for Lord John. If this is right, then Normanby's appointment was meant to put Canada on ice for a year, and Lord John disregarded pleas for speedy legislation from both Ellice and Peel,[175] and took the house of commons no further in 1839 than a resolution expressing approval of the plan for union.

Normanby would not have been Normanby had he not, at the same time that he began to talk of leaving Ireland, made suggestions as to his replacement. In the summer of 1838 he suggested offering the post to the Duke of Sussex. 'It would be very popular here *at first* and would ensure the Government against any dissatisfaction on the part of the Irish people at my removal.'[176] The proposal was not well timed, since Lord John had only recently opposed an increase in the duke's allowance and was at that moment engaged in an angry, snubbing altercation with him.[177]

In February 1839 Melbourne offered Ireland first to Tavistock, who declined,[178] and then to Clarendon, who refused on grounds of inexperience.[179] The choice then fell on Ebrington, who went to work with less vanity and with no less efficiency than Mulgrave. At the same time, as a reward for his four years' excellent service as chief secretary, Morpeth was brought into the cabinet at Lord John's request, and henceforward took much of the Irish work off Lord John.

On 4 February 1839, the day before parliament assembled, there also met in London the Chartist Convention (or people's parliament), and the first anti-corn-law conference. Lord John's attitudes to the two movements were different. Chartism came up like a demand for civil rights from the kitchen, and was time-consuming, and contrary to order. Like the rest of the cabinet, Lord John attributed the movement to the bad harvest and the depression of trade, and to a vague 'spirit of disaffection'. There is no evidence that at this period he ever seriously asked himself how far the movement had its origin in disappointment with his Reform Act of 1832 or with his finality speech of 1837.

Thus far Lord John was scarcely true to the Whig principle of his youth that people do not agitate·unless they have something to complain about. But when, within six months of the publication of the charter by the London Working Men's Association in May 1838, reports began to reach the home office of torchlight meetings on the moors and of incendiary speeches by Stephens and O'Connor, Lord John made a better showing. Even Melbourne feared a 'heated mode' of dealing with the chartists 'upon the part of the magistrates and country gentlemen',[180] and Lord John resolved that, come what might, he would not be responsible for another Peterloo. But that did not mean doing nothing. While Lord John was shut away in mourning, the cabinet, with Samuel March Phillipps the permanent under-secretary in attendance, decided to prosecute Stephens.[181] Lord John may have suggested and certainly supported their decision, which was not taken in panic, or even in haste. As he said, one wouldn't prosecute speeches against the poor law or the government, or for universal suffrage, but only speeches which encouraged the poor to use arms to deprive the rich of their property.[182] It was a sensible distinction: the government kept calm, and at the end of the year Lord John wrote to Lady Holland, simply, that there was 'a good deal of bad spirit among the workmen in the North' but that he did not expect any real mischief would come of it.[183] That, of course, was written to a lady, but to that lady's husband, Lord John wrote with only a little more anxiety, that arming was going on, and added, in words that a chartist might have used, 'I know no law against it – or how it is possible to make having arms an offence consistently with the old maxims of our laws.'[184]

In the demands of the anti-corn-law league, on the other hand, Lord John saw a way of stepping out of the impasse caused by his finality speech. From the time the government was formed the corn laws had been an open question. But towards the end of 1838, when Lord John was warned the Radicals wished to cast him off,[185] he began to press Melbourne upon the corn law issue more insistently than he had yet done upon any other. The league was gaining strength, and Lord John argued that if the country gentlemen wanted to save some remnant of the corn laws, they must make concessions at once. If they persisted

> till the harvest has been far more deficient, or till it shall have failed generally, and wheat reached famine prices, it will be impossible to legislate in any other way than by refusing to interfere at all, or by acceding to the total repeal.[186]

Hence the proposal for a moderate or small fixed duty. On 7 January 1839 Lord John told Melbourne that he was convinced there would be a very strong division on the corn laws this year, and that 'next year the question of fixed moderate duty will be carried'.[187]

Melbourne dreaded the corn question, and in order to forestall

Lord John, he wrote with shortening temper, on 19 January that he was not prepared to put himself at the head of this corn law movement; on 20 January that he was determined the corn laws should remain an open question; and on 21 and 23 January that he did not care how many people were for a fixed duty, he was not prepared to pledge himself to one.[188] Melbourne won his point, but in the middle of March when Villiers brought on his annual motion for repeal, he secured 172 votes instead of the 95 he had secured the year before. He then moved for a committee of the whole house to inquire into the operation of the law of 1828. Melbourne thought it mad, but 195 members voted for it, including Lord John, Baring, George Grey, Hobhouse, Howick, Labouchere, Morpeth, Palmerston, Rice and Charles Wood. The free traders were gaining: but Lord John was wrong to suppose that at this stage the Whigs could have taken up the proposal for a fixed duty, for the Whig county members and the Irish 'generally' voted with the majority.[189] The party was split, and from this moment the government's majority on other issues fell, and the life of the administration became more precarious than ever.

Every session began with Ireland. For over two years Drummond had been hatching a plan for the state to construct the lines of railway in Ireland 'as National Works',[190] and Morpeth now brought in a bill to provide a loan of £2·5m to begin work. Torrens said later that Peel 'denounced the project as unsound in principle, vicious in detail, and likely to prove perilous as an example'.[191] This was an exaggeration. Peel referred to the dangers of state interference, and played with the effect Morpeth's bill would have upon Mr Bianconi, an immigrant from Milan, who, starting with one car plying between Clonmel and Cahir, now had ninety-four going all over Munster.[192] The government abandoned the bill, and Ebrington was sorry the scheme had ever been introduced, if they were not prepared to push it harder.[193]

In their annual municipal corporations bill for Ireland, the government began by proposing an £8 franchise, which was the same as their compromise offer of the year before. But they now proposed that, after the poor law had been in operation for three years, the franchise should be assimilated to the English ratepaying franchise, and that any town of over 3000 inhabitants should be able to apply to the lord lieutenant for incorporation. The bill passed the commons, but in the lords the Irish interest was in an ugly mood. O'Connell had just launched a new and strangely named Precursor Society. Lord John dismissed it as humbug,[194] and felt sure O'Connell's object was to keep his followers out of the arms of O'Connor.[195] But it was too much to expect the ascendancy to take the same view. Nettled by a lecture from Drummond on the duties of property, nervous after the first elections of guardians under the poor law act of 1838, and alarmed by the murder of Lord Norbury, the lords reacted by appointing a select committee to inquire into the whole state of Ireland since 1835. Thus was Normanby welcomed back into the upper house, with what was tantamount to a vote of censure, which would have to be met by a motion in the commons.

In asking for a vote of confidence in the government's Irish policy, Lord John made one of his greatest speeches. Lord Roden, the Grand Master of the Orange Society, and his kind had ruled Ireland for seventy-five years, and in that time, almost alone among the countries of the world, Ireland had made no progress.

> The statute book is full . . . of Insurrection Acts, and of the Suspension of the Habeas Corpus Act . . . all tending to punish Whiteboy outrages, and all using the utmost severity against the poor, and all taking care to pursue crimes with penalties, but I can find none providing permanently for the welfare of the people. I can find none admitting the Irish Catholics to be treated as the free subjects of a free country – none speaking in the spirit of mercy or in the language of conciliation.[196]

Lord John could still be formidable in support of a colleague and in defence of a policy which he believed to be right, and he obtained his vote of confidence by 318 votes to 296. Nor was his speech ill-judged, for on this occasion Peel, who thought he had Lord John at a disadvantage and was in no mood to let him off, went down to the house with two speeches in his pocket, and replied to Lord John with the more moderate one. Perhaps, in his heart, Peel already agreed with Lord John that the evils had not been sown in a day, and that it would require not four years, but forty to eradicate them.[197]

At the lords' inquiry, Drummond, and Colonel McGregor the new inspector general of police, were cross-examined. Their lordships' questions revealed their fears that the government was withholding police in cases of distraint, that the roman catholics recruited into the police were disloyal, and that both Dublin castle and the roman catholic clergy were insincere in their denunciations of ribandism.[198] Drummond countered with statistics, which showed that though there had been variations in the crime rates between 1835 and 1839, almost all the peculiarly Irish crimes were down. Illegal processions were down and the class of persons taking part in them was getting lower every year;[199] riots and faction fights were down; and cattle stealing and cattle maiming were down. There were a few statistical crumbs for the lords, for firing into dwellings was on the increase,[200] but in general the lords' inquiry recoiled upon its authors. Never mind, they could always end the session meanly, by once again amending the municipal corporations bill at all points so that it was dropped, and lay all through another winter like an encumbrance on friend and foe alike.

Ireland still united the ministry with its supporters, but Lord John's declaration of finality still divided them, and the lead in agitating for a new reform bill now passed to the chartists. May 6 was fixed for the presentation of their petition to the house of commons, and in the weeks preceding many people expected a revolution. Even Lord John was at times inclined to see all Radical proposals as part of a comprehensive scheme of a revolutionary character.[201] Tavistock advised him to stick to his declaration, but added that it was impossible to disguise from oneself what the consequences must be:

> loss of popularity certainly; the weakening and perhaps dissolution of the Whig party in its present state . . . as a popular leader and I fear as a Minister, your days are numbered. You may struggle on for a time, but everything portends a downfall.[202]

Unlike his brother, Lord John was never supine, and in an inspired moment he now sent for Fox's nephew, General Sir Charles Napier, to take command of the troops in the northern districts. Napier was pleased to find that Lord John spoke without violence against the chartists, and accepted the commission.[203] Napier went to work with this advantage, that he was known to share the chartists' objects, and to differ only as to the manner in which they were to be obtained. He believed 'that the men with whom we have to deal, did in 1830–1, get up a powerful organised force' of 8000 men, which kept the field with military discipline for four months.[204] To the alarm of the local magistrates, but to the comfort of the country as a whole, he withdrew isolated detachments which might be assassinated in their billets, and concentrated his forces at Nottingham, Manchester, Leeds and Newcastle. It is difficult to know how many of the melodramatic stories of his attending chartist meetings in plain clothes to believe, but he clearly spent a lot of time making the chartist leaders realise that he would shoot them if he had to. All in all, he was a credible deterrent, and although he sometimes doubted it, he received steady, if not absolutely unwavering support from Lord John in his many quarrels with the magistrates.

At this moment the ministry had cause once again to congratulate itself upon its Irish policy. O'Connell lent no countenance to chartism, and Ireland was so quiet that the administration in Dublin volunteered to send troops to reinforce those in England. Two regiments were actually sent, and Ebrington and Drummond repeatedly offered more.[205] With these reinforcements, Napier went on alternately keeping the troops out of sight to avoid provocation, and in sight to act as a deterrent.

While this was going on Lord John wrote a *Letter* to his electors at Stroud. His object was to side-step his finality speech, by saying that he did not rule out improvements and alterations in detail. But upon the issue of the ballot he still made no concession, and the pamphlet conveyed the unfortunate impression that Lord John thought the Radicals ought to defer to him rather than have minds of their own. As Melbourne said, much as he personally liked it, 'What they want is a retraction of your former declaration, and this is in fact a reiteration of it, explained certainly, but not modified or altered.'[206]

Lord John's letter did nothing to stop the excitement mounting as the day approached for the presentation of the chartist petition. There was no certainty that Napier's policy would succeed, and on 30 April while still keeping silence in parliament, Lord John asked the cabinet for permission to issue a

proclamation against illegal drilling, and for leave to call out
the yeomanry.[207] The country was close to insurrection, and
the cabinet decided that *in extremis*, loyal citizens should be encouraged to organise local defence forces. Some cutlasses were
issued, but Lord John said later that he had refused requests for
muskets.[208]

In this supercharged atmosphere the presentation of the
petition was put off by an unexpected event. For reasons best
known to himself Peel suddenly launched a full-scale attack
upon the government's proposal to suspend the constitution of
Jamaica. Lord John spoke animatedly in favour of ensuring that
a negro population of 300,000 was not oppressed by 2200 con-
stituent planters, and characterised the members of the assembly as floggers of females.[209] The government scraped home
by 294 votes to 289. Six Tories voted in the majority,[210] but
Ellice said that eleven of 'our people' voted against the government.[211] It was a bitter disappointment, and on an issue like
this where agreement between the two parties was always sought
and often obtained, the cabinet were unanimous that the vote
was an invitation to every colony to rebel, and that a government which could not legislate for Jamaica could not hope to
legislate for Canada either.

Melbourne resigned, and Lord John composed a swan song
on four years of Whig government. He addressed it to O'Connell
and thanked him and his party for their 'constant and disinter-
ested support'.[212] The contrast with the Radicals was obvious.
There was nothing wrong in this except that it was premature.
Peel would not take office unless there were changes among the
ladies of the bedchamber. The Queen refused, and the Whigs
came back, congratulating themselves on their gallantry to a
young girl. Spencer and Ebrington both said that as gentlemen
ministers could not have done anything else.[213] Only Howick
disapproved,[214] but then Howick disapproved of everything, so
no one listened to him even when he was right. The government
had been in a mess before, and it was to be in a humiliating
mess henceforward.

Abercromby seized the opportunity to resign, and Rice
wanted to become speaker in his place. But the Radicals would
not purchase his removal from the exchequer at that price,
and Shaw Lefevre was elected. Charles Grove, who had been

Lord John's private secretary since 1830, was appointed to the woods and forests, and Lord John replaced him with his half brother, Lord Edward Russell, who as the Duke of Bedford said, would do the job well when he had settled in.[215]

When the ministers dragged themselves back to finish the session, the Radicals let it be known that they would give the government quiet possession for a time in return for the penny post, which they received the next year.[216] But they insisted on going on with Fleetwood's motion to extend the occupation franchise in the counties to £10, and with Grote's motion for the ballot. The first was the easier to deal with. The Reform Bill had been distorted by the Chandos clause, and the cabinet agreed that Lord John would resist Fleetwood's motion, but announce that the government might be willing to consider it at some future date. This brought Howick out in a passionate fit of devotion to his father, and it was settled that he would resign the next day if he disapproved of Lord John's speech.[217] Howick's wife knew her husband well and wrote in her diary 'So there we are almost *out* again'.[218] But Lord John picked his words with skill, and Howick did not go out this time.

In dealing with Grote's motion for the ballot there was now only one thing to do, and that was to let ministers vote as they liked. The point was carried in the cabinet against Lord John, who continued, with a mixture of subtlety and ill humour, to deny that it had become an open question.[219] When the vote was taken 333 members opposed the ballot, including 287 Tories and Lord John, and 216 members voted for it including Campbell, George Grey, Fox Maule (Lord John's under-secretary at the home office), and Poulett Thomson.

It was with diminished authority, then, that Lord John strove to carry his education bill through the commons. He had introduced the bill in February, by contrasting the lamentable deficiency of education in England with the provision made both in the more autocratic countries of Europe and in the more democratic U.S.A.[220] The bill provided for the appointment of a committee of the privy council, or board of education. The committee was to appoint inspectors, and the inspectors' reports upon church schools were to be made available to the bishops. A normal school was to be established where children of all denominations could be taught together on the 'united' system.

The annual grant from public funds was to be increased from
£20,000 to £30,000, and in future the grant would come before
parliament every year. The subject of education would then
receive 'that care, that interest, and that concern on the part
of the State, which it never hitherto has received'.[221]

Educationally, the chief interest of Lord John's arguments
lies in the stress he laid upon the provision of infant schools,
upon the new methods of instruction which 'instead of burden-
ing the memory, and rendering learning irksome and disagreeable, taught the child to instruct himself, and to follow with
curiosity the lesson which he learnt',[222] and upon the need to
incline the teaching towards a trade.[223] Children's habits were
to be fitted to their station. If the last point seems conservative,
it is as well to remember that, with the country convulsed by
chartism, it would have been hopeless to have come to parliament to ask for money for education with any other argument.

Lord John's own favourite proposal for the normal school fell
a victim to Anglican jealousy, and when the decisive vote was
taken in June the increased grant was secured, in the face of
objections from economists of all colours, by a vote of 275 to 273,
with O'Connell and his supporters once again loyally voting
for the government. Despite the narrow majority in the commons the bill passed the lords, and the reason was that unlike
some of Lord John's other measures, this one had a real advocate. Lansdowne was a very moderate Whig, and on Irish
measures he was scarcely a Whig at all. But upon this subject of
education he shared Lord John's enthusiasm,[224] and with independent assistance from Brougham he got it through. The system
thus established grew every few years for thirty years, until the
point had at last been reached in 1870, when the state could step
in, and compel every district to provide schools in the manner
contemplated by Lord John in 1837.

The vote upon the Jamaica bill and the ministerial crisis that
followed, put off the presentation of the chartist petition, and
with that postponement the high tide of chartism passed. The
charter had brought the various working-class groups under one
flag. The convention showed what disparate stuff they were made
of, and in May the convention lost heart, and moved from
London to Birmingham. When Attwood finally asked for leave
to present the petition on 12 July, Lord John scored an easy

debating point by contrasting Attwood's own specific of paper money with the views of O'Connor, Lovett, Collins and Frost. The chartists as a whole he had the good taste not to score off, though he very properly challenged their presumption in speaking for the 'nation'. There were a million signatures to this petition. But then one million people already had the vote. 'Observe how differently this number of a million is treated, according to the side it happens to be at.'[225] In more conventional vein, he refuted the notion that there could be any easy solution to economic problems through universal suffrage. The U.S.A. had universal suffrage, and trade depressions too, and 600 kinds of forged paper money by which the working man could lose his all. The best one could do in the United Kingdom was to encourage the 'political freedom, commercial freedom, and religious freedom' which tended to increase the riches of every class 'by not directly growing riches, or directly creating property, but by allowing men to use their own energies, in their own ways'.[226]

Leave to present the petition was of course refused. This led to a riot in the Bull Ring at Birmingham, and the opposition thought they could blame the delay in calling out the police, who had been sent down from London, upon Muntz, the Radical magistrate appointed by Lord John. Lord John turned that off easily enough,[227] brought in bills accelerating the establishment of police forces in Birmingham and Manchester, and persevered with his carefully matured plan to set up a rural police. In August when the chartist leaders were arrested the country stayed quiet.

Lord John had brought the country through the chartist crisis without asking for special powers. It was an achievement of which he was justifiably proud, and in the education debate he allowed himself to say as much.[228] Congratulations come better from other people, and in October 1839 Samuel March Phillipps wrote that the home office was entitled to much credit for its handling of the chartists.

> There can only be one opinion on this subject, . . . How happy that we had no gagging bill no arms seizing Bill, not one single Bill put upon the statute Book. And what a signal triumph followed. Lord John in his quiet way, without parade, but with a steady decided hand, and a most undisturbed temper, steered the

ship among the breakers, and the breakers have died away with a perfect calm.[229]

By the time that was written Melbourne had reconstructed the ministry, and Lord John had left the home office. Admittedly Lord John's appointment of Sydney Smith's son, Wyndham Smith (Thackeray's Spavin the Turfite) to a clerkship had not been well advised.[230] That apart, it was an office which Lord John had occupied with conspicuous success: getting on well with the established staff, and adding his own drive to every aspect of their work. A book could be written about the impetus he gave to the reform of the criminal law; he drastically reduced the number of offences, including forgery, punishable by death; he took the chair at the meetings of the select committee on transportation; he pursued a policy of dividing serious offenders, who should be transported for not less than ten years, from less serious offenders who should be sent to prison for not more than five; he established a prison inspectorate, and a prison for juvenile offenders at Parkhurst; and he opened the way to the abolition of the hulks and the construction of a model prison at Pentonville.[231]

It was not altogether without reason, then, that towards the end of the 1839 session, when someone said the Whigs had a host of enemies, the Duke of Wellington replied that that was true, but that Lord John Russell was a host in himself.[232]

CHAPTER X

The Noblest Man, 1839–41

i. Office, 1839–40

TOWARDS the end of the session of 1839, Melbourne and Lord John began to look about them for a strong man to send to Canada to impose the union. They turned first to Clarendon, and then to Dunfermline.[1] Both refused, and the invitation then went to Poulett Thomson. Like Lord John, Thomson was short of stature, courageous, and relatively Radical. His weak spot was his wish to become a lord, and his first reaction was to ask for a peerage before he would consent to go. This, as Lord John said to Melbourne, would not do,[2] but Melbourne promised him one as soon as the union of the two provinces was completed, and his appointment was announced early in August.

Lord John then pressed Melbourne to reconstruct the ministry. Rice was ready to retire,[3] and Melbourne and Lord John agreed upon Baring to take his place. Howick was asked if he would go to the lords as postmaster general and implement the penny post, but he refused.[4] Lord John referred next to his own position, and when Melbourne demurred at his going to the colonial office, he insisted.[5] It seems likely that, after what had happened to Durham, Thomson then made it a condition of his going to Canada that it was Lord John he would be responsible to. But where was Normanby to go? Lord John's first thought was to move Minto to the home office, and to send Normanby to the admiralty.[6] But Minto would not agree to that,[7] and in the end it was agreed that Lord John and Normanby should change places. As Normanby said to Greville, since Lord John was bent upon Poulett Thomson's appointment, there was nothing left to do but to change offices, and to let Lord John administer the colony with a governor of his own choice.[8]

The exchange was known at the end of August and aroused much opposition. Ellice feared Normanby would not be popular with judges and lord lieutenants.[9] Palmerston objected that the colonial office would ruin Lord John's health: Glenelg wrote or revised 30,000 despatches in four years; Lord John 'by his Promptitude and Decision' would do the same quantity in less than half the time, but even he would not be able to cope during the seven months in which the house was sitting.[10] Holland said the home office suited Lord John and was agreeable to the lead.[11] The Duke of Bedford teased his son with his willingness to take command of the Channel Fleet.[12] Rice thought the plan would be fatal to Lord John, the government, and the public interest;[13] and Lansdowne wrote that one half of the public would think the exchange of seals unaccountable, and the other half highly objectionable.[14]

Howick carried his objections further. He was egged on by his father, who stigmatised Lord John as 'a little animal engrossed by an inordinate ambition, of the most narrow and selfish kind', and regretted having brought him on by entrusting him with the management of the Reform Bill.[15] Howick complained that Melbourne and Lord John had not told him what they had in mind. Lord John said 'I thought he knew it'.[16] Ellice, striving to patch things up, reminded Howick that Lord John was never very communicative, even to his best friends.[17] It was no use. Canada, the exchequer, the colonial office, and the home office – Howick believed himself competent to undertake any of these, and feeling one of them ought surely to have come his way, he resigned. He had always been a difficult colleague, and by this time Melbourne and Lord John were tired of trying to please him. Ellice warned Howick that he had a way of pressing his opinions which was hard to bear,[18] and told Durham that with all his great and good qualities, Howick's 'contentious and obstinate temper, and the differences in which he involves himself . . . *with the whole Cabinet*, diminish, and detract from his weight and consequence.'[19]

The Grey family's connections were both extended and strong: Howick succeeded in making his brother-in-law Charles Wood as 'discontented and angry as himself', and Wood went too.[20] Lord John cheerfully remarked that 'September is the most incurious month of the year',[21] but the resignations were bound to do the ministry harm. Since 1832 Durham had gone, Stanley and Graham had gone, Grey had gone, Spencer had retired and Brougham had been excluded. Spencer was still a friend, but Stanley and Graham had passed into opposition, Grey was moody and hostile, Durham lawless and Brougham vengeful. Howick now told Ellice that he would abstain from opposition, but Ellice knew better: 'Fudge!', he said, 'He will be Brougham the 2nd.'[22]

Time would show the truth of Ellice's prediction. For the moment the thing to do was to fill up Howick's place. George Grey declined to come in upon his cousin's going out,[23] and Melbourne inclined to Macaulay. Lord John regretted that this would start a contest on the treasury bench as to ballot, but he agreed it could not be helped.[24] There were so many '*dumb dogs*' in the cabinet,[25] and Macaulay would at least be able to speak in the house of commons, where help was much needed following the departure of Rice, Thomson, Howick and Wood. Lord John thought that if Macaulay were promoted, Clarendon ought to be invited to join the cabinet too.[26] He was conceited, but that was 'the vice of the age'.[27] In fact Melbourne brought Macaulay in at once, and offered Clarendon the mint, without a seat in the cabinet. Clarendon refused, and was lucky, therefore, to come in as lord privy seal in October, when Duncannon resigned.

Lord John moved into the colonial office at the beginning of September, and Thomson set sail for Canada on the thirteenth. The two men must have been busy coming to a final understanding. Thomson had to do two very different things: he had to impose union on lower Canada, which was still being governed under special powers, and he had to sell union to upper Canada, where there was vociferous opposition to it. It was essential, therefore, to leave much to his discretion. He was to take with him two draft bills, one drawn up by the British cabinet, and the other by Sir John Colborne, who had been in charge of Canada since Durham left, and whose part in saving Canada from dissolution never receives the praise it deserves. But Thomson was not to treat either bill as more than a guide. He went out 'holding forth Union as our plan, but not any one kind of Union, should he find another mode of effecting the object more popular'.[28]

In order to pave the road to union Thomson was told that he might offer a loan of £1·5m to the new united province. He insisted upon having this in writing. He also chose, in a businesslike and demanding tone, to drive a hard bargain for his services. The cabinet agreed to a salary of £6000. They also agreed to pay him £1000 for journeys and removals. Thomson understood he was to have £7000, and was to have all his expenses paid in addition, and alleged that many members of the cabinet had told him they thought even that too low. By the time the misunderstanding came to light, the cabinet had separated, and Lord John took upon himself the responsibility of letting Thomson have what he asked.[29] The extra money was well spent, if, as seems possible, it finally cemented the confidence of the new governor in the new colonial secretary.

Thomson liked to have everything cut and dried. This makes it certain that upon the most important question of all he must have insisted upon knowing exactly how far he might go. In upper Canada everything would depend upon how far Thomson might meet the inhabitants' wishes for 'responsible government'. Against the phrase itself Lord John still set his face. But in June 1839, when Charles Buller asked him point blank whether he contemplated carrying on the government in Canada with the support of a minority in the assembly, Lord John replied that

> what he really said was, that the executive should be carried on in such a way, as that their measures should be acceptable and agreeable to the representatives of the people, and that he saw no reason why the Government should not agree to adopt the measures approved of by a majority of the colonists.[30]

This was the first indication that Durham's proposals were sinking in, and that if the Canadians would not insist upon the name, they might in fact get what they wanted. Before Thomson left for Canada, there was drawn up in the colonial office on 9 September, the 'circular despatch' of 16 October 1839. The trouble in Canada stemmed from the fact that the governor's appointments to his executive council, though nominally at pleasure, were in fact made for life. Lord John therefore determined that in future a governor was to be free to ask for resignations from the executive council whenever public policy made it expedient, and pointed out that a governor would be in a particularly good position to do this at the beginning of his administration.

Although a good deal of mystery still surrounds both the drafting and the interpretation of this despatch,[31] it is impossible to believe that it was not drawn up with Thomson's concurrence. On 18 September the editor of the *Colonial Gazette* undertook to establish 'by legal evidence' if necessary, that Thomson had told him that Lord John, in spite of his denunciation of responsible government by name, was nevertheless preparing to carry into effect the substance of Durham's recommendations. Nobody knows who leaked the news, or whether its publication was intended to help, or to stimulate, or to embarrass.

It is a curious fact, then, that Lord John sent Thomson out and kept the despatch back. But it had been drafted in a hurry, it was bound to give an impulse to notions of self government all over the empire, and Lord John presumably wanted time to consider the implications for other colonies and other continents.[32] He had a month in which to make up his mind, for in the first month after his arrival, Thomson would be at work in lower Canada, where he could make what settlement he chose. What mattered was that the despatch should reach Thomson in time for him to deal with the reluctant unionists and ardent constitutionalists of upper Canada. It was sent, accordingly, on 16 October, to all the governors of the North American colonies, and for safety's sake it was preceded by a letter of 14 October, in which Lord John once again blasted the formal notion of responsible government as being contrary to the relations between a mother country and its colonies.

Having got Thomson off to Canada, and knowing that it must be two months before he heard from him, Lord John took stock of the rest of his new duties with the aid of the long memoranda prepared for him on the establishment of the colonial office, and on the various colonial legislatures.[33] Lord John soon found that those of his colleagues who had objected to his taking the colonial office, on the ground that it would involve too much work, had a point. It was not his way to divide the work, as Normanby suggested, into matters which required immediate decision, and matters 'which might by postponement dispose of themselves – a process to which you will find after a little

practice many Colonial questions are not unapt to yield'.[34] He
had, indeed, taken the labouring oar,[35] and on 20 September he
admitted that it was quite as much as he could do to get through
the daily task.[36]

But Lord John enjoyed his work that autumn, picking up the
other end of the problem of the transportation of convicted
criminals; establishing the Colonial Land and Emigration
Board; trying to make the white Jamaican planters see reason;
extending British anti-slavery activity further up the Niger;
contemplating the introduction of free institutions into New
South Wales and the desirability of ridding that colony of its
penal character; and wondering what to do next in New
Zealand now that the government had at last (in August) decided to annex it. He brought fresh energy to the whole office,
and on 18 October Stephen, the permanent under-secretary,
wrote of his new minister:

> He is one of the very few men in the World, who in the exercise of
> great political power, is filling the precise function for which
> nature designed, and education qualified him. He is far better
> fitted for Statesmanship, than for any calling to which he could
> have betaken himself, and except Mr. Huskisson, he is the only
> Statesman I ever knew, of whom I could say as much.[37]

In other ways, though, it was not a happy autumn. Lord
John's home was still desolate, and his children were recovering
but slowly from whooping cough.[38] Then in October his father
died. Lord John's grief was 'not a little aggravated by his recol-
lection of the loss which he sustained just at the same time
in the last year,'[39] and he was too distressed to attend the
funeral.[40]

Private grief contributed to an overall feeling of despondency.
Melbourne thought the Whigs were losing ground,[41] and Lord
John doubted whether the ministry could get through another
session without a dissolution.[42] He began to wonder whether
the old Whig party might not be left as a rump,[43] and for the
first time, perhaps, he felt resentment at Melbourne's easy life
chatting up the Queen.

Justice-to-Ireland Melbourne was evaporating, and all that
was left was cold-water Melbourne. Lord John had always
known that if he wanted to bring in a bill to admit dissenters to

the university, Melbourne would ask whether it was 'absolutely necessary';[44] that if he wanted to bring in a bill to establish a poor law in Ireland, Melbourne would 'accede to' it rather than approve it;[45] and that if he wanted to bring in an education bill, Melbourne would 'differ'.[46] That he had been prepared for, and had often been able to get round. But Melbourne was now beginning to speak lightly and provocatively of every great cause the party had espoused since 1830. He told Lord John that he could not 'entertain a doubt' that the Reform Bill was 'in itself an unjustifiable experiment and only rendered necessary by the public feeling and by the apparent, rather than real defects of the old system'.[47] He twitted Lord John for being upset at a temporary rise in the crime statistics in Ireland:

> How unreasonable you are. I never thought that these crimes and outrages had much to do either with former misgovernment or with present politics. I believe them to arise from the natural disposition of the people.[48]

Lord John identified himself with the Reform Bill and the policy of justice to Ireland, and Melbourne, of all people, ought to have known better than to pull his leg about them.

The session of 1840 was set aside for Canada. The government's claim to life now rested upon the need to deal with an emergency – and that, as the Tories noted with glee, was an emergency of its own creating. The Reformers were running out of initiatives, and the Tories might not think Canada worth a truce. That being so, this year's municipal corporations bill for Ireland had better be a conciliatory one, for if they left it any longer there might not be any corporations at all. Accordingly, when Morpeth brought in the sixth bill in six years, he cast the schedules in the form in which they had already been accepted by both houses the year before, and conceded to the house of lords by restricting the franchise in what were now the ten towns on schedule A to £10. The only attempt which the government made to save face lay in the retention of the clauses providing for the franchise in the towns on schedule A to be changed automatically to a ratepaying franchise after the poor law had been in operation for three years, and for a majority of the rated inhabitants in any of the thirty-eight towns on schedule B to apply to the lord lieutenant for corporate status.

The events of the last two parliamentary sessions of the Melbourne government have scarcely received the attention they deserve. And yet the contest between the two parties was keen, and the behaviour of their leaders was characteristic. For five years the Tories had been kept out of office by a slender margin of votes. Peel might be content to wait for the government to crumble, but many of his supporters were impatient. So short a distance seemed to stand between them and office, and yet, at the end of every session the Whigs were still in and they were still out. Now, at the beginning of 1840 they thought they had the government at a disadvantage: for all Lord John's conceit that chartism would be put to sleep by an education act, there had been a serious rising led by Frost at Newport. Graham reminded the house that Lord John had appointed Frost to the bench at Monmouth, and moved a direct vote of no confidence. But the cabinet, which was at that moment mercifully deciding to transport Frost rather than take his life, parried the attack by a majority of 308 votes to 287.[49]

A few days later Lord John cut a sorry figure when coming to the house for an allowance for Prince Albert. In order to demonstrate to the Queen that the Tories were no friends of hers, he bad-naturedly asked the house for more than it could possibly be expected to give. In the course of the debate he lost his temper, and taunted Peel 'like a sulky boy flinging rotten eggs'.[50] Greville blamed him for going on to encounter a mortifying defeat,[51] and the Queen was furious about the mismanagement and the publicity. It was a most unfortunate start to Lord John's relations with the Prince.

In the meantime, in Canada, Thomson had done all that was expected of him. The story of how, armed with his two draft bills, the loan, Lord John's despatch of 16 October, and Melbourne's promise of a peerage if he succeeded, he secured some semblance of acquiescence to the union from lower Canada, and then went on to secure something more like a genuine assent first from the legislative council and then from the assembly of upper Canada, forms part of his life, not of the life of Lord John. But one point must be noticed. The new policy of letting the Canadians have what they wanted if only they would not call it responsible government was immediately put to the test. The prime cause of party animosity in lower Canada was race: the union, it was hoped, would look after that. But the prime cause of party animosity in upper Canada was the land set aside for 'the clergy reserves', and the proportions in which it should be divided among the denominations. Thomson's private view was that the lands should be 'swept into the Atlantic'. But that was not possible, and the question had to be settled before the union was established, otherwise 'you would throw the agitation of it into the Lower Province, where amongst all its ills, the greatest of all, religious dissension is hitherto unknown'.[52]

Thomson determined, therefore, to let the Canadians tell him how they wanted the matter settled. The Canadian Radicals wanted to appropriate the lands for education, and the Canadian Conservatives wanted to keep them for the church. Warned by the Whig government's experience in Ireland, Thomson sided with the Conservatives, and his bill provided for one-half to be allotted to the Church of England and the Church of Scotland. But he let the Canadians settle how the other half was to be divided, and his bill then passed through the assembly and the legislative council of upper Canada. As Thomson said, 'it is the greatest work that ever has been done in this Country, and . . . worth ten Unions and was ten times more difficult'.[53] By 13 February 1840 Thomson was able to report that he had carried his union and his clergy reserves 'the Reform Bill and Irish Church of Canada', and that when he had finished his house of commons had given him three cheers – 'I wonder when you will say as much of *your* parliament'.[54] The ball thus passed into Lord John's court, to bring the union bill and the clergy reserves bill before the imperial parliament, and to pass them if he could. As Thomson said of the clergy reserves bill, he could not trust it back again.[55]

Lord John began with the union bill, which he introduced on 23 March, after writing to Durham that all the general principles of his report 'which can be embodied in a bill' had been adopted. Durham generously assented to this, and added that Thomson was lucky to have at the colonial office a man of spirit to support him.[56] But for all Durham's commendation, the union bill is not, at its vital point, easy to evaluate. In his speech Lord John reiterated his conviction that the official servants of the governor could not be subject to exactly the same responsibility as ministers in the United Kingdom. But he went on to spell out the evils of irresponsible government from which upper Canada had suffered. There had been one set of men, the executive council, 'enjoying the confidence of the Governor', and 'distributing the revenues of the Colony', and there had been another set of ambitious and talented men in the assembly 'totally excluded from all share in the administration'.[57] Members of the assembly, who had the power to propose money votes, had no responsibility for the executive government of the country, and were perpetually proposing votes of money for parochial interests of their own.

The union bill of 1840 was a bill to bring irresponsible government to an end. It took away the direct power of the assembly to propose money votes. That was in the act. In return the leaders of the majority in the assembly were in future to be included in the executive council. That was not in the act, and the Canadians must rely upon the discretion of the governor.[58] Money votes would then originate with the executive, and the executive would be representative and popular. In order to raise the deliberations of the central assembly of the united provinces to a high plane, Thomson dearly wanted and Lord John proposed to turn local affairs over to municipal councils with power to levy taxes.[59]

The Canadians were being asked to take a good deal on trust, and an unkind critic might have described the union bill as a municipal corporations bill for Canada. It was at this point that the government's proposals could be seen to bear too much resemblance to British politics to pass without danger through the British parliament. In the house of commons the union was not contentious, but Ellice objected to the municipalities being able to tax the 'wild' lands,[60] and Peel objected to being asked to legislate in such detail. If Lord John once let a discussion on municipal corporations start in the commons, there was no knowing where it might end in the lords, where Wellington was all set to make an impassioned resistance to the union. Lord John decided to drop municipal institutions from the bill, which then passed the commons without difficulty. There was only one vote, when the ministry romped home by 156 votes to 6, and Lord John thanked the house for having taken the bill without party feeling.[61]

Three days later Lord John carried the second reading of the

clergy reserves bill by 152 votes to 35. This was encouraging,
but at a time when echoes of the appropriation clause were still
reverberating round Westminster, and priests of all denominations were 'running a race for power of proselytism in the
Colonies',[62] there was no knowing what mischief the bishops
might get up to in the lords. A party which insisted upon the
inviolability of the established church in Ireland might yet insist in Canada upon the clergy reserves being divided between
the Church of England and the Church of Scotland, to the exclusion of the roman catholics and the other denominations.
Peel, Stanley, Graham, Gladstone and Sandon were all at the
archbishop's elbow, and rather than lose the bill Lord John
went direct to the archbishop of Canterbury himself.[63]

He had good reason to expect a favourable reception. He was
on the verge of passing a new church leases bill, which he had
conducted with patience and ability;[64] and he was presently
meeting the archbishop's wishes in the matter of the ecclesiastical commission by agreeing to find places for all the bishops.[65]
Peel, whose conduct Lord John described as 'fair and upright',[66]
gave the archbishop moderate counsel, and on 6 July Lord John
introduced a new set of proposals which he understood would
have the archbishop's support. Two-thirds of the proceeds of
the lands already sold under an act of 1827 were to go to the
Church of England, and one-third to the Church of Scotland.
The remaining lands were to be sold and the proceeds divided
into two parts. The first part was to be allotted two-thirds to the
Church of England and one-third to the Church of Scotland.
The second part was to be allotted, at the discretion of
the governor and his council, for religious worship and education.[67]

It was not what the Canadians had asked for, and it justified
the stand Lord John had always taken against any formal commitment to responsible government. But it was not too bad a
bargain, because it left the door open to the Canadian government to aid the catholics. On 4 August, when the bishop of
Exeter tried to insert the word protestant into the relevant
clause, he was defeated by 27 non-contents to 17 contents. In
Ireland Lord John had failed to vindicate the state's right to
dispose of church property, and his proposal for concurrent endowment had never got off the ground. In Canada he had some

success. At three thousand miles distance the established churches gave up their claim to a monopoly of resources.

By the time the new clergy reserves act reached Canada, Thomson had re-established confidence in the regime, and the act was accepted. As for the municipal councils, the Canadians, as Lord John pointed out to Thomson, could set them up for themselves.[68] The union was proclaimed on 10 February 1841, and Thomson became Lord Sydenham. Sydenham's health was not good and he did not survive long. On 4 September 1841, he fell off his horse and broke his leg. The wound became infected with tetanus, and he dictated his will and left a legacy of £500 to Lord John. After a night spent in prayer, he asked to have his will read out to him. When they came to the point at which Lord John was mentioned, he stopped, and said of him that 'he was the noblest man, it ever was my good fortune to know'.[69] Before the news of his death reached England Peel was prime minister.

While Lord John was busy in 1840 with Canadian legislation, the opposition were springing their mine against the government. For five years the Whigs had been in power with the support of about 70 out of the 105 Irish M.P.s. Everyone knew that the system of registering voters in Ireland led to fraud, and there had already been several abortive attempts to improve the system, before O'Connell began a campaign to register more voters.[70] This seems to have suggested to Stanley the idea that, in the guise of a bill for putting an end to abuses, he might drastically reduce the electorate. A reduced electorate would return fewer Irish Liberals and more Irish Tories, and the political balance of power in the United Kingdom would be tipped from the one party to the other. The plan was opened to Peel,[71] and approved.

Stanley introduced his bill on 25 February, and gave an added twist to the knife by the form in which he cast his proposals. English and Irish registration laws were different: in England claims had to be proved afresh every year, while in Ireland they only had to be made good every eight years, and Stanley turned the tables on Lord John by professing his anxiety to assimilate Irish institutions to English ones, and to have equal laws throughout the United Kingdom.[72] This change, alone, would have led to many names dropping off the registers.

But just to make certain that his bill would succeed in doing what he blandly denied it was intended to do, and effectively alter the franchise,[73] Stanley included a provision for sending claimants on from the revising barristers in their own districts to the judges sitting in towns many miles away.[74]

The bill was at once denounced by the Irish, who invoked the Lichfield House compact, and called upon the government to throw it out. The difficulty was how to do so. Stanley had impressed the house with his illustrative catalogue of Irish impurity, and nobody could deny that there was a real problem. When the bill was introduced, Morpeth offered no opposition,[75] and when ministers opposed the second reading Stanley won the day by 250 votes to 234. Lord John was then forced to play for time, by trying to defeat the bill in committee. It is a tactic that does not read well, whether it is employed by him against Stanley in 1840, or by Derby against him in 1866.

Before the committee stage came on, Thomas Drummond died. The Irish turned his funeral into a demonstration of support for the ministry's Irish policy, and tempers grew short on both sides of the house. On 18 May Lord John was accused of encouraging repeal. In reply he denounced Stanley's bill for unsettling the Reform Act. It was the commencement of a series of attacks designed to take the franchise away from a people that 'are as easily governed as any on the face of the globe'.

> But let this bill pass. Show that you are determined, step by step, to take away the franchise from the people of Ireland, to disable them from sending Roman Catholics as Members of this House; . . . indulge in the triumph which the minority would then indulge in over the majority; insult, vilify, and abuse the Roman Catholics; tell them that the people are ignorant, degraded, and priest-ridden, and speak of those priests in a tone of contumely and contempt; do all this, and you will have done more for repeal [than any thing O'Connell has ever been able to do].[76]

Lord John's anger did not save the government from a humiliating defeat on the motion to adjourn, by 281 votes to 262. Howick and Wood abstained. Two days later the government did better, but were again defeated by 301 votes to 298. This time Howick and Wood actually voted against their former colleagues, and as Lord John said had they acted with the government the bill would have been thrown out.[77] After that the only way to stop Stanley was for Lord John to offer to take the matter up himself: he would bring in a new registration bill for England and Wales, and the solicitor general would bring in a new bill for Ireland.[78] Wood, at least, was now sorry for what he had done, and moved that the registration bill for England be taken before that for Ireland. The house did not like his tactics, and he was defeated by 206 votes to 195. Stanley himself, however, then made a mistake by unaccommodatingly pressing his bill for the day Lord John wanted to take the second reading of the Canadian clergy reserves bill.[79] This time Lord John got his way, and on 19 June, when Stanley's registration bill came up again, the government were at last in a majority. On 6 July Stanley gave up for the session.

Lord John thought the cause justified his tactics,[80] but even he knew that, deplorable as Stanley's motives were, Stanley had in many ways had the better of this battle. Howick might have sunk to zero,[81] but the ministry was now weaker than ever, and it was in the atmosphere left by this struggle that the last act in the long drama of the Irish municipal corporations was played. The lords refused to contemplate a time when the Irish cities would enjoy a ratepayers' franchise, and made the £10 franchise permanent in both schedule A and schedule B. When the commons amended the lords' amendments, and sent the bill upstairs again, Lyndhurst announced that he was sick of discussing the bill, and (in the words of *Hansard*) those amendments 'which Lord Lyndhurst objected to were negatived without a division'.[82] Melbourne rather shamefacedly supposed Lord John would not insist on them.[83] Lord John capitulated. He had no alternative. Halevy thought the act established 'islands of representative democracy', but nowadays more people agree with Maitland who called it a scheme of disfranchisement whereby fifty-eight corporations vanished.[84] The high franchise inserted into schedule B proved an effective bar to more towns acquiring corporate status, and in 1878 there were still only twelve towns in Ireland administered under the act of 1840.[85]

ii. Office, 1840–1

In 1840 Lord John became involved in foreign affairs for the first time, and we can now see how his adolescent attitudes to the outside world developed in practice. He made no objection to the invasion of Afghanistan, and over the opium question he agreed with Palmerston that it was time to say 'we mean to knock the Chinese Emperor down for this impudence'.[86] When the opposition attacked the China policy Lord John said nothing peculiarly offensive to the Chinese, but it is to Stanley's speech against the war that an Englishman must turn for comfort today.

Lord John had not been at the colonial office long before he came into much more frequent contact and friction with Palmerston, who was now married to Melbourne's sister. Between Canada and the United States there was a boundary problem. War with the United States would put the Canadian union in jeopardy. In October 1839 Lord John thought the foreign office was dragging its feet,[87] and in April 1840 the Americans were pressing for war with an eagerness that President Van Buren might not be able to withstand. Lord John then appealed to Melbourne to get Palmerston to send instructions by the next boat 'to sign a convention by which this Boundary question may be settled'.[88] Palmerston thought Lord John was panicky, and replied that 'with such Cunning Fellows as these yankees it never answers to give way because they always keep pushing on their Encroachments'.[89] Thanks largely to Thomson there was no invasion, but the boundary problem wore on, and in April 1841 Palmerston sent Lord John a memorandum on the best way of carrying on a war against the United States, which would be to raise the South against the North.[90]

In 1839–40 the revolt of Mehemet Ali in Egypt, the invasion of Syria, and French intervention on Mehemet Ali's side against the Porte, brought Lord John and Palmerston into much deeper conflict. Palmerston could never get it out of his mind that the French were seeking to avenge Waterloo and overthrow the 1815 settlement, while Lord John saw in France the only other power in Europe with Liberal institutions. Right up to the last moment, in July, Lord John emphasised that Britain could not

separate from France without danger, and without danger, as
he persuasively put it, to Palmerston's achievement in Belgium.
Louis Philippe must be allowed to 'repress the vanity and ambition of his subjects without humiliation to his government'.[91]

As the Eastern crisis developed Palmerston became excited
and absurd, looking upon the question

> to be whether England is to remain a substantial Power, or is to
> declare herself a Dependency of France. In the event of the latter
> Decision you had better abolish the office of Secy of State for
> Foreign Affairs and have in London an under Secy for the
> English Department from the Foreign Office at Paris.[92]

But at the same time he skilfully won the support of Austria,
Prussia, and Russia for his policy of maintaining the Ottoman
empire. When he brought his projected quadruple alliance before the cabinet, Holland and Clarendon both objected to it as
an unnecessary rebuff to France. They had reason to hope that
Lord John would agree with them, but Lord John had changed,
and was at that moment convinced that Thiers was determined
to set the world at defiance.[93] He spoke in favour of the alliance,
and his voice, as Palmerston reminded him afterwards, was
decisive.[94]

The treaty made, ministers separated at the end of the session,
and Lord John went North to stay with Lord Minto, whose
second daughter attracted him. Fanny was born in 1815. She
was slim and upright, with dark hair, dark eyes, freckles that
were not disfiguring, and a white neck,[95] and when Lord John's
first wife died, she wrote in her diary of 'the sad, sad news of the
death of Lady John Russell. God give strength to her poor unhappy husband, and watch over his dear little motherless
children.'[96] It is easy for a man of forty-eight to be in love with
a girl of twenty-four. But when that man is a widower with four
step-children and two children, the girl must always be in
danger of mistaking compassion for love. Fanny Elliot did not
make that mistake. She liked Lord John, but she was not in love
with him, and when he proposed on 3 September, she refused
him.[97] Lord John returned to London feeling that there was
nothing left to him 'but constant and laborious attention to
public business, and a wretched sense of misery, which even
the children can never long drive away'.[98] Minto reflected that

he had never thought of Lord John as an old man until he heard that he wanted to marry Fanny.[99]

While Lord John was at Lady Fanny's feet, Palmerston was busy organising British warships and marines, and Turkish soldiers, to enforce the terms laid down by the four powers, and to secure the withdrawal of Mehemet Ali from Syria. The French press reacted strongly, and while the danger of war increased day by day, 'the peace party' in England were hard at work behind Palmerston's back. Holland was in correspondence with Thiers, and Ellice was in Paris promising French newspaper editors that there would be no war. Lord John was not in the conspiracy, but the peace party rightly supposed that they might be able to make an impression upon him, and a stream of letters reached him at Minto. Holland pointed out that Palmerston's proposed methods of blockade and search were illegal:[100] Spencer thought them criminal.[101]

Lord John respected Spencer's opinion more than that of any other man, and he returned to London solitary, in no good humour, and much alarmed by fears of war. Instead of going straight to Palmerston, he dined on 8 September with Clarendon and Guizot at Holland House. On 10 September he wrote to Melbourne proposing that a special mission be sent to give the Sultan temperate advice, and that an overture be made to France. Melbourne hesitated, and on 15 September Lord John wrote again, threatening to resign. Melbourne demurred at Lord John's breaking up the cabinet, and Lord John replied that he knew not why his proposals should have such an outcome 'unless it is to be laid down that one member of the Cabinet is to conduct matters simply as he pleases without concert or control'. Peace was worth more than the present ministry.[102]

Melbourne agreed to summon the cabinet, and before it met on 28 September, it became known that Ponsonby, the British ambassador at Constantinople, exceeding his formal instructions but not perhaps misreading the mind of his chief at the foreign office, had advised the Sultan to stiffen his terms. Lord John, in a fury, said that Ponsonby ought to be disavowed, and that unless the cabinet agreed he would resign. The cabinet adjourned for three days, and this gave Melbourne time to invoke the wishes of the Queen, and the necessity to spare her a crisis immediately before the birth of her first child. Lord John agreed to do nothing until he had seen the Queen,[103] who told him she thought he was acting to some extent from personal animosity against Palmerston.[104] Lord John then made a serious attempt to clarify and narrow his differences with the foreign secretary,[105] and agreed to consider any proposal put forward by Palmerston and Melbourne on its merits. At the same time he rounded angrily and impotently on Melbourne, telling him that the entire want of control had spoiled Palmerston, 'But for that you are more to blame than he is.'[106]

When the cabinet met again on 1 October, Melbourne suggested that Palmerston should be instructed to summon the representatives of the four powers, and invite them to make a fresh overture to France. It was a victory for Lord John. Simple cabinet – they did not yet know their man: Palmerston made no objection, and it turned out that Brunnow, at least, would have to refer the matter back to his own court. In the meantime, Ponsonby advised the Porte to 'depose' Mehemet Ali. Thus, as Lord John said, 'while difficulty and delay are interposed to every proposition that may tend to maintain peace, those which lead to war are at once adopted'.[107] Lord John demanded another cabinet, which took place on 11 October. Once again, it was satisfactory to Lord John. The cabinet agreed that Palmerston should speak in a conciliatory way to Guizot, and to the French government. But Palmerston moved slowly, and in the meantime Lord Holland died. Before Lord John had time to recover either personally or politically from this loss, Thiers fell, and success attended the Turkish and allied arms in Syria. Palmerston had judged accurately, if not well, when he said that as the French had no army and no fleet, they must knock under.[108]

But the crisis did not end without one more angry remonstrance from Lord John. Before the month was out it transpired that instead of communicating the cabinet's decision of 1 October, Palmerston had told Lord Beauvale, the British ambassador in Vienna, that the government did not consider a meeting of the four powers expedient, and that Ponsonby had encouraged the Turks to blockade Alexandria. Once again Lord John wrote to Melbourne to resign: 'it is much better that Palmerston should lead in the House of Commons than that I should degrade myself by pretending to an influence which I do not possess'.[109] Melbourne could not talk him round, and invited Palmerston to do so. Palmerston found Lord John 'very cross and somewhat sour', but 'he relaxed and softened' as the conversation went on.[110] Palmerston frankly admitted his fault, and then pointed out that Ponsonby must remain in service until December to qualify for a pension. Faced with that argument Lord John could scarcely insist on Ponsonby's being recalled at once.[111] When Palmerston left him he seemed to be in a good humour, 'and so I think this little Cloud has blown over – we must try to keep the sky clearer in future'.[112] Palmerston could afford a little humour at Lord John's expense, for by this time Mehemet Ali had been defeated and there was nothing left for Lord John to do but to admit that Palmerston's policy had been successful.[113]

The Eastern crisis was an unhappy experience for Lord John, who had been in a false position from the day he supported the quadruple alliance. Melbourne pointed out that having been a party to the convention Lord John could not 'upon slight . . . grounds' withdraw himself from the consequences of it,[114] while Palmerston fairly argued that all he wanted to do was to implement the treaty of July.[115] Lord John then lost his temper and confused the essential facts of the case. He allowed himself to drift into what was in the circumstances a ludicrous dispute with Palmerston for the command of the troops engaged in the operations in Syria. Their command, he said, belonged to him, as secretary of state for war and colonies.[116] Quite so, agreed Palmerston, when we are at war, but until we are at war their command belongs to the secretary of state for foreign affairs.[117] Finally Lord John failed, even when he had a good case, to carry out his threats. Palmerston did not change his course, and Lord John did not resign.

The whole crisis marked a deterioration in Lord John's relations with Melbourne, in whom, according to his brother the Duke of Bedford, he no longer had any confidence.[118] Worse than that it brought a significant change in his relationship with Palmerston. Palmerston was an older man than Lord John, and he did not think of himself as a lesser one. Lord John relied upon good feelings and high principles to guide him in politics. Palmerston studied the men he dealt with. There is no reason to

suppose that, when it was all settled, Lord John stopped to
consider where he had gone wrong. There is every reason to suppose Palmerston could have supplied an answer to that question. It would be interesting to know when Palmerston went
through his papers, re-read the letter of 31 July from John
Russell, which had been endorsed, 'Thinks Louis Philippe will
support Thiers in armed Interference in Favor of Mehemet Ali
and that Thiers will support Louis Philippe in establishing ar-
bitrary govt in Spain,' and added, crushingly, 'He was wrong
on both Points – P.'[119]

In his speech at the opening of parliament in 1841, Lord John
passed over the Eastern crisis lightly, and even claimed, on behalf of the government, some credit for the success of Palmerston's policy.[120] The house then got down to the renewal of
the English poor law, and to the eternal topic of Ireland. The
opposition were in great heart. They had just won a seat at a
by-election at Carlow, and in five contests in England and Wales
the Whigs had lost four seats and only won one. On 2 February
Stanley asked for leave to bring in his registration bill again.
Lord John remarked that it reminded him of something Durham had once said. A franchise could seem wide and be narrow.
'You may say that every £10 householder shall have a vote, but
you may also say that he shall only have such vote on condition
of his being able to construe the first book of Homer.'[121] It was
his happiest hit at Stanley. Lord John then asked for leave to
bring in his English registration bill, and Morpeth asked for
leave to bring in the government's bill for dealing with the registration of voters and for amending the franchise in Ireland.
The pawns advanced across the board.

The government's Irish bill took precedence. Now that the
Irish poor law was working, the government proposed to put
the franchise on a new footing. Henceforth a combination of
£5 rating with a fourteen-year lease would qualify a man for a
vote. The fourteen-year lease was a guarantee that the plan
would not be revolutionary; the £5 rating was a guarantee that
the franchise would not be illusory. Lord John was driving down
the middle, but as had happened so often since 1835, he was not
to be allowed to reach his destination. He knew it, and he ended
his speech with an appeal to reason as the term was understood
at Woburn. Our measure, he said,

may be met by prejudice in the first place, or by indifference; but my belief is, that if the change be urged strenuously and peaceably – I do not say without vehemence, because I believe that vehemence may be rightly used in a just cause . . . the proposal will be ultimately adopted by this House . . . Whatever be the immediate fate of the present measure, justice will make it prevail in the end . . .[122]

The government carried the second reading, after a division in which both sides brought down the sick and the dying,[123] by 299 votes to 294. Faced with the certainty that the bill would never get through committee, let alone the house of lords, Lord John postponed further consideration of it until 23 April, when he would have more facts available, illustrating the relation of the poor rating to the value of property in Ireland.[124]

Before the debate was resumed, two things happened. First, the government yielded ground, and the proposed franchise was amended to £8 rating with a fourteen-year lease.[125] Then Howick and Wood let it be known that they were going to play a game of their own. To do him justice Wood was no doubt sincere when he told Lord John that he was afraid 'you are again about to embark in one of those struggles on Irish measures, which after long contention, and exasperated feelings will end either in concession as before, or in a tory government doing as they please'.[126] Howick and Wood believed that they, in their turn, could drive down the middle between Stanley and Lord John. They proposed to keep the £5 rating, but to abolish the leasehold qualification and substitute a simple occupation franchise – parliament to decide the amount of the occupation.[127] To the Tories, this would have the attraction, or so they supposed, of resemblance to the Chandos clause; to the Whigs it would have the merit of producing a large electorate. They miscalculated. To the opposition, Stanley's bill was a stick to beat a dog, not a serious attempt to settle a disputed question. On the other side, Ebrington admitted that many of 'our Irish friends' would prefer a simple occupation franchise, 'because the requirement of a lease must leave the *future* extension or contraction of the franchise wholly at the discretion of the landowners' and reduce some constituencies to nothing.[128] Lord John was wiser. He did not wish to reduce the whole of Ireland to hold land by occupation. If Ireland was ever to know something of the peace of the English countryside, long leases must be encouraged, not discouraged. Lord John was not interested in a large electorate if it was dominated by the landlords of the ascendancy,[129] and he denounced the whole scheme as tortuous. But in committee the government were defeated on 26 April by 291 votes to 270, with Howick and Wood acting as tellers for the majority, and on 29 April they were defeated again by 300 votes to 289. There was no alternative but to drop their bill. Howick had turned out to be Brougham the second.

The struggle over the Irish registration bill was about a real issue. It was, as Lord John said, to decide whether millions of people were to have what they could accept as parliamentary representation, or whether they were to express their voice through secret clubs and combinations.[130] It was to decide whether, when foreign powers were in negotiation with the United Kingdom they were to know that they had to deal with a united kingdom, or with a country where between one-quarter and one-third of the queen's subjects were on the point of rebellion.[131] There was much at stake, and the next few years were to throw light upon the motives of the principal actor. When the Tories came back into office, nothing more was heard about an Irish registration act. Stanley's bill had served its purpose, and was then 'thrown like a worthless weed away',[132] and the Duke of Bedford condemned Stanley's conduct as the most bare-faced piece of profligacy of his time.[133]

Budgets were things in which Lord John took little interest. As a statesman you employed a chancellor of the exchequer as your elder brother might employ a land agent or a steward. If one agent kept the accounts badly, you tried another. If the second did likewise, you were in a mess yourself. There is no need, in a biography of Lord John, to go into the details of the budget deficits of 1838, 1839 and 1840. Suffice to say that Rice failed, and that in 1840 Baring had bad luck when he increased the existing duties, and the crises in Canada and Syria led to a continuing depression in trade. By the time parliament met in 1841, the deficit had reached six millions. Baring may have been right when he said that his estimate of last year would turn out right for the year after next,[134] but he was not going to be allowed to prove his point. In 1841 it was inescapable that the whole cabinet address itself to the budget.

The cabinet reviewed the possibilities. They rejected a loan, they rejected an income tax, they rejected another small increase in duties,[135] and they came to the conclusion that the best thing to do would be to lower the protective duties and to try and recoup more revenue from increased consumption. Next they must decide which duties to reduce. There were over 1200 items on the tariff, but of these a mere dozen or so brought in 90 per cent of the revenue, and the key items were sugar, timber and corn. It would have been more prudent to have attacked the smaller monopolies first.[136] But bravery was forced upon the government, for if they were to solve the deficit they must attack the duties on items for which there was a large unsatisfied consumer demand. Sugar was one such, and tales were rife of the poor man going into the grocer's shop, and after hearing the price of sugar, turning away in sorrow;[137] and of the villagers who were obliged to let their fruit go to waste because they could not afford the sugar to preserve it.[138] Timber was another, because cheaper timber would mean more houses. When the cabinet met in February, these were the interests that Baring proposed to attack.

It was at this stage that Lord John threw corn into consideration too. He was, after all, colonial secretary and sugar and timber were both colonial interests. In his inmost heart, he was probably not averse from having a crack at the planters in the West Indies. But a change in the duties on foreign timber just at the moment that his Canadian union act came into force would be a serious matter, and Lord John had cause, if he was to be required to sell a reduction in imperial preference to the Canadians, to ask for a *quid pro quo*. Nobody yet knew the potential of the Canadian prairies, but it was already apparent that the Canadians might to some extent make up in corn what they lost in timber. Over and above this, Lord John had a nose for a breeze. The Whigs had just lost a seat at Walsall, thanks to the intervention of an anti-corn-law league candidate; and Ward, the original genius behind the appropriation resolution, was pressing him to have the courage to deal with the corn laws. Lord John submitted to the cabinet a memorandum in which he asked them to add corn to Baring's list.[139]

Instead of recommending the fixed duty he was already known to prefer, Lord John suggested a graduated scale with smaller steps and lower duties than the present one. Why? Because by retaining the sliding scale, 'the principle proclaimed by Sir Robert Peel and Sir J. Graham would be adhered to'. Peel had on several occasions in 1838 and 1839 intervened to save the Whigs from their Radical friends. Might he not now support them in a moderate reform of the corn law? It was a question which he would be well advised to have out of the way, before he came to power himself. Furthermore, if the Whigs could secure Peel's support, it would save them from the consequences of a revolt among their own landowners. Lord John had in front of him a list of the fifty-seven Liberal members who had voted against the house going into committee on the corn laws on 26 May 1840.[140] Some of those fifty-seven members would, of course, come back into line, but others might not, and a middle-of-the-road settlement could only be obtained by middle-of-the-road men from both parties.

There is no record of what happened at the cabinet, but it scarcely matters. Long before Baring rose to introduce his budget on 30 April, it was apparent that Lord John's plan of drawing Peel in was a non-starter, because the debates on the Irish registration bill had made it certain that the government could no longer stand. Swinging right round, Lord John then persuaded the cabinet to stay on in order to spell out their difference from Peel. He dropped his plan for a graduated scale, and before Baring rose on 30 April to introduce his proposals for sugar and timber, Lord John announced that on 31 May he would move the house into a committee on the corn laws, and that the government would then propose a moderate fixed duty as a final solution to the problem.[141] What mattered to the Whigs now was not whether they fell, but how they fell. They would inevitably be beaten in the present house of commons, but by taking up corn, they were bound, or so Lord John thought, either to gain at the polls, or to fasten Peel with a problem he dare not tackle. From far away in Canada Sydenham echoed Lord John: if beaten upon sugar, give them timber; if beaten on timber, give them corn; 'the discussions *must* benefit you, and *must* injure them'.[142]

Even at this moment, which brings the politics of the 1830s to an end, Lord John did not, as might at first glance appear, sacrifice Ireland, which was the part of the United Kingdom to benefit most from the existing corn law. The Irish executive warned Lord John that there would be an outcry against any change, and also warned him to disregard it. It would be better for the Irish to learn to eat corn, which they would do if the price were low, than to have their present artificially high share of the English market under the present 'vicious' system.[143]

The stage was now set for the ministry's execution. On 7 May, before the debate on the sugar duties began, Lord John announced that what the government had in mind for corn was a fixed duty of 8s a quarter.[144] There could have been no surer way of making certain that the representatives of the great interests would support each other. The house then listened to an impassioned debate about sugar, which lasted for eight days. Sugar was an exception to the general rule that Peel was more knowledgeable than Lord John on tariff matters. But then sugar was an exception to every rule, because it was tied up with the question of slavery.

Sugar brought out in Lord John the academic philosopher who loved exposing sophistries. Most foreign sugar came from plantations worked by slaves. The British planters in the West Indies having been compelled to emancipate their slaves, now employed free labour which, they argued, was dearer. Therefore the British parliament had a moral duty to help them, and to preserve the prohibitive duty of 63s a hundredweight on foreign sugar. Lord John started with the argument advanced to the select committee on import duties, that a duty of 63s on foreign sugar was equivalent to an extra 63s taken out of the purse of the British consumer and paid into the pockets of the West Indian planters who had already received £20m compensation for emancipating their slaves. He then turned on the moralists. Did they apply the same argument to cotton, or to coffee? Did they refuse to wear cotton garments? Did they refuse to drink coffee? Yes, if it came direct from Brazil; but not if it came from Brazil by way of the Cape, and arrived as 'colonial' produce. What could you gain by refusing to trade with Brazil? If you traded with Brazil, at least you had influence there. If you refused to trade with Brazil, Brazil did not give up slavery, Brazil merely sold her coffee to other countries which were not so squeamish. Why, even the planters in the West Indies themselves imported refined slave-grown sugar from

Europe in order to re-sell it as free sugar to the United Kingdom.[145]

Sydenham considered Lord John's speech 'the crowning work even of his mind'.[146] But Peel too, as Lord John said, 'made a magnificent speech',[147] and at the end of the debate on 18 May Peel won by the large majority of thirty-six, by 317 votes to 281. Among the Whigs, nine county M.P.s and six borough M.P.s voted against their party, and nine more county M.P.s abstained.[148]

On the day the sugar debate began, Lord John received a memorandum on 'The Question of *Resignation* or *Dissolution*'. Parkes thought that by dissolving, the Whigs would keep 300 seats, and that by resigning, and leaving Peel to dissolve, they would retain only 250 or 260.[149] All through the debate the cabinet were trying to persuade Melbourne to dissolve, because, as Palmerston said, neither '*we*' nor '*they*' could go on in the present parliament.[150] Melbourne demurred, and referred to 'the united panic of all the interests we are about to affect'.[151] But Melbourne had no support, and when the defeat on the sugar duties was announced, Lord John wrote that it was impossible to postpone a decision any longer because 'no one would bear a further suspense'.[152] Melbourne had lost his power of veto at last, and he capitulated.

It remained to settle the tactics to be adopted before the dissolution took place. The vital thing now was to achieve time to try and trap Peel into discussing the ministry's proposals for dealing with the corn law. On 20 May Baring blandly announced that the government's proposals for overhauling the sugar duties not having met with approval, he would move that the house go into committee to consider the annual sugar duties – i.e. the old ones – which were to be renewed. The announcement caused a surprise, as well it might. On 31 May Lord John was due to open the ministry's proposals on corn. In order to deny him this advantage Peel moved a motion of no confidence, and argued that ministers could no longer get their measures through the house. Much was said against this, but it was no more than ministers themselves had known since February. Lord John spoke on the fifth day of the debate, on 4 June. He made play with Peel's record in 1828–9, 'and this was your strong Government!' – and then asked one of the deserters

among the Whig county members whether he thought Peel
intended to stand upon the principle of the present corn law?

> I confess I did not so understand him . . . I believe if he had the
> power, he would make a very great alteration. The hon. Member
> . . . and I have read the oracle, and we read it differently. It is to
> be sure a very obscure and mysterious oracle, but I gather, from
> a statesman of the right hon. Baronet's prudence and long experi-
> ence intimating that he was not satisfied with the present law, and
> would not adhere to its details, that he intends some day or other,
> if he has the power, to make a considerable alteration – always
> reserving, however, the sliding scale. How far that scale may slide
> may depend upon . . . circumstances.[153]

Lord John knew that in the long run Peel could not win. If he
adhered to the existing laws he must soon alienate the new
middle-class electorate: if he changed them he would be broken
by the squires, who had never forgiven him for his apostasy in
1829.

Peel won his motion of no confidence by 312 votes to 311.
Three days later on 7 June Lord John announced the dissolution, and after he had promised that the new parliament would
meet as soon as possible, members left Westminster for the constituencies. Ministers stayed in office until the end of August,
but this was, in effect, the end of the Melbourne administration.
For over six years Melbourne had presided over a government
to which Lord John supplied the reforming impulse. To this day
Lord John's enemies call him a giant among pygmies. The real
question is whether Lord John was also a giant among giants.
William IV had said that Lord John would cut a wretched
figure when opposed by Peel and Stanley. But in fact, as Gladstone said in 1890, 'no man ever led the House of Commons
with a more many-sided activity, or a more indomitable
pluck'.[154] For over six years, while Peel and Stanley possessed a
veto in the house of lords, and Lord John had nothing to rely on
but a 'three-legged' party of Whigs, Radicals, and Irish in the
commons;[155] for over six years while Melbourne ruled out the
creation of peers, and Peel and Stanley had the power and Lord
John had the responsibility; for over six years, while Lord John
suffered more than his share both of public obloquy and of
private misfortune, Lord John had kept the Tory party at bay
in single combat. No wonder then, that before the results of the

election were known, Parkes, who expected the Whigs to come
back 300 strong, 'for Lord John to make 301', could add that
'Johnny counts for 25 himself, which so balances parties';[156] and
that Sydenham could exclaim 'He is, indeed, a LEADER', and
argue that the Liberal party ought to erect him a statue of
gold.[157]

Part Three, 1841–52

CHAPTER XI

The Poisoned Chalice, 1841–6

i. Office, 1841

ON THE day Lord John announced the dissolution of parliament he became engaged to Lady Fanny Elliot, who had refused him nine months earlier. Fanny had gone on thinking about Lord John; in March she told her mother that 'she was too old to think it necessary to be what is called desperately in love',[1] and on 7 June she accepted him.[2] William called Lord John a perfect salamander: 'You set fire to the Country and to a Lady's heart at the same time and you flourish in the general conflagration.'[3] Lord John hastily made sure that a marriage in Scotland was as good as a marriage in England,[4] and the wedding was arranged for 20 July. The Minto children left London and went home to prepare for it. Posting back along the road from Carlisle, they threw pieces of bread and cake to the labourers' children who stood to watch the carriage pass, 'and told them it was cheap bread from Lord John Russell'.[5]

The marriage might easily have turned out a disaster. Fanny was no more physically in love with Lord John in July 1841 than she had been in September 1840, and according to Bertrand Russell, 'puritan inhibitions' made her incapable of passionate love.[6] She found begetting, carrying, bearing, and nursing children very difficult. As she herself said to her sister-in-law in 1848,

> We must buy every great blessing at a great price, that of children perhaps at the greatest, and you and I have often lamented together over the loss of our *careless* days – in short we have wished to shake ourselves free of husbands and children . . .[7]

Four children were born: John, later Lord Amberley, in December 1842; Willy, in April 1848; Rollo, in July 1849; and

Agatha, in March 1853. In addition Lady John suffered mis-
carriages, and year after year, for months on end she would be
laid up on a couch, husbanding her strength 'for the great
squeezes, wch were necessary but not agreeable',[8] or making a
slow and painful recovery, whose trials 'are many and great,
and less known by all around than those of the more critical
phase of illness'.[9] Fanny would have been happier had she been
able to plan her family. As it was, she was censured for making a
fuss, and her health always gave way in a political crisis.[10]

Nor was Lady John a good manager. Seven months after her
marriage, her father noticed that she still had not brought herself to believe 'that there is anybody in the world so wicked as
really to intend to cheat, or to overcharge'.[11] Thereafter, Minto
kept her supplied with fresh, honest, country servants from the
estate in Scotland. Even so, the bills kept on mounting, and the
family, when travelling, resembled an army on the march.

Fortunately Fanny's failings did not antagonise her husband.
Lord John was solicitous for her health, and he was not censori-
ous. They shared simple tastes, and a detestation of theology
'as the greatest enemy of true religion'.[12] Fanny made Lord
John and his children a home which endured, and what strains
there were seem to have been between the two families. The
marriage was the first between a Russell and an Elliot, and when
Fanny's first child was born, the Duchess of Bedford, 'like her
own silly self', asked Fanny why she and Lord John had not yet
asked the duke to be godfather. 'W[d] you believe that the D[ss] of
B. actually said to me "you know it may be a very good th[g] for
the little boy – the Duke may leave him someth[g]".'[13] The
duchess whispered and contrived until Fanny gave way.

Fanny enjoyed Scottish dancing, but she was solemn, and
lacked the talents to further her objects. Her lightest humour,
when Lord John became prime minister, was to say that (her
name being Fanny Anna Maria Elliot) she looked after the
FAME of the ministry, not its fate.[14] But she did hold some part
of the fate of future Whig ministries in her hands, for now that
he was married again, Lord John would be expected to entertain. Lady John was as shy as he was, and even so commonplace
a compliment as being asked to drink a glass of wine embarrassed her.[15] In a moment of depression nineteen months after
her marriage, she wrote that she was reckoned 'cold, dull, and

unworthy of such a husband', and concluded that it was quite
right, for she never appeared anything else.[16] She could never
rise to the role of a political hostess, and occasionally fell far
below it. Lord and Lady John had not been married long before Fanny was writing to her brother that

> Ly Holland has ever since we came to town coaxed and begged,
> and begged and coaxed us to give her a dinner. *I* always flatly
> refused, tell[g] her the easy truth that we do not give dinners to any-
> body – however she last time tried her power on the weaker sex
> . . . and gett[g] hold of Ld John alone actually made him, against
> his will, consent to have her this day. I scolded him well, and so
> far improved upon the plan as to delay the fatal hour for one
> week.[17]

One can understand her reluctance to share her husband with
Lady Holland, but it was no way to treat Lord John's oldest
surviving friend, or to promote his political fortunes. And as
she was earnestly ambitious for Lord John, she found herself
day-dreaming about the patriotic anti-corn-law harangues in
which she fancied herself at Lord John's side,[18] and the Whig–
Radical ministry to come when he was prime minister;[19] and
impressing upon her husband that it was her wish that he
should become 'the head of the most moral and religious government' the country had ever known.[20]

Equally damaging to Lord John was the fact that marriage
necessarily connected him with the whole Elliot clan. Carlisle
once referred scathingly to the Minto family as the Scots
Greys.[21] Fanny's grandfather was viceroy of India, and her
father was ambassador at Berlin before he took the admiralty
in Melbourne's government. Now, it seemed as though there
was an Elliot in every embassy and in command of every fleet.
Nepotism was not unusual, but there was a universal feeling
that the Elliots were below standard. It is a verdict which is
borne out by the evidence of the Minto papers. As official
appointments scattered them over the face of the earth, the
family kept together by correspondence. But, alas, every member of the clan was drilled never to set pen to paper without
filling four full sides and ending up at right angles and in a
crush. The result is a disaster. They inflated trifles, and kept
news back until too late. It was not an able family, and when

Lord John became prime minister there was great apprehension lest the government be 'over-*Ellioted*'.[22]

The general election of 1841 went badly. Lord John was asked to stand for the city of London. The opportunity to promote free trade as a member for the city was too good to miss, but the contest was close. His agent reported that the Whigs had polled 500 to 600 '*within our promises*', and advised him not to come to the declaration on 30 June.[23] Lord John was elected at the bottom of the list of four successful candidates, with two Conservatives and one Radical for company, and only nine votes above the next candidate. Elsewhere, 'our best exertions in a public cause' produced no corresponding exertions among the people:[24] the Radicals virtually disappeared, and even in Ireland, the Tories made gains. In England the Whigs suffered a net loss of fifteen in the boroughs, and a net loss of twenty-three in the counties, where they had, in any case, held only forty-five seats before.[25] Parkes walked ruefully among 'the tombs of the County dead'.[26] Ellice bewailed their losses, but thought that if Lord John had not taken up the corn laws, the minority of seventy-five would have been 150.[27]

It was a complete defeat, and from 5 July Lord John was in communication with Stanley, his successor at the colonial office, to ensure a smooth change over.[28] But Melbourne and Lord John did not resign, and waited to meet parliament. Lord John wanted to secure the advantage of drawing up the Queen's speech, to direct the attention of the new parliament to the question of corn, and to make another attempt to fasten upon Peel the responsibility for rejecting a moderate fixed duty. Lord John had promised Peel there would be no delay in calling the new parliament together. Strictly speaking, the promise was not kept. If it had been, parliament would have met towards the end of July, and not towards the end of August. In 1835 Lord John was obliged to abandon his honeymoon with his first wife in order to help Melbourne form a government. Now Peel had to wait a month to become prime minister, while Lord John got married at Minto and enjoyed a honeymoon at Bowhill.

When Lord and Lady John returned to London to face their new responsibilities, Lady John soon took stock of hers. On 14 August the children arrived from Ramsgate – one boy and five girls: the next day Baby Toza and Georgy both called her mama, and a great weight was taken off h'er mind when, after talking to her about the children, Lord John spoke of their mother too.[29] A few days later Lord John faced the new house of commons. In the address he invited parliament to consider whether the existing duties on corn did not 'embarrass trade, derange the currency, diminish the comforts, and increase the privations of the great body of the community'.[30] Peel moved an amendment; Lord John developed his views upon the corn laws, and at the end of the debate the government was defeated by 360 votes to 269. At last Melbourne resigned. But even after Peel had taken office, Lord John continued to try and bring before the public the difference between the two parties. He did not wish, he told Duncannon, that the new ministers should be opposed at their elections on taking offices of profit under the crown, 'but that they should be required to give some answer at the hustings as to their intentions, especially relating to corn'.[31]

The Whigs' tactics of hanging on in 1841 have not had a good press. Lord John's discovery that the graduated scale was 'the main cause of the evils under which the country is at present suffering',[32] came, as Peel pointed out, in haste at the end of a period of five or six years in which he could have done something about it.[33] Nobody listens to a dying ministry, even when it has something new to say, and Lord John mistook the time at which to argue. He was also, as Melbourne told the Queen, 'very angry and very bitter' at being turned out of office.[34] But his behaviour can be interpreted in terms rather more to his credit than panic and bad temper. His actions were intended to have an effect both upon his own position and upon Peel's. Throughout 1841 Lord John was changing his ground. In 1835 he had rushed into alliance with the Radicals and the Irish. His understanding with the Radicals came to an end in 1837, and long before 1841 he had concluded that the Irish connection too 'impaired his usefulness'.[35] Now, in tariff reform, Lord John had found a new flag to fight under, and an intelligible policy which 'does *not* meddle with religious prejudices', and 'does *not* relate to Ireland'. As Sydenham said, it could scarcely be expected 'to give you a majority', but it would at least range 'parties under new banners . . . and enable you *to force your measures on another government*'.[36]

The process of getting off with the old love went fairly

smoothly. The Radicals almost disappeared at the general election, and in his election speeches O'Connell abused the Whigs so ungratefully that Lord John even considered answering him back in public.[37] Fortunately, he held his peace, and when the new parliament met, he made it clear that one of the main differences between the parties was still 'the practical Administration of the Government of Ireland'.[38] Lord John was not going to drop his policy of justice to Ireland, but the Whig party was to be rid of visible and humiliating dependence on Irish support. The Irish were left out of the resignation honours, and were indeed, as O'Connell complained, 'not *well treated*'.[39] O'Connell then said he was not prepared to act in future with any party that refused to make repeal an open question, and Lord John consulted Palmerston about the Whigs' relations with O'Connell in opposition.[40] Palmerston replied that 'To act with him will often be impossible, to break openly with him would be hurtful.' He suggested thanking him for his support when he gave it, and not supporting him when the Whigs disapproved of what he was doing.[41]

By taking up the corn laws Lord John also affected the Whigs. The proposal for a moderate fixed duty was announced by Russell in his capacity as leader of the house. It committed that unruly party in a way that no announcement made by Lord John after Peel took office could have done. No party actually courts losses: but on 24 July Lord John wrote that despite the election results the party stood better than it had done with a majority of twelve.[42] What he meant was that the fewer county seats the Whigs had the better. Only five of the nine Whig county rebels on the sugar vote, and the son of one more, got back into the new parliament. Of these six, two now called themselves Conservatives. Lord John had simultaneously reduced the number of his own potential rebels, and added to those of Peel, and early in August he boasted to Melbourne that by his conduct of the election he had laid upon the county members of England 'the burden of standing singly in the way against Corn Law Reform'. He added that he meant to play upon this string until he made them give up their monopoly.[43]

It was one thing to move away from the left of politics. It was another to move over to the middle, for that was the ground already occupied by Peel. There were times when the Whigs toyed with the idea of taking an independent position in support of Peel,[44] and in October 1841 Ellice thought there was no significant point of difference between the Conservative party and the Liberal party.[45] But that was not often Lord John's way of looking at things. At this time he felt no personal regard for Peel to moderate the bitterness of party warfare. He agreed with the view Brougham expressed in 1828–9, that Peel was 'too great an impostor';[46] he never could forget how Peel had taunted him that the Reform Bill would be 'some miserable measure';[47] and he had taken a wry interest, as home secretary in 1839, in warning Sir Robert that a chartist mob had left Birmingham to sack his country house at Drayton.[48] Lord John had no cause to spare Peel, and if he was right that the corn law question could no longer be avoided, then he was bound to gain either way: either Peel would succeed in carrying his supporters with him or he would not. If he did, he could be exhibited as the shameless turncoat of 1828–9; if he did not, his party would split. Peel was to be humiliated or broken.

Lord John was not required to say which outcome he thought more likely, but in his public utterances he pretended to suppose that Peel would carry his supporters with him. Lord John devoted his address to the city electors to free trade, and his speech in the house on 27 August to nailing Peel up on his corn law cross. Dissenters in office, roman catholics in parliament, and the reform of parliament: all these Peel had formerly opposed, and all these Peel had subsequently agreed to. Now Peel told us he would never abandon the sliding scale on corn. That meant the monopoly of corn would go the way of the anglican monopoly. In office or out of office, the Whigs (and public opinion) would dictate the government's measures.[49] For six years since 1835 Peel and the house of lords had exhibited the party of movement reduced to move at a speed dictated by the party of resistance. Now Lord John looked forward to the party of resistance being compelled to advance at a speed dictated by the party of movement.

In his private correspondence, too, Lord John made the same point. In October he told Melbourne that the 'next session must either destroy the Tory Ministry, or give a heavy blow to Tory principles. I should think the last the most likely, and perhaps the most to be desired . . .'[50] To Ellice, Lord John wrote,

> No one can tell how far Peel may be inclined to go himself, and still less how far he may be able to carry the representatives, as he called them, of the heavy lands of England . . . [If we avoid] putting forward or countenancing . . . plans so democratic that all prudent men will prefer a lagging, backward, bigotted conduct of affairs . . . there may be a conduct of affairs far more liberal than the majority of the Lords would like . . .[51]

Ellice himself thought the Whig minority might prove all powerful for purposes of good,[52] and the Duke of Bedford said Lord John might do more good in opposition than as a minister 'exposed to . . . the malice of a large and powerful party determined not to let you govern'.[53]

But the dominant note of Lord John's correspondence is that he expected Peel's party to break up. He assured Melbourne that if Peel proposed a real alteration of the corn laws the squires would turn against him.[54] He wrote to Lansdowne that if Peel did much the squires would raise a cry that they had been betrayed,[55] and to Clarendon that Peel's supporters 'will give him some rare kicks and plunges if not an upset before he gets to his journey's end'.[56] To Lady Holland, he wrote once that Peel would do very well if he could only 'drag his bumpkins after him',[57] a second time that 'The blockheads of their party will make their insurrection',[58] and a third time that the Tories were made of sterner stuff than Peel supposed.[59] Parkes, too, thought Peel could not settle the corn law question without shivering his Conservatives to pieces – 'the outdoor men have always scattered the Tories'.[60]

There is enough in all this to show that Lord John foresaw Peel's being caught between the squires and the league. Peel would then start by keeping his sails furled and waiting the squall, and end by running before the storm.[61] Or as Lord John put it much later, in 1866, to lord Grosvenor, Peel would meet the demand for repeal 'by stout resistance followed by unqualified concession'.[62] The Whigs knew their Peel, and his policy of 'waiting till there is a crash, and then conceding everything at once'.[63] In due course Disraeli said that in December 1845 Lord John returned the poisoned chalice to Sir Robert. But the chalice was already poisoned when Lord John passed it over in 1841. That is why, when the new parliament was prorogued in October 1841, Lord John wrote that he did not think more could have been made of the past session.[64] To change the metaphor, Lord John had moved his shop into the same street as Peel's, and with his unique line of Irish goods available but no longer advertised, and with his new cut-price offer on corn, he had reason to hope that Peel could soon be driven out of business.

ii. Opposition, 1842–5

The next few years were to show that Lord John had been too sanguine when he told Prince Albert that he hoped to run into Peel within a year.[65] Lord John had over-estimated himself and under-estimated Peel. In the first place, Lord John had difficulties of his own. Melbourne complacently took the view that 'A party never yet has been entirely broken up by defeat',[66] and continued to condemn every lead Lord John took on the corn laws.[67] Melbourne was ageing fast, but as late as 1844 he still clung to the idea that, if Peel were defeated, he would be asked to succeed him.[68] His attitude did nothing to diminish the small hard core of protectionist Whig peers, and in 1843, when the policy of a fixed duty was put to a vote in the house of lords, only 31 peers took the trouble to attend and vote for it.[69] Nor were things much better in the house of commons. Contemporaries spoke of the utter demoralisation and apathy of the party. They exaggerated, but the position was bad enough. When Lord John sent notes to his followers before the beginning of the session in 1842, one of the newspapers 'commented on the style, the seal &c.', and pronounced them a forgery.[70] As the session went on Lord John was 'a good deal vexed at finding himself so little followed and attended to',[71] and he left London before the session came to an end.[72] Year after year the opposition mustered low votes in the division lobbies, by-elections increased Peel's majority from ninety to one hundred, and worst of all Lord John's policy made no impression upon Cobden, who showed no desire to help the Whigs turn the Conservatives out.

As for Peel, even while he spoke in favour of a sliding scale in 1841, he was careful not to commit himself to the existing one. In 1842 he presented his new scale with a wonderful equivocation which left him free to move backwards to protection or

forwards to free trade. He then introduced his budget, and profiting from the Whigs' experience, he attacked the tariff from the
other end, rubbing out the small monopolies first, and bringing
in his income tax, which Lord John supposed he could not even
get through his cabinet,[73] to balance the revenue. Peel got away
with nothing worse than the resignation of the Duke of Buckingham, and a danger signal when eighty-six Conservatives
voted against the reduction in the duties on imported cattle.
Vernon Smith thought the session brought free trade principles
to their zenith, and the Whigs to their nadir.[74] In the summer of
1842 renewed chartist disturbances consolidated opinion behind the government, and after that Peel was able to coast
along on a succession of good harvests. In November 1842
Ellice recognised that the Whigs had lost the initiative, and that
the only chance of power falling into 'our' hands was by its
falling out of 'their' hands.[75] A year later still, Lord John, while
continuing to believe that Peel's party only accepted him as a
pis aller, was obliged to admit that there was no immediate prospect of his overthrow.[76]

There was little for Lord John to do except wait. The Irish
Repealers attended Whig meetings for a time in 1842,[77] but the
new model moderate Lord John refrained from getting up a
debate on Ireland. In 1843 Peel brought in an arms bill. Lord
John called a meeting of Liberal members at Smith O'Brien's
request,[78] but the Irish received little help from the official opposition in their filibuster against the bill, and Lord John contented himself with pressing the government to give the healing
as well as the restrictive medicine.

As for the revision of the sliding scale and the budget, all Lord
John could do was to point to the contrast between everything
Peel said about the tariff as a whole, and the manner in which
he dealt with the corn problem;[79] to hint that Peel was going,
not as far as argument would carry him, but as far as his supporters would allow him; and to get in a shrewd hit or two at
Peel's style of legislation. Peel's style (consciously modelled in
contrast to the Whigs') was to wait until he could bring before
parliament, with certainty as to its passing, a well-thought-out
measure as broad and deep as the problem it was to solve. In
1842 Lord John begged Peel to consider what the event would
be, if his new sliding scale had no sooner received the royal

assent than the agitation against the corn laws began afresh.[80]
'To concede, but not to conciliate, to disturb the existing
state of things, and yet to settle nothing, would be . . . of all
courses . . . the most imprudent.' In place of finality, Peel was
offering us the double disadvantage of what Bacon called 'the
froward retention of custom' coupled with the mischiefs of
innovation.[81]

Lord John also began to express his fear that a fixed duty
might no longer settle the question. In December 1842 he wrote
to Fox Maule that he now thought an 8s duty too high. Fox
Maule's reply, which was unexpected and which no doubt
helped to keep Lord John on the move, was that he was now in
favour of total repeal.[82] When the session of 1843 began, Lord
John asserted that if Peel had settled for an 8s fixed duty in 1841,
many of the anti-corn-law league's wealthiest and most influ-
ential subscribers would have fallen off. Now it was too late.[83]
Four months later Lord John made his last public exhortation
to the league to accept a compromise,[84] and before the end of
the year Parkes wrote to Cobden that Lord John 'could not
without gross inconsistency jump from 8s out of all Fixed Duty,
that he had to convert the interested *aristocratic* members of his
party'.[85] Lord John was already looking for a way of escaping
from his own commitment to a fixed duty.

While the house was quiet, Lord John's brother invited him
to edit the *Correspondence of John, Fourth Duke of Bedford*.[86] More
significantly, Lord John picked up books by Adam Smith,
Malthus, Ricardo and McCulloch, and pamphlets on the corn
question by Greg and Hubbard, and the effect of his reading
began to appear in his speeches.[87] His attachment to free trade,
or with a fixed duty to 'certainty' of trade,[88] stemmed from the
general principle of not legislating at all on the subject,[89] from
the fact that the United Kingdom already depended on imports, and from the observation that if you derive your corn
from only one kingdom, the fluctuation will be much greater
than if you derive it from many kingdoms, from Poland, Russia,
Germany and America.[90] Time and again Lord John returned
to this theme of opening up a supply from America,[91] but he
was careful not to hold out any hope that when Britain did draw
her supply from the new world, corn would be cheaper. There
was a rising population, and Lord John always stressed that he

looked not so much to cheapness of corn, as to regularity of supply, and to employment for the people.[92]

The extent to which America had now taken hold upon his imagination is revealed in his correspondence with Palmerston over the Webster Ashburton treaty. While Palmerston fulminated against the sacrifice of British interests and prestige,[93] Lord John thought that we might have got better terms, but that the great thing to do was to exploit the opportunity of selling British goods and buying American corn.[94] He informed Palmerston that when parliament met, he would 'urge the opportunity of letting in American bread stuffs at a moderate duty',[95] and he told Melbourne that a good treaty of commerce would be the best medicine for the suffering country.[96] It must have been a temptation, after their clash in 1840, for Lord John to go along with Palmerston, and denounce the treaty. Instead, he reassured Ellice that he was 'for peace with America, beyond any other nation',[97] and he told Palmerston that the opposition ought not to irritate either France or America.[98]

Lord John's reading meant that by 1843, he could advance much more strictly economic arguments against the sliding scale, which operated like a gardener who left his ground unwatered during arid heats, and soaked it when the rain fell.[99] In illustrating this point, he now felt able to interpret what had happened in 1838–9 when he was home secretary. As the summer came on, and home supplies became scarce and the price went up, the corn dealers put best-quality imported corn on the market in such a way as to obtain the double benefit of a high price and a low rate of duty. Then, just as the new harvest was coming along, they put the lower-quality imported corn on the market in order to bring the price of corn down before making their new season's purchases from the British farmer. In the first operation they deprived the consumer of the benefit of cheap, or moderately priced corn, and in the second they deprived the farmer of his expected reward.[100] Peel defended the sliding scale on the ground that the second variable, the duties, moved in time with and in the opposite direction to the first, the price. But in fact this did not happen, and all that did happen was that the dealers took advantage of both. The moral was clear: you could not stop fluctuations in the price, because the harvests varied, but you could show that you had done what you could to reduce them, by abolishing the sliding scale and letting 'persons . . . send their orders abroad, to bring the article into the market, and to dispose of it like any other commodity'.[101]

For all Lord John's growing expertise in economics, it was Peel who dominated the house, and in 1843 it began to look as though the difference between the two parties might after all continue to be Ireland. Peel's policy stopped short of the Whig principle of equality in all matters ecclesiastical and civil. No catholics were appointed to office, and, as Lord John said, Peel could not send a Drummond to Ireland.[102] The repeal agitation began again, and this time the anti-repealers among the catholics were fast yielding to the cry, while those who did not join in became silent.[103] By June 1843 things had come to such a pass that, as Lord John dramatically put it, 'France and Russia may do as they please East and West, while O'Connell hangs on the rear of our forces'.[104] At this point Peel appointed a commission under Lord Devon to investigate the problems of landlord and tenant. Lord John reacted with chagrin: 'If we had thus thrown the subject loose . . . we should have been charged with endangering all property'.[105] But he had the honesty to admit that on this topic, at least, Peel was likely to go as far as he would.[106]

Lord John could not bear to think of Peel closing the gap between the parties on Ireland, but he still refused O'Connell's invitation to issue 'a magnificent epistle' declaring that the Whigs would put down the church nuisance and give Ireland additional M.P.s.[107] Then Peel had O'Connell arrested, and Lord John concluded that the security and confidence established by the Whigs had all been thrown away,[108] that Peel and the good government of Ireland were a contradiction in terms,[109] and that the great object must now be 'to prevent the establishment of a settled hatred between the two nations, which Lyndhurst and O'Connell have laboured so hard to create'.[110] Lord John decided that, early in 1844, for the first time since he left office, he must force a debate upon Ireland. While he was busy wondering whether there was anything he could do about the revenues of the Irish church that would not raise the ghost of appropriation,[111] Charles Buller approached O'Connell, and asked him what the Irish wanted.

O'Connell's answer – perfect religious equality, paying all
the clergy, or better still paying none; changes in the law of
landlord and tenant; an extension of both the county and the
borough franchise; municipal institutions equal to those in
England and Scotland; and a tax on absentee landlords, – was
not ill calculated to appeal to Lord John. But O'Connell then
went on to say, bitterly, that Lord John

> will never permit anything like justice to be done to the Catholic
> people of this country. I know him well. He has a thorough, con-
> temptuous, Whig hatred of the Irish. He has a strong and, I
> believe, conscientious abhorrence of Popery everywhere, but, . . .
> particularly of Irish Popery.[112]

Lord John did abhor Popery, but the rest, as Clarendon said,
was stupid, ungrateful accusation.[113] Nevertheless, it spurred
Lord John on, and the three-and-a-half-hour speech in which
he opened the opposition's debate on Ireland on 13 February
1844 was one of the best speeches that even he ever made on
Ireland.

Lord John began by saying that when the Whigs took office
in 1835, 'every precedent on the file was a model for partiality;
. . . the clerks were familiar with nothing but Protestant ascendancy and Catholic degradation'.[114] The Whigs had not cured
all the evils in six years, but Ireland had been delivered into
Peel's hands 'tranquil and undisturbed'.[115] Why was it now in
such an alarming condition? Ireland was occupied and not
governed. 'In England the Government as it should be . . . is a
government of opinion; the government of Ireland is notoriously
a government of force.'[116] No catholic had been placed in a
situation of trust, and some catholic magistrates had been dismissed. Now O'Connell was charged with endeavouring to stir
up the people of Ireland against the people of England, and all
ten catholics had been struck out of the panel of forty-eight
jurors for his trial. Were there no others who endeavoured to
stir up the people of England against the people of Ireland? Lord
Lyndhurst, for example? Was he put on trial? No, he was put
at the head of the magistracy and law of England.

Greville thought the speech very good, though he deplored
Lord John's attack upon Lord Lyndhurst as having been too
personal.[117] Even the more moderate among us today may not

think that was so very out of place. The debate went on for nine nights. In the middle, O'Connell, who had been released pending sentence, re-entered the house to a storm of applause from the Liberal benches, and Lord John shook him by the hand.[118] But at the end, Lord John's motion for a committee of inquiry was defeated by 324 votes to 225.

The opposition's attack upon the Irish front had ended in a low vote. But 1844 was not a comfortable year for Peel, who got caught in two nasty cross-currents. First, Ashley's ten-hour amendment was carried against the government, with Lord John and Palmerston both voting in the majority, and Peel was forced to whip his followers back into line by threat of resignation. Next, when Peel attempted to adjust the sugar duties, and to distinguish between foreign free and foreign slave-grown sugar, Lord John moved to put them on an equality. Lord John was defeated by 197 votes to 128, but a Conservative then made a new proposal to lower the duties still further. Lord John decided to support this as an improvement,[119] and it was carried by 241 votes to 221. In order to counteract this, Peel was obliged to move an amendment himself. The government was then in danger of defeat, and it was saved, Gladstone thought, by a magnificent speech by Stanley.[120] But, in fact, Lord John did not send out notes to his followers to attend.[121] He could not yet take Peel's place, and the government got home by 255 votes to 233.

At the end of the 1844 session Stanley was promoted to the house of lords, where Campbell looked forward to him and Brougham firing into each other,[122] and Peel began to map out a new policy for Ireland. The result was that for the first time it became possible to consider that there might not be much in it for Ireland whether Peel or Russell were in power, for Peel's lesser measures might at least be expected to pass the house of lords. One man, at least, was quick to get the point. In September 1844 Prince Albert said that he thought Peel would now govern Ireland upon the most liberal principles, and that he hoped one day to see Peel and Lord John in the same cabinet.[123] That was running on a bit, but Lansdowne, too, believed in Peel's conversion.[124] Peel now stood only a little further away from O'Connell than Lord John, and Lord John dare not draw any closer. In September 1844 he refused to countenance

O'Connell's new cry for Federal Union, and agreed with Bessborough that it meant either repeal or double debates.[125] In 1844 Lord John was not, as Hartington supposed even as late as 1874, to be tempted into a renewal of the old alliance with O'Connell.[126] It required steady nerves to go on driving along the road he had followed since 1841, when, with every year that passed, Peel was narrowing the gap between the two parties. But Lord John reflected that Peel was too distrusted by all parties in Ireland to succeed in his new course,[127] and wrote to Brougham that it was a great obstacle to good measures in Ireland that the present ministers brought them forward.[128]

The situation was made all the more piquant by the changes which were now taking place over corn, where the conviction was beginning to go out of the ministers' defence of the sliding scale. Until 1844 Peel fought the battle for the landlords stoutly, but he received no help from them either in or out of the house.[129] Then, in 1844, he found himself unable to answer Cobden, and Lord John expressed what everyone was thinking, when he doubted whether Peel was prepared 'to stand the test of three bad harvests, or of two, or even of one'.[130] Lord John watched Peel's progress with very mixed feelings. One side of him rejoiced to see Peel 'efface the old tory fleur de lis from his state carriage'.[131] Another resented the apparently inexhaustible credit extended to him by Liberal public opinion, and in this mood Lord John did not see why he should go an inch out of his way to support Peel's government.[132]

And yet, when the session of 1845 began, that was precisely what Lord John was obliged to do, and what he received credit for doing. Peel brought in three bills for Ireland: one to regulate the relations of landlord and tenant, another to establish three Queen's Colleges, and a third to increase the grant to the catholic seminary at Maynooth. The landlord and tenant bill disappeared in the house of lords where it was introduced. The university bill passed and was to cause Lord John many headaches in the future. The increased grant to Maynooth raised a storm of protest, and split the Tory party from top to bottom. The protestant interest had not defended the established church against Lord John in order to be sold by Peel.

However much Lord John might think that Peel was causing 'a great outcry for a very small benefit',[133] this was one of the specific measures he himself had suggested the year before, and on 18 April he came to Peel's rescue with one of the best speeches of his life.[134] Hitting a note he could not often reach, he rose clean above party politics, and was temperate, conciliatory and firm. Hobhouse was delighted, and recorded that Lord John had spoken with the tone of 'a moderator and a master, like the head not only of a party, but of the House, which in the present state of the Ministers he has a right to assume'.[135] Although he fell below this high level five days later, his contribution to the debate was impressive. When the vote was taken, 148 Conservatives voted for the measure, and 149 against. Thirty-five Liberals voted against, and the bill was carried by the 169 Liberals who followed Lord John. In 1838–9 Peel had propped Lord John up against the balloteers: now Lord John had performed an equal service for Peel against the protestants. With this in mind, it irritated him to the end of his life that people went on praising Peel for his strong government.[136]

The year 1845 brought another of Peel's great free trade budgets, and raised in ever more acute form the contrast between Peel's general policy of free trade, and his continued inactivity over the corn laws. The war of nerves intensified. What if Peel's next move was to leave Lord John stranded on his fixed duty, and to come out in favour of total repeal? Lord John became increasingly anxious to keep one step ahead. But he still had a shadow cabinet to consider, and they were not in favour of any further move. Throughout the winter of 1844–5, then, Lord John meditated bringing in a series of resolutions for the permanent improvement of the conditions of the labouring classes. It would not be a bad move to subordinate the corn laws to the condition of England question, and to show that he could look at the latter more comprehensively than Peel. In December 1844 Lord John drew up a plan commending free trade generally and emigration specifically.

He submitted his plan to Melbourne and Palmerston, who treated him 'as the old man was treated by his two wives, who pulled out one the black hairs, and the other the white, till they left him bald'. Melbourne objected to the free trade, and Palmerston to the emigration.[137] Lord John then shelved the plan, and tried once more to persuade the shadow cabinet to drop the fixed duty and come out in favour of total repeal.[138] When they refused, he took his plan down, rounded off his resolutions with a proposal to extend the benefits of education to those who were left behind, and introduced them to the house of commons. In his speech, Lord John announced more than eight months before Peel that he had come to the conclusion that the argument that wages follow the price of food was erroneous;[139] and he also, for the last time, proposed to substitute a fixed duty of 4*s*, 5*s*, or 6*s* for the present sliding scale.[140] By 182 votes to 105 the house declined to let Lord John put his resolutions to the test.

In what remained of the session, Lord John declared that when he compared the arguments used by ministers to defend the corn laws with the arguments that were used to attack them, it was certain that the present law could not last for long. 'No one can deny', he said, 'that the present Corn Law is intended to, and does in the opinion of political economists, add to the rent of the landlords. Only conceive the effect of this impression working on the minds of the people for many years.'[141] Lord John then defied his colleagues, and voted for the first time in favour of Villiers' annual motion in favour of total repeal.

If this final gesture meant that Lord John ended the session of 1845 one jump ahead of Peel, it also meant that he ended it one jump ahead of his own party. To all intents and purposes Peel and Lord John already appeared at the point of conjuncture in which they were to stand before the public in December. By the time the potato crop failed Peel and Russell were pretty equally determined to effect reforms in Ireland, and to repeal the corn laws. Prince Albert was not the only one to speak of the two men in one breath. Russell himself took up the idea of a junction, in a letter to Brougham, written on 1 May 1845, though, admittedly only to discount it: 'People distrust our *opinions* – they distrust Peel's *conduct*, and if the two parties were joined the double distrust would operate with increased force.'[142] In point of fact, as Lady Russell said on 9 December 1845, John would not dream of a coalition, and neither would Sir Robert.[143] But it is not without significance that when Lady John's sister Lady Mary Abercromby heard about the Edinburgh letter, she at once jumped to the conclusion that before it was written, Lord John and Peel must have understood one another.[144]

There was another, and from Lord John's point of view, a menacing possibility emerging in 1845. If, by adopting Lord John's opinions, Peel broke his own party, there were already those who would like to see not Lord John as prime minister at the head of the Liberal party, but Peel. First among them came the Prince. As Lord John wrote to Palmerston, the Prince likes Liberal policy, but he likes Peel better than either the Whig or Tory party.[145] When the time came, there would be others ready to take the same view. There was in fact no serious risk that if Lord John drove Peel out of business, Peel would emerge triumphant as the manager of Lord John's shop. But it was very disheartening to have people talk as though that was the result they would like to see.

iii. The Edinburgh Letter and the attempt to form a Ministry in December 1845

Among the malcontents was Howick, who was to play such an unattractive part in the next phase of the duel between Peel and Lord John. After his conduct over the Irish registration bill, Lord John behaved with extraordinary good nature to Howick, having, as he told Ellice, a very high regard for him.[146] Following Howick's defeat at the general election of 1841 Lord John went out of his way to try and find him a seat,[147] and when Howick did get back into the house of commons, as M.P. for Sunderland, the Duke of Bedford paid £500 towards his election expenses.[148] Howick resisted his father's recommendation to throw in his lot with the Tories, but he put an active intelligence at the service of disgruntled emotions, and throughout Peel's ministry, he was toying with the idea of a realignment of parties from which he and Peel would emerge on the same side.[149] That was the position when his father died in July 1845, and Howick became the third Earl Grey. Lord John had always held Howick's father in high regard, principally because he admired his approach to the conduct of foreign affairs, which was (or so Lord John supposed) in the true tradition of Fox, who would hazard neither the country's fortunes by isolationism, nor its reputation by 'brinkmanship'.[150] The new earl wrote understandingly enough to Lord John that he was sure 'you will sincerely lament the loss of a person to whose character I know that you have always done justice',[151] but he was jealous of Lord John, and without, perhaps, actually meaning to, he was now about to do both Lord John and the party an injury.

The death of the second Earl Grey was followed at the beginning of October by the death of Spencer. Within a few days Lord John was busy writing an appreciation of the careers of both Grey and Spencer for the *Edinburgh Review*. The article appeared in January 1846, and brought him £50.[152] It was one of the most attractive things he ever wrote, because in estimating the character and achievements of these two men, he really got outside himself. And while he was writing, events at last began to progress towards the drama for which Lord John had been waiting since 1841.

In 1845 the potato crop failed, and the anti-corn-law league became irresistible. There was no logical reason why it should have done so, for it was the Irish who were going to starve, and there was no reason to think that the Irish would benefit from repeal. But a conjunction of two simple facts caused the landslide: men were starving, and bread was taxed. In September Peel began to fear the potato had failed; in October he knew it had. When the cabinet met at the beginning of November, Peel proposed to suspend the duties on corn, and to summon parliament. But ministers fell out among themselves, and finally they separated, with nothing decided except that they were to meet again towards the end of the month. Lord John was at Edinburgh, where Lady John, who had been ill almost continuously for over a year, was at present under the treatment of Dr Simpson. On 6 November Cobden, disappointed in Peel, wrote to Parkes to ask what Lord John was going to do. Parkes began in his own style: 'What have you to do, at this critical juncture, with Whigs, or with the Sayings or Doings of so minute a political Philosopher as Lord John Russell . . . Steer your ship against the *Common Enemy* – in power.' But his answer was not sent until 12 November, and in the interval he showed it to Lord John. When it was posted, there was a postscript:

> Leave Lord John alone. You have all but weaned him from 'Fixed Duty'. If you insult him, at this juncture, you will create difficulties in his onward path towards you. But really the back-

water of the Whig Lords on Corn Law Repeal is *not* worth your thought at this moment.

Then followed a paragraph on Luther, the Commonwealth, and the French Revolution which must have been suggested by Lord John.[153]

At first, while rumour credited Peel with intending some great coup on corn, Lord John expected him to dictate to his colleagues and to pull through.[154] But as the days and weeks went by without a summons to parliament, the world became impatient. Here at last was an opportunity for Lord John to be rid of the party's commitment to a fixed duty. At that distance he did not consult Melbourne or Palmerston, or indeed any of his more important colleagues, before writing his Edinburgh letter. All he did was to take Minto and Rutherfurd into his confidence, both of whom approved.[155] The letter was addressed to Lord John's constituents in the city, and was not in Lord John's best style.[156] It contained too much self-justification and some quite unworthy jibes at Peel, and four years later Lord John himself admitted that it was spoiled by party allusions.[157] But it made three points very clearly: (1) there was a crisis; (2) the government was doing nothing about it, and (3) it was 'no longer worth while to contend for a fixed duty'.

Lord John wrote his letter on 22 November and left it in Edinburgh for Lady John, who rejoiced to think that it would reunite her husband to the Radicals, to copy and send to the *Morning Chronicle*. He then set off for London to attend the funeral of Lady Holland, who had died calmly, 'whatever', as Lady John unkindly remarked, 'it was that enabled her to do so'.[158] On 24 November Lord John told Lansdowne what he had done. Lansdowne hoped there was still time to stop it. Two days later when the letter appeared, the Duke of Bedford reflected 'what a bold little fellow' his brother was,[159] and Parkes wrote to Cobden that he trusted 'you will receive the convert as the Apostles received Saul'. Parkes added that Lord John was 'an honest if a slow man'.[160] Lord John was annoyed by this, and wrote sharply to Parkes that what he and Cobden reckoned very slow 'has been in my opinion a fair time allowed for the Ministry and the Tory gentry to lay down their arms, and march out of the citadel'. He further betrayed his feelings when he ended by saying that he hoped 'the fulsome flattery of the Peel administration by the liberals' would now cease.[161]

The letter had a mixed reception. Melbourne objected, though in so illegible a hand that it took two men to decipher what he had written.[162] Palmerston regretted Lord John had handed the leadership of the party over to Cobden.[163] Baring thought Lord John ought to have waited until parliament met,[164] Fortescue still preferred a low duty but would support Lord John,[165] Cottenham thought the timing right,[166] and Wood wrote with unusual brevity 'Well done Johnny'.[167] From among the rank and file Ward thanked Lord John 'for making us a *Party* again, which we certainly have not been for the last four years'.[168] Lord John had changed party policy without consultation, but he got away with it because he had expressed what many people thought. On the day Lord John's letter was published, Morpeth independently announced his conversion to the anti-corn-law league. 'I wish to record . . . my conviction that the time is come for a final repeal of the Corn Laws, and my protest against the continued inaction of the State in the present emergency.'[169] Morpeth thought 'the coincidence of our appearances was rather remarkable, and I . . . can only surmise that some magnetic influence must have been at work'.[170]

Lord John's letter embarrassed Peel. Labouchere saw it as a heavy blow,[171] and one correspondent wrote that had Lord John been a member of the prize ring instead of the brightest ornament of the senate he could not have known better when to deliver his knockdown blow.[172] It is impossible to say whether, when Lord John wrote his letter, he did it with the intention of ousting Peel. But that was the effect, and on 6 December, after Peel had failed to wield the rod over the protectionist and still 'boyish' Stanley,[173] he resigned. A few days later, when the retiring ministers went over to the Isle of Wight for their last council, a steamer called *The Little Wonder* raced their boat. 'They all got excited. Ld. Stanley said, "Little Wonder, that must be Johnny, I'll bet £10 he distances us" '.[174] The story does Stanley credit. In Lord John's life, however, it is a dispiriting milestone, for this was one of the last occasions on which anyone alluded appreciatively to his physique.

When Peel resigned the Queen did not send for Melbourne,

but for Lord John, who thus became the head of the party. The summons was despatched on 7 December, and as the events of the next fortnight are difficult to follow, they must be set out day by day. The Queen's letter reached Lord John at Edinburgh on 8 December: Lady John was in two minds; she dreaded losing her husband while she was ill, and she felt obliged to urge him to accept office as 'a great duty'.[175] Lord John set out on 9 December, spent the night at Newcastle, and then came on by train, meeting John Bright on the way. He reached London at 8.30 p.m. on 10 December, and went down to Osborne the next day. The Queen thought he might have done the journey more quickly.[176] Lord John's first interview with the Queen and the Prince took place on the evening of 11 December. The Prince handed Lord John a paper from Peel, who promised to support a measure based upon the last paragraph of the Edinburgh letter, and to do what he could to secure its passage through the house of lords. Lord John thought this very fair, and asked for time to consult his friends.[177] He spent the night at Osborne, and went back to London on 12 December, where he met Lansdowne, who was the senior Whig peer fit for active service, Clarendon, Cottenham and Macaulay.[178]

Down at Osborne, Peel's promises seemed genuine to Lord John. But Lord John's colleagues suspected a ruse. As Dr Dreyer has said, they commanded the votes of less than one-third of the house of lords, and of a minority not more than 250 strong in the commons.[179] They felt, like Minto, that in office the Whigs would be in Peel's power, while Peel in office would be in theirs.[180] Minto thought Peel and Graham 'the two most insincere and artful men upon earth'.[181] Against this was the fact that Lord John would like to go down in history as the man who repealed the corn laws,[182] and the result of the meeting was that they decided to ask Peel for a more detailed statement of his intentions.

At 5.30 p.m. on 12 December Lord John and Lansdowne saw Graham, and asked Peel to clarify his position. Early the next day Graham sent a letter, the burden of which was that Peel refused to elaborate. Lansdowne thought he detected some signs of drawing back. Macaulay said they all thought Peel's original communication was too vague, and the Whig leaders, who had now been joined by Baring, agreed, at Lord John's suggestion, to draw up a plan of their own, and to take it to Peel and ask him if he would support it. Lord John then wrote to Grey that he did not want either to accept or to refuse without his assistance, and invited him to come up to town.[183] On the same day, Ellice, who was with Grey in Northumberland, wrote to Lord John to say that Grey would be particular as to the arrangements at the foreign office. Ellice did not name Palmerston, but when his letter reached Lord John it was endorsed, presumably immediately after it had been read, 'Grey will make difficulties about Palmerston at the foreign office'.[184]

On 14 December Lord John showed Baring a plan for opening the ports at once, and for gradually abolishing the duties thereafter. For Lord John it was a step back, but it was a step back to the path Peel was believed to be following. On 15 December many more of Lord John's friends arrived in London. Grey was extremely averse and cantankerous,[185] and when Lord John outlined the proposed measure to him, he was 'more hasty than was necessary'.[186] At this stage, Lord John would have preferred to let Grey drop out,[187] and he sent the Whig plan to the Queen and asked her to find out if Peel would support it.

On 16 December the Whigs learned that Peel refused even to look at their plan. They then turned right round, dropped their scheme for immediate suspension and gradual extinction of the duties, and agreed instead to propose the immediate repeal of the corn laws. This change did not take place out of deference to Grey, for men do not defer to the mood Grey was in. The point was that if Peel would not support his plan, when brought in by Lord John, it would be better to let Lord John bring in a plan of his own with an eye on the constituencies. The comparison with 1831 at once came to Lord John's mind, and Clarendon was instructed to analyse the prospects for a dissolution. The *Westminster Review* later claimed that a snap dissolution in January 1846 might have secured a majority,[188] but Clarendon's own evaluation was not a hopeful one. He argued that the comparison with 1831 was false. At that time the middle classes and the working classes had been united, and what ministers had now to deal with was a purely middle-class movement.[189]

Clarendon's pessimism was notorious and not infectious, and on 16 December it began to look as though the Whigs would, after all, make the attempt. They agreed that Lord John should explain to the Queen that immediate suspension followed by gradual abolition would alarm the farmer and irritate the merchant and manufacturer, and ask her to find out whether Peel would now support immediate repeal. Grey then wrote to Lord John warning him to guard against giving the impression that his ministry was a revival of the last Whig government. 'That Government had, justly or unjustly, totally lost the confidence of the public, and had become so unpopular, that even now the recollect^n of it is one of the chief difficulties with which you have to deal.' He made various hints about men and offices, but he did not refer to Palmerston.[190]

On the evening of 17 December the Queen and the Prince communicated Peel's latest answer to Lord John. It was evasive, but not improperly so, and Lord John wrote to Lady John that Peel refused to pledge himself to anything, but gave the 'fairest assurance of general support'.[191] When the Whig leaders met again on 18 December Lord John, Baring, Cottenham, Ellice, Grey, Sir George Grey, Hobhouse, Labouchere, Macaulay, Morpeth and Palmerston (11) voted in favour of accepting the commission, while Auckland, Bedford, Clarendon, Lansdowne and Monteagle (5) voted against.[192] Disregarding the objectors, all of whom were peers, Lord John went to Windsor to accept the Queen's commission. The Whigs had been a long time making up their minds, and the Tories thought they had flown in the face of every precedent, for hitherto a man had either accepted the sovereign's commission, or refused it. That was not quite fair, for the Whigs were in an exceptional position, and any irregularity would soon have been forgotten had the matter ended there.

Unfortunately it did not. Lansdowne waited until the evening and then put in a claim for £1m compensation to the landed interest as the price of his acquiescence in the majority decision.[193] Early on 19 December Lord John began the serious work of filling up the offices. All sorts of people had already written to him, asking for places – not least his relatives. The Duke of Bedford disapproved of the whole thing, and wouldn't go into the cabinet himself, but thought Wrio was amiable enough to make a bishop, while Hastings would make an efficient private secretary.[194] Minto jocularly offered to take the

admiralty, as the government would not 'endure long enough
to produce any serious wear and tear of health'.[195] Lord John
had more serious matters to attend to. The feeling against Palmerston's going back to the foreign office was 'almost universal',[196] and Lord John offered him the colonies instead.
Palmerston refused, and held out for the foreign office, where-
upon Lord John gave way.[197]

Next, Lord John and Palmerston both went to a meeting
called to consider Lansdowne's ultimatum. The other people
present were Auckland, Baring, Clarendon, Grey and Labouchere. It was agreed to give £700,000 relief at once, and the
rest as soon as possible. Immediately after this meeting Lord
John saw Grey. When Grey heard that Palmerston was to have
the foreign office, he refused to serve. Palmerston again refused
to take any other office, but offered to stand out if Lord John
would go on. That was out of the question, and Lord John
called in Auckland and asked him whether the Whig peers
could get on in the lords without Grey. Auckland said they
could not, and Clarendon and Ellice agreed.[198] Lord John then
sent Ellice to try and talk Grey round. Palmerston alleged later
that Ellice 'pretending to go to Grey to convince him he was
wrong, told him in plain terms that he thought him right'.[199]
However that may be, Grey did persist, and without calling his
colleagues together again, Lord John wrote to the Queen and
resigned the commission he had accepted the day before. He
did not mention Grey by name, but said that unanimity had
been essential, and that in one case a difficulty had arisen. To
Lady John he wrote that he 'could not make a Cabinet without
Lord Grey'.[200] From that day to this, people have wondered
why, and have been surprised, as Normanby put it, that after
what had occurred in 1839, Lord John had let his conduct
depend on Grey's.[201]

One thing is clear: Grey's colleagues were struck by his
general disposition to make trouble. Grey's vanity led him to
suppose that he might even be asked to mediate between Peel
and Lord John,[202] and he came to London in the sort of ill
temper men reserve for the occasions on which they are about
to injure their friends. The testimony on this point is over-
whelming. Emily Eden wished Grey 'would stay in the North
during times of crisis, and not come South at other times'.[203]

Morpeth commented on Grey's 'insufferable arrogance and self-sufficiency':[204] Minto heard that Grey 'had exhibited from first to last . . . such a preparation for dissention as must have rendered it quite impossible to act with him in the cabinet':[205] Lansdowne wrote that 'without being there you could scarcely conceive what provision our refractory ally had made for future as well as present disagreement. It was quite Howick as we knew him formerly, with the additional sense of importance of having become Lord Grey.'[206] Lord John himself said simply that 'with Howick as he was in 1840, we could not go on'.[207] It scarcely mattered what Grey's objection was, and Minto understood that had the difficulty over Palmerston been resolved, there would have been others.[208]

To the effect of Grey's behaviour we must add that Lord John was aware of the sheer length of time he had taken making up his mind. In his Edinburgh letter he had accused Peel of delay in an emergency. The letter had provoked a new emergency in which Lord John himself, and his colleagues, appeared to be wasting time. They could not see 'their way clear',[209] and Lord John threw the government up on 19 December for the same reason that he had taken it on 18 December, because the pantomime could not be allowed to go on any longer.[210] Once the decision to form a government had been taken, any new objection would compel him to reverse his decision. If the issue had not, after all, been settled one way, it must be settled the other.

There was one further consideration, which may have been the last straw. On 14 December Lady John wrote that she was lying on her sofa 'a broken-down useless bit of rubbish'.[211] Clarendon told Hobhouse that worrying about Lady John's health, Lord John had not had any sleep for three nights, and that this finally unnerved him so that he gave up.[212] On 21 December, when Morpeth went to reproach his leader, Lord John told him that he had received a letter in which Lady John said she had not long to live. 'He then burst into an agony of tears. What could I say, or do, but speak kindly.'[213] There was not one, but there were many reasons why Lord John gave up.

When Lord John threw in his hand 'all those who did not want office' were glad.[214] The Duke of Bedford wrote of his 'inexpressible relief'.[215] Minto congratulated Lord John on his escape from 'this most hopeless undertaking',[216] Lansdowne thought the result was good,[217] and Fox Maule thought Lord John was well out of it.[218] No amount of satisfaction, however, could put a stop to the inquest that now took place in the corridors of impotence as Peel resumed the premiership, Lord John returned to Lady John at Edinburgh, and the rest of his colleagues went off to spend Christmas in the country.

Naturally there was a war against Grey.[219] Ellice found 'our friends . . . loud in their complaints of Howick'.[220] Lansdowne thought it unpardonable that Grey had not made his objection known a week earlier.[221] Lord John himself was indignant, and was resolved never to act with Grey again.[222] Unwisely, he allowed himself to be drawn into a long dispute over the technical point whether Grey had given warning of his objection to Palmerston in advance.[223] Fortunately, it did not become irreparably acrimonious, and the reason may have been that both men knew they were in the wrong. Grey had not made himself plain, but Lord John (warned by Ellice's letter of 13 December) had understood more than he admitted, and the best verdict on this aspect of the case is that of Charles Wood, who said that he could not acquit either man of blame in having failed to make clear something 'which two minutes conversation between two people, who lived two doors apart would have made so'.[224]

The inquest did not stop at Grey. The Duke of Bedford wondered if he had any backers,[225] and Bessborough said

> He never took any decided opinion of that sort six or seven years ago, and I cannot think he would now have taken so decided a line unless it had been urged upon him.[226]

The obvious suspect was Ellice. The Oregon boundary dispute was coming to a head, and with his investments in the new world Ellice had reason to prefer truckling with Aberdeen to menace with Palmerston. Palmerston, of course, was sure of it, 'the objector was Ld. Grey, urged on by Ellice'.[227] When Ellice dropped in at Bowood early in January he was discomfited to find the Palmerstons there. Lansdowne reported that from what he saw and heard 'of the explanations that passed between them, they were anything but satisfactory to either',[228] and Palmerston wrote to Lord John that Ellice looked like a foxhound who had been caught chopping a hare in cover.[229]

Lord John himself could scarcely be brought to entertain these suspicions at all.[230] He dealt with other people as though they were honest, and both Minto and Morpeth recorded that after they had heard what Ellice had to say, their suspicions dropped away.[231]

Thanks in part, at least, to Lord John, the feeling against Ellice gradually died. But the same could not be said of the feeling against Lord John. Ellice himself assured Lord John that he did not hear a murmur.[232] It can scarcely have been true. Clarendon blamed Lord John for not having called another meeting before abandoning his commission.[233] Greville and the Duke of Bedford agreed,[234] and so, on reflection, did Lord John. Charles Howard thought this showed 'much candour'.[235] What was not so easy for Lord John to overcome was the impression that he had been feeble. Few people expressed this as kindly as his sister-in-law, who wrote that he was a better undertaker than cabinet maker.[236] Morpeth thought it a 'lame and mournful' story,[237] and the Queen wrote to King Leopold on 23 December, 'They have indeed cut a sorry figure, and have, I am certain and I must add *I hope* removed themselves from Office for years and years. Ld John I am sure never *can* be Prime Minister for he has not a shadow of Authority.'[238] Lord John now stood even further below Peel in the estimation of the court and of the public than before.

At this moment, when Lord John had nobody else to turn to, he received little practical support from his own family. While the once reliable William wrote bitterly to Lady John accusing her of being the cause of Lord John's failure,[239] the Duke of Bedford forwarded every accusation that came to his notice, on the ground that unless Lord John knew what was said he would not know how to defend himself. The duke industriously answered every charge himself, but then complained to Lord John that the effort 'will probably shorten my life', and added, 'If all the letters and papers I have written for your defence in the last 15 years cd be put together, I wonder how many volumes they would fill!'[240] Lord John's nearest relations did Lord John no service, either, by the manner in which they combined to put the blame on Peel. William called Peel Sir Slippery Eel, and the duke took this up, saying Peel was slippery by nature, 'and the fault is so confirmed by long habit, that he knows not how to walk straight, or to act in a plain straight-forward manner'.[241] The result was that Lord John himself once unworthily complained to Hobhouse that Peel had deliberately refused to co-operate in December 1845 in order to prevent him taking office.[242]

iv. Opposition, 1846

At the end of December it was clear that Peel was to repeal the corn laws, supported by Lord John, and not vice-versa. It was also virtually certain that when he did so, he would break his party. Disraeli told Hobhouse in 1848 that, had Peel assembled his party 'and told them openly his opinions they would have given way and followed him'.[243] Disraeli was in a position to know, but this seems an instance of a man being foolish after the event. Many of the letters of commiseration which Lord John received after his failure to form a government made the point that it was not for long, and Lord John himself seems to have looked forward to an early return to power.[244] Even so, the first six months of 1846 were not an easy period for him, because his party was almost as feverish as Peel's.

Early in January Lord John received the freedom of Glasgow. On that occasion he touched on the Oregon problem:

> I think nothing of the questions which are at present in dispute – (loud cheering) – questions of territory, in which, as they now stand, the honour of neither country is engaged – (cheers) – and regarding which, I think calm men . . . might . . . come to an amicable agreement.[245]

Three weeks later, however, when he received a message from Everett, he consulted Palmerston and then rebuffed the former American ambassador ferociously, saying that he was 'at a loss to account for the rage of hostility against England and aggression agst all the world wh. seems on a sudden to have seized so many of your Senators and Representatives'.[246] This was strong language, but it was for public consumption only. Lord John now wanted the question out of the way, and in private he promised Aberdeen that he would not oppose the surrender of the British claims to the Columbia river, and then told Palmerston what he had done.[247]

The parliamentary session began with the 'explanations' of the December crisis. Lord John did not allude to the late hour of Grey's objection, and thus took the blame upon himself. In the upper house, Lansdowne, too, handled Grey gently. Wood conveyed Grey's thanks to Lord John,[248] and Minto heard that Grey was now in a much more conciliatory mood.[249]

Peel then introduced one bill to repeal the corn laws, and another to prevent assassination in Ireland. Both caused Lord John trouble. Peel did not propose immediate suspension of the corn laws, but reverted to gradual reduction of the duties over a period of three years. Lord John had already told Villiers that if Peel did not propose immediate repeal, he would,[250] and on 28 January Cobden attended a meeting of Whig M.P.s at Lord John's house.[251] But in fact Lord John was disqualified by the events of December from manoeuvring to alter Peel's plan. On 5 February he informed the Prince's secretary that he would support Peel,[252] on 6 February he rebuffed Cobden,[253] and on 7 February he secured the consent of his followers in the commons to vote for Peel's bill without amendments.[254] On the second reading the bill was carried by the votes of 112 Peelites and 227 Whigs and Radicals against 231 Protectionists and 11 Whig Protectionists. Once again, as on Maynooth, Lord John had lent Peel decisive aid.

For Lord John the real crisis was yet to come in the house of lords, where the Whig peers were restive. For eleven years, while the Whigs were in office, there had been a peer as prime minister, and in 1843 Normanby represented to the court that the next Whig prime minister ought also to be a peer (though he lessened the effect by suggesting himself for the post).[255] In 1845 the 'backwater' of the Whig peers had still not been reconciled to the proposal for a fixed duty when Lord John wrote the Edinburgh letter. In 1846 a substantial number of Whig peers were openly flirting with the idea of doing a deal with the Protectionists, and reverting to a fixed duty. Many different motives were at work, and the revolt had no recognised leader, but Normanby and Bessborough came to the front while Palmerston was prominent at the back of it.[256] We may conjecture that Normanby's efforts were directed against Lord John's leadership, Bessborough's to obtaining a better deal for Ireland from the Protectionists, and Palmerston's to securing his own position, which would be threatened by a junction between Lord John and the Peelites.

The differences between the Whig party in the commons and the Whig lords were accentuated by their reactions to Peel's coercion bill for Ireland, according to which any one caught out of doors between sunset and sunrise in a proclaimed district could be taken into custody and transported. The bill was introduced first to the house of lords, where, without consulting Lord John, Lansdowne and Bessborough welcomed it. When Lansdowne asked Lord John how he liked his speech, Lord John answered honestly '*not at all*'.[257] Although Cottenham, Campbell, Grey and others moved an amendment, there was, as Bessborough said, not one person in the house of lords connected with Ireland who opposed the bill,[258] and Clanricarde and Clarendon both wrote to Lord John begging him not to oppose it when it came before the commons.[259] At the same time More O'Ferrall wrote to Lord John urging him to come to the same understanding with Peel over Ireland that he had already done over the corn laws.[260] That was all very well, but when the coercion bill came before the commons for its first reading in April, ministers insisted on obtaining a vote of confidence on the first reading, and put Lord John in a quandary. The bill would serve the purposes of the 'enemies of Emancipation' in Ireland for years to come,[261] but he dare not upset Peel, and he dare not set the Whig peers at defiance until the bill to repeal the corn laws had passed. He assented, therefore, to the house giving a first reading to the coercion bill, but went on to say 'that in the future stages of it, I shall have objections to offer going to the foundations of some of its principal provisions'.[262] He could never consent to a clause which made it possible for a man who went out at night to visit a sick relative or to secure a stray animal to end up in Australia. No greater provision could have been made for confusing the innocent and the guilty – the government's maxim was not *fiat justitia, ruat coelum*, but *ruit coelum, fiat justitia*. If the bill reached the committee stage, he would amend it so as to define the circumstances which would justify arrest. In the meantime Lord John did not oppose, and the Protectionists actually voted for the bill.

By the beginning of April the Protectionists were ready to make almost any overture to Lord John's party, and Lord John

decided that much greater confidence between himself and Peel
was essential. On 10 April he had a long conversation with
Aberdeen, a record of which was sent to the Prince. Lord John
said

> the Protectionists have made overtures to me, that they would be
> ready to support me and that they would prefer me as Minister to
> Sir R. Peel, but they cannot be relied on, they would readily join
> in upsetting Peel, but could give us no safe support. Ld. A.
> replied: 'the only chance you have is *our* support and therefore
> you must take care, that in turning us out, you do not make it
> impossible for us to support you'. Ld. John (laughing), I have
> heard it said that Sir Robert wanted killing with a silver bullet;
> to say the truth: I don't think the bullet is cast yet, which is to
> kill him. Ld. A. repeated his assurances and added: 'in fact there
> is nothing which divides us, and I would as readily support you
> as Sir R. Peel; a coallition is impossible, but I think we perfectly
> agree with each other on every point, the Irish Church perhaps
> excepted'. Ld. John; and not even that, for I don't think the times
> would allow for any experiments with that.[263]

Thereafter Lord John snubbed Bentinck's approaches[264] and
scoffed at the Protectionists' wooing Smith O'Brien,[265] and
when Palmerston brought forward a motion on the sugar duties,
with the object of bringing Peel down before the corn laws were
repealed, Lord John sent Ellice to Peel to get the sugar duties
put off until the corn bill was safe.[266] Week after week the Duke
of Bedford kept Peel informed of his brother's intentions.[267]

Now that the Tory party was breaking up, Lord John was
determined to incline his party to the Peelites and not to the
Protectionists. The decision was consistent with his conduct
since 1841, but that did not mean that the Whig peers would
follow him. At the beginning of May they were still divided,
and Morpeth found the Melbournes and Beauvales very protectionist.[268] On 9 May Hobhouse, who sympathised with the
mutineers, learnt that the Duke of Buckingham and the Duke
of Richmond were both in favour of a fixed duty.[269] Palmerston
was inclined to go with them, and Lady Ashley thought Lord
John could be induced to follow in Palmerston's wake.[270] On
20 May, Hobhouse thought it almost certain the peers would
vote for a fixed duty.[271] It was time for Lord John to act. On 21
May he asked Lansdowne to call a meeting of the Whig peers.

At the same time he wrote to Melbourne that he hoped he would not be a party to the revolt. Throwing out the bill 'must lead to that violent agitation on this subject which you have always apprehended . . . and stir up society to the bottom'.[272] No letter Lord John wrote had a more beneficial influence. Melbourne agreed with Lord John,[273] and two days later he came to the meeting to say so. Lord John told the peers that if they voted for a fixed duty he would give up the lead of the party. Then Melbourne said,

> Sir Robert Peel has damned himself to all eternity, your Lord-
> ships seem about to do the same thing, for as my noble friend tells
> you a different course would break up the party, I am prepared to
> take my share of the disgrace.[274]

What followed can be summarised in Palmerston's words, 'all unanimous against the bill and all unanimous not to oppose it'.[275]

The revolt collapsed. Bessborough does not seem to have been present, and Normanby, Vivian, De Mauley and Clanricarde, whom Morpeth named as the ringleaders,[276] were quite unable to overcome the fact that their protest came too late. Normanby had always recognised that Lord John's Edinburgh letter made their position very difficult, and when Hobhouse recorded that he never spoke to anybody who did not prefer a fixed duty, he added that 'Russell's letter seems to preclude a choice'.[277] Lord Lilford said, 'what could we do?'.[278] As for Palmerston, who Greville thought was at the centre of the intrigue,[279] he was cautious in conspiracy, and he left it to Lady Palmerston to re-buke Lord John and tell him that she was sure the Protection-ists were honest 'and would have given you a sincere support if you could have accepted a compromise'.[280]

Greville was delighted at this 'bold, judicious, and successful move of John Russell's'.[281] So, too, was Lord John. Elated by his victory over the Whig peers, he announced that it would be more honest in him to oppose the second reading of the coercion bill than to amend it in committee.[282] The Protectionists, who had voted in favour of the first reading of the bill, at once saw that by changing their opinions on the ground that they no longer had confidence in the government, they could throw Peel out. On 6 June there was a meeting of 70–80 Liberal members at Lord John's. 'The good little man mounted a chair and addressed us', and the meeting agreed to follow their leader.[283] Brougham was furious, and said they had imperilled the passage of the corn bill.[284] But Brougham was wrong, and the corn law bill went on its way through the lords. The danger lay rather in the commons, where the Protectionists were too obviously determined – to use their own language – that the fox should be killed in the open, and where they might easily mistake the cry of their own pack for the voice of the house.[285]

The debate was duly spun out until the corn law bill had passed through all its stages in the lords on 25 June. Then, in the early hours of 26 June, the coercion bill was defeated on its second reading in the commons by 291 votes to 218. The result, as Morpeth noted with relief, was received without a cheer, except for the seventy Protectionists who voted with the majority.[286] When Peel entered the house to make his resignation speech, he 'walked up the House; colder, dryer, more introverted than ever; yet to a close gaze showing the fullest working of a smothered volcano of emotions'.[287] For once he fell below his own high estimate of a prime minister's duty, and mischievously attributed all the credit for the repeal of the corn laws to Cobden. Some Whigs thought it a deep design 'to take the crown of laurels from Lord John's head'.[288] It was not that, for the crown of laurels did not belong there. But Lord John did deserve credit for keeping his party steady in May, and Peel's 'egotistical' speech,[289] was 'not friendly to the Whigs'.[290] Monteagle condemned it as a bitter party speech, adding to Lord John's difficulties.[291]

Lord John's behaviour over the coercion bill has never been understood. Prince Albert called the vote a 'factious combination'.[292] Morpeth thought it betrayed an avidity for office,[293] and Charles Wood told Lord John that it was 'a bad return to Peel for all that he has done in carrying our measures especially the corn bill, to turn him out *the next day*'.[294] It might have been better to have given Peel time to resign, but the parties were in turmoil, every possible combination was being canvassed, and there were good reasons for acting quickly to bring the confusion to an end.

Even so it was not dignified to ally with the Protectionists, and in order to see why Lord John did it, we must go back to the conduct of the Whig peers between December 1845 and June 1846. The peers' preference for inclining the party towards the Protectionists did not come to an end with the meeting on 23 May. As Minto said 'many of our friends wish Lord John to play the rogue and the fool and unite with the protectionists after carrying the corn bill'.[295] On 9 June Normanby was still harping on this theme. He wrote to Lord John that he had seen Stanley who had repeated 'that they must not think of a Government themselves, that what he should most wish to do was to support your Govt.'.[296] On 23 June Denison admitted having had informal discussions with Bentinck, Portland and Manners, and forwarded a list of the constituencies where co-operation might help at an election,[297] and on 29 June Lansdowne gave a dinner to Beaufort, Bentinck, Eglinton, Malmesbury, Richmond and O'Brien.[298]

All this was anathema to Lord John, who knew he had nothing in common with the Protectionists, and much in common with the Peelites. The most he could say to the Duke of Portland was that the Whigs would welcome independent support, so that they could keep clear of the English Radicals and the Irish Repealers.[299] But he was not in Peel's confidence, and he could never be quite sure what Sir Robert intended. Lord John half feared that if Peel were left in office for a few weeks after the repeal of the corn laws, he would find some way of reuniting his party, or of stealing Liberal supporters. Lord John had every incentive to cut Peel down as soon as possible, and he could only do it in alliance with the Protectionists. A night out with the Protectionists would take some explaining away, if, as Lord John intended, he was going to make an offer of marriage to the Peelites next day. That being so, the coercion bill was of all issues surely the best. The combination was so obviously unnatural that it could lead to nothing: it was the exact opposite of the appropriation clause of 1835. And need the Whigs lose credit by it? Lord John had reserved his position; the Protectionists, on the other hand, who had previously voted for the bill, would be condemned to acting from spite.[300] So be it, that was what they were like, and it would facilitate Lord John's future approaches to the Peelites if that was the reputation they enjoyed.

Lord John's conduct in 1846 is by no means the least of his

FIG. 1 POLITICAL ECONOMY; OR, LORD JOHN
IN PEEL'S CLOTHES *Punch* 1846

The Queen: Well! It is not the best fit in the world, but we'll see how he
goes on!

claims upon his country's gratitude, but it went unrecognised, and it was Peel who enjoyed the respect of the middle-of-the-road public for which both men had been bidding since 1841. Lord John was about to become prime minister, but there could be little doubt which of the two men the country would prefer. When the change took place, Prince Albert opened a new file, 'Formation of Lord John Russell's Government (continuation of Sir Robert Peel's free trade policy . . .)'.[301] *Punch* put the whole thing in a nutshell with a cartoon of the diminutive Lord John trying on Peel's voluminous clothes, while an anxious Queen and Prince looked on and asked whether they would fit. There was a rumour that Loyd, who had invited Lord John to stand for the city in 1841, would now ask Peel to run against him.[302] Hobhouse noted 'that Peel must return all say is certain'.[303] Fortescue wrote to Lord John that, considering Peel's return to power out of the question for three years at least, the new government was the best that could be formed.[304] The public then, like historians since, took Peel at the value he set upon himself, and Russell at the value Peel set upon him.

It was a mystery Russell never solved, and because he knew that for five years Peel had guided the ship by the charts left by the Whigs in the cabin,[305] Lord John found it difficult, even in his public utterances, to hide his feelings. On 29 January Greville thought he praised Peel's bill to repeal the corn laws very coldly,[306] and on no fewer than four occasions in 1846 Morpeth noted that Lord John's speeches betrayed jealousy.[307] Morpeth condemned Lord John for 'twitting' Peel and his party on past misdemeanours; 'perhaps my rustic fastidiousness made me see in this a little want of generosity – which I sometimes think is Ld John's only political fault'.[308] Lord John was provoked that 'a man of whom he has so bad an opinion should have outstripped him in popularity and public consideration'.[309] It was not a good note on which to begin his own administration, and unless Lord John soon rose superior to it, he would be in danger of becoming, as Greville said, 'a very clever, ingenious, but *little* man, full of personal feelings and antipathies'.[310]

CHAPTER XII

The Minister of Necessity, 1846–7[1]

i. Lord John and his cabinet

PEEL resigned on 27 June, and the Queen sent for Lord John the next day. A prime minister must always be lonely, but Lord John was to be more lonely than most. When he first came into politics he was supported by the affectionate and steadying influence of his father, and of Lord and Lady Holland. Now he was nearly fifty-four, there was nobody to take their place, and straight away a new blow fell upon him, when his brother William died at Genoa. For some years things had not gone well with William. He had quarrelled with his wife, fallen in with 'an abandoned Jewish woman',[2] and been thrown out of the embassy at Berlin by Aberdeen, along 'with all the Diplomatic Palmerston rubbish'.[3] Thereafter he had lived abroad, and the brothers scarcely met, but his death meant that the new prime minister now had no intimate to fall back on but the Duke of Bedford.

The part played by the seventh Duke of Bedford in politics will never be fully known. He had long since made up his mind not to accept a post of responsibility, and in 1847 he declined even to enter the cabinet without office.[4] He took no part in the debates in the house of lords, where the government was weak, and what he did was done by visits and by writing letters. No man, according to Greville, ever had a more interesting correspondence, but the duke inherited a habit of burning letters, not just occasionally, but wholesale when the mood took him.

The details, therefore, are a mystery, but the outline is clear, and the duke had already, between December 1845 and June 1846 chosen the line he would follow. Believing Lord John to be simple, the duke would guide him away from the traps set by his enemies. Knowing his brother was deficient in knowledge of

the world, the duke would supply some of it for him. Knowing
his brother was deficient in courtesy and social grace, the duke
would supply some of those too. Where Lord John was cold, he
would be warm; where Lord John was vacillating, he would
supply the ballast in the ship of state. There is no reason to
doubt that the duke played a sincere part, but that is not to say
that he was well equipped for it, or that he did it well. As Palmerston once said, when he was ruminating on what a strange
mixture of talent and foolishness the Russells were, Lord John
had a good deal more talent than his brother, while the duke
was even more foolish than Lord John.[5] In short, it might have
been better, as Lady John thought in 1852, if the duke had not
meddled at all.

The duke was always a very lordly elder brother, advising
Lord John to get Ribblesdale 'out of a bad habit of lolling back
in his chair after dinner',[6] and hinting that he hoped young
Johnny would not be spoilt – 'they tell me there is much danger
of it'.[7] In the same spirit he now attempted to guide Lord
John's political footsteps – 'I am sorry you did not answer
Fitzwilliam. Let him find an apology from you on his return to
England.'[8] To be fair to the duke, Lord John was well advised
to write an account of the events of December 1845 for posterity, and to be firm with his colleagues.[9] But the duke took
delight in pointing out Lord John's mistakes, and month after
month the confidence-sapping letters came in: 'I wrote to Col.
Phipps last night to set you quite right with the Prince';[10] 'if I
had been quite satisfied with your explanation . . .';[11] I have
seen C. Greville and we agree 'that the main fault you committed was in suffering crude Bills to be brought in so late. It
gave the appearance not only of weakness, but of incapacity. I
told you so beforehand, but you disregarded my advice';[12] I am
glad your speech in the house of commons has been commend-
ed, it is 'a relief to me, as I have of late seen you so perpetually
abused in all the newspapers, Tory . . . Whig, and Radical.'[13]

On top of all these letters came the whole question of money.
Lord John's father secured him an interest of £40,000 in the
estate,[14] which must have brought him in about £2000 p.a.
From a note in Lord John's papers it appears that in 1836, after
his first marriage, his expenses for the first half of the year came
to £1247.[15] Even after allowing for the fact that the bills for

Lord John's elections probably went straight to his father, and that his father left Lord John an additional legacy of £10,000 when he died,[16] it is clear that Lord John was not well off.

The sixth duke spent money freely, and the seventh was obliged to retrench the family expenditure in order to save the family estate. He sacked his librarian, bought no more books, and lived off less than one-fifth of his rental,[17] keeping a mere £20,000 for household, stable, and personal expenses.[18] As soon as his economies began to show results, and he had some money in hand, he spent it like a good landlord in building new cottages and in the erection of schools, as anyone can see to this day who will walk round his estates. The duke's priorities do him credit, but the price was that he became so mean that, as Clarendon put it, every time he came to see you, he asked you for the money to pay the cab.[19]

The duke probably continued his father's practice of paying Lord John's election bills, and from time to time he stepped in and set Lord John right with his bankers.[20] But he accompanied the action with a homily on Lord John's style of living, which was certainly careless, but which was also extremely modest, and we shall not be far out if we assume that the duke paid the bills, but that he did it grudgingly and that he did it late. The results were seen in Downing Street, where the rooms were dingy,[21] and the food was always cold before it reached the table;[22] and Lord John's position became notorious after he testified to a select committee of the house of commons in 1850 that he had never been in debt before he became prime minister.[23]

The duke would bail Lord John out, but what he would not do was to endow Lord John with an estate suitable to his status. That being so, it was left to Lady Holland to supplement Lord John's income. Before she died in November 1845, she made Lord John one of her executors. She also left him a legacy of £1000 and a life interest in her Lambeth estate, which yielded him an additional £1200–£1500 p.a.[24] Lord John needed the money, and he accepted it. It might have been better for him if he had not. There was, as Morpeth noted, about Lady Holland's will, as about her life, 'more of the friendly than the family virtues'.[25] Lady Holland's children were outraged by her alienating their father's property, and although they could

not dispute Lord John's right as beneficiary, they challenged
his conduct as executor, and twelve years later he still had a
chancery suit hanging over him.[26] The will was a *cause célèbre*,
and did nothing to raise the Russell family in the eyes of the
world.

Finally there was the episode of the prime minister's house.
Lord John had a house in Chesham Place, but every party
leader needs a house in the country too. In 1844 he and Fanny
went to look at two houses for sale, one at Leith Hill, which was
too small, and another in Sussex, which was too remote.[27] In
1846 they rented a house at Wimbledon, which Lord John's
colleagues condemned as being 'too far from Town', but which
was really 'just far enough to be out of reach of being plagued'.[28]
Before the lease ran out, they looked at a house in Chorley
Wood.[29] This time they liked it, but the deal fell through, presumably because Lord John could not afford it. Months went
by, and as the prime minister could not solve the problem for
himself, there were only two people who might be expected to
solve it for him. These were the Duke of Bedford and the
Queen, and a slow race took place between them. On one
occasion, Sir George Russell, who was an admirer but not a
relation, drove over to Woburn intending to tell the duke that
he would like to offer Chequers to the prime minister, but the
duke received him so coldly that he went away again without
making the offer. Lord John used to say thereafter that he had
lost Chequers 'for want of a glass of sherry and a biscuit'.[30] One
can almost feel the chill creeping out of the archives at Windsor
Castle as the Queen realised that the duke was shameless and
was not going to do the decent thing. In March 1847 the Queen
offered Lord and Lady John a house at Petersham, Pembroke
Lodge, on the border of Richmond Park. There, as Lady John
put it in a poem addressed to the Queen, her husband could
unbind the weary shackles of the week, and find the sabbath he
had come to seek. With some insight into her husband's faults,
which, however, never enabled her to help him overcome them,
Lady John went on, 'Here lay the babbling, lying Present by,
And Past and Future call to counsel high. To Nature's worship
say a loud Amen And learn of solitude to mix with men.'[31] Lord
and Lady John appreciated the Queen's generosity, and lived
at Pembroke Lodge for the rest of their lives, but it seems un-

likely the Queen and the Prince liked Lord John any the better
after having had to provide a house for the brother of the Duke
of Bedford.

Lord John was determined that it would be no fault of his if he
could not establish the government on a broad basis.[32] Accordingly he consulted Lansdowne, Palmerston, Bessborough,
Clarendon and Cottenham about an offer to the Peelites. Only
Palmerston objected,[33] and Lord John approached Peel with
an invitation to three of the ministers in the late government,
Dalhousie, Herbert, and Lincoln, to retain office. Peel undertook not to dissuade them, but did not expect them to accept.
The Peelites, as Lord John already realised, would combine
with the Whigs in the end, but nobody can blame Peel's lieutenants for refusing to join Lord John at this stage. Old animosities, which Lord John had done nothing to soften, cannot
be buried overnight.

By making this offer, Lord John forced Palmerston back into
line in support of the free trade policy, and upset the Protectionists, who were furious at being thrown over after the hopes
some of the Whigs had held out to them.[34] Only one thing that
Lord John could have done would have offended the Protectionists more, and that was to have made an offer to Cobden.
He considered this, but Cobden was no favourite with the
Irish, and it turned out that he had taxed his health, and
emptied his pocket in the service of the league. He was now
about to go abroad to repair the first, and to receive a public
subscription to refill the second. Both were sufficient reasons
against an offer. The cabinet considered sending him as consul
to Egypt, or something of that sort.[35] Finally it was agreed at
Clarendon's suggestion[36] that Lord John should write him a
letter 'without an immediate, but with prospective cabinet
offers'.[37] Lord John's letter was abrupt, and the public thought
Cobden had been slighted by Whig exclusiveness. Adminis-
tratively, however, Cobden was no loss. Peel said later that he
was 'nobody' on the commission preparing the Great Exhibition, where 'he showed no talent for business'.[38]

Once it was settled that it was to be a purely Whig government, Lord John's cabinet-making went on apace. Everyone
was on his best behaviour, and Ellice actually went out of town

in order to avoid a repetition of the suspicions of six months earlier.[39] Grey's challenge having failed, Palmerston must 'of course' be foreign secretary.[40] Fortunately Aberdeen had settled the Oregon question before he left office, and it was open to Wood, therefore, to press upon Lord John the value of having Grey in.[41] Almost up to the last moment Lord John seems to have been determined not to work with Grey again. But after a talk with Lansdowne,[42] he decided that as Grey would be a difficulty either way, he would probably be better in than out, and if he went to the colonial office, he would at least 'get work enough' to keep him quiet.[43]

Having made up his mind about Palmerston and Grey, Lord John had little room for manoeuvre in filling up the rest of the posts. Something had gone wrong with the breeding habits of the Whig species early in the nineteenth century, and there were few young ones to bring on. There were sixteen members of the cabinet, eight in each house, and thirteen of them had served in the cabinet under Melbourne.

Prime minister and first lord of the treasury, Lord J. Russell.
Lord chancellor, Lord Cottenham.
Lord president of the council, Marquis of Lansdowne.
Lord privy seal, Earl of Minto.
Chancellor of the exchequer, Sir C. Wood.
Home secretary, Sir G. Grey.
Foreign secretary, Viscount Palmerston.
Secretary for war and colonies, Earl Grey.
First lord of the admiralty, Earl of Auckland.
President of the board of trade, Earl of Clarendon.
President of the board of control, Sir J. C. Hobhouse.
Chancellor of the duchy of Lancaster, Lord Campbell.
First commissioner of woods and forests, Viscount Morpeth.
Chief secretary for Ireland, H. Labouchere.
Postmaster-general, Marquis of Clanricarde.
Paymaster-general, T. B. Macaulay.

At the top of the government there were three men, Lord John, Palmerston, and Lansdowne. Palmerston stood second to Lord John in the house of commons, and led the house and wrote the daily letter to the Queen whenever Lord John was away. It is not easy to read Palmerston's mind at this time. He was not one of the cabinet's talkers, and like the diplomat he was he knew how to hide his own thoughts while he studied other people's. But he was eight years older than Lord John, and he had already been in office for twenty years before Lord John became paymaster in 1830. In 1830 Palmerston proposed himself to Grey for the lead,[44] and in 1834, when Melbourne said that henceforth Lord John ought to lead the party in the commons, Palmerston looked grave, and turned away to finish his despatches.[45] Thereafter he was never quite 'with' Lord John. In 1842 the Duke of Bedford thought he was trying to 'give a direction to the party, and to public opinion thro' the newspapers',[46] and in 1846 he was certainly testing how much support there was for an alternative policy. But Palmerston was not related to any of the great Whig families, and at the time the government was formed he was still constrained to be cautious in party affairs, and to avoid any direct challenge to Lord John. He compensated for this at the foreign office, where he refused to keep within the bounds of either discipline or decorum.

Lansdowne stood above Palmerston in the administration, and led the government in the house of lords. To him whiggery was a matter of civilisation, of tolerant behaviour and of the cultivation of the mind. He commanded respect on both sides of the house, and for many years now it had been inconceivable that anyone would form a Whig administration without him. But he was not quite ambitious enough, as Lord John put it in 1829, to 'be stamped with the king's head, and pass current throughout the country',[47] and Grey and Melbourne had both invited him to serve as lord president of the council. From that office he and Lord John had fought the 1839 education campaign together, and their ties were deep. The fact that Lansdowne stood well to the right of Lord John was no bar between them, and every time Lord John became embroiled with Palmerston over foreign affairs, he looked to Lansdowne for assistance. But because Palmerston and Lansdowne were both Irish landlords, Lord John was obliged to trim his Irish policy, in order to be certain of Lansdowne's support in keeping the governmental triangle the right way up.

In the house of lords, Lansdowne's aides fell into three categories, the old, the young, and the lawyers; Auckland, and Minto; Grey, Clarendon, and Clanricarde; and Cottenham and

Campbell. Auckland had been governor general of India in Melbourne's time, but he had been relieved by Peel after the disaster at Kabul, and his return to high office was unexpected. But he had been at the admiralty before, for a few months in 1834, and in one sense at least he was a good, Liberal service chief. He was 'ready to depart from a senseless competition [with France] in the exhibition of strength',[48] and he met Palmerston's incessant memoranda on the defenceless state of the country with reasoned estimates of the difficulties which a French expeditionary force would encounter.[49]

Auckland did not make much impression in the cabinet. Minto, on the other hand, did, and made a bad one. He was very wrapped up in local Scots politics and feuds, and on one occasion Lord John reminded him that a cabinet was more important that a county meeting.[50] When he did attend,Morpeth found him 'tiresome', and regretted how much of him they were subjected to.[51] Sometimes a cabinet dinner passed pleasantly even 'tho' Ld Minto was strong in talk', but on other occasions he engrossed the conversation,[52] and when Hobhouse objected to the Minto mission, Wood said that 'Minto was no good at home and might as well be abroad'.[53] The cabinet did not blame Lord John for being his son in law and put up with Minto's having an ornamental office, but there would be trouble if Lord John ever came to rely upon Minto's judgement.

Grey joined the cabinet with the determination that he would not be the person to originate resistance to Palmerston's conduct of foreign affairs.[54] But his general behaviour was still the same as ever. He grumbled and shook his head, and 'prognosticated ill'.[55] His tone was violent, his language was burning and blustery, and ever and anon he could be seen clenching and unclenching his fists'.[56] On one occasion he 'did all but fly out' at Labouchere and was heard to say as he left the room that he would not come again,[57] and on another he 'flew into a fury and shook his fist at George Grey – at which we all burst out laughing'.[58] He did much good for the colonies, but his despatches were 'peppery, irritating, and injudicious', and the cabinet once suggested that Palmerston, who was supplying Grey with softening phrases, should write Grey's despatches, and he Palmerston's.[59]

Clarendon already had a career in the diplomatic service behind him before he became lord privy seal in 1839. He had friends in the Household and upon *The Times*, and in many ways he was a courtier rather than a politician. Ideologies meant little to him, but he had negotiated a commercial treaty with France in 1831, he was the elder brother of Charles Villiers who stood third in the anti-corn-law league, and he was one of the few out-and-out free traders in the cabinet. He was probably given the board of trade in preference to Labouchere, who had held it before, because it was desirable to have one such generally popular free trader in the upper house.

Clanricarde was bald and bland. He was married to Canning's daughter, and he had been under-secretary for foreign affairs in 1826–7, and ambassador at St Petersburg from 1838 to 1841. No stigma of immorality yet attached to his name, and he was a resident, protestant Irish landowner. Unlike Lansdowne and Palmerston, he did not also possess estates in England, and he was brought into the cabinet to strengthen the government's hand in Irish debates, which were likely to be fierce. At this time his approach to Irish problems was of that litmus paper brand of common sense and good feelings which looked blue in the company of Lord John, and pink in the presence of Stanley and the house of lords.

Cottenham and Campbell were both old, and were brought into the cabinet as a pair. Cottenham had been lord chancellor under Melbourne, and in Campbell's *Lives of the Lord Chancellors* he is lost between Lyndhurst and Brougham. It is a fair summary, for he 'could scarcely put two sentences together in the House of Lords', and he avoided any conflict with Brougham 'as with an evil spirit'.[60] Lord John brought him back because there was no acceptable alternative. But it was a pity: he had no interest in the reform of the law, and he remained at heart an austere judge. Campbell had been attorney general under Melbourne, and he was brought into the cabinet because Cottenham could not speak.

In the house of commons, in addition to Lord John and Palmerston, there were Hobhouse, Macaulay, Morpeth, George Grey, Charles Wood, who came into the cabinet for the first time, and Labouchere.

Hobhouse seemed to have burned his radicalism at the same time as Byron's memoirs, and he now belonged to the right wing of the cabinet. He had been president of the board of control from 1835 to 1841, and like Palmerston he wished to go back to his old office. Lord John agreed, but was reluctant,[61] and after that the two men never hit off a happy working relationship. At first Hobhouse found Lord John wanted to 'appear to know and to direct everything',[62] and he accordingly laid everything on the premier's desk. Lord John then reacted against being used: 'I spoke to Russell about the great difficulty I had in preparing the Punjaub paper for parliament. R. replied "I dare say you have, but that is your affair".'[63] The Duke of Bedford, who cared for Hobhouse more than for all the rest of Lord John's colleagues put together,[64] hastily assured him that his office was the only one which Lord John felt confident would be properly conducted.[65] Hobhouse himself doubted if this was true, and in fact he aged to the point where he had 'such bad repute for efficiency' that Lord John did not choose to have an inquiry into the East India charter under his management.[66]

By Whig standards Macaulay was an upstart, and great things had been hoped for from him. But he turned out not to be a success as a speaker in parliament, and he had, in fact, already made up his mind that if he had to choose between literature and politics he would choose literature. Mackintosh had fallen between two stools, and Macaulay was determined not to do the same. He came in to oblige, and after he lost his seat at Edinburgh at the general election in 1847, he resigned, and concentrated upon his *History*.

Morpeth first came into the cabinet as chief secretary for Ireland in 1839, and in December 1845 when he heard that Lord John intended to send him to the woods, he felt 'let down'.[67] Now he wrote that 'having received an office of less importance gives me rather the feel that I was going out instead of coming in'.[68] He acquiesced, but in 1847 he asked to become lord-lieutenant of Ireland, and in 1849 he requested the admiralty.[69] His reaction to successive disappointments was an excellent 'oh for more docility of resignation',[70] but he was upset when Lord John invited him to accept an early promotion to the house of lords and to give up the conduct of the health of towns bill.[71] Morpeth rallied George Grey and Wood to write to Lord John in his support.[72] Lord John underestimated Mor-

peth's determination, but he was not so far wrong about his
capacity, and in 1850 it was George Grey who had to try and
make a practical measure out of Morpeth's 'project for burying
every body agst their will'.[73]

George Grey had hitherto achieved only moderate recognition as under-secretary for the colonies from 1835 to 1839, and
as judge advocate general from 1839 to 1841. Elevated to a
major office, he now became the best home secretary Richmond
had ever seen.[74] He reorganised his department, and like Lord
John before him, he was interested in the reform of the penal
system and in the gradual abolition of transportation. In the
cabinet he was patient, reasonable and firm, and as he was
without a trace of Palmerston's ambition, Grey's jealousy, and
Morpeth's feeling that he was under-valued, he was usually a
rock of strength to Lord John. In the commons, however, he
did not make such a good impression, and nobody has ever been
able to say why. As Morpeth put it, 'everything is so good,
voice, manner, look, language, feeling, character, one is a little
surprised why it is not even better as a whole, it is not very impressive, and never gives the thrill'.[75]

Charles Wood, like Grey, was lucky to be rewarded for his
rebellious course in 1839–41 by being raised to the cabinet,
particularly as he at once donned Grey's mantle, and stood sen-
tinel over Palmerston, ostentatiously 'making signs' whenever
foreign affairs were discussed, and taking notes of what had
been agreed in cabinet.[76] But Baring did not want to come back
to the exchequer,[77] and Wood's known sympathy with Peel was
a guarantee of continuity in fiscal policy. Wood was not altogether inhuman: he had a curious habit of going down on his
knees at a table in order to make a draft, and at a discussion on
the corn trade he once brought a tuft of sprouting wheat out of
his pocket with green blades two inches high.[78] But he took his
job seriously: in an orthodox way he preached the necessity for
a surplus, and for the sphere of government activity to be kept
to a minimum. He gave an unusual slant to a common dogma
by the emphasis he placed upon local government. Following
the poor law amendment act of 1834 he feared that Britain was
gradually approaching the condition of continental countries
where the state was responsible for everything.[79] This was
dangerous because:

It is evidently wise to put as little on the Govt whose overthrow causes a revolution as you can, and to have as much as you can on local bodies which may be overthrown a dozen times and nobody be the worse.[80]

Like every chancellor of the exchequer, Wood was, in his own words, 'like Cain, his hand was against every body and every body's hand was against him',[81] and on one occasion after he had been pruning the estimates, Minto woefully remarked that his will must be done at home as it was abroad.[82] Nowhere was this more true than in Ireland. Finance not being Lord John's field, he came to place 'a blind confidence' in Wood's judgement,[83] and this was unfortunate, for Wood was not as skilful as circumstances made him important, and his budgets were a recurrent source of weakness to the administration.

Before coming to Labouchere, who became chief secretary for Ireland, it will be as well to mention his superior officer, the lord lieutenant. There was a lot to be said in favour of Bessborough. He was connected by family to the right of the Whigs, and for all his flirting with the Protectionists in 1846, he leaned to the left of the party.[84] He was an Irish landlord, and a resident one. He had been one of the committee of four which drew up the Reform Bill, and he had negotiated the Lichfield House compact. His name inspired confidence in Ireland, and was perhaps the only name that could have done. But there was also much to be said against him. He was 'a fool in regard to women'.[85] He was discreet neither in his liaisons,[86] nor in his choice of the persons whom he allowed to read and even to open his correspondence,[87] and he had 'another unfortunate weakness', which was that he drank.[88] His handwriting betrayed his condition, and the Whigs had not been in office long before it became apparent that the government of Ireland by Whitehall and Dublin meant 'double discussion'.

Bessborough's weaknesses were complemented by those of his assistant. Labouchere was descended from a Dutch Huguenot, and his mother, who provided him with his ticket of entry to the Whig club, was a Baring. He was the sort of man the Whigs needed to bring on, if they were to recover the confidence of the commercial classes, and he had already been president of the board of trade under Melbourne. But he was new to Ireland, and he was not prepared for what he found. In the face of starvation and death, he lost his calm, and complained that the government was not doing enough to save life. His colleagues found the chief secretary importunate, and his appointment was 'the least felicitous' in the whole cabinet.[89]

Lord John did not display all the tact he might have done in forming his cabinet. Melbourne was too old, but he still clung to the notion that he might hold office once more, and it was a pity that Lord John had to be prompted to write him a letter. The letter was brusque, but Melbourne was pleased, or had the kindness to pretend to be.[90] Others, however, were not so easily satisfied. Thinking to do good, Lord John wrote to a number of those whom he was obliged to disappoint. Several of them actually answered him back. More O'Ferrall replied bitterly that 'les absens ont toujours tort',[91] while H. F. Berkeley snorted indignantly that he represented Bristol, the third city of the empire.[92]

Nor was Prince Albert impressed by the way the Whigs behaved while the ministry was being formed. He was irritated by the demanding way in which 'every great family claims what it considers to be its due',[93] and when the new ministers arrived he was amazed by the way in which they spoke of all their differences. From their conversation he concluded that there were two parties among the Whigs,

> There is the *Grey* party consisting of Lord Grey, Lord Clarendon, Sir George Grey and Mr. Wood; they are against Lord Lansdowne, Lord Minto, Lord Auckland, and Sir John Hobhouse, stigmatising them as old women.

Lord John, he thought, leaned entirely to the second group, while Palmerston would even forget last December to join the Grey party against Lord John personally.[94] The Prince was an observant man; George Grey and Earl Grey were cousins, Wood was a brother in law of Earl Grey, and the three men often acted together. But they were scarcely a party within a party. Much the most significant thing about the cabinet was, as Lord John himself said in parliament, that there were too many people in it 'connected by family entirely with land'.[95]

ENGLAND IN 1869.

From the " Gazette " of the period.

YESTERDAY LORD JOHN RUSSELL entertained at dinner, at his mansion in Great Russell Street, the SECRETARY FOR FOREIGN AFFAIRS and the COUNTESS GREY; the SECRETARY FOR THE COLONIES and LADY WILHELMINA ELLIOT; the ARCHBISHOP OF CANTERBURY and MRS. GREY; the LORD CHANCELLOR and LADY GREY (of Greybeard); the MARQUIS OF MINTO and the LADIES FREDERICA and ANASTATIA ELLIOT.

After the banquet, LADY JOHN RUSSELL held an assembly, at which her ladyship had the honour of receiving their ROYAL HH. THE PRINCE CANUTE and PRINCE HENGIST; the DUKE and DUCHESS OF BEDFORD ; the DUKE and DUCHESS OF PALMERSTON ; EARL and COUNTESS DISRAELI ; the COUNTESS OF STOCKPORT and the LADIES COBDEN ; RIGHT HON. SIR B. and LADY HAWES; the VICE-CHANCELLOR OF ENGLAND and LADY P. ELLIOT ; the FIRST LORD OF THE ADMIRALTY and LADY (GREGORY) GREY ; the BISHOP OF VAN DIEMAN'S LAND and MRS. X. ELLIOT; H. E. SIR GRIMES GREY, Governor of Canada, and LADY GREY; MESSRS. R. GREY, OXFORD GREY, FRENCH GREY, J. GREY, F. GREY, and L. GREY; MESSRS. L. S. D. and F. R. S. ELLIOT; MESDAMES A. GREY, G. ELLIOT, S. GREY, L. ELLIOT; MESDAMES A. B and F. ELLIOT; MISSES S. P. Q. R. GREY; MR. JONES; MR. SMITH.

Dancing occurred in the course of the evening, when H. R. H. PRINCE CANUTE opened the ball with MISS Z RUSSELL, having for his *vis-à-vis* H. R. H. THE PRINCE HENGIST and LADY KATINKA ELLIOT.

The ARCHBISHOP OF CANTERBURY danced a Scotch strathspey with LADY ROBINA ROY GREY ; and the festivities were kept up until a late hour.

FIG. 2 ENGLAND IN 1869 *Punch* 1849

Many observers were struck by the exclusive self-sufficiency of the great Whig families and by the number of Russells, Elliots and Greys in Lord John's administration. In this glimpse into the future notice who has joined the club.

ii. Office, 1846

First the cabinet must decide whether to hold a general election. Grey and Wood spoke in favour, and Hobhouse supported them.[96] Their argument was that the poor law was coming up for revision in 1847, and that this would make the Whigs unpopular, as it had done in 1837 and 1841. But the rest of the cabinet agreed with Lord John that a general election in the summer of 1846 would lead to dangerous excitement, and they decided to carry on with the 1841 parliament for another year.

With a minority in both houses, the Whigs were sustained by Wellington's promise of the same support he had given Peel,[97] and by the hatred felt for each other by the Peelites and the Protectionists. Peel rather pretentiously claimed that he would not have consented to hold office upon sufferance.[98] But no man had done more to break up the party system, and to make it certain that the next government must be a weak one. Lord John, who had to carry on the administration, made the best case he could. He argued that Peel had

> aimed at a much greater agreement of opinion, and at a much greater identity of conduct on the part of the Members of his Administration, and of his party generally, than was aimed at by Mr. Pitt, Mr. Fox, or Lord Liverpool; but I own that though the right hon. Gentleman, from his great talents, . . . for a time succeeded in that attempt, I do not think that it is an attempt likely to be very successful again, or to be advantageous to the country.[99]

In future men must be brought together who agreed in their general opinions, but not necessarily upon every question. Lord John did not agree with Earl Grey about the Irish church, and George Grey would vote for the factory bill, Labouchere not. As Bernal Osborne acidly commented, 'all questions, it seemed, were to be open questions'.[100]

That was one side of the picture: the other was that for the time being, at least, the government had two kinds of strength. In the first place the house of commons was not going to overthrow two administrations in one year. As Hobhouse wrote to Lord John, 'a vote more or less is nothing to you and you may laugh at the idle menaces of any man or set of men'.[101] That

being so, Lord John began his career with a coup. Peel's reduction of the duties on foreign free sugar in 1844 had solved
nothing, because very little foreign free sugar was available, and
the British market was still unsatisfied. Lord John had always
denounced the distinction between foreign free and foreign
slave-grown sugar, and he decided to do away with it. In place
of the prohibitory duty of 63s on foreign slave-grown sugar, and
the duty of 23s 4d on foreign free, there was to be a single duty
of 21s, and this was to be reduced year by year until it fell to
14s in 1851, when it would be equal to the duty on colonial
sugar. By way of compensation the British colonies were to be
allowed to purchase manufactured goods where they chose.

Lord John's proposals for sugar had much in common with
his proposal for a small fixed duty on corn in 1841, and were a
bold attempt at a final solution. Peel disapproved, but announced that he would vote for the measure rather than turn
Lord John out after six weeks.[102] Some Protectionists, even,
voted with the government, and many abstained. The bill
passed. This was a considerable achievement, but there was an
uncomfortable feeling that the house of commons was being
punished for the sugar vote of 1841, the West India interest
rallied, and in 1848 the 'final' solution had to be amended in its
turn.

The second and much greater strength of the government's
position lay in the crisis in Ireland. The famine began with the
failure of the potato in 1845. In 1846 there was a second and
even more complete failure, and the cereal crops, which had
been good in 1845, were poor all over Europe. Peel had got out
just in time. In bare outline, a population of ten millions faced
the winter, spring, and early summer of 1846–7 with no more
than four-fifths of their normal food supply. Within that population, 2m were normally unemployed, and one-third lived off
their potato patches at subsistence level. These groups were already enfeebled by the first failure, and had no reserves to face
the second successive dearth. The truth will never be known,
but in round figures 1m or more people perished in the two
years after Lord John took office, and another 1m emigrated
between 1847 and 1850. It was 'an evil unknown in the history
of modern Europe',[103] or as Lord John said in a famous phrase,
it was like a famine of the thirteenth century acting upon a

population of the nineteenth century.[104] That is not in dispute, the real question is whether the famine was met with the resources of the nineteenth century or with those of the thirteenth.

Lord John Russell did not, as the Irish juries asserted, starve 1m Irish to death. What he did do was to preside over a government in whose tenure of office 1m Irish starved to death. It is a sober thought, and it is not easy to put the case for Lord John. But in December 1845 he and Lady John looked beyond the repeal of the corn laws to 'a golden age for Ireland',[105] and when the champion of justice for Ireland became prime minister he wrote to Bessborough, 'circumstances have given you a power over the Irish people which no one has held since the Revolution'.[106] He himself, therefore, must be judged by his success or failure in dealing with the crisis in Ireland.

Even without a famine things in Ireland would have been immeasurably more difficult than they had been in the period from 1835 to 1841. As Ellice said in 1845, Peel had given further power to the repeal movement.[107] His new course had come too late, and O'Connell had already raised 'a spirit which no one can lay again'.[108] In December 1845 Lord John was assured that most of the Repealers would rally to his support,[109] but three months later More O'Ferrall warned him that there was a new generation to deal with in Ireland, and that

> men, without large measures will no longer succeed in governing Ireland. It would be impossible to return to the govt of Lord Normanby with the same success, not even if you placed an Irishman in every office, and bestowed the patronage of the Empire.[110]

When Lord John took office he told the commons that with the exception of the appropriation clause he still contended in 1846 for what he had contended in 1836,[111] and an Irish franchise bill and an Irish municipal bill were among the first measures to be concerted between London and Dublin. But Lord John had not been in office long before he saw that the famine changed the problem, and required a new order of priorities. In July 1846 he told the commons that 'the social grievances of Ireland are those which are most prominent'.[112] Votes were no use without employment and food, and before the end of the year the franchise and municipal bills dropped to the end of the queue.[113] In November 1847 Lord John went much further and actually wrote to the lord lieutenant, 'I think we may now assume that the political franchises on which we so long pondered and legislated were not directed to the case of the specific evils of Ireland.[114]

In the face of chaos Lord John soon formulated an overall concept of what he wanted to achieve, and throughout the crisis he tried to ensure that even immediate measures of relief went in the direction of his long-term plans. Ireland was an agricultural country, and Lord John aimed to establish there the harmony of interests which he supposed to prevail in the English countryside.[115] The so-called small farmers were to be allowed to fall through to their 'natural' position as labourers. Labourers were to be put on wages, and a new middle class of shopkeepers and merchants would then spring up to supply them. Labourers, when old or ill, and perhaps also when unemployed, were to be supported out of rates paid by the landowners and tenants. Insolvent landowners, most of whom were protestant, were to be sold up. Their places would be taken by catholic merchants anxious to invest in land. Landlord, tenant, priest and labourer would then be of the same religion, and the priests' exclusive allegiance to the poor would be gradually widened to include the landowners by a land tax for the payment of the catholic clergy. Finally tenant farmers would be attached to their landlords by being given security. All would then be in harmony with each other, and with the state, the lord lieutenant would be abolished, and Ireland would be ruled by a secretary of state.[116]

Lord John wanted to change the habits of a whole people,[117] and although he once said that there were three bad classes in Ireland, the landlords, the tenants, and the labourers,[118] it was the landlords he was really after (so that by some modern notions at any rate, his antipathies were in the right place). As he wrote in 1848:

> Time out of mind the Landlords of Ireland have exercized the rights of property, squeezing by means of agents, police and military the utmost rents out of their tenants, and performing none of the duties of property. If a farm house was wanted they did not build it; if gates were broken down they did not put up new ones; if the labourers were reduced to beggary they did not feed them; if the people had no place of public worship for their own creed

they did not contribute to erect one. In receiving rent, and in collecting rent, began continued and ended their part as proprietors.[119]

We shall come back to this theme repeatedly, and find that on a
number of occasions Lord John's animus against the landlords
made him lose sight of the famine.

He who will understand why Lord John's achievement fell
short of his objectives must now consider that his cabinet was a
cabinet of landowners, and not least the owners of land in Ireland. In answer to Roebuck Lord John agreed that two or three
or four members of the cabinet owned land in Ireland.[120] He
was presumably counting aloud. There were Lansdowne and
Palmerston, both of whom were named in debate;[121] there was
Clanricarde; and then there was Cottenham – did he count or
not? – for he was a mortgagee on encumbered estates. These
are the names to watch in this and the next chapter. They were
not in a majority, and they did not act as an organised group,
but they were in a powerful position, and what happened was
this. Everything was scrutinised by the Irish landlords, and
passed or rejected by the English and Scots landlords in the
cabinet. The Irish landlords could not afford to meet every proposal with outright rejection, but they could try and substitute
the word voluntary for the word compulsory in all acts. They
could also protest too much, and if they gave the impression
they were trying to shirk duties which English and Scots landlords carried, and which according to the ethics of landlordism
every landowner ought to carry, they were outvoted. Hence the
new Irish poor law of 1847, and the encumbered estates acts of
1848 and 1849. Landlords ought to support their poor by rates,
and they ought to be solvent in order to do so. But when Lord
John came up with a proposal that might cross the water, then
it was rejected, even if it went to the root of the problems of
Ireland, like his proposal for security of tenure.

There was thus a stranglehold upon Lord John in his own
cabinet. The great clashes of the 1830s between Lord John and
the house of lords were not repeated (though there were
clashes), because the lords were, in effect, able to abort measures in the cabinet. And when, a month after the formation of
the ministry, the Duke of Bedford feared that Lord John's
policy might bring him to an open breach with his cabinet, he

altered his will to leave an Irish estate at Ardsalla, which had
come to him from the third Earl Ludlow and was worth £5000
p.a.,[122] to Lord John, and in the event of his earlier death to
young Johnny.[123] This was the duke's master stroke, to keep
Lord John short of cash, and to appeal to him through his
expectations.

It is time now to return to the problem of the relief of famine
as it appeared to Lord John and to his cabinet when they took
office in 1846. There had been famines in Ireland before, just
as there had been depressions of trade in England, and the
recognised unit for the alleviation of distress was the locality,
where the leading inhabitants would set up a committee to receive contributions and to distribute bread or meal. Peel had
met the famine of 1845–6 in three ways. First, the government
subscribed to the relief committees pound for pound. Secondly,
Peel encouraged landowners to originate schemes of public
works. These were to be paid for half by a loan to be repaid by
the locality and half by an outright grant from the state. The
idea was that with the wages he earned on the works, the
labourer would be able to buy food. Thirdly, in order to keep
the price of food down in the crisis months of May and June,
Peel provided depots for storage and distribution. To these
depots were delivered the £100,000 worth of American maize
purchased in the autumn of 1845 (Peel's brimstone).

Peel's measures looked good on paper. But there were many
areas where no relief committee could be formed because there
were no leading inhabitants; the public works were offered on
terms so generous that the landowners went at them and upset
the normal pattern of employment; and the only part of the
scheme which worked at all satisfactorily was the provision of
food from the depots in May and June. When the Whigs took
over, the whole scheme was about to expire, and by that time
the economy was over-heated by the railway boom, the British
public had built up a year's immunity to Irish suffering, and the
officials of the treasury had experience of the waste and fraud
inseparable from public works.

Lord John had not been in office four weeks when it became
clear that the potato had failed for a second time. While the
public took the view that this must be the fault of the Irish
themselves, the government's relief measures for 1846–7 were
drawn up by Trevelyan, the permanent official at the treasury,

in the light of the mistakes that had been made the year before. The new scheme was brought before the house of commons by Lord John on 17 August. The government's contribution to the relief committees was to be cut from a pound for a pound to ten shillings for a pound. The reasoning behind this was that voluntary contributions had fallen below the level of the problem. This was true, but for that very reason the amounts involved were small, and the cut was mean. The public works were to be continued and reorganised by a new labour rate act, whose object was to compel (rather than to encourage) the landowners to take responsibility for the welfare of the populations on their soil.

How was this done? In the first place, in order to discourage landlords from making unnecessary applications and from swamping the board of works, outright grants of public money came to an end. But in order to make sure that works were put in hand, where there was destitution baronies were required to undertake them, and the lord lieutenant was given power, if the baronies refused, to compel them. The entire cost would be met in the first instance by a treasury loan, and the entire cost was to be repaid over ten years by a rate levied on every person rated to the relief of the poor. It was, as Morpeth noted, the nucleus of a compulsory poor law,[124] and the all-important word 'required' was inserted into the bill by Bessborough and Labouchere against the opposition of Palmerston and Clanricarde.[125]

The landowners were thus to be compelled either to employ the people at wages, or to pay rates which would be used to pay wages.[126] To enable the wage labourer to purchase food, the government decided not to repeat Peel's state purchase of American maize, and indeed not to make any state purchases at all. This needs some explaining. According to Lord John, Peel did not purchase maize in order to feed the Irish, but to introduce a new commodity to the Irish market;[127] Labouchere quoted Peel as having said that such a purchase ought never to be made again,[128] and Wood alleged that Peel 'said to me that . . . it was hard upon us having to withdraw.'[129] There being no trade in maize, Peel's government had not gone into direct competition with any established interest. But in the heated atmosphere surrounding the repeal of the corn laws, the corn merchants were unusually sensitive on this point. They accused Peel of having accentuated the famine by interfering with the ordinary channels of trade, and professed to believe that if, in 1846–7, the government bought any corn, private enterprise would buy none. They conned Russell's government into believing that there was no *via media*: either the government must take over the entire supply of corn to Ireland, or it must supply none. In these circumstances the government decided to supply none, and when the merchants demanded a specific undertaking, Wood gave it. The same argument applied to the distribution of corn, and it was agreed that all the government depots were to be closed with the exception of those in the West of Ireland where there was no established system of retail trade.

Russell's plan passed quickly through parliament. But it contained false assumptions and was a source of confusion. Even before the session came to an end young Daniel O'Connell wrote that there was actual famine in county Cork.[130] One after another the Irish peers reported that there would not be a potato left by Christmas – Shannon on 5 August, Enniskillen on 12 August, Bessborough himself on 5 September.[131] At the beginning of September Lord John was told that three-quarters to five-sixths of the potato crop had been lost; by mid-September that six-sevenths had gone.[132] At that time Wood still claimed that there was every account from Ireland ranging from 'can't get the harvest in for want of hands' to 'people dying of starvation',[133] but three months later there was no room for doubt. Labouchere wrote that deaths from starvation were multiplying, that the people were being turned away from the workhouses to perish, and that half the population of Skibereen would die. Before the end of the year deaths from starvation were routine, and on Christmas eve he reported 'many well authenticated cases . . . today'.[134]

The government knew what was happening. How did they react? On 20 September Wood told Lord John that they would need iron nerves to go through with it.[135] At the treasury Trevelyan had iron nerves, and Wood an iron heart. In Ireland, Bessborough resented the British administration's perpetual lectures on how much better the loss of the potato was being handled in Scotland than in Ireland,[136] and Labouchere thought he could espy Trevelyan's 'cloven foot' in every treasury minute.[137] When Bessborough sent Redington, the confidential secretary, over to put the Irish point of view, 'Trevelyan gave him a great deal of sound political economy' totally inapplicable to Ireland.[138] As the scarcity grew worse, Labouchere implored Lord John not to be misled by the abuses mixed up with the relief works into doubting the reality of the misery.[139] When deaths became frequent he wrote 'that the time has arrived when we must take decisive measures to mitigate this appalling amount of human suffering'.[140] He went on, in a way that Lord John cannot have liked, in two instances to compare what was being done by Lord John's government with what had been done by Peel's.[141] Under the new ten shillings in the pound system the government had contributed to the relief committees less than one-sixth of what had been contributed the year before;[142] and the depots in the South and West which contained 8000 tons of food in the winter of 1845–6, now held only 4500.[143]

Lord John was thus caught between the iron nerves of the treasury, and the good but agitated feelings of Labouchere. How did he respond? He accepted Wood's assurances that British merchants had bought up 'every atom of Indian corn in the market',[144] and that there was 'no corn now in the world *unbought*'.[145] British merchants were in competition with those from France, where there was a shortage of from 19 to 42 days' consumption,[146] and government intervention would only raise the price still higher. The government could not convert 'a period of scarcity into a period of abundance',[147] and Lord John told Bessborough that 'we cannot feed the people. It were a cruel delusion to pretend to do so.'[148] The government had taken all the short-term measures it felt able to recommend. There was to be no autumn meeting of parliament – in this crisis an Irish M.P.'s place was in Ireland[149] – and in January the ministry would be ready with its long-term measures of reconstruction.

While parliament stood prorogued there was a tug of war going on between Dublin and London over the interpretation of the labour rate act. Bessborough complained that the restriction to public works was too narrow. On 13 September he asked to be allowed to approve public works which benefited private people: on 19 September he wanted landlords to be allowed to spend their rates upon their own land.[150] Lord John could not sanction this:

> It is a proposal for advances of public money to improve private estates, only excepting ploughing and sowing . . . if we are to advance public money to improve gentlemen's property, the whole landed property of England and Scotland must be drained, fenced, and furnished with farm buildings from the Consolidated Fund.[151]

But he agreed to call a cabinet. Bessborough was a good landlord, and his case was simple: since a rate was going to be levied, the landowners 'ask only to lay it out upon profitable works instead of unprofitable'.[152] Labouchere sided with Bessborough: normally, he thought, employing the poor on unproductive works would stimulate landowners into taking them into productive employment, but in the present case there was a danger of the land being mortgaged for a vast expenditure that would yield no return.[153]

In the cabinet, Lansdowne expressed surprise at 'the strange preference evinced . . . at the Treasury for useless rather than useful works',[154] and Cottenham ruled that the act could be construed to mean that work that was considered of public utility was a public work even though it was for the advantage of private persons.[155] On his authority the cabinet agreed to put the most liberal construction upon the term public works, though with the proviso that no government could directly subvent Irish landlords.[156] Bessborough's immediate reaction was that this gave him all he asked for. But the Irish government's lawyers disagreed with the lord chancellor's interpretation of the law,[157] and the officers of the Irish government all signed a memorial to Lord John saying that they must have the modification Bessborough asked for, even if it meant calling parliament in November.[158] George Grey invited them to make a draft of the bill they wanted, and Lord John promised to hold another cabinet to consider it.[159] It did not take Bessborough long to draft his bill. All he sought was to omit one word from the act, so that instead of public money being advanced for public works, public money would be advanced for works. The cabinet refused, but went some way to meet Bessborough by agreeing to adopt his principle when lending money under Peel's drainage act.[160] This would require fresh legislation.

Bessborough supposed he must acquiesce,[161] but this was not the end of the story. No sooner was the decision known than the Irish landlords wanted any landlord who applied for public money to drain his own land to be exempted from paying the rate under the labour rate act,[162] and asked for the unit of rating to be reduced from the barony to the townland,[163] which would accentuate the differences between rich and poor areas – the rich looking after themselves and the poor having no one to look after them. Bessborough did not condone this, but embarrassed the government in his own way, by leaving the word public out of his instructions to the localities on the interpretation of the labour rate act. When taken to task by Lord John he disingenuously explained that he had done it in order to encourage applications under the act, and that the board of works would sort the applications out in accordance with the cabinet's instructions.[164] It was a flagrant breach of discipline, and Bessborough seems to have looked forward to sanctioning everything, and employing two million people on the works.[165] Lord John dare not sack him, but the treasury fought back, and the number employed on the works never reached 1m. In the meantime, the cabinet, who had been out-manoeuvred, were trying to make up their minds what to do after 15 August 1847 when the labour rate act expired. They had already agreed as early as December 1846 that there would be no more public works.

In this drama over the public works lay an insoluble conflict of right with right. The Irish administration exaggerated when they supposed that all public works must be unproductive and all private works must be productive, but they, like the treasury, had a case, and it can be argued that in the short run they had a better one. Deplorable as it would have been for the state to subsidise a body of men who consistently took money out of Ireland, the fact was that in this crisis you could either work through the Irish landlords, or you could work against them. Peel's system of outright grants had the merit of working through them. But Lord John identified the Irish landowners as the authors of the famine, and he bitterly accused his old colleague Monteagle and his fellow Irish landlords, of seeking reward for the duties they had neglected.[166] In giving way to Cottenham's interpretation of the labour rate act he expostulated that the change was 'for the benefit of the rich – of the proprietors . . . and gives the poor not a shilling beyond the original act', and he agreed with Wood that 'the Irish proprietors . . . have contrived to work the distress of the people for their own pecuniary benefit.'[167] Even in the short term, the Irish famine thus degenerated into a squabble between Lord John and Charles Wood on one side and a few hundred Irish landowners on the other. Lord John's attitude was correct, and in its own way it was high-minded, but it was the starving millions who suffered. From the Irish point of view, the best government they could have had would have been, as Bessborough saw in May 1846, a Protectionist government – a government by Tory landlords for Irish ones.

While the battle over the labour rate act continued, and while the numbers employed on the works rose from 110,000 on 6 November, to 200,000 on 19 November, and 300,000 on 23 November,[168] the fatal defect in the act became apparent. As George Grey said, 'wages at 8d a day with meal at a "famine price" will not keep the people alive'.[169] Even in September the merchants in Mayo and Galway were 'not providing a sufficient quantity of meal at any wages',[170] and by December 'many of the people who had the *means* were almost starving for want of food'.[171] Early in January 1847 Bessborough reported that the price of provisions was now so high that wages were almost 'nugatory', and that 'all attempt at giving employment to enable the poor to purchase food is out of the question.'[172] And if the wage-Irish could not afford food, how much worse off were all those others out in the West, who had neither potatoes nor wages?

Corn was being imported into the United Kingdom on a scale never before known, and the government's decision not to interfere with the importers was justified by results. The difficulty was to make sure that the corn which came into the United Kingdom crossed over to Ireland. Irish wages could not draw it over, and the refusal to interfere in the distributive trades was a disaster. Without rationing, the result was inevitable. As Lord John himself wrote to the Duke of Leinster, a smaller amount of food is to be divided among the same number of human beings. It must be scarcer – it must be dearer. Any attempt to feed one class of the united kingdom by the government would, if successful, starve another part – would feed the producers of potatoes which had failed by starving the producers of wheat, barley and oats which had not failed.[173]

It was no wonder that, before the year was out, Clanricarde heard 'a great outcry agst the Govt and our measures',[174] while Labouchere reported that 'we are violently assailed for not providing Depots and feeding the whole country'.[175]

iii. Office, 1847

The parliamentary session of 1847 thus began in precisely the manner Lord John had hoped it would not begin, with an attack upon the government's short-term measures. This came, not from the Peelites, but from the Protectionists. The Duke of Newcastle had been on a tour round Ireland, making notes with a view to a hostile motion in the house of lords. But on laying his case before Peel, the advice he received was 'to do nothing'.[176] It was just as well: the Peelites' expert on Ireland was Lord Devon, who had headed Peel's commission of inquiry into the condition of Ireland. According to the Duke of Bedford, Devon was absent from his estates in Ireland for a whole year at the height of the famine,[177] but that did not discourage Charles Wood from having long conversations with him at Bowood, and finding that he 'concurs in *all our views*, and goes the full length of all that *even I* have suggested'.[178] This was no misunderstanding. Clarendon, who joined in their conversations, reported that

> Ld Devon has been here for two days very well disposed towards the Govt. . . . C. Wood has told him unreservedly all that has been done and all that is intended, and no one could express himself in terms of more unqualified approbation. He assured me before he went away that he was perfectly satisfied, that he did not see how a Govt. cd. do more, and that C. Wood had a knowledge of Ireland such as few Irishmen possessed.[179]

It was only proper, therefore, that criticism was left to the Protectionists and to the Irish. In the lords Stanley attacked the

government for 'too rigid attention to the principles of competition in trade, and . . . the abstract doctrines of political
economy'.[180] In the commons Bentinck said that this was a
time when Ministers should have broken through these harsh
and severe rules of political economy, and should themselves
have found the means of providing the people of Ireland with
food'.[181] Smith O'Brien went further and argued that 'it was
the duty of the Government . . . to ransack every part of the
civilised world' for food.[182]

Wood replied with the stock answer that 'a partial interference would have paralysed the exertions of private individuals'.[183] But even Labouchere thought the notion that the
government should have fed the people 'so absurd that it will
not stand discussion in parliament',[184] and argued with conviction that, had the government turned importers on a large
scale, a short period of artificial abundance would have been
followed by an aggravated famine.[185] Lord John spoke for the
whole cabinet, and impressed the house, when he said that
government interference in the corn trade

> would lead to a greater number of deaths from famine than the
> course we thought it our duty to pursue . . . I think . . . it is evident
> that no sooner had that intention been declared . . . [than] there
> would have been an end at once of all private enterprise . . . and
> that everything would have been abandoned to the care of the
> Government which had been so presumptuous as to undertake
> such a task . . . But suppose that by means of our vessels a supply
> had been brought into Ireland, then the next thing to have been
> undertaken would have been what would, in fact, have amounted
> to the whole retail trade of that country . . .[186]

Lord John's speech was a high-water mark of *laissez-faire*. He
had not been reading the political economists for nothing, and
when deputations came from Ireland to represent to him the
state of famine existing in their districts, they were presented
with extracts from the fifth chapter of the fourth book of Adam
Smith's *Wealth of Nations*.[187] Or, as he put it in 1863, 'what
Adam Smith wrote in 1775 began to be acted upon in 1825 and
was finally adopted as true and useful in 1848'.[188]

Strange to say, even while ministers were defending the
policy they had pursued since August, they were preparing to

abandon it. In the face of the manifest fact that, as Bessborough put it, 'the merchants who last July made promises of all sorts about the stock of meal &c that they would bring into the country, . . . have done as little as they could have done even if the Government had entered on the trade',[189] the government decided to bring forward the extinction of the last import duties on corn and to suspend the navigation laws; to purchase imported corn, 'always following, but never leading the market',[190] and to ship it from Liverpool and Plymouth in government vessels to the depots in the West of Ireland;[191] and to prohibit the use of grain in distilleries and breweries, where sugar was to be used instead.

Above all, while the numbers on the relief works were rising to 450,000 in the middle of January and to 734,000 in March, the government was obliged to think again about the labour rate act. Costs rose from £298,799 in November to £545,054 in December, to £736,125 in January, and to £944,141 in February,[192] and Wood was obliged to raise £10m to cover the whole year from August 1846 to August 1847. Parliament complained bitterly about the expense, but the main reason for the change of policy which now took place was that it was no use enforcing a transition to a wage economy, if before the transition was over, the people were dead. Hence the change to soup. The money could be better spent, and on 17 January, at Bessborough's recommendation, the cabinet adopted the soup kitchen plan for future relief.[193] Palmerston may have approved for the rather personal reason that the priests, who had been getting a penny in the shilling out of the wages of the superstitious labourers on the relief works, could not dip their spoons in other people's soup.[194] The destitute persons (Ireland) bill was introduced and passed accordingly, and it was because this change was made from works to soup that Lord John subsequently felt able to resist charges that the government had allowed anyone to starve. For the rest of his life he indignantly denied that the government had carried *laissez-faire* principles too far, and contrasted the attitude of the government with that of 'some philosophers' who calmly advocated that 2m Irish should be allowed to perish 'without interference'.[195]

The flurry of short-term bills consequent upon the change in policy got in the way of the long-term measures of reform which had been under discussion since the autumn. The Irish government lawyers were not the most efficient part of the machinery of state at the best of times, and on 31 December Lord John asked Bessborough to tell the attorney general to drop his private business and attend to matters of state.[196] It is not surprising, therefore, that the government's three main bills were not ready in time for the opening of parliament on 19 January, and that they had to be finished in a hurry.

The waste lands bill owed something to the Devon report. There were 4,600,000 acres of virgin soil in Ireland. The government proposed to start acquiring them by compulsory purchase, and to divide them into small farms, which were to be let on leases of thirty-one years in order to prevent subdivision. Lansdowne assented, provided it was understood that interference with property was not to be had recourse to on every occasion,[197] and Labouchere showed the bill to Devon,[198] who approved.

Lord John himself attached more importance to the poor law, and he was determined to extend the act of 1838. For the first time, the aged and the infirm were to be given a right to relief. In the cabinet Lansdowne agreed to that,[199] but when Lord John reached the clause empowering the commissioners to relieve the aged and the infirm out of doors, and explained that there might then be room in the workhouses for the able-bodied, Lansdowne began to talk 'rather earnestly' about the law going too far.[200] That being so, there could be no right to relief for the able-bodied poor, but the cabinet accepted a clause by which, when the workhouses were full, the commissioners were to be empowered to order the guardians to supply food to the able-bodied poor outside.

It would have been hopeless to have shown the house of lords these two sticks of compulsory purchase and a right to poor relief without offering them a carrot too. It was at this point that the cabinet's undertaking to extend Peel's drainage act to allow any landowner to borrow money from the state came in. By borrowing money to drain marginal land a man could escape compulsory purchase. The only condition under this new landed property bill was that a landowner must pledge his estate as security. Wood thought the proposal went too far, and looked forward gloomily to the day when the state would own all the land in Ireland,[201] but the scheme was essential to the success of Lord John's plans.

Before describing what happened to these bills, it is worth noticing that the government rejected any large-scale scheme of emigration. Labouchere and Clanricarde urged Lord John to deal with emigration in a liberal spirit.[202] But Lord John and Grey considered that the Irish reproduced the faults of their existing social system on arrival in America and Australia, and that it would be better to improve their condition 'before we people our colonies with them'.[203] In any case, it was too late. There was 'no use in sending men from starving at Skibereen to starve at Montreal',[204] and a 'sweeping hurricane' of emigration would both choke the market in Canada,[205] and make the country catholic.[206] The poor law authorities were to be encouraged to sponsor families, after having received from the emigration commissioners an assurance that upon landing they would be provided for,[207] but that was all. Bessborough agreed: the emigration would be enormous without any aid,[208] and the only thing the government did not do, which it might have done, was to regulate the conditions on board ship.

When Lord John rose to introduce the government's long-term measures, he still enjoyed some advantages from being the minister of necessity. The Duke of Wellington wrote of his anxious wish to avoid embarrassing the government.[209] Peel thought the ministry as weak as water, but detected a general disposition to help them through the crisis.[210] Stanley recognised that 'the present Government do not hold office under ordinary circumstances',[211] and Disraeli proclaimed his wish to offer no obstacle to her majesty's ministers.[212] Even the Irish M.P.s, Bessborough thought, would be 'exceedingly friendly', if Lord John would only hear a little what they had to say, and tell them his wishes.[213] Thus encouraged, Lord John rose to Peel's level of comprehensiveness, presented the government's measures as being equal to the problems with which Ireland was faced, and restored the government's fortunes. His speech won praise from men as far apart as Bentinck, Inglis, and Roebuck, and Disraeli said it was the best he had ever heard Lord John make.[214] Charles Villiers wrote that Lord John

gains every day wonderfully upon the House . . . and the absence of the Peel egotism . . . was much remarked upon. I have had a

great many people from the Country with me today. They all say
that this week has given the Govt a character for *durability* wch it
had not before and that the idea extends that *it will do*.[215]

It was a good start, but within a few days lord George Bentinck brought in a plan to solve the Irish crisis by spending
£16m of public money on building railroads in Ireland. Bentinck helpfully offered his scheme as filling a gap in the government's proposals, but Lord John thought his speech had been
written by Hudson, the 'railway king'. He told Prince Albert
that

> these Railroads are *most of them* bubbles and extravagant specula-
> tions . . . got up . . . 2 years ago, the speculators have lost their money
> and the shares are nearly worthless. This measure would of course
> raise their value again and enable the holders to sell them at a
> great profit,[216]

and reminded him that in 1839 Morpeth's plan had provided
for the state to take over the railways at their current value.
But Lord John dare not speak so plainly in the commons, and
it was not until Bentinck's scheme came up for its second
reading that he felt strong enough to announce his outright
opposition.

In the meantime he consulted Brunel, who pointed out that
the scheme would not provide the short-term relief Lord George
claimed, because in building a railway only 25 per cent of the
cost was spent on the ground in labour, 30 per cent went in
articles in whose manufacture Ireland would not participate,
and the rest went in the purchase of land.[217] Peel supported
Lord John, and on 16 February the government was able to
dispose of the scheme by 332 votes to 118. Fifty-eight Protectionists actually voted with the government,[218] but Lord John wrote
to Bessborough that Lord George was now fairly in opposition,
and welcomed this as a first step towards getting the house
back into two parties.[219]

Next, Lord John was able to proceed with the government's
own measures. The waste lands bill aroused much opposition
and (despite Devon's involvement) Peel begged Lord John to
pause before spending so much on such an object.[220] This was
unexpected: and Lord John therefore dropped the bill. It was
a blessing in disguise, for the state was well out of the purchase

of marginal land, and it meant there was more money available
to bait the landed property bill.

The poor law bill was the main measure of the session, and it
turned out to be, as Bessborough forecast, 'the most difficult
subject'.[221] This was not surprising, for ministerial statements
wavered round the critical point, Lansdowne declaring that
giving outdoor relief to the able-bodied would mean the end of
all property in Ireland and denying that the bill provided for it,
while Lord John laid stress on the fact that it did. Scarcely had
the bill been introduced before Lord John received a deputation
from 64 peers and 43 M.P.s protesting that it went too far. He
refused to give way,[222] and the bill then underwent three crises,
the first in the commons, the second in the lords, and the third
in both houses.

In the commons, Mr Gregory, who was an Irish M.P., moved
an amendment that no one in possession of more than one-
quarter of an acre of land should receive relief unless he surrendered his holding. The amendment was harsh, and Lord
John was told later that out of the 681,794 persons relieved in
the week ending 4 July 1847, no fewer than 335,535 possessed
more than a quarter of an acre of land.[223] But there could be no
doubt that it would facilitate the complete reorganisation of
Irish society by forcing independent cottiers to become labourers. The government gave no clear lead, and decided to hear
what members had to say.[224] Both the feeling of the house, and
the reluctance of most members to attend Irish debates, were
shown by the vote of 117 to 7 by which the amendment was
carried. Not even the Irish M.P.s voted against it, and indeed
one small group of them, led by John O'Connell, made it clear
all through the debate that they acquiesced in a poor law rather
than supported it.[225]

In the lords, where Bessborough hoped to avoid a landlords'
debate,[226] Monteagle successfully moved an amendment to
stop payment of outdoor relief to the able bodied after 1 August
1848. Next, in both the commons and the lords the Protectionists attempted to pass a detailed amendment which would have
had the effect of making sure that the payment of poor rates
did not lead to a diminution of rent. The government resisted
this, but Protectionists and Peelites combined, and in the house
of commons the government scraped home by 79 votes to 76.[227]

This made it virtually certain that they would be defeated in the lords. Lord John muttered under his breath that the debates and divisions in the lords created much discontent against that house,[228] and then made it clear that the poor law and the loans stood or fell together. If the landlords would not agree to pass the poor law bill as he had drafted it, then they would not be allowed to vote themselves the landed property bill. The Protectionists withdrew their motion, and at the report stage Lord John persuaded Lansdowne to have Monteagle's amendment struck out by 54 votes to 42. The result was that when the bill became law it still had teeth in it.

Much has been said against the Irish poor law of 1847, but it was no mean achievement. Palmerston called it 'a most drastic Black Dose',[229] and Lady Palmerston said her husband, who had 10,000 cottiers on his Irish estate would now be obliged to send money there.[230] George Grey announced that £121,000 was raised in rates in October 1847 compared with the £26,000 which had been raised in October 1846,[231] and overall, the yearly burden on property was increased, Russell thought, from £400,000 to £1,800,000.[232] Not all went smoothly, and in 1847 twenty-two of the 130 unions were too impoverished to manage their own affairs, but Lord John had some justification for claiming in his memoirs that the act of 1847 had contributed to the greatly improved state of Ireland twenty years later.[233]

Before the session was over the government in their turn brought in a bill to assist the Irish railways. Wood did not like it, but gave way because it was a pet scheme of Lord John's.[234] The bill provided for £620,000 to be advanced to three railways of known financial solidity, and it was carried by votes of 218 to 75 on introduction and of 175 to 62 on second reading. It was opposed by Peel, and Lord George Bentinck naturally accused Lord John of theft. But there was a difference between advancing £16m indiscriminately, and giving a small amount of aid in the right places. It was the right thing to do, and it was of a piece with the line the government had followed since January of augmenting the sum available to help emigrants through the poor law, but not promoting emigration in general; and of providing some food, but not undertaking to feed the people.

While the Irish poor law was passing through parliament, Bessborough fell ill, and on 16 May he died. It was impossible to supply his place, but Morpeth asked for the appointment, and Stanley wrote to Lord John to say how pleased he would be if the Duke of Bedford could be prevailed upon to take it.[235] Lord John's first thought was to abolish the office,[236] but after opening his mind to Lansdowne he concluded that famine and the forthcoming general election made the step premature.[237] The Duke of Bedford had not escaped in 1839 when Ireland was calm in order to be caught when Ireland was clamant, and Lord John and Lansdowne favoured Clarendon, and only if he refused, Morpeth. Clarendon accepted the post on the understanding that the office would be extinguished in the first session of the new parliament, and that he would then become a fourth secretary of state. When the matter came before the cabinet, and someone objected to Clarendon's being offered a job and told that it was to be abolished as soon as possible, Clarendon raised a laugh by saying that he would not have accepted the post on any other terms.[238]

Clarendon's appointment would be acceptable to both Whig and Tory parties, but he had no other obvious qualification for the post, and it is a question why he was chosen. The most obvious things about him were that he was indiscreet, and that he was far too friendly with the editors of newspapers. Lord John had already dropped him a hint about this in December 1846.[239] In 1847 the government's Irish policies were attacked in *The Times*. This was something to which Lord John was peculiarly sensitive, and it may have occurred to him that it might do much harm to leave Delane's favourite in England, and equal good to send him to Ireland. Cabinet secrets would be better kept, and the government might receive a better press for its Irish policy.

One other advantage of Clarendon's appointment should not be overlooked. Clarendon was vacating the board of trade, an office which Labouchere had already held, and for which he was fitted. Labouchere had not been a success in Ireland, and he was glad to make the change. He threw himself into the study of the navigation laws, and quickly adopted a 'nec vitia nec remedia pati possumus' attitude to Ireland[240] and ultimately became a hard liner. Labouchere's place as chief secretary was taken by Sir William Somerville, an Irishman, who was not taken into the cabinet. Finally, just as the new team took over, O'Connell died, and there were new men on both sides.

In 1847 there was also a full programme of legislation for England. First there was the factory bill, which was not a government measure; then there was the reorganisation of the English poor law, which could not be avoided; and finally there were the issues of public health, education, and the Manchester bishopric, which Lord John chose to take up.

In the 1840s factory legislation proved almost as embarrassing to governments as sugar. But by 1847 the heat was going out of the controversy. Ashley told Lord John that the masters were coming round to a limitation of hours, and that the operatives would settle for an eleven-hour day.[241] As Ashley himself was out of parliament, the bill of 1847 was brought in by Fielden. The Protectionists, on the whole, were in favour: the Peelites, on the whole, were against. All depended on the attitude of the Whigs, who were themselves divided, Lord John being in favour, and Wood against. Profiting from Peel's experience in 1844, Lord John was careful not to commit the government against any decision parliament might make. But he himself spoke decisively in favour of limitation:

> I cannot look with indifference to the statement that the great proportion of the people of this country have only to work, to sleep, to eat, and to die. In my opinion, it is the duty of the State to endeavour that you should have a population, in the first place, aware of the doctrines of religion; that, in the next place, they should be able to cultivate domestic habits and domestic affections; and that, in the third place, they should be likely to look up to the laws and Government of the country as their protectors from undue inflictions upon the young of this country . . . I cannot see how a girl of 14 years of age, actually employed for twelve hours in a mill, and engaged there for two hours more, coming home tired and exhausted . . . can be brought up to be a good wife and a good mother.[242]

It was no embarrassment to Lord John when the house of commons carried ten hours as opposed to the eleven which he would have preferred.

The reorganisation of the English poor law was another problem which could easily have led to the loss of a whole session.

After a decade of experience, almost every interest in parliament had reason to dislike the system established in 1834. Old-fashioned Radicals attacked its inhumanity – new-fashioned ones its cost. The Protectionists still disliked the unions, which stood outside the traditional framework of local government, and many Whigs joined them in distrusting the centralising tendencies of the commissioners. M.P.s generally were inclined to make a constitutional issue out of the fact that the commissioners were independent of parliament, and time and again ministers found themselves in the unenviable position of being obliged to defend repugnant decisions rather than repudiate their authors.

Lord John invited the house to proceed by way of a select committee, and persuaded the committee to reconstruct the commission so that in future it would consist of a president and two secretaries. The president and one of the secretaries were to be members of parliament. Duncombe ironically suggested that the new officers ought to be given seats *ex officio*, 'for he believed that before a Poor Law Minister was able to obtain a seat in that House, . . . the new poor law must be made much more popular'.[243] But it was the kind of political problem that Lord John had a flair for, and his solution was accepted. In due course Lord John wanted to offer Cobden the presidency of the board with a seat in the cabinet. But the Queen objected,[244] and he appointed Charles Buller instead.

In his address to the city electors on seeking re-election as prime minister, Lord John had announced that 'great social improvements' were required, and referred specifically to the problems of public health and education.[245] If that was a promise, he kept his word. The health of towns bill was drafted by Morpeth, and introduced on 30 March. It was met by protests against the omission of London, which was attributed to the influence of the city upon their member. Lord John said that the metropolis would be dealt with in due course: in the meantime there was no reason to refuse to cleanse Exeter and Hull.[246] The bill passed its second reading, but it soon became clear that the government could not hope to steer it through committee. At the cabinet dinner on 23 June Hobhouse began to urge his colleagues to drop the bill. 'Labouchere put his hand before my mouth and whispered that it would be dropt by itself in the natural course of business.' He was right, and on 7 July the cabinet agreed without discussion to give the bill up and bring in a new one next year.[247]

The education measure arose out of the new privy council minutes of 1846, which were prepared by Kay Shuttleworth (of whom Lansdowne said 'intelligent, zealous, indefatigable, but write short, he *cannot*'),[248] and adopted by Lord John and Lansdowne soon after the Whigs came back into power. The system of grants had remained unaltered since 1839, though the amount had gone up to £100,000 p.a. The year 1847 was not the time to ask for more money but it was time to overhaul the machinery. The use of the two societies as the channels for public aid meant that two bodies, the methodists and the roman catholics, were excluded. The government started negotiations to bring them in. But the religious rivalries of the 1830s had been succeeded by the religious animosities of the 1840s: Puseyism provoked voluntaryism among the dissenters and new fears of the tendencies of state education, which fed upon the fact that the greater part of the grant still went to church schools which taught the catechism. Ashley, who was moving over to the Whigs, obligingly held meetings in support of state education: the quarter from which the government received support increased the suspicion and the alarm, and the dissenters countered with meetings to oppose state education, or to plead for it to be secular.

By the time Lord John brought on the education vote it was a fact that 'In most of the large towns, the very best friends we have had, are the persons now leading the anti-government-education movement'.[249] With a general election to come, this was too dangerous, and Lord John abandoned the plan of aiding the roman catholics for that year. This was unfortunate because the methodists reversed their decision of 1839, and agreed to accept government money. The new proposals, therefore, gave the impression of a bargain between the government and the methodists to shut the catholics out. There was no bargain, and stung by the charge that he had lost his moral courage, Lord John stated publicly that he hoped to be able to include the catholics next year[250] (which was done).

In every other way the proposals laid before parliament in 1847 were excellent. Hitherto the grants had been spent on schools; some money was now to be spent on schoolmasters:

it has always been my view that you never could effectually raise education in this country till you raised the condition and prospects of the schoolmaster . . . the best of them, seeing what were the rewards offered in this country to persons of intelligence . . . soon found other occupations far more valuable than that of teaching.[251]

Lord John made two main proposals: teachers with fifteen years' exemplary service were to receive retirement pensions; and the best teachers were to be allowed to select apprentices from among their pupils. The teachers would be paid for the apprentices, who would be sent on later to college at the state's expense. They, and other trained and certificated teachers would receive higher salaries. For once, a government had the right priorities, and Lord John and Lansdowne deserve much more credit for this than they have ever yet received.

Speaking to such an issue, Lord John warmed to his theme. Contrasting crime with education, he attacked the opposition's concept of the criminal classes for whom 'the means of education are not to be provided', and for whom there was to be only 'imprisonment, transportation, and the gallows'.[252] One-third of the nation's children were at school, one-third attended Sunday school only, and one-third attended no school at all. Forty out of every one hundred adult men could not write their names. In bringing forward the same estimates as last year

I feel . . . that the most natural observation would have been . . . 'Is this all? . . . your plan is not equal to the immensity of the evil, and a larger and a greater plan ought to be proposed.'[253]

In face of the opposition that had been aroused, he could not hope to succeed if he presented larger estimates, but 'it will, nevertheless, be a consolation to me that I have made an attempt to diminish the empire of ignorance'.[254] Lord John never made a more inspiring speech, and at the end of a long debate, the vote was carried by 372 to 47. The size of the majority must have made him wish he had asked for more. In retrospect his speech seems too big for the measure he had to propose, but we have to remember the confused state of parties in 1847, and the fact that under the forms of the house, any virulent group could spin out a debate almost endlessly.

The last fact was clearly illustrated in the painful debates

which took place towards the end of the session over the creation of a new see. Disraeli hoped to see an angel at Manchester:
Lord John more realistically settled for a bishop. The question
had been left unresolved because Peel agreed with Lord John
that the times were not propitious for an addition to the ecclesiastical members of the house of lords, and thought it undignified to create new bishops without seats in that body. Lord
John argued more sensibly that the church, like any other
institution, ought not to be left 'without the principle of life and
extension'.[255] He envisaged new sees at Manchester, St Albans,
Southwell, and Bodmin or Truro, and proposed that in future
bishops were to go up to the lords in rotation as vacancies occurred. The last three sees dropped out of sight for the time
being, but Lord John persevered with the Manchester one
against an intolerant group of Radicals supported by Sir James
Graham. It was the last act of a dying parliament.

When the session began the government held a trump card
in the crisis in Ireland: long before it came to an end, parliament had become intractable. In November 1846 Ellice had
told Lord John that he was 'the proximate author of all our
great reforms',

> and I have no doubt the fame of being that of the last and most
> important, a social one, also awaits you. But what a House of
> Commons to rely upon for support! . . . how are you to adapt wide
> and important changes – especially affecting landed property, to
> the digestion of landlords, disappointed and discontented parti-
> zans, coxcomical philosophers, and old and young Ireland, all
> looking to popularity with their constituents at an expected
> election?[256]

Ministers had been compelled to spend an unusual proportion of
their time ascertaining the feelings of the house. Twelve days
elapsed before Lord John dare announce his opposition to
Bentinck's railway scheme, and the education debate went on
for three nights before he felt confident that he would carry his
vote.[257] The relaxed party discipline is well illustrated by Sir H.
Douglas's apologising for his opposition to the short service bill
in April and excusing it on the ground that he had voted for
the government on every other important measure so far that
session.[258]

FIG. 3 THE BOY-OF-ALL-WORK *Punch* 1847

Lord John: Here's a precious lot of dirty boots I've got to clean! *I never* was
in such a house.

This cartoon appeared during the last session of the parliament of 1841–7
when the parties were still in confusion following the repeal of the corn laws.
In the new parliament elected in 1847 things were even worse: ministerial
patronage had been reduced to its lowest point, party discipline was slack,
and the house of commons was far too independent for the comfort of the
government.

Ministers made the best case they could: in the commons
Lord John said

> we do not pretend to force a compulsory measure, or a set of com-
> pulsory measures . . . to be adopted by Parliament . . . I considered
> it expedient that we should propose measures which were gener-
> ally well calculated for the end; and I did expect that some of
> those measures, with modifications, would be adopted by Parlia-
> ment . . . but with regard to others, I expected that we should be
> obliged to change or even to abandon them.[259]

In the lords, Lansdowne argued that even bills which did not
pass, 'left seeds behind them which never failed to fructify'.[260]
Lord John and Lansdowne had a point, but in July when Lord
John dropped all the bills he could not hope to pass, and announced the dissolution of parliament, there was an uneasy
feeling, to which Brougham gave expression

> that the conduct of the Ministry argued a systematic and whole-
> sale degree of impotency on their parts which would induce in the
> public mind the belief that a strong Government, which was not
> to be much liked, . . . was, on the whole, to be preferred to a weak
> one. . . . Any Ministry was better than a Ministry without
> power.[261]

Brougham had a point too, and the only hope was that the
general election would do something to get the house back into
two parties again, and that the Whigs would be returned with a
disciplined majority.

CHAPTER XIII

In the shadow of Peel: the bad workmen, 1847–9

i. Office, 1847–8

LORD JOHN's great object was to assimilate the Peelites, and just before the election he offered India to Graham. Graham refused, ostensibly on the ground that it would look too much like the price for the Peelites' restraint towards Palmerston's policy in Portugal.[1] But in private, Graham told Hobhouse that Lord John had behaved harshly to him on 'an occasion which nearly destroyed him', apparently referring to Duncombe's attack on the opening of letters by the post office in 1845.[2] Lord John then offered the post to Dalhousie, who complained that 'Peel never gave him a word of thanks or encouragement, but treated him like a schoolboy'.[3] Dalhousie accepted, but the appointment came too late to influence the elections, and nobody followed his lead.

The Peelites had no mind to give up their separate identity. In 1847 Peel still received assurances that nobody expected the Whig government to pull Ireland through the present crisis, and that everybody looked to him.[4] His position was an extraordinary one, and he was 'determined to enjoy it'.[5] Delane thought Peel's hopes lay in breaking up the Liberal party,[6] and for months *The Times* had made no secret of the fact that it would prefer Peel to Russell. In the present state of the constituencies, this could not do Peel much good, but it might do Russell harm. Le Marchant tried, therefore, to put this point of view to Delane. Surprisingly enough, he had some success:

It seemed that a panegyrical article on Peel had already been prepared for tomorrow. *This* I stopped, and obtained an assurance that during the Elections he would write no more in that strain.

He offered to wage war agst the Protectionists, but was silent as to Peel. I dwelt on the necessity of *positive support* at a moment like this, and he promised to give it, and engaged that an article should appear tomorrow which should satisfy me.[7]

It was a confused election, and many strange pacts were made wherever the local Whigs leaned to one side or other of the divided Conservative party. Lord John himself was returned at the head of the poll in the city, but Rothschild was elected too, who was a Jew, and would be unable to take his seat. Lord John was thus saddled with a delicate constitutional problem right at the beginning of the new parliament. The author of the repeal of the test and corporation acts would gladly bring in a bill to remove Jewish disabilities. But to an overworked prime minister, in poor health, unable to impose his will upon an independent cabinet and an undisciplined house of commons, it was an extra burden.

Not all ministers fared as well as Lord John. In Ireland, the solicitor general was defeated – that was a blow rather than a loss, for the transmission of bills from London to Dublin and back had not done much good.[8] But Hobhouse was defeated at Nottingham, and Macaulay at Edinburgh. Both carried on for the time being, and Hobhouse was returned at a by-election for Harwich in March 1848. Macaulay waited until April and then gave up politics altogether. He had fallen a victim to the new dissent, which Lord John thought so 'disgraceful'.[9] It was not an isolated manifestation, and from Yorkshire Wood reported that at Bradford the Whig candidate only got in by promising the nonconformists not to vote in favour of more education grants.[10] It was one of the most protestant general elections of the reign,[11] and everywhere, Lord John thought, 'the absence of any party contest, or of any great question has led to results of a very unfortunate character – the indulgence of caprice, ingratitude and injustice'.[12]

Attempts to estimate the results only showed how confused the parties had become. The government whip, Tufnell, thought the new parliament would contain 336 Liberals, 225–30 Protectionists, and 85–90 Peelites, but added that 40 of the Liberals were doubtful. Dod gives the figures as Liberals 324, Protectionists 199, and Peelites 117.[13] It is scarcely possible to resolve the differences, for far from having got the house back into two parties, the election had divided it still further into four.[14] The Protectionists were as far apart from the Peelites, and the Peelites were as far apart from the Whigs as they had been before; while the Whigs were estranged from the 'shoals' of out-and-out free traders, rabid economists, and fanatical dissenters who comprised the new Radical party.[15] Graham thought all rules for calculating numbers were at an end.[16] Lord John spoke of a gain of 52 seats, but told the Queen that he could not command a regular party majority. However, by lumping the Peelites with the Whigs, he thought he could count upon 395 supporters of moderate progress. This meant that the government would be strong enough to resist both a reaction against free trade, and a democratic movement against the church and aristocracy. There was no reason why the parliament should not last five years, and there was no reason, therefore, why members should stand 'in servile awe of their constituents'.[17] Two years later Lord John wrote that the Protectionists exceeded 200, that the Radicals could usually muster 80 to 86 votes, and that 'the number who do not go to any extreme are thus about 360'.[18]

Nowhere were the results of the election more difficult to interpret than in Ireland, and Lord John could not fit the Irish elections into any system 'Linnaean or Natural'.[19] There were 29 Whigs, 23 Whig Repealers, 10 Repealers, 2 Tory Repealers, 1 Young Ireland, 8 Peelites, and 32 Protectionists.[20] The growth of the repeal movement did not pass unnoticed in England, and Lord John probably expressed the general feeling when he said that 'the Irish seem always to act in the manner most opposite to that which is usual in other countries. The expenditure of ten millions to save the People from starving has thus raised a bitter spirit of hostility . . .'[21] He realised that the demand to establish Ireland as a separate nation could not be dismissed as the 'mere ravings of a distempered fancy',[22] and had O'Connell lived, he thought there would have been 70 Repealers.[23] But Young Ireland, which he admitted, had the great merit of speaking 'openly and undisguisedly',[24] had made no headway, and he still hoped that within a few years the repeal cry would die away altogether.[25]

The full consequences of Peel's actions could now be seen. Parties derive their cohesion from each other, and with the

Conservative party in ruins why should the Liberals keep their ranks? In these circumstances Lord John was not left without good advice. Fortescue thought that, on balance, the result was favourable:

> difficult as it will certainly be to unite the support of all the jarring elements composing the *liberal* party, it will I suspect be even more difficult to bring together Protectionists, Peelers and Radicals into any efficient combination against Your Government.[26]

Fitzwilliam thought that if Lord John would only 'hold rather higher language' to the house of commons all would be well.[27] C. R. Fox advised Lord John to let the members for '*wide awake* constituencies' 'know a little before hand what is to be done'.[28] The Duke of Bedford urged his brother to insist on his colleagues 'having their measures better prepared'.[29] Every man had his own answer, and Wood was right when he said that getting a good majority had a lot to do with the success of measures.[30] The difficulty in this parliament would often lie in persuading the government's nominal supporters to vote at all.

Graham, with his oft-remarked capacity for looking on the dark side, was worried lest the house of commons lose public respect from the sheer difficulty of getting government business through.[31] That did not mean, however, that he and his friends had any intention of helping the Whigs. The Duke of Bedford warned Lord John that Lincoln would be on the watch for bills that were ill-prepared, and that he and his fellow Peelites were waiting to attack the government as bad workmen.[32] Then, as Wood said, there will be Peel and his party 'ready to avail themselves of the opportunity, and to say again "we are the only people to do business" '. Wood thought that if Peel came back into office again, it would be 'as the unquestioned head of our side of the House',[33] and Lord John himself knew that if the Queen and the Prince had their way, the Peel party would be called 'to the entire direction of affairs'.[34]

While Lord John was allowing these apprehensions to undermine his morale, a new crisis was arising of a kind likely to show him off, however unfairly, to disadvantage with respect to Peel. Peel's reign ended in a mania of railway speculation. Lord John took an interest in the various schemes that were suggested for stopping it, and both in 1846 and in 1847 he was attracted to the notion of limiting the amount of capital which could be applied to railways in any one year.[35] But from the banker Loyd in 1846, and from Wood in 1847, came the verdict that any interference would be undesirable.[36] The alternative was to put all the railway bills for the year in a single act to be passed at the end of the session.[37] No line would then be voted on until all the bids for the current year were on the table. This would have helped parliament to construct an order of priority. The proposal won no support, schemes continued to be introduced and voted on pell mell, and by 1847, under the existing railway legislation, which required a deposit of 5 per cent on every scheme to be paid in bank notes into chancery, between £11m and £12m had been withdrawn from the currency.[38] At the same time, capital was running out of the country to finance new railways overseas.

There were signs of trouble, then, even before the disastrous harvest of 1846. The release of corn in bond, under the act to repeal the corn laws, kept the price of corn down to 60s in 1846. Thereafter prices rose, and before the end of May 1847 wheat was being sold at over 100s. The British merchants on whom the government relied to solve the famine in Ireland, responded all too successfully. They sent for corn from Odessa, and they sent for corn from New Orleans, and in the first half of 1847 gold drained out of the country to pay for these costly imports. At this point Peel's bank act of 1844 failed. Peel intended it to act as a regulator, automatically. As gold went out of the country, notes were to be withdrawn from circulation, prices were to fall, British goods become more competitive overseas, and gold return. But Peel had not taken sufficient account of the ingenuity of man to manufacture credit. 'The Manchester and other banks (including that of Jones Loyd and Co.) completely evaded the limitation to the circulation of Bank notes; by putting into circulation their own notes, in the shape of three months Bills.'[39] Simultaneously the Bank of England, having been encouraged by the act of 1844 to compete in the discount market, used its power not in the national interest, to raise the discount rate and to restrict speculation, but to scoop up business. The reserves fell rapidly until April, when the market rate for bills was seven per cent, and the Bank reluctantly went up to five. Belated and half-hearted as it was, this restriction of credit stopped the drain of gold and restored confidence – for the time being.

It was not for long. In August there was a bumper corn harvest. Wheat fell to 50s, and the corn importers, who had patriotically responded to the famine by importing all they could at no matter what price, were ruined. In September the panic spread to the East and West India houses, in October to the banks themselves. Finally it reached the symbols of financial purity, the Scottish banks. Jones Loyd came to the government to say the mischief must be stopped. If Littledales in Liverpool went, every East India house would follow, while the collapse of 'the great bank at Glasgow' (which had liabilities of £6m and only £300,000 to £400,000 to meet them) would bring down the whole of Scotland.[40] A deputation from Liverpool waited on the prime minister and the chancellor of the exchequer. They were amazed at the questions asked by Lord John, and by his 'total want of knowledge of the operations of trade'. Wood, on the other hand, was 'sharp as a needle'.[41] Sharp he may have been, but when the cabinet met on 21 October he advised them that things were mending, and the next day they agreed to disband, because frequent meetings added to the panic.[42] They were too late to ride the crisis out by a display of cool nerves. When trading ended for the day on Saturday 23 October, there was only £1,547,000 in notes and £447,000 in coin left in the banking reserve of the Bank of England. The Bank told Lord John that when trading began again on Monday it must contract its advances.

Thus far Lord John seems to have taken the view that the crisis was weeding out the houses which had been badly conducted.[43] He was now compelled to recognise that 'the prospect of . . . multitudes thrown out of work at the beginning of winter' was too appalling to contemplate.[44] He and Wood at last decided to write to the directors of the Bank encouraging them to break the law of 1844, and to accommodate anyone who really needed credit by 'an unrestricted issue of bank notes at 8 per cent interest'.[45] While Wood called on Peel, who gave his opinion 'as if he were a colleague',[46] Lord John was busy writing to the Queen that he thought the named rate of interest was the point most likely to be attacked. 'The motive however is a very strong one . . . The Bank Directors might otherwise fix the rate of interest so low, as to endanger the currency, and prevent the return of gold.'[47] Prince Albert, who had spent the last week sending Lord John cuttings from the *Economist*,[48] completely misunderstood Lord John's letter, and thought the Bank was 'to issue paper against gold paying 8 p. ct. for it'. He then sent for Peel. 'On my observing that Ld John's explanation had not been very clear Sir R. thought this not unlikely, as in fact Lord John did not understand these money matters thoroughly.'[49] Peel passed the rest of the week-end writing a memorandum for the Prince on the working of the 1844 Act, while the cabinet met to endorse their chief's letter advising the Bank to break it. The Prince forwarded Peel's memo to Lord John, who kept it for a day, and then returned it with an encomium on its clarity.[50] For his part, Lord John sent the Prince a copy of the letter of 25 October to the Bank: but he drily sent no accompanying explanation, and suggested the Prince show it to Peel, who 'will explain more clearly than I can do by letter'.[51]

On 28 October Wood still thought the Glasgow bank was going,[52] but in fact the letter signed by Lord John and Charles Wood worked like magic. Hoarding of notes stopped at once, and the Bank never did have to break the law. But a government which had encouraged it to do so must summon parliament at once to ask for an act of indemnity. The question then arose whether to modify the act of 1844, or to refer the investigation of the whole crisis to a select committee. Wood could get no sense out of Peel,[53] and when the cabinet met, George Grey proposed a committee. 'Russell for the first time since the formation of his government, took a paper and asked our opinions seriatim, and marked down our names. We all agreed with G. Grey.'[54] When the new parliament assembled in the middle of November the Protectionists tried to widen the issue, and put Peel's free trade policy in the dock, but the government confined the issue to Peel's bank act, the matter was referred to select committees of each house, and there, in a life of Lord John, we may leave it.

The financial crisis of 1847 had cast a long shadow over the cabinet's discussions of future measures for Ireland. The public works were due to come to an end on 15 August, and the soup kitchens on 1 October. In February 1847 Lord John reminded

FIG. 4   DOMBEY AND SON   *Punch* 1847

(Lord John Russell   Peel)

Mr Dombey was in a difficulty. He would have liked to give him (the boy) some explanation involving the terms circulating-medium, currency, depreciation of currency, paper, bullion, rates of exchange, value of precious metals in the market, and so forth.

Bessborough that England could not go on advancing £12m p.a.,[55] and Bessborough agreed that the people were beginning to think they were to be provided for, and must be disillusioned.[56] In April Wood warned that 'bad money times' were coming, and that 'a second loan to be spent upon Irish paupers will not be so easily raised'.[57] In July, before the crisis grew worse again, Lord John wrote to Clarendon that his plan for next year was to 'give very little for relief, and much for permanent improvement',[58] and that he hoped to supply funds to the colonies to enable them to employ immigrants upon public works from the moment of their arrival.[59] But thereafter, as things became worse, Lord John was obliged to tell Clarendon that the falling off in the revenue 'deranges all my views of being able to help Ireland', and to warn him not to be surprised if Downing Street had 'no heart'.[60]

In July Lord John recognised that they had an awful winter before them,[61] and he drew the attention of the cabinet to the fact that in the South and West of Ireland 'there are huge masses of population without any capital in the hands of landowners, farmers, or themselves sufficient to maintain them'. Notwithstanding, he concluded that aid should be confined to donations in aid of subscriptions, and to keeping depots on the West coast.[62] The Irish were to be thrown upon the new poor law and to be supported by rates. Even in 1847 the crops in Ireland were worth about £40m. 'The landlords and tenants wish to divide this sum among them, and to charge the poor on the tea and sugar taxes of the English and Scotch.'[63] This must be resisted, and where the land could not at present support the people and pay rent,

> rent should be sacrificed. Proprietors and their tenants have raised up, encouraged, and grown rich upon a potato fed population. Now that the question is between rent, and sustenance, I think rent must give way, and the whole rental if necessary, given to support the people.[64]

Lord John believed that if the government stuck to this line sufficient rates could be levied in three parts of Ireland. In the fourth part, where 'there must be much misery',[65] the primary responsibility was still to fall upon the landlords. 'It is not enough to say that a landlord has no rent for 1847, while between 1836 and 1846 he received £10,000 a year, and has the means of borrowing for 1847-48'.[66] The government would give a little relief to insolvent unions, but that was all.

Clarendon could scarcely believe Lord John meant what he said. In August he wrote praising the relief given the year before, and added casually that there would still be 1m or 1½m Irish to provide for this winter.[67] In October, just as the financial crisis reached its peak, he wrote that whatever the state of trade or credit '*Ireland cannot be left to her own resources*',[68] and he challenged Lord John to consider whether he dare announce that 'in certain districts . . . deaths by starvation are daily taking place, but that the Govt has no measure of relief to propose?'[69] Finally, he became angry and sarcastic: 'I know that we can't get on without further aid, not because men who won't till the ground, and won't cut turf don't deserve to starve, but because the Govt *cannot allow above a certain number to do so*'.[70] Ireland could no more get on unaided than it could fly into the air.[71]

Clarendon's sarcasm did no good to him or to the Irish. The potato had failed, and the government had provided a poor law.[72] Most of the guardians had money, and where they did not it was the fault of the Irish. In 1847-8, as in 1846-7 Lord John denied that the government allowed the Irish to starve. The question was

> should rent be paid as before, and . . . three millions starve? Or, part of the remaining produce support the 3 millions leaving rent either unpaid or diminished? The landlords wished for the first course – the Govt took the second.[73]

Wood, in turn, said that starvation arose from the misconduct of the Irish officers and guardians on the spot.[74] He and Lord John have not had a good press. The world saw a million human beings starving, not in Ireland – one of the most impoverished countries in Europe, but in the United Kingdom, which was the richest country in the world. As Grattan said, 'mankind in future ages would never believe that, with £53,000,000 of money annually in the English Exchequer, that country could not save the dying Irishman'.[75] It is difficult not to agree with him.

When every allowance has been made for the difficulty of squeezing money out of that parliament, and for that purpose, it is impossible not to recognise that behind the refusal to try lay something stronger even than Lord John's dislike of Irish landlords – a Malthusian fear about the long-term effects of relief. In October 1846 Lord John wrote to Grey that 'we all know that if the Irish are not socially improved the vacuum caused by Emigration will be speedily filled'.[76] In his cabinet memorandum of July 1847 he spoke of the risk of 'dragging the better classes into the same abyss of misery with the lower',[77] and in May 1849 he specifically asked Clarendon whether 'pauperism was advancing on capital?'[78] Clarendon himself admitted that doling out food merely to keep the people alive would do nobody any permanent good,[79] and Morpeth agreed that money would do 'no lasting good'.[80] The Irish were the victims of deep fears engendered by doctrine.

As the famine took hold, in the winter of 1846–7, landlords began to evict their cottiers, and there were rumours that the Irish were arming. In December 1846 Lord John asked Bessborough whether they were arming for any purpose.[81] Bessborough thought not, and was determined to do without an arms act if he could.[82] Eight months later, when the cabinet decided to bring the relief works to an end, disaffection became a certainty and insurrection a possibility. The continuation of law and order in Ireland would now depend upon the attitude of the priests. But the Irish hierarchy was hostile to the British government, and the question naturally arose whether the British government could go over their heads and appeal successfully to the Pope. Hitherto the court of St James had not been represented at the Vatican. But Lord John's return to power succeeded the election of Pius IX, and as early as 30 July 1846 Palmerston was busy wondering how a Whig government could encourage a Liberal Pope.[83]

Palmerston concluded that the thing to do was to try and establish diplomatic relations, and in the meantime to use British influence to discourage Austria from invading the Pope's dominions. Negotiations with the Vatican were carried on through the British ambassador in Vienna, and towards the end of March 1847 Ponsonby reported that he had arranged for the Pope to encourage the Irish to be peaceful, and 'to confide in the good intentions of the Queen's government to succour and protect them'.[84] As the situation in Ireland worsened the government decided to send a special mission to Rome. With his love of Italy, and his confidence – not to say vanity – in his own powers as a diplomat, Minto was an obvious choice.

Lord John did not hope for much from the Pope, and he was worried, as he told Minto, lest the Pope 'suppose that we are in such need of his assistance that we have sent you to Rome for that purpose'.[85] But he did hope for 'authentic means of refuting the lies by which the Irish malcontents seek to turn the Papal authority against us',[86] and he hoped that Minto would be able to break the deadlock over Peel's Irish colleges.[87] Minto was instructed to assure the Pope that the British government disapproved 'of the movement for Italian Unity ... whether ... kingdom or republic';[88] to warn the Italian patriots that unless they went slowly, they would 'give Metternich an occasion for driving back reform for another ten years'; and to convince the Italian sovereigns 'that their only safety consists in the boldness with which they institute useful sound reforms'.[89] Minto's mission was three-sided, and it was not incompatible with a genuine concern for the future of Italy. But it is difficult to rid one's mind of the suspicion that Lord John and Palmerston compromised themselves in their anxiety to install an ambassador in the Vatican who could tell the Pope

> that he is misled by the mischievous party in Ireland – that they aim at rebellion and separation. That we do not object to any measures he may take to secure his own faith, but that he ought to discountenance the seditious and rebellious harangues of priests. He ought to feel that we are his friends.[90]

Minto had not been away long before Clarendon reported that 'Irish' crimes were increasing. Homicides were up from 68 in 1846 to 98 in 1847; firings at the person from 55 to 136; and firings into dwellings from 51 to 116.[91] The autumn of 1847 brought a wave of assassinations which made a deep impression on the British public. Major Mahon was a harsh landlord, who had sent 900 of his tenants overseas, 300 of whom perished in one vessel.[92] But, as Clarendon reported, 'Two Sundays before Major Mahon was murdered he was denounced from the altar, called *worse than a Cromwell*, and yet said the Priest *this man lives*'.[93] The moral was obvious and the danger acute.

The reactions of the different members of the administration could have been predicted. Palmerston thought there would soon be an end to the trouble if a priest were hanged every time a landlord was shot.[94] Clarendon sent over an arms bill and a prevention of crimes bill according to which localities were to be made to pay for their crimes, and the lord lieutenant was to be given a discretionary power to impose heavier fines for the murder of a good landlord than for the murder of a bad one.[95] Lord John did not like arms bills, and he did not want to start a new parliament with one. His immediate reaction was that the evils of Ireland could not be eradicated by coercion or they would have disappeared long ago.[96] He admitted that things had reached the point where the multitudes considered the landlords as enemies to be shot, the priests denounced them as heretics to be cursed, and the assassin having public opinion and religion in his favour, had no remorse.[97] But this enmity arose from the mischievous custom of growing paupers and potatoes in the same soil, and from the violent means taken by the landlords to extirpate the evil.

> It is quite true that landlords in England would not like to be shot like hares and partridges. But neither does any landlord in England turn out fifty persons at once, and burn their houses over their heads, giving them no provision for the future. The murders are atrocious, so are the ejectments. The truth is that civil war between landlords and tenants has been raging for 80 years . . .[98]

Sir George Grey sympathised with Lord John,[99] and Clarendon then became nearly hysterical. On 15 November he said he was convinced there was a systematic plan to shoot landlords that winter; on 17 November he demanded to know how Lord John could maintain an arms bill was not necessary when 300,000 firearms were in the hands of the most ferocious people in Europe who were starving; on 18 November he threatened to resign; and on 19 November he claimed to have information that lists were in circulation with the names of the landlords to be shot.[100]

Lord John then had no alternative but to take the whole case before the cabinet, where Palmerston took Clarendon's part:[101] Irish rents were low, the country was full of 'ferocious blood thirsty Ruffians', and landlords were being told that they must give up their property to their tenants.[102] Lord John countered by saying there was nothing new about the present atrocities, and adjourned the cabinet for two days. When it met again Lansdowne said they must legislate, Grey said tenants must be made to pay rent even if they had to be stripped to the skin, and a majority 'thought the outrages had assumed a new form'[103] and voted to go on with Clarendon's bills. All Lord John could do was to mutter that 'if stringent laws are required, they must bear on both sides in the contest',[104] and to tell the cabinet that unless reform accompanied coercion, he would resign.

This brings us to the long-term remedial measures for 1848. The original proposal for a landlord and tenant bill came from Clarendon, and it was unfortunate that right from the beginning there was a difference of opinion between him and Lord John. Clarendon wanted a bill to secure compensation for improvements. Lord John was interested in security of tenure, or Ulster tenant right.[105] Clarendon objected to Ulster tenant right as a mischievous invasion of the rights of property,[106] and when Lord John tried the subject out on the cabinet, they were all against it.[107] Clarendon then sent over his compensation bill, which was prospective but compulsory.[108] Lansdowne at once objected to making the landlord responsible for any improvements to which he had not given a previous assent,[109] and when the bill came before the cabinet, nobody spoke up in its support except Clanricarde.[110] The cabinet amended the bill to make it voluntary – that is to say, parties making contracts could decide whether to put themselves under the provisions of the act or not:[111] it was, as Lord John wrote to Clarendon, all they could think just to the landlord.[112] Clarendon replied that he would rather have no bill than that bill.[113] Lord John himself doubted whether any compensation bill could help the cottiers – 'you might as well propose that a landlord should compensate the rabbits for the burrows they have made on his land'[114] – and the landlord could still say, 'if you use this bill against me I will turn you out'.[115] What was wanted was to stop the evictions. It was at this point that the cabinet agreed to Clarendon's request for a coercion bill, and Lord John demanded measures bearing on both sides in the contest. To show what he meant, he drew up a new bill to interpose a judicial authority between landlord and tenant in every case of ejectment.[116] His idea was that where rent had been paid, or there was not more than one year's rent in arrear, ejectment could be stayed. He and George Grey then agreed to make it apply to existing leases.[117]

Simultaneously the cabinet was discussing a bill to facilitate the sale of encumbered estates. Distressed landlords obstructed that sovereign remedy for Irish society, the Irish poor law, and even a cabinet of landowners recognised that the difficulty of unravelling Irish mortgages was now so great that prospective purchasers were put off, and there was no free market in land. Clarendon was apprehensive about the consequences of throwing half the property of Ireland onto the market at the same time.[118] Lord John agreed that the sales might go on too quickly, but believed the risk was worth running for the sake of the ultimate object, which was to substitute solvent catholic merchants and tradesmen for embarrassed protestant noblemen. The encumbered estates bill would recreate 'the natural order' of landlord and priest in alliance.

> This is a very serious change. The new proprietors will not be separated from the clergy and the people by religion and habits: but they will not be united to the Govt. by the feeling that English connexion is their only security. We ought not therefore to adopt this change, without looking forward to the ultimate consequences – the Roman Catholic Church united with the State and the displacement of 'one stratum in the social hierarchy' of Ireland – viz. the Protestant gentry.[119]

For just one moment, then, in the late autumn of 1847 light shone through the gloom over Ireland. Parliament was going to be summoned early to pass an indemnity act for the Queen's servants and a coercion act for Ireland, but with the prime minister insisting on a genuine landlord and tenant bill, and with an encumbered estates bill on the stocks, it looked as though Lord John might be able to secure something for Ireland from the famine after all.

At this point public attention was switched from the meeting of parliament to the appointment of Hampden as bishop of Hereford. Stockmar once said that 'as strongly as Lord John *can feel* he does upon this *matter*' of church appointments.[120] With his affection for the reformed church and his antipathy to the Tractarians, Lord John looked for learning, a Liberal vote in the house of lords, and a willingness to promote the cause of public education. His first recommendation was of Dr Graham, whom he described to the Queen as a scholar and a man of science.[121] His first appointment, which was to the see of Sodor and Man, was of the Rev. Robert Eden, who had been 'very active and useful in the cause of education at Battersea, where a training school is established'.[122] The next see to come Lord John's way was his own creation of Manchester, and it was then that he first considered the name of Dr Hampden. Hampden was a man of latitudinarian views that would not have caused offence in the eighteenth century, and even in 1832 his Bampton lectures passed without notice. But in 1836 when Melbourne appointed him to the regius chair of divinity at Oxford, Newman and Pusey persuaded the university to condemn him.

The university's action caused Melbourne to tread the path of prudence. The professor was not further promoted to be a bishop, and at that time Lord John agreed with Melbourne that 'Any scandal, such as a Memorial from the Clergy is to be avoided, and . . . Hampden may as well remain where he is'.[123] In 1846 Lansdowne called Lord John's attention to Hampden's claims for preferment.[124] Next year Hampden himself solicited a bishopric on the ground that he had been persecuted by a party 'then but little known . . . but whose views and intentions have since been fully developed'.[125] Lord John must have hoped he had earned some credit with the church by establishing the new bishopric. Even so, he still proceeded cautiously, and wrote to the archbishop of Canterbury, who assured him that in the ten years Hampden had been a professor he had seen 'no reason to believe that he has taught from the Chair any doctrine at variance with the articles of our Church'.[126] Lord John then considered an alternative candidate, Lee, the headmaster of King Edward's School, Birmingham. Morpeth said his father favoured Hampden, but George Grey, who thought both men suitable for bishops, thought Lee would be the better among an industrial population, and Lord John chose Lee.[127]

The announcement was greeted with an accusation of insobriety, which Lord John was obliged to ask Lee to refute before he could be consecrated. This was undignified, but the charge was false and the refutation easy. Then, on 5 November the archbishop of York died. Lord John wrote to Lansdowne that he did not find it easy to make another one.

> The B. of Durham has declined by anticipation. The A. of Canterbury writes to me in favour of the bishop of Lincoln. You know more of him than I do – I fear he is timid, and shabby – but a gentleman and only occasionally a bigot.

Whoever was chosen for promotion, 'at all events Hampden must be the new Bishop'.[128] Finally, Lord John selected Musgrave, the bishop of Hereford, for York. He 'has the merit of judgement, integrity and Whig politics. A Whig Archbishop will be a novelty'.[129] As for Hampden,

> The Archbishop of Canterbury says he thinks it right to warn me that the appointment of Hampden will occasion an outcry, but he thinks it will be unjust, as for the last 12 years his writings have been without reproach on the score of Orthodoxy.[130]

In subsequent correspondence, the archbishop thought that 'explosion' was the word he had used,[131] and the Duke of Bedford said his brother 'had not the least notion of the opposition that would be made to Hampden'.[132] They may both have been right, for there was no precedent for what followed. Thirteen bishops led by the bishop of London protested, and the bishop of Oxford, Samuel Wilberforce, incited three of his clergy to put Hampden on trial for heresy in the court of arches.

Nobody cuts a good figure in a quarrel, and Lord John can be blamed for having thought too highly of Hampden in the first place, for his erroneous supposition that the outcry came entirely from 'that portion of the Clergy who share Mr Newman's opinions, but have not had the honesty to follow Mr Newman in his change of profession',[133] for the liberty he took in subsequently quoting the archbishop of Canterbury in his support, and for the unconciliatory manner in which he conducted the controversy. Macaulay was right, 'Pugna est de paupere regno'.[134] But there was something noble about Lord John's refusal to 'sacrifice the reputation of Dr Hampden, the rights of the Crown', and what he believed to be 'the true interests of the Church' to a ban imposed eleven years earlier by the university of Oxford,[135] and it would be a mistake to suppose that Lord John came out of the incident any worse than his opponents.

From the beginning Lord John's enemies displayed such a disposition to believe that he had only made the appointment in order to shock the church,[136] that Prince Albert credited a rumour that the whole agitation had been prepared for Lee and switched to Hampden at the last moment.[137] The only bishop who took the trouble to read the Bampton lectures refused to sign the letter of protest. As for Samuel Wilberforce, having got up a prosecution which he pretended would provide Hampden with a welcome opportunity to clear his name, he offered himself as a 'peacemaker' because he was not a 'partisan',[138] and then from fear of royal displeasure withdrew the prosecution. All Hampden's enemies achieved was that Parker, the bookseller at Oxford, who had ordered 1000 copies of Hampden's lectures, and had hitherto sold only 150, quickly sold every copy.[139] Palmerston summed the whole episode up, when he wrote to Lord John that when it was all over 'the State may be none the worse for the misconduct of the church'.[140]

But first, fanaticism must run its course. While the bishop of Exeter took Lord John tendentiously through his answer to the bishops' protest, the dean of Hereford postponed the election by the cathedral chapter, and, braving the penalties of *praemunire*, announced his intention of voting against the nomination. Lord John thereupon wrote one of his shortest letters. 'Sir, I have had the honour to receive your letter of the 22nd inst., in which you intimate to me your intention of violating the law.'[141] By this time the betting was two to one on Lord John against the whole field of bishops,[142] and when the chapter met on 28 December, Hampden was elected by a majority of votes. But even that was not the end of the matter. Dr Phillimore applied for a writ of *mandamus* to compel the archbishop of Canterbury to hear the objections against Dr Hampden, and in the meantime Dr Hampden's consecration had to be postponed. It was not until 1 February 1848 that the *mandamus* was refused, and on 11 February the archbishop, whose conduct had been exemplary throughout, died, leaving Dr Hampden unconsecrated.

As Lord John said, it will be difficult to find another archbishop 'who is so good and mild and charitable a Christian'.[143] That was not the only difficulty. Lord John must also find an archbishop willing to consecrate Dr Hampden. By the time the thirteen bishops who had protested against his appointment had been eliminated there was not much choice. The Duke of Bedford and the bishop of Durham agreed that Sumner, the bishop of Chester, would be best.[144] It was he who had read the Bampton lectures and refused to sign the protest:[145] he who had informed the bishop of Durham that the outcry against Hampden was unfair.[146] Sumner would be 'gall to the Tractarians' but he was 'not disposed to place one party in the church in power over the rest',[147] and he promised to be impartial.[148]

Lord John was scarcely out of this hornets' nest before the new parliament escaped his control. When parliament met in November 1847, the act of indemnity was a formality. The house of commons then turned to the crime and outrage bill for Ireland. Inevitably the Whigs were criticised for bringing in a coercion bill after throwing Peel out for trying to pass one in 1846. But the circumstances were worse and the bill was not so bad. As Sir George Grey said, it would be a crime to carry arms about, not to possess them, and nobody was to be transported for being caught out at night.[149] Justices and constables were to have the power to call out all males between the ages of sixteen and sixty to hunt for a murderer, and refusal to turn out was to be a punishable offence. The debate was enlivened by O'Connor, who quoted Lord John's book on the constitution to the effect that repression defeats its own object. [150] But J. O'Connell admitted he had anticipated something much more severe,[151] and the bill passed through all its stages before Christmas.

Lord John was left rueing the ease with which parliament could be persuaded to pass a coercion act, and contrasting it with the difficulties he encountered over every measure of permanent improvement for Ireland. Each of the three measures for 1848 came to a bad end. Following the Minto mission, the government's bill to establish diplomatic relations with Rome placed no restriction upon the Pope's choice of representative. The bill was welcomed by English roman catholics, and denounced by the Irish hierarchy. It passed into law but not without an amendment, introduced by Eglinton, restricting the Pope's choice to a layman. The Pope refused to accept this, and the act remained a dead letter.

When the cabinet met to consider the new landlord and

tenant bill drafted by Lord John and George Grey, the prime
minister was ill, and his colleagues 'ran riot' in his absence.[152]
The cabinet condemned compulsory arbitration, while Lansdowne, who did not object to this, concentrated his fire on the
proposal to make the bill retrospective.[153] Two weeks later,
when Lord John was back in harness, he handled the situation
with good humour; 'no doubt the bill was meant to be a boon
to tenants not to landlords . . . it was against all principle, and
there was no use in attempting to make it conform to principle'.[154] The cabinet gave a cheer and a laugh, and the teeth
were put back in the bill, which was introduced into the commons. But it was not long before Lord John spotted a new
danger. The bill contained provisions bearing stringently upon
both landlords and tenants: the first could not be carried, and
the second would be carried all too easily. Clarendon had
warned him all along that any attempt at taking up security of
tenure would fail because the English landowners would think
their turn was coming next,[155] and Lord John was not sorry to
see the bill end up in a select committee, where, as he said
lamely, the subject at least got an airing.[156]

The encumbered estates bill was as large as Cottenham could
be induced to make it.[157] The owner himself, or the first encumbrancer, or any encumbrancer who held the deeds of an
estate, could put it into the Irish court of chancery. The estate
would then be sold up, the proceeds divided among those with
claims upon it, and any balance paid over to the former owner.
The new owner was to receive an indefeasible parliamentary
title to the land.[158] The bill passed, and in July Normanby congratulated Lord John on salvaging it from the storms of the
session. He had 'always said' that such an act was needed.[159]
Alas, praise was premature: the act proved unworkable because
the Irish court of chancery was incompetent, and the whole
thing had to be done again next year. All in all, the government's long-term legislation for Ireland in 1848 fell far short of
what Lord John had insisted upon as the price of his agreement
to a coercion act.

For much of the session of 1848, however, finance took precedence over Ireland. The problems were so serious that when
parliament reassembled in February Lord John brought in the
budget himself. In 1847 the money for relieving the Irish had

been raised by borrowing, and immediately before a general election this was probably the only way the government could have obtained it. Now any deficiency in the revenue must be met by increased taxes. In 1847–8 the country was in the grip of a panic about French armaments and the construction of steamers at Cherbourg. Lord John was not immune from these fears, and in November he read the cabinet a draft paragraph from the Queen's speech about the need to improve the defences: 'there was a general shriek of laughter, and he laughed himself and gave it up'.[160] But early in the new year, Palmerston threatened to resign unless something were done,[161] and the cabinet agreed to increase the navy estimates and to do something about the militia (though nobody knew what).

In round figures receipts for the past year were £1m less than expected, and expenditure was £2m more. In the coming year expenditure would be £3m more than the yield from the existing taxes. Lord John proposed, therefore, to continue the income tax for five years after it ran out in 1849, and to raise it from 7d to 1s immediately and for the next two years. His speech was clear, but 'perhaps not over judicious in presenting certainly all the dark hues of the picture, and dwelling on the military topics',[162] and his announcement was met by a storm of protest from the country. The Duke of Bedford forwarded a letter comparing Lord John to Napoleon, and his speech to the drum that roused the soldiers to arms the night before Waterloo.[163] A few days later Lord John told the Queen that the Protectionists reckoned upon being able to combine with the Radicals to throw the government out.[164] There could be little doubt if that happened whom the Queen would send for; Stanley first, perhaps, but then Peel. The Queen would then ask Lord John to lend Peel his supporters. Lord John panicked, and invited the cabinet to abandon the proposals he had just made. When he put the question, most of them, as Hobhouse records, reluctantly assented:

> Labouchere was very much against giving way. Ld Lansdowne was for the 5% for one year, but gave way. So was Clanricarde. So was I . . . but Lord John said 'we cannot carry it' which settled the matter. Charles Wood . . . gave way like the rest.[165]

The upshot was that ten days after Lord John introduced one

budget, Wood introduced a second. The house now learnt that the existing taxes would suffice, and that the income tax need only be continued for three years. The only excuse Wood made was that in the meantime with the departure of Louis Philippe the danger of French invasion was over, and that could not disguise the fact that the government had lost their nerve upon the first appearance of the enemy, and run away. Thereafter there was to be no peace in that parliament. The Radicals set themselves up as a separate party, and Cobden joined them. Horsman proposed an amendment to equalise the burden of taxes upon the different kinds of property, Sir B. Hall moved to apply the income tax to Ireland, and Hume moved to grant the income tax for one year only. In opposing Hume's motion Lord John recovered some of the authority he had lost. He placed himself as refusing to give way to either Protectionists or Radicals, and as Greville said gave 'the concern an immense lift'.[166] Tufnell told Lord John that 'Up to the last moment there was a large *floating* balance of Votes, great part of which was turned over to our side of the account by your speech'.[167] Sir George Grey confirmed this, and wrote to Clarendon that he had never heard Lord John speak better.[168] A few days later he brought along Clarendon's reply, praising Lord John's speech, and read it to the cabinet. 'Ld. John Russell put the newspapers before his face. Though not indifferent to praise he is "modest as a maid" in that respect.'[169]

The Whigs' financial troubles did not end with the success of their rearguard action to save the income tax. Bentinck drew attention to the plight of the planters in the West Indies, and asked for a select committee on the sugar duties, as a bridge of retreat for ministers from the 'final' solution of 1846. In addition to recommending the invasion of Cuba, he proposed an increased duty of 10s a cwt on foreign sugar.[170] Ministers agreed to the committee, but pointed out how both consumption and revenue had already increased. In 1845 consumption was 244,000 tons: in 1847 (despite the financial crisis) it was 290,700 tons. Revenue was up from £3,743,362 in 1845 to £4,596,696 in 1847, and Lord John announced that he would not increase the duties on foreign sugar, but that he would decrease those on colonial sugar still further, and lengthen the period allowed till complete equalisation until 1854.

It was an ingenious riposte, but even so there were doubts as to its success. Tufnell expected to be beat,[171] and Lord John feared the Irish might vote as a bloc against the government, and warned the Queen that he would have to resign if he were defeated.[172] The vote of 260 to 245 was, as his brother pointed out, 'close shaving'.[173] Peel voted for the government, but Lord John observed that he took only Graham and three other Peelites with him.[174] The ministry was probably saved by abstentions among the Protectionists, who made fun of the revised duties as budget number three, and the amended final settlement did not become law without a celebrated clash between Bentinck and Lord John. Bentinck alleged the colonial office had withheld information from the select committee. Lord John accused Bentinck of the morals of the turf, and Disraeli crushingly capped this with a reference to 'the Chairman of the meeting held to compliment Ld. George upon the successful issue of his Turf investigations, who was the Duke of Bedford'.[175] A lamentable year's housekeeping came to its predictable end in August, when Wood announced that in order to keep in balance the government would have to borrow £2m. That was budget number four.

The Radicals' attack on the income tax left no doubt who was now represented in parliament, and it had scarcely begun before the chartists gave another reminder of who was not. Previous outbreaks of chartism had occurred after a general election followed by a depression in trade, and trouble was to be expected in 1848. The chartism of 1848 was a less dangerous movement than that of 1838–9 and that of 1842. But there were features about it which gave the government a different impression: revolutions were taking place all over Europe, chartism at last reached the English capital, and for the first time there was evidence that the chartists were in touch with revolutionary leaders abroad. The situation was in some ways more like 1792 than 1838–9, and as one of its precautions the government passed an aliens act.

The demonstrations began in March and were still going on in June, but they reached their height in April when Lady John was in the last stages of pregnancy. It was a mercy for the country that the man the chartists had to deal with was calm George Grey. In March when windows and lamps were broken in Trafalgar Square, he thought the offenders were 'chiefly lads'. Then, when tricolor cockades were worn at a meeting on Clerkenwell Green, and the speakers expressed an intention of raiding the gunsmiths for arms, he wrote, 'this is very disagreeable and troublesome, but I hope it will go no further'.[176] But it did, and the chartists arranged for a monster meeting to assemble on Kennington Common on 10 April and march on the houses of parliament. The government made its own preparations quietly: Lord John reported that many building workers refused to be sworn as special constables,[177] but the shopkeepers were sound, and there could be little doubt, as Trevelyan infelicitously put it, that the middle classes could keep the chartists down.[178] Wellington attended the cabinet and assured them he could stop the procession wherever they chose.[179]

On 9 April Morpeth still expected some loss of life the next day.[180] But the troops were loyal, and when the roman catholic soldiers asked their priests if they were to fire on the crowd, they were told to do their duty as soldiers.[181] That evening Sir George Grey heard that the chartist leaders were frightened. The police urged them to call off the meeting. But

> Jones thought this impossible, saying the leaders would gladly do so, but that the people could not be controlled. He went on however to say that if the meeting was allowed to take place, and some sort of demonstration to be made on condition that the procession shd not come near the H. of Commons, he thought the people would be satisfied, and that the affair might pass off quietly.

No wonder, then, that Sir George Grey expected 'a quiet termination to this business'.[182] The only question was whether the chartists could acquire a few martyrs. Lord John told the Prince that 'any loss of life will cause a deep and rankling resentment',[183] and Wellington promised to leave 'plenty of room for the chartists to run away'.[184] When the day came, Lord John's windows were blocked up with blue books,[185] and he had a posse of constables in the house.[186] The meeting on Kennington Common numbered (according to the authorities) only 12,000 to 15,000 persons, and after addressing the crowd, O'Connor went off to the home office in a cab 'where he repeated to Sir George Grey his thanks, his fears, and his assurances that the crowd should disperse quietly'.[187] The soldiers had been kept out of sight, and in the evening, O'Connor, Sir George Grey, and Lord John Russell all took their places in the house of commons, where Sir George Grey was loudly cheered, as he deserved to be.[188]

Although a rumour went round at midsummer that the chartists were going to burn London,[189] that was the end of the English revolution. Alarm was succeeded by self-congratulation. The Queen hoped that 'the bright and glorious Example of this Country' would be 'a check to the wild notions and wicked example set by France'.[190] Morpeth thought 10 April had been 'a remarkable day for England',[191] and Lord John gleefully forwarded to the Prince the story of a Frenchman who was vociferating in Trafalgar Square 'that the English do not know how to fight. "Don't they?", said a butcher's boy, and knocked him down. This is English patriotism'.[192] In more tasteful vein, Lord John turned a deaf ear to pleas from the Queen and the Prince for prosecutions,[193] and instead of the day of thanksgiving suggested by his new archbishop, which was inappropriate for deliverance from civil war, got up a subscription for a free hospital.[194] Finally in June, when O'Connor heard of a plot to assassinate Lord John, he told Hobhouse, who told Lord John, who told George Grey. In the commons, O'Connor spoke to Lord John, 'who thanked him for his attention'.[195]

It was too much to hope that Ireland would escape the year of revolutions. In March Smith O'Brien went to Paris, and in April Clarendon expected an outbreak to follow the chartist meeting on the tenth.[196] But by this time Clarendon had achieved an unenviable reputation as an alarmist, and everyone knew that he was only told what he wanted to hear.[197] He travelled little, and stayed in Dublin Castle, where he slept until far into the day, and stayed awake until far into the night. His secretary told Lord John that they divided the day between them; Clarendon seldom went to bed before 4 a.m., and he got up about that hour.[198] The cloistered lord lieutenant wore 'dark glasses and magnifiers',[199] and when Lord John responded to his pleas to avert revolution by coming before the cabinet to propose emergency legislation to control ejectments, to provide £1m for relief works, and to suspend *habeas corpus*,[200] his only support came from Lansdowne and Palmerston.[201]

When the topic of ejectments was first raised Clanricarde said there was no remedy for the evil.

> If the tenant is not ejected by a certain day he claims to stay another year, and if he cannot be persuaded to go away by daylight, nothing is left but to force him out by night, and so he is forced out on a winter night and dies of cold and starvation by the roadside.

Hobhouse noted that 'there was a general shudder . . . But I did not hear a remedy suggested'.[202] Palmerston then joined in, writing that

> Ejectments ought to be made without cruelty . . . but it is useless to disguise the Truth, that any great Improvement in the Social System of Ireland must be founded upon . . . a long continued and systematic ejectment of Small Holders and of squatting Cottiers.[203]

The cabinet did, in fact, allow Lord John to bring in a bill to 'control' ejectments, but its scope and its fate are interesting. The bill required a landowner to give the poor law guardians seven days' notice of his intention to evict. The house of lords amended seven days before eviction to twelve hours after, and in the confrontation which followed the commons congratulated themselves on securing a compromise of 48 hours before.

As for relief, Labouchere took the lead in arguing that it was inexpedient, and he was joined by Grey, George Grey, Hobhouse and Wood.[204] Lord John reported to Prince Albert that the cabinet found insuperable objections to most of the remedial measures proposed by Clarendon.[205] All they would do was to re-advance any money which the Irish repaid from former loans.[206] Immediately after this Lord John had a long meeting with J. O'Connell, at the end of which he admitted to Clarendon that there was one good argument in favour of repeal of the union, in the want of time and inclination at Westminster to discuss Irish or any other problems.[207]

Fortunately, Lamartine refused Smith O'Brien's request for aid, and the Irish did not rebel in April. But in May Clarendon's 'plaintive' letters started again, and by July he was 'in a fever'.[208] This time he had some reason. The *Nation* newspaper and the *United Irishman* were preaching disobedience, the clubs were multiplying, and for weeks Smith O'Brien could be heard talking himself into an insurrection. Clarendon repeated his request for the suspension of *habeas corpus*; Grey, George Grey, and Wood still opposed it, but the cabinet over-ruled them. George Grey then refused to introduce the bill in the commons,[209] and Lord John was obliged to bring it in himself. It was passed in a day, and on 24 July Wellington came to the cabinet and recommended sending Hardinge over to Ireland to take command of the troops. Before he arrived Smith O'Brien appeared in arms. The country did not rise with him and 'the poor crazy creature'[210] cut a sorry figure when arrested by the constables.

While O'Connor denounced O'Brien for running away, O'Brien himself admitted he had taken the field too early, and had the bravado to claim that six weeks later he would have been master of Ireland.[211] Lord John could have been forgiven for congratulating himself upon the outcome. But that was not the line he took: the rebellion was the bitterest moment in his life. As Lady John wrote to her sister; Ireland, '*there* is the weight that almost crushes John, who opens Lord Clarendon's daily letters with an uneasiness not to be told'.[212] To Lord John, failure as prime minister did not lie in bringing in two budgets in ten days or even in bringing in four budgets in one session. Failure lay in the fact that he who had refused to adopt 'ripening measures' to force on a rebellion in Ireland,[213] was still unable to save that country from the disaster, and was forced to write successively to Clarendon to tell him *in extremis* not to rebuff offers of help from the orange associations, and to envisage arming the protestants.[214] The fates themselves seemed to be condemning his crusading zeal of the 1830s.

It had been the most miserable session Lord John could remember. On top of everything else, the bill to admit Jews to parliament, which he introduced so warmly,[215] was thrown out by the lords; while the bill to repeal the navigation laws was held up by the debates on the income tax and introduced too late to go through all its stages that year. The one success of real moment was Morpeth's second health of towns bill, which struck a delicate balance between the centralising tendencies of the general board of health and the initiative of the localities. Where the death rate exceeded 23 per thousand, the act was to be compulsory: where it was under 23 per thousand the board could not impose, but the local ratepayers could assume the

responsibility. Ashley became president of the board, where he
was convinced he was carrying out 'all the wise, beautiful, and
sanitary regulations of the Levitical Code',[216] and within five
years nearly 2m people came under the beneficial influence of
the act.

The year 1848 was not a good year for legislation, and the
fact was widely noticed. Disraeli indicted 'the almost sublime
coolness' which characterised the prime minister, made play
with the four budgets, and read the 'bills of mortality' for the
session. Ministers had no confidence their measures would pass:

> the success of their measures in this House depends on a variety of
> small parties, who, in their aggregate, exceed in number and in-
> fluence the party of the Ministers . . . a measure is so altered, re-
> moulded, remodelled, patched, cobbled, painted, veneered, and
> varnished, that, at last, no trace is left of the original scope and
> scheme.[217]

'Sublime coolness' was a mistake: Lord John was dogged by ill
health from the beginning of the session. Before Christmas he
had an influenza, which he could not throw off. In his budget
speech his manner and voice showed that he was fagged out.[218]
Thereafter, late nights prevented him getting well,[219] and in
March he was obliged to go away to St Leonards to try and re-
gain his health. When he broke his holiday to speak in the
house, Morpeth thought he had 'a blighted look',[220] and in
April he still had not got rid of his 'flu.[221] Enfeebled by illness,
and buffeted by crisis after crisis, while the whole of Europe
stood between 'the triumph of absolute Governments and the
triumph of Jacobin principles',[222] Lord John had not succeeded
in stamping his own image upon the statute book. It was no
wonder, and it was not all his own fault.

Grey might moan that ministers were not equal to their difficulties, 'the principal fault being in our chief',[223] but others
pointed an accusing finger at the forms of the house of commons. Dunfermline wrote that the rules had broken down since
the majority of members ceased to be aristocratic and passive,
and added that this was the deliberate opinion of an ex-
speaker.[224] Normanby wrote that Lord John was unfairly
abused: parliament was a machine with insufficient power. He
went on to suggest separate meetings of the Irish, Scots,

English and Welsh members, to prepare legislation for their own countries two months before the imperial parliament met.[225] Lord John did not take this up. But he did do one thing. In 1848 the government had only two days a week for its business. In 1849 Lord John asked the house to devote one day a month more to public business, and so jealous was parliament of its independence that he had some difficulty in securing even that.

ii. Office, 1848–9

The rebellion in Ireland was a fiasco; and 'so prompt a finish to so formidable a preparation was never before seen'.[226] But the consequence for Ireland was the final alienation of public opinion in England and Scotland. From the moment Lord John became prime minister he had to contend with the argument that the English and the Scots paid higher taxes and received fewer benefits than the Irish.[227] After the success of the repeal candidates at the general election of 1847, Lord John noticed that the clergy, who had previously preached in favour of subscriptions to Irish distress, now mostly preached against subscribing.[228] Lord John himself once wrote that 'we cannot be more abused, if we give nothing',[229] and after the rebellion he hoped some of the Irish would at last see 'that it is not the best course to freeze the current of English benevolence'.[230] In 1848–9 the rage against Ireland on account of its faction, its mendicancy and its ingratitude was extreme.[231] As Lord John said, the great difficulty this year does not spring from Trevelyan or Wood,

> but lies deep in the breasts of the British people. It is this. We have granted, lent, subscribed, worked, visited, clothed the Irish millions of money, years of debate &c., &c. – the only return is calumny and rebellion. Let us not grant, lend, clothe &c., &c. any more, and see what that will do. Such is the result to which Machale, J. O'Connell and S. O'Brien have brought us.[232]

But Lord John's reactions were, in other ways, more creditable than this. In March 1848 he had told Clarendon not to pack a jury, even if the result was no verdict.[233] Now, he wrote that it would be barbarous to wait until March 1849 to try

O'Brien.[234] In September, after a second small outbreak, he wrote a little too light-heartedly that he did not mind if Clarendon hanged a few rebels by court martial, but immediately reminded him that he must not start a war of atrocities like 1798.[235] In October, when he heard that O'Brien was not to be hanged, he was glad: it was true that in that case they could never hang another rebel, 'but I don't mind that'.[236]

Above all, Lord John made up his mind to visit Clarendon, and as soon as the session was over he set off for Dublin. The Irish greeted him with 'some cry for Repeal, but great civility and apparent good humour'.[237] He found Clarendon was still expecting a French invasion at any moment, and with that, as Charles Wood said, 'we really are getting beyond all reasonable bounds of apprehension'.[238] Lord John's discussions with the Irish government ranged over the whole field of future reform from a bill to establish an £8 rating franchise everywhere, to a plan for converting leaseholds into perpetuities.[239] But the great measure which he had in mind for 1849 was the endowment of the priests. This had been considered before, and rejected as impracticable. What had changed now? The revolutions of 1848 had not stopped at nationalism, and as Lord John said to Clarendon, 'the priests and we are in the same boat to row against the current of infidelity and communism setting in with Mitchell and Duffy'.[240] Normanby advised Lord John that the time had come to make the attempt,[241] and Redington, who held Drummond's old office in Ireland, thought the Pope would accept.[242] As for the Irish clergy themselves, 'The Pulpit's laws, the Pulpit's Patrons give, And those who live to please, must please to live'.[243] The clergy had encouraged the Irish to rebel. They had then flinched from the conflict, and for the moment their influence was low and their dues had dried up. They would welcome state endowment.[244]

The policy was still not without risks. Lord John heard a curious story of Peel when he was staying at Nuneham.

> He is said to have been talking to five or six of the guests among whom was Sheil. Peel declared that it must be done, but that probably it would cost the Ministry who proposed it their offices, and then their adversaries would be obliged to carry it. Sheil with an equivocal compliment said 'Perhaps it is reserved for you Sir Robert'.[245]

Lord John himself anticipated a clamour, and knew that if that clamour was successful, 'no subsequent measure nor even the same measure carried another year would reconcile Protestant and Catholic'.[246] But the attempt had to be made because

The great problem . . . remains: How are the Roman Catholic Masses to be attached to Imperial Rule? All the franchises we have granted, all the relief we have bestowed have failed to do so. The middle and lower classes are against us – the higher afraid of what may happen, and unwilling to act.[247]

When the conference in Dublin Castle considered how the money was to be raised, Redington wanted to re-open the whole question of the established church. Lord John insisted that this was now 'quieta movere',[248] and reverted to his favourite plan for a land tax. Redington in turn feared opposition from the protestants of Ulster to any land tax to endow the catholic clergy.[249] Lord John then proposed – as he had in 1838 – to disguise the dose. Part of the proceeds of the land tax would be applied to drainage, and the surplus would be paid into the consolidated fund, which would be used to endow the clergy.[250] Hitherto, all plans for the endowment of the catholic church had envisaged contributing to the upkeep of churches and providing the clergy with glebes, and had stopped short of actually paying the priests. Brushing aside Redington's doubts,[251] Lord John insisted that payment of stipends must form part of the plan. A scale was to be attached in a schedule to the act, and the whole sum was to be voted in perpetuity and placed in the hands of a body of roman catholic commissioners, who were to be bound by no other fetter than that of laying an account before parliament annually.[252]

The cabinet met on 24 October, when Clarendon came over to London for the occasion. First Lord John announced that there was no need for parliament to meet before Christmas – a cheer, and that for 1849 they would confine themselves to Ireland and the navigation laws – another cheer. Then he unfolded his plan for putting £340,000 p.a. at the disposal of the catholic hierarchy for the support of the priests. His speech 'seemed to please generally'. Minto having long since come home, Palmerston volunteered to ask his brother, Mr Temple, to approach the Pope, and the cabinet agreed to drop the plan if the Pope objected. Grey observed that they would carry it, and be turned out after. Lord John replied that 'It was the duty of government to apply a great remedy to a great evil at all risk to themselves'. Wood alone objected that it had already been refused by anticipation, but Hobhouse noticed that while Lord John was speaking, 'Clarendon smiled in his peculiar way'.[253] Perhaps that was because, as he told the Prince a few days later, he thought the Irish clergy would accept endowment, but dare not avow it as their bishops were against it.[254]

The result was an anti-climax. The Pope, who had just re-affirmed his ban on Peel's ungodly colleges, raised no objection, but insisted upon consulting the Irish bishops.[255] Clarendon went back to Ireland and found Archbishop Murray and the Irish hierarchy hostile.[256] In the middle of November he and George Grey went to Lord John, and persuaded him it was impossible,[257] and when the cabinet met again on 5 December, Lord John announced sheepishly that he had given it up for the time being. Shutting his eyes to the likelihood of refusal, he had pinned his hopes upon the endowment of the catholics. When that fell through his plans collapsed. As he said, it would have been nice to have met parliament with a plan for permanent improvement. 'But the Catholic clergy question formed an essential part of such a settlement . . . Thenceforth everything else was lame and imperfect'.[258] The cabinet agreed to give some relief to insolvent unions, and allowed Lord John to save face by bringing in again, without hope as to its passing, the landlord and tenant bill of the previous session.[259] But it insisted upon extending the suspension of *habeas corpus*, and at this point Lord John lost credibility as the Whig party's expert on Ireland.

In the autumn of 1848 the Earl of Carlisle died, and Morpeth went up to the lords. At the beginning of 1849 Auckland died, and Lord John made another attempt to woo the Peelites. It had never been far from his mind, but a year earlier, when he made Argyll an offer not of office, but of honour, it was refused.[260] Now he wanted to introduce three of the younger Peelites gradually.[261] As he said to Palmerston, 'Whigs and Peelites ought to govern the country and not to quarrel about trifles'.[262] He asked Wood to consult Peel in confidence.[263] Peel said his followers must make up their minds for themselves. The younger Peelites would do nothing without a lead, and so on 9 January a unanimous cabinet agreed to Lord John's seeing Graham and offering him the admiralty.[264]

The interview lasted two hours, and according to Graham was 'conducted throughout with the freedom of former colleagues and old friends'.[265] Graham objected to Palmerston's foreign policy, to the scale of government expenditure, and (contradictorily) to the absence of large plans for Ireland. Lord John wrote to Clarendon that Graham had 'declined for fifty different reasons, but all ending in one, viz. that he is afraid',[266] and Carlisle thought Graham refused to join a sinking ship.[267] Lord John was compelled to fall back upon the Whigs. Carlisle had already offered himself for the post, but Lord John said 'he thought the same thing about me that Lord Melbourne had once said, that I might have too much facility in giving way to wishes which ought not to be complied with. Little Johnny!'[268] The place went to Francis Baring, who was married to Sir George Grey's sister.

While these negotiations were going on the public cry for economy was growing. Wood was committed to a reduction of 7000 men in the army,[269] but even so, as Baring said, 'we have not the confidence of the country that we shall keep a surplus'.[270] Simultaneously, from Ireland, came loud complaints that the poor law was bringing landlords and tenants to universal ruin.[271] Farmers were leaving Ireland on account of the rates,[272] and Lansdowne and Clanricarde pressed for a maximum of 5s to be set to the poor rate,[273] even though, as Lord John said, if we adopt that we abandon the claim that no one is to starve.[274] Wood then announced that he would do nothing for Ireland but what was cheapest, which was to help the guardians to buy food.[275] Lord John was not interested in rations, which would only make things worse in the long run, and Wood was amused to find the prime minister thought there was a danger of his giving too much to the Irish. 'I have always feared that you thought me too stingy. I am perfectly ready to give them as near nothing as may be.'[276]

When Lord John saw Graham and told him there was nothing in the pipeline for Ireland except the suspension of *habeas corpus*, Graham said 'That is only putting on the strait waistcoat; you must think of curing the patient, and for that

purpose employ large remedies'. Lord John admitted to Clarendon that 'this is true',[277] but without borrowing and lending
there could be no great plan for Ireland.[278] Clarendon, however, continued to press for money for emigration:

> assuming that the people are not to die of starvation and that the
> P[oor] Law after 3 successive years of scarcity is inadequate for
> their relief . . . the Govt has to determine whether it is not better
> to make a great effort and get rid of those who under a non
> potato system must continue to be a burden.[279]

Although Clarendon and Lord John were still at odds, Clarendon wanting Britain to pay, and Lord John insisting that Ireland must, Lord John did his best by his lord lieutenant. Five
days before the new session began he undertook to propose an
emigration scheme for districts where the poor rate exceeded
5*s*, and told Clarendon that if the resistance of the cabinet was
invincible he would throw up the government.[280]

On 27 January Lord John asked the cabinet to approve a rate
in aid of emigration, which would compel the more prosperous
areas of Ireland to contribute to the cost of removing the surplus
population from the depressed areas. 400,000 people had already left Ireland in the last two years, and with £600,000 the
unions could get rid of 300,000 more.[281] Nine ministers, including Clanricarde and Palmerston, voted in favour, while
Grey, Hobhouse, Labouchere, Lansdowne, and Wood voted
against.[282] Lansdowne then demanded another cabinet,[283]
which agreed instead to ask for a select committee of each house
upon the poor law. Clarendon did not like this, and when parliament met Lord John found it very difficult to speak.[284] On 8
February he came back to the cabinet for an outright grant of
£50,000, for a rate in aid of the distressed unions, and for a 6*d*
rate on all Ireland for emigration. He again told Clarendon that
if he could not get the cabinet to agree the government was at
an end.[285]

The cabinet found that nothing whatever could be proposed
which was not exposed to insuperable objections,[286] and broke
up without a decision. Two days later they met again. Lansdowne, who was still 'in favour of any grants that can be
obtained from the Treasury, but against any rate or tax on
Ireland',[287] made it clear that if there had to be a tax on Ireland

he would prefer an income tax to a rate, and out of deference to him an income tax was considered at length.[288] But when it came to a vote only Lansdowne, Lord John, and one other voted for an income tax, while eleven ministers voted for a rate in aid.[289] The cabinet decided to ask parliament for the grant of £50,000, and for a rate of 1s in the £ in aid of both relief and emigration: in return they would be prepared to concede a limit of 5s on the poor rate. Lord John had not done badly, but he was disappointed, and wrote apologetically and weakly to Clarendon that 'having nobody to give me real support, I was obliged either to submit, or break up the Cabinet'.[290]

The cabinet's discussions had been confused, and those in the house of commons were scarcely less so. The government secured its grant, and when the principle of the rate in aid was tested, it was carried by 206 votes to 34. This brought murmurs from Ulster, which Lord John called 'the loyal but too favoured portion' of Ireland,[291] and Peel and Wellington doubted whether the rate in aid would pass the lords. Interpreting this as a threat, Lord John suggested throwing it up.[292] The cabinet sensibly decided not to do anything so sudden, and two days later the commons passed the second reading by 193 votes to 138. But throughout April opposition to the rate in aid continued to mount among the Irish M.P.s. Thereupon 'we . . . had a slight trial of "Repeal". Lord JOHN RUSSELL, with his wonted urbanity, resolved to give Ireland a treat':[293] he attended a meeting of the Irish members and told them that they could have either the rate in aid or the income tax, whichever they preferred. According to Lord John, they did not like either, and pretended to have been affronted.[294] Finally, the house of commons was invited to vote upon both proposals. There voted for income tax 146, and against 194: for the rate in aid 201, and against 106. Even that was not the end of the matter, and in May the rate in aid was opposed in the lords by the archbishop of Dublin, Fitzwilliam, and Monteagle, and only carried by 48 votes to 47. The lords were never slow to see when Lansdowne was not whole-heartedly behind a government measure.

In the protracted debates on the rate in aid, the limelight was stolen by Sir Robert Peel, in 'two great speeches', as Prince Albert called them,[295] on 5 and 30 March. Realising that Lord John had large aspirations for Ireland, but that the 'economical

ague' had chilled them,[296] Peel broke his long silence. He
pleaded for a government commission to manage the distressed
areas, and pointed to the ineffectiveness of the encumbered
estates act of 1848. Redington thought Peel's speeches could
only have come from an opposition bench,[297] but Clarendon,
who was bitter against his colleagues, went to see Peel, and
asked him for details of his proposal to place the encumbered
estates in the hands of a new tribunal. At first Lord John was
annoyed.[298] But Lansdowne wrote to say that he hoped Lord
John would adopt 'so much at least of Peel's plan as consists in
brushing away with a vigorous hand all legal hindrances to the
transfer of property in Ireland',[299] and within a few days open-
mindedness triumphed over anger, and Lord John instructed
Romilly, the solicitor general, to draw up a new bill.

In his *Recollections and Suggestions* Lord John said that it was
while he was in Dublin in 1848 that he realised the encumbered
estates act of 1848 was not going to work and instructed Romilly
to prepare another one that would,[300] and it is true that
further measures for setting land free for sale and purchase
featured in his discussions with the Irish government.[301] But
there is little doubt that twenty-five years later his memory
misled him, or that he was guilty of a jealous lie, for there is no
evidence in his papers that he gave the matter another thought
until April 1849.[302] If this is right, then we must add that the
government now moved with an exemplary sense of urgency.
The new encumbered estates bill was introduced on 26 April,
and this time it was draconian. In place of the court of chancery,
a special body of three encumbered estates commissioners was
set up, in a 'court' of their own. Any encumbrancer for any
amount could now bring an estate before the commissioners.
Here was government interference with a vengeance, and here,
too, was 'administrative law'. Although the lords referred the
bill to a select committee, and amended it to keep estates out of
the hands of the commissioners which were mortgaged for less
than one-half of their value, the bill passed, and the lawyers for
once found a way round the lords' amendment.[303]

The act, which was one of the largest measures ever passed,
achieved what both its friends and its enemies expected. Land
came on to the market, and by 1858 one-tenth of the land of
Ireland had been transferred through the agency of this court

FIG. 5 PEEL'S PANACEA FOR IRELAND *Punch* 1849

Russell: Oh! This dreadful Irish toothache!
Peel: Well, here is something that will cure you in an instant [the sale of
    encumbered estates].

alone. Furthermore, many of the new owners were, as Lord John hoped, roman catholics. The act went a long way to returning the soil of Ireland to the native Irish, and in 1871 Mill described it as 'the greatest boon ever conferred on Ireland by any government'. Against this it must be admitted that for some years the land was sold at ridiculously low prices, and that both the former owners and the mortgagees suffered. The answer to this is that they were meant to. Professor Burn's criticism is that there was no provision for selling the encumbered estates to the tenants, but we may be sure that if there had been the bill would not have passed. And if time revealed that the new owners were more rapacious than the old ones, that was not the fault of the act – it was a consequence for which a new remedy was needed, and for which one was ultimately found.

Lord John had said that in 1849 they would confine themselves to Ireland and to the repeal of the navigation laws. In dealing with the latter, Labouchere decided against reciprocity. As he said in November 1848, how could the United Kingdom negotiate with either France or Germany in their present state?[304] Britain was to do what was right: let other nations follow. Lord John was staunch upon the free trade question, and the bill therefore dealt with the ocean-carrying trades upon the most extended free trade principles. It rattled the Protectionists, but rallied the Peelites to the Whig side, and the second reading passed by 266 votes to 210. Labouchere then, almost casually, proposed an amendment to throw open the coasting trade as well.

His action provoked the most strenuous opposition in the lords. As Lord John told the Queen, there were 'strong class interests' in arms against the bill, and the prejudice of two centuries was in favour of the present law, which was believed to be the foundation of maritime supremacy.[305] Lord John warned the Queen of the possibility of defeat, to be followed by Derby, dissolution, agitation, Bright, and chaos.[306] The Queen and the Prince undertook to do all they could to secure the passage of the bill, and Lord John then asked members of the cabinet to use their influence with individual peers, because the government was going to stand or fall by the result. 'No one remarked on this decision, but an ominous silence prevailed.'[307] Palmerston wrote to Lord John imploring him not to make the outcome a matter of confidence. The Queen would send for Peel:

> But how is Peel at present to command a majority in either House? only by the support of the Whig party. Could you under such Circumstances of Difficulty created by your own act, refuse to do your best to obtain for him that support? Join him yourself... you could not . . . but you would be bound almost, and obliged to hand your Party over to Peel and to abdicate your own Position in his Favour . . .[308]

Palmerston could not have touched Lord John upon a more sensitive nerve, and no doubt knew it. But the situation was not like that in February 1848. Prince Albert had already written to Wellington asking him to save the country from a lords versus commons election,[309] and to Peel, who had approached Aberdeen who would vote for repeal, and Hardinge who would vote for the government.[310] The Duke of Cambridge, the Marquis of Abercorn, the Marquis of Ormonde, the Earls of Denbigh, Howe, and Morton, and Samuel Wilberforce the bishop of Oxford, would all do whatever the Prince asked them.[311] After consulting Lansdowne, Lord John replied to Palmerston, therefore:

> We both agree that after hav^g brought forward the Navigation Bill in so solemn a manner for two sessions we ought to resign if we are beaten by a considerable majority in the Lords . . . the probable case is that we shall carry the Bill if we show ourselves in earnest upon it.[312]

Right up to the last moment, however, Lord John still feared that 'impressions taken up during the debate' might turn a close vote against the government.[313] As the Whig ambassadors made their way back from Brussels, Paris, and Vienna, advance calculations showed first that the voting would be 171 in favour and 155 against, and then that it would be 180 in favour and 169 against.[314] The debate was exciting because it was novel. The methods used by the ministry to secure attendance led Protectionist peers to question the powers of the monarchy, the composition of the upper chamber, and the value of proxies. They had a point: a majority of those present voted against the repeal, but when the proxies were counted, the government won by 173 to 163. With a mixture of royal influence and resolution, the Whigs had won, and in July the cabinet all rather considered it a prosperous session.[315]

When parliament rose, the famine was officially brought to an end by the Queen's visit to Ireland. The Whigs had long since thought the Queen ought to visit her Irish subjects. Lord John mentioned it to Palmerston in 1843,[316] and no sooner was the party back in power than Bessborough issued an invitation. As the Queen wrote to Lord John, 'It is a journey wh must one day or other be undertaken, and wh the Queen wd be glad to have accomplished, because it must be disagreeable to her that people shd speculate whether she *dare* visit one part of her dominions'.[317] But the visit must not be made to look like a party move, and anyway who would pay? In 1847 Lord John suggested an impromptu visit,[318] and in the spring of 1848 Clarendon again urged the Queen to come, and even envisaged her holding a parliament in Dublin, though the cabinet thought this of doubtful policy.[319] Now, in 1849, the visit could no longer be put off – the Queen had, after all, been on the throne for over twelve years. Even then Prince Albert made a last attempt to downgrade a state visit into a yachting excursion, and Lord John had to insist on a visit of several days.[320]

Up to the last moment Lord John and Clarendon were anxious how she would be received. But Palmerston was confident: 'I shall be very much mistaken in Paddy's character, if the Queen is not satisfied with the demonstrations of Joy and Loyalty with which her arrival in Ireland will be greeted'.[321] He was right, and the Irish were warmer than they might have been had they known how reluctant the Queen had been to come; the soldiers were kept in the background, and finally the Queen was able to drive round Dublin 'without escort or police'.[322] At the end Clarendon reported that she had been 'radiant with pleasure' the whole time, and hoped the visit would have taught the Irish that tranquillity was better than rebellion. At all events he was satisfied the Irish no longer felt on a different footing from the Scots and the English.[323]

When the Queen's visit to Ireland took place, Lord John had been prime minister for just over three years. From the day he took office his administration had been marked by 'famine, commercial revulsion, and a state of political agitation both at home and abroad such as the world has scarcely ever witnessed'.[324] Or, as Dalhousie put it, 'these are hard times for Prime Ministers'.[325] Now this was true, and Lord John would have had an easier time had he been content just to preside over the government. It is easy, as Palmerston showed later, to look impressive if you do not wish to do anything. But Lord John still belonged to the movement, and he attempted much, and with parties in the state Peel left them it is not surprising that the sugar duties, the health of towns bill, the encumbered estates act, and the repeal of the navigation laws all had to be re-worked. This gave the public a poor impression of the Whig ministers, but in their improved form these acts were not a negligible legislative achievement.

It might appear that we could give the same guarded approbation to Lord John's government's handling of the famine in Ireland. There was a logic in the succession of their measures: first they gave aid in the form of works and soup, then they passed a poor law, and finally they passed a rate in aid of the distressed unions. But here we must be more cautious: in round figures their relief saved 1m lives and their logic contributed to as many deaths. Lord John must take his share of the blame for this, because his approach to the Irish problem was as doctrinaire as any, but it is only fair to him to remember that at all times he wished to attempt more for Ireland than did his cabinet. He could not carry out his threats to resign, because the only Whigs he could resign in favour of were Lansdowne and Palmerston, and by giving place to them he would only make things worse. Compelled to continue, his real failure was his inability to apply himself regularly and steadily to the problem in hand. In his papers one misses the carefully-thought-out and closely reasoned memoranda which Peel prepared for his cabinet. No doubt Peel's memoranda would not have made the same impression upon Lord John's friends that they did upon his own, but Lord John gave up too easily, and tried to guide his colleagues by hasty judgements, whose limitations were exposed by the first objection.

Because Lord John could not impress himself upon his cabinet, a strain was set up. This was not yet apparent on the surface. Lord John handled his cabinet as a committee of friends and equals, and good humour predominated. In January 1847 when the cabinet were going through the phrasing of

the Queen's speech, an alternative was suggested: Lord John
said with a smile, 'if you please I had rather have it my own way',
at which Hobhouse could not help laughing aloud 'as did R.
himself'.[326] On 1 April 1848 they all laughed boisterously when
it was discovered that somebody had played a hoax on the Duke
of Wellington by imitating Lord John's hand, and inviting him
to attend.[327] In December 1849 Carlisle recorded his experience that 'Cabinets very seldom quarrel'.[328] Outwardly all was
well, but Lord John had not found it fun starving the Irish to
death, he was not plucking out of this catastrophe the reconciliation between the kingdoms of which he had always dreamed,
and worst of all, since he was jealous of Peel, it was Peel who in
1849 stepped in and pointed this out to the world. Lord John
did not pretend to be Peel's equal as to budgets, but he had
always regarded himself as Peel's superior on Ireland, and this
upheaval in the political firmament told upon his temper, with
the result that between 1841 and 1849 Russell beat Peel and
then lost to himself.

CHAPTER XIV

In the shadow of Palmerston: a most harassing warfare, 1849–52

i. Office, 1849–50

THE prime minister of movement was constrained by his cabinet and saddled with an unworkable parliament, and the situation grew worse until the point was reached, in January 1851, when Lord John exclaimed that 'a Government ought not to be the only body of politicians in the country who proposed nothing'. Hobhouse answered for Lord John's colleagues, 'Good heavens, I am sure you are always bringing forward something new about every thing'. Lord John joined in the laugh,[1] but he had long ceased to find his situation amusing, and his reaction to it, which decided the fate of his ministry, was to reopen the question of the reform of parliament.

In 1841 Parkes had thought the great majority of the people deemed the Reform Bill 'a Cheat'. At that time Lord John refused to move on – it would be the 'Road to Ruin',[2] and Parkes concluded that he was totally identified with 'retrospective great questions of Liberalism'.[3] There the matter rested until 1848. But immediately after the chartist meeting Bannerman, Macaulay, and Normanby all wrote to Lord John to say that further reform could not be delayed much longer.[4] Lord John observed that action might bring on a revolution, but that in the long run inaction must.[5] Then, in June 1848, he dropped a hint that the time might soon come when the freemen's franchise could be altered to make it really representative of the industrious classes.[6]

The experience of another session finally convinced Lord John that the Reform Act of 1832 left two great defects in the constitution, the exclusion of the working classes, and the imbalance between the houses. The time to remedy these defects was when the country was quiet. Merely to admit the working classes would make the imbalance still worse, and in order to preserve the two-chamber system Lord John preferred to start with a reform of the lords. At first sight this is surprising: Lord John himself said that Grey and Melbourne had created over seventy new peerages, that the Whigs now had their share of bishops, and that on ordinary occasions the government could get by.[7] But this was not the whole story. Legislation was now concerned with social questions. After every general election the Tory majority chose the representative peers for Scotland, and every time an Irish representative peer died the Tories elected another in his place. There were forty-four representative peers, and only thirty bishops. Stanley created more peers than Lord John did,[8] and the opposition could still command a majority upon any question on which they thought it safe to beat the government.[9]

When he became prime minister Lord John still hoped that with 'light sails' the house of lords could go on for a long time.[10] He had no wish to 'shut up the House of Lords like the Great Council of Venice', but he was sparing of new creations, as he reminded the Marquis of Westminster in a characteristically sharp letter in 1847,[11] and his policy was to create a new hereditary peerage only when an old one became extinct. But in 1849 the lords' opposition to the bill to repeal the navigation laws compelled him to think again. Hobhouse heard a rumour that Lord John was ready, if he was defeated, to create a hundred peers,[12] and after the excitement was over Lord John returned to the proposal he had first made in 1837 for life peers. In June 1849 he tried the idea out on Lansdowne, who thought life peers should be confined to Liberal Scots and Irish peers who were excluded from the house of lords under the present system.[13] Prince Albert was worried lest Lord John bring the hereditary principle into disrepute and weaken the monarchy, but thought the scheme worth a cautious trial,[14] and Cottenham ruled that, although it had not been used for a long time, the crown possessed the prerogative.[15] Lord John then opened his mind to the cabinet, which was not enthusiastic. Cottenham had already objected that the lords would be afraid of swamping, and even those who agreed with Lord John that there was a problem, did not like the remedy.

Once again, Lord John had failed to carry his colleagues with him, and this time the reason is not far to seek. There were great public objects to be served by the proposal, but they were not the only ones he had in mind. Ever since his health broke down in 1848 he had been thinking of accepting a peerage himself, and he had even gone so far as to speak to his brother about his title.[16] But every time he thought of going to the lords, he also thought about young Johnny. In 1849 Lord John was fifty-seven, and young John was seven. By the time young John was twenty-one, Lord John would be seventy-one. Constituencies never liked being asked to elect the eldest sons of aged peers, and if Lord John became a peer, young John might not find a seat in the house of commons. A life peerage would be the answer,[17] though delicacy no doubt prevented Lord John from saying this to his cabinet.

Lord John's setback did not deter him from bringing forward the other wing of his reform proposals, and in September he told Lansdowne that he thought of adding largely to the number of voters. No plan would satisfy the Radicals, but he was confident he could draw up a bill which they would support.[18] On 9 October, when the cabinet met, Carlisle records that

> Ld John made one announcement which may become historical – that he should wish to introduce next session a measure of considerable enfranchisement of voters for Members of Parlt. . . . He did not require any immediate opinion, but when we meet again in Nov[r], he would wish G. Grey, Ld. Campbell, and myself to consider with him the details of such a measure.

Carlisle thought the proposal of 'a safe and proper tendency', but he noted that the announcement was 'not very cordially received'.[19] The cabinet was taken completely by surprise, and as it was a topic upon which ministers were still accustomed to defer to Lord John, no immediate bar was placed upon his proceeding. Lord John began to frame a measure on the understanding that there was to be no schedule A, but that in order to overcome 'the blot in the present system', which was the very small number of voters in the smaller boroughs, the borough franchise was to be reduced to £5 and the occupation franchise in the counties to £20.[20]

Lord John asked G. C. Lewis for a return of all the £10

householders, £5–£10 householders, and under £5 householders in the boroughs, and for information about the cases in
which the landlord paid the rates.[21] Widening the issue, he told
Grey that he wished to give members to the colonies, at the rate
of one member for every £30,000 'secured as permanent payment' to British military expenditure.[22] In the meantime Palmerston warned Lord John that reform was a rock on which his
government was likely to be shipwrecked,[23] and when the
cabinet met again in the middle of November they decided not
to have a Reform Bill.[24] Immediately afterwards, in what some
members of the cabinet interpreted as an attempt to strengthen
his hand for the future, Lord John brought into the cabinet Fox
Maule, who had been under-secretary at the home office from
1835 to 1841, and was personally attached to his chief. He held
the office of secretary at war.

As the cabinet refused to join Lord John in creating a new
parliament, he must go on with the old one. This was a matter
of balance among the four parties, and in 1850 the administration's fate would depend, as it had done in 1848 and 1849, upon
the attitude of the Peelites. But corn prices were still low, the
Protectionists were gaining confidence, and rumours began to
get about that Lord John was thinking of reverting to a fixed
duty. Peel was invited to Woburn,[25] where the Duke of Bedford asked him what he would think of an extension of the
franchise, and the reimposition of a fixed duty. Peel apparently
gave a guarded approval to the first, and expressed total opposition to the second.[26] Lord John thereupon let it be known that
he and Peel would have nothing to do with any new plan for a
fixed duty of 5s on wheat.[27]

Everything was now conditioned by the Radicals' campaign
for economy, and by Wood's demand for a surplus.[28] It was
scarcely worth attempting anything, for it was virtually certain
that nothing could be achieved. The health of towns problem
was downgraded to a bill to stop interments in city churchyards,
and in due course, when Campbell retired, Carlisle moved to the
duchy of Lancaster. The great cause of education was reduced
to a definition of the functions of Kneller Hall. Lord John's
correspondence went into a minor key. Ashley and the bishop
of London complained about Sunday work in post offices,
Inglis of the omission from the new florin (introduced with a

view to decimal coinage) of the words *dei gratia*.[29] The Queen and the Prince asked for a pay rise; the Duke of Wellington opposed the abolition of brevet promotions; and Sir Erasmus Williams wanted Lord John to appoint a man who could speak Welsh to the see of Llandaff. Then there was the man who asked £8000 for the secrets of the French percussion shell;[30] J. W. Green who had once bought the copyright of a seditious pamphlet and burned the manuscript;[31] and, in due course, Thos Keightley who threatened, unless his merits received official recognition, to condemn Lord John's administration in the next edition of his *History of England*.[32]

However, there was always the problem of Irish relief. Lord John feared that this winter the state of the West and South of Ireland would be worse than ever before.[33] With a touch of honesty denied to most politicians, he now told Clarendon that it was idle to talk of natural causes:

> the acts of parl[t] of 1846 and 1847 are no doubt the efficient causes of much of the present difficulty. And tho' I maintain stoutly the wisdom both of the repeal of the Corn Law, and the enactment of the Poor Law, the first pressure of free trade prices and poor rate burthens must be felt severely.[34]

He wondered whether to go it alone, brave the Irish hierarchy, and offer the priests salaries, hoping that the scheme would catch on.[35] Nobody would join him in such a venture, and the only alleviation he could now propose was that the Irish should be given longer to pay their debts. Lansdowne supported him, but the two of them had such a hard time persuading the cabinet to agree to an extended period of forty years that any request for more money was out of the question.[36]

All that could be done for Ireland was what cost nothing. The cabinet agreed to introduce another landlord and tenant bill, but nobody expected it to pass when English landlords would be joined in opposing it by English Radicals like Bright, who asked to see Lord John, and told him that he disapproved of both tenant right and compensation for improvements.[37] A more hopeful line lay in a new Irish franchise bill. The Irish constituency had been hit by the famine, and there was general agreement among the parties that it ought to be restored. Lord John wanted to lower the borough franchise to £5, for that was what he thought it ought ultimately to be in England.[38] The cabinet preferred a bill to establish an £8 franchise in counties and boroughs alike, and agreed to allow Lord John to bring in the bill he had meditated for so long to abolish the lord lieutenant, and to rule Ireland through a fourth secretary of state in London.

Everyone was glad to push Ireland down into second place for 1850, and to find a new subject in the colonies. In many ways Grey had been an admirable appointment at the colonial office, and the choice of Elgin for Canada was a master stroke. After the Canadian general election in December 1847, Elgin admitted the Liberals, Baldwin and La Fontaine, to power. Where Durham and Sydenham had sought to submerge the French Canadians, Elgin took them into his confidence, and when the new ministry introduced their rebellion losses bill, he refused to 'reserve' it, and braved the anger of the Tory mob of Montreal.[39] Thus was Canada brought safely through a period in which the Canadian farmer was getting less for his wheat than his American neighbour,[40] in which upper Canada merchants and lower Canada irreconcilables still looked to union with the United States, and in which Irish immigrants were ready for any mischief.

But Grey was a man in whom independence of mind never ceased to appear contrariety, and his despatches contrived to insult even when he meant to show confidence. He was closely watched in the lords by his predecessor Stanley, and by Brougham, who was envious of a fellow renegade who had climbed back. In the commons, too, jealous eyes watched his every step, and in 1849 his Canadian policy was attacked in both houses. In the commons, thanks to Lord John, the opposition were defeated by 291 votes to 150. In the lords Grey himself scraped home by 99 votes to 96, and this narrow vote must also have been in Lord John's mind when he made his proposal for life peers.

Next, the opposition got hold of a much bigger stick with which to beat the government. Lord John had sent Torrington out to Ceylon with a recommendation to read Adam Smith on the way.[41] Upon his arrival Torrington changed the tax system, and in 1848 there was a rebellion which he suppressed by executing the ring-leaders and by insulting the Buddhist religion.

In 1849 the Radicals attacked the executions, and Gladstone befriended the Buddhist religion. Lord John found it very difficult to defend Torrington,[42] and Grey described his first speech as feeble and noted how much his chief had changed for the worse.[43] Later Lord John recovered, and made a stout defence,[44] but he was unable to put a stop to a bitter debate which continued on and off for three years.

Grey's performance under attack won him an unfortunate reputation 'for being untrustworthy in his statements', and he became known to the Radicals as Bouncing Ben.[45] In the summer of 1849 he offered to resign.[46] Lord John did not agree that he had been unsuccessful, but admitted that great prejudices had been raised, and did not at once refuse to release him.[47] But it would have been repugnant to let a colleague go in that way, and while the Radicals and Tories counted upon being able to unite for a new assault upon the ministry's colonial policy in 1850,[48] the prime minister was busy getting ready to rehabilitate a colleague who was down on his luck.

Grey had prepared a scheme for the Australian colonies. In the autumn of 1849 a committee of the cabinet, consisting of Lord John, Grey, Campbell, G. Grey, and Labouchere,[49] modified it and made it into the main plank of the government's programme for 1850. The various Australian colonies of New South Wales, Victoria, South Australia, and Van Diemen's Land already possessed separate institutions of their own. Australian nationalism was non-existent, and there was a danger that if the colonies were allowed to govern themselves they would erect customs barriers against each other. The ministers' object was to allow each territory to develop its own institutions as it chose, and to retain the authority of the Westminster parliament solely in order to stop the colonies harming each other. But they also went further, and in order to phase Westminster out, they proposed to set up a new general assembly of the Australian colonies, which was to phase Australia in.

When the session began, and the Protectionists' plea for agricultural relief had been defeated by the narrow margin of 273 votes to 252, parliament turned to the colonies. In the lords there was, as Carlisle noted, 'a regular Grey-hunt, which seems to be the favourite sport of the times'.[50] In the commons Lord John introduced the Australia bill, and threw his whole weight behind the colonial secretary. There was, according to Charles Wood, nothing very new in his speech,[51] but he raised the debate to the level of great principles applicable to the government not of Australia only, but of the whole empire.

Lord John said that in dealing with the empire we must make up our minds what we would 'preserve, or amend, or abandon'. He would not attempt to retain a reluctant colony, nor would he sever connections with any colony which valued them. Colonies were of two kinds, British and native. Henceforth British colonies were to be given British freedom, and it would be impossible to draw a line between laws passed by the colonial legislature which required imperial sanction and those which did not. Accordingly, the government proposed to hand over the sale of Australian lands to the colonial governments, and to leave it to the new assembly to enact a common tariff. In other words, in a period of about twelve years, Lord John's insistence that self-government was incompatible with the relations between a mother country and her colonies had been turned inside out. The colonies were to have self-government, and the imperial parliament was to be left only with the residual right of intervening to restore order if need be.

In the second class of colonies where there were native races, we were there – never mind how. What we had to calculate was not the advantage we derived from being there, nor (as was more likely) what it cost us to be there, but the consequences which would ensue if we left. In New Zealand and Natal self-government was not desirable so long as there was a danger of one race oppressing the other. Only when 'the processes of civilisation' had brought the different races up to the same level, and had brought them into harmony, could complete self-government be granted.[52]

The prime minister had got the session off to a good start. Gladstone and Sidney Herbert joined Disraeli, and even Roebuck in opposition, but their amendments were defeated by votes of 165 to 42, 187 to 102, and 226 to 128, and the bill passed. But in other ways it was not an easy session. The government's Irish legislation fared no better than before. The landlord and tenant bill quickly disappeared. The bill to abolish the lord lieutenant passed its second reading, but for all Lord John's arguing that railroads and steamers had solved the problem,[53] there was too much legerdemain in pretending that when this bill passed the Irish problem would cease to exist. The Irish had no reason to look forward to being governed as well as legislated for from Westminster, Peel objected to the additional secretary of state, and Ellice pointed out that a fourth secretary would be a minister 'as there are already others, beyond yr control, and with more power than yourself'.[54] The bill was dropped, and the only one of the three Irish measures to pass the commons was the franchise bill. Even this was mutilated before it reached the statute book. The lords changed the £8 franchise to £15, and Stanley carried an amendment to prevent the rate book being used as a register of voters and to compel an elector to make a claim to get on the register. When the bill came back to the commons, Lord John proposed £12 as a compromise figure, estimating that it would produce an electorate of 172,000 in place of the 264,000 originally proposed and the 144,000 conceded by the lords.[55] He rejected Stanley's amendment. The lords accepted the £12, but insisted upon the registration clause. The great struggle of 1840–1 thus ended in a whimper, and the Irish electorate remained almost exactly what it was before the famine.

At home, Fielden's factory act of 1847 had to be reworked with a government bill drafted and steered by Sir George Grey, which provided for a ten-and-a-half-hour day. Finance remained a weak spot: the Radicals obtained a committee on public salaries; the government carried the window tax by three votes and was defeated on the stamp duties by twenty-nine; and in March defeat seemed imminent on Hutt's motion to reduce the West Africa squadron.[56] Lord John treated this as a blatant attempt to reintroduce the slave trade, and the cabinet was roused from its 'usual flaccidity' when he said he wanted to make the vote an issue of confidence,[57] and announced that Palmerston would say the same. Palmerston supported him, but not very stoutly.[58] Lord John then called a meeting of his followers. Hume with cordiality, Lord Harry Vane with mildness, and E. Denison with bitterness, announced that they must oppose the government.[59] Denison complained of having received five lines of dry threat from Lord John instead of the three minutes' conversation he had asked for.[60] But the general feeling of the meeting was with Lord John, and when the debate took place the government won by 232 votes to 154. The majority consisted of 176 Liberals, 23 Peelites and 33 Protectionists, and the minority of 48 Liberals, 17 Peelites, and 89 Protectionists.[61] Carlisle thought the vote showed that Lord John still had 'considerable power among his own party'.[62]

Ireland was Lord John's greatest worry, but Palmerston ran a close second, and in 1850 the problem of Palmerston came to a head. On his return to the foreign office in 1846 Palmerston pursued a vendetta with Aberdeen. In a mild moment he referred to Aberdeen as 'a good natured, easy tempered, apathetic and yielding man',[63] but what he really thought was that Aberdeen had made himself under-secretary to Guizot,[64] and that he had sold Britain short all over the world. The Whigs had not been in office more than a few weeks when the announcement of the Spanish marriages seemed to prove him right. The French had not scored such a notable diplomatic success since 1815, and Palmerston sought to reverse the humiliation by diplomatic intervention in the internal affairs of Spain and Portugal. Strong feelings clouded his judgement, and early in 1848 the Spanish government dismissed Bulwer, the British ambassador at Madrid, and Palmerston looked foolish. After the revolutions of 1848, however, Palmerston gradually found a surer touch in heaping abuse upon the sovereigns of Europe and resting himself upon the Liberal British press. The new course nearly led him to disaster in January 1849, when it transpired that he had given orders for guns to be delivered out of the Queen's ordnance to the rebels in Sicily, but before the end of 1849 he scored a popular triumph by persuading Turkey to resist Austrian demands for the surrender of rebel Hungarian refugees.

Right or wrong, Palmerston's policies, Palmerston's language, and Palmerston's habit of sending despatches off before they had been approved by the Queen, all led to continuous friction. Normanby had scarcely taken up his post as ambassador at Paris before he reminded Lord John that it would require his constant vigilance 'to soften down the tone of communications in which (if not inserted by you) *conciliation* is never *studied*'.[65] Wood, too, drew Lord John's attention to the necessity of taking more into his own hands 'the *detailed steps* of foreign matters with France'.[66] Above all, of course, Lord John found himself caught in 'a most harassing warfare' between Windsor and Broadlands.[67] As umpire, he played an honest part, representing to the Queen and the Prince that Palmerston had no other object but the honour of Great Britain and that he was at all times a most agreeable colleague,[68] and reminding Palmerston that the Queen's request to see the despatches before they were sent was not part of an international conspiracy hatched by Clarendon, Reeve, Delane, Princess Lieven, and Guizot to thwart British diplomacy.[69]

In December 1845 both the Duke of Bedford and Fox Maule professed to believe that with Lord John at the helm, Palmerston would be different from what he had been in Melbourne's day.[70] It was a delusion. Not even the second Earl Grey had been able to control Palmerston. The colonial secretary might believe that if Palmerston had played such tricks in his father's day, he would have been dismissed,[71] but the truth was that in 1831 the prime minister used to go along to the foreign office, to the room where Talleyrand was kept waiting every time he asked for an interview, and sit with him there to prevent him taking offence.[72] Grey and Melbourne were older than Palmerston, and it was much harder, as Charles Wood admitted, for Lord John to control him.[73]

But there was another reason for Lord John's failure. There were two separate issues in the policies, and the courtesies, and upon the first of these Lord John was never quite sure what he wanted to achieve. He agreed pretty generally with Palmerston in opinion,[74] and he enjoyed giving the Cobdenite Radicals a drubbing. But he knew they sometimes had a better case than Palmerston, and when the episode of the Sicilian guns came before the cabinet Lord John argued that, 'we ought as a strong Power to do voluntarily that which we should enforce upon a weaker state – we are bound to express to the Neapolitan Government our regret . . .'[75] When Palmerston was drafting a note to the Austrian government about the Hungarian refugees, Lord John urged him to leave out the bit about shooting in cold blood, in case the Radicals used it against Torrington.[76] Taken individually, many of Lord John's attempts to influence the conduct of foreign affairs do him credit, but looked at in the mass and over the years, they do not make such a good impression because he could never follow a distinct line of difference from Palmerston. Nor did he know how to press home an advantage, and when the indiscretion over the Sicilian guns leaked out, he missed a wonderful opportunity to bring Palmerston to trial before the cabinet. He countermanded Admiral Parker's orders without consultation, and thereby put himself in the wrong and presented Palmerston with the chance to be magnanimous.[77] Thereafter it was left to the Queen and the Prince to make the running. They had already suggested that Clarendon and Palmerston change places.[78] Now they returned to the charge, only to discover that Lord John's main concern was lest Palmerston throw up his office in a huff.[79] But the Prince did not give up, and in the summer of 1849 he succeeded in manoeuvring Lord John more directly into the firing line, by insisting on a new procedure whereby all foreign office drafts were to be sent to the prime minister before they were submitted to the Queen. If Palmerston committed another indiscretion, it would be impossible for Lord John to slip out of the predicament as easily as he had in the past.

At the beginning of 1850 Lord John first heard about the case of Don Pacifico. He wrote to Palmerston that it was 'hardly worth the interposition of the British Lion', and added that Baring 'somewhat remonstrates' against the constant employment of his ships to support British diplomatic agents.[80] Palmerston replied by asking what British ships were for,[81] and on 2 February acquainted the cabinet with 'a slight scrimmage which had got up on the shores of Athens'.[82] A few days later there was, as Lord John said, a despatch gone 'w$^{\underline{ch}}$ is not in conformity with the Q's opinion, or mine, or that of the cab^t', ordering the British admiral to seize merchant vessels and force the Greek government to pay their debts to Don Pacifico.[83]

This was the challenge for which the Queen and the Prince had been waiting. On 25 February Lord John called on Palmerston to have a very serious talk.[84] A week later, after consulting Lansdowne, Lord John saw the Queen and the Prince.[85] He explained his wish

> to adopt a plan by which Lord Palmerston's services could be retained with his own goodwill, and the Foreign Affairs entrusted to other hands. The only plan he could think of was to give Lord Palmerston the lead in the House of Commons – the highest position a statesman could aspire to – and to go himself to the

House of Lords . . . Lord Palmerston appeared to Lord John willing to enter into this agreement.

The Queen asked who would take the foreign office, and Lord John replied Lord Minto. The Queen was startled '(! ! !)',[86] and asked why Lord John had not proposed Clarendon. Lord John said that 'somehow or other he never could agree with Lord Clarendon on Foreign Affairs', and the Queen then urged him to take the foreign office himself. There was a good deal of discussion about the office Palmerston was to take, and the conversation ended with Lord John saying that the change would take place at the end of the session, and that in the meantime the utmost secrecy must be observed. Curiously enough, it seems to have been Lord John himself who could not keep the secret, for on 25 March he told Carlisle and Wood that he thought of taking the foreign office himself 'which would be a great coup'.[87]

If Lord John was in earnest it was a mistake to postpone the change until the end of the session, for Palmerston now played his hand with recklessness, sagacity, and luck. The cabinet accepted the mediation of the French: Palmerston delayed passing this information on to the British minister in Athens, and instead instructed him to bring further pressure on the Greek government. The Greeks capitulated to Palmerston's demands, and the French withdrew their ambassador. When the cabinet met on 16 May 'both P. and R. had a serious manner',[88] but Palmerston went over the whole case 'with his usual self-possession'.[89] Grey, to everyone's surprise, was stout in his support,[90] and the cabinet agreed to back Palmerston up. Lord John defended the decision as best he could to Prince Albert,[91] and then wrote to Palmerston on 22 May to confirm that at the end of the session there must be a change at the foreign office. England was 'encountered by more hostile feelings in her course than was natural and necessary . . . if you were to take some other department, we might continue the same line of foreign policy without giving the same offence'.[92]

Palmerston did not reply – he still had a few weeks in which to turn the tables, and luck was with him. In the lords, Protectionists and Peelites combined to pass a vote of censure on the government's handling of the Greek affair. The cabinet met to consider whether to take any notice. Palmerston opened the proceedings by offering his resignation, 'perhaps not very strenuously, but this we all held was inadmissible'. Lord John then turned to Lansdowne, who thought the lords' vote ought to be met by a vote of confidence in the commons. Carlisle agreed. Grey objected to this. Others thought a vote might only be carried by a small majority. 'Wood was for a vote or immediate resignation. Ld Jn asked Labouchere for his opinion, who gave it very strongly for immediate resignation. Hobhouse and George Grey were inclined for the same . . .'[93] Lord John then looked a little discomposed and said 'very well then, I shall resign, and shall state that I was prepared to go on . . . but was deserted by my colleagues'. Hobhouse immediately retracted, and so did the others.[94] Lansdowne then veered round and said he would be content with something being said in the commons, and this seemed to be the final decision.[95] Two days later when the cabinet met again, Lord John said Lansdowne had written to say that on reflection he thought some action must be taken.[96] The cabinet agreed, and Roebuck was put up to introduce a motion supporting the government's foreign policy in general. Russell and Palmerston, only, were to speak for the government. 'R. to P. "what will you say?". P. "I suppose I must say something about Greece" '.[97]

Protectionists, Peelites and Manchester Radicals combined, and Peel himself spoke against the government. Then Lord John spoke up for Palmerston, and dubbed him the Minister of England.[98] Clarendon praised his speech as a 'perfect' exposition of broad principles by the head of the government.[99] But everyone forgot what Lord John had done for Palmerston when Palmerston showed what he could do for himself. Lord John told the Queen beforehand that they needed a majority of forty if they were to go on.[100] Palmerston's speech may not have made the difference between victory and defeat, but it certainly made the difference between a majority of under forty and the majority of forty-six which the government obtained in a vote of 310 to 264. Palmerston had achieved two things that Lord John had been conspicuously unable to do since 1847, he had nearly filled the house, and he had mustered a solid Whig majority. At the end of the debate, he was fêted at the Reform Club, and though still without 'the prestige and generalissimo position of Lord John', he had 'the most numerous personal adherency' in the commons.[101]

The day after Palmerston's triumph, Peel fell off his horse. Four days later he died. Between the two men, Peel and Palmerston, Lord John never enjoyed a day's independent existence at the head of affairs. Peel had been the court favourite, but for four years he had assisted Lord John in his own way, and, as it now appeared, without any idea of embarrassing Lord John for his own ends. That support was now at an end. Palmerston was no favourite at the court, but he was a much more dangerous because a much more unorthodox man than Peel. As for Lord John, he was worn out, and in June he wrote to Clarendon that he wondered whether he would get through the year. Fox and Canning had both broken down at his age, and he could not get the relaxation his fragile body required.[102]

When Clarendon heard the result of the Don Pacifico debate he realised that the plan to move Palmerston from the foreign office must be abandoned.[103] When Prince Albert heard of the death of Peel, he concluded that the Queen dare not let Lord John go to the lords, because there would then be no moderating influence left in the commons.[104] Lord John himself did revert, tentatively, to the plan that had been drawn up in March, and met with a double rebuff. Palmerston refused to leave the foreign office, on account of the approbation his policy had received from one end of the country to the other, as he wrote on the back of Lord John's letter of 22 May;[105] and Prince Albert, who had already objected to Palmerston's being given the lead in preference to Sir George Grey, played his trump card, took Lord John to one side, informed him of Palmerston's alleged attempt to rape a lady-in-waiting at Windsor Castle, and said that after that it was impossible for the Queen to agree to give him the lead.[106]

There was no alternative but to leave Palmerston where he was. Lansdowne admitted the evil, but knew no remedy.[107] Early in August the Duke of Bedford went to Osborne and explained to the Queen 'Lord John Russell's views on . . . the Foreign Office'.[108] They amounted to this – that he could now neither control Palmerston nor risk turning him into opposition.[109] This was too much for the Queen, and on 12 August she

Fɪɢ. 6 SAUCY JACK RUSSELL; OR, WHO'S TO
TURN HIM OUT?

Punch put this question in 1850, and a year later it was on everybody's lips.

laid down new rules for Palmerston's conduct: he was to 'distinctly state what he proposes', and not to alter arbitrarily anything to which the Queen had given her assent.[110] While the Queen was selecting her position for the future, Lord John decided that in order to keep in front of Palmerston, he must take up the question of reform next year.[111] He went to the cabinet with another proposal for life peers. It was the lords who had amended the Irish franchise bill and censured Palmerston, and Lord John argued that Stanley was now ready to throw out anything he disapproved of. Grey said the present house of lords could not be worse. But Lansdowne said nothing about the remedy, and indeed 'no one . . . said anything very decided against it' except Hobhouse. Lord John was met by uninterested disapproving silence, and with that the cabinet dispersed for the holidays.[112]

ii. Office, 1850–1

In October the Pope divided England into twelve sees, and bestowed upon Wiseman the title of archbishop of Westminster. In November Lord John wrote publicly to the bishop of Durham 'blaming the Pope much, the Puseyites more'[113] – the Pope for his 'aggression' and the Puseyite spies 'within the gates' for reintroducing 'the mummeries of superstition'.[114] Not the least of the many things that were wrong with this letter was the confusion of the Pope and Puseyism. How did this come about?

Pius IX had been thinking of establishing an English hierarchy as far back as 1847, when he had handed Minto a paper about it. Minto may never have read the paper, and he gave the Pope no reason to suppose the British government would object.[115] In 1848 there was a revolution in Rome, and when the Pope reappeared he was a changed man supported by French bayonets. The Irish colleges then became the test of the relations between the British government and the Pope. Lord John himself would have preferred to leave Trinity College alone in Dublin, and to set up a roman catholic university in Cork and a presbyterian one in Belfast.[116] But nobody else agreed with him, and he went on trying to secure the consent of the Pope to the mixed colleges founded by Peel. Pius IX maintained the ban on the colleges, and in 1849 affairs took a turn for the worse with the appointment of Dr Cullen, the former rector of the Irish College in Rome as archbishop of Armagh. In 1850 Cullen summoned the first national synod since the twelfth century, which met at Thurles, in August, and condemned the Queen's colleges. Lord John set much store by higher education as a means to put Ireland on her feet, and the continued ban was a poor reward for his long career espousing the roman catholic and the Irish causes.[117]

Ingratitude stirred Lord John deeply. This is apparent in the Durham letter: paragraph 1, I am indignant; paragraph 2, 'I . . . promoted to the utmost of my power the claims of the Roman Catholics to all civil rights'. Nothing is more corrosive than old suspicion reawakened. The Pope seemed to have reverted to type, and Lord John wrote to Clarendon:

> I fear an angel from heaven would have little effect at Rome if he brought credentials from our Queen. Our crime is not the Colleges, or the Eglinton clause; it is the belief that we are in favour of the religious liberties and civil rights of nations.[118]

Lord John was falling back upon the instincts of his youth: 'mummeries' was a word freely used in his family,[119] and even before he wrote the Durham letter he characterised the Pope's attitude to the colleges as an 'aggression'.[120]

In the meantime the affairs of the church of England were also coming to a head in 1850. Lord John took care not to appoint another Hampden, but there was opposition to his choice of Dr Hinds, whom he recommended to the Queen as having written works upon the early history of the church,[121] for Norwich. The high church party were not alone in feeling that the prime minister ought not to be able to appoint 'heretic' bishops, and relations between church and state were already being questioned before the Gorham judgement of 1850. Gorham was a clergyman whom the bishop of Exeter refused to institute to a living on account of his views on baptism. Gorham appealed to the privy council, and the privy council, without offering any opinion as to his views on baptism, said that the bishop had no right to refuse to institute him. Lord John was not responsible for the Gorham judgement, but he no doubt agreed with his half-brother who wrote that 'we have gained our point'.[122] It was a summary vindication of the state's control over the reformed church.

Churchmen met the Gorham judgement by demanding the revival of convocation. The archbishop of Canterbury forwarded to Lord John a plan drawn up by the bishop of London for questions of heresy to be tried by the upper house of convocation. Carlisle came into the room when Lord John was drafting his reply, which 'is likely to be a smart one, to the effect that this would probably dispossess one half of the clergy from their livings'.[123] So far so good, but Lord John himself felt that something was necessary 'separating Tractarianism from Protestantism and treating Tractarianism as the Romish Church in disguise', and in October he was meditating setting up a committee of twenty-five clergymen 'for maintaining within the Church the principles of the Reformation'.[124] He would scarcely have started a purge, but as he said to Brougham,

> I shall be sorry if the Tractarians leave the Church, but if it can only remain Protestant at the cost of their secession, I shall be ready for one to pay the price. Like Arnold, I prefer the Roman Catholic foe to the Tractarian spy.[125]

Things having reached this point, it is not altogether surprising that when the Pope's bull was published, Lord John misinterpreted it as a take-over bid for the Church of England. This was a serious error of judgement, for, as G. C. Lewis pointed out, the Pope regarded even a Puseyite bishop as no better than a layman.[126]

On 30 October the bishop of Durham wrote to ask what Lord John and the government thought about 'the late aggression of the Pope upon our Protestantism'. Lord John did not reply at once. He found that the bishop of London considered the bull took possession of English territory and defied the supremacy of the Queen, and that Dr Ullathorne on the other hand represented it as a mere regulation of the relations of the catholics with their spiritual head. On 2 November Lord John wrote to Palmerston, 'The tone of the document favours the first interpretation; what is actually done, the second . . . It seems to me that we ought neither to leave the matter alone, nor to proceed in a hurry', but to ask the Pope for an explanation.[127] It was a

great pity he did not stop at that. But outside the storm was
rising; Lord Edward Howard, who was a catholic, offered to
resign his place in the Household before the clamour reached
the Queen;[128] and two days later Lord John wrote his fatal
letter, and missed two birds with one stone.

The letter brought Lord John cheap applause, and a cynic
might suppose that after the Don Pacifico debate this was what
he wanted. But it laid him open to the charge that he had
thrown away the principles of his political life.[129] The roman
catholic bishops in Ireland already used territorial titles, and in
October 1847 Lord John had written to Clarendon that the
law against their doing so was 'legislative humbug'.[130] He had
ordered Clarendon to address them by their titles in public, and
subsequently defended the obedient lord lieutenant in parliament.[131] He could not now escape by saying that Ireland was
not like England, when his whole political career had been devoted to showing that it could be made to be so. No argument
in his favour can escape this dilemma, and for years afterwards
men commented on 'the Durham letter *versus* Lord John's
theory of toleration'.[132]

The Peelites and the Irish were offended by the contents of
the Durham letter, and Lord John's colleagues were furious
that they had not been consulted before it was sent. For over
four years Lord John had been trying to woo the Peelites. The
Peelites were hard to get, but this made certain that he could
not win them. From Ireland Clarendon complained that 'the
"aliens" of Lord Lyndhurst were as nothing compared with the
"mummeries" of Lord Jn and we shall never hear the end of
it'.[133] Somerville, the chief secretary, received a requisition to
resign his seat.[134] As for the cabinet, when they assembled on 6
November, Hobhouse came into the room before Lord John
arrived, and 'Clanricarde asked me if I had seen Lord John
Russell's letter, and opened a cabinet box to show it to me. I
read it, as did others, and made no remark. I do not believe
any of the Cabinet had seen it before'.[135] When Lord John
entered, and asked whether they should refer the papal proceedings to the law officers, Grey and Carlisle thought not.[136]
Lord John then said such acts could not be passed over, 'and
some one (Labouchere I think) said "that question is decided
for us, look here", and he then read the passage of Russell's

letter in which he says that the matter shall be enquired into'.[137] The cabinet agreed that Truro, who had just succeeded Cottenham as lord chancellor, should be asked to report on the law,[138] but as Hobhouse said, they were unable to help themselves.

When the cabinet met again early in December, Grey, Carlisle and Labouchere were against doing anything.[139] Baring was for prosecuting under the act of 13 Elizabeth, but the law officers said that would not do. Then Lord John found an important ally in George Grey, who urged them to bring in a bill for fear of having a worse one forced upon them, and said that he would resign if nothing was done. 'George Grey read a draft, the Lord Chancellor read one, Lord Lansdowne wrote one, but there were great differences of opinion amongst us'.[140] Hobhouse thought the majority expressed a disinclination to do anything, but Lord John and George Grey carried the day, and finally discussion centred on a bill which provided for a fine of £100 upon assuming a title, and for all bequests left under the titles to be forfeited to the crown. Carlisle, who was 'stronger and more serious' than Hobhouse had ever heard him before,[141] never consented to anything which he thought 'so unworthy of ourselves, and of the nation'.[142]

Lord John had fallen into an error to which men who cannot get their own way are prone, and some of his colleagues now began to recall that five years earlier they had not been consulted about the Edinburgh letter. How was Lord John to cast the first stone at Palmerston now? It was no wonder that as Carlisle walked away from a cabinet with Wood and Labouchere, 'we all rather criticised Lord John'.[143] The prime minister himself tried to rationalise what he had done. He told Clarendon that what he had feared all along was that

> the young Tractarian clergy by the weakness and connivance of the Bishops would get possession of the Churches, and establish a religion of the higher classes, from which the middle and lower would separate,[144]

and that unless the government had taken the matter up there would have been such an outcry that all the roman catholics then in office, Bellew, Monaghan, O'Ferrall, Pigot, and Sheil, would have been driven out.[145]

It is fair to add that as time passed Lord John became calming. He admitted that it would have been better if he had left out the mummeries of superstition.[146] He toyed with his sister in law's idea of writing a second letter inculcating charity, in order to undo the harm done by the first one.[147] He considered trying to reopen negotiations with the Pope.[148] He disregarded a letter from Chadwick to the effect that in matters of public health the commissioners received every assistance from the clergy of the established church and none from the priests of Rome,[149] and he spurned an assurance volunteered by the bishop of Oxford that in five years he had never yet appointed to any post 'any one, who, even in these days of evil speaking, has been charged with being a Tractarian'.[150] He declined to set apart the day of Wiseman's enthronement as a day of national thanksgiving for deliverance from the yoke of Rome,[151] and he refused to consider making the dean of Westminster into a bishop.[152] He did not take advantage of the no Popery cry to hold a general election, and when the new session began in 1851, he told the cabinet that if anything more penal was forced upon the government they ought to resign.[153] He refused to exempt Ireland from the bill, but he conceded that in Ireland the law would have to be differently administered. In England a roman catholic bishop who assumed a title would be prosecuted, but in Ireland the law officers would not prosecute the titles the bishops already assumed.[154]

While the cabinet were digesting the Durham letter Lord John returned to the topic of parliamentary reform, and proposed to lower the franchise to £6 in the boroughs and £20 in the counties. His timing could not have been worse. There was 'a chorus of opposition against having any extension at all at present',[155] 'Grey stated his objections very forcibly', and Hobhouse followed suit. George Grey confirmed that there was no demand for reform, and Palmerston asked for a year's delay. Charles Wood, on the other hand, said he would not object if it could be carried,[156] and Truro and Minto spoke in favour, the latter 'very decidedly', which, Carlisle thought, meant that Lord John must be 'much bent on it'.[157] Both Carlisle and Hobhouse noticed that the premier seemed to think he had a pledge to redeem, and were puzzled how he could interpret his 1848 speech as a binding commitment. Nothing was settled, and as the cabinet broke up, Hobhouse, who was 'much struck by this second proposal of an organic change without any apparent necessity', told Grey that if they had to do it he would much rather start with the reform of the lords, for that, if successful, might enable Lord John to carry the other.[158]

In January 1851 Lord John brought the subject up again, and this time the scene in the cabinet was distressing. His scheme 'was strenuously backed by father in law Minto, faintly by Clanricarde, and strongly objected to by everyone else'.[159] Somebody pointed out that it would be inexpedient to run the risk of a clash between the houses in the year of the Great Exhibition, and Palmerston again asked for delay. Lord John then referred to his pledge. Hobhouse thought that would have been a reason 'if he had settled with his Cabinet that he should make his declaration, but he did not, any more than he consulted them as to his late letter'.[160] Lord John was not pleased, and at one time 'it looked a little serious', as he talked of bringing in a Reform Bill as a private member of parliament.[161] Finally, Lord John said he would give way if the cabinet agreed to a measure next year. 'No one took part with our master',[162] and there the matter stood adjourned.

Before the cabinet met again, Lord John asked the Queen for leave to confer a life peerage on Dr Lushington.[163] Then, on 28 January, he told his colleagues that he had been thinking during the week about reform. 'As he said this we were all silent and looked down.' Lord John said he now realised there were reasons for not attempting it that year. Palmerston then asked whether the cabinet were supposed to be agreeing to a measure next year. Grey and Hobhouse objected to any promise, and the latter felt that 'whenever the measure was really brought forward it would break up the government'.[164] Carlisle noticed that Lord John was bitter, and confided to his diary that 'it looks as if we might have a squall on the subject next year'.[165] To complete a bad start to the year, Lord John heard from Dr Lushington on 6 February that he was not prepared to become the first life peer.[166]

After this, the government faced the new session almost empty-handed except for the ecclesiastical titles bill. Lord John made a last attempt to persuade the cabinet to introduce a landlord and tenant bill for Ireland, but soon concluded that the subject was an impossible one.[167] The bill to abolish the lord lieutenant was to be wheeled out again, and there was to be another attempt to admit the Jews to parliament. But that was all; Lord John and the reformed parliament of 1832 had reached bottom dead centre. As Mr Slaney said, since the beginning of the century the work of 'the Liberal Party' in abolishing slavery, removing religious disabilities, reforming parliament, and freeing trade had been completed. Fresh ground must be taken up, and he suggested social reforms in favour of the middle and lower classes who thought the present laws prevented their working their way up.[168] Lord John would have agreed with much of this, but knew that until there was a further extension of the franchise, parliament could never be got on the move again.

At the opening of parliament there was an unusually large attendance, and casting his eye over the peers Carlisle 'felt the poor Pope to be an unequal match with the throne of Britain thus begirded'.[169] Lord John unveiled the ecclesiastical titles bill in a temperate speech in which he dwelt upon the appointment of Cullen, the synod of Thurles, and the attitude of the roman church to the Irish colleges.[170] But he made a mistake he often made when he knew he had the house behind him, and both Palmerston and Carlisle noted that his speech was 'too big for our bill'.[171] After strenuous opposition from Gladstone and the Irish, the government was given leave to introduce the bill by 395 votes to 63. But nothing else went well. Disraeli's annual motion on agricultural distress was only defeated by 281 votes to 267, and Wood's budget disappointed everyone. Locke King then brought on his annual motion to equalise the county and the borough franchise. Last year he had been beaten by 161 votes to 102, and the 161 had been made up of 32 official members, 99 Peelites and Protectionists, and 30 Liberals, and this time Hayter, the whip, sent out 172 circulars. But the government's supporters stayed away, and so did the Peelites and Protectionists. In an almost empty house, and without consulting his cabinet, Lord John tried to stave off defeat by promising to bring in a government measure next year. His speech had no effect, and the government was defeated by 100 votes to 54. This time the 54 were made up of 27 official members, 17 Peelites and Protectionists, and 10 Liberals.[172]

When the defeat was announced 'Russell gave no sign of disappointment', and nobody expected a serious result.[173] But overnight Lord John saw an opportunity to turn the tables on his cabinet, and the next day he said he felt he had lost the confidence of the house and must resign. He had been at the palace, and the Prince agreed.[174] Palmerston and Labouchere thought they had been beaten by accident, but George Grey and Hobhouse agreed with Lord John, who then said 'I *can't go on*'.[175] The government was out. Greville blamed it excessively, Lady Clanricarde thought they had been brought in by one letter of Lord John's and turned out by another,[176] and Truro commented that 'there was a good deal of temper' even in Lord John's resignation.[177]

A prolonged crisis followed. The Queen sent for Stanley, who declined to form a ministry until everything else had been tried. The Queen and the Prince then tried to bring about the longed-for coalition of Whigs and Peelites. They sent for Lord John and put him in touch with Aberdeen and Graham. Lord John offered the Peelites a complete reconstruction of the ministry, and a cabinet of eleven, chosen solely for fitness. The present commercial policy was to be inviolable, the year's financial measures were to be open to revision, the preamble and the first clause of the ecclesiastical titles bill (condemning the bull and imposing a fine for the assumption of titles) were to be persevered in and the remaining clauses dropped, and a Reform Bill was to be brought in after Easter.[178]

Now was seen the full folly of the Durham letter. For the first time the Queen and the Prince were backing a Whig-Peelite coalition with Lord John at the head of it. But so long as Ashley was imploring Lord John not to abandon 'a charge to which God has specially called you in this resistance to the Papacy',[179] Aberdeen and Graham resolved to have nothing to do with the ecclesiastical titles bill. Lord John explained that the bill was to assert national independence, not to restrict religious liberty.[180] The Queen took his part,[181] and Lansdowne thought the Peelites would find it difficult to maintain in public that the aggression could be passed over in silence.[182] But Lord John's tone was not persuasive, and there was transparent irritation in his letters to Aberdeen and Graham, who hastily closed the correspondence before it became a '*polémique*'.[183]

Lord John concluded that Graham wanted Stanley to take office and the Whigs and Peelites to fuse in opposition,[184] and he abandoned his attempt to form a new administration. The Queen then sent for Stanley again. Lord John was told that Stanley approached the Irish and offered to modify the poor law, and to bring encumbered estates on to the market more slowly.[185] But the Protectionists were even more protestant than the Whigs, the Irish were wary, and Stanley gave up. A few days later he was in high spirits after his two failures, and said to Lady John, 'you know they cannot come to me again; I am *l'homme impossible*'.[186] It is a good Stanley story, but it was naughty of Lord John to pass it on to the Queen.

Politics were in a tangle, as Lord John showed in an over-simplified memorandum which he prepared for the Prince.

Questions	*Agreed on them*
1. the budget	Whigs and Radicals
2. establishments of army and navy	Whigs and Tories
3. papal aggression	Whigs and Tories
4. parliamentary reform	Whigs and Radicals partially
5. economical reform	Peelites and Radicals.[187]

A bewildered Queen then sent for Lansdowne and Wellington. While a rumour went round that Clarendon was to be asked to form a ministry,[188] Wellington settled the matter. 'Is your majesty dissatisfied with your ministers?' 'No.' 'Then you had better keep them.'[189] The Queen still thought that if papal aggression was the sole ground of difficulty between Lord John and Aberdeen and Graham, he should take them in and make it an open question. When Lord John said this was not prac-tical, she suggested the Whigs might pass the ecclesiastical titles bill, and then reconstruct the ministry to include the Peelites.[190] Not surprisingly Lord John's colleagues reacted vio-lently against this,[191] especially Grey, who was sick of Peelite attacks upon his colonial policy, and was now backing towards the Protectionists.[192]

The Whigs came back as before, except that Hobhouse was made a peer with the title of Lord Broughton. The moral of the episode, Carlisle thought, was how much the Queen must miss

Peel.[193] *The Times* compared the government to Indian fakirs who bury themselves for a week and come out exhausted but alive.[194] Lord John came back in 1851 weaker even than Melbourne in 1839, and his speech announcing that ministers had returned to their places was not well received by the house,[195] where the party's 'lower limits' were 'in a state of absolute paralysis'.[196] His supporters began to ask for favours before it was too late, and there was now much more open grumbling among the members of the cabinet. Wood said all their difficulties stemmed from Lord John's letter.[197] Truro said Lord John had 'the great defect of taking up opinions and measures rashly, and abandoning them capriciously'. Broughton thought there was truth in this, but with his peerage in his pocket, added more kindly, 'when a minister begins to lose credit with the country his faults become more perceptible to his Cabinet than during his palmy days'.[198]

The first thing the government must attend to on coming back into office was the ecclesiastical titles bill. They were under much pressure to put Ireland outside the scope of the act. G. C. Lewis pointed out that the bull only referred to England, and asked why the defence should be greater than the attack.[199] Minto told Lord John that he was harnessing two horses to his carriage 'which will pull in opposite directions'.[200] But George Grey thought Ireland must be in,[201] and once again his view was decisive. In his negotiations with the Peelites, however, Lord John had offered to drop all but the preamble and the first clause, and when he took up his pen, the cabinet voted unanimously in favour of abridging the bill.[202] Two days later they decided not to proceed with the bill to abolish the lord lieutenant.[203] Presumably Lord John wanted to remove an obstacle to future junction with Graham, who had vowed war against a fourth secretary of state: the rest of the cabinet had never cared for the bill anyway.

Lord John then consulted Stanley about the ecclesiastical titles bill.[204] Stanley thought its loss after it had been introduced would be a great evil. He saw Disraeli, and promised Lord John the undivided support of the Protectionists for the second reading,[205] which was carried by 438 votes to 95. While the world flocked to the Great Exhibition in Hyde Park to see the wonders of modern industry, the British parliament was busy with the committee stage of a bill more worthy of the sixteenth century than of the nineteenth. Three amendments were introduced to make the declaratory clause apply to all rescripts, to give the prosecuting power to an individual, and to make the introduction of bulls a penal offence. Lord John resisted them, but the Irish M.P.s walked out, and they were all carried.[206] The bill thus passed into law more irritating, but no more effective, than he had anticipated.

Even before the bill passed the government's chief hope seems to have been that they could use it as a lever in diplomacy. They would leave it in abeyance in return for the Pope making nominations to bishoprics by domestic election and giving the crown a right of veto.[207] Nothing came of this, and in October, when Campbell went to Rome, he noted that upon the issue of the Irish colleges the Pope was still in the hands of the Propaganda and the McHale interest.[208] The act contributed nothing to British diplomacy, and there was little else it could have contributed to. Although Lord John did once think of prosecuting Cullen,[209] he was aware that 'a modern martyr professes one of the easiest and most gainful of trades',[210] and he decided to wait until he could get an English prosecution.[211] None took place, and all that ever happened was that in 1866 Lord John objected to Longmans putting the words archbishop of Westminster on the title page of a book.[212] The act was repealed in 1871 by Gladstone, who had been its principal opponent in 1851, and by that time even Lord John admitted it had been a mistake.

There was nothing else in the session to bring the ministers much cheer. The Jew bill passed the commons but was lost in the lords by 144 votes to 108. Hume carried a vote to restrict the income tax to one year, and in April Disraeli again raised the question of agricultural distress and ran the government closer than ever before with a vote of 265 to 252. With fatal timing, Grey proposed a new Canada clergy reserves bill favourable to the catholics and 'eminently calculated to swamp us',[213] and the whole conduct of colonial affairs was again called into question when the Radicals reopened the debate on Ceylon. Before the session ended there were signs that the British were about to become embroiled with the Kaffirs in South Africa.

iii. Office, 1851–2

On 7 August 1851, in what was now an annual end-of-session ritual, Lord John again drew the attention of the cabinet to life peers. Attendance was 'scanty',[214] for George Grey was seriously ill, and Baring, Maule, Minto and Wood were absent. Broughton records that

> Ld Grey thought if such peers were created they should be legal personages. Labouchere thought that any such plan would lower the House of Lords. The Chancellor said nothing, but shook his head. I observed that life peers would inevitably lower the character of the House . . . Russell said he entirely differed from me, so did the Prince . . . Ld Carlisle and Labouchere hinted that the Prince's opinion in such matters was not worth much. Russell's views were not supported by any one . . .

Lord John then spoke about the government's commitment to a Reform Bill next session.[215] Broughton did not think he pressed it as earnestly as before, and the meeting ended with Lord John's saying that he wished to make a new approach to Graham, and perhaps to Gladstone, and if that failed, to bring in Seymour and Granville.[216]

Five days later, however, Lord John set out his plans for a Reform Bill at length, in a memorandum written for the Queen and the Prince. Small boroughs were to be retained because they had tempered extremes by carrying the repeal of the corn laws against the counties and keeping up the army and navy estimates against the large towns. But there were anomalies and there ought to be a small redistribution of seats. The franchise should be lowered to £20 in the counties and £5 in the towns, and at the same time a new attempt should be made to create a real representation for the working classes. 'The manner in which this object can probably be best attained is by working on the ancient principle of Guilds or Companies.' Lord John proposed to divide the persons following any trade or profession mentioned in the population returns into guilds. In any town there were to be between two and twelve guilds, which would elect master citizens who would have the right of voting for members of parliament.[217]

The Queen and the Prince were taken aback, and the plan

has not been highly thought of since. Yet it was a serious attempt
to remedy the exclusion of the working classes by the 1832 act,
and had it been accepted it would perhaps have delayed the
eventual formation of a Labour Party. The Prince urged Lord
John not to lay so startling a plan before his colleagues for the
time being, but 'to ask each to submit to you his views as to the
nature of the reform *he* would propose'. The Queen, he added,
would like to see these views.[218] This was of doubtful constitutional propriety, and was something to which Lord John could
not agree,[219] not least because the answers would all have said
that there was at present no need for reform at all. The position
in the middle of August was summed up by Ellice, who told
Parkes that he doubted whether Lord John had had any defined notions in February when he readily promised a measure
for the future: 'By this time of course he has, but not so his
colleagues, who are as innocent of his views as you or I'.[220]

Before the end of August Lord John wrote to Lansdowne and
to Palmerston that Broughton was ready to give up the board of
control and that he would like to offer it to Graham, who would
be a great help in planning the new Reform Bill.[221] Neither
raised any personal objection,[222] and Lord John sent G. C.
Lewis to Graham to invite him to join the government. The
ecclesiastical titles act was on the statute book, there were no
other differences, and Lewis took with him a personal letter
from Prince Albert. It was all to no avail, as it always had been.
Graham replied that as one of the authors of the Reform Act of
1832 it ill became him to propose another one.[223] He could
hardly have rebuked Lord John more personally, and Minto
thought he had done it 'simply from his instinctive preference
for an insincere and dishonest reason'.[224]

Wood suggested approaching Newcastle, who was the person
Peel had desired his friends to look to.[225] But Newcastle had
already warned Lord John off,[226] and the prime minister
quickly fell back upon his plan of bringing in Seymour and
Granville. Seymour had a beautiful wife,[227] and Granville was
'suaviter in modo'.[228] It was two more peers,[229] and the appointments brought no tail and no new tone.[230] Next, Lord John
offered young Frederick Peel the under-secretaryship of the
colonies. Peel asked for an assurance about the new Reform Bill,
Lord John referred him to his speech of 1848,[231] and when he

joined, Minto hoped that now the ice was broken other Peelites would follow.[232]

In the first week of October Lord John consulted Palgrave, who was an expert on the guild scheme.[233] In the second week he received the electoral statistics of nearly 8000 parishes.[234] On 14 October the cabinet assembled and Seymour and Granville took their places for the first time. Lord John announced that parliament was not to meet until February,[235] and then said that

> one of the first measures would be the extension of the suffrage. He had not formed his plan entirely, but he had resolved what he could not do, he could not get rid of small constituencies. Here Lord Lansdowne applauded. Little or nothing was said by others . . .[236]

Lord John then named a committee – Carlisle, Minto, Wood and himself. Carlisle thought it a great honour, but grudged 'any abridgement of my country'.[237] Clarendon, who had come over for the occasion, then said that in Ireland the franchise ought to be lowered to £5, and the meeting came to an end: 'very little was said on this most important subject at all'.[238]

On 15 October the committee set to work. They agreed to reduce the borough franchise to £5, and Lord John then began to expound his 'additional industrial franchise'. The committee foresaw difficulties.[239] The next day there was another meeting of the full cabinet, and Broughton asked why they should extend the suffrage: 'at which there was a general cheer from almost every body, and R. said rather testily "you were not one of those who made the Reform Bill" '. Lord John then went on to say that many were frightened in 1831. No one dared to ask how that applied to them, and Broughton concluded that they were to have a Reform Bill 'merely because Ld J.R. without consulting any one promised one'.[240] No more was said, and the next day the committee of the cabinet met again, and got on 'rather sweetly'. Three days later they met for the third time, and then adjourned until the last week in November.[241]

On the face of it, Lord John had driven a reluctant cabinet into agreeing to bring in a new Reform Bill. But in fact his position was still precarious. It was not a strong committee. Wood was of consequence, but Carlisle was light-weight, and

Minto was disliked, and more than half the cabinet would have refused to serve on this committee had they been asked. Everything now depended on whether there was anyone courageous enough to brave Lord John's extreme ill temper, and it was not long before Ellice heard that the foreign office and the treasury were not of one mind on reform. He then composed Lord John's epitaph: 'I was well. I would be better. Here I am'.[242]

Palmerston did not waste time on the Reform Bill, but expressed himself in his own language, that of foreign affairs. All through 1851 the tone of his letters to Lord John had been menacing, and he now put himself beyond restraint. The reform committee met for the third time on 20 October. On 23 October Kossuth was due to arrive at Southampton. Kossuth was, according to one's beliefs, a patriot or a rebel. Palmerston the man regarded him as a patriot, and invited him to his house. But Palmerston the foreign secretary was responsible for relations with the government of Austria who regarded Kossuth as a rebel. Lord John's immediate reaction was to suggest quite mildly that Palmerston ought not to receive him.[243] Then, when this had no effect, he forbade Palmerston to receive him, first in a letter expressing incredulity which left Palmerston a line of retreat,[244] and then in a way that left him none.[245] Palmerston answered the first letter by saying that he expected 'to see the Day when the City of London will require their Member to shew some Courtesy to their Guest',[246] and the second, with Lord John's messenger waiting, by saying that he did not choose to be dictated to, and that he would use his own discretion – 'You will of course use yours as to the Composition of your Government'.[247]

The Queen wrote scathingly to Lord John that if he was content to go on with a minister who answered him like that, she might even dismiss Palmerston herself.[248] Lady John then took fright. She revered Kossuth, and thought that if there were a breach on this issue Palmerston would emerge at the head of the Liberal party. She begged her father to persuade Lord John to climb down.[249] Lord John summoned the cabinet for 3 November and informed each member that he had got into 'a disagreeable altercation' with Palmerston.[250] Then, he wrote to Palmerston himself that the question between them must be decided by argument and not by passion, and added that if his letter had been too peremptory, Palmerston's had been quite unjustifiable.[251]

When the cabinet met, Carlisle, G. Grey, and Fox Maule were absent. Lord John spoke quietly, and then called on Palmerston. Broughton records that 'P. smiled and said being so called upon he must speak'. He spoke well, but he did not persuade the cabinet that he was right. Lansdowne was not convinced. Grey was not. Minto was not. Granville was not, and 'was a little too decisive for a young Cabinet minister'. Broughton himself said it would be funny if Kossuth having failed to bring down the Austrian government brought down the British one, but gave his voice against any reception. Truro, Labouchere, and Baring all agreed with Lord John, and the cabinet decided that Palmerston was to give a hint to Kossuth not to come.[252]

Lord John was vindicated, and Palmerston was not humiliated. The foreign secretary could have left the matter there, but he was not the man to lie down under a defeat, and on 19 November he received an address presented by a delegation from the constituency of Finsbury and Islington. This was the Radical part of London, and it is a remarkable fact that this delegation went not to Lord John to congratulate him upon his new Reform Bill, but to Palmerston to congratulate him upon his championing the Liberal cause overseas. In the address the emperors of Austria and Russia were called 'Despots and Assassins'. Lord John was at first inclined not to take the escapade very seriously, but the Queen forced him to remonstrate with Palmerston,[253] whose answer appeared meek, though its substance was an excuse which no man could have taken at face value.

> If I had been as much in the Habit of receiving Deputations as you and Charles Wood are, I should probably have stipulated when they entered my Room, that our Interview should not be manufactured into a Commodity to be sold to the Newspapers.[254]

Palmerston was not a junior minister in his first scrape, and Lord John must have felt very small as he professed to accept this.[255]

In the meantime the members of the reform committee continued to correspond, the industrial franchise was replaced by a 40s direct taxes franchise, and by the time they met again on 27, 28, and 29 November, the main question concerned the redistribution of seats. Lansdowne would resign if they attempted

much, and they decided at Wood's suggestion that there was to
be no complete disfranchisement, but that the smallest boroughs
were to be paired, and turned into 'contributory boroughs'.[256]
Lansdowne missed the cabinet on 2 December,[257] which came
to no decision about the bill and adjourned for two days. That
night Napoleon carried out his *coup d'état* in Paris, and on 3
December, without consulting anyone, Palmerston saw the
French ambassador, Walewski, and told him that he approved
of the emperor's action. Even by Palmerston's standards this
was a surprising thing to do. On 4 December the cabinet met
again. Lansdowne was there, and after going over the case of
the Finsbury and Islington delegations, they moved on to the
Reform Bill. Lansdowne objected to the contributory boroughs,
but was not, Carlisle thought, 'likely to oppose any desperate
resistance'.[258] Last of all they discussed the *coup d'état* in France,
and decided to instruct Normanby to be neutral. Palmerston
did not object, and from that moment was guilty of deception
as well as insubordination. On 5 December the cabinet agreed
to the scheme for contributory boroughs; and on 6 December
they considered the Scots and Irish Reform Bills, and decided
against the ballot. Before the day was out they had finished the
Reform Bill,[259] and Lansdowne and George Grey were added to
the committee to steer it through parliament.[260] Palmerston
does not seem to have said anything, but on 10 December he
wrote to Lord John that he was sorry they were going to disturb
so many boroughs.[261]

By that time Palmerston had passed on the cabinet's official
instruction to remain completely neutral to Normanby in
Paris. Normanby communicated it to Turgot, and was astonished to be told that Palmerston had already expressed his
approval of the *coup d'état* to Walewski. Normanby had never
got on well with Palmerston, and their correspondence now degenerated into a quarrel. Normanby laid the case before Lord
John,[262] and Lady Normanby took it to the Queen. On 13
December the Queen demanded an explanation of Lord John,
and on 14 December Lord John demanded one of Palmerston.[263] By the morning of the sixteenth no explanation had
arrived. Lord John wrote to Minto to say that Palmerston had
got into fresh trouble: 'I cannot get from him any explanation
of his conduct . . . I am tired of this battle, and of these con-

tinual scrapes – so that I think of finishing the affair suddenly.'[264] Lord John made one last attempt to approach Palmerston, and said his silence was disrespectful to the Queen.[265] Palmerston at last replied soberly, and at length, not explaining his conduct, but justifying it.[266] His answer reached Lord John at Woburn on 17 December, and without making any further attempt to see him Lord John dismissed Palmerston from the foreign office: 'misunderstandings perpetually renewed, violations of prudence and decorum too frequently repeated have marred the effects which ought to have followed from a sound policy and able administration'.[267] Lord John offered him Ireland in place of Clarendon. It was a forlorn hope, and in a 'cold and careful'[268] answer Palmerston preferred to be dismissed.[269]

He would be a bold man who would presume to say exactly what Palmerston was up to in the autumn of 1851. In his life of *Lord Palmerston* H. C. F. Bell, who knew all about Palmerston's foreign policy, but nothing about Lord John's Reform Bill, described Palmerston's rashness as 'almost incomprehensible'.[270] We, who know about the Reform Bill, may be inclined to agree with Joseph Parkes that it was 'wilful bedmaking to fall upon'.[271] At any rate, as soon as he knew Palmerston had gone, Lord John summoned the cabinet for 22 December. With characteristic carelessness he omitted to say what the meeting was for, and Lansdowne and Wood both assumed that it must be about the Cape, where Grey's colonial policy was ending in ruins at the hands of Sir Harry Smith.[272] When Lansdowne heard what the summons was for he wrote that there was not a member of the cabinet who would suppose Palmerston ought to have spoken to Walewski.[273] And so it proved: the cabinet was unanimous and very kind to Lord John.[274] The only person who expressed any doubt was Clarendon, who wrote from Ireland to ask whether it was really worse than anything Palmerston had done before, and whether it was not, in any case, only doing what the whole world would do in six weeks' time.[275]

Everyone knew that Palmerston's departure would lead to the defeat of the ministry. Parkes described it as 'a shot in our hull',[276] Lansdowne was afraid the public would never believe Lord John's story,[277] and Clarendon wondered whether the cabinet would think it worth while even trying to go on with

Palmerston in opposition.[278] That was too pessimistic for Lord John, who started to look for a replacement. He offered the foreign office first to Clarendon, who did not want to succeed Palmerston,[279] and then to Granville, who accepted.

Members of the cabinet then talked of strengthening the ministry. Wood suggested making yet another offer to the Peelites,[280] and Clarendon volunteered to give up Ireland to the Duke of Newcastle.[281] But George Grey thought Gladstone's accession would alarm the rank and file, and added that it was no use supposing one could neutralise him by bringing in Shaftesbury at the same time;[282] Minto argued against making any offer at all to the Peelites, because it would look as though Lord John had turned Palmerston out to get them;[283] and Lady John was all for 'a good fight and a good fall'.[284]

Lord John himself invited the Duke of Newcastle to come and see him, and wrote to Broughton to say that he wanted to offer the board of control to Gladstone, and that he counted upon his generosity.[285] Broughton was willing, but Newcastle objected to the ecclesiastical titles act, to Lord John's distribution of patronage which he thought would lead to a secession from the church, and to the Whigs' colonial policy. Even so the cabinet thought the negotiations ought not to be allowed to fail until the Peelites had actually been offered places, and Lord John was empowered to say that they had all put their offices at his disposal.[286] Prince Albert summoned Newcastle, but could make nothing out of him,[287] and the negotiations ended with a sharp and almost rancorous exchange of letters between Lord John and Newcastle.[288]

In desperation the cabinet considered making a last effort to recover Graham. After the last rebuff, Lord John was extremely reluctant to do this.[289] Minto, too, deprecated 'the catching at foul weeds to keep our heads above dirty water';[290]

> a long discussion arose, which ended in the Cabinet deciding, *Pintone nonobilante*, that a *large* offer should be made to Graham; the two Greys, Wood, and Francis Baring putting their places at the disposal of the Premier.[291]

Lord John agreed to invite Graham to come and see him, but only on condition that Lansdowne was present too. Sir James' answer to Lord John's letter was 'coy'. Lord John and Minto

wanted to take this as final: the rest of the cabinet still wanted
Lord John to see Graham. 'At last Lord John said that he *would
not* . . . so the matter is at an end'.[292]

Lord John lived 'in misery',[293] and as Clarendon said, he had
some reason to:

> Look at the position of J.R. – is that a desirable one for a man who
> has no call to jump naked into a nest of hornets? He may have
> faults, and certainly has committed errors, but who is perfect? . . .
> He has, however, great talents and great virtues . . . and he is, by
> common consent, the only man fit to lead the H. of Commons;
> yet there he is, accused of numberless . . . offences, not a friend
> coming forward in his defence – badgered, insulted . . . asking for
> aid and meeting with refusals, compelled to carry on the govern-
> ment . . . if anxiety such as he undergoes did not destroy my intel-
> lect, it would soon take me to the receptacle in Watford Church.[294]

But over in Dublin, Clarendon scarcely knew how bad things
had become. The cabinet was verging on dissolution. On 14
January Broughton walked away with Seymour, who 'complained of the irritability of these Cabinets'.[295] Broughton
attended the cabinet on 15 January, but he ignored the summonses for 17, 20, 21, and 22 January. He then received a letter
from Lord John telling him that Fox Maule was to have the
board of control. He was upset by this, having agreed to vacate
for Gladstone, not Maule, and after a painful interview with
Lord John on 25 January, he did not come again, although he
continued to receive summonses as usual.[296]

It was a disintegrating ministry which put the final touches
to the Reform Bill for 1852, and to the long overdue militia bill.
Lansdowne renewed his objection to the swamping of the small
boroughs,[297] and refused to introduce the Reform Bill in the
lords.[298] Seymour said he hated the whole thing, but would not
be the one to break up the government. Granville was the only
one 'who ventured to hint that I was not in perfect despair at
there being such a thing as a Reform Bill'. Lord John handled
Lansdowne 'with temper and tact',[299] agreed it was hard on
him having to propose a bill he did not like,[300] but queried
whether his part was as difficult as he supposed. If the bill
passed the commons, all he had to do was to recommend it
as the bill which the commons had passed.[301] Lansdowne

acquiesced, but wished they had all gone out together with
Palmerston, and foresaw that it would not last long.[302]

When parliament met, the great question was how Palmerston would behave. Normanby had warned Lord John that
Palmerston 'never forgives'.[303] After the cabinet on 22 December, Lord John had written to Palmerston, who endorsed the
letter

> Cabinet regret my loss, but agree with him on the subject* . . .
>   * This assertion was totally untrue. P.[304]

Palmerston was very cool in all he wrote to Lord John;[305] and
Lady Palmerston spoke of treachery,[306] and stopped inviting
Lord and Lady John to her Saturday evening receptions. For
his part, Lord John found the parting with Palmerston 'a blow
to me, which few would suspect, and which I did not expect',[307] and when Clarendon represented Palmerston's policy
as 'a signal failure',[308] Lord John reminded him of Palmerston's
energy and Englishness.[309] Lord John refused even to consider
offering a place to Aberdeen, because it would be too humiliating to Palmerston.[310]

At the beginning of the session, there had to be an explanation. Lord John warned Palmerston in advance that he might
refer to the Queen's letter of 12 August 1850.[311] Palmerston
later complained that Lord John had not behaved like a
gentleman,[312] but he was not taken by surprise, and if Lord
John made a good speech and Palmerston made a bad one, that
may have been because Lord John had a good case and Palmerston had none. Two days later Lord John introduced the
Reform Bill. Carlisle thought that on the whole it was well received, though not with rapture.[313] However that may be, Lord
John was not to be allowed to proceed with it. Lord Naas was
ready with an attack on Clarendon, Palmerston had his eyes on
the militia bill, and there was almost universal dissatisfaction
with the state of affairs at the Cape. On 19 February, when
Naas' motion came on, Carlisle records, 'Ld John spoke admirably – he put his whole heart into it, being as I believe very
fond of Clarendon; the house warmed up to him completely'.[314]
It was Lord John's last great effort in parliament, made in defence of his record in Ireland and on behalf of a colleague. The
very next day Palmerston moved an amendment to the militia

PLATE 9   The Politician's Portfolio

(John Bull   Palmerston   The Queen   Lord John
The Russian Emperor   The Pope)

This caricature was published at the beginning of 1852. Palmerston
professed to believe that his dismissal was known in advance in
Vienna, and at the very least did nothing to correct the impression
that he had been sacked to please the autocrats of Eastern Europe.
Notice that Lord John is here portrayed as having taken too
un-Protestant a line against the Pope.

bill, and carried it by 136 votes to 125. Lord John at once announced that the government would resign, and the next morning *The Times* published a funny article on the chances of Palmerston's being sent for, and offering Lord John the foreign office with the Queen's letter of August 1850 for guidance.[315]

On 21 February the fallen cabinet met, and 'no one dissented respecting the propriety of resignation, and the impossibility of dissolution'. The whip said their defeat made no difference, for they would in any case have been beaten the very next day, by fifteen, on the Cape. The cabinet then ended as it had latterly gone on:

> Ld. Grey rather flew out about the crude state in which the Militia Bill had been brought forward – to which Lord John 'every body tells me we should have done very well if a certain despatch had not been written to Sir Harry Smith'. I had scarcely ever heard such sharp sayings . . . Fox Maule deprecated any further indulgence in them, and all ended with their acquiescence in my proposal to have one more cabinet dinner with me . . .

The good Carlisle poured oil over the wounds. He also delivered the administration's funeral oration:

> So ends the Administration, by an inadequate blow, but the body had become too weak for dignified existence. Many causes have co-operated . . . above all the Ecclesiastical Titles Bill. I cannot regret the termination of the Administration; on that occasion I thought it not true to the cause of religious liberty, and I have always been inclined to question the vote against the Irish Disturbance bill upon which it was originally founded.[316]

Part Four, 1852–78

CHAPTER XV

A Pitch of Wilfulness, 1852–5

i. Opposition, 1852

LORD JOHN had been prime minister for five years and eight months, and it was inevitable, as Clarendon assured him, that people had become tired and wanted novelty, even though the new men might not get on so well.[1] This was an understatement: there was hardly one member of Lord John's cabinet who would be in a hurry to serve under him again, and Grey actually told the Queen that if he were invited to, he would refuse.[2] Ellice said that

> The public soon discovered . . . more departmental independence, and stronger self-will on the part of individual members of that Cabinet, than was consistent with an energetic and homogeneous administration,[3]

and the Duke of Bedford told his brother bluntly, 'The complaint is that you were not sufficiently Prime Minister'.[4]

Looking back over the whole period from 1846 to 1852 it is clear that there had been a decline in Lord John's capacity since the 1830s, and indications of this are to be found in his correspondence. Lord John had never been businesslike, and when he became prime minister, he escaped from the discipline of a department. Wherever he went, papers were mislaid,[5] letters became separated from the enclosures to which they referred,[6] and laboriously compiled statistics were lost and had to be copied again.[7] In 1846 the lord lieutenant received a letter from Lord John headed:

mislaid
Sept. A~~ug~~ 12   Woburn Abbey
               J.R.   Sept. 8 1846[8]

FIG. 7   THE RHYME OF YE ANCIENT MINISTERE

Punch 1852

From Treasury Bench condemned to fly,
  Their salaries forego:
Each seem'd to say, as he pass'd me by,
  'It's all your fault, you know'.

Official boxes were left lying around for days on end when Lord John forgot to give them to the messenger,[9] and papers which ought to have been in one box turned up in another.[10] Sometimes a letter from Lord John ended abruptly where he had left a whole sheet out of the envelope.[11] Amendments to bills would be circulated to the cabinet without explanation,[12] and towards the end of 1850, when the ecclesiastical titles bill was being prepared, members of the cabinet received a printed, confidential paper 'respecting our "griefs" certainly not over-stated against the Pope, and nothing accompanied it to show whether the statement was your own, or one you had received and thought it right to circulate'.[13]

Some of Lord John's correspondents were fortunate to receive their letters at all. One letter to Lord Erroll was addressed simply to Paris.[14] Another, to Lord Lansdowne, went first to Colne, and when it finally reached Bowood drew from the recipient the tactful advice that 'without reflection upon the a's of my correspondents I always recommend to add Wilts to the direction'.[15] Baron Brunnow opened an envelope brought by special messenger from Lord John, and found inside a letter addressed to Mme de Lieven.[16] Finally, even when you received a letter, you might be asked next day to have a copy made and send it back because Lord John had not kept one, and Bessborough, Clarendon, Palmerston, and in due course Aberdeen, all suffered in this way.[17]

These bad habits extended to other aspects of Lord John's official life. Ministers would call on Lord John in Downing Street at a time he had named, and find he had gone out.[18] He once fixed a day to do business in London, and stayed at home all day at Pembroke Lodge. On another occasion friends who could not find him in London, where he had arranged to meet them, went down to Pembroke Lodge, and could not find him there either.[19] As Lord Minto said, 'You are the best of Prime Ministers, but you would have been a bad postmaster general: the calculation of time and space being evidently beyond your powers'.[20] All this carelessness was tolerable so long as it stemmed from absent-mindedness. But when Lord John felt overworked, or found himself at odds with his colleagues, he became wilful and capricious. In January 1852 the cabinet met to hear an account of Lord John's negotiations with the Duke

of Newcastle. Lord John expected to be censured,[21] and it
turned out he had not got the papers with him – they were
coming up from Pembroke Lodge by the carrier.[22]

No one felt Lord John's deficiencies more than the Queen and
the Prince. Lord John's daily reports on the proceedings in
parliament were perfunctory, apprehensive for his own position, and ungenerous to anyone, like Stanley, who might deprive him of it. Lord John told Palmerston that he made his
reports brief because there were newspapers.[23] Newspapers or
not, the Queen and the Prince can be forgiven for being dissatisfied with anything as brusque as this: 'The Transportation
Bill was then committed, and the usual nonsense was spoken
upon it till past one in the morning.'[24] Lord John did not wish
to insult the Queen and the Prince, but he never took the
trouble to please them, and on 11 January 1852, Prince Albert

> found him very inattentive and almost unwilling to listen to me,
> breaking off the conference in the midst of the most important
> subject by looking at his watch and expressing his fears that he
> would be too late for the train.[25]

In a man who year by year came before his recalcitrant cabinet
with very familiar letters from the Prince beginning 'My dear
Lord John',[26] in support of his proposals to give more aid to
Ireland, for life peers, and for reform, this was ill-mannered
folly.

The kindest explanation of all this is that prime ministers are
exhausted after three years. But Lord John did not go entirely
without relaxation, for he had Pembroke Lodge, where the
peace was not disturbed by the man taken in the shrubbery,
who confessed to being a thief in the petty larceny line.[27] Down
at Petersham Lord John was quite the squire. He and Lady
John set up a school for the children of the village.[28] Morpeth
allotted Lord John a paddock in Richmond Park, out of the
woods and forests.[29] Two heifers arrived,[30] and Lord John kept
poultry – though with the ill fortune which attends the imprac-
tical it turned out that 'when well fatted . . . they were too old
to be eaten'.[31]

When Carlisle went down to Pembroke Lodge in 1851 he
found it 'a most simple and primitive ménage: we had no
dinner, but tea at 8 with a boiled chicken'.[32] Lord and Lady

John generally ate with their children, and Johnny always appeared to advantage 'domestically'.[33] Young John was coming on well 'malgré his papa's efforts to coddle, and cut him off from the danger of a through draft or of a drop of rain water',[34] and was already showing signs of the family's precocity in religion, asking his aunt Mary in Turin why monks should think it pleased God not to eat meat, and not to speak.[35] Willy was even more advanced, and when he was not yet four years old, he was walking with his mother in the garden one day when he said, 'Soon God will call us all. But only my soul will go up, my body will be eaten by worms'. Lady Russell asked him who had told him that. 'Dada did tell me.' Was William glad to hear it? 'No, I would like my soul to be eaten by worms, and my body to go up to God.'[36]

Life at Pembroke Lodge gave Lord John the rest he needed, but at the price of finally cutting him off from his supporters. During the session he and Lady John came up to London, and did their best to entertain, but when they held an assembly, the company consisted largely of 'Diplomats and Elliots'.[37] Carlisle, who was not a hostile witness, generally stayed 'about three minutes', and like many other people who abused Lord and Lady John when they did not entertain, he also complained when they did, saying that Lady John had grown 'awfully recipient'.[38] The rank and file continued to feel that no notice was ever taken of them,[39] and when Lord John fell out with his cabinet as well, the breakdown in communication between the prime minister at Pembroke Lodge and the rest of the party was complete. Johnny came, as Parkes said, to 'dwell in a Wigwam', and the trouble was that 'not only does not Truth reach him, but that he is ever surrounded only by those who dare not tell it him'.[40]

When the ministry fell, Lord John was nearly sixty, and he should have retired with his two and a half dozen bottles of Australian wine and his Colt's revolving firearm from the Great Exhibition.[41] He had, after all, as H. G. Ward told him, done more in twenty-five years than was ever done before by any British statesman,[42] and had he given up at this point posterity would have recognised this. But he was understandably reluctant to hand the party over to Palmerston, and he dug his heels in over reform, behaved as though he had a divine right to go

on leading the party, and rounded angrily on any former colleague whose loyalty was not unconditional. The result was that
before he died Lord John had thrown away a great reputation,
and done it, moreover, in such a way that no one has ever been
able to restore it since.

When Derby and Disraeli succeeded Lord John in 1852 they
were in a minority. Their government was expected to last only
so long as the divisions among their opponents, and was known
as the Derby militia – called out for twenty-eight days, and then
to be sent home.[43] Lord John attempted to reunite the Whig
party, and invited Palmerston to a meeting at his house.[44] But
Palmerston refused, and when Lord John imprudently attacked the new government's militia bill, Palmerston handled
him with savage contempt. Lord John then turned to the Peelites and resumed his friendship with Graham upon the opposition benches. But Gladstone thereupon severed all connection
with Graham, and the prospect of the younger Peelites ever
serving under Lord John seemed as remote as ever.

In the summer, Derby asked for a dissolution. Lord John
made free trade and reform the planks of his election address,[45]
and held a meeting at Chesham Place which raised apprehensions that under the guise of defending the one he intended to
ally with Cobden and Bright to secure the other.[46] Lord John
came second in the poll in the city, but the honours of the campaign went to the Protectionists, who came back about 315
strong,[47] while the Peelites suffered heavily.

The result put free trade in jeopardy, and immediately after
the election, Lord John wrote to Aberdeen and asked him what
he and the other Peelites proposed to do.[48] Aberdeen replied
cautiously that fusion, which he favoured, must come from circumstances and not from previous discussion.[49] But Gladstone
recalled the manner in which Lord John had turned Sir Robert
out in 1835, and Newcastle objected to becoming a Whig, and
said he hoped Aberdeen would take the lead of a Conservative-
Liberal government. Lord John concluded that Gladstone was
'strongly for Free Trade, but evidently wishes it to be in the
keeping of the Protectionist party',[50] and dismissed Newcastle's
scruples with the observation that 'The term Whig has the
convenience of expressing in one syllable what Conservative

Liberal expresses in seven'.[51] He added bitterly that 'Sir Robert Peel while he lived did all he could to maintain the late Ministry in power. After his death his followers in the House of Commons have thought it best to contribute to its fall'.[52]

The consultation was a charade. Parkes, who expected the house of commons to range in two parties only, 'Standstill or Progress',[53] neglected to add that the Irish held the balance between the two. In England, Wales and Scotland the ministry had 274 seats and the opposition 275,[54] and the vital question was who could bring the Whigs and Peelites together and add the Irish to them. It was impossible for Lord John to do so, because the Peelites and the Irish were still smarting under the ecclesiastical titles act, and the Whigs from the way in which they had found themselves committed to it by the Durham letter. Roebuck said summarily that 'Lord John will never again unite us'.[55] Tufnell told Graham that 'a great portion of the old Whig party would not serve in a Government, or support it if Lord John were the head'.[56] Ellice heard that the Whig aristocracy talked of the impossibility of Lord John.[57] Aberdeen, who still thought Lord John 'the fittest person to be at the head of any Liberal Government', found that 'he appears by common consent to be out of the question at this time', and wondered if the Peelites could supply his place.[58] The Queen thought that only a knot of Elliots and Russells would accept office under Lord John,[59] and even Lord John himself came to realise that there were fifty Peelites, thirty Irish brigade, and twenty high Whigs and low Radicals who would not serve under him.[60]

In these circumstances Lord John was once again badly served by his nearest relations. The Duke of Bedford, who understood that the cry against his brother was 'pretty general',[61] foolishly spoke of 'a scheme for deposing John'.[62] Minto went further and spoke of an intrigue,[63] and Lord John himself began to lament his 'degradation'.[64] But there was no intrigue. As Clarendon said:

> I believe I am pretty well acquainted with all that has been doing and saying lately, and I think no one of your friends *can* be more vigilant than myself upon whatever concerns your honor and interests, but I affirm that nothing has taken place to wch the denomination of intrigue can be correctly applied . . .[65]

While Minto encouraged Lord John not to stand aloof and let the intrigue destroy the party,[66] Clarendon wrote to G. C. Lewis that he wished to inspire Lord John with more confidence in himself, 'and, above all, to prevent his knocking on every man's door, as he has done lately in obedience to Lady J's mandate of always to be doing *something*, in total forgetfulness of his own dignity'.[67]

Parliament was to meet before Christmas, and in September Palmerston said openly that he would never consent to serve under Lord John again. He was not, as he frankly recognised, in a position to bid for the lead himself,[68] and he began canvassing the name of Lansdowne. The Duke of Bedford's first reaction to this was that it 'wd never do',[69] but after seeing Palmerston the duke thought that 'I cd manage the whole case if it were put into my hands'.[70] It is not clear what he meant by this, but within a few days the notion of Lansdowne as a person under whom everybody might act gained acceptance.[71] Lord John informed Minto that he no longer thought serving under a peer would be a degradation,[72] and when Lansdowne came back to town Lord John told him he would take office under him.[73] A few days later Lord John took it for granted that Lansdowne would be at the head of the next government.[74]

But Lansdowne himself wrote to Palmerston that he still thought Lord John ought to lead the party, and told Lord John that he had done so.[75] Perhaps that is why Lord John once again appeared to his friends to be spoiling for a fight. When he and Lady John dined with Emily Eden,

> he was, as he always is in that quiet way, pleasanter than most people and entirely unlike anybody else . . . Lord John said '. . . There are now thirty men in this country who *have* been cabinet ministers'. 'And can you bring thirteen of them together?', I asked. 'Certainly', quoth he, 'I see no difficulty about it'. I did not pursue the subject, as Lady John was present; and though the Dial spoke not, it made shrewd signs and pointed full upon the hour of *office*.[76]

Disregarding the advice of his friends, who thought that all would still be well if 'our little Chief, could only be persuaded . . . to listen to the suggestions of patience',[77] Lord John sent out invitations for a dinner on 10 November on the eve of the session. Graham at once took fright, and refused.[78] Ellice accepted, but confided to Parkes that Johnny was 'sour, discontented with his party, [and] dissatisfied with himself',[79] and wrote to Lord John himself and accused him of intending, if he were excluded, to break everything to pieces 'like a bull in a china shop'.[80]

ii. The Aberdeen coalition, 1852–5

When parliament met, Palmerston drafted the free-trade amendment upon which the opposition groups combined, and Gladstone demolished Disraeli's budget. Anticipating Derby's defeat, the Queen then turned to the Duke of Bedford for confidential advice about the succession. The duke invited Lord John, Lansdowne, Clarendon, Aberdeen, and Newcastle to confer with him at Woburn.[81] Lord John came for one night, on 15 December, and the duke asked him what he thought the Queen should do when Derby was defeated. Lord John said he thought she should send for Lansdowne and Aberdeen, and was indignant afterwards when he discovered that the question had been put to him at the Queen's request and that his brother had concealed the fact.[82]

The duke thought his 'little meeting' had been of 'infinite use' in 'putting the parties in good humour with each other'. In the early hours of 17 December Derby's government was defeated, and the Prince's secretary, Colonel Phipps, set off for Woburn. He arrived just as the hunt breakfast was coming to an end, and the duke's horse was ready for the meet to move off.[83] The duke, who was 'so afraid of and unfit for responsibility',[84] was now required to give decisive advice. He was in an 'agony of mind at the responsibility thrust upon him . . . and . . . flew to Aunt Emma for counsel and support'.[85] His horse was kept waiting a long time while he covered '5 sheets of paper'[86] saying that his brother did not wish to be sent for, and recommending the Queen to consult Lansdowne and Aberdeen.[87] Lansdowne had gout and could not go, and Aberdeen decided that delicacy forbade his going to see the Queen alone, and stopped in London to await further instructions. While he was there, Graham pressed him to hold out for sole power, and Lord John, whom he met in the Park, told him that he thought he would serve under him as leader in the house of commons and foreign secretary.[88]

On 19 December the Queen invited Aberdeen to form a government, and the power exclusively confided 'fluttered the dove-cot'.[89] Lady John despised the 'solemn old Athenian pet', whom the Queen and the Prince had long wished 'to see at the head of all things',[90] and the Russell children thought that asking Lord John to serve under Aberdeen was like asking a housekeeper to take a scullery maid's place.[91] Lord John had much to gain from taking office under Aberdeen, but he could not keep this steadily in mind, and the pattern for the entire ministry was set in the days of its formation. One day, when he was with Aberdeen, Lord John would be 'magnanimous and happy', and the next, after Lady John had had a night to rouse his wounded feelings, he would come back 'jealous and jibbing badly',[92] and Aberdeen, who could not get on without him, was driven to expedients which at other times would have been quite incomprehensible.

When Aberdeen came down to breakfast on 20 December he found a letter from Lord John saying that he could not manage the burden of the foreign office with the lead. Next, Lord John himself arrived, and said that he would rather stay out and give the administration independent support.[93] Aberdeen then enlisted the Queen, who appealed to Lord John's patriotism, and the Duke of Bedford, who wrote 'Do not, for God's sakes, allow any personal feeling to prevent this arrangement'.[94] Lansdowne, Clarendon, and Macaulay all pleaded with Lord John, and the decisive moment came when Aberdeen intimated that as soon as the temporary objections to Lord John's becoming premier had been overcome, he would retire in his favour. Aberdeen's biographer doubted whether such an undertaking was ever given.[95] Lady John, on the other hand, had no doubt: 'No oath was taken, no pen and ink used, but the agreement as between gentleman and gentleman was . . . as binding as if there had been twenty oaths . . . *On this agreement* alone John consented to take office'.[96] Lady John was a partial witness, but the arrangement seems to have been understood by the court and by the cabinet, both of whom strongly disapproved of it.[97]

Lord John was thus talked round into joining the administration, and Aberdeen renewed his offer of the foreign office.

But the despatches had increased from 5000 in 1828 to 32,000 in 1852, and Lady John dreaded the work. Finally, she sent her husband back with the proposal that he should take the lead of the house of commons and a place in the cabinet, but not hold office. It would be 'both *grander* and more useful . . . to work at Reform, Education &c.',[98] and it would give him the opportunity to 'maintain his influence in the House, cabinet, and country'.[99]

There was no precedent for this, and Aberdeen's friends at once raised objections to Lord John's being left without an official salary, and without the necessity to vacate his seat. Lord John then said that if he took office at all, he must have second place, meaning the foreign office, which he had already refused on account of the work. If things went on like this, Aberdeen would never be able to form a ministry at all, and the arrangement the two men finally came to, on 22 December, was that Lord John would take the foreign office and vacate his seat, and that as soon as he found it too much for him (which he expected to be in February when the session began),[100] he would give it up to Clarendon. It is difficult to see how anyone could have acquiesced in such an arrangement, and Palmerston warned Lord John that it would look like legerdemain, 'the Reason of which will not be apparent; and Things not understood are apt to be misinterpreted: at all events it might look like Instability of Purpose'.[101] But Lord John was not in a mood to listen to Palmerston, and Lady John now supposed that in six weeks her husband could get rid of Westmorland, the ambassador at Vienna,[102] and give the pro-Austrian Clarendon a lecture on foreign affairs.[103]

Even after Lord John had finally agreed to join Aberdeen there were still misunderstandings. Aberdeen thought he was the head of a Peelite administration, while Lord John thought of himself and Aberdeen as the twin heads of a coalition, and 'the arrangement of offices under the Junction Company'[104] turned out to be very difficult. Aberdeen estimated 'the persons and the offices they fill'[105] while Lord John naturally referred to the strength of the two parties in the house of commons, and feared that the administration would 'break down from the weakness of the old Liberal party (I must not say Whig) in the Cabinet'.[106] Aberdeen proposed to give seven seats in the cabinet to the 30 Peelites, five to the 270 Whigs and Radicals, and one to Palmerston. Lord John protested that the shame would overwhelm him.[107] Wood thought that Lord John having been discontented and dissatisfied with his own position, and having reconciled himself to submitting to that . . . very much abandoned everything else'.[108] But this was not fair. Lord John asked for three more Whigs in the cabinet, and the genuine difficulties of his position are apparent when we consider that though he fought the point 'pertinaciously'[109] he only secured one, Granville, who unappreciatively condemned Lord John for having let himself be 'overjockeyed' by Aberdeen.[110]

When the cabinet was complete, the worst of it was, as Lady John said, that the Liberal ministers in the cabinet were hardly the ones she would have chosen

> either to give effect to liberal opinions or to support J personally. At least if I had been asked to name those who wd answer both these purposes, I shd have said Lds Minto, Carlisle, Granville, Sir G. Grey, and Sir F. Baring – of these but one is in office, and instead of the others, alas, alas, Lds Clarendon, Lansdowne, Palmerston, and Sir C. Wood.[111]

Clarendon, who incidentally was not yet in, but was only to come in when Lord John gave up the foreign office, was, as Panmure said, but a milk-and-water reformer,[112] while Lansdowne, Lady John thought, only took a part in the ministry with a view to beating Lord John down upon reform.[113] As for Wood, it was not long before Lady John was complaining that he was 'saucy' to Lord John's face, 'grumbling behind his back, contemptuous in the cabt., and obstructive at all times'.[114] Lady John exaggerated, but Broughton, too, noted that Lord John went into the cabinet 'with scarcely a personal or even a party friend in it',[115] and Lady John was not altogether without wisdom when she wrote 'that we had better have kept aloof from Ld Aberdeen',[116] and expressed her fear that the junction would lead to loss of character and reputation.[117]

Any chance there ever was of Lord John settling down happily under Aberdeen was destroyed by *The Times*. As prime minister Lord John had been inclined to make a virtue out of having nothing to do with editors: but what he called high principle, journalists called being snubbed. Lord John's increasing waywardness had not passed unnoticed in the press, and *The Times* now chose Christmas day to publish an article which Clarendon considered 'evidently intended to bring Lord John into contempt'. Clarendon had never seen Lord John 'so mortified and annoyed, because the friendship between Lord A and Delane is, as he said, well known, and nobody will suppose that attacks on him would find their way into the *Times* unless they were agreeable to Lord A'.[118]

After this, it was not surprising that the ministry ran into John-trouble. The foreign office sent 'boxes on boxes all day long' so that even before parliament met, Lord John could never reckon on a quarter of an hour's relaxation during the day.[119] Lord John just had time to write one curt letter to Sir Henry Wynne at Copenhagen, telling him he was to be replaced after fifty-four years' service,[120] and another to Lewis Hertslet rebuking him for the irregularity of his attendance at the office,[121] and to send Stratford de Redcliffe back to Constantinople with Aberdeen's reluctant consent, when the time arrived for him to hand over the office to Clarendon.

At this point the Queen intervened, and Aberdeen tried to persuade Lord John to stay on until the end of the session. Lord John appealed to the performance of their agreement 'as a matter of good faith'.[122] Aberdeen, who had just given a dinner to the representatives of foreign powers at which he had spoken of them to Clarendon as 'your future flock',[123] accepted this, but reopened what he called a 'very grave question', which was whether Lord John could constitutionally hold the lead without office. Lord John replied that unless he thought this question had been settled, he would never have joined the government. Thus far he had the better of the exchange. But he added that he never would have agreed to 'descend' to another office, and to vacate his seat again. Aberdeen correctly rebuked him: 'Surely you take a wrong estimate of your own position and character. For you there can be no ascending or descending in the Government', and went on, 'you know perfectly well it is not my fault that you do not now occupy the position in which I am placed'.[124]

The correspondence ended there, and Lord John had his way. But he drew down upon himself a stinging remonstrance from the Queen, which he answered, truthfully, but not tactfully, by pointing out that

> Lord John Russell has done all in his power to contribute to the
> formation of a Ministry in which he himself holds a subordinate
> situation; from which nearly all his dearest political friends are
> excluded, and which is held by some to extinguish the party which
> for eighteen years he has led.[125]

After that, the Queen never even acknowledged Lord John's
daily reports on the proceedings in the house of commons, and
communicated to him only through Aberdeen.[126]

With both Aberdeen and Clarendon in the lords, Lord John
had plenty to do. The session did not go badly. Relations within the cabinet improved when Lady Clarendon established a
singing class for twenty children of cabinet ministers in the
Russell's house.[127] There was no time to bring in a Reform Bill,
and the government's attempt to extend the educational system
collapsed, but the privy council grant was increased, and
Oxford University was given notice to put its house in order
that year or be reformed the next. The ministry patched up the
old company-government of India, though not, as Lord John
wished, for a period of five years only.[128] Above all, Gladstone's
first budget was a triumph, and Lord John rejoiced at a scheme
that was 'large, honest, and framed for duration',[129] and generously told the Queen that 'Mr Pitt in the days of his glory might
have been more imposing, but he could not have been more
persuasive'.[130]

Lord John did, however, get into one scrape during the
session. The Irish catholics asked for a select committee to find
out how far the ecclesiastical revenues of Ireland were applied
to the benefit of the people. It was the sort of inquiry Lord John
himself had pressed upon parliament twenty years earlier. But
his judgement had been affected by the establishment of the
hierarchy in England in 1850, and he argued that membership
of the roman catholic church was incompatible with loyalty
both to the crown and to the general cause of liberty. His
speech was loudly cheered, and nobody rose from the government front bench to contradict him. The three roman catholic
members of the government thereupon handed in their resignations. Aberdeen employed Newcastle to talk them round in
return for a public letter assuring them that Lord John's views
were not shared by most of the rest of the cabinet.[131]

Long before the session ended the cabinet found itself in a

crisis over the guardianship of the holy places, and Russia's occupation of the principalities. The cabinet divided between those who supported the *'paix à tout prix* minister',[132] Aberdeen, and those who wanted to save Turkey from Russia in the interests of the balance of power, led by Palmerston. Clarendon came between the two camps, and as Lord John inclined to the second group, it is interesting to speculate what would have happened if he had remained at the foreign office, as Aberdeen wished. Lord John was genuinely alarmed lest the cabinet end by having no policy at all, but he found it hard to follow a consistent course himself. In March he wrote to Clarendon that the emperor of Russia 'is clearly bent on accomplishing the destruction of Turkey, and he *must be resisted*';[133] and in August, when the four neutral powers agreed on the Vienna note, to be presented to both Russia and Turkey, Lord John wanted the British government to tell the Turks they must sign it.[134]

When the Russians accepted the neutrals' terms, Aberdeen wrote to Lord John that he believed this settled the affair.[135] The session was over, and Aberdeen, who never left the office until nine o'clock 'and does nothing',[136] took Lord John on one side,[137] and explained to him what he had already discussed with Graham,[138] his wish to retire, and subject to the consent of the Queen and of their colleagues, to hand the government over to Lord John. It was an unfortunate conversation. Gladstone had already expressed strong objections to Aberdeen's proposal,[139] and within a few days the Turks refused to accept the Vienna note. The renewed diplomatic crisis gave the court a decisive argument for dissuading Aberdeen from stepping down.

Lord John was up in Scotland with his father-in-law when he heard about the Turkish answer. Under Minto's influence he now thought that the government ought to show the Turks some indulgence when they were wrong-headed. He therefore agreed to Aberdeen's proposal that pro-Turkish modifications should be pressed upon Russia, and by this change of front incurred his own personal responsibility for the outbreak of the Crimean war. He came down to London, saw Aberdeen, Clarendon and Palmerston, and gave it as his opinion that in the event of Russia rejecting the modifications, Britain should revert to the prime cause of quarrel, and take sides with Turkey against Russia. He then returned to Scotland.[140]

Russia refused to accept any change in the Vienna note, and Aberdeen, Clarendon and Palmerston met in London, turned about, and agreed to press the Turks to accept the original terms. Forgetting that this was what he himself had wanted to do a few weeks earlier, Lord John now felt that he had been double-crossed, and at once flared up. He told Aberdeen that he hoped the Turks would instantly reject such a proposal, and then, confusing his griefs with matters of public importance, unburdened his mind to Clarendon in a way that wounded a hitherto staunch friend deeply:

> you have made me feel my degradation more than I ever felt it before. You assumed that I was to be the chief organ for defending in the House of Commons that which I had no share in deciding, and of which I had previously recorded my disapproval. It was impossible that I could so lower myself, or that I should not feel the blow you had inflicted on me more than all the other humiliations I have endured.[141]

It is impossible not to see behind this outburst Lord John's increasing awareness that Aberdeen was not, after all, going to make way for him. Within a month Minto noticed that 'with a pretty general belief in Aberdeen's early retirement, great pains are taken to prepare the public for a successor *other than you* . . .' Minto added that Lord John would know best how to deal with this.[142] He could not have made a greater mistake, and when the cabinet met again at the beginning of November 'J. allowed himself to say . . . what I know he has long thought – that if he had been Prime Minister and Ld Palmn at the F.O., all wd have been settled 4 months ago.[143]

Lord John's wounds were inflamed by his wife and his father-in-law, who pointed out that if Aberdeen was not going to give way to Lord John, it must be because the Queen and the Prince would not allow him to. For some time now there had been an antipathy between the Queen and Lady John. At the time of the Hampden affair, Prince Albert had written that Lady John was 'very clear sighted and enlightened upon religious matters',[144] and in 1849 he stood godfather to little Rollo, who was named Francis Albert after him.[145] But long before Lord John's ministry came to an end, the Queen had learned to despise Lady John, as only women who bear many

children easily can despise women who bear a few with difficulty. The Queen thought that 'the quiet passing off of the late
Cabinet' in February 1852 'was mainly owing to *her* not having
come up to town with Ld. John'.[146] Every month in 1853 their
relations grew worse. In January Lady John wrote indignantly
to her sister-in-law before setting off to join the Queen at
Windsor, 'stand *I will not*, even at the risk of her think^g me lazy
or affected, one of wch epithets . . . she applies to every woman
less strong than herself'.[147] In September Lord John upset the
Queen by refusing to attend her at Balmoral,[148] and in October, when the Queen returned to Windsor, she paid the Russells
out in their own coin. Lady John asked if they might bring the
new baby Agatha with them on a visit. No answer came, and
Lord and Lady John were actually in the carriage with the
baby, when a note arrived on H.M. service, which Lady
Russell paraphrased as '*no room* for Baby in Windsor Cottage!'[149]

In order to avert a war, Aberdeen must keep control of
foreign affairs in his hands rather than those of Palmerston, and
in order to keep the ministry together, he must find some way
of preventing Lord John from breaking it up. The answer was
to take up reform 'pour les beaux yeux de Master Johnny',[150]
and accordingly, on 11 November a committee of cabinet was
formed including Lord John, Granville, Graham, Newcastle,
and, in order to take the bull by the horns, Palmerston.[151] Lord
John then proposed a £20 franchise in the counties and a £6
franchise in the boroughs, and announced that he thought of
redistributing seventy seats.

Palmerston now pursued a course almost as wavering and
incomprehensible as Lord John was accustomed to do. Three
days after the committee was formed he wrote to Lord John, to
ask whether there was any demand for reform. 'The necessity
arises principally if not solely from Declarations made by you
in the House of Commons in former years without any previous
concert or agreement with the other Members of your Government'. Palmerston argued (correctly) that the discovery of gold
in 1849 would lower the franchise automatically through infla-
tion, and (fantastically) that the interests of the working men
'as a Class are efficiently cared for by their employers'.[152] In
the committee he was temperate and reasonable,[153] but when the
committee's proposals came before the cabinet he was difficult,

and asked for the bill to be confined within the narrowest possible limits.[154] Next, he wrote to Lansdowne to say that he would not be a party to the bill, and that he did not choose to be dragged through the dirt by John Russell. Aberdeen and Graham both thought that with his 'Love of War and Hatred of Reform',[155] Palmerston was ready to leave the cabinet and to put himself at the head of the pro-war and anti-reform parties, which were nearly the same.

The Queen wanted to let Palmerston go on this issue, which would not be popular.[156] Aberdeen himself was ready to 'extrude' Palmerston, and after consulting Graham and Lord John, he wrote to Palmerston to say that the three of them could not agree to modify or drop the Reform Bill to please him.[157] Palmerston thereupon resigned, and the Queen accepted his resignation. But Newcastle and Gladstone were both afraid that without Palmerston Lord John would soon acquire a mastery over Aberdeen in the cabinet. They asked Aberdeen to take Palmerston back, and the press assumed that Palmerston had resigned because he thought the government too weak upon the Eastern question, and attacked the Prince for interfering in matters of state. Aberdeen asked Lord John if he should give way, and tell the Queen it was a political necessity. 'Yes', said Lord John thinking of his Reform Bill, 'owing to the shabbiness of your Colleagues'. 'Not shabbiness', Aberdeen replied thinking of the dangers of war, '*cowardice* is the word'. Palmerston was allowed to withdraw his resignation, but Aberdeen refused to let him set any conditions, and believed his return would damage him more than the government. Lord John foresaw that 'it would ruin anybody but Palmerston'.[158] Parkes thought that Palmerston had only come back because war was now certain and because he knew reform could be put off,[159] and Ellice, with his talent for political prophecy, said that henceforth the cabinet would find Lord John 'at single combat, under any circumstances which may annoy him',[160] and that if the cabinet broke up Palmerston would be the new premier.[161]

Even now, had Lord John heeded Graham's advice that 'those who agree on Reform must not quarrel on the Eastern question',[162] and thrown in his lot with Aberdeen, Palmerston would never have become prime minister. But Lord John had 'always liked' Palmerston and had 'a leaning to his policy':[163]

he was still quarrelling with Aberdeen about the original distribution of offices upon the formation of the government;[164]
and when Palmerston resigned and Aberdeen asked Lord John
to take the home office, Lord John went home, and after seeing
Lady John, declined,[165] because the government was so unpopular for its peace policy that he would lose his seat in the
city upon seeking re-election.[166] No sooner was Palmerston
back than news arrived that the Russians had sunk the Turkish
fleet at Sinope, and Lord John promptly presented 'the repelling
end of the magnet' to Aberdeen again.[167] Lord John was in such
complete ignorance of his own position that he thought he
could carry both a Reform Bill against Palmerston and a declaration of war against Aberdeen.

Lord John did, however, have enough sense to try and keep
Lansdowne on his side, and early in the new year he modified
his redistribution scheme in favour of the counties. Aberdeen
then thought the bill less liberal than he expected,[168] but Làns-
downe accepted it, and rather than oppose it alone, Palmerston
did too.[169] Lord John's relief did not last long. On 22 January
Palmerston wrote to condemn what he called 'a Leap in the
Dark',[170] and a week later he exclaimed angrily that 'workmen
are not *free* agents', and that 'a thousand can be swayed by 5 or
6 agitators'. He then went on, in a way he sometimes used with
Lord John, to deliver candid advice with a blow below 'the belt,
'you can hardly be aware of the Feelings of personal Hostility
towards you which are daily spreading through all the Party
which has hitherto acknowledged you as their Leader.'[171]

When parliament met, Lord John bravely defended the
Prince from the slanders spread against him by the press in
December, and for the first and only time in Aberdeen's ministry earned the Queen's gratitude. He then announced that he
would introduce the Reform Bill on 13 February. But time was
running out. Early in February, the Russian ambassador was
recalled. On 10 February an M.P. related to Palmerston by
marriage asked Lord John whether it was his intention to proceed with the measure,[172] and two days later Palmerston himself wrote wildly to Lord John to ask whether he really supposed
that 'men who murder their Children to get nine Pounds to be
spent in drink, will not sell their vote for whatever they can get
for it?'[173] At this point Aberdeen showed much more real moral

courage than he is usually given credit for, and told Palmerston firmly that it was too late to change the bill. The cabinet had met three or four times upon it, and Palmerston had said nothing.[174] The next day Lord John duly brought the bill in, and even Lady John, who was present, admitted that it was received without enthusiasm.[175]

The second reading of the bill was fixed for 13 March, but on 24 February Palmerston came to Aberdeen and said he must vote for Dering's motion to postpone the bill. 'It is evident', the Prince thought, 'that Ld. Palm: has been playing a deep game all along.'[176] The Prince agreed with Lord John that the outbreak of war would not be a sufficient reason for dropping the bill,[177] and Lord John asked Aberdeen to go on with it in April.[178] Aberdeen thought it would be more dignified to go on with the bill, as arranged, in March, and warned Lord John that it was indefinite postponement which its opponents aimed at.[179] At this time Aberdeen was deeply afflicted by a sense of responsibility for the war which was now inevitable, and was himself in need of sympathy and reassurance.[180] Lord John thanked him for his support with the Reform Bill, but brusquely dismissed his self-reproaches,[181] and got on with the task, which Aberdeen willingly left to him, of drafting the declaration of war. While he was doing this, Lady John came into the room: Lord John said

> he had tried to lower it down to the tone of the cabt. He read it to me and when he came to the sympathies of the people for right against wrong, remarked 'Depend upon it the Cabt won't let that stand.' Accordingly when it was read in the cabt., there was an immediate outcry against that sentence – he was half amused and half indignant and exclaimed that he had foreseen the Cabt. wd not bear to be supposed to prefer right to wrong: this made them ashamed and it was allowed to remain . . . J had put in that the Empr did so and so in defiance of the 'protest of the civilised world' on wch our matter of fact old chief said there had been no protest . . . the word was voted 'poetical', and 'opinion' substituted, and so on, with every strik\\g expression and every sentence that contained a high sentiment or a distinct mean\\g.[182]

As soon as the war began, it became apparent that Palmerston had judged the feeling of the house of commons correctly.

Prince Albert saw Lord John,[183] who agreed to give up the Reform Bill provided he was allowed to commit the government to bring it in again as soon as possible. Palmerston then told Aberdeen that 'neither *under present nor any future circumstances could he vote for the 2d reading of the Bill!*'.[184] Lord John said that in that case he must resign; the Queen wrote to King Leopold that they had a crisis due to personal feelings between Lord John and Palmerston;[185] and Aberdeen, who thought Lady John was aiming at Palmerston's resignation, warned Lord John that he was cutting his own throat.[186] The Queen, the Duke of Bedford, and Lansdowne each made a personal appeal to Lord John,[187] and Sidney Herbert wrote him an admirable letter which shows how much more sympathy the Peelites had for Lord John and for his Reform Bill than his own Whigs did.[188] Palmerston refused to allow Lord John to commit the government in public, but Aberdeen promised that 'whenever Ld John said "the Reform Bill is to come on", and Ld Palmerston opposed it he should go'.[189] Lord John then gave way, and with tears in his eyes announced to the house that the government would withdraw the bill.[190] But the incident did not end without another bitter letter from Lord John to the Queen, which, as Aberdeen said, must have been written after his return home.[191]

Lord John now turned with a mixture of genuine statesmanship and wounded feelings to the problem of getting the government in trim for the war, and on 24 April he wrote to Aberdeen urging the separation of the war department from the colonial office.[192] Aberdeen took no notice, and on 5 May Lord John complained that there was a question to answer in the house that night about the conduct of the war, and that he could neither defend the existing system, nor promise that a better one would be adopted.[193] So far so good, Lord John was the only member of the cabinet, apart from Sidney Herbert, to urge the prosecution of the war as a matter of urgency. But he foolishly supposed that the war made it more than ever necessary for the public service that he should take Aberdeen's place. He told Aberdeen that he could feel no confidence in the administration,[194] and wrote to Clarendon that the great want 'is a head of the English Cabinet'.[195] It was no use; Clarendon was not going to help Lord John into Aberdeen's place, and from now on the harder Lord John hinted that Aberdeen ought to retire, the more Lord John became the lone juror.

But the cabinet did agree to separate war and colonies, and on 20 May Lord John specifically suggested that Palmerston should take the war department, that Newcastle should keep the colonies, and that George Grey should be invited to return to the home office.[196] Aberdeen countered that it would be unfair to remove Newcastle from the war department, and urged Lord John to take the colonies himself.[197] Lord John weakly agreed to Newcastle's keeping the war department,[198] and George Grey accepted the colonies. George Grey was, or if Lord John had behaved himself, would have been, another ally in the cabinet. But unfortunately, Lord John repeated his demand for the cabinet to be 'more press'd to decide matters of urgent importance than it has hitherto been',[199] and now insisted upon taking office himself as lord president of the council. This was foolish, not because he was, as the Queen complained, the first commoner to hold this office since the reign of Henry VIII,[200] but because it meant pushing Granville out of the cabinet. Granville owed his original promotion to Lord John, he was friendly to reform, and as Aberdeen said, the current business of the house of lords was mostly in his hands and 'he does it remarkably well'.[201] Gladstone thought the whole transaction worthy of a set of clowns, blamed it all on Lady John, and doubted 'if there is any man in England, except Lord Aberdeen, who could have borne what he has had to bear during the last seventeen months from *Lady* John', who had brought her husband 'to a pitch of wilfulness and to an abyss of vacillation and infirmity of purpose' which were 'a chapter in the history of human nature'.[202]

At this point Lord John's relations with Gladstone became of importance to the coalition as a whole. The two men had not been thrown much into each other's company until December 1853, when the ministry's ultimatum to Oxford University expired. Aberdeen then entrusted the preparation of a bill to Lord John, who had appointed the commission of inquiry in 1850, and to Gladstone, the member for the university. Suspicion evaporated, and some kind of understanding originated between the two, but it was too early for it to develop into confidence. Lord John wanted to follow the reform of the university by an inquiry into the great schools, while Gladstone wanted to establish a system of competitive entry into the Civil Service. Lord John asked Gladstone, in a few crisp sentences, how he thought it would be possible to carry on the executive government without the present system of patronage. Gladstone overwhelmed him with ten pages of argument which even Peel could not have improved upon.[203]

Shortly after the outbreak of war, Lord John heard that Gladstone had dismissed an official in the woods and forests. Kennedy was a Whig, and a very old friend of Lord John, who had appointed him to what he believed to be a permanent office.[204] The incident reminded Lord John of all his former grievances, and aggravated them. He took the matter up with Gladstone, and for the time being both men behaved in an exemplary manner. Lord John admitted that Kennedy had brought charges against a subordinate which he could not substantiate,[205] and Gladstone correctly offered to refer the whole case to the prime minister, and to reinstate Kennedy if Aberdeen so decided.[206] But Lord John felt certain that Aberdeen would take Gladstone's part, and by the time the session came to an end he had still not made up his mind how to proceed in the case, which thus remained open. It had not been so easy a session as the one before: the Liberal party was restless, and in July Lord John asked to be relieved of his duties as leader of the house, and had to be talked back into harness.

During the summer the expedition sent to the Crimea ran into trouble, and by October it was evident that the British and French forces faced a winter siege. The press began to grumble, and Lord John wrote to Graham at the beginning of October, laying 'many points as foundations for future quarrels'.[207] Every day that passed brought Lord John more ammunition. There were rumours that the house of commons would ask for an inquiry into the Kennedy affair, and ominous reports began to reach England about the supplies in the Crimea. In both cases Minto roused Lord John, by referring to the case of Kennedy as an exposure 'of the bare-faced jobbing of your devout Chancellor of the Exchequer and your virtuous Premier',[208] and by assuring him that out at Pembroke Lodge he could scarcely appreciate 'how very great is the clamour of indignation' at the misconduct of the war, and how strongly 'the want of . . . a commanding spirit in the cabinet is rung in one's ears from all quarters'.[209]

In November Lord John urged Aberdeen to put an end to the ancient division of authority between the secretary for war and the secretary at war.[210] It was a sensible suggestion, and the change was made the moment the Aberdeen government fell. Aberdeen's difficulty was that Newcastle occupied the first office and Sidney Herbert the second. Both were Peelites, and in the case of the duke, at any rate, there was reason to suspect that Lord John had never forgiven him for his refusal to join the Whig government in January 1852 and for the part he had played in bringing Lord John's own reign as premier to an end. As for Lord John's proposal to make Palmerston the first holder of the unified department, that, as Prince Albert said, looked too much like an attempt to put Palmerston into a siding.[211]

To do Lord John justice, he did not act behind Newcastle's back, and asked Aberdeen to tell Newcastle what he had said.[212] But Newcastle was 'deeply mortified at the heartless manner' in which Lord John contemplated ruining his reputation,[213] and Aberdeen asked for time, and 'demurred at Palmerston's age.[214] Lord John countered this by going to see Palmerston to try and secure his support for an early meeting of parliament.[215] He did not take Palmerston into his confidence, but while he was with him, looked him over, and detected no signs of deterioration in mind or body. He then wrote to Aberdeen that it was clear 'either that the Prime Minister must be himself the active and moving spirit of the whole machine, or the Minister of War must have delegated authority to controul other departments'.[216] Lord John then took up much more specific complaints about Newcastle's handling of the troops, and forced Aberdeen to say that Lord John's proposal resolved itself into 'a personal preference, and the substitution of one man for another', and that he could not agree to it.[217]

Lord John responded by promising to bring the matter before the cabinet when they met early in December, and by saying that he expected to resign on it.[218] But before then Palmerston got wind of what Lord John had in mind, and refused to accept the part cast for him.[219] So there, as Lady John said, 'was poor J a peg lower in the Cabᵗ, from havᵍ expressed very strong opinions upon wch he cd not act'.[220] Poor J. was now so 'way-ward, uncertain, [and] querulous' that it was impossible to imagine what he might or might not do next.[221] When the cabinet met on 6 December he said he would not go through with another session, and all but came to an open rupture with Aberdeen.[222] Palmerston then turned on him and asked him, when he had 'succeeded in overthrowing the Govt which has difficulty enough to hold its ground even with your assistance', what he would say to the country.

> Will you say; 'Here I am – I have triumphed and have displaced in the midst of most hazardous operations all the ablest men the Country has produced, but I shall take their place with Mr Vernon Smith, Lord Seymour, Lord Minto, and others whose ability the country despises?'

And then, later, when the cabinet moved on to the Queen's speech, and Lord John inserted an alteration about strengthening the institutions of the country,

> Lord Palmerston started up and asked: 'Does that mean Reform?' Lord John answered 'it might or might not'. 'Well then' said Lord Palmerston . . . 'I wish it to be understood that I protest against any direct or indirect attempt to bring forward the Reform Question again!'[223]

The storm was not finished yet, for there was still Kennedy. Aberdeen tried to placate Lord John by offering to take him on to the emigration board.[224] Lord John was not satisfied, and at the cabinet dinner on 8 December he violently attacked both Gladstone and his chief. Clarendon's account was that

> John Russell was wrong in his facts, insolent in his assertions, and most ill-tempered in his replies. No spoilt child could have been more perverse or inaccessible either to kind or firm words, and his look was as if he had plied himself with wine in order to get courage for doing what he felt was wrong . . .[225]

A few days later Lord John received a letter from Minto, inviting him to give his father-in-law's proxy to 'a man who is for Kennedy against Gladstone, for Russell against Aberdeen, and against truckling to Nicholas'. Lord John forwarded the letter to Granville, and even he can hardly have been surprised when Granville returned it.[226]

Graham and Gladstone wanted Aberdeen to turn Lord John

out at once.[227] Aberdeen admitted to 'a sense of self-degrada-
tion, by submitting to such an unprecedented state of relations
among Colleagues',[228] but he was still afraid of the Liberal
party making Lord John a martyr.[229] And so he carried on,
knowing full well, as his son said, that 'We cannot exist with or
without him',[230] and suspecting, too, that the royal family had
at last made up their minds, in the event of the government's
falling, to send for Palmerston, even if he were going to look for
subterfuges to evade the 'four points' and for excuses to extend
the war against Russia.[231]

Lord John's friends now made their last attempts to bring
him to his senses. Wood reminded him, tactfully, that he had
been 'a good deal out of the way', recalled the 'uniform straight-
forwardness' of the Peelites, and warned Lord John that if he
persevered in his present course he would be deserted by 'your
own old Whig party'.[232] Lansdowne, too, 'altho in a very mild
way, gave Ld John an idea of his position of which he seemed to
be quite unaware',[233] and urged him to take care that 'no
break up should appear to originate in personal feeling on your
part. It would never be forgiven'.[234]

Lord John took part in the cabinet on 16 December, and his
colleagues understood that he had withdrawn his threat not to
go through with another session. But Aberdeen knew that there
could be no security even for a week.[235] At the beginning of 1855
Lord John once again made up his mind to resign, and communicated his decision to Granville and Sir George Grey, who
talked him out of it.[236] He then wrote another excellent memorandum on the state of affairs in the Crimea, where the
soldiers were one night out of two in the trenches,[237] and again
spoilt the effect by complaining to Aberdeen that 'Nothing
could be less satisfactory than the result of the recent Cabinets'.[238]

There was then a short interval while Lord John took Lady
John over to Paris to see her youngest sister, who was ill.[239]
Upon their return, Lord John attended a meeting of the cabinet,
but the talk of the town was that the ministry could not stand,
'the discontent with the Minister of War being so great',[240] and
when parliament met, Roebuck gave notice of a motion to inquire into the conduct of the war. Without consulting anyone,
Lord John wrote simultaneously to the Queen and to Aberdeen,

that he could not resist the motion, and that he must, therefore, resign. Even Lady John thought this was going too fast, and the cabinet, of course, were disgusted.[241] But the last actions of the Aberdeen administration underlined the paradox of the previous nine months, which was that all along Lord John had been both wrong and right. Newcastle offered to resign, and Palmerston agreed to take the war department. But when Clarendon said that in that case Lord John might perhaps be induced to remain, Aberdeen cut in and said that while they might be justified in sacrificing the duke to the wishes of the country, they could not sacrifice him to Lord John.[242] The Queen persuaded them to stay in office and to meet Roebuck's motion. They did, and in those few days Palmerston led the house. The Queen also wrote to Lord John, and her letter made him so angry that instead of abstaining, he decided to vote for Roebuck's motion and against his former colleagues. The motion was carried on 29 January 1855 by 305 votes to 148, and the coalition fell with a crash that might have been heard in the Crimea.

iii. The Vienna mission, 1855

According to his mood, Lord John now pretended that what he had done was 'one of the wisest and most useful acts of his life',[243] and blamed George Grey and Wood for having been determined there should be 'no mistake' about his resignation.[244] But the truth was, as the Queen said, that he had 'entirely ruined himself',[245] and he was now to be made to feel it. The Queen sent first for Derby, who gave up when he could not persuade Palmerston to join him; and then for Lansdowne, who was too old. Then she turned to Lord John. Lady John misunderstood the call, and told her husband that he had it in his power 'to purify and to reform much that is morally wrong – much that you would not tolerate in your own household',[246] and Lord John spoke to the Prince of going to the lords himself, and asking Palmerston to lead the commons.[247] He was quickly disillusioned. He sent for Palmerston, Lansdowne, and Clarendon. It is impossible to improve upon Palmerston's account of what followed: 'I went. Lansdowne sent an excuse. Clarendon spoke his mind'.[248] After twenty-four hours Lord John gave up, and the Queen sent for Palmerston.

Lord John was not invited to join the new government, which comprised the old coalition, less Aberdeen, Lord John, and Newcastle. But it was still a question what was to be done with him. There was no knowing what mine he might spring under the new ministry, nor what way the Palmerstonian rank and file in the house of commons would find of reminding him that he had not 'acted on those principles which are taken for granted as the foundation of the intercourse and combination of public men with each other'.[249]

There was an answer to hand. On 2 December 1854, the Austrian government had entered into a treaty with Britain and France to call a conference at Vienna, to press the 'four points' upon Russia, and if Russia refused to make peace on these terms, to join the allies in the field. It had at once occurred to Clarendon that, as he put it to Lord John, 'For European effect you wd be the best man to negotiate a peace (altho the H. of C. wd go to the dogs in 10 days without you) . . .'[250] When Palmerston re-formed the government, he weighed this proposal carefully:

> the reasons against are his habit of acting upon sudden impulse, his rather dry and stiff habits, his aptitude to be swayed by others, and the circumstance that, if he came back with success, he would be more inconvenient to the government than he would otherwise be; . . . Nevertheless, I have no objection; and if he would go to the H. of Lords on his return, with an olive branch round his temples, that would be a good arrangement.[251]

Lord John agreed to go, and Palmerston said that his acceptance was 'plain proof to all the world that England goes into the negotiation in earnest and in good faith'.[252] Lord John received many congratulatory letters upon his appointment, most of whose authors probably meant, though only Graham said, that 'Your temporary absence from the House of Commons, as matters at present stand, is not to be regretted either by you or your friends'.[253] But it was one thing to get Lord John out of the way: it was another to send him to Vienna, for he had no experience of diplomacy, and low as he had already sunk, he was now to fall much further. The story can be quickly told.

When the three powers signed the treaty on 2 December, the Austrian offer to join the allies in the field was conditional upon no new points being added to the terms, and the definition of the vital third point, concerning Russian armaments upon the Black Sea, was deliberately left vague. Lord John understood his task as being either to secure peace, or to show such a desire to make peace upon the basis of the four points that Austria would be left with no honourable alternative but to join the allies as she had promised. Lord John took the view that Buol had 'given his hearty assent to the principle of putting an end to Russian preponderance in the Black Sea', and believed he would be allowed some discretion to concert with Buol '*at the moment of negotiations* the mode of carrying this principle into effect.'[254] Clarendon, on the other hand, formally instructed Lord John to insist upon the Russian navy in the Black Sea being limited to four police boats, to reject outright any alternative plan for a counterpoise, and if the Russians refused to accept this limitation, to insist upon an Austrian declaration of war.[255] This left ample room for misunderstanding between the foreign office and the British representative at the conference.

Lord John set out suspecting that 'the Emperors at Paris and Petersburg will both wish for another throw of the dice that they may rise winners'.[256] He went first to Paris, where he saw Napoleon III, the British ambassador Cowley, and the French foreign secretary Drouyn de Lhuys. Meantime, back in London, Roebuck pressed his inquiry. Palmerston accepted that there had to be one, and the remaining Peelites, Graham, Gladstone, and Herbert all resigned at what they took to be a slight upon Aberdeen. Clarendon condemned their attitude as 'Fiat *quirk* ruat coelum',[257] and Palmerston wrote inviting Lord John to join the administration. Lord John lectured Palmerston about his appointments, just as though he were still prime minister, and accepted the colonial office.[258] Lady John heard the news with regret,[259] and there were ominous signs when Layard refused to serve as Lord John's under-secretary,[260] and when a plan was spoken of to unseat Lord John at his election upon taking office.[261]

From Paris, Lord John proceeded to Brussels, where he saw King Leopold, and to Berlin, where he tried in vain to persuade the King of Prussia to join the conference. While he was at Berlin the Emperor Nicholas I died, and it was with renewed hopes of a change in Russian policy that Lord John travelled on

to Vienna, which he reached on 4 March. Lady John and the
children joined him there, and the whole family stayed with the
Westmorlands, whom Lady John had tried to persuade her
husband to remove from the embassy in January 1853. It was
just as well the Westmorlands were so hospitable, for Lord John
was tired. As Lady John wrote, her husband's adviser

> has but two topics, Foreign Office and Nursery: on the Nursery he
> and I get on very well, and on F.O. he and J. ought but do not, J
> be^g apt to shut his eyes . . . He complained that J had gone to
> sleep 3 times one day while he was comment^g to him on the 4
> points, and yesterday ev^g after persever^g for half an hour, he left
> him in despair to his armchair and his nap and came to the tea-
> table say^g he found the Principalities had the same effect.[262]

Before the conference opened on 15 March, Clarendon repeated the British government's ban on a patch-up peace. But
Lord John soon found that Austria would not force the British
terms upon Russia, and that she would not take up arms beside
Britain and France if Russia turned them down. Gorchakov
refused to consider limitation, and Buol proposed instead that
the allies be allowed to keep as many ships on the Black Sea as
the Russians – i.e. a counterpoise. To Lord John, on the spot,
this seemed reasonable, and he asked the British government
how far it was willing to modify its 'preconceived opinions'.
The answer was, not at all. The conference was thus heading
for breakdown, and Buol suggested that the Russians should
simply be asked not to increase their forces on the Black Sea.
On 20 March Lord John told the British government that he
thought this was acceptable, if it would bring Austria over to
the allied side, and that he expected to receive further instructions in good time for the conference session of 26 March.[263]

Palmerston and Clarendon were horrified, and could not
agree to perpetuate and legalise the Russian armaments they
were fighting to destroy.[264] But instead of at once forbidding
Lord John to proceed, they sent over to Paris, where Drouyn de
Lhuys came up with an entirely new proposal for neutralising
the Black Sea. Palmerston and Clarendon jumped at this, as
providing even better security for peace in the future than
limitation, and their change of course was sprung on Lord John
only hours before the conference met again on 26 March.[265]

Buol at once ruled that neutralisation fell outside the scope of the conference, where it was never formally discussed, and from that day to this people have suspected that Palmerston and Clarendon only took it up in order to widen the field of conflict and to bring the conference to an end. Lord John himself thought that it was 'bad faith' on the part of the British and French governments to have introduced it at this stage,[266] while Lady John wrote that 'the entire transformation of Ld Clar[n] under the Palmerstonian wand is discreditable in the highest degree'.[267]

Drouyn de Lhuys then set out for Vienna, to lay his plan before the powers. Upon arrival, he discovered for himself that it was unacceptable, and gave it up. In a last effort to keep the conference alive, Buol returned to his original notion of counterpoise, and suggested that the allies should be allowed to increase their strength in the Black Sea *pari passu* with the Russians, and that Austria should join Britain and France in a treaty to defend Turkey from aggression. Drouyn de Lhuys and Lord John agreed that the adhesion of Austria gave the allies what they wanted, and set out for home to press the latest Austrian proposal upon their governments.[268]

In the meantime the Queen and Palmerston had been busy fêting the French emperor upon his visit to England, and when Drouyn de Lhuys and Lord John reached home they were met by an united front.[269] The emperor dare not bring his army back from the Crimea until it had won a victory, while Palmerston had fallen completely in love with the neutralisation proposal,[270] which he must have known there was no hope of forcing upon the Russians until Sebastopol had fallen. Neither government wanted peace, and Drouyn de Lhuys resigned. Lord John said Drouyn's resignation must be followed by his own, and then very foolishly allowed Palmerston to persuade him to continue.[271] When Disraeli started asking questions about the Vienna conference, Lord John made no reference to Buol's final proposal, and lined himself up behind Palmerston who said that the war ought to be prosecuted with vigour.[272]

Buol then let the cat out of the bag, and Lord John was done for. The press attacked him for having been willing to truckle to Russia and for having deceived the house, and Bulwer gave notice of a motion of no confidence. Palmerston offered to stand by Lord John,[273] and Clarendon confessed he could not bear to throw over a colleague who had 'done nothing except make a bad case for himself when he had a good one'.[274] But Lowe persuaded the junior ministers in the government to sign a round robin against Lord John, and there was then no alternative but to let Lord John go, for, as Palmerston put it to him, 'The storm is too strong at this moment to be resisted'.[275]

Lord John was ruined: harshly if we have regard only to the part he took between February and July 1855, but not surprisingly if we have regard to his behaviour in the Aberdeen coalition. Parkes thought Lord John's greatest mistake was in undertaking the Vienna mission before Sebastopol had fallen,

> and when the Country here did not understand his and his Colleagues differences between *limitation* and *counterpoise*; and so his Downing Street Friends made a Jonah of Johnnie. He lost and they kept their places.[276]

Lord John himself blamed Clarendon. It was Clarendon who had sprung the neutralisation proposals on him, Clarendon who had prevailed upon Napoleon to refuse the terms Lord John and Drouyn de Lhuys approved of, and Clarendon who did not print Lord John's letters from Vienna sufficiently fully to do justice to Lord John's point of view. Before the session came to an end Lord John made a bitter attack on Clarendon in the house of commons.[277] It was a mistake. To a later generation the solution which Buol put forward and which Lord John and Drouyn de Lhuys approved does not seem unreasonable. But it is not difficult to imagine Lord John, at home, insisting at least as strongly as Palmerston and Clarendon upon the capture of Sebastopol; and the reason Clarendon did not publish more of Lord John's despatches was that they were written in such a peculiar and undiplomatic language that he thought they would do Lord John more harm than good.[278]

CHAPTER XVI

The Two Terrible Old Men, 1855–65

i. Out of office, 1855–9

LORD JOHN was on the verge of a breakdown. He could not sleep at night, and he repeated expressions 'Blood, Blood', as of terrors of war.[1] In August he went off for a month's holiday, without Lady John, to Lord and Lady Fortescue.[2] But his misfortunes were not over yet, and in October it turned out, as Parkes put it, that he carried no single point in Vienna:

> A week last Saturday fresh accoucheurs were called into Pembroke Lodge, and after examination, and her Ladyship having kept her bed 11 weeks, . . . she was informed . . . that she had not been in the Family Way and consequently could not miscarry and must take up her bed and walk.[3]

For her sake, as well as for his own, Lord John then bought Rodborough Manor, at Amberley in Gloucestershire. But even here he had no luck: buying it 'in propria persona, without legal advice, the "parcels" did not comprehend adjacent domain he had been showed over on view', and he was swindled.[4] Lord and Lady John liked the place, but they only lived there for one winter, and the house was afterwards let in succession to Lord John's step-son, Lord Ribblesdale, and to his eldest son, Viscount Amberley.[5]

In the meantime Lord John hardly knew what to do. He had only one public engagement that autumn, when he was invited to lecture to the Y.M.C.A. on the causes which have retarded moral and political progress.[6] The lecture was a success, but winter came and the acceptance of office by one old friend after another left him increasingly isolated.[7] He rejoiced at the fall of Sebastopol, but kept a jealous eye on the negotiations for peace,

which he expected to end 'on a chimerical basis'.[8] He continued
sour with Palmerston, and could never forget the behaviour of
the junior members of the government, who 'thought it best to
forswear me, who had made the fortunes of most of them'.[9]

Finally, Lord John's grievances came to a point: he had been
ruined by the newspapers, and especially by *The Times*. Lord
John's relation by marriage, Gilbert Elliot, the dean of Bristol,
said that '*The Times* has done it all'.[10] In order to eliminate
Palmerston, the usurper, and to restore Lord John to the head
of his party, the dean, who was a 'Goose on a common' about
the London press,[11] got up a scheme for buying a newspaper
and putting it at Lord John's disposal. But Lord John had no
money, and the dean approached both Ellice and Parkes to ask
if they could open the purse strings of the party. Parkes tactfully
pointed out that the present 'macadamisation of parties' was
not the best time to buy a paper,[12] but Ellice told Lord John
'the truth',[13] that he was surrounded by 'women and Elliots'.[14]
Ellice's letter was 'strichnine',[15] and the plan was given up.

As the new session approached, in 1856, men wondered what
Lord John would do. Would he write some bitter memoirs,[16]
or would he stick to his Reform Bill 'hobby',[17] throw in his lot
with Bright, and lead the democracy against the aristocracy?[18]
Right up to the last moment Parkes feared that 'the Little Man
will burn his fingers, and that on the meeting of Parliament no
Day Nurse can keep him from the Grate'.[19] But he need not
have worried. All Lord John did was to move resolutions in
favour of putting education within the reach of every child.[20]
He spoke admirably, but a great cause suffered because the
house was in no mood to listen to Lord John, who concluded
that the session had brought the country back to 'the old do-
nothing days of Castlereagh'.[21] He then turned to the task
which he had inherited under Lady Holland's will, of editing
Fox's letters, and preparing his *Life and times of Charles James Fox*.

Lord John decided to go abroad, to Switzerland and to Italy.
He gave instructions for his house in Chesham Place to be
leased for five years, and 'On the servants taking leave of him
. . . he shed tears.'[22] From his villa at Lausanne he contemplated
appearing 'as a second Gibbon'.[23] But when he moved on into
Italy, where he met Cavour,[24] the call of parliament proved too
strong, and in January 1857 he set off for home. Upon his

arrival in London, he asked if he could have his house back. Fortunately, it had been let to Panmure, who was now his best friend in the government,[25] and for once a landlord had no difficulty getting rid of his tenant.[26]

Lord John had got wind of the fact that time was beginning to work in his favour. Westmorland thought Lord John had been very unjustly treated,[27] and Greville soon concluded that the negotiations at Vienna were a sham, 'and that our Govt never intended to make peace at all',[28] Palmerston never quite hit off the mood of the house,[29] and with the return of peace Ellice foresaw that Lord John might yet recover the lead.[30] He had done 'enough to render his countrymen sceptical of his common sense',[31] but the newspapers began to hint at his joining the ministry in the lords.

Lord John was seriously 'talked to' before the new session began,[32] and Minto advised him to give the ministry cordial but independent support.[33] But Lord John joined forces with the Peelites and with a large part of the opposition, and spoke in support of Cobden's motion on the second China war. 'We have heard much of late – a great deal too much, I think – of the prestige of England. We used to hear of the character, of the reputation, of the honour of England.'[34] His plea for Britain, when she had committed an injustice, to admit it, was consistent with the advice he had given Palmerston in 1849. But the Liberal party noticed 'the increased bitterness of his tone',[35] and regarded 'all his criticism as from a deliberate mischief',[36] and his former colleagues resented his share in their defeat by 263 votes to 247.

Parliament was dissolved, and Lord John was warned that if he stood for the city, he would almost certainly be defeated. He gave his supporters the impression he would not stand,[37] and they invited Mr Raikes Currie to take his place. This brought out what Greville called 'the gallant little fellow' in Lord John. He contested the election, happily stigmatised Mr Raikes Currie as 'a young man from Northampton', and retained his seat even though he only managed to come third in the poll.[38] The public, who knew nothing of Lord John's vacillation, warmed to his courage in resisting an attempt to oust him, and cheered his success.

Palmerston returned from the general election with an

increased majority. It was a triumph for chauvinism, and both Cobden and Bright lost their seats. But the parliamentary re- formers also made some headway, and Lord John thought that in the new parliament 'The attempt lately made to carry on a conservation policy with the reform party, bribed by places, must fail.'[39] He would not play the ministers' game for them,[40] and he told Ellice that he was all for giving Palmerston a 'very large locus poenitentiae'.[41] When the new parliament met, news reached England of the Indian mutiny. Palmerston had a very inadequate idea of the scale of the emergency, and in private Lord John said of ministers 'what Ld. C. says of me – they did not think seriously enough about it'.[42] But he realised that people still 'have faith in Palmerston, in spite of facts', and that if he found fault he would be called 'jealous, envious, factious, &c, &c, &c',[43] and he actually spoke up for the government in the house.

After the election Clarendon found that the Queen 'expects to have to *subir* Lord John one of these days',[44] and in the autumn Palmerston himself set up a committee of cabinet to consider a Reform Bill. The rumour spread that Lansdowne was to be made a duke, which could only mean that Calne was to be dis- franchised.[45] The Duke of Bedford, who knew that Lord John overestimated himself, took alarm, and at last gave his brother an annuity of £2000 p.a. to enable him to accept a peerage.[46] Lord John did not accept the hint: reform was in the air; it was certain that the government of India would have to be re- modelled, and Johnny began to 'chuckle at his possible change out of the new rupee'.[47] He entered into much more frequent correspondence with Graham, and even began to contemplate, when parliament reassembled, moving his seat close to the Peelites.[48]

Parliament was called up early, in November, on account of the financial crisis. So there, as Lord John put it, were 'three most important questions – India, Finance, Reform, and a Prime Minister with little knowledge to inform him, and no principle to guide him, upon any of these subjects'.[49] Lord John confided to the dean of Bristol that he had made up his mind 'not to serve under *any* one again';[50] wrote to Vernon Smith telling him what kind of India bill he expected to see;[51] can- vassed an Indian bill of his own, and a Reform Bill among the

Peelites;[52] and treated the government with what Wood called hostility.[53]

When parliament reassembled early in 1858, the ministry just had time to introduce its India bill before it was overtaken by a new crisis which nobody had anticipated. Orsini threw a bomb at Napoleon III, and when the pieces were examined it was found that the bomb had been made in England. The French asked the British to strengthen their laws, and Sir George Grey took the precaution of opening the proposed legislation to Lord John. But there was intense indignation in England at the violence of the French press, Lord John saw his chance for a tit for tat with Palmerston, and he answered George Grey curtly that he would oppose the bill to the utmost of his power.[54] Palmerston doubted whether Lord John would find much support for an opposition 'founded upon pique and anger',[55] and when Lord John rashly spoke against the introduction of the bill, he was defeated by 299 votes to 99. He had moved too soon, but he had not misjudged the strength of the opposition. Even before the second reading, the Peelites, the Manchester Radicals, and a large body of Conservatives joined forces to defeat the government by 234 votes to 215, and Palmerston, of all people, was dismissed by the house of commons for truckling to the French.

Ellice thought that in assisting to throw out the late government, Lord John 'acted upon the impression that he must inevitably be asked to try and make one of his own'.[56] The Queen sent for Derby instead. Derby was in a minority, and would be defeated whenever the forces arrayed against him were able to unite. But that was not a thing which could be achieved in a day. Lord John himself alleged that he had no quarrel with Palmerston, who had offered to serve under him in February 1855, and to fall with him in July in the same year. But it was a different case with the rest of the Whig leaders. 'After 20 years faithful service they discarded me because I was for a constitutional inquiry. I can never serve or act with them till I am restored to my proper position. There is *my* point of honour.'[57] He refused to help 'the Loweing herd . . . back to their stalls and provender',[58] and for the time being he was much more friendly to Derby's government than he had been to Palmerston's.

Derby's new India bill incongruously vested the election of some of the members of the council in large English cities, and Lord John was told that if he moved to oppose the second reading he would be warmly supported by Palmerston and by his late colleagues.[59] But the trouble was that if he threw the bill out, the Liberal party would have Palmerston back.[60] Lord John took counsel with Aberdeen, and through him with Gladstone, both of whom disliked this new bill, and neither of whom wished to reinstate its predecessor or its author.[61] Then, rather than overthrow Derby, he invited him to proceed by resolutions in a committee of the whole house.[62] It thus became possible to keep India out of party politics, to amalgamate the best features of both bills, and to pass an act that year; but the change of tactics led to 'a general clamour' against Lord John 'on the part of the late Government and their friends'.[63] Lord John met this by agreeing to see Palmerston at Wood's house, and by offering to join forces on Cardwell's motion of censure upon the government's handling of the confiscation of the lands of the rebels of Oudh.[64] But the motion never came to a vote, Derby and Disraeli survived, and in the recess Lord John actually went to see Derby at Knowsley.[65]

As Gladstone said, no government could now stand 'which blinked the question' of a Reform Bill.[66] But this was not a topic upon which Lord John and Derby could see eye to eye, and Lord John concluded that any future 'performances of the School for Reform by actors who have hitherto only appeared in Speed the Plough' would be farcical.[67] Reform was his child, and he was not going 'to consent to see it hacked at the request of a sham mother'.[68] He passed the autumn in urgent correspondence with Aberdeen and Graham, and his state of mind nearly worried the Duke of Bedford to death;

> who says he immediately puts his letters in the fire in order that there may be no record of such foolishness and injustice. His father years ago said that John's failure thro' life would be want of judgement, and his brother considers that the prophecy has been strictly fulfilled.[69]

This was true, but events were in fact continuing to raise Lord John relatively to his rivals. Palmerston and Clarendon went to Paris to pay a private visit to the emperor, and Lord

John was not alone in thinking that henceforth they must be considered 'rather as courtiers of the Tuileries than subjects of St. James's'.[70] Then, at home, Bright gave notice that if Derby brought in one Reform Bill, he would bring in another. Lord John saw Bright, or 'Free-born John' as he was called,[71] and was relieved to find that he had not hoisted the republican flag.[72] But Bright's plan would set the towns over the country, just as Derby's would undoubtedly set the country over the towns.[73] Lord John was understandably alarmed lest Bright's extremism stampede middle-of-the-road Liberals into voting for Derby's bill, and Parkes, for one, thought that though Lord John had set the house on fire, he would now be the best fireman to put out the combustion.[74]

Lord John could hardly wait to bring in his own bill, and he came up for the session of 1859 in a state of feverish excitement, scarcely knowing 'à quel saint se vouer', [75] for Palmerston was aloof, and Graham could see no prospect of the broken fragments of the old Whig party being pieced together again.[76] Derby's bill proposed to enfranchise the £10 tenant at will in the counties, and to leave the borough franchise untouched, except for the addition of some fancy franchises. Lord John called a meeting, where he 'rather *frightened* the Lieges' by condemning the government's bill for failing to enfranchise 'the *great Body* of the working Classes'.[77] Sidney Herbert hastily warned him that this was going too far,[78] and Lord John emerged with an amendment 'that no re-adjustment of the Franchise will satisfy this House or the Country which does not provide for a greater extension of the Suffrage in Cities and Boroughs than is contemplated in the present Measure'.[79] Even Palmerston did not care to oppose that, and the amendment was carried by 330 votes to 291. It was a decisive majority, and Ellice and Parkes both thought that Lord John would go to the lords as premier.[80] But they reckoned without the Queen. She condemned 'Little Johnny' for a factious vote,[81] and remarked that he was 'ever ready to *make* mischief and do his country harm',[82] and thus encouraged, Derby decided not to resign, but to dissolve.

To Lord John's disappointment the election which followed was not fought upon reform. Napoleon had attacked the Austrians in Italy, and Derby drew attention to the danger of

an invasion of England. It was not enough to win him a majority, but the Conservatives came back stronger than before, and
this time they could only be thrown out if all the opposition
groups from the Peelites to the 'advanced Liberals' agreed to
act together. Palmerston and Lord John must bury the hatchet.
But Lord John was difficult: Palmerston 'has moved back to
1821 and I have moved forward from 1831'.[83] If Palmerston
would serve under him, well and good. If not, it would be
better for Palmerston to form a government, and for him to
stay out.[84] But that, as Sidney Herbert said, would never do –
'You must be in'.[85] G. C. Lewis and Granville then took over
the functions hitherto performed by the Duke of Bedford, and
began to smooth away the difficulties. On 18 May Lord John
wrote to Palmerston that the time had come to shut the mouths
of the underlings 'who themselves were instrumental in separating us'.[86] Two days later Palmerston came down to Pembroke
Lodge, and in two hours it was agreed that Derby would be
turned out on a motion of no confidence, and that a broad-
bottomed ministry would take his place, committed to a Reform
Bill that would satisfy Lord John.[87] This meant, as Lord John
explained to Bright, a borough franchise of six pounds. Nothing was said as to the lead, but on 29 May Palmerston proposed to Lord John that they should each say they would serve
under the other, as the Queen chose, but not under a third.[88]

Lord John agreed to this, and on 6 June the opposition
assembled in Willis's rooms. Palmerston and Lord John announced their reconciliation, and Bright 'upon the whole
promised co-operation'.[89] Derby was defeated by 323 votes to
310 and the Queen then sent for Granville and asked both
Palmerston and Lord John to serve under him. Granville
offered Palmerston the lead in the house of commons. Palmerston accepted; and Granville then approached Lord John, who
insisted on taking the lead himself. Palmerston refused to surrender it, and Lord John refused to take third place. Granville
was obliged to give up, and the Queen was compelled, as Lord
John discourteously put it, to 'encounter the difficulty of
making a choice'.[90] It was nearly five years since she and the
Prince had come to the conclusion that Palmerston was the
less of two evils, and the Queen was virtually certain to choose
Palmerston rather than 'selfish, peevish Johnny'.[91]

ii. Foreign Secretary, 1859–61

When Palmerston became prime minister, Lord John demanded the foreign office. Both the Queen and Palmerston would
rather have given it to Clarendon, but Lord John was adamant,
and he got his way. But this was the last concession Palmerston
made, and he quickly disabused Lord John of the idea that they
were to be joint heads of the administration. Palmerston did
not consult Lord John about the rest of his appointments, and
when Lord John accused him of assembling a caucus,[92] Palmerston told Granville what Lord John had said, and 'added
with that peculiar twinkle he sometimes had in his eye, "A
pretty mess I would have been in with Johnny alone, and ob-
jecting to all his proposals with no one to back me up" '.[93] It
was not a promising beginning, but in fact no sooner was Lord
John back in office than he recovered his good humour, and it
was not long before people began to remark with astonishment
upon 'the complete cordiality upon every thing between him
and Pam'.[94]

Nobody who wishes to raise Lord John in the eyes of posterity
will dwell for long upon his tenure of the foreign office from
1859 to 1865. Johnny thought he was 'the right man in the right
place', but, as Clarendon said, 'even his best friends in The City
are of a totally different opinion'.[95] In the first place, by insisting upon having that office, and no other, Lord John had once
again shown a complete misunderstanding of the true dignity
attaching to a former prime minister. In the second place, the
foreign office was not the best department from which to launch
the Reform Bill, or to pursue the expanded policy of state education, which were the two most important objects Lord John
had in mind. In the third place, Lord John was uniquely un-
fitted for the foreign office itself. In 1859 he was sixty-seven: he
was still active, but his appointment brought him out in the
guise of the lecturer at exactly the age at which a don now re-
tires, and his ink was 'abundant'.[96] His lectures, moreover, were
reminiscent of the inexperienced ideologue of the 1820s, and
quite unworthy of what ought to have been the mature statesman of the 1860s. Lord John explained to Queen Victoria both
brusquely and at length 'the connexion between the present

position of Italy and the doctrines which have been held by
every Minister of the Crown since 1688':[97] he referred the
emperor of Austria to the authority of 'that eminent jurist
Vattel' for his opinion on the subject's right to resist his sovereign;[98] and he instructed British ambassadors all over Europe
to help curb 'the ruthless tyranny of Austria and the unchained
ambition of France'.[99]

Palmerston himself drew Lord John's attention both to the
importance of despatches being 'an Instruction to say or to do
something, or an Explanation of the Policy of the British
Government',[100] and to the danger, if they were written in a
style that would find favour with the readers of the *Edinburgh
Review*,[101] of touching on hypothetical cases,[102] and offering
speculative opinions,[103] and thereby starting 'Doubts as to the
validity of subsisting diplomatic engagements the maintenance
of which is for our advantage.'[104] But that was all: generally
speaking Palmerston handled Lord John gently, and the reason
is not far to seek, for only the style was Lord John's own – the
substance was not. Clarendon, who was jealous, may have been
exaggerating when he said that 'John Russell has neither policy
nor principles of his own, and is in the hands of Palmerston',[105]
but Prince Albert found that Lord John's 'inefficiency in the
office . . . and fear of Ld Palmerston' made him a ready tool,[106]
while Gladstone recorded that Lord John 'leans so much upon
Palmerston in regard to foreign affairs that he is weaker in other
subjects when opposed to him, than might be desired'.[107] Their
judgement is borne out by Lord John's and Palmerston's papers.
Lord John laid his problems on Palmerston's desk: Palmerston's
advice was decisive, and Algernon Cecil was not far out, when,
in his book on British foreign secretaries, he dealt with Lord
John in an appendix to the chapter on Palmerston.

The best excuse that can be made for Lord John is that he
took the foreign office because his wife was 'Italianissima',[108]
and because his own feeling for Italy went back forty-five years
to his first visit in 1814, and was shared by Palmerston and
Gladstone and not by other members of the cabinet. The case
of Italy was urgent: a week before Derby resigned, the French
defeated the Austrians at the battle of Magenta; a week after
the new government took office they defeated them again at the
battle of Solferino. Palmerston and Lord John both preferred

French government to Austrian, but they had no wish to see the French take the Austrians' place. Before they could do anything about it, however, Napoleon double-crossed Cavour and did a deal with the Austrians. Austria was to retain Venice, but to cede Lombardy to France, which, in turn, would cede it to Piedmont; Tuscany was to be returned to its duke; and the Pope was to become the head of an Italian confederation in which Austria would be represented. The prospects for Italy were then much worse: the Austrians were not out, the French were in, and the Pope was in a fair way to being aggrandised.

Palmerston and Lord John both thought the situation called for diplomatic intervention. A majority of the cabinet doubted whether the author of the Durham letter could intervene effectively between two catholic powers and in Italy. And so, within a few weeks of its formation, Clarendon was speculating on the break-up of the government on foreign policy 'wh. Johnny thought no one but such an Atlas as himself had shoulders broad enough for'.[109] When Palmerston asked for fuller powers to act during the recess, he was met 'by a general assurance of readiness to come up by night trains',[110] and the Queen offered Lord John a house at Abergeldie for the summer, where his family could have a holiday at her expense, while he remained under her eye.[111] This did not solve all her problems, because 'He is not the moving power in all this but *Some one else*',[112] but at least it separated the pliable foreign secretary from his chief.

Palmerston soon saw that the terms of the armistice at Villafranca, and of the treaty of Zurich which followed it, were unworkable. The Italians were in revolt: the Pope was unable to reoccupy the Romagna, Austria dared not intervene to restore the dukes to Tuscany, Parma, and Modena, and Napoleon scarcely wished to. There was thus plenty of room for the Italians to determine their own fate, and for the British to support them. At this point a difference of emphasis appeared between the Queen and the majority of the cabinet. The Queen was for Austria: the cabinet was against risk. So long as France held Austria in check, and was herself held in check by the engagements she had undertaken at Villafranca, there was little danger in Lord John's encouraging the people of Tuscany to elect a representative assembly just as Lord Holland had encouraged the Spaniards to in 1808–9. Palmerston and Lord John were then able to beat the Queen down by sheer persistence, and when the Tuscan assembly declared in favour of union with Piedmont, Lord John openly encouraged Piedmont to act.[113] Britain thus played a part second only to France in sponsoring a greater Piedmont. But all through the summer and autumn of 1859 it was impossible for the two Liberal powers to co-operate, because it was impossible to discover what Napoleon's object was. At one moment he appeared to be for the Italian patriots against Austria; at a second for the Pope against the Italian patriots; and at a third he seemed to be ready to guarantee the Austrian position in Venice in return for a free hand on the left bank of the Rhine.

In any case British relations with France were conducted on a wide front. Napoleon's mind floated between 'great ideas of revenge against us for 1815', and 'great ideas of peace and commerce',[114] and both evoked a response on the British side of the channel. Palmerston threw his whole soul into the evaluation of shot and shell and armour plate,[115] and, perhaps because he lived so close to the south coast, went in continual dread of a French expeditionary force being landed in one night, and seizing the British naval arsenals from the land side. He began to press for fortifications. Simultaneously, Cobden, who had turned down Palmerston's offer of a place in the administration, decided to play a hand on his own. The free traders had come a long way since the 1840s. Cobden no longer condemned reciprocal arrangements, and he knew the emperor had the power to conclude treaties without reference to the French chambers and their multitude of protectionist interests. Early in October, therefore, he approached Gladstone, announced that he was on his way to Paris, and asked the chancellor of the exchequer whether he would give his blessing to a free-trade treaty. Gladstone was enthusiastic, and since the negotiation must necessarily involve the foreign office, he passed Cobden on to Lord John.

At this point Lord John's attitude became of some importance. Palmerston wanted to arm against the French, and Gladstone to trade with them. Lord John saw that the two approaches were not exclusive. He assured Palmerston that he was in favour of keeping the army and navy in 'a state of thorough preparation',[116] and gave his blessing to Cobden's amateur diplomacy. The French made only one half-hearted attempt to make the commercial treaty conditional upon the British following their line in Italy,[117] and early in January, when Cobden's negotiations had reached the point where a draft treaty could be drawn up, Lord John hustled it through the foreign office, in order to have everything ready in time for the beginning of the new session.[118]

In the meantime Lord John had his own iron in the fire. He had taken office on the understanding that there was to be a Reform Bill,[119] and in November, when he was trying to decide whether to attend Napoleon's proposed conference on the affairs of Italy, Palmerston appointed the usual cabinet committee. G. C. Lewis took the chair and obtained the statistics,[120] Lord John received some support from Gladstone,[121] and the cabinet accepted a bill which would reduce the county franchise to £10 and the borough franchise to £6. Clarendon now thought that Gladstone, Bright, and Lord John had fraternised completely,[122] and when parliament met, and Gladstone announced the terms of the commercial treaty, and the reduced rates of duty on French wines, Lord John backed Gladstone 'cordially and well'.[123] But when it came to his turn, Lord John asked to bring forward his Reform Bill on 1 March, which was the day fixed for going on with Gladstone's budget. Gladstone said he would go down on his knees to Johnny not to bring in his Reform Bill then,[124] but Lord John met all entreaties with the remark that he thought he had the same right to be heard as the licensed victuallers.[125] The little man was inexorable, and as Clarendon said, 'why do you think?' 'it is because 29 years ago on the 1st of March il a accouché laborieusement of his first reform Bill and it is therefore indispensable that he shd be brought to bed of the 2nd on the anniversary!!!'[126] Lord John had his way, and the bill was received with indifference.

At the beginning of May Lord John's bill was read a second time without a division. But before the month was out, Brand, the whip, reported growing alarm at any addition to the franchise,[127] and it became clear that the only way to save the bill was to raise the proposed new franchises to £15 and £8.[128] Lord John swallowed this, but in June a motion was tabled in favour of putting the question off until after the census of 1861. There was no chance of passing the bill, which achieved nothing, and brought a sharp exchange of letters with Grey, in which even Lord John's own son thought his father went too far.[129] The bill was buried in a familiar way, when the Duke of Bedford referred to the mistake Lord John had made the year before in not allowing Derby's bill to go into committee,[130] and ended by reminding Lord John, who had caught a summer cold, that he could not help thinking these colds 'might in some measure be avoided'; 'If you sleep with bed curtains drawn, and a night cap . . . opening your window at 5 was sure to bring mischief.'[131]

While the Reform Bill was still alive the house of lords rejected Gladstone's bill abolishing the paper duties, and Palmerston jauntily took the line that even though it was a money bill, the upper house had acted within its rights. Lord John told Granville that if Gladstone went, 'he should take an early opportunity of following him',[132] but at the same time he urged Gladstone to consider where he would now find 'any set of men with whom you are more likely to act to promote great public objects which we have in common',[133] and begged Bright not to say anything that would compel Gladstone to resign.[134] When the session came to an end, Gladstone, who could now be backed even against Lord John for upsetting a ministry,[135] was still there. Thanks partly to Lord John, Gladstone had got his French treaty, and Palmerston had got his fortifications and still had a chancellor of the exchequer. Lord John, on the other hand, who had not got his Reform Bill, was not in a bad humour, because he was engrossed in the affairs of Italy, and still hoped through them 'to connect his name with something'.[136]

Lord John's success did not come easily. Early in the year, when he was still encouraging the Italians to summon representative assemblies, Napoleon trumped his hand, and advised them to hold plebiscites. Then, in March, Napoleon took Nice and Savoy. Public opinion in England was outraged, and Lord John spoke rashly of seeking other alliances. He added that he hoped to see the two tiny districts of Chablais and Faucigny, neutralised by the treaty of Vienna in 1815, ceded to Switzerland, and then wrote, with timid, cocky vanity that he had just made a speech which would redound throughout Europe.[137] Finally, in May Garibaldi sailed for Sicily, and Palmerston suspected that Cavour had made another bargain with Napoleon, to cede Genoa in return for a free hand in the south.

In fact a successful invasion of Sicily was bound to be followed by an assault upon Naples, and in the summer the British and French governments drew closer together. Palmerston feared that an attack upon Naples would be followed by a demand for Malta, and Napoleon that it would be followed by an attack upon Rome, which was defended by French troops. The French invited the British to consider joint action to stop Garibaldi crossing the straits of Messina. Palmerston's immediate reaction was to accept, and on 24 July Lord John was actually closeted with the French ambassador in Chesham Place, when Sir James Lacaita arrived with a personal message for Lord John from Cavour. Lacaita asked to see Lady John. Lady John was ill, in bed. Lacaita forced his way past the maid, ran upstairs to Lady John, and explained the case to her. Lady John sent down to her husband, who thought her illness must have taken a turn for the worse, and hurried upstairs. Lacaita explained that Italy was to be made now or never; Lady John took his part, and when Lord John came down he blandly announced that the British government was not yet ready to make up its mind.[138] Palmerston made no objection: the French could not act alone, and Garibaldi duly conquered Naples.

Cavour then occupied the whole of the Papal territories, except Rome, and before the end of October he annexed the whole of central and southern Italy. The continental powers thereupon withdrew their ministers from Turin, and victorious Piedmont was left without a friend. Lord John saw his chance, and on behalf of her majesty's government, and without consulting either her majesty or the government, he penned his famous despatch of 27 October 1860.

Her Majesty's Government do not feel justified in declaring that the people of Southern Italy had not good reasons for throwing off their allegiance to their former Governments. Her Majesty's Government, therefore, cannot pretend to blame the King of Sardinia for assisting them . . . Her Majesty's Government can see no sufficient grounds for the severe censure with which Austria, France, Prussia, and Russia have visited the acts of the King of Sardinia. Her Majesty's Government will turn their eyes rather to the gratifying prospect of a people building up the edifice of their liberties, and consolidating the work of their independence, amid the sympathies and good wishes of Europe.[139]

This time Lord John really had said something which re-dounded throughout Europe. It was 'le monument le plus curieux d'une littérature diplomatique tout à fait nouvelle',[140] and hostile observers thought it was Lord John's revenge for papal aggression in 1850. But it was also read, as Odo Russell reported with pardonable exaggeration, by twenty million Italians, every one of whom blessed Lord John 'night and morning'.[141]

Parkes thought the despatch was 'of a piece of other former rash acts – a day too late' to help Cavour.[142] But Cavour him-self would hardly have published it had he thought that, and four months later when the British government's blue book of the Italian despatches came out, even Clarendon admitted that ever since Lord John took office he had 'only intervened to pre-vent the intervention of others'.[143] Early in 1861 Britain offici-ally recognised the new kingdom of Italy. Lord John had managed to identify his country with the birth of the Italian state, and his behaviour had all along been manifestly disinter-ested compared with that of the French.

Venice and Rome remained as problems for another day, and Lord John continued to dissuade Piedmont from going at them 'with a crowbar and jemmy'.[144] But the specific task which had tempted him to take the foreign office was complete. As for reform he confessed to Palmerston that 'the apathy of the country is undeniable',[145] and early in the session of 1861, to Bright's fury,[146] he announced that for the time being at least, he must give it up. Palmerston was 'as fresh as a four year old' [horse],[147] and Gladstone had become the strength and glory of the real Liberals.[148] Lord John had insisted on second place, but now, as Clarendon unkindly put it, 'he is nobody and sinking fast'.[149] He began once again to think of going to the house of lords, and in May he made a definite request.[150] Palmerston persuaded him to stay on till the end of the session, but any lingering doubt Lord John may have had was removed when his brother died, and he inherited the Ardsalla estate in Ireland.[151] A life peerage was out of the question, because Pal-merston had tried once before to make one in 1856 and failed, and at the end of the session Lord John became Earl Russell of Kingston Russell, and young John became Viscount Amberley of Amberley and Ardsalla. When Gladstone sent Lord John his patent for the Chiltern hundreds he thanked him for many 'acts of courage and kindness'.[152] Palmerston, on the other hand, waited a bit, and then cheeked him by saying that the history of the world showed 'that Power in the Hands of the Masses throws the Scum of the Community to the surface, and that Truth and Justice are soon banished from the Land'.[153]

iii. Earl Russell, 1861–5

Earl Russell spoke of resting and being thankful,[154] but he did not surrender the foreign office, which he liked, and where, as he honestly said, with Palmerston's help, he felt he could do the work.[155] For another four years he continued to follow too hard upon the heels of events, to lean heavily upon Palmerston for his policies, and to lard his despatches with well-meant but empty homilies, and sharp rebuffs. Both in America and in Europe Palmerston and Russell were tempted to intervene, and year by year the collective weight of the cabinet had to be employed to restrain what Queen Victoria called the 'two terrible old men' from committing the country to anything disastrous.

Lord John's immediate reaction to the outbreak of the American civil war in 1861 was to deplore the collapse of a free state, and recall that it was the British who had saddled America with this disruptive slavery.[156] But when the North declared a blockade of Southern ports, and interrupted the supply of raw cotton to Britain, the British government found itself in the unusual situation of taking an interest in neutrals' rights, and decided to recognise the belligerent rights of the seceded states. The South then appointed two agents, Mason and Slidell, to Britain and France, and a Northern cruiser stopped a British ship, the *Trent*, in which they were travelling to Europe, and took the two men prisoner.

Palmerston thought it was time 'to read a lesson to the United States which will not soon be forgotten',[157] and the cabinet instructed Russell to demand both an apology and the release of the two agents, and if this were not forthcoming, to withdraw the British ambassador from Washington. Russell's despatch was unconciliatory, and from his death-bed the Prince Consort persuaded the Queen to ask the cabinet to modify it. 'She should have liked to have seen the expression of a hope that the American captain did not act under instructions, or, if he did, that he misapprehended them.'[158] The cabinet accepted this, and Russell himself informed Seward, the American secretary of state, that the British government set more store by the release of the commissioners than they did by the apology.[159] Seward was unmoved, but Lincoln realised that he must either give up Mason and Slidell or lose the Southern states, and he gave way.

Following the release of the two agents, the British and French governments were lobbied continuously by both sides. In June 1862, Adams, the Northern ambassador in London, drew Russell's attention to no. 290, a ship which was building in Laird's yard at Birkenhead, and which he had reason to believe was being modified for sale as a cruiser to the South. Russell referred the matter to the commissioners of customs at Liverpool, who reported that there were no grounds for arrest. It did not cross his mind that the commissioners might have been bribed. Adams then forwarded a legal opinion that if the British government allowed this ship to fall into Southern hands, they would be liable for any damage it might cause. Adams' case reached the foreign office on 24 July, and Russell ought to have detained the vessel pending inquiries. But there was a delay and a muddle, and the papers did not reach the law officers until 28 July. The same day no. 290 left dock, and the next day she put to sea. Russell made frantic efforts to stop her – when it was too late.[160] Thereafter Palmerston and Russell kept their eyes open, and the next year when suspicion fell upon two more ironclads which were building at Birkenhead, they were detained.[161] But the one error cost Britain dear. No. 290, the *Alabama*, took sixty-eight prizes in twenty-two months. Russell denied liability because he had acted in good faith, and set his face against arbitration, which would be decided against Britain solely on the ground that she was rich. The case was still open, therefore, when he left the foreign office in 1865. Thereafter each successive foreign secretary moved a stage nearer to arbitration, until finally in 1872 Britain paid the United States $15m.[162]

While the *Alabama* was fitting out for sea, on land the two armies remained in deadlock. As the North must conquer the South to win the war, while the South need only remain in the field to survive, this result was, as Russell said, favourable to the Southern cause. In September 1862 Palmerston gave his preliminary blessing to a plan for Britain, France and Russia to make a joint offer of mediation. Thereupon Russell was all for quick action, and saw himself cast in the role of a second Canning.[163] Fortunately Palmerston decided to await the result of one more battle, the North prevailed at Antietam, and Lincoln emancipated the slaves. Gladstone missed the turn of the tide, and rashly announced in public that Jefferson Davis had made a nation. But Palmerston and his cabinet declined to join France in an offer of mediation, and when France made one on her own it was refused. The British government left the North to finish the war in its own way, and not even his worst enemies supposed Russell wished to imitate Napoleon, and take advantage of American embarrassments to set an Elliot on the throne of Mexico.

In 1862 Bismarck came to power at Berlin. It is often said that Palmerston and Russell ought to have anticipated the diplomatic upheaval of the next nine years, and formed a common front with France. But events in Italy and America had not created a basis of trust upon which the two nations could act together, and Russell's original attitude to Poland was the same as Palmerston's to Hungary in 1849 – that much as he would like to help the Poles, they were too far away.[164] It was a pity he did not stick to it. But when Bismarck offered to assist Russia repress the Polish revolt, and France threatened to attack Prussia in order to help Poland, Palmerston and Russell could not resist informing Russia that Britain might allow herself to be drawn into a war for the sake of Poland by France. France thereupon invited Britain to send a joint note to Berlin, and Palmerston became alarmed for the Rhine frontier. The result was that the British government lost all the way along the line. Russia called Britain's bluff, and Napoleon complained of British pusillanimity. Worst of all, in Berlin Bismarck weighed the whole case, and drew the correct conclusion from what had happened.[165]

Napoleon was humiliated, and towards the end of 1863 he fell back upon an old plan to invite the sovereigns of countries which had been parties to the treaty of Vienna to attend a new congress and settle all the disputed questions in Europe. The British cabinet decided unanimously that such a conference would raise more problems than it solved. Even so, it was not wise to snub Napoleon. Russell's despatch was shown to the cabinet, which made no objection at the time, but regretted afterwards that 'a little more soft powder was not used'.[166] It was sent on 25 November, and reached Cowley the next day. Cowley did not deliver it at once, and in the meantime it was published in London. When Cowley at last saw Napoleon on 28 November, the emperor was angry, and said that England would soon want France's help in dealing with the Schleswig Holstein question, and that it would not be forthcoming.

The relations between the two duchies of Schleswig Holstein, with their predominantly German population, and Denmark on the one hand and the German confederation on the other were regulated by the protocol of 1850, negotiated by Palmerston, and by the treaty of London of 1852 to which all the powers were parties. The whole arrangement was brought into question in 1863, when the Danish king promulgated a new constitution under which Schleswig and Holstein would be separated, and Schleswig would be incorporated into Denmark. Thus far, the Danes were in the wrong, but instead of appealing to the treaty of 1852 the German states decided to carry out a federal execution against Denmark. Palmerston and Russell were then in a quandary. According to the principles of Lord John's despatch of 27 October 1860, they ought to have sided with the Germans. But it was two years since Palmerston had first taken note of Prussia's 'aggressive Policy against Denmark', and of her 'anti-English Policy all over the world'.[167] Now he observed that Prussia, the big boy, thought she had got the little boy in a corner,[168] or, as Russell told the Queen, it was a case of two and a half million people against forty millions.[169]

The original and greatest mistake in the British government's handling of the affair was Palmerston's declaration in the house of commons on 22 July 1863, that if Denmark were attacked she would not stand alone. Even at this stage Palmerston ought to have realised that it would be difficult for Napoleon to pursue one line of policy on the Po, and another on the Eider and the Schlei. But once Britain had turned down Napoleon's favourite project for a conference, the plight of the Danes was hopeless. Bismarck realised this, but because he was still not sure that Palmerston did, he advanced by stages. First the Germans invaded Holstein, in December 1863: then at the beginning of February 1864 they invaded Schleswig; then in the middle of February they entered Jutland; and finally, in March, they occupied the whole peninsula. Palmerston and Russell ought to have offered their good offices, and uttered no more threats. But Russell was caught between the majority of the cabinet who wanted him to restrain Copenhagen, and Palmerston who wanted him to warn Frankfurt and Berlin. For a time he wavered between the two, and then, instead of sensibly taking up a position on the peaceful side of Palmerston, he seems to have thought that he had served his apprenticeship to the master craftsman of 1850, and he became more bellicose than his chief. Finally, in a manner reminiscent of his behaviour in 1852–5, he ill-temperedly defied the rest of the cabinet to desert the prime minister in the position the foreign secretary had taken up.

At one moment, in February, after the Danes had formally asked Britain for help, and a rumour went round that the Austrians were sending a fleet up the English channel, it looked as though Britain might still have some influence over affairs. Palmerston urged Somerset to despatch a British squadron to Copenhagen, and the German powers agreed to attend a conference in London. But the French refused to act with the British, and when the conference opened Russell was stranded without a plan. The Germans agreed to an armistice, but started the conference by tearing up the treaty of London of 1852. The conference broke up without achieving anything, and on 11 June the cabinet met to decide what to do if the war was resumed. They agreed to support the proposal for a new frontier drawn by arbitration, and Russell told the Queen that they had decided, if this was rejected by Germany, to give material aid to Denmark. This was a misrepresentation, and it left the cabinet with no choice but to take Russell's decisions for him. When the Danes refused mediation, the cabinet decided on 24 June not to make war either in conjunction with

Napoleon, who had had a last-minute change of heart, or single-handed, and next day they decided not to send a fleet to Copenhagen even if Austria sent hers.[170]

As soon as the fighting began again, Denmark had to sue for peace, and Disraeli and Malmesbury moved votes of censure in the two houses. Both dwelt upon the hopes so carelessly held out to Denmark, and the threats so lightly uttered to the Germans. In the commons one future foreign secretary, Stanley, doubted whether the government ever had 'a deliberate determination to adopt a policy either of war or of peace', while another, Lord Robert Cecil, pointed out that if British policy had been conducted on the principles of Cobden and Bright, the result would have been the same and would have been more dignified.[171] In the lords Malmesbury denounced Russell for paying too little heed to the larger questions, and twitted him with recommending Reform Bills to the Danes.[172] Russell himself spoke calmly and without a trace of the folly which marred his despatches. But ministers were defeated in the lords by 177 votes to 168, and they only survived because they scraped home in the commons by eighteen votes. Russell remained at the foreign office for another year, but the debate was decisive for British foreign policy in the nineteenth century. The great body of the Liberal party, led by Gladstone and Granville, henceforth sought to avoid continental entanglements even if it meant jeopardising the balance of power.

Russell did not add to his reputation by staying at the foreign office from 1861 to 1865, and in apeing Palmerston he unnecessarily lowered his character below that of his chief. There were many ways in which Palmerston was a greater man than Russell, but it was impossible not to notice, as Palmerston passed into his eighties, that he stood for nothing. He subscribed to no intelligible, enlightened principles, and he had neither legitimate children nor disciples. When he dined at Pembroke Lodge he ate enormously, 'and seemed to enjoy his food more than talking'.[173]

Russell, on the other hand, did stand for something, and in 1861, when Jowett first got to know him well, he found that notwithstanding his shyness Lord John 'talks to you on any subject of history or philosophy like a real man'.[174] The foreign secretary was still busy writing his three-volume *Life and times of Charles James Fox*, and he was identified with the living causes of constitutional development, civil and religious liberty, and the ultimate triumph of reason over prejudice. A cynic would say that ambassadors of foreign countries came down to Pembroke Lodge because Russell changed his mind so often that they dare not let him out of their sight. But they were not the only visitors. Dickens came, and esteemed Russell more than any other prime minister;[175] John Stuart Mill came, and accepted one of Amberley's puppies for his step-daughter Helen Taylor;[176] and in due course Lecky came, and found that the charm of Russell's talk

> lay mainly in his admirable terseness and clearness of expression, in the skill with which, by a few happy words, he could tell a story, or etch out a character, or condense an argument or statement.[177]

As they dined in the little room painted with trellis and green leaves,[178] played croquet on the lawn, heard Lord John regret his son could not give time to Dugald Stewart's moral philosophy because 'the Little-go is always coming and never gone',[179] and listened to a reading aloud from Sydney Smith on Bentham's *Book of Popular Fallacies*,[180] they came to understand, as Jowett said, how it was that Lord John had been ' "bowled over" by Palmerston, and yet is really the better and greater man of the two'.[181]

Unlike Grey and Melbourne, Lord John did not become crabbed and cynical with age, and in the 1860s he became elder statesman to the intelligent. As the parliament of 1859 grew old, convinced reformers began to make themselves heard again. In May 1864 Gladstone startled the country with a guarded, but apparently unequivocal speech in favour of universal suffrage: then, in September, he began to doubt whether any solution to the Irish problem could be obtained from the present constituency.[182] Politics had come back to the problems of the 1830s. Lord John had been the best guide then. Now he could, in any case, not live long to guide the footsteps of another administration. But at least he had a son. Amberley was educated at Harrow. Afterwards he went first to Edinburgh, where he lived for a year with Professor A. C. Fraser, and then to Trinity College Cambridge, where he was unhappy. Amberley was

serious, and more than a bit of a prig, until he met the deft and
vivacious, equally Radical, charming and winning Kate
Stanley, and after an enforced six-months cooling-off period
which increased the ardour on both sides, married her in
November 1864, when he was only twenty-two.

In January 1865 Amberley received an invitation from the
Working Men's Parliamentary Reform Association to speak at
Leeds. Jowett was glad he was beginning among the working
men – 'that is the right place for the Politics of the Future'.[183]
Amberley's début was closely watched by the press, and his
unqualified advocacy of universal suffrage caused a sensation.

> While in the Lords Papa
>   Rests, and is thankful,
> Or at the F.O. wastes
>   Ink by the tankful,
> Lecturing Pruss and Russ,
>   Dane, Turk, and Hun, Sir –
> Prattling away at Leeds,
>   Hark to 'my Son, Sir!'[184]

The Times gave Amberley two leaders, and after making the
obvious point that he had been 'thoroughly indoctrinated in
the logic, the controversy, and the history of Reform', alleged
that he had been told whom to look to – 'Mr. Gladstone is the
mentor of the young Telemachus'.[185] This was running on a
bit. Russell himself was still in favour of the £6 franchise, and
when he received a report of the speech, laughed at Amberley's
agreeing with Gladstone.[186] But the beneficiaries of mid-
Victorian prosperity did not know that. For nearly ten years,
now, they had supported Palmerston and even Derby to spare
themselves the agitation of great questions by Russell. In 1865
they became aware that, when Palmerston died, there would be
another Reform Bill, and that there might even be another
Irish church bill, and that this time it would not be Russell
alone with whom they would have to contend, but Russell and
Gladstone.

CHAPTER XVII

Lord Russell's Rapidity, 1865–6

IN THE spring of 1865 Palmerston was ill, and Clarendon thought that if he died the 'patch-up' would be attempted of Russell prime minister, with Gladstone leading in the house of commons.[1] But Palmerston recovered, and lived to hold a general election in the summer. For several years Derby had tacitly supported Palmerston so long as reform remained a dead issue. The truce of parties appealed to the electorate, and at the election reform was dealt with on Palmerston's terms, vaguely. Liberal candidates stressed that an extension of the franchise must be 'safe', and Palmerston was returned with about 360 supporters compared to Derby's 290. The results were a triumph for Palmerston, and were to prove an insuperable handicap to Russell, for among the 360 were some forty nominal Liberals whose loyalty would cease with Palmerston's death. From Russell's point of view the only favourable sign was that among the 150 new members was a distinguished group of intellectuals including Fawcett, Thomas Hughes, John Stuart Mill and G. O. Trevelyan, but not, alas, Amberley, who lost his contest at Leeds.[2]

Palmerston never met the new parliament. He died on 18 October, leaving the rest of the cabinet, as Bagehot put it, like the solar system without the sun. *The Times* hoped the Queen would entrust the government to a younger man, and favoured Gladstone,[3] but Gladstone himself had no doubt that Russell would be sent for,[4] and he was right. The Queen felt for 'poor Ld Russell; to begin at his age afresh after *13 years* as Prime Minister is very trying'.[5] But after all she was not asking him to form a new government, but only, as a crestfallen Russell told Gladstone, to carry on the present one.[6] Clarendon had an obvious claim to succeed Russell at the foreign office, and there was no call to disturb the rest of the cabinet.

Gladstone delicately waived all claim to the lead in the commons, if Russell preferred to entrust it to Sir George Grey.[7] But for ten years now Russell had been closer to the Peelites than to the Whigs, and Sir George Grey 'heartily and unreservedly concurred', as he wrote to Gladstone, in Russell's proposal '(the only one in fact that he could make) that you should lead the House of Commons'.[8] Here, at last, was the alliance of Whigs and Peelites under Russell's leadership for which Russell had hoped since 1846. But Russell himself could not do much because the house of lords was 'an idle and nearly useless body unless in a crisis, when it is apt to be mischievous'.[9] He required someone of Gladstone's energy to do the work in what Tierney had taught him 'never to call the Lower House',[10] and he wrote to Gladstone that 'the most frequent and unreserved communications must take place between us – such as always took place between Ld Grey and Ld Althorp, and between Ld Melbourne and me'.[11]

Russell was fortunate in his lieutenant. In the first place Gladstone knew he could handle Russell, and was therefore not put out by Russell's sudden coups and frequent foolishnesses to the extent that most of their colleagues were. In the second place the two men shared a mood. Russell's last political intimate, Lansdowne, had died in 1863, and at seventy-three the prime minister was in a hurry. Gladstone had been separated by death from Sidney Herbert and the Duke of Newcastle, and had since lost his seat at Oxford university and fallen back upon South Lancashire, where he was 'unmuzzled'. Above all, Gladstone acknowledged that his career was carrying him closer to the Lord John Russell of the 1830s whom he had opposed, and for that reason he refused to thrust himself forward in succession to Palmerston.[12]

Palmerston's death changed everything, and even before he had been buried, after a delay which threw Russell under the suspicion of grudging, in Westminster Abbey, men on both sides of parliament were taking note of the fact. Harcourt wrote to Russell that under Palmerston the Liberal party had been in a false position.[13] Lyttelton assured Gladstone that he was unable to join in the apotheosis of Palmerston, that he could support a Russell government better, and a Russell and Gladstone government better still.[14] Gladstone himself said cautiously that any government now to be formed 'cannot be wholly a continuation; it must be in some degree a new commencement',[15] and Disraeli forecast eagerly that 'If Johnny is the man, there will be a Reform Bill – very distasteful to the country. The truce of parties is over.'[16] The opposition at once began to count the Liberal dissidents who might be expected to follow Lowe, Horsman, and Elcho, and upset the balance of parties.[17]

Disraeli had spies or second sight. Russell's first act was to tell the Queen that he would want to bring in a Reform Bill, and his second was to tell Gladstone that it would be a life-or-death question.[18] At the very first meeting after Palmerston's death, Russell and Gladstone apparently had no difficulty in persuading the cabinet to take up the question of reform, and ministers arranged the heads under which they would need information in order to frame a bill.[19] A few days later Gladstone addressed a meeting of the Parliamentary Reform Union at Glasgow, and praised Her Majesty's choice of Earl Russell (loud cheers), 'whose career was a guarantee for the future'.[20] Any remaining doubt that an era had come to an end was dispelled when Russell discovered that in Ireland the chief secretary, Sir Robert Peel, had been working against the government at the elections.[21] Russell dismissed him, and in an attempt to recover the support of the Irish M.P.s offended by the ecclesiastical titles act, replaced him with Chichester Fortescue, who lost no time in promoting a land bill in 1866, and later played a decisive part in drafting Gladstone's first land act of 1870.

The first thing to concern the two leaders was the 'lob sided' condition of the government.[22] Palmerston never looked beyond his own time, and made little effort to plant out 'young trees'.[23] Now, in addition to the prime minister and the foreign secretary, the heads of the two great spending departments, Somerset at the admiralty and de Grey at the war office, were in the lords, and there was an urgent need to bring on young house of commons men. Clarendon had vacated the duchy of Lancaster, and Russell looked at the question of a successor in the light of the necessity of winning support for the proposed Reform Bill. He wanted to make room in the cabinet for Horsman, who might bring as many as twenty-five of the Liberal dissentients over with him.[24] But Gladstone thought Lowe was more powerful,[25] and Granville later claimed that if Lowe had

been asked to support a moderate bill, he would have accepted.[26] Gladstone himself, however, queried Lowe's *'digestion'*,[27]
while Russell could not forget the round robin of 1855, and was
understandably hurt by the stinging leading article in *The
Times* with which Lowe greeted his second premiership.[28] Both
names were allowed to drop while Russell made an approach
to the open-minded young Stanley, and when Stanley refused
to accept office, understandably enough, on the ground that his
father was the leader of the opposition,[29] Gladstone asked
Russell to leave the duchy vacant for the time being.[30]

Russell and Gladstone then turned to the consideration of
posts outside the cabinet. Russell favoured Goschen, a city man,
whom he made vice-president of the board of trade. Gladstone
then suggested offering Chichester Fortescue's old place as
under-secretary for the colonies to Forster, an advanced Liberal, and 'a very good man, whom you have not known much in
the H of Commons'.[31] Russell was not averse, but Forster's
promotion was intricately bound up with another question,
which was whether reform was to be approached cautiously, by
way of a commission of inquiry. Clarendon, de Grey, George
Grey, Somerset, Stanley of Alderley and Wood were all in
favour of this. Russell himself referred to the proposal as 'the
resort of delayers',[32] but Gladstone had learned his politics from
Peel, and never liked to bring in a bill until he could see his
way to passing it. He was fearful of 'Lord Russell's rapidity',[33]
and for a few days Lady Russell thought he was 'all for putting
off reform, tho' that was the question on which he was supposed to go further . . . than any of the others'.[34]

The cabinet was still evenly balanced between Whigs and
Reformers when Russell saw Forster on 16 November. Russell
said that 'Gladstone and he would bring in a bill', and spoke of
an inquiry. Forster refused to accept office if there were to be a
commission, and publicly urged the government to bring in a
real measure of reform next year. On 24 November Russell told
Forster he liked his speech, and added that 'you must trust in
Gladstone and me'. Forster accepted office, and no more was
heard of the proposed commission.[35] Brand, the chief whip,
warned Russell that in that case he was bound to be beaten,[36]
but the prime minister cannot on this occasion have got himself
too far out in front of his colleagues, because the day after

Forster accepted office Clarendon wrote that he had 'never assisted at cabinets more entirely harmonious than those held since Earl John put his little hand to the helm'. Even Gladstone, Clarendon noticed, who used to be 'ever and anon minatory and overbearing' under Palmerston, was now 'meek and gentle'.[37]

In the meantime Stanley of Alderley made another attempt to persuade Russell to invite Lowe to join the government. Lowe said later that Russell offered him everything 'short of the Governor General of India, out of England',[38] but in fact Russell simply said that if Lowe came in he would go out.[39] That was decisive, but one day when Russell was absent, and Gladstone was in the chair, an apprehensive cabinet resolved to send a propitiating letter to Lowe.[40] Lady Russell condemned 'this abject fear of *The Times*',[41] but her husband did not object, and merely remarked that Granville would be the best person to convey the message.[42] Curiously enough, even after Lowe had dropped out of consideration, Gladstone was still wondering whether it would be possible to make an offer to Bright. Russell was more level-headed, and knew that if he was not willing to have Lowe, he dare not have Bright,[43] and finally Gladstone admitted that at that moment Bright's name 'would sink the Government and their bill together'.[44]

As for the bill itself, Russell's original notion was to go for a £12 rating franchise in the counties and a £6 rating franchise in the boroughs,[45] and to postpone redistribution until 1867.[46] The statistics collected by the poor law board would be complete by the time ministers met at the beginning of January, and a committee would then sit three times a week to get the bill ready in time for the opening of parliament in February.[47] But Russell's timetable was soon thrown into disarray. The argument for a Reform Bill rested upon the assumption that the working classes were not represented in parliament, and each set of returns as it came in showed that between one-fifth and one-quarter of the existing electorate was working class,[48] and that since 1832 the electorate had kept pace with the population.[49]

Russell himself, 'shut up at Pembroke Lodge and taking Amberley for public opinion',[50] was not disturbed by these discoveries, and still thought 'we can have a good measure by which we can stand or fall'.[51] But Gladstone at once saw the use to which opponents would put them, and queried the accuracy of the figures.[52] Gladstone was preoccupied with schemes for the reorganisation of the Treasury, he wanted 'mind and time more free' for the Reform Bill, and on 1 January 1866 he wrote to Russell that he would gladly have seen the franchise bill in the house of commons in other hands than his.[53] This letter can be misinterpreted to mean that the two leaders did not see eye to eye upon reform, and it was at this period that Gathorne Hardy was told that Gladstone was talking conservatism and sneering at Lord Russell.[54] But Gladstone never sneered, it was not his habit to write a new year's day letter in order to set himself at a distance from a colleague, there is no evidence that the reluctant reformers in the cabinet ever expected help from Gladstone, and this letter meant simply that Gladstone wished Russell, with all his accumulated expertise upon this subject, was still in the house of commons. Gladstone was understandably afraid that Russell was going too fast, but that was a different thing.

Gladstone was, indeed, overworked, for the main burden of deciding whether the government should compensate farmers affected by the cattle plague rested upon him, and it was sad that he and Russell now fell out over the manner in which he was to be relieved. At Gladstone's request, Russell had not filled the post at the duchy of Lancaster. Week after week went by, and still Gladstone would not say what he wanted. Clarendon suspected Gladstone wished to bring the private revenues of the Queen under public control and to suppress the duchy altogether,[55] and Brand told Russell the government must use all the patronage at its command if it was to carry its Reform Bill.[56] The matter was raised in the cabinet one day when Russell was absent. Afterwards Sir George Grey reported that he had suggested linking the duchy to the treasury in order to help Gladstone, and that he thought Goschen would be the best man for the place.[57] But Goschen was only thirty-four, and Gladstone himself objected strongly to 'disturbance of the order of promotion in the official body'.[58]

When ministers met on 11 January, there was much concern at the statistics produced by the poor law board, and the cabinet rejected the franchises proposed by Russell and Gladstone, and insisted on further inquiries.[59] Immediately afterwards Russell appointed Goschen to the duchy and brought him into the cabinet.[60] Gladstone was very angry, but knowing that the act had been intended to help him with his work, he refused to take Russell to task.[61] Wood, therefore, took Lady John to one side, and talked 'about John, his occasional sudden acts without consulting colleagues, and the bad effect of so acting'.[62] Clarendon interpreted the appointment as an act of power, bringing another convinced reformer into the cabinet, and said that it was done 'in the most thoro'ly Johnian style. Nobody was thought of by John but John'.[63] From this moment every rumour of disaffection in the cabinet was seized upon by London society, injected with malice, and magnified a hundred times. Even so, the bill was still alive. The cabinet appointed a committee of Russell, Gladstone, Milner Gibson, Villiers and one other,[64] and towards the end of January Russell wrote with true kindness to Gladstone:

> If I bring in or contribute to bring in a measure which I think right it will be to me a satisfactory close of my political life, whether carried or defeated. But you have . . . a long parliamentary life before you and I should be very sorry to hang a millstone about your neck. So pray do not commit yourself to £6 rating unless you think it is the best measure we can propose in present circumstances.[65]

Gladstone was touched by this, and replied that he confidently hoped to fight by Russell's side.[66]

It was now the end of January: the bill could not be ready in time for the opening of parliament, and the delay, as Bright said, was very damaging.[67] Russell did what he could. He appointed Monsell, who was a roman catholic, to succeed Goschen at the board of trade, and then, when Wood had an accident and was obliged to retire, he seized the chance to rejuvenate the ministry. He moved de Grey from the war office and made him secretary of state for India. He appointed the Marquis of Hartington, who was a member of the house of commons, to succeed de Grey, and he made Stansfeld, another prominent young Liberal, under-secretary of state for India. The government then had a much fresher look, and Russell rounded off his good work by persuading the Queen to open

parliament, for the first time since the Prince Consort died; by
offering Lady Palmerston a peerage (which was refused);[68] and
by ordering 800 yards of new carpet and getting Downing
Street ready for parties.[69] It was all to little avail, and he must
have been sad when Broughton, and the contemporary Durham, and Lansdowne, among others, all refused to attend his
dinner on the eve of the session.[70]

Parliament met on 6 February, and ministers were confronted
by a spoiling bill, which provided for an 'extension' to the suffrage by means of an educational test.[71] On 12 February they
met to consider their own bill, and after hearing how much the
rates varied from place to place, and discussing the problem of
the compound householder (whose rates were paid for him by
his landlord), they decided to abandon the rating qualification,
and to plump for rental instead.[72] No figure was settled, but on
the eve of their next meeting Bright dined with Russell,[73] and
when Russell and Gladstone proposed a £14 county and a £7
borough rental, there was a chorus of complaint that they were
going too far. A rumour went round that Clarendon, de Grey,
and Somerset had walked out of the meeting,[74] and on 28
February *The Times* maliciously and falsely announced that the
ministry was at an end, and that the Queen had sent for
Somerset.

On 1 March Gladstone asked Russell whether the new
borough franchise was to be over £7 rental or at and over £7.[75]
The distinction would make a difference between enfranchising
109,000 and 144,000 people,[76] and Gladstone thought even the
larger number 'by no means too large'.[77] Russell did not call
the cabinet together, but circulated a memorandum, and thus
gave the impression that he was afraid of meeting his colleagues.[78] Somerset spoke of resignation, and the whole cabinet
became mutinous.[79] The back-door communications to Windsor Castle, which had gone on when Russell was foreign
secretary, now began again, and Granville wrote to the Queen,[80]
while Sir George Grey wrote to her secretary, his cousin General
Grey.[81] Clarendon's language was loose, if not actually disloyal,[82] and enough harm was done to make it virtually certain
that the bill would not be allowed a fair hearing when it was
brought into the commons on 12 March.

The subsequent history of the bill belongs more to the life of

Gladstone than to that of Russell. Gladstone showed an unwise degree of commitment to their proposals as being perfect, and it at once became evident that the attempt to steer between Lowe and Bright had failed. Bright had urged the government not to bring in a redistribution bill at this stage, but to enlarge the franchise in order to secure a 'lever'. There was no redistribution bill, and Lowe accused Russell and Gladstone of having taken the mass of their supporters and laid them at Bright's feet,[83] while Horsman said it was the old battle revived, Bright and Russell against the majority of the cabinet and the country.[84] At this stage the opposition all came from the Palmerstonians, whom Bright dubbed the cave of Adullam. It was not until 16 March that Disraeli made up his mind to ally with the cave to wreck the bill with an amendment on the second reading.[85]

The terms of Grosvenor's amendment asking the government to bring in their redistribution bill before the house would consider the franchise bill were known well in advance, and Gladstone doubted whether it had powder enough to kill.[86] But he was taking no chances: he spoke to a public meeting at Liverpool of having crossed the Rubicon,[87] and Argyll joined him on the platform 'just to show that *all* the Peerage is not dragged reluctantly *"to the scratch"* '.[88] Russell himself called a meeting of his supporters at Downing Street. He found it difficult to address the house of lords, because 'one cd not speak of truth and justice to an assembly who did not care for such things at all', but now he spoke for nearly an hour. The government could not give way to Lord Grosvenor, but they would lay a redistribution bill on the table before going into committee. It was like one of his speeches of old:[89] he was much applauded, and even Granville congratulated him upon a great personal and political success.[90] But Disraeli reckoned upon 290 votes plus 40 seceders,[91] and Russell remained low at the prospects, and consoled himself with the thought that 'it is fine weather to go out in'.[92]

The debate upon the second reading began on 12 April and lasted until the twenty-seventh, when Gladstone wound up with a generous tribute to Russell 'whose name has been associated for forty years . . . with every measure of beneficent legislation'.[93] Brand's latest estimate was for a majority of between fifteen and twenty,[94] but when the vote was taken thirty-five Liberals voted against the bill, and the ministry only won by 318 votes to 313. Kate Amberley at once spotted that the majority of the thirty-five were young lords or the eldest sons of peers.[95] When the cabinet met, the left wing wanted to dissolve, and the right wing wanted to resign. Gladstone spoke in favour of carrying on.[96] Russell supported him, and pointed out that the majority was five times as great as that for the first Reform Bill in 1831.[97] Sir George Grey went home and wrote to his cousin the General, and the next day the Queen asked Russell not to annoy the house of commons.[98] Russell, who had been very angry with Lord Grosvenor at first, and would call him an insincere man, then allowed, 'as an improvement [that] he is a puzzle headed insincere man'.[99] Russell was ready to concede every point except the £7 franchise,[100] and the government announced that they would bring in their redistribution bill on 7 May.

The redistribution bill was finished in a hurry. Russell gave the guidelines, and in order to minimise the opposition, he proposed to disfranchise only the very small boroughs of fewer than 5000 inhabitants. The rest of the boroughs affected were to be grouped. Russell had never cared for grouping, but he had no alternative, and his plan, which would make sixty-nine seats available for redistribution, was scrupulously honest in the sense that 55 out of the 112 members who would be affected were supporters.[101] This was too much for Brand, who said he could not carry it, and what finally emerged was a decision to group single-member boroughs of under 8000 inhabitants, and to take one member away from two-member boroughs of under 8000 inhabitants. This would make forty-nine seats available for redistribution, and the cabinet proposed to allot twenty-six of these to the English counties, fifteen to the English boroughs, one to London university, and seven to Scotland.[102] Gladstone introduced the scheme on 7 May, in a speech in which he threatened to go on into the autumn if need be, in order to avoid the loss of a whole year.[103]

On 10 May Overend and Gurney failed and precipitated a financial crisis, in the course of which Gladstone had to suspend the bank charter act and raise the bank rate to 10 per cent. On 11 May Amberley was at last returned to the house of commons

at a by-election in Leeds, and Russell skipped the house in order
'to enjoy the nightingales at Pembroke Lodge.'[104] Amberley
was in time to witness the last seven weeks of his father's second
ministry, in which one event now followed rapidly upon
another.

On 14 May Gladstone agreed to combine the redistribution
bill and the franchise bill, and the second reading of the redistribution bill then went through without a division. The next
day Gladstone allowed Russell to send a conciliatory letter to
Grosvenor.[105] A few days later it became clear that Prussia was
about to attack Austria, and the Queen, in between sending
Russell medical certificates to say that she was not fit to leave
Balmoral,[106] wrote both to Derby pleading with him not to
mount a factious opposition,[107] and to Russell inviting him not
to go on with the bill.[108] Both leaders refused to be deflected,[109]
and Disraeli planned to strike at the bill through Hayter, the
son of a former Whig whip, who would stigmatise the redistribution plan as 'not sufficiently matured'.[110] The motion went
off at half-cock and was withdrawn at the last moment. But the
same evening Knightly carried an instruction to the committee
of the house to add to the bill clauses dealing with corruption.
This was too much for Gladstone. He had fourteen hours a day
'other work',[111] and was trying, for the first time in his life, to
sleep in the house of commons, but without success because the
members behind, seeing him nodding off, put their feet upon
the bench and shook it.[112] He had already appealed to Russell
for more help from other members of the cabinet, and on 28
May he wrote that the multitude of points which would now
arise upon the combined measure would be too much for him.[113]

The next attempt to defeat the bill came on 7 June, when the
Adullamite leaders persuaded Stanley to move, without warning, that redistribution be taken first. But this was too low a blow
for the rebel rank and file, twenty-one of whom went back to the
government,[114] and on the same evening ministers successfully
resisted an opposition amendment to raise the new county franchise from £14 to £20. Derby was upset by these setbacks, and
told General Grey, who was very sorry to hear it, that the
government might now carry its bill through the lower house.[115]

While Derby began to plan how to defeat the bill in the
lords,[116] and found that his forces would be considerably

strengthened by the apprehensions aroused by the government's Irish land bill,[117] Disraeli continued to look for a formula which would reunite the opposition in the commons with the cave. He found it in an amendment to substitute rating for rental in the county franchise. The amendment was defeated by 280 votes to 273, but twenty-five Liberals voted with the opposition,[118] and it was obvious that if the same motion were brought forward in relation to the new borough franchise it would really cut into the working-class vote. Disraeli tried again, and entrusted the motion to Dunkellin, Clanricarde's heir, whose brother in due course became known as the worst landlord in Ireland. On 18 June the amendment was carried by 335 votes to 304. The cave had recovered all but two of those who had voted for Grosvenor's motion in April, and polled fifteen more besides.[119]

When the cabinet met, Gladstone, who started from the conviction that what they had proposed 'should be regarded as a *minimum* of enfranchisement', and who now thought that a general election which would somewhat reduce the party would be of use if it also had the effect of purging it,[120] spoke in favour of dissolution. He was supported by Russell, Argyll, Milner Gibson and Goschen (5). Cardwell, Clarendon, de Grey, Sir George Grey, Somerset and Stanley of Alderley (6) voted in favour of resignation, and Cranworth, Granville, Hartington and Villiers (4) were undecided.[121] The decision taken, therefore, was to resign. But already, the house of commons was talking about a resolution which would dispose of the bill but not the ministers, and the Queen commanded her servants to stay at their posts.[122]

A week of confusion followed. Brand scotched the idea of dissolution, by pointing out how many members were embarrassed by the financial crisis. Gladstone then suggested that he and Russell resign, and leave their less rigid colleagues to carry on and help the Queen. Sir George Grey drew up a resolution which he believed the house would pass in order to enable the government to survive. But Gladstone rejected it, and when Russell and Gladstone drew up another one Grosvenor rejected that. On 23 June the Queen at last agreed to come down to Windsor from Balmoral. On 24 June Russell and Sir George Grey revised the saving resolution eight times, and Gladstone rejected it each time.[123] On 25 June Clarendon complained to

Russell about Gladstone's desire to humiliate the house of commons, and said he could not bear to think that the last act of Russell's political life should be to break up the party.[124] Russell endorsed Clarendon's letter 'Abuse of Gladstone', and replied that he could not wonder Gladstone refused to accept 'a resolution which was intended to mean one thing to us, and another thing to Lord Grosvenor.'[125]

Russell himself then devised a formula which would enable the ministry both to accept Dunkellin's motion and to put the occupier with a £7 rental on the register. Gladstone agreed to this, and he, Argyll, Milner Gibson, Goschen, Granville, Stanley of Alderley and Villiers (7) voted in favour. Cardwell, Clarendon, Cranworth, de Grey, Sir George Grey, Hartington and Somerset (7) voted against, and Russell gave a casting vote in favour, after which the discussion broke out again.[126] Next day Russell and Gladstone went down to Windsor to see the Queen. In the train Gladstone said to Russell:

> it is singular that the same members of the Cabinet (generally speaking) who were prematurely eager for resignation after the division on Lord Grosvenor's motion are now again eager to accept almost anything in the way of a Resolution as sufficient to warrant our continuing in office. He replied 'yes but I am afraid at the root of both proceedings there is a great amount of antipathy to our Reform Bill. They were anxious to resign when resignation would have been injurious to it, and now they are anxious to avoid resignation because resignation will be beneficial to it'.[127]

At the audience it was arranged that after another cabinet meeting Russell should send one of two telegrams; either 'Proposition No. 1' (Lord Russell), or 'Proposition No. 2' (resignation). Later that day, when the Queen opened her telegram, it read 'Proposition No. 2', and she sent for Derby the same evening.[128]

Russell had started with a majority of seventy, his ministry had lasted just over eight months, and on the face of it he had achieved nothing. He had rushed upon his fate, and he was condemned by London society. But at this distance of time his conduct does not appear to have been unwise, or lacking in nobility. He was old, but his spirit was reminiscent of his better days in the 1830s, and had he not been guilty of so many follies in the interim, the eight-months ministry would have been treated more leniently. As it was, Russell knew from the moment he took over that he would be met by a rebellion in his party as 'utterly destitute of consistent principle' and 'patriotic end' as that which had driven Sir Robert Peel from office in 1846.[129] But he was much struck by the intelligence of the working men who came to see him,[130] and in parliament he kept his eye firmly upon the faithful three hundred rather than the revolting forty. Above all he discerned that, even if he were beaten, his successors would be obliged to bring in 'a bill like ours' with 'some of Dizzy's elixir' infused into the dose.[131] In those eight months, when he was supported by Gladstone, Russell recovered his political character. The tragedy was that had he only kept his temper under Aberdeen, he and Gladstone might have been at the head of the government ten years earlier, and with ten times better prospects.

CHAPTER XVIII

The Victim of Infirmities, 1866–78

WHEN the government fell, Russell did not retire. Gladstone was being criticised for his 'rigid obstinacy',[1] and London was full of malicious rumours that he had gone mad and went every day to buy the contents of Kremer's toyshop, which Mrs Gladstone took back every evening.[2] All Russell could do was to defend Gladstone from the charge of having shown excess of warmth,[3] and to call a conference with him and with the party whips at Woburn in September, after which Brand paid a round of visits to the Adullamites, almost all of whom were now 'more or less ashamed of themselves'.[4]

The two leaders then set off independently for Italy with their families. The Russells reached Florence in time for the opening of the new Italian parliament, and on 4 December Clarendon reported from Florence that

> Ld John has been confined to his hotel with a bad cold and Lady J with an *extinction de voix* ever since they came here and neither of them seem in good spirits *14 colds* having been distributed among the family since they left Eng^d.[5]

Russell asked Gladstone to come and see him, but Gladstone said they were so watched in Italy that he thought it better to keep apart,[6] and Clarendon wrote that Russell 'seems quite to understand the reasonableness of your declining his unreasonable request to come and confer with him here about nothing at all'.[7] This was not quite fair: Russell was already looking ahead to what was to happen after the Reform Bill, and he wanted to have a talk about the Irish church. Gladstone relented, and when they met Russell discovered that Gladstone was 'as little disposed as I was to maintain Protestant ascendancy in Ireland'.[8]

The year 1867 was not an easy one for Gladstone, who found

Russell acorn.   Gladstone acorn

FIG. 8   THE RUSSELL ACORN AND THE
GLADSTONE ACORN

In 1867 the Duke of Argyll picked up two acorns, one at Pembroke Lodge and the other at Hawarden, and took them back to Inverary and potted them. On 15 October 1868 he sent Gladstone this sketch of their 'relative success'. He added that when Russell came to see him he showed him '*his acorn* . . . but thought it wd be cruel to show him yours'. It was still not certain that Russell's career was over, and the drawing was not without political significance.

it impossible to unite the Liberal party in opposition to Disraeli's bill. Russell did his best to cheer Gladstone up, saying that the house of commons 'having behaved to us with great prejudice and unfairness are resolved to make up for it by showing to Disraeli undue favour and immoderate credulity'.[9] He agreed with Gladstone that Disraeli's bill went too far, and at one moment flirted with the notion of using his position in the lords to oppose household suffrage.[10] But he made no attempt to lead the party himself, and looked 'complacently at the piles of dust-collecting and ever-increasing letters on his table', and said, 'it does very well, I don't answer them'.[11] When the session came to an end, he took his children off to show them the beauties of Ireland.

But Russell did not look for repose – the questions were too exciting,[12] and he continued to the end of his life to take a 'feverish and fidgetty' part in affairs.[13] Upon his return from Ireland he told Jowett that he felt his time was short, and that he was 'determined to make a move about Education'. Jowett furnished him with a paper on the education of the poor in primary schools, of the middle classes in grammar schools and commercial schools, and of the higher classes and the clergy at the university, and Russell drew up a series of resolutions, in which he asserted the 'moral Right' of 'Every Child' to 'the Blessings of Education'. In December he insisted on bringing these resolutions before the house of lords, even though Gladstone warned him it was premature.[14]

Then, at Christmas, Russell wrote to Gladstone to say that he had more or less made up his mind not to take office again.[15] Gladstone at last gave the old man a gentle push, and replied that his title to repose could not be questioned.[16] Russell, who was busy penning the first of three *Letters* to Chichester Fortescue about the Irish church, undertook to announce his decision at the end of his pamphlet.[17] But publication day came, and nobody could make out whether he had retired or not. All through 1868, while Gladstone prepared to disestablish and disendow the Irish church, Russell argued in favour of his old formula for the concurrent endowment of the three churches.[18] In April a rumour went round that, in expectation of another Liberal government, Russell would waive his right to chieftainship on condition that he was again to be foreign minister.

Disraeli told the Queen that in that case the Liberal commercial class would vote even for the Irish church.[19]

Russell took no part in the general election of 1868, but stayed at home and read the newspapers, or as he put it, he took 'a quart bottle of Gladstone every morning' and found it 'pure, and light and well flavoured, and strong bodied into the bargain'.[20] Amberley was defeated, but it was clear that the Liberals would have a majority in the new parliament. Russell was getting deaf, but he was still completely 'absorbed in politics', and when he went to see Granville 'he gave no signs of retirement from Political life'.[21] Gladstone did not propose to give a dinner before the opening of the session, because his house was being redecorated. Russell seized his chance, and spoke of giving one himself. As Granville wrote to Gladstone,

> J.R.'s power of self assertion is one of the strong points of his nature, which as someone said is compounded of a giant and a little child . . . I suspect that his present ambition is to be sent for by the Queen (which he expects but I do not) – to have the credit of magnanimously recommending you to H.M. – to build on that recommendation a right to dictate a policy by which his name will be connected with the disestablishment of the Irish Church, and to have a potential voice in the selection of the persons who are to form the new administration.[22]

Gladstone reminded Russell that 'the hours you so genially propose to dedicate to Bacchus ought to be consecrated to the severe study of concocting a poison tipped amendment'.[23] Russell accepted this, but asked to be allowed to hold the conclave at his house. Granville told him it would not do, and Russell escaped neatly by saying that the paint was the only thing he had ever had in mind, and that he 'had presumed that the smell of paint being bad for friends at dinner, would not be innocuous to friends in Council'.[24]

When Gladstone became prime minister, he thought Russell might be less trouble in the government than out of it,[25] and he invited him to come into the cabinet without office.[26] Russell declined, which was sensible, and later grumbled at not having been offered an office, which was unworthy.[27] He wanted to be loyal to Gladstone, and on many occasions he wrote to him affectionately about his labours, which were too great for any

man,[28] and his education act of 1870, which was as good a law
'as Solon ever gave to the Athenians'.[29] But Russell had never
understood restraint, and it was too late to learn. He could not
resist getting up in the lords, or writing to the newspapers, to
say how much better he could have done in Gladstone's place,
and when the government sent the *Alabama* claims to arbitration, he tried to raise a motion of censure, and 'offered a spectacle melancholy to those who have known and admired him
when he was himself'.[30] He opposed the ballot act; and said
some hard things about Gladstone's new course in foreign
politics.[31]

Gladstone wrote that it was deplorable 'to think of Lord R.
who has done such great things, and whom individually I have
only known as a faithful and generous colleague, performing
such petulant acts'.[32] But he was 'more sorry than surprised to
see Lord Russell leading the mad'.[33] Russell was 'the victim of
infirmities',[34] and Gladstone told Granville that in no circumstances would he give Russell 'other than a soft answer'.[35]
Gladstone went patiently into every complaint, and even found
time during a ministry which 'has been the most laborious as a
whole that I have ever seen',[36] to write long letters to the former
premier about the progress of the sessions. Above all, Gladstone
did something which nobody else was prepared to do: he gave
Russell credit for his great achievements. At the general election
of 1868 he informed the electorate that 'the proper basis of
national policy in Education' lay in Lord John Russell's
speeches in 1839.[37] In 1869 he told Russell that the Irish church
bill was 'really founded upon principles of which you were the
expositor long ago'.[38] In 1869–70 he opened his mind to Russell
about the Irish land bill,[39] and may even have understood that
in going for something more than mere compensation for improvements he was following where Lord John had tried to lead
in 1847.[40] In 1873 he told Russell that in all that related to the
constitution, he looked upon him as his 'oracle and master', and
added that 'I can most truly say that I have been governed by
feelings and motives which I have thought would be your
feelings and motives, had you been, once again, in the place I
hold.'[41]

In 1869–70 and again in 1871–2 Lord and Lady Russell
spent the winter in the south of France, and early in 1872

Russell crossed the border into Spain, where he was delighted to find that he could still remember some Spanish after an interval of nearly fifty years.[42] But in 1873 he got no further than Dieppe.[43] He was ageing rapidly, and never went abroad again. In 1874 he finished dictating his *Recollections and Suggestions*, which were published the next year. He had left it too late, and it is a disappointing book, but it is a revealing one, because it shows that even at eighty-two he still did not really understand why the public had given its accolade to others. All he knew was that Peel had run off with the credit for the free trade policy, Palmerston for the conduct of foreign affairs, Disraeli for the second Reform Act, and Gladstone for the policy of justice to Ireland, and the flavour of the writing is a little sour.

Perhaps the thing that hurt most in these years was the fact that no constituency could be found willing to adopt Amberley as a parliamentary candidate. Gladstone soothed that wound by offering, if Russell wished it, to give Amberley an early promotion to the upper house.[44] But not even Gladstone could avert the series of tragedies which God inflicted upon Lord Russell in his extreme old age. First Rollo's eyes gave way, and he had to leave his place at the foreign office. Then, in June 1874, Kate Amberley and her daughter caught diphtheria and died. Before the year was out, Willy went mad, and was put under restraint. In January 1876 Lord Amberley died: little Bertrand Russell was taken away from the atheistic guardian chosen for him by his father, and came to live at Pembroke Lodge, where he soon learned to hide from his grandmother among the shrubs in a garden that was already beginning to run wild.[45]

Finally, in January 1878 Earl Russell himself caught a fever. After March he never left his room again.[46] On 20 April the faithful Gladstone came down to see him for the last time, and found him 'a noble wreck';[47] and on 9 May when a deputation of nonconformists went to Pembroke Lodge to congratulate Earl Russell upon the repeal of the test and corporation acts fifty years earlier, he was too ill to receive them.[48] Russell was 'quite ready to go now',[49] and dying said to Lady Russell, who was holding his hand, that he fell back on the faith of his childhood.[50]

The end came on 28 May, and Disraeli at once offered a

funeral in Westminster Abbey. But Earl Russell had left instructions that his body was to be laid in the family vault at Chenies, and his wish was respected.[51] Letters of appreciation came from the King of Italy and from the Italian senate, the protestant dissenting deputies, the British and Foreign School Society, the National Union of Elementary Teachers, and from Liberal associations all over the country.[52] Ungrateful Ireland did not condole with Lady Russell, but the Fox Club acted with discrimination and added a fourth toast to the immortal memory of Charles James Fox, Earl Grey and the Reform Bill, and the memory of the late Lord Holland, and drank to 'the memory of Lord John Russell'.[53]

APPENDIX 1

Lord John Russell's Elections

1813 autumn, Tavistock
Vacancy on death of Col. Richard Fitzpatrick, unopposed.
1818 June, Tavistock
General election: Lord William Russell and Lord John returned unopposed.
1820 March, Huntingdonshire
General election: W. H. Fellowes and Lord John returned unopposed.
1826 June, Huntingdonshire
General election: Lord Mandeville   968
                 W. H. Fellowes   911
(defeated)   Lord John Russell   858
1826 November, Bandon
At the instance of the Duke of Devonshire, unopposed.
1830 August, Bedford
General election: W. H. Whitbread   503
                 Capt. Fred. Polhill 483
(defeated)   Lord John Russell   475
1830 November, Tavistock
At the general election Viscount Ebrington had been re-turned for both Tavistock and Devonshire. He chose to sit for the county, and Lord John was now returned unopposed for Tavistock. After the writ was issued, but before the return took place, Lord John accepted an office of profit under the crown (Paymaster general).
1831 May, Devonshire
General election: Lord William Russell and Lord John were returned unopposed for Tavistock, and Viscount Ebrington

and Lord John were returned unopposed for Devonshire. Lord John chose to sit for the county.

1832 December, South Devonshire
General election: Lord John Russell (L)   3782
                  J. C. Bulteel (L)   3684
(defeated)   Sir J. Y. Buller (C)   3217

1835 January, South Devonshire
General election: Lord John Russell (L) and Sir J. Y. Buller (C) were returned unopposed.

1835 May, South Devonshire
Election upon Lord John's accepting an office of profit under the crown (Home Secretary).
                  E. Y. M. Parker (C)   3755
(defeated)   Lord John Russell (L)   3128

1835 May, Stroud
Vacancy created by Col. Fox who accepted the Chiltern Hundreds, Lord John returned unopposed.

1837 July, Stroud
General election: G. P. Scrope (L)   698
                  Lord John Russell (L)   681
(defeated)   Serjeant J. Adams (C)   297

1839 September, Stroud
Election upon Lord John's accepting an office of profit under the crown (Colonial Secretary), unopposed.

1841 June, City of London
General election: J. Masterman (C)   6339
                  Sir M. Wood (L)   6315
                  G. Lyall (C)   6290
                  Lord John Russell (L)   6221
(defeated)   M. W. Attwood (C)   6212
                  J. Pattison (L)   6070
                  W. Crawford (L)   6065
                  J. Pirie (C)   6017

1846 July, City of London
Election upon Lord John's accepting an office of profit under the crown (Prime Minister and First Lord of the Treasury), unopposed.

1847 July, City of London
General election: Lord John Russell (L)   7137
                  J. Pattison (L)   7030

	Baron L. de Rothschild (L)	6792
	J. Masterman (LC)	6722
(defeated)	Sir G. Larpent (L)	6719
	R. C. L. Bevan (C)	5268
	Ald. J. Johnson (C)	5069
	J. W. Freshfield (C)	4704
	W. Payne (L)	513

1852 July, City of London
General election: J. Masterman (C)   6195
                  Lord John Russell (L)   5537
                  Sir J. Duke (L)   5270
                  Baron L. de Rothschild (L) 4748
(defeated)   R. W. Crawford (L)   3765

1853 January, City of London
Election upon Lord John's accepting an office of profit under the crown (Foreign Secretary), unopposed.

1854 June, City of London
Election upon Lord John's accepting an office of profit under the crown (Lord President of the Council), unopposed.

1855 March, City of London
Election upon Lord John's accepting an office of profit under the crown (Colonial Secretary), unopposed.

1857 March, City of London
General election: Sir J. Duke (L)   6664
                  Baron L. de Rothschild (L) 6398
                  Lord John Russell (L)   6308
                  R. W. Crawford (L)   5808
(defeated)   R. Currie (LC)   4519

1859 April, City of London
General election: Sir J. Duke, Baron L. de Rothschild, Lord John Russell, and R. W. Crawford were returned unopposed.

1859 June, City of London
Election upon Lord John's accepting an office of profit under the crown (Foreign Secretary), unopposed.

Sources: *The Times*, and after 1832 McCalmont's *Parliamentary Poll-Book*. The party affiliations L=Liberal and C=Conservative are taken from McCalmont.

APPENDIX 2

The Edinburgh Letter

To the Electors of the City of London

Gentlemen, – The present state of the country, in regard to its supply of food, cannot be viewed without apprehension. Forethought and bold precaution may avert any serious evils; indecision and procrastination may produce a state of suffering which it is frightful to contemplate.

Three weeks ago it was generally expected that Parliament would be immediately called together. The announcement that Ministers were prepared at that time to advise the Crown to summon Parliament, and to propose on their first meeting a suspension of the import duties on corn, would have caused orders at once to be sent to various ports of Europe and America for the purchase and transmission of grain for the consumption of the United Kingdom. An Order in Council dispensing with the law was neither necessary nor desirable. No party in Parliament would have made itself responsible for the obstruction of a measure so urgent and so beneficial.

The Queen's Ministers have met, and separated, without affording us any promise of such seasonable relief.

It becomes us, therefore, the Queen's subjects, to consider how we can best avert, or at all events mitigate, calamities of no ordinary magnitude.

Two evils require your consideration. One of these is the disease in the potatoes, affecting very seriously parts of England and Scotland, and committing fearful ravages in Ireland.

The extent of this evil has not yet been ascertained, and every week, indeed, tends either to reveal unexpected disease, or to abate in some districts the alarm previously entertained. But there is one misfortune peculiar to the failure in this particular crop. The effect of a bad corn harvest is, in the first place, to diminish the supply in the market, and to raise the price. Hence diminished consumption, and the privation of incipient scarcity, by which the whole stock is more equally distributed over the year, and the ultimate pressure is greatly mitigated. But the fear of the breaking out of this unknown disease in the potatoes induces the holders to hurry into the market, and thus we have at one and the same time rapid consumption and impending deficiency – scarcity of the article and cheapness of price. The ultimate suffering must thereby be rendered far more severe than it otherwise would be. The evil to which I have adverted may be owing to an adverse season, to a mysterious disease in the potato, to want of science or of care in propagating the plant. In any of these cases Government is no more subject to blame for the failure of the potato crop than it was entitled to credit for the plentiful corn harvests which we have lately enjoyed.

Another evil, however, under which we are suffering, is the fruit of Ministerial counsel and Parliamentary law. It is the direct consequence of an Act of Parliament, passed three years ago, on the recommendation of the present advisers of the Crown. By this law grain of all kinds has been made subject to very high duties on importation. These duties are so contrived that the worse the quality of the corn the higher is the duty; so that when good wheat rises to 70s a quarter, the average price of all wheat is 57s or 58s, and the duty 15s or 14s a quarter. Thus the corn barometer points to fair, while the ship is bending under a storm.

This defect was pointed out many years ago by writers on the corn laws, and was urged upon the attention of the House of Commons when the present Act was under consideration.

But I confess that on the general subject my views have in the course of twenty years undergone a great alteration. I used to be of opinion that corn was an exception to the general rules of political economy; but observation and experience have convinced me that we ought to abstain from all interference with the supply of food. Neither a government nor a legislature can ever regulate the corn market with the beneficial effects which the entire freedom of sale and purchase are sure of themselves to produce.

I have for several years endeavoured to obtain a compromise on this subject. In 1839 I voted for a committee of the whole House, with the view of supporting the substitution of a moderate fixed duty for the sliding scale. In 1841 I announced the intention of the then Government of proposing a fixed duty of 8s a quarter. In the past session I proposed the imposition of some lower duty. These propositions were successively rejected. The present First Lord of the Treasury met them in 1839, 1840, and 1841 by eloquent panegyrics of the existing system – the plenty it had caused, the rural happiness it had diffused. He met the proposition for diminished protection in the same way in which he had met the offer of securities for Protestant interests in 1817 and 1825 – in the same way in which he met the proposal to allow Manchester, Leeds, and Birmingham to send members to Parliament in 1830.

The result of resistance to qualified concessions must be the same in the present instance as in those I have mentioned. It is no longer worth while to contend for a fixed duty. In 1841 the Free Trade party would have agreed to a duty of 8s a quarter on wheat, and after a lapse of years this duty might have been further reduced, and ultimately abolished. But the imposition of any duty at present, without a provision for its extinction within a short period, would but prolong a contest already sufficiently fruitful of animosity and discontent. The struggle to make bread scarce and dear, when it is clear that part, at least, of the additional price goes to increase rent, is a struggle deeply injurious to an aristocracy which (this quarrel once removed) is strong in property, strong in the construction of our legislature, strong in opinion, strong in ancient associations, and the memory of immortal services.

Let us, then, unite to put an end to a system which has been proved to be the blight of commerce, the bane of agriculture, the source of bitter divisions among classes, the cause of penury, fever, mortality, and crime among the people.

But if this end is to be achieved, it must be gained by the unequivocal expression of the public voice. It is not to be denied that many elections for cities and towns in 1841, and some in 1845, appear to favour the assertion that Free Trade is not popular with the great mass of the community. The Government appear to be waiting for some excuse to give up the present

corn law. Let the people, by petition, by address, by remonstrance, afford them the excuse they seek. Let the Ministry propose such a revision of the taxes as in their opinion may render
the public burdens more just and more equal; let them add any
other provisions which caution and even scrupulous forbearance may suggest; but let the removal of restrictions on the ad-
mission of the main articles of food and clothing used by the
mass of the people be required, in plain terms, as useful to all
great interests, and indispensable to the progress of the nation.
I have the honour to be, Gentlemen, your obedient servant,

J. RUSSELL.

Edinburgh: November 22, 1845.

APPENDIX 3

The Letter to the Bishop of Durham

Downing Street: November 4, 1850.

My dear Lord, – I agree with you in considering 'the late aggression of the Pope upon our Protestantism' as 'insolent and insidious', and I therefore feel as indignant as you can do upon the subject.

I not only promoted to the utmost of my power the claims of the Roman Catholics to all civil rights, but I thought it right and even desirable that the ecclesiastical system of the Roman Catholics should be the means of giving instruction to the numerous Irish immigrants in London and elsewhere, who without such help would have been left in heathen ignorance.

This might have been done, however, without any such innovation as that which we have now seen.

It is impossible to confound the recent measures of the Pope with the division of Scotland into dioceses by the Episcopal Church, or the arrangement of districts in England by the Wesleyan Conference.

There is an assumption of power in all the documents which have come from Rome; a pretension of supremacy over the realm of England, and a claim to sole and undivided sway, which is inconsistent with the Queen's supremacy, with the rights of our bishops and clergy, and with the spiritual independence of the nation, as asserted even in Roman Catholic times.

I confess, however, that my alarm is not equal to my indignation.

Even if it shall appear that the ministers and servants of the

Pope in this country have not transgressed the law, I feel per-suaded that we are strong enough to repel any outward attacks. The liberty of Protestantism has been enjoyed too long in England to allow of any successful attempt to impose a foreign yoke upon our minds and consciences. No foreign prince or potentate will be at liberty to fasten his fetters upon a nation which has so long and so nobly vindicated its right to freedom of opinion, civil, political, and religious.

Upon this subject, then, I will only say that the present state of the law shall be carefully examined, and the propriety of adopting any proceedings with reference to the recent assump-tion of power, deliberately considered.

There is a danger, however, which alarms me much more than any aggression of a foreign sovereign.

Clergymen of our own Church, who have subscribed the Thirty-nine Articles and acknowledged in explicit terms the Queen's supremacy, have been most forward in leading their flocks 'step by step to the very verge of the precipice'. The honour paid to saints, the claim of infallibility for the Church, the superstitious use of the sign of the cross, the muttering of the liturgy so as to disguise the language in which it is written, the recommendation of auricular confession, and the administra-tion of penance and absolution – all these things are pointed out by clergymen of the Church of England as worthy of adoption, and are now openly reprehended by the Bishop of London in his charge to the clergy of his diocese.

What then is the danger to be apprehended from a foreign prince of no great power compared to the danger within the gates from the unworthy sons of the Church of England herself?

I have little hope that the propounders and framers of these innovations will desist from their insidious course. But I rely with confidence on the people of England; and I will not bate a jot of heart or hope, so long as the glorious principles and the im-mortal martyrs of the Reformation shall be held in reverence by the great mass of a nation which looks with contempt on the mummeries of superstition, and with scorn at the laborious endeavours which are now making to confine the intellect and enslave the soul. – I remain, with great respect, &c.,

J. RUSSELL.

APPENDIX 4

The Cabinet of 1865–6

Prime Minister and First Lord of the Treasury, Earl Russell.
Lord Chancellor, Lord Cranworth.
Lord President of the Council, Earl Granville.
Lord Privy Seal, Duke of Argyll.
Chancellor of the Exchequer, W. E. Gladstone.
Home Secretary, Sir G. Grey.
Foreign Secretary, Earl of Clarendon.
Secretary for War, Earl de Grey, succeeded in February 1866
    by Marquis of Hartington.
Secretary for the Colonies, E. Cardwell.
First Lord of the Admiralty, Duke of Somerset.
President of the Board of Trade, T. Milner-Gibson.
Secretary for India, Sir C. Wood, succeeded in February 1866
    by Earl de Grey.
Chancellor of the Duchy of Lancaster, vacant, filled in January
    1866 by G. J. Goschen.
Postmaster-general, Lord Stanley of Alderley.
President of the Poor Law Board, C. P. Villiers.

Sources

THE RUSSELL PAPERS

At his death in 1878 Earl Russell's papers were found divided between Pembroke Lodge and his town house in Chesham Place. In 1887, when Spencer Walpole agreed to write the *Life of Lord John Russell* (2 vols, 1889), Lady Russell promised to place all Lord John's 'private as well as public papers, letters, diaries' at his disposal, and Russell's executor, G. S. Elliot, sent the papers to him at Government House, Isle of Man, where the *Life* was written. Lady Russell also made available 'diaries and letters of a much more private nature', which presumably meant Lady Russell's own papers, upon which, since she did not wish to appear in the biography, Spencer Walpole drew sparingly.

Spencer Walpole returned the papers to Lady Russell and to G. S. Elliot towards the end of 1889. Lady Russell died in 1898, and her papers, which have never been made available to the public, were used in a *Memoir* edited by Desmond MacCarthy and Agatha Russell, first published in 1910. In 1913 Lord and Lady John's surviving son, Rollo, published two volumes of the *Early Correspondence of Lord John Russell 1815–1840*. These volumes supplement Spencer Walpole's *Life* to some extent, but the work was badly done. Rollo funked difficult hands, like those of Brougham and Melbourne, and he made mistakes even in extracts which Spencer Walpole had already printed correctly.

Rollo died in 1914, and many of the papers used for the *Early Correspondence* were deposited in the Public Record Office by his widow. Other papers, which Rollo had hoped to work upon, were ultimately put into the hands of G. P. Gooch, who published two haphazardly edited volumes of *The Later Correspondence of Lord John Russell 1840–1878* in 1925. Mrs Russell then added more papers to the deposit in the Public Record Office, and upon her death in 1942 the entire deposit was made into a gift.

From that day to this the Russell Papers have been a disappointment to historians. All private papers have been removed: there are many conspicuous gaps – in the years up to 1841 especially; and a number of papers used by Spencer Walpole and Rollo Russell have disappeared.

From time to time, however, small collections of Lord John's papers appear in the sale rooms. Some of these, like the solitary volume in the British Museum (Add Ms 38080), consist of assorted letters addressed to Lord John and apparently selected for their interest as autographs. These albums were very likely assembled by Lord John himself or by Rollo Russell, and given as presents to grandchildren, nephews and nieces. None of these collections signifies much in itself, but each was a chip off the block, and as the chips were many the block has been diminished to the point where it is not always easy to carve a lifelike image of Lord John out of what remains. Other bundles are occasionally sold, containing private letters from Lord John. They derive from one and another of the innumerable descendants of Lord John's relations, as the turning out of an attic leads them to realise their capital assets in the former prime minister.

MANUSCRIPT SOURCES

Aberdeen Papers, British Museum
Babbage Papers, British Museum
Brougham Papers, University College London
Broughton Papers, British Museum
Carlisle Papers, Castle Howard
Clarendon Papers, Bodleian Library
Derby Papers, Knowsley
Ellice Papers, National Library of Scotland
Gladstone Papers, British Museum
Grey Papers, University of Durham
Halifax Papers, British Museum
Holland House Papers, British Museum
Lansdowne Papers, Bowood

Melbourne Papers, Royal Archives and National Register of
    Archives
Minto Papers, National Library of Scotland
Ogden Manuscripts, University College London
Palmerston Papers, National Register of Archives and British
    Museum
Parkes Papers, University College London
Peel Papers, British Museum
Royal Archives, Windsor
Spencer Papers, Althorp

PRINTED SOURCES

Works of Lord John Russell (This is not a complete list of his
    printed works)
*The Life of William lord Russell; with some account of the time in
    which he lived*, 1819
*Essays and Sketches of Life and Character, by a Gentleman who has
    left his lodgings*, 1820
*An Essay on the History of the English Government and Constitution,
    from the reign of Henry VIII to the present time*, 1821; second
    edition, enlarged, 1823; new editions 1865 and 1873
The Nun of Arrouca, a novel, 1822
Don Carlos; or Persecution, a tragedy in five acts, 1822
Memoirs of the Affairs of Europe from the Peace of Utrecht, vol. I
    1824, vol. II 1829
*A Letter to Viscount Althorp on the resolutions of the late House of
    Commons respecting Bribery at Elections*, 1827
The Establishment of the Turks in Europe; an historical discourse, 1828
A Letter to the Right Honourable Lord Holland on Foreign Politics,
    fourth edn 1831.
The Causes of the French Revolution, 1832
Letter to the Electors of Stroud on the Principles of the Reform Act, 1839
*Correspondence of John, fourth Duke of Bedford, selected from the
    originals at Woburn Abbey*, edited with an introduction, 3 vols,
    1842–6
Article on Grey and Spencer, *The Edinburgh Review*, CLXVII
    January 1846
Hon. H. Grove, *The Calendar of Nature*, edited with a preface,
    1849–50

Address to the Members of the Leeds Mechanics' Institution and Literary Society, 1852

Memorials and Correspondence of Charles James Fox, edited, 2 vols, 1853

Memoirs, Journal and correspondence of Thomas Moore, edited, 8 vols, 1853–6

The Obstacles which have retarded Moral and Political Progress. A lecture delivered to the Young Men's Christian Association, 1855

The Life and Times of Charles James Fox, 3 vols, 1859–66

The Official Correspondence on the claims of the United States in respect of the Alabama, *with a preface by Earl Russell*, 1867

A Letter to the Right Hon. Chichester Fortescue, on the state of Ireland, 1868

A Second Letter to the Right Hon. Chichester Fortescue, on the state of Ireland, 1868

A Third Letter to the Right Hon. Chichester Fortescue on the state of Ireland, 1869

Selections from Speeches of Earl Russell 1817 to 1841, and from Despatches 1859 to 1865, 2 vols, 1870

The Foreign Policy of England 1570–1870, 1871

Recollections and Suggestions 1813–73, 1875

Parliamentary Papers

The select committees in which Lord John appears to have taken most interest were:

1827	IV	Election Polls for Cities and Boroughs.
1835	VII	Education in England and Wales.
	VIII	Bribery at Elections.
	XVIII	Rebuilding Houses of Parliament.
1836	VIII	State of Agriculture.
	XXI	Houses of Parliament.
1837	XIII	Committee of Privileges.
	XVII	Poor Law Amendment Act.
	XIX	Transportation.
1837–8	IX	Church Leases.
	XVIII	Poor Law Amendment Act.
	XXII	Transportation.
1839	VIII	Church Leases.
	XIII	Stockdale v. Hansard.
1842	XI–XII	West Coast of Africa.
1849	XV	Poor Laws (Ireland).

Books

E. Abbott and L. Campbell, ed., *Letters of Benjamin Jowett*, 1899.

A. R. Ashwell, *Life of the rt. rev. Samuel Wilberforce, D.D., lord bishop of Oxford, with selections from his diaries and correspondence*, 3 vols, 1880–2.

A. Aspinall, *Lord Brougham and the Whig Party*, 1927;
ed., *The correspondence of Charles Arbuthnot*, Camden series 1941;
ed., *Three early nineteenth-century diaries*, 1952.

Lady Frances Balfour, *The Life of George, Fourth earl of Aberdeen*, 1923.

H. C. F. Bell, *Lord Palmerston*, 2 vols, 1936.

A. C. Benson and Viscount Esher, ed., *The Letters of Queen Victoria 1837–1861*, 3 vols, 1908.

G. F. A. Best, *Shaftesbury*, 1964.

R. N. W. Blake, *Disraeli*, 1966.

Noel Blakiston, ed., *The Roman Question*, 1962.

Kenneth Bourne, *Britain and the Balance of Power in North America 1815–1908*, 1967.

Asa Briggs, *Victorian People*, 1954;
The Age of Improvement, 1959.

O. J. Brose, *Church and Parliament, the reshaping of the Church of England 1828–1860*, 1959.

G. E. Buckle, ed., *The Letters of Queen Victoria*, second series, 3 vols, 1926–8.

J. K. Buckley, *Joseph Parkes of Birmingham*, 1926.

E. G. E. L., *Bulwer Lytton, The new Timon, a Romance of London*, 1846.

W. L. Burn, *The age of equipoise, a study of the mid-Victorian generation*, 1964.

J. R. M. Butler, *The passing of the Great Reform Bill*, 1914.

John, first Baron Campbell, *The Lives of the Lord Chancellors*, vol. 8, ed M. S. Hardcastle, 1869.

Edmund Cartwright D.D. inventor of the power loom, a Memoir of his life, writings and mechanical inventions, 1843.

A. Cecil, *British Foreign Secretaries 1817–1916*, 1927.

Lord David Cecil, *The Young Melbourne*, 1939;
Lord M., or the later life of Lord Melbourne, 1954.

O. Chadwick, *The Victorian Church*, pt 1, 1966.

Basil Champneys, *The hon. Adelaide Drummond, retrospect and memoir*, 1915.

J. H. Clapham, *An Economic History of Modern Britain*, 3 vols, second edn repr. 1950.

G. S. R. Kitson Clark, *Peel and the Conservative Party 1832–1841*, 1929;
Peel, 1936.

J. B. Conacher, *The Aberdeen Coalition 1852–1855*, 1968.

B. Connell, ed., *Regina v. Palmerston*, 1962.

L. Cooper, *Radical Jack, the life of the first earl of Durham*, 1959.

Sir Reginald Coupland, *The Durham Report, an abridged version, with introduction and notes*, 1945.

M. Cowling, *1867, Disraeli, Gladstone and Revolution*, 1967.

Homersham Cox, *A history of the reform bills of 1866 and 1867*, 1868.

M. Creighton, *Memoir of Sir George Grey*, 1884.

B. Disraeli, *Whigs and Whiggism*, ed. William Hutcheon, 1913.

Sir George Douglas and Sir George Dalhousie Ramsay, ed., *The Panmure Papers; being a selection from the correspondence of Fox Maule second baron Panmure, afterwards eleventh earl of Dalhousie*, 2 vols, 1908.

A. L. Dunham, *The Anglo-French Treaty of Commerce of 1860 and the progress of the industrial revolution in France*, 1930.

R. Dudley Edwards and T. D. Williams, ed., *The Great Famine, studies in Irish history 1845–52*, 1956.

H. E. Egerton and W. L. Grant, *Canadian Constitutional Development*, 1907.

Frank Eyck, *The Prince Consort, a political biography*, 1959.

G. B. A. M. Finlayson, *England in the eighteen-thirties, decade of reform*, 1969.

Lord Edmond Fitzmaurice, *The life of Granville George Leveson Gower, second Earl Granville 1815–1891*, 2 vols, 1905.

N. Gash, *Politics in the age of Peel, a study in the technique of parliamentary representation 1830–1850*, 1953;
Mr. Secretary Peel, the life of Sir Robert Peel to 1830, 1961;
Reaction and Reconstruction in English Politics, 1832–1852, 1965.

F. E. Gillespie, *Labor and politics in England 1850–1867*, 1927.

A. H. Gordon, baron Stanmore, *The Earl of Aberdeen*, 1893;
Sidney Herbert, Lord Herbert of Lea, a memoir, 1906.

Henry George third earl Grey, *The Colonial Policy of Lord John Russell's administration*, 2 vols, 1853;
ed., *The Reform Act 1832. The correspondence of the late Earl Grey*

with His Majesty King William IV and with Sir H. Taylor from November 1830 to June 1832, 2 vols, 1867.

Joseph Hamburger, *James Mill and the art of revolution*, 1963; *Intellectuals in politics. John Stuart Mill and the Philosophic Radicals*, 1965.

J. L. Hammond, *Gladstone and the Irish Nation*, 1938.

J. L. and B. Hammond, *Lord Shaftesbury*, 1923.

H. J. Hanham, *Elections and party management, politics in the time of Disraeli and Gladstone*, 1959.

M. S. Hardcastle, *Life of John lord Campbell, lord high chancellor of Great Britain*, 2 vols, 1881.

G. B. Henderson, *Crimean war diplomacy, and other historical essays*, 1947.

F. H. Hitchens, *The Colonial Land and Emigration Commission*, 1931.

Christopher Hobhouse, *Fox*, 1934.

J. C. Hobhouse, baron Broughton, *Recollections of a long life*, ed. Lady Dorchester, 6 vols, 1909.

E. Hodder, *The life and work of the seventh earl of Shaftesbury*, 3 vols, 1886.

W. D. Jones, *Lord Derby and Victorian conservatism*, 1956.

A. L. Kennedy, ed., *My dear duchess. Social and political letters to the Duchess of Manchester, 1858–1869*, 1956.

O. A. Kinchen, *Lord Russell's Canadian Policy*, 1945.

P. Knaplund, ed., *Letters from Lord Sydenham, Governor General of Canada 1839–1841, to Lord John Russell*, 1931; *James Stephen and the British Colonial System 1813–1847*, 1953.

Andrew Lang, *Life, letters and diaries of Sir Stafford Northcote, first earl of Iddesleigh*, 2 vols, second edn 1890.

Lady Caroline Lascelles, ed., *Extracts from journals kept by George Howard, earl of Carlisle*, 1864.

E. C. P. Lascelles, *The life of Charles James Fox*, 1936.

D. Le Marchant, *Memoir of John Charles Viscount Althorp, third Earl Spencer*, 1876.

G. Le Strange, ed., *Correspondence of Princess Lieven and Earl Grey*, 1890.

N. McCord, *The anti-corn-law league 1838–1846*, 1958.

G. I. T. Machin, *The Catholic Question in English Politics 1820 to 1830*, 1964.

Angus Macintyre, *The Liberator*, 1965.

B. L. Manning, *The Protestant Dissenting Deputies*, ed O. Greenwood, 1952.

L. A. Marchand, *Byron, a biography*, 3 vols, 1957.

A. P. Martin, *Life and letters of the right honourable Robert Lowe, viscount Sherbrooke*, 2 vols, 1893.

F. C. Mather, *Public Order in the age of the Chartists*, 1959.

Sir H. E. Maxwell, ed., *The Creevey Papers*, 2 vols, 1903;
The life and letters of George William Frederick fourth earl of Clarendon, 2 vols, 1913.

A. Mitchell, *The Whigs in Opposition 1815–1830*, 1967.

J. Morley, *The life of Richard Cobden*, 2 vols, 1881;
The life of William Ewart Gladstone, 2 vols, 1905.

W. P. Morrell, *British Colonial Policy in the age of Peel and Russell*, 1930.

W. E. Mosse, *The European Powers and the German Question 1848–1871, with special reference to England and Russia*, 1958.

Sir William Napier, *The life and opinions of General Sir Charles James Napier*, 4 vols, 1857.

C. W. New, *Lord Durham*, 1929;
The life of Henry Brougham to 1830, 1961.

E. R. Norman, *The Catholic Church and Ireland in the age of rebellion, 1859–1873*, 1965.

K. B. Nowlan, *The politics of repeal*, 1965.

C. S. Parker, *Sir Robert Peel*, 3 vols, 1891–8;
Life and Letters of Sir James Graham 1792–1861, 2 vols, 1907.

Ethel Peel, *Recollections of Lady Georgiana Peel*, second edn, 1920.

V. J. Puryear, *England, Russia, and the Straits Question 1844–1856*, 1931.

The Queen and Mr. Punch 1897.

L. Radzinowicz, *A history of criminal law and its administration from 1750*, 4 vols, 1948–68.

A. Ramm, ed., *The Political Correspondence of Mr. Gladstone and Lord Granville 1868–1876*, 2 vols, 1952.

A. A. W. Ramsay, *Sir Robert Peel*, 1928.

S. J. Reid, *Lord John Russell*, 1895;
Life and letters of the first earl of Durham 1792–1840, 2 vols, 1906.

B. Russell, third earl, *The Autobiography of Bertrand Russell*, vol. I, 1967.

B. and P. Russell, ed., *The Amberley Papers*, 2 vols, 1937.

G. W. E. Russell, *Collections and Recollections*, seventh edn, 1904.

John Robert Russell, thirteenth duke of Bedford, *A Silver Plated Spoon, 1959*.

L. C. Sanders, ed., *Lord Melbourne's Papers*, 1889.

G. P. Scrope, *Memoir of the life of Charles Lord Sydenham*, 1844.

H. Senior, *Orangeism in Ireland and Britain 1795–1836*, 1966.

F. B. Smith, *The making of the Second Reform Bill*, 1966.

Sydney Smith, *Works*, 4 vols, 1850.

D. Southgate, *The Passing of the Whigs 1832–1886*, 1962; *The Most English Minister, the policies and politics of Palmerston*, 1966.

D. Spring, *The English Landed Estate in the Nineteenth Century, its administration, 1963*.

L. Strachey and R. Fulford, ed., *The Greville Memoirs*, 8 vols, 1938.

The History of The Times, 4 vols, 1935–52.

A. W. Tilby, *Lord John Russell*, 1930.

W. M. Torrens, *Memoirs of William Lamb, second viscount Melbourne*, 1890.

G. M. Trevelyan, *Garibaldi and the making of Italy*, 1911; *The life of John Bright*, 1913; *Lord Grey of the Reform Bill*, 1929.

Sir G. O. Trevelyan, *Life and letters of Lord Macaulay*, 2 vols, 1876.

George J. T. H. Villiers, *A vanished Victorian, being the life of G. Villiers, fourth earl of Clarendon*, 1938.

J. R. Vincent, *The formation of the Liberal Party, 1857–1868*, 1966.

John Wade, *The extraordinary black book*, 1831.

R. A. J. Walling, ed., *The diaries of John Bright*, 1930.

J. T. Ward, *Sir James Graham*, 1967.

Sir C. K. Webster, *The Foreign Policy of Palmerston 1830–1841*, 2 vols, 1951.

W. E. Williams, *The rise of Gladstone to the leadership of the Liberal Party 1859–1868*, 1934.

C. Woodham-Smith, *The Great Hunger*, 1962.

E. L. Woodward, *The Age of Reform 1815–1870*, corrected edn 1946.

G. M. Young, ed., *Early Victorian England*, 2 vols, 1934.

Articles and pamphlets

Olive Anderson, 'The Wensleydale peerage case and the position of the House of Lords in the mid-nineteenth century', *English Historical Review*, 1967.

W. L. Burn, 'Free Trade in Land, an aspect of the Irish Question', *Transactions of the Royal Historical Society*, 1949.

David Close, 'The formation of a two-party alignment in the House of Commons between 1832 and 1841', *English Historical Review*, 1969.

M. Cowling, 'Disraeli, Derby and fusion, October 1865 to July 1866, *Historical Journal*, *1965*.

F. A. Dreyer, 'The Whigs and the Political Crisis of 1845', *English Historical Review*, 1965.

G. B. A. M. Finlayson, 'The Politics of Municipal Reform 1835', *English Historical Review*, 1966.

J. Gallagher, 'Fowell Buxton and the New African Policy 1838–1842', *Cambridge Historical Journal*, 1950.

W. E. Gladstone,
  A chapter of autobiography, 1868;
  'The Melbourne Ministry', *The Nineteenth Century*, 1890.

A. H. Graham, 'The Lichfield House Compact', *Irish Historical Studies*, 1960–1.

Spencer Johnson, *Some remarks on Lord J. Russell's Life of William Lord Russell, and on the times in which he lived*, 1820.

D. Large, 'The House of Lords and Ireland in the age of Peel 1832–1850', *Irish Historical Studies*, 1954–5.

F. Merk, 'British Party Politics and the Oregon Treaty', *American Historical Review*, 1931–2.

D. C. Moore, 'Concession or Cure: the sociological premises of the first Reform Act', *Historical Journal*, 1966.

W. E. Mosse, 'Queen Victoria and her ministers in the Schleswig-Holstein crisis 1863–64', *English Historical Review*, 1963.

J. M. Prest,
  'Jowett's correspondence on education with Earl Russell in 1867', a supplement to the *Balliol College Record*, 1965;
  'Gladstone and Russell', *Transactions of the Royal Historical Society*, 1966.

William Thomas, 'Whigs and Radicals in Westminster, the election of 1819', *The Guildhall Miscellany*, 1970.

C. N. Ward-Perkins, 'The Commercial Crisis of 1847', *Oxford Economic Papers*, 1950.

James Winter, 'The Cave of Adullam and parliamentary reform', *English Historical Review*, 1966.

Theses

F. A. Dreyer, 'The Russell Administration 1846–1852', D.Phil. thesis presented to the University of St Andrews, 1962.

R. Job, 'The Political Career of Henry, third Earl Grey' (1826–1852), M.Litt. thesis presented to the University of Durham, 1959.

Abbreviations

AP	B. and P. Russell, ed., *The Amberley Papers*, 2 vols, 1937.
BM Add Ms	British Museum Additional Manuscript: 38080 refers to Russell Papers; 40424, 40426 and 40602 to Peel Papers; 43066–8 to Aberdeen Papers; 44100, 44133, 44162, 44165, 44193, 44239, 44291–4, 44534, 44537–8, and 44755 to Gladstone Papers; 48581 to Palmerston Papers; 49531 to Halifax Papers; and 51677–80 and 51751 to Holland House Papers.
BP	Brougham Papers, University College London.
Broughton diary	Diary of J. C. Hobhouse, first Baron Broughton, BM Add Mss 43748–43756.
C and R	G. W. E. Russell *Collections and Recollections*, seventh edn, 1904.
Clar. P	Clarendon Papers, Bodleian Library.
CP	Carlisle Papers, Castle Howard.
DNB	Dictionary of National Biography.
DP	Derby Papers, Knowsley.
E and S	JR anon. *Essays and Sketches of Life and Character, by a Gentleman who has left his lodgings*, 1820.
EC	Rollo Russell, ed., *Early Correspondence of Lord John Russell 1805–1840*, 2 vols, 1913.
EP	Ellice Papers, National Library of Scotland.
ETE	JR *The establishment of the Turks in Europe; an historical discourse*, 1828.
FR	JR *The causes of the French Revolution*, 1832.
G and S	JR article on Grey and Spencer in *The Edinburgh Review* CLXVII January 1846.

GP	Grey Papers, University of Durham.
HEGC	JR *An Essay on the History of the English Government and Constitution, from the reign of Henry VIII to the present time*, 1821.
Howick diary	Diary of Viscount Howick, third Earl Grey, Grey Papers, University of Durham.
Journal	JR's journal of his visit to Ireland in 1833, Ogden MSS, University College London.
JR	Lord John Russell.
Lady JR *Memoir*	D. MacCarthy and A. Russell, ed., *Lady John Russell: a Memoir with selections from her diaries and correspondence*, 3rd edn, 1926.
LC	G. P. Gooch, ed., *The Later Correspondence of Lord John Russell 1840–1878*, 2 vols, 1925.
LFP	JR *A Letter to the Right Honourable Lord Holland on Foreign Politics*, 4th edn, 1831.
Life	Spencer Walpole, *The Life of Lord John Russell*, 2 vols, 1889.
LP	Lansdowne Papers, Bowood.
MAE	JR *Memoirs of the Affairs of Europe, from the Peace of Utrecht*, 2 vols, I 1824, II 1829.
Morpeth diary	Diary of Viscount Morpeth, seventh Earl of Carlisle, Carlisle Papers, Castle Howard.
MP	Minto Papers, National Library of Scotland: Fanny is Lady John Russell: her sisters were Charlotte, Lady Portal = Lotty = Bobm; Mary, Lady Abercromby; Elizabeth, Lady Romilly=Lizzie or Lizzy; Harriet=H.E.: her brothers were William, Viscount Melgund=Billy; Charles; George=Doddy; Gilbert=Gibby; and Henry: Nina was Lady Melgund.
MPNRA	Melbourne Papers, National Register of Archives.
MPRA	Melbourne Papers, Royal Archives.
Ms	Manuscript.
n.d.	no date.
PD	Parliamentary Debates.
PP	Palmerston Papers, National Register of Archives.

RA   Royal Archives.
R and S   JR first Earl Russell, *Recollections and Sugges-*
            tions, 1813–1873, 1875.
RLGP   Ethel Peel, *Recollections of Lady Georgiana Peel*,
            second edn, 1920.
RP   Russell Papers, Public Record Office.
SP   Spencer Papers, Althorp.
SPS   John Robert Russell, thirteenth Duke of
            Bedford, *A Silver Plated Spoon*, 1959.
TS   Typescript.
WLR   JR *The Life of William lord Russell; with some*
            account of the time in which he lived, 1819.

Notes

INTRODUCTION

1 Abbott and Campbell, *Letters* 58, Jowett to Morier 10 May 1861.
2 RP 118A, Spencer Walpole to G. S. Elliot 1 Mar 1889.
3 *AP* I 33.
4 MP, Lizzy to Mary n.d. [early 1846?].

CHAPTER I

1 *SPS* 74–5.
2 *DNB* article on Francis Russell, 5th duke of Bedford 1765–1802.
3 *Life*, I 3.
4 RP 1A, Lady Georgiana Russell to 'dearest Isabella' n.d. [1800–1?].
5 *EC* I 131.
6 *DNB* article on Lord John Russell, 1st earl Russell 1792–1878.
7 *Life*, I 1.
8 RP 118A, *Lord John Russell, by one who knew him in his later years*.
9 Butler, *Great Reform Bill*, 194.
10 RP 118A, *Lord John Russell, by one who knew him in his later years*.
11 RP 13H, Bedford to JR 14 Jul [1859].
12 *C and R* 11.
13 *Life*, I 3.
14 *RLGP* 81.
15 *Life*, I 4.
16 Morpeth diary 29 Oct 1848 says £1m, but see Spring, *English Landed Estate* 24–5.
17 RP 3A, Bedford to JR 21 Mar 1838.
18 *Life*, I 16.
19 *EC* I 164.
20 *EC* I 199.
21 *EC* I 313.
22 EP E47, Tavistock to Ellice 7 Sep 1839.
23 BM Add. Ms 51680, JR to Lady Holland 1830.
24 BM Add. Ms 51677, JR to Holland 23 Oct 1839.
25 *Life*, I 164.
26 *EC* I 225.
27 *EC* I 303.

28 *EC* II 102.
29 *Life*, I 371.
30 *Life*, I 19.
31 *Life*, I 7.

CHAPTER II

 1 *Life*, I 4.
 2 *Life*, I 10.
 3 *Life*, I 11.
 4 RP IA, Cartwright to JR 6 Jul 1807.
 5 RP IA, JR to Lady A. M. Stanhope 12 Apr 1807.
 6 RP IA, JR to Lady A. M. Stanhope 24 Mar 1807.
 7 RP IA, JR to Lady A. M. Stanhope 12 Apr 1807.
 8 *Life*, I 13–14.
 9 RP IA, Clare to JR 2 Aug 1810.
10 *Life*, I 17.
11 *SPS* 113.
12 E. Lascelles, *The Life of Charles James Fox* (1936) 17.
13 *PD* 3 ser. XXXVI 210, 7 Feb 1837.
14 RA D22, 12, JR to the Queen 18 Sep 1864.
15 *Life*, I 23.
16 *EC* I 144–6.
17 *R and S* 343.
18 *RLGP* 72.
19 BM Add. Ms 51679, JR to Lady Holland 24 May [1820].
20 *Life*, I 42–3.
21 William Allen, *Suggestions on the Cortes* (1809).
22 *Life*, I 44.
23 *Life*, I 43.
24 BM Add. Ms 51678, JR to Lady Holland 19 Oct 1809.
25 BM Add. Ms 51678, JR to Lady Holland 23 Nov 1809.
26 RP IA, Playfair to JR 13 Aug 1810.
27 BM Add. Ms 51678, JR to Lady Holland Dec 1809.
28 BM Add. Ms 51678, JR to Lady Holland 4 Feb 1810.
29 BM Add. Ms 51678, JR to Lady Holland 6 Jan 1810.
30 BM Add. Ms 51678, JR to Lady Holland 4 Feb 1810.
31 BM Add. Ms 51678, JR to Lady Holland 6 Jan 1810.
32 BM Add. Ms 51678, JR to Lady Holland 13 May 1810.
33 BM Add. Ms 51677, JR to Holland 7 Aug 1810.
34 *EC* I 131–9.
35 BM Add. Ms 51677, JR to Holland 29 Aug 1810.
36 BM Add. Ms 51677, JR to Holland 25 Sep 1810.
37 *Life*, I 53.
38 BM Add. Ms 51678, JR to Lady Holland 25 Dec 1810.
39 Ms recently acquired by Bodleian Library.
40 *Life*, I 48: *EC* I 21: and BM Add. Ms 51677, JR to Holland n.d. [1811?].
41 *Life*, I 48.

42 *Life*, 1 54–6.
43 *Life*, 1 45.
44 BM Add. Ms 51678, JR to Lady Holland 5 Jun 1812.
45 *Life*, 1 ch. III.
46 BM Add. Ms 51677, JR to Holland 23 Nov 1812.
47 BM Add. Ms 51677, JR to Holland 16 Jul 1813.
48 *E and S* 49–51.
49 *Life*, 1 70 and 73.
50 BM Add. Ms 51678, JR to Lady Holland n.d. [1814?].
51 BM Add. Ms 51678, JR to Lady Holland 28 Nov 1814.
52 RP 17A memo dictated to Lady Russell in 1869: and Lady JR, *Memoir* 51–6.
53 *EC* I 26–7.
54 *MAE* I 54.
55 *Life*, 1 77.
56 *Life*, 1 78.
57 *Life*, 1 78–80.

CHAPTER III

1 *PD* xxxv 742, 26 Feb 1817.
2 *EC* I 195.
3 BM Add. Ms 51677, JR to Holland 23 Feb 1818.
4 William Thomas, 'Whigs and Radicals in Westminster, the election of 1819', *The Guildhall Miscellany*, III 3 (Oct 1970), 194, Lambton to Grey 21 Nov 1818.
5 *Life*, 1 163 n.2.
6 Broughton, *Recollections*, III 122–3.
7 BP, JR to Brougham 28 Sep 1828.
8 BP, JR to Brougham 26 Nov 1828.
9 BM Add. Ms 51678, JR to Lady Holland n.d.
10 *E and S* 21.
11 *E and S* 3 and 7.
12 *E and S* 77.
13 BM Add. Ms 51678, JR to Lady Holland 26 May 1817.
14 BM Add. Ms 51678, JR to Lady Holland 24 Oct 1817.
15 BM Add. Ms 51679, JR to Lady Holland n.d. [1820?].
16 Benjamin Disraeli, earl of Beaconsfield, *Whigs and Whiggism*, ed. with introduction by William Hutcheon (1913) 266.
17 *Life*, 1 96.
18 *EC* I 222.
19 *Life*, 1 112.
20 MPNRA, Melbourne to JR 14 May 1835.
21 *Life*, II 148.
22 *Life*, 1 103 and 113.
23 *WLR* preface.
24 *WLR* 228.

25 *WLR* preface.
26 *Life*, I 104.
27 *EC* I 203.
28 Spencer Johnson, *Some remarks on Lord J. Russell's life of William Lord Russell, and on the times in which he lived* (1820).
29 *FR* 91.
30 *ETE* 2.
31 *ETE* 26.
32 *MAE* I 50 and 68.
33 *LFP* 20–4.
34 *LFP* 25–9.
35 *LFP* 22.
36 *HEGC* 9–10.
37 *MAE* I 48.
38 *FR* 271.
39 *FR* 126.
40 *FR* 3.
41 *PD* 3 ser. IV 345, 24 Jun 1831.
42 *MAE* I 37.
43 *MAE* I 63–4.
44 *PD* new ser. VII 85, 25 Apr 1822.
45 *MAE* I 70.
46 *MAE* I 71.
47 *DNB* article on Lord John Russell, 1st earl Russell 1792–1878.

CHAPTER IV

1 *E and S* 22–3.
2 GP, JR to Grey 20 Jan 1823.
3 *PD* new ser. X 1235, 18 Mar 1824.
4 *PD* XL 513, 18 May 1819.
5 *PD* XXXII 32, 1 Feb 1816.
6 *PD* XXXII 845, 26 Feb 1816.
7 *PD* new ser. V 613–14, 9 May 1821.
8 *E and S* 180.
9 *E and S* 144.
10 *G and S* 242.
11 *PD* new ser. VII 62, 25 Apr 1822.
12 *HEGC* 257.
13 *PD* new ser. VII 64, 25 Apr 1822.
14 *PD* new ser. VII 71, 25 Apr 1822.
15 *PD* new ser. VII 72, 25 Apr 1822.
16 *PD* new ser. VII 69, 25 Apr 1822.
17 *PD* new ser. V 607, 9 May 1821.
18 *E and S* 148.
19 *Life*, I 85.
20 *HEGC* 289.
21 *PD* XXXV 745, 26 Feb 1817.

22 *PD* XL 1496, 1 Jul 1819.
23 William Thomas, 'Whigs and Radicals in Westminster, the election of 1819', *The Guildhall Miscellany*, III 3 (Oct 1970) 210.
24 *EC* I 205.
25 *PD* XLI 1091, 14 Dec 1819.
26 *PD* XLI 1091–107, 14 Dec 1819.
27 *PD* new ser. V 604–22, 9 May 1821.
28 *PD* XLI 1103–4, 14 Dec 1819.
29 *HEGC* 266.
30 *PD* new ser. VII 83, 25 Apr 1822.
31 *PD* new ser. VII 73–5, 25 Apr 1822.
32 Mitchell, *Whigs in Opposition* 166–7.
33 *PD* new ser. VIII 172–4, 20 Feb 1823.
34 *PD* new ser. VII 60, 25 Apr 1822.
35 *PD* new ser. XV 651–63, 27 Apr 1826.
36 Mitchell, *Whigs in Opposition* 16.
37 *R and S* 41.
38 Mitchell, *Whigs in Opposition* 168.
39 Mitchell, *Whigs in Opposition* 30–1.
40 *EC* I 250.
41 *Life*, I 132.
42 Mitchell, *Whigs in Opposition* 200–1.
43 GP, *JR* to Grey 8 Sep 1827.
44 *PD* new ser. XVII 543–4, 3 May 1827.
45 *Life*, I 135.
46 *Life*, I 137.
47 GP, JR to Grey 8 Sep 1827.
48 At this point I had the kind help of Mr Trevor Burchell, who was writing a thesis for Oxford University on 'Political opinions and activities of Dissenters 1828–47': see too B. L. Manning, *The Protestant Dissenting Deputies*, ed. O. Greenwood (Cambridge, 1952) 217–53.
49 *PD* new ser. XVIII 692, 26 Feb 1828.
50 *EC* I 275.
51 *EC* I 272.
52 *EC* I 272.
53 *PD* new ser. XIX 1538, 27 Jun 1828.
54 *EC* I 277.
55 GP, JR to Grey 18 Oct 1828.
56 GP, JR to Grey 24 Oct 1828.
57 *EC* I 283–4.
58 GP, JR to Grey 2 Nov 1828.
59 *PD* new ser. XX 126, 6 Feb 1829.
60 *PD* 3 ser. IV 335, 24 Jun 1831.
61 BP, JR to Brougham 30 Jan 1830.
62 *PD* new ser. XXII 863, 23 Feb 1830.
63 *MAE* II bk IV ch. II 551–87.
64 *Life*, I 156–7.

CHAPTER V

1 *The Times* 1 Oct 1830.
2 BM Add. Ms 51677, JR to Holland 18 Oct 1830.
3 On this and many other points in this chapter I have received invaluable help from the Vice President of Wolfson College, whose book on the Reform Bill had not appeared at the time I was writing.
4 RP 15D, JR reminiscence 6 Mar 1865.
5 BM Add. Ms 51751 fos 46–8, Holland to his son Henry 5 Nov 1830.
6 *Life*, 1 158–9.
7 *Life*, 1 160.
8 G. M. Young, ed., *Early Victorian England* (1934) 1 86.
9 EP E49, JR to Ellice 1 Oct 1839: and GP, JR to Howick 27 Aug 1839.
10 RP 1C, Durham to JR 21 Oct 1834.
11 *EC* II 52.
12 Butler, *Great Reform Bill* 178–9.
13 *Daily News* 4 Dec 1872.
14 RP 1A draft headed *No. 1 Lord John Russell's Plan.*
15 *EC* II 52.
16 BM Add. Ms 38080 fol. 15, John Edwards to JR 18 Oct 1822.
17 RP 1A, G. W. Woods to JR 11 Jan 1830.
18 *EC* II 53.
19 *EC* II 52–3.
20 RP 1B, Durham, Graham, Russell and Duncannon to Grey n.d.
21 Sydney Smith, *Works* (1850) 570.
22 *PD* 3 ser. IV 341, 24 Jun 1831.
23 See BM Add. Ms 51677 and *EC* II 9–14.
24 RP 15D, JR reminiscence 6 Mar 1865.
25 RP 1C, Durham to JR 21 Oct 1834.
26 GP, JR to Durham 13 Feb 1831.
27 RP 1B, JR memo 4 Apr 1831.
28 *PD* new ser. IV 618–19, 9 May 1821.
29 *HEGC* 265.
30 *PD* 3 ser. III 314–15, 9 Mar 1831.
31 *EC* II 13.
32 Greville, *Memoirs*, II 112, 6 Feb 1831.
33 Greville, *Memoirs*, II 65, 20 Nov 1830.
34 RP 1C, Durham to JR 21 Oct 1834.
35 Le Marchant, *Althorp* 296–7.
36 Le Marchant, *Althorp* 297.
37 *PD* 3 ser. II 1061, 1 Mar 1831.
38 *R and S* 72n.
39 *PD* 3 ser. II 1062, 1 Mar 1831.
40 *R and S* 70–1.
41 Le Marchant, *Althorp* 298.
42 Butler, *Great Reform Bill* 194–5.
43 Le Marchant, *Althorp* 298.
44 Butler, *Great Reform Bill* 194.

45 Le Marchant, *Althorp* 298: and Butler, *Great Reform Bill* 195 n 1.
46 Le Marchant, *Althorp* 299n.
47 RP 1B, memo n.d.
48 *EC* II 14.
49 The Queen and Mr Punch 1897, IX Jul 1846, an improved version of a familiar story.
50 *EC* II 19.
51 BM Add. Ms 51677, JR to Holland 1 May 1831.
52 *EC* II 20–1.
53 RP 1B, Bedford to JR 24 May 1831.
54 *PD* 3 ser. IV 338, 24 Jun 1831.
55 *PD* 3 ser. IV 331, 24 Jun 1831 and see *PD* 3 ser. III 305, 9 Mar 1831 and *PD* 3 ser. VI 1225, 7 Sep 1831.
56 Le Marchant, *Althorp* 335.
57 *PD* 3 ser. V 39, 19 Jul 1831.
58 *PD* 3 ser. V 102, 20 Jul 1831.
59 *PD* 3 ser. III 1241–2, 12 Apr 1831.
60 *PD* 3 ser. IX 164–5, 12 Dec 1831.
61 *C and R* 11.
62 Le Marchant, *Althorp* 338.
63 Le Marchant, *Althorp* 344.
64 LP, JR to Lansdowne Thursday [1831 or 32].
65 *PD* 3 ser. VIII 611–14, 12 Oct 1831.
66 Clar. P, Irish box 43, JR to Clarendon 12 Oct 1848.
67 *Life*, I 173n.
68 *PD* 3 ser. VIII 599, 12 Oct 1831.
69 EP, TS, Ellice to Durham n.d.
70 Le Marchant, *Althorp* 375.
71 Le Marchant, *Althorp* 378.
72 GP, JR to Grey 28 Feb 1832.
73 GP, JR to Grey 26 Mar 1832.
74 GP, JR to Grey n.d.
75 *R and S* 95–6.
76 *R and S* 102–3.
77 EP E43, Ellice to Parkes 31 Jul 1852.
78 A. Aspinall, ed., *The Correspondence of Charles Arbuthnot* (Camden Series) (1941) 154, Hardinge to Mrs Arbuthnot.
79 *Life*, I 178n.
80 *Life*, I 178.
81 *G and S* 255.

CHAPTER VI

1 SP box 7, Althorp to Grey 6 Aug 1832.
2 RP 15D, JR reminiscence 5 Jun 1865.
3 PP, JR to Palmerston 23 Sep 1832.
4 *Life*, I 162.
5 *EC* I 237.

6 *EC* I 253.
7 *PD* 3 ser. IV 346, 24 Jun 1831.
8 *PD* 3 ser. XLI 681, 7 Mar 1838.
9 Broughton diary, 12 May 1850.
10 Angus Macintyre, *The Liberator* (1965) 36.
11 Angus Macintyre, *The Liberator* (1965) 29.
12 *PD* 3 ser. XIV 377, 13 Jul 1832.
13 SP box 7, Althorp to Grey 6 Aug 1832.
14 SP box 8, Grey to Althorp 21 Oct 1832.
15 *Life*, I 188.
16 SP box 7, Althorp to Grey 20 Oct 1832.
17 *Life*, I 189.
18 *Life*, I 190–1.
19 *Life*, I 191.
20 RP IB, Tavistock to JR 27 [Oct 1832?].
21 GP, JR to Howick 16 Oct 1836.
22 SP box 7, Althorp to Grey 6 Aug 1832 and 3 Nov 1832.
23 DP box 130 bundle 12, JR to Stanley 30 Dec.
24 DP box 130 bundle 12, JR to Stanley [11?] Jan 1833.
25 SP box 8, Althorp to Grey 1 Jan 1833.
26 SP, TS, Althorp to Spencer 2 Jan 1833.
27 *PD* 3 ser. XV 286–7, 6 Feb 1833.
28 *PD* 3 ser. XVIII 1095, 21 Jun 1833.
29 GP, JR to Grey 8 Jun 1833.
30 Greville, *Memoirs*, II 372 n, 19 May 1833.
31 SP box 11, JR to Althorp 29 Aug 1833.
32 Journal, Ogden Mss, University College London, Ms 84.
33 *Life*, I 195–6.
34 Journal 8 Sep.
35 Journal 16 Sep.
36 Journal 8 Sep.
37 GP, JR to Grey 2 Oct 1833.
38 *Life*, I 197 n 1.
39 Journal 7 Sep.
40 *PD* 3 ser. XXXIII 74, 21 Apr 1836.
41 Journal 7 Sep.
42 SP box 11, JR to Althorp 14 Sep [1833].
43 J. T. Rutt; information from Mr Trevor Burchell, see above Ch. IV, n 48.
44 *PD* 3 ser. XXII 1049, 21 Apr 1834 and XXIII 507–8, 5 May 1834.
45 *R and S* 116.
46 *G and S* 265.
47 DP box 130 bundle 12, JR memo Feb 1834.
48 BM Add. Ms 51677, JR to Holland 15 Feb [1834].
49 DP box 130 bundle 12, JR to Stanley 12 Jul 1834.
50 *R and S* 120.
51 *Life*, I 199.
52 SP box 7, Althorp to Grey 2 Dec 1832.

53 Robert Blake, *Disraeli* (1966) 114.
54 GP, Grey to JR copy 7 May 1834.
55 DP box 130 bundle 12, JR to Stanley 28 May 1834.
56 SP TS, Althorp to Spencer 12 Jun 1834.
57 *PD* 3 ser. xxiv 33, 2 Jun 1834.
58 *PD* 3 ser. xxiv 804, 23 Jun 1834.
59 *Life*, I 203.
60 *PD* 3 ser. xxiv 1202, 4 Jul 1834.
61 *Life*, I 204.
62 Journal 9 Sep.
63 *Life*, I 205.
64 MPRA, Melbourne to JR 23 Aug 1834.
65 GP, JR to Grey 3 Sep 1834.
66 MPRA, JR to Melbourne 6 Sep 1834.
67 Howick diary 12 and 13 Nov 1834.
68 SP box 10, Brougham to Spencer 13 Nov 1834.
69 *Life*, I 208.

CHAPTER VII

1 E. Bulwer Lytton, *The new Timon – A Romance of London* (1846) 36.
2 *RLGP* 33.
3 EP E38, Parkes to Ellice 21 Nov 1853.
4 Robert Blake, *Disraeli* (1966) 76.
5 *The Creevey Papers*, ed. by Sir Herbert Maxwell (1903) II 198.
6 *EC* I 295.
7 *Life*, I 150.
8 *Ibid.*: Walpole did not print Lady Emily's name but it occurs in RP 118A, Spencer Walpole to G. S. Elliot 22 Jan 1890.
9 BM Add. Ms 51680, JR to Lady Holland 20 Apr 1830.
10 *Life*, I 164n.
11 RP 118A, Spencer Walpole to G. S. Elliot 22 Jan 1890.
12 GP, JR to Grey 12 Nov 1834.
13 GP, Grey to JR copy 15 Nov 1834.
14 EP E19, Grey to Ellice 14 Nov 1834.
15 *EC* II 61.
16 *Life*, I 208.
17 Sanders, *Lord Melbourne's Papers* 232–3.
18 EP E38, Parkes to Ellice 16 Sep 1841.
19 Lady JR, *Memoir* 58.
20 *Spectator* 29 Jan 1870.
21 *SPS* 17.
22 Abbott and Campbell, *Letters* 56, Jowett to Miss Elliot 16 Apr 1861.
23 *Spectator* 29 Jan 1870.
24 *C and R* 13.
25 RP 4E, Lady William Russell to JR n.d.
26 Le Marchant, *Althorp* 378.
27 *Life*, I 287n.

28 *R and S* 346.
29 *EC* II 51–4.
30 GP, Grey to JR copy 31 Oct 1834.
31 BM Add. Ms 51677, JR to Holland 26 Oct [1834].
32 BM Add. Ms 51677, JR to Holland 29 Oct [1834].
33 LP, JR to Lansdowne 24 Aug 1837.
34 Sanders, *Lord Melbourne's Papers* 219.
35 *Daily News* 4 Dec 1872.
36 *R and S* 221.
37 S. J. Reid, *Lord John Russell* (1895) 335.
38 RP 1A, Playfair to JR 4 Apr 1819.
39 RP 9G II, Palmerston to JR 30 Oct 1851.
40 *Spectator* 29 Jan 1870.
41 RP 8F, Lord Holland to Sir Robert Adair 15 Dec 1850.
42 RP 7C, Normanby to JR 20 Jul 1848.
43 *MAE* II 483.
44 S. J. Reid, *Lord John Russell* (1895) 364.
45 *FR* 129–30.
46 RP 5G, Bishop of Durham to JR 21 Dec [1846].
47 Ogden Mss, University College London, Ms 84.
48 *PD* 3 ser. XXXIII 1277, 1 Jun 1836.
49 *PD* 3 ser. XXVII 766, 2 Apr 1835.

CHAPTER VIII

1 Basil Champneys, *The Hon. Adelaide Drummond* (1915) 61–70: and *Life*, I 229–30.
2 *EC* II 78.
3 RP 1E, Howick to JR 3 Feb 1835.
4 *PD* 3 ser. XXVI 471–2, 2 Mar 1835 and EP TS, Ellice to Durham 14 Apr [1835].
5 *EC* II 103.
6 Sanders, *Lord Melbourne's Papers* 251.
7 For this period see especially David Close, 'The formation of a two-party alignment in the House of Commons between 1832 and 1841', *English Historical Review* (1969).
8 Sanders, *Lord Melbourne's Papers* 239–43.
9 Sanders, *Lord Melbourne's Papers* 236.
10 EP, TS Ellice to Durham 8 Mar 1835.
11 *PD* 3 ser. XXVI 43, 19 Feb 1835.
12 GP, JR to Howick 1 Feb 1835.
13 Sanders, *Lord Melbourne's Papers* 243.
14 Sanders, *Lord Melbourne's Papers* 251.
15 Sanders, *Lord Melbourne's Papers* 244.
16 Sanders, *Lord Melbourne's Papers* 248.
17 Sanders, *Lord Melbourne's Papers* 245.
18 *EC* II 76.

19 *EC* II 72.
20 *EC* II 81.
21 DP box 20 bundle 1, list dated 23 Feb 1835.
22 *EC* II 84.
23 DP box 130 bundle 12, JR to Stanley 3 Feb 1835.
24 BP, JR to Brougham 18 Feb 1835.
25 GP, JR to Grey 28 Feb 1835.
26 LP, JR to Lansdowne 28 Jan 1835.
27 Sanders, *Lord Melbourne's Papers* 237.
28 LP, JR to Lansdowne 28 Jan 1835.
29 Sanders, *Lord Melbourne's Papers* 248.
30 LP, JR to Lansdowne 28 Jan 1835.
31 *EC* II 82.
32 A. H. Graham, 'The Lichfield House Compact', *Irish Historical Studies XII* (1960–1).
33 *Life*, 1 220.
34 MPNRA, Melbourne to JR 5 Feb 1835.
35 Sanders, *Lord Melbourne's Papers* 255.
36 MPNRA, Melbourne to JR 12 Feb 1835.
37 MPNRA, JR to Melbourne 13 Feb 1835.
38 *Life*, 1 220.
39 *Life*, 1 221–3.
40 GP, JR to Howick 1 Feb 1835.
41 *Life*, 1 221.
42 GP, JR to Grey 10 Feb 1835.
43 For this and later details see A. H. Graham, 'The Lichfield House Compact', *Irish Historical Studies XII* (1960–1).
44 MPNRA, JR to Melbourne 13 Feb 1835.
45 *PD* 3 ser. XXVI 44, 19 Feb 1835.
46 *PD* 3 ser. XXVI 287–94, 25 Feb 1835.
47 *Life*, 1 225 n.
48 RP 1E, H. G. Ward to JR 18 Feb 1835.
49 *PD* 3 ser. XXVII 365, 30 Mar 1835.
50 A. H. Graham, 'The Lichfield House Compact', *Irish Historical Studies XII* (1960–1).
51 *Life*, 1 229 and 231.
52 Sanders, *Lord Melbourne's Papers* 233.
53 E. Bulwer Lytton, *The New Timon* (1846) 37.
54 EP, TS Ellice to Durham 8 Mar [1835].
55 A. H. Graham, 'The Lichfield House Compact', *Irish Historical Studies XII* (1960–1).
56 *EC* II 89.
57 *EC* II 113.
58 *Life*, 1 229.
59 EP E38, Parkes to Ellice 22 Dec 1853.
60 EP, TS Ellice to Durham [13 Apr 1835] and 14 Apr [1835].
61 *Life*, 1 234.
62 Sanders, *Lord Melbourne's Papers* 243.

63 GP, Grey to JR copy 11 Mar 1835.
64 *RP* 1E, handbill *To the Electors of Devon etc.*
65 *Life*, 1 239–40.
66 Broughton, *Recollections*, v 36.
67 Sanders, *Lord Melbourne's Papers* 237.
68 MPNRA, JR to Melbourne 17 Feb 1835.
69 MPNRA, JR to Melbourne 14 Dec 1835.
70 Sanders, *Lord Melbourne's Papers* 196–8.
71 MPNRA, Melbourne to JR 12 Feb 1835.
72 MPRA, Melbourne to William IV 15 Apr 1835.
73 MPNRA, JR to Melbourne 9 Oct 1835.
74 G. B. A. M. Finlayson, 'The Politics of Municipal Reform, 1835', *English Historical Review* (1966).
75 Buckley, *Parkes* 121.
76 *PD* 3 ser. xxviii 557, 5 Jun 1835.
77 Buckley, *Parkes* 122.
78 *PD* 3 ser. xxviii 549, 5 Jun 1835.
79 Greville, *Memoirs*, iii 247, 1 Sep 1835.
80 *PD* 3 ser. xxx 1407, 7 Sep 1835.
81 Buckley, *Parkes* 129.
82 MPRA, William IV to Melbourne 29 May 1835.
83 MPNRA, Melbourne to JR 3 Feb 1837.
84 MPNRA, Melbourne to JR 7 Apr 1838.
85 MPNRA, Melbourne to JR 5 Jul 1838.
86 RP 2A, Mulgrave to JR 17 Jan 1836.
87 RP 3A, Morpeth to JR 17 Mar 1838.
88 *PD* 3 ser. xxviii 1330, 26 Jun 1835.
89 RP 1E, William IV to JR 15 Aug 1835.
90 *PD* 3 ser. xxxvi 207, 7 Feb 1837.
91 *PD* 3 ser. xlii 1199, 14 May 1838.
92 *PD* 3 ser. xlvii 33, 15 Apr 1839.
93 D. Large, 'The House of Lords and Ireland in the age of Peel 1832–50', *Irish Historical Studies IX* (1954–5).
94 H. Senior, *Orangeism in Ireland and Britain 1795–1836* (1966) ch. XI.
95 BM Add. Ms 51677, JR to Holland 28 Sep 1835.
96 RP 1E, JR to Sir Herbert Taylor copy 30 Sep 1835.
97 *Life*, 1 250.
98 *Life*, 1 247–8.
99 BP, JR to Brougham 11 Sep 1835.
100 MPNRA, JR to Melbourne 30 Sep [1835].
101 *EC* II 139.
102 MPNRA, JR to Melbourne 9 Oct 1835.
103 BM Add. Ms 51677, JR to Holland 9 Oct 1835.
104 *PD* 3 ser. xxxi 371, 12 Feb 1836.
105 O. J. Brose, *Church and Parliament* (Stanford, 1959) 126–7.
106 RP 1E, archbishop of Canterbury to Melbourne copy 5 May 1835.
107 RP 1E, Melbourne to archbishop of Canterbury copies 12 May 1835 and 18 May 1835: and archbishop of Canterbury to Melbourne copy

19 May 1835: and Melbourne to archbishop of Canterbury copy
23 May 1835.

108 MPNRA, JR to Melbourne 25 Jul 1836.
109 Owen Chadwick, *The Victorian Church*, 1 (1966) 129 and 133.
110 *R and S* 142.
111 MPNRA, JR to Melbourne 12 Dec 1835.
112 RP 1E, Morpeth to JR 28 Nov 1835.
113 RP 2A, Ebrington to Tavistock 10 Jan 1836.
114 *EC* II 143.
115 *Life*, 1 265.
116 *R and S* 142.
117 Angus Macintyre, *The Liberator* (1965) 241.
118 RP 2B, Mulgrave to JR 15 Apr 1836.
119 EP, TS Ellice to Durham 16 May 1836: and RP 2B, Mulgrave to JR
3 May 1836.
120 Angus Macintyre, *The Liberator* (1965) 245–6.
121 RP 2B, Mulgrave to JR 15 Apr 1836.
122 *PD* 3 ser. xxxiii 1274–90, 1 Jun 1836.
123 *PD* 3 ser. xxxiv 1257–8, 4 Jul 1836.
124 *PD* 3 ser. xxxiii 1284, 1 Jun 1836.
125 *PD* 3 ser. xxxiv 1259, 4 Jul 1836.
126 *PD* 3 ser. xxxv 764, 1 Aug 1836.
127 *PD* 3 ser. xxxv 527, 25 Jul 1836.
128 RP 2B, Mulgrave to JR 15 Apr 1836.
129 RP 2B, Melbourne to JR 18 Apr 1836.
130 RP 2B, Mulgrave to JR 7 Jun 1836.
131 *Life*, 1 266–7.
132 *Life*, 1 267.
133 *PD* 3 ser. xxxv 1293, 18 Aug 1836.
134 *PD* 3 ser. xxxv 1341, 20 Aug 1836.
135 BM Add. Ms 38080, O'Connell to James Abercromby 5 Sep 1834.
136 *Life*, 1 269–70.
137 MPRA, JR to Melbourne 22 Aug 1836.
138 BP, JR to Brougham 2 Oct 1836.
139 RP 2C, Parkes to JR 6 Oct 1836.
140 RP 2D, Howick memo on JR's plan 29 Nov 1836.
141 RP 2D, Melbourne to JR 27 Dec 1836.
142 *PD* 3 ser. xxxviii 1364, 9 June 1837.
143 *EC* II 120.
144 *Life*, 1 249.
145 EP, TS Ellice to Durham n.d. [1835].
146 *EC* II 115–16 and 140–2.
147 *EC* II 158.
148 GP, JR to Grey 13 Dec 1835.
149 Reports Committees 1839, XII, Evidence of Drummond 17 Jun
1839.
150 RA 2476, 50550–2, JR to Sir Herbert Taylor copy 5 Jan 1836.
151 *PD* 3 ser. xxxiii 1287, 1 Jun 1836.

152 Reports Committees 1839, XII, questions 12,499: 12,501, 12,504; *PD* 3 ser. XLVII 201, 17 Apr 1839.
153 Reports Committees 1839, XI, questions 1508–9.
154 *EC* II 171.
155 RP 2D, O'Connell to Henry Warburton 29 Dec 1836.
156 RP 2E, Mulgrave to JR 12 Apr 1837.
157 RP 2D, Mulgrave to JR 5 Nov 1836.
158 *Life*, I 278.
159 MPNRA, JR to Melbourne 31 Dec 1836.
160 MPNRA, Melbourne to JR 9 Jan 1837.
161 RP 2D, Morpeth to JR 19 Nov 1836: and JR to Mulgrave 4 Dec 1836.
162 RP 2B, Tavistock to JR 12 Jun 1836.
163 MPNRA, Melbourne to JR 19 Sep 1837.
164 RP 2A, Lord Killeen to JR 5 Feb 1836.
165 *Ibid.*
166 RP 2C, Morpeth to JR 5 Oct 1836.
167 RP 2C, Mulgrave to JR 22 Sep 1836.
168 RP 2C, Nicholls to Mulgrave 23 Sep 1836.
169 RP 2D, Stanley to JR 18 Dec 1836: and DP box 130 bundle 12, JR to Stanley 20 Dec 1836.
170 *Life*, I 276.
171 *PD* 3 ser. XXXVI 223, 7 Feb 1837.
172 *Life*, I 278 n 3.
173 RP 2E, Melbourne to archbishop of Canterbury copy 20 Mar 1837.
174 RP 2E, Spencer to JR 12 Apr 1837.
175 *PD* 3 ser. XXXVIII 694, 8 May 1837.
176 PP, JR to Palmerston 24 Jul 1843.
177 RP 4C, Palmerston to JR 26 Nov 1843.

CHAPTER IX

1 RP 2E, JR to Mulgrave draft 18 Jul 1837.
2 RP 2F, Mulgrave to JR 20 Aug 1837.
3 RP 2F, Mulgrave to JR 6 Oct 1837.
4 MPNRA, Melbourne to JR 7 Jul 1837.
5 *Life*, I 282.
6 RP 2F, JR to Melbourne 13 Aug 1837.
7 GP, JR to Howick 16 Aug 1837.
8 *Ibid.*: and MPNRA, JR to Melbourne 29 Aug [1837].
9 MP, Lansdowne to Minto n.d.
10 RP 2F, Mulgrave to JR 9 Aug 1837.
11 EP, TS Ellice to Durham 15 Aug 1837.
12 RP 2F, Mulgrave to JR 17 Aug 1837.
13 MPNRA, Melbourne to JR 24 Aug 1837.
14 MPNRA, Melbourne to JR 2 Aug 1837.
15 MPNRA, JR to Melbourne 4 Aug 1837.
16 MPNRA, JR to Melbourne 2 Aug 1837.
17 GP, JR to Howick 16 Aug 1837.

18 MPNRA, Melbourne to JR 18 Aug 1837.
19 *Ibid.*
20 MPNRA, JR to Melbourne 4 Aug 1837. ʹ
21 RP 2F, JR to the Queen copy 15 Aug 1837.
22 MPNRA, Melbourne to JR 7 Sep 1837.
23 *Ibid.*
24 SP, JR to Abercromby copy 4 Sep 1837.
25 RP 2F, Mulgrave to JR 17 Aug 1837.
26 RP 2F, JR to Melbourne 9 Sep 1837.
27 *Ibid.*
28 MPNRA, Melbourne to JR 30 Aug 1837.
29 RP 2F, JR to Melbourne 9 Sep 1837.
30 MPNRA, Melbourne to JR 7 Sep 1837.
31 CP 7 Carlisle ser. II bk 27, JR to Morpeth 24 Sep 1837.
32 RP 2F, JR to Melbourne 13 Aug 1837.
33 *Life*, I 282–4.
34 MPNRA, JR to Melbourne 10 Aug 1837.
35 BP, JR to Brougham 10 Sep 1837.
36 RP 2F, JR to Melbourne 13 Sep 1837.
37 RP 2D, O'Connell to Henry Warburton copy 29 Dec 1836.
38 RP 2F, Mulgrave to JR 20 Aug 1837.
39 MPNRA, Melbourne to JR 13 Aug 1837.
40 RP 2F, Melbourne to JR 4 Sep 1837: and Mulgrave to JR 20 Aug 1837.
41 MPNRA, Melbourne to JR 2 Aug 1837.
42 MPNRA, JR to Melbourne 1 Aug 1837.
43 RP 2F, JR to Melbourne 13 Sep 1837.
44 MPNRA, JR to Melbourne 7 Jul 1837.
45 MPRA, JR to Melbourne 9 Jan 1838.
46 MPNRA, Melbourne to JR 17 Jan 1838.
47 GP, JR to Grey 26 Jan 1847.
48 MPNRA, Melbourne to JR 3 Jan 1837.
49 BP, JR to Brougham 1 Aug 1837.
50 MPNRA, JR to Melbourne 15 Aug 1837.
51 RP 13F, JR to dean of Bristol 27 Oct 1858.
52 *PD* 3 ser. XXVIII 451, 2 Jun 1835: and XL 1184, 15 Feb 1838.
53 *PD* 3 ser. XXXIX 106, 20 Nov 1837: and XL 1187–9, 15 Feb 1838.
54 MPNRA, JR to Melbourne 11 Aug 1837.
55 MPNRA, Melbourne to JR 13 Aug 1837.
56 MPNRA, Melbourne to JR 15 Sep 1837.
57 MPNRA MEL/RU 532, Melbourne to JR n.d.
58 BM Add. Ms 40424 fos 138–9, JR to Peel 17 Sep 1837: and Peel to JR draft 22 Sep 1837.
59 MPNRA, Melbourne to JR 27 Sep 1837.
60 MPNRA, Melbourne to JR 28 Sep 1837.
61 BP, JR to Brougham 25 Nov 1837.
62 PD 3 ser. XXXIX 65–73, 20 Nov 1837.
63 *Life*, I 289.
64 *EC* II 209.

65 RP 2F, Tavistock to Duke of Grafton 29 Nov 1837.
66 *Life*, I 289.
67 RP 2F, Abercromby to JR 23 Dec 1837.
68 RP 3A, Spencer to JR 11 Feb 1838: and Tavistock to JR 21 Feb 1838.
69 RP 3A, Mulgrave to JR 9 Feb 1838.
70 Sanders, *Lord Melbourne's Papers* 370.
71 Southgate, *The Passing of the Whigs 1832–1886* 91.
72 MPNRA, Melbourne to JR 10 Feb 1838.
73 RP 3A, Sir H. Vivian to JR 5 Feb 1838.
74 MPNRA, Melbourne to JR 23 Jan 1838.
75 RP 3A, Tavistock to JR 18 Feb 1838.
76 RP 2F, Henry Warburton to 'My dear Lord' 16 Nov 1837.
77 RP 2F, JR memo 11 Nov 1837.
78 RP 3A, Mulgrave to JR 21 Feb [1838].
79 RP 2F, Mulgrave to JR 23 Dec 1837.
80 RP 3A, Drummond to JR 20 Mar 1838.
81 RP 3A, Mulgrave to JR 21 Feb [1838].
82 RP 3A, Thompson memo 24 Feb 1837 [1838].
83 RP 3A, Drummond to JR 6 Jan 1838..
84 *PD* 3 ser. XLI 1319, 27 Mar 1838.
85 RP 3B, Mulgrave to JR 11 May [1838].
86 *PD* 3 ser. XLII 1192, 14 May 1838.
87 *PD* 3 ser. XLII 1194–5, 14 May 1838.
88 RP 3B, E. G. Stanley to JR n.d.
89 *PD* 3 ser. XLIII 460–6, 29 May 1838.
90 *PD* 3 ser. XLIV 233, 16 Jul 1838.
91 *PD* 3 ser. XLIV 355, 19 Jul 1838.
92 RP 3B, Normanby to JR 29 Jul [1838].
93 *Life*, I 300.
94 Angus Macintyre, *The Liberator* 222.
95 RP 3C, Ebrington to JR 26 Jun 1839.
96 Angus Macintyre, *The Liberator* 223.
97 *PD* 3 ser. XLIV 879–83, 2 Aug 1838.
98 MPNRA, JR to Melbourne 20 Jul 1838.
99 RP 3B, Tavistock to JR 29 Jul [1838].
100 RP 3B, Normanby to JR 29 Jul [1838].
101 *PD* 3 ser. XLIV 886–7, 2 Aug 1838.
102 *PD* 3 ser. XXXIII 949–53, 16 May 1836.
103 Kinchen, *Lord Russell's Canadian Policy* 32 n 27.
104 *Life*, I 12 n 2.
105 *PD* 3 ser. LII 1326, 23 Mar 1840.
106 *PD* 3 ser. XXXVI 1294, 6 Mar 1837: and XXXVII 1277, 14 Apr 1837.
107 MPRA, JR to Melbourne 26 Dec 1837.
108 MPNRA, Melbourne to JR 31 Dec 1837.
109 Kinchen, *Lord Russell's Canadian Policy* 52.
110 RP 3A, JR memo n.d.
111 *PD* 3 ser. XVI 56, 1 Mar 1833.

112 DP box 130 bundle 12, JR to Stanley 6 Jan 1838: and Stanley to JR copy 8 Jan 1838.

113 RP 3A, Mulgrave to JR 2 Jan 1838.

114 RP 3A, Mulgrave to JR 6 Jan 1838.

115 *PD* 3 ser. XLIV 826–8, 30 Jul 1838.

116 *Life*, I 297.

117 RP 3B, JR to Melbourne copy 9 Jul 1838.

118 Campbell, *Lives of the Lord Chancellors*, VIII 117.

119 RP 3B, Tavistock to JR 10 Aug [1838].

120 *PD* 3 ser. XLIV 1228, 14 Aug 1838.

121 *PD* 3 ser. XLIV 1228–9, 14 Aug 1838.

122 *Life*, I 307.

123 RP 3B, Normanby to JR 29 Jul [1838].

124 EP, TS Ellice to Lady Durham 11 Aug 1838.

125 RP 3B, Bedford to JR 24 Aug 1838.

126 S. J. Reid, *Lord John Russell* 348.

127 RP 2F, Mulgrave to JR 16 Sep 1837.

128 RP 3A, Spencer to JR 11 Feb 1838.

129 RP 3B, Bedford to JR 24 Aug 1838.

130 E. Bulwer Lytton, *The New Timon* 37.

131 *Life*, I 310.

132 MPRA, Melbourne to JR 2 Sep 1838.

133 RP 3B, JR to Melbourne 25 Oct 1838.

134 RP 3B, JR to Melbourne 7 Sep 1838.

135 MPRA, Melbourne to JR 25 Aug 1838.

136 RP 3B, JR to Melbourne 18 Oct [1838].

137 *EC* II 227.

138 RP 3B, JR to Melbourne 22 Oct 1838.

139 PP, JR to Palmerston 25 Oct 1838.

140 MPRA, Melbourne to JR 26 Oct 1838.

141 RP 3B, JR to Melbourne 23 Oct 1838.

142 RP 3B, Palmerston to JR 24 Oct 1838.

143 RP 3B, JR to Melbourne 25 Oct [1838].

144 *Life*, I 308.

145 *Life*, I 310–11.

146 Moore, *Memoirs*, VII 170.

147 RP 3B, Elizabeth Villiers to JR n.d.

148 RA Y89, 21, the Queen to the King of the Belgians 6 Nov 1838.

149 *Life*, I 312.

150 BM Add. Ms 51680, JR to Lady Holland 28 Nov [1838].

151 RP 3B, Tavistock to JR 21 Nov [1838]: and *Life*, I 311–12.

152 RP 3C, Bedford to JR n.d.

153 RP 3C, Bedford to JR 23 Jun 1839.

154 MPNRA, JR to Melbourne 11 Aug 1837.

155 BP, JR to Brougham 15 Aug 1837.

156 BP, JR to Brougham 27 Aug 1837.

157 *Life*, I 329 n.

158 RP 3B, Rice to JR 29 Oct 1838.

159 RP 3B, Henry Dunn to JR 5 Oct [1838].

160 RP 3B, Rice to JR 29 Oct 1838.

161 Broughton, *Recollections*, v 168.

162 MPRA, Melbourne to JR 27 Nov 1838.

163 RP 3B, JR to Melbourne 28 Nov [1838].

164 RP 3C, JR to Melbourne 20 Dec [1838].

165 EP E49, JR to Ellice 10 Dec 1838.

166 MPNRA, JR to Melbourne 6 Jan 1839.

167 *PD* 3 ser. XLVII 1260, 3 Jun 1839.

168 *Life*, I 312–13.

169 MPRA, JR to Howick copy 31 Jan 1839.

170 *Life*, I 313.

171 RP 3B, Normanby to JR 29 Jul [1838].

172 RP 7A, Normanby to JR 8 Feb [1839].

173 MPRA, Melbourne to JR 12 Feb 1839.

174 MPRA, Palmerston to Melbourne 25 Aug 1839.

175 Kinchen, *Lord Russell's Canadian Policy* 94.

176 RP 3B, Normanby to JR 6 Sep [1838].

177 RP 3B, Jul 1838.

178 *Life*, I 314.

179 Maxwell, *Clarendon*, I 159–62.

180 MPRA, Melbourne to JR 1 Dec 1838.

181 MPRA, Melbourne to JR 28 Nov 1838.

182 MPNRA, JR to Melbourne 30 Nov 1838.

183 BM Add. Ms 51680, JR to Lady Holland 29 Dec 1838.

184 BM Add. Ms 51677, JR to Holland 1 Jan 1839.

185 RP 3C, Tavistock to JR 8 Dec [1838].

186 *PD* 3 ser. XLVI 698, 14 Mar 1839.

187 MPNRA, JR to Melbourne 7 Jan 1839.

188 MPRA, Melbourne to JR 19, 20, 21 and 23 Jan 1839.

189 RA A6, 64, JR to the Queen 19 Mar 1839.

190 RP 3A, Drummond to JR 20 Mar 1838.

191 Torrens, *Melbourne* (1890) 475–6.

192 *PD* 3 ser. XLV 1083–4, 1 Mar 1839.

193 RP 3C, Ebrington to JR 26 Jun 1839.

194 MPNRA, JR to Melbourne 27 Aug 1838.

195 MPNRA, JR to Melbourne 23 Sep 1838.

196 *PD* 3 ser. XLVII 17, 15 Apr 1839.

197 *PD* 3 ser. XLVII 13, 15 Apr 1839.

198 Reports Committees 1839, XII, questions 14,203: 13,120: 13,234: and 13,375.

199 Reports Committees 1839, XII, answer 12,319.

200 Reports Committees 1839, XII, table of evidence handed in on 19 Jun.

201 Greville, *Memoirs*, IV 142, 6 Apr 1839.

202 *Life*, I 317–18.

203 Napier, *Life of Napier*, II 5.

204 Napier, *Life of Napier*, II 17–18.

205 RP 3C, Ebrington to JR 1 May, 23 May, and 26 Jun 1839.

206 MPRA, Melbourne to JR 3 May 1839.
207 MPNRA, JR to Melbourne 30 Apr 1839.
208 MPNRA, JR to Melbourne 30 Jun 1839.
209 *PD* 3 ser. XLVII 955 and 959–60, 6 May 1839.
210 D. Southgate, *The Passing of the Whigs* 71.
211 RP 3C, Ellice to JR n.d.
212 *Life*, I 321.
213 RP 3C, JR to Melbourne 12 May [1839]: and Ebrington to JR 20 May 1839.
214 D. Southgate, *The Passing of the Whigs* 73.
215 RP 3C, Bedford to JR 23 Jun 1839.
216 RP 3C, Warburton to JR 30 May 1839.
217 *Life*, I 324–5.
218 Job, thesis, 115–16.
219 *Life*, I 326.
220 *PD* 3 ser. XLV 274–5, 12 Feb 1839.
221 *PD* 3 ser. XLVIII 664, 20 Jun 1839.
222 *PD* 3 ser. XLVIII 663, 20 Jun 1839.
223 *PD* 3 ser. XLV 281, 12 Feb 1839.
224 *EC* II 269.
225 *PD* 3 ser. XLIX 239, 12 Jul 1839.
226 *PD* 3 ser. XLIX 244, 12 Jul 1839.
227 *PD* 3 ser. XLIX 410–13, 17 Jul 1839.
228 *PD* 3 ser. XLVIII 665, 20 Jun 1839.
229 RP 3D, S. March-Phillipps 17 Oct 1839.
230 Communication from Mr A. P. Donajgrodski.
231 The best account of JR's career at the home office is in Leon Radzinowicz, *A History of English Criminal Law* vol. IV.
232 Broughton, *Recollections*, V 221.

CHAPTER X

1 *Life*, I 335.
2 MPNRA, JR to Melbourne 19 Jul 1839.
3 MPRA, Rice to Melbourne 27 Jan 1839.
4 *Life*, I 336.
5 MPNRA, JR to Melbourne 16 and 19 Jul, and 19 Aug 1839.
6 MPNRA, JR to Melbourne 16 Jul 1839.
7 MPRA, Minto to Melbourne 17 Jul 1839.
8 Greville, *Memoirs*, IV 206, 4 Sep 1839.
9 RP 3C, Ellice to JR n.d.
10 MPRA, Palmerston to Melbourne 25 Aug 1839.
11 MPRA, Holland to Melbourne 23 Aug 1839.
12 RP 3C, Bedford to JR 24 Aug 1839.
13 MPRA, Rice to Melbourne n.d.
14 MP, Lansdowne to Minto 6 Sep [1839].
15 Job, thesis 319.
16 RP 3C, JR to Melbourne 29 Aug [1839].

17 RP 3D, Ellice to JR n.d.
18 Howick diary 19 Oct 1839.
19 EP, TS Ellice to Durham 29 Aug 1839.
20 EP E49, JR to Ellice 24 Aug 1839.
21 RP 3C, JR to Melbourne 31 Aug 1839.
22 EP, TS Ellice to Durham 8 Sep 1839.
23 MPNRA, Melbourne to JR 29 Aug 1839.
24 RP 3C, JR to Melbourne 29 Aug 1839.
25 *EC* II 264.
26 RP 3C, JR to Melbourne 28 Aug 1839.
27 RP 3C, JR to Melbourne 31 Aug 1839.
28 EP E49, JR to Ellice 26 Aug 1839.
29 Knaplund, ed., *Letters from Lord Sydenham to Lord John Russell* 26–8.
30 *PD* 3 ser. XLVII 1287, 3 Jun 1839.
31 Kinchen, *Lord Russell's Canadian Policy* 124–30.
32 Kinchen, *Lord Russell's Canadian Policy* 132.
33 RP 3C.
34 RP 3D, Normanby to JR 2 Sep 1839.
35 RP 3D, Ebrington to JR 8 Sep 1839.
36 MPRA, JR to Melbourne 20 Sep 1839.
37 Knaplund, *James Stephen and the British Colonial System 1813–47* (Madison 1953) 16.
38 BM Add. Ms 51680, JR to Lady Holland 4 Nov 1839.
39 MP, Melbourne to Minto 24 Oct 1839.
40 RA Z505, 28, JR to Sir T. Martin 16 Dec 1874.
41 MPRA, Melbourne to JR 16 Sep 1839.
42 MPNRA, JR to Melbourne 30 Oct 1839.
43 EP E49, JR to Ellice 23 May 1840.
44 MPNRA, Melbourne to JR 15 Dec 1836.
45 MPNRA, Melbourne to JR 4 Sep 1837.
46 MPRA, Melbourne to JR 27 Nov 1838.
47 MPNRA, Melbourne to JR 24 Oct 1837.
48 MPRA, Melbourne to JR 5 Sep 1838.
49 *Life,* I 341–2.
50 Greville, *Memoirs,* IV 231, 29 Jan 1840.
51 Rightly, see RA Z270, 43, JR to the Queen 27 Jan 1840.
52 Knaplund, *Letters from Lord Sydenham to Lord John Russell* 42–3.
53 Knaplund, *Letters from Lord Sydenham to Lord John Russell* 44.
54 Knaplund, *Letters from Lord Sydenham to Lord John Russell* 47.
55 Knaplund, *Letters from Lord Sydenham to Lord John Russell* 45.
56 S. J. Reid, *Life and letters of the first earl of Durham 1792–1840* (1906) II 367.
57 *PD* 3 ser. LII 1333–4, 23 Mar 1840.
58 *PD* 3 ser. LII 1334, 23 Mar 1840.
59 *PD* 3 ser. LII 1334–5, 23 Mar 1840.
60 *PD* 3 ser. LIV 1132–5, 12 Jun 1840.
61 *PD* 3 ser. LIV 1146, 12 Jun 1840.
62 DP box 130 bundle 12, JR to Stanley 14 Sep 1841.

63 RP 3D, JR memo 30 Jun 1840.
64 Broughton, *Recollections*, v 282–3.
65 Chadwick, *The Victorian Church*, 1 139.
66 GP, JR to Howick 14 Jul 1840.
67 *PD* 3 ser. LV 464–5, 6 Jul 1840.
68 H. E. Egerton and W. L. Grant, *Canadian Constitutional Development* (1907) 288.
69 RP 4B, G. P. Scrope to JR 12 Oct 1841.
70 RP 3D, Ebrington to JR 8 Sep 1839.
71 Angus Macintyre, *The Liberator* 165 n 3.
72 *PD* 3 ser. LII 624, 25 Feb 1840.
73 *PD* 3 ser. LII 623–4, 25 Feb 1840.
74 *PD* 3 ser. LIV 210–11, 18 May 1840.
75 *PD* 3 ser. LII 629–32, 25 Feb 1840.
76 *PD* 3 ser. LIV 213, 18 May 1840.
77 EP E49, JR to Ellice 23 May 1840.
78 *PD* 3 ser. LIV 507–8, 22 May 1840.
79 *PD* 3 ser. LIV 1092, 11 Jun 1840: and 1169–70, 15 Jun 1840.
80 *PD* 3 ser. LV 461–3, 6 Jul 1840.
81 RP 3D, Lord William Russell to JR 3 Jun 1840.
82 *PD* 3 ser. LV 1356, 6 Aug 1840.
83 MPRA, Melbourne to JR 6 Aug 1840.
84 Angus Macintyre, *The Liberator* 259–60.
85 Reports Commissioners 1878, XXIII, 750.
86 MPNRA, JR to Melbourne 6 Nov 1839.
87 RP 3D, Palmerston to JR 25 Oct 1839.
88 RP 3D, JR to Melbourne 26 Apr 1840.
89 RP 4A, Palmerston to JR 19 Jan 1841.
90 PP, JR to Palmerston 22 Apr 1841.
91 PP, JR to Palmerston 5 Jul 1840.
92 RP 3D, Palmerston to JR 4 Jul 1840.
93 MPNRA, JR to Melbourne 8 Jul 1840.
94 *Life*, 1 362.
95 Lady JR, *Memoir* 33.
96 Lady JR, *Memoir* 29.
97 Lady JR, *Memoir* 35–6.
98 *AP* I 31.
99 Lady JR, *Memoir* 38.
100 RP 3D, Holland to JR 28 Aug 1840.
101 *Life*, 1 347–8.
102 *Life*, 1 348–50.
103 *Life*, 1 352–3.
104 MPNRA, JR to Melbourne 29 Sep 1840.
105 PP, JR to Palmerston 30 Sep 1840.
106 MPNRA, JR to Melbourne 29 Sep 1840.
107 *Life*, 1 307.
108 RP 3E, Clarendon to JR 1 Nov 1840.
109 *Life*, 1 359.

110 MPRA, Palmerston to Melbourne 1 Nov 1840.
111 PP, JR to Palmerston 2 Nov 1840.
112 MPRA, Palmerston to Melbourne 1 Nov 1840.
113 PP, JR to Palmerston 2 Dec 1840.
114 MPRA, Melbourne to JR 16 Sep 1840.
115 *LCI* 22.
116 PP, JR to Palmerston 14 Sep 1840.
117 *LC* I 20.
118 EP E47, Bedford to Ellice 25 Nov 1840: and nd.
119 PP, JR to Palmerston 31 Jul 1840.
120 *PD* 3 ser. LVI 75, 26 Jan 1841.
121 *PD* 3 ser. LVI 238, 2 Feb 1841.
122 *PD* 3 ser. LVI 1125-6, 25 Feb 1841.
123 Greville, *Memoirs*, IV 356, 27 Feb 1841.
124 *PD* 3 ser. LVI 1151-3, 27 Feb 1841.
125 *PD* 3 ser. LVII 970, 22 Apr 1841.
126 RP 4A, Wood to JR 15 Apr 1841.
127 *PD* 3 ser. LVII 1091, 26 Apr 1841.
128 RP 4A, Ebrington to JR 19 Apr 1841.
129 *PD* 3 ser. LVII 1116-21, 26 Apr 1841.
130 *PD* 3 ser. LVII 1202, 28 Apr 1841.
131 *PD* 3 ser. LVI 1125, 25 Feb 1841.
132 Hardcastle, *Life of Lord Campbell* (1881) II 140.
133 EP E47, Bedford to Ellice 13 Oct [1841].
134 RP 4A, Baring to JR 13 Apr 1841.
135 *PD* 3 ser. LVIII 21, 7 May 1841.
136 *R and S* 205.
137 *PD* 3 ser. LVIII 33, 7 May 1841.
138 RP 4A, Bedford to JR [Jun 1841].
139 *Life*, 1 368-9.
140 RP 3D.
141 *PD* 3 ser. LVII 1326-8, 30 Apr 1841.
142 G. P. Scrope, *Memoir of Lord Sydenham* (1844) 90 n.
143 RP 4A, T. F. Kennedy to JR 3 May 1841.
144 *PD* 3 ser. LVIII 16, 7 May 1841.
145 *PD* 3 ser. LVIII 16-53, 7 May 1841.
146 G. P. Scrope, *Memoir of Lord Sydenham* (1844) 90 n.
147 RP 4A, JR to Melbourne 19 May 1841.
148 Norman Gash, *Reaction and Reconstruction in English Politics 1832-52* (1965) 214-15 n 3 and 4.
149 Norman Gash, *Reaction and Reconstruction* 206-11.
150 MPRA, Palmerston to Melbourne 14 May 1841.
151 MPRA, Melbourne to JR 14 May 1841.
152 RP 4A, JR to Melbourne 19 May 1841: see too BM Add. Ms 44294 fos 53-6, JR to Gladstone 2 May 1868.
153 *PD* 3 ser. LVIII 1198 and 1211, 4 Jun 1841.
154 *The Nineteenth Century* (Jan 1890) 40.
155 GP, JR to Grey 1 Sep 1852.

156 EP E38, Parkes to Ellice 5 Jul 1841.
157 G. P. Scrope, *Memoir of Lord Sydenham* 91 n.

CHAPTER XI

1 Lady JR, *Memoir* 40.
2 MP, diary of H. E. 7 Jun 1841.
3 RP 4A, Lord William Russell to JR 16 Jun 1841.
4 RP 4A, Dr S. Lushington to JR 22 Jun 1841.
5 MP, diary of H. E. 4 Jul 1841.
6 *AP* I 31.
7 MP, Lady JR to Nina 23 Nov 1848.
8 MP, Lady JR to Lady Minto 22 Nov 1852.
9 MP, Lady JR to Lotty 27 Oct 1849.
10 Morpeth diary 27 Jun 1846.
11 Lady JR, *Memoir* 64.
12 Lady JR, *Memoir* 66.
13 MP, Lady JR to Bobm 17 Jan [1843].
14 MP, Lady JR to Lotty 6 Jan 1852.
15 MP, Lady JR to Lotty 20 Dec 1849.
16 Lady JR, *Memoir* 67.
17 MP, Lady JR to Billy 2 Apr [1842].
18 MP, Lady JR to Bobm 8 Oct [1842].
19 MP, Lady JR to William 25 Nov [1842].
20 Lady JR, *Memoir* 72.
21 Morpeth diary 17 Jan 1851.
22 RA C25, 10, C. Wood to Anson 30 Jun 1846.
23 RP 4A, John Barnes [?] to JR 29 Jun 1841.
24 CP 7 Carlisle ser. II bk 44, JR to Morpeth 11 Jul 1841.
25 Southgate, *The Passing of the Whigs* 122.
26 EP E38, Parkes to Ellice 15 Jul 1841.
27 EP E41, Ellice to Parkes 16 Jul 1841.
28 RP 4B, JR to Stanley 5 Jul 1841: and DP box 130 bundle 12.
29 Lady JR, *Memoir* 60.
30 *PD* 3 ser. LIX 535, 17 Sep 1841.
31 RP 4B, JR to Duncannon 8 Sep 1841.
32 *PD* 3 ser. LIX 440, 27 Aug 1841.
33 *PD* 3 ser. LIX 542, 17 Sep 1841.
34 RA A4, 40, Melbourne to the Queen 1 Dec 1841.
35 *Glasgow Constitutional* 12 Jan 1846.
36 G. P. Scrope, *Memoir of Lord Sydenham* (1844) 89–90 n.
37 *Ibid.*
38 *PD* 3 ser. LIX 436, 27 Aug 1841.
39 RP 4B, O'Connell to the O'Connor don 29 Aug 1841.
40 PP, JR to Palmerston 4 Oct 1841.
41 RP 4B, Palmerston to JR 12 Oct 1841.
42 EP E49, JR to Ellice 24 Jul 1841.
43 *LC* I 42.

44 Greville, *Memoirs*, IV 142–3, 6 Apr 1839.
45 RP 4B, Ellice to JR 28 Oct 1841.
46 BM Add. Ms 38080 fos 39–40, Brougham to JR [1829].
47 Greville, *Memoirs*, V 53, 22 Nov 1842.
48 BM Add. Ms 40426 fo 419, JR to Peel 14 May 1839.
49 RP 4A, address 12 Jun 1841: and PD 3 ser. LIX 429–49, 27 Aug 1841.
50 MPRA, JR to Melbourne 16 Oct 1841.
51 EP E49, JR to Ellice 31 Oct 1841.
52 RP 4B, Ellice to JR 28 Oct 1841.
53 RP 4B, Bedford to JR 19 Jul 1841.
54 MPRA, JR to Melbourne 6 Nov 1841.
55 LP, JR to Lansdowne 12 Nov 1841.
56 Clar. P C523, JR to Clarendon 3 Oct 1841.
57 *LC* I 49 20 Oct 1841.
58 *LC* I 49 27 Oct 1841.
59 BM Add. Ms 51680, JR to Lady Holland 23 Nov 1841.
60 EP E38, Parkes to Ellice 16 Sep 1841.
61 *LC* I 72.
62 RP 16C, JR to Grosvenor copy 15 May 1866.
63 Clar. P Irish box 44, JR to Clarendon 26 Aug 1851.
64 PP, JR to Palmerston 4 Oct 1841.
65 RA Y54, 58.
66 MPRA, Melbourne to JR 19 Jul 1841.
67 PP, JR to Palmerston 23 Jul 1842.
68 Sanders, *Lord Melbourne's Papers* 527.
69 Southgate, *The Passing of the Whigs* 125.
70 PP, JR to Palmerston 15 Jan 1845.
71 RA A4, 62, Melbourne to the Queen 11 Apr 1842.
72 *Life*, I 385.
73 PP, JR to Palmerston 12 Jan 1842.
74 *Life*, I 385.
75 RP 4C, Ellice to JR 6 Nov 1842.
76 EP E49, JR to Ellice 6 Oct 1843.
77 A. Macintyre, *The Liberator* 263.
78 PP, JR to Palmerston 15 Jul 1843.
79 *PD* 3 ser. LXV 1353–4, 11 Jul 1842: LXVI 107–8, 2 Feb 1843: LXVI 873 and 876, 17 Feb 1843: and LXXV 1426, 25 Jun 1844.
80 *PD* 3 ser. LX 59, 3 Feb 1842.
81 *PD* 3 ser. LX 336 and 356, 14 Feb 1842.
82 *The Panmure Papers*, I 21–2 and 22–4.
83 *PD* 3 ser. LXVI 108, 2 Feb 1843.
84 *PD* 3 ser. LXIX 1460–4, 13 June 1843.
85 RP 4D, Parkes to Cobden copy 25 Nov 1845.
86 RP 4B, Bedford to JR 19 Jul 1841.
87 References to Adam Smith in *PD* 3 ser.; LX 337, 14 Feb 1842: LXVI 877, 17 Feb 1843: LXIX 1459–60, 13 Jun 1843: LXXII 691, 13 Feb 1844: LXXX 865 and 870, 26 May 1845: LXXXI 367, 10 Jun 1845.
   To Malthus; LX 338 and 350, 14 Feb 1842.

To Ricardo; LX 337 and 350, 14 Feb 1842: LXIX 230, 11 May 1843:
and LXIX 1460, 13 Jun 1843.
To McCulloch; LX 350, 14 Feb 1842: LXIX 230, 11 May 1843: LXXX
863 and 866, 26 May 1845.
To Greg and Hubbard; LX 343–4, 14 Feb 1842.

88 *PD* 3 ser. LIX 440, 27 Aug 1841.
89 *PD* 3 ser. LX 336, 14 Feb 1842.
90 *PD* 3 ser. LIX 444, 27 Aug 1841.
91 *PD* 3 ser. LX 347, 14 Feb 1842: and LXI 387, 9 Mar 1842.
92 *PD* 3 ser. LIX 445, 27 Aug 1841: and LXIX 1455–6, 13 Jun 1843.
93 RP 4C, Palmerston to JR 24 Sep 1842.
94 PP, JR to Palmerston 19 Sep 1842.
95 PP, JR to Palmerston 16 Oct 1842.
96 MPRA, JR to Melbourne 3 Feb 1843.
97 EP E49, JR to Ellice 11 Oct 1842.
98 PP, JR to Palmerston 11 Nov 1842.
99 *PD* 3 ser. LXVI 106–7, 2 Feb 1843.
100 *PD* 3 ser. LIX 443, 27 Aug 1841: and LXIX 1451–2, 13 Jun 1843.
101 *PD* 3 ser. LIX 443, 27 Aug 1841.
102 PP, JR to Palmerston 19 Aug 1843.
103 MP, JR to Minto 22 Aug 1843.
104 MPRA, JR to Melbourne 5 Jun 1843.
105 PP, JR to Palmerston 26 Aug 1843.
106 BP, JR to Brougham 19 Aug 1843.
107 PP, JR to Palmerston 15 Sep 1843.
108 *LC* I 67.
109 *LC* I 65.
110 *Life*, I 395.
111 PP, JR to Palmerston 23 Nov 1843.
112 *Life*, I 396.
113 *Ibid.*
114 *PD* 3 ser. LXXII 691, 13 Feb 1844.
115 *PD* 3 ser. LXXII 684, 13 Feb 1844.
116 *Ibid.*
117 Greville, *Memoirs*, V 162, 15 Feb 1844.
118 *Life*, I 397.
119 *Life*, I 398–9.
120 Morley, *Gladstone*, II 802.
121 Broughton diary 15, 16 and 17 Jun 1844.
122 RP 4D, Campbell to JR 17 Jan 1845.
123 RP 4C, Le Marchant to JR 20 Sep [1844] retailing the words of G. E.
    Anson who had come up to town with Prince Albert that morning.
124 RP 4D, Minto to JR 6 Dec 1844.
125 RP 4C, JR to Duke of Leinster Sep 1844: and RP 4C, Bessborough to
    JR 20 Sep 1844.
126 RP 17A, Hartington to Russell 22 Jun 1874.
127 CP 7 Carlisle ser. II bk 51, JR to Morpeth 17 Dec 1844.
128 BP, JR to Brougham 20 Apr 1845.

129 RP 8D, extract from Lord Hatherton's Journal.
130 *PD* 3 ser. LXXV 1426, 25 Jun 1844.
131 EP E49, JR to Ellice 28 Nov 1844.
132 MP, JR to Minto 12 Dec 1844.
133 MP, JR to Minto 14 May 1845.
134 *PD* 3 ser. LXXIX 1004–16, 18 Apr 1845.
135 Broughton diary 18 Apr 1845.
136 *R and S* 421–2.
137 PP, JR to Palmerston 24 Dec 1844.
138 Broughton diary 25 Apr 1845: and MP, JR to Minto 20 Feb 1851.
139 *PD* 3 ser. LXXX 878, 26 May 1845.
140 *PD* 3 ser. LXXX 880, 26 May 1845.
141 *PD* 3 ser. LXXXI 368, 10 Jun 1845.
142 BP, JR to Brougham 1 May 1845.
143 MP, Lady JR to Minto 9 Dec 1845.
144 MP, Lady Abercromby to William 18 Dec 1845.
145 PP, JR to Palmerston 15 Jan 1845.
146 EP E49, JR to Ellice 1 Oct 1839.
147 GP, JR to Howick 15 Jul 1841.
148 RP 5A, Bedford to JR 1 Jan 1846.
149 F. A. Dreyer, 'The Whigs and the political crisis of 1845', *English Historical Review* (1965) 523–4.
150 *G and S* 253.
151 RP 4D, Grey to JR 18 Jul 1845.
152 RP 5A, Macvey Napier to JR 3 Jan 1846.
153 RP 4D, Parkes to Cobden copy 12 Nov 1845.
154 EP E49, JR to Ellice 9 Nov 1845.
155 EP E47, Bedford to Ellice 25 Nov 1845.
156 See Appendix.
157 RP 8C, JR to Bedford copy 18 Dec 1849.
158 Lady JR, *Memoir* 71.
159 EP E47, Bedford to Ellice 25 Nov 1845.
160 RP 4D, Parkes to Cobden copy 25 Nov 1845.
161 Parkes Papers, University College Library, JR to Parkes n.d.
162 RP 4E, Melbourne to JR 13 Dec 1845 and following fos.
163 PP, Palmerston to JR copy 3 Dec 1845.
164 RP 4E, Le Marchant to JR n.d.
165 RP 4E, Fortescue to JR 4 Dec 1845.
166 RP 4E, Cottenham to JR 2 Dec 1845.
167 MP, Wood to Minto 5 Dec 1845.
168 RP 4D, H. G. Ward to JR 29 Nov 1845.
169 CP 7 Carlisle ser. II bk 52, Morpeth to E. Baines jun 24 Nov 1845.
170 RP 4E, Morpeth to JR 4 Dec 1845.
171 RP 4E, Le Marchant to JR n.d.
172 RP 4E, Sir J. V. Shelley to Bedford 30 Nov 1845.
173 The phrase is in EP E 49, JR to Ellice 17 Aug 1845.
174 Morpeth diary 13 Dec 1845.

175 *Life*, I 410.
176 RP 4E, Graham to JR 10 Dec 1845.
177 *Life*, I 410.
178 For this and later details of the crisis *LC* I 102–7.
179 F. A. Dreyer, 'The Whigs and the political crisis of 1845', *English Historical Review* (1965) 520.
180 MP, Lady JR to Billy 16 Jan 1846.
181 RP 4E, Minto to JR 18 Dec 1845.
182 BM Add. Ms 44165 fos 181–8, Granville to Gladstone 8 Oct 1868.
183 GP, JR to Grey 13 Dec 1845.
184 RP 4E, Ellice to JR 13 [Dec 1845].
185 Morpeth diary 14 Dec 1845.
186 *LC* I 105.
187 Greville, *Memoirs*, v 259, 16 Dec 1845.
188 Gash, *Reaction and Reconstruction* 191 n 4.
189 RP 4D, Clarendon memo Dec 1845.
190 RP 4E, Grey to JR 16 Dec 1845.
191 *Life*, I 411.
192 Morpeth diary 18 Dec 1845.
193 RP 4E, Lansdowne to JR Thursday evening [18 Dec 1845].
194 RP 4E, Bedford to JR 14 Dec [1845].
195 RP 4E, Minto to JR 14 Dec 1845.
196 RP 4E, Bedford to JR 14 Dec [1845].
197 *Life*, I 415, Grey to JR 19 Dec 1845.
198 Maxwell, *Clarendon*, I 260–1.
199 PP, Palmerston to JR copy 11 Jan 1846.
200 *Life*, I 416.
201 RP 5A, Normanby to JR 24 Jan 1846.
202 F. A. Dreyer, 'The Whigs and the political crisis of 1845', *English Historical Review* (1965) 533.
203 Morpeth diary 14 Dec 1845.
204 Morpeth diary 19 Dec 1845.
205 MP, Minto to Lady Minto 19 Jan 1846.
206 F. A. Dreyer, 'The Whigs and the political crisis of 1845', *English Historical Review* (1965) 525.
207 EP E49, JR to Ellice 30 Dec 1845.
208 MP, Minto to Lady Minto 18 Jan 1846.
209 EP E41, Ellice to Parkes 22 Dec 1845.
210 See CP 7 Carlisle ser. II bk 52, C. Howard to Morpeth 31 Dec 1845.
211 *Life*, I 410.
212 Broughton, *Recollections*, VI 158.
213 Morpeth diary 21 Dec 1845.
214 RP 4E, Ellice to JR Tuesday [23 Dec 1845].
215 RP 4E, Bedford to JR 20 Dec 1845: and CP 7 Carlisle ser. II bk 52, C. Howard to Morpeth 31 Dec 1845.
216 RP 4E, Minto to JR n.d.
217 RP 4E, Lansdowne to JR 21 Dec [1845].

218 RP 4E, Fox Maule to JR 22 Dec 1845.

219 RP 4E, Bedford to JR fragment n.d.

220 RP 4E, Ellice to JR Tuesday [23 Dec 1845].

221 RP 4E, Lansdowne to JR 21 Dec [1845].

222 *Life*, 1 417.

223 *Life*, 1 414—16.

224 RP 4E, Wood to JR 31 Dec 1845.

225 RP 4E, Bedford to JR 22 Dec 1845.

226 RP 4E, Bessborough to JR 27 Dec [1845].

227 PP, endorsement on JR to Palmerston 19 Dec 1845.

228 RP 4E, Lansdowne to JR 30 Dec [1845].

229 RP 5A, Palmerston to JR 5 Jan 1846.

230 See CP 7 Carlisle ser. II bk 53, C. Howard to Morpeth 1 Jan 1846:
    PP, JR to Palmerston 18 Jan 1846: and RP 5A, JR to Wood copy 3 Jan
    1846.

231 MP, Minto to Lady Minto 19 Jan 1846: and Morpeth diary 11 Feb
    1846.

232 RP 4E, Ellice to JR Tuesday [23 Dec 1845].

233 CP 7 Carlisle ser. II bk 52, C. Howard to Morpeth 28 Dec 1845.

234 RP 4E, Bedford to JR 26 Dec 1845 and 31 Dec [1845].

235 CP 7 Carlisle ser. II bk 53, C. Howard to Morpeth 1 Jan 1846.

236 MP, Charlotte Elliot to Mary 11 Jan 1846.

237 Morpeth diary 20 Dec 1845.

238 RA Y92, 36, the Queen to the King of the Belgians 23 Dec 1845.

239 MP, Lizzy to Mary [early 1846].

240 RP 4E, Bedford to JR 26 Dec 1845: and RP 5A, Bedford to JR 12 Feb
    1846.

241 RP 4D, Bedford to JR fragment n.d.

242 Dreyer, thesis 39.

243 Broughton diary 22 Dec 1848.

244 Morpeth diary 9 Feb 1846.

245 The *Glasgow Constitutional* 12 Jan 1846.

246 RP 5A, Palmerston to JR 2 and 3 Feb 1846, and JR to Everett copy
    3 Feb 1846.

247 F. Merk, 'British Party Politics and the Oregon Treaty', *American
    Historical Review* xxxvii, 1931—2.

248 RP 5A, Wood to JR [22 Jan 1846].

249 MP, Minto to Lady Minto 26 Jan 1846.

250 Greville, *Memoirs*, v 288, 28 Jan 1846.

251 Dreyer, thesis 39.

252 RA C23, 44, to Anson 5 Feb 1846.

253 RP 5A, Cobden to JR 6 Feb 1846.

254 Morpeth diary 7 Feb 1846.

255 RA Y55, 41, Anson memo 27 Oct 1843.

256 Greville, *Memoirs*, v 313—14, 319 and 323.

257 Dreyer, thesis 48.

258 RP 5A, Clarendon to JR 11 Mar [1846].

259 *Ibid.*: and RP 5A, Clanricarde to JR 11 Mar 1846.

260 RP 5A, O'Ferrall to JR 17 Mar 1846.
261 EP E49, JR to Ellice 8 Apr 1846.
262 *PD* 3 ser. LXXXV 548, 3 Apr 1846.
263 RA C24, 27, Prince Albert memo 10 Apr 1846.
264 C. S. Parker, *Sir Robert Peel*, III 346.
265 EP E49, JR to Ellice 26 Apr 1846.
266 Broughton diary 13 May 1846.
267 C. S. Parker, *Sir Robert Peel*, III 344.
268 Morpeth diary 3 May 1846.
269 Broughton diary 9 May 1846.
270 Greville, *Memoirs*, v 322, 21 May 1846.
271 Broughton diary 20 May 1846.
272 MPRA, JR to Melbourne Friday n.d.
273 MPRA, Melbourne to JR 22 May 1846.
274 Broughton diary 25 May 1846.
275 Broughton diary 23 May 1846.
276 Morpeth diary 23 May 1846.
277 Broughton diary 21 May 1846.
278 Broughton diary 23 May 1846.
279 Greville, *Memoirs*, v 323, 1 Jun 1846.
280 RP 6H, Lady Palmerston to JR [1846].
281 Greville, *Memoirs*, v 323, 1 June 1846.
282 *PD* 3 ser. LXXXVI 1201, 25 May 1846.
283 Broughton diary 6 June 1846.
284 Morpeth diary 6 Jun 1846.
285 RP 5A, J. G. Denison to JR 23 and 16 Jun 1846.
286 Morpeth diary 25 Jun 1846.
287 RA C25, 9, S. Wilberforce to Anson 29 Jun 1846.
288 RA C25, 35, Prince Albert memo 4 Jul 1846.
289 Broughton diary 29 Jun 1846.
290 Morpeth diary 29 Jun 1846.
291 Broughton diary 29 Jun 1846.
292 RA C25, 35, Prince Albert memo 4 July 1846.
293 Morpeth diary 6 Jun 1846.
294 RP 5G, Wood to JR Monday morning.
295 MP, Minto to Lady Minto 18 May 1846.
296 RP 5A, Normanby to JR 9 Jun 1846.
297 RP 5A, J. E. Denison to JR 23 Jun 1846.
298 Dreyer, thesis 88.
299 RP 5A, JR to Duke of Portland copy 10 Jun 1846.
300 RP 5A, Monteagle to JR 2 Jun 1846.
301 RA C25.
302 C. S. Parker, *Sir Robert Peel*, III 352.
303 Broughton diary 22 May 1846.
304 RP 5D, Fortescue to JR 29 Oct 1846.
305 *PD* 3 ser. LXXXVII 513, 15 Jun 1846.
306 Greville, *Memoirs*, v 289, 29 Jan 1846.
307 Morpeth diary 9 and 18 Feb, 27 Mar, and 3 Apr 1846.

308 Morpeth diary 9 Feb 1846.
309 Greville, *Memoirs*, v 286–7, 22 Jan 1846.
310 Greville, *Memoirs*, v 292, 30 Jan 1846.

CHAPTER XII

1 RP 5A, Bedford to JR 23 May 1846.
2 RP 2C, George Grace to JR 21 Oct [1836].
3 RP 4B, Lord William Russell to JR 10 Sep 1841.
4 See RA C54, 5, JR to the Queen 14 Oct 1847.
5 RA L13, 16, Palmerston to Clarendon copy Jan 1859.
6 RP 4E, Bedford to JR 31 Dec [1845].
7 RP 6A, Bedford to JR 4 Jan 1847.
8 RP 6D, Bedford to JR [Jul 1847].
9 RP 4E, Bedford to JR 22 Dec 1845: RP 5A, Bedford to JR 1 Jan 1846:
   and RP 6E, Bedford to JR n.d.
10 RP 6D, Bedford to JR 5 Jul [1847].
11 RP 6A, Bedford to JR 4 Jan 1847.
12 RP 6E, Bedford to JR n.d.
13 RP 6B, Bedford to JR 24 Mar [1847].
14 Spring, *The English Landed Estate* 35.
15 RP 2B.
16 Spring, *The English Landed Estate* 190.
17 RP 5F, Bedford to JR 7 Dec 1846.
18 RP 6A, Bedford to JR 22 Jan 1847.
19 Maxwell, *Clarendon*, II 194.
20 See MP, JR to Minto 10 Mar 1857.
21 Morpeth diary 21 Jun 1848 and 21 Mar 1849.
22 Morpeth diary 18 Jan 1847 and 22 Nov 1847.
23 Reports Committees 1850, XV, question 1228.
24 RP 4D, Mr Currey to JR 17 Nov 1845.
25 Morpeth diary 17 Nov 1845.
26 BP, Holland to JR copy 10 Aug 1857.
27 MP, Lady JR to Lotty 25 Nov 1844.
28 RP 5G, Duchess of Somerset to Lady JR 28 Dec 1846.
29 MP, Lady JR to Mary 28 Nov 1846.
30 *RLGP* 43.
31 RA A21, 44, 30 Jun 1850.
32 RA C25, 10, Wood to Anson 30 Jun 1846.
33 Broughton diary 1 Jul 1846.
34 RA C25, 35, Prince Albert memo 4 Jul 1846.
35 RP 5B, Beauvale to JR n.d.
36 RA C25, 6, Prince Albert memo 30 Jun 1846.
37 Morpeth diary 2 Jul 1846.
38 RP 8D extract from Lord Hatherton's journal 28 Mar 1850.
39 RA C25, 10, Wood to Anson 30 Jun 1846.
40 RA C25, 6, Prince Albert memo 30 Jun 1846.

41 RP 5B, Wood to JR n.d.
42 Morpeth diary 2 Jul 1846.
43 RA C25, 6, Prince Albert memo 30 Jun 1846.
44 Le Marchant, *Althorp* 260.
45 W. M. Torrens, *Melbourne* 315.
46 RP 4C, Bedford to JR 6 Nov 1842.
47 *Life*, I 148.
48 RP 7D, Auckland to JR 17 Dec 1848.
49 RP 7A, Auckland to JR 17 Jan 1848.
50 MP, JR to Minto 5 Jan 1849.
51 Morpeth diary 21 Mar and 28 Apr 1849.
52 Morpeth diary 24 Apr 1850 and 16 Oct 1851.
53 Broughton diary 28 Jan 1848.
54 Job, thesis 414.
55 Broughton diary 23 Jan 1849: and Morpeth diary 24 Oct 1847.
56 Broughton diary 23 Jan 1849, and 6 Jun 1850.
57 Morpeth diary 13 Jan 1847.
58 Broughton diary 26 Mar 1849.
59 Morpeth diary 30 Nov 1849.
60 Campbell, *Lives of the Lord Chancellors*, VIII 110, 121, and 479.
61 Broughton diary 27 Jun and 2 Jul 1846.
62 Broughton diary 14 Apr 1847.
63 Broughton diary 31 Mar 1849.
64 Broughton diary 26 Jun 1846.
65 Broughton, *Recollections*, VI 201, 9 Jan 1848.
66 GP, JR to Grey 25 Jan 1852.
67 Morpeth diary 19 Dec 1845.
68 Morpeth diary 3 Jul 1846.
69 Morpeth diary 2 May 1847 and 9 Jan 1849.
70 Morpeth diary 12 May 1847.
71 CP, 7 Carlisle ser. II bk 56, JR to Morpeth 22 Dec 1847: and RP 6H,
   Morpeth to JR 23 Dec [1847].
72 RP 6H, G. Grey to JR 23 Dec 1847: and Wood to JR 25 Dec 1847.
73 MP, JR to Minto 20 Dec 1849.
74 RP 6D, Bedford to JR 27 Jul 1847.
75 Morpeth diary 29 Nov 1847.
76 Broughton diary 7 Dec 1848 and 8 Jun 1850.
77 RP 5A, Baring to JR 26 Jun 1846.
78 Broughton diary 15 Oct 1847 and 28 Aug 1848.
79 RP 8G, Wood to JR 31 Dec 1850.
80 RP 8C, Wood to JR 1 Jan 1850.
81 Broughton diary 6 Dec 1848.
82 RP 7F, Minto to JR 6 Apr 1849.
83 MP, F. Romilly to Minto 5 Dec 1851.
84 Broughton diary 18 May 1847.
85 *Ibid.*
86 Morpeth diary 28 Oct 1846: RP 6D, K. C. Maberly to JR 19 Jun
   [1847]: and JR to K. C. Maberly copy 19 Jun 1847.

87 RP 5D, JR to Bessborough 21 Oct 1846.
88 RP 5D, Fortescue to JR 29 Oct 1846.
89 Hardcastle, *Life of Lord Campbell*, II 210.
90 MPRA, Melbourne to JR 3 Jul 1846.
91 RP 5B, More O'Ferrall to JR 6 Jul 1846.
92 RP 5B, H. F. Berkeley to JR 7 Jul 1846.
93 RA C25, 35, Prince Albert memo 4 Jul 1846.
94 RA C25, 42, Prince Albert memo 6 Jul 1846.
95 *PD* 3 ser. LXXXVII 1176, 16 Jul 1846.
96 Broughton diary 26 Aug 1846.
97 RP 5B, Wellington to JR 12 Aug 1846.
98 *PD* 3 ser. LXXXVII 1041–2, 29 Jun 1846.
99 *PD* 3 ser. LXXXVII 1178–9, 16 Jul 1846.
100 *PD* 3 ser. LXXXVII 1187, 16 Jul 1846.
101 RP 5D, Hobhouse to JR 8 Oct 1846.
102 *PD* 3 ser. LXXXVIII 99 and 103, 27 Jul 1846.
103 RP 5D, Monteagle to JR 4 Oct 1846.
104 *PD* 3 ser. LXXXIX 428–9, 25 Jan 1847.
105 MP, Lady JR to Billy 16 Jan 1846.
106 RP 5D, JR to Bessborough 10 Oct 1846.
107 RP 4D, Ellice to JR 31 Mar 1845.
108 BP, JR to Brougham 1 May 1845.
109 RP 4E, Pigot to JR n.d.
110 RP 5A, More O'Ferrall to JR 26 Mar 1846.
111 *PD* 3 ser. LXXXVII 1180, 16 Jul 1846.
112 *PD* 3 ser. LXXXVII 1179, 16 Jul 1846.
113 RP 5G, JR to Bessborough 28 Dec 1846.
114 Clar. P Irish box 43, JR to Clarendon 10 Nov 1847.
115 RP 5E, JR to Bessborough unfinished 6 Nov 1846.
116 Some of this has to be inferred from what was actually done, but
      particularly suggestive points are made in RP 5E, Bessborough to
      JR 3 Nov 1846: RP 5G, Bessborough to JR 22 Dec 1846: and RP 6B,
      JR to Bessborough 28 Feb 1847.
117 *PD* 3 ser. XCII 539, 7 May 1847.
118 Clar. P Irish box 43, JR to Clarendon 3 Dec 1847.
119 Clar. P Irish box 43, JR to Clarendon 20 Dec 1848.
120 *PD* 3 ser. XC 1260, 12 Mar 1847.
121 *PD* 3 ser. XCV 81, 23 Nov 1847.
122 RA G23, 66, Prince Albert memo 2 Feb 1855.
123 RP 6A, Bedford to JR Aug 1846, 4 Jan 1847 and 13 Jan 1847.
124 Morpeth diary 13 Aug 1846.
125 Broughton diary 13 Aug 1846.
126 RP 5C, Wood to Bessborough 9 Sep 1846 and JR to Earl of Dunraven
      28 Sep 1846.
127 *PD* 3 ser. XCI 309, 22 Mar 1847.
128 *PD* 3 ser. LXXXIX 91, 19 Jan 1847.
129 RP 5D, Wood to JR 14 Oct 1846.
130 RP 5B, O'Connell to JR 12 Aug 1846.

131 RP 5B, Earl of Shannon to JR 5 Aug 1846: Enniskillen to Bessborough 12 Aug 1846: Bessborough to JR 5 Sep 1846.

132 RP 5C, JR to archbishop of Canterbury copy 8 Sep 1846: and enclosure in bishop of Durham to JR 15 Sep 1846.

133 RP 5C, Wood to Bessborough 9 Sep 1846.

134 RP 5F, Labouchere to JR 9 and 11 Dec 1846, and RP 5G 22 and 24 Dec 1846.

135 RP 5C, Wood to JR 22 Sep 1846.

136 RP 5D, Bessborough to JR 6 Oct [1846].

137 RP 5G, Labouchere to JR 22 Dec 1846.

138 RP 5C, G. Grey to JR 28 Sep 1846.

139 RP 5E, Labouchere to JR 6 and 11 Nov 1846.

140 RP 5F, Labouchere to JR 11 Dec 1846.

141 RP 5G, Labouchere to JR n.d.

142 RP 6A, Labouchere to JR 1 Jan 1847.

143 RP 5F, Labouchere to JR 16 Dec 1846.

144 RP 5C, Wood to Bessborough 26 Sep 1846.

145 RP 6A, Wood to JR 5 Jan 1847.

146 RP 6A, JR to Bessborough 30 Jan 1847.

147 LP, JR to Lansdowne 11 Oct 1846.

148 RP 5D, JR to Bessborough 11 Oct 1846.

149 RP 5C, Wood to JR 22 Sep 1846: and RP 5D, Lansdowne to JR 15 Oct [1846].

150 RP 5C, Bessborough to JR 13 and 19 Sep 1846.

151 RP 5C, JR to Bessborough 20 Sep 1846.

152 RP 5C, Bessborough to JR 23 Sep 1846.

153 RP 5C, Labouchere to JR 24 Sep 1846.

154 RP 5D, Lansdowne to Bessborough 10 Oct [1846].

155 RP 5C, Bessborough to JR 23 Sep 1846.

156 RP 5C, JR to Bessborough 25 and 26 Sep 1846.

157 RP 5C, Bessborough to JR, 23 Sep 1846.

158 RP 5C, 27 Sep 1846.

159 RP 5C, G. Grey to JR 28 Sep 1846: and JR to Bessborough 29 Sep 1846.

160 RP 5D, JR to Bessborough 1 Oct 1846.

161 RP 5D, Bessborough to JR 2 Oct [1846].

162 RP 5D, Wood to JR 7 Oct 1846.

163 RP 5E, Bessborough to JR 14 Nov 1846.

164 RP 5D, Bessborough to JR 12 Oct 1846.

165 RP 5D, Bessborough to JR 23 Oct 1846.

166 RP 5C, Wood to JR enclosing letters from Monteagle 22 Sep 1846.

167 RP 5D, JR to Bessborough 4 Oct 1846: and Wood to JR 7 Oct 1846.

168 RP 5E, Labouchere to JR 6, 19, and 23 Nov 1846.

169 RP 5C, G. Grey to JR 23 Sep [1846].

170 RP 5C, Bessborough to JR 13 Sep 1846.

171 RP 5G, Morpeth to JR enclosure 24 Dec 1846.

172 RP 6A, Bessborough to JR 6 and 8 Jan 1847.

173 RP 5D, JR to Duke of Leinster 17 Oct 1846.

174 RP 5F, Clanricarde to JR 17 Dec 1846.

175 RP 5G, Labouchere to JR 23 Dec 1846.

176 Le Marchant, *Althorp* 51.

177 RP 6C, Bedford to JR 25 May 1847.

178 RP 5F, Wood to JR 9 Dec 1846.

179 RP 5F, Clarendon to JR 10 Dec 1846.

180 *PD* 3 ser. LXXXIX 28, 19 Jan 1847.

181 *PD* 3 ser. LXXXIX 103, 19 Jan 1847.

182 *PD* 3 ser. LXXXIX 78, 19 Jan 1847.

183 *PD* 3 ser. LXXXIX 226, 21 Jan 1847.

184 RP 5G, Labouchere to JR 23 Dec 1846.

185 *PD* 3 ser. LXXXIX 90, 19 Jan 1847.

186 *PD* 3 ser. LXXXIX 138–9, 19 Jan 1847.

187 Smith O'Brien, *PD* 3 ser. LXXXIX 83, 19 Jan 1847.

188 *AP* I 267.

189 RP 6A, Bessborough to JR 23 Jan 1847.

190 *PD* 3 ser. LXXXIX 227, 21 Jan 1847.

191 RP 5G, JR to Labouchere copy 28 Dec 1846.

192 *PD* 3 ser. XC 1245, 12 Mar 1847.

193 RP 6A, Bessborough to JR 14 Jan 1847: and JR to Bessborough 17 Jan 1847.

194 RP 6E, Palmerston to JR 19 Aug 1847.

195 *PD* 3 ser. XCII 282–3, 30 Apr 1847: and XCVII 521, 13 Mar 1848.

196 RP 5G, JR to Bessborough 31 Dec 1846.

197 RP 5E, Lansdowne to JR 1 Nov [1846].

198 RP 5E, Labouchere to JR 23 Nov [1846].

199 RP 5F, JR to Bessborough 3 Dec 1846.

200 Broughton diary 30 Jan 1847.

201 RP 6A, Wood to JR 6 Jan 1847.

202 RP 6A, Labouchere to JR 8 Jan 1847: and Clanricarde to JR 8 Jan 1847.

203 GP, JR to Grey 15 Oct 1846.

204 RP 5G, JR to Bessborough 29 Dec 1846.

205 GP, JR to Grey 3 Apr 1847.

206 RP 7D, Grey to JR 4 Sep 1848.

207 RP 5G, JR to Bessborough 29 Dec 1846.

208 RP 6B, JR to Bessborough 25 Feb 1847.

209 RP 6C, Wellington to JR 12 Apr 1847.

210 C. S. Parker, *Sir Robert Peel*, III 476.

211 *PD* 3 ser. LXXXIX 19, 19 Jan 1847.

212 *PD* 3 ser. LXXXIX 257, 21 Jan 1847.

213 RP 6A, Bessborough to JR 16 Jan 1847.

214 Broughton diary 25 Jan 1847.

215 RP 6A, Clarendon to JR 26 Jan 1847.

216 RA D16, 33, Prince Albert memo 11 Feb 1847.

217 RP 6B, Brunel to Hawes 10 Feb 1847.

218 Dreyer, thesis, 85.

219 RP 6B, JR to Bessborough 14 Feb 1847.

220 *Annual Register* (1847) 33.
221 RP 6B, Bessborough to JR 15 Mar [1847].
222 *PD* 3 ser. xc 1249, 12 Mar 1847.
223 RP 6D, report 4 Jul 1847.
224 LP, JR to Lansdowne 15 Mar 1847.
225 *Annual Register* (1847) 45.
226 RP 6C, Bessborough to JR 10 Apr [1847].
227 *Annual Register* (1847) 48.
228 RP 6C, JR to Bessborough 8 May 1847.
229 RP 6G, Palmerston to JR 20 Nov 1847.
230 Broughton diary 29 May 1847.
231 *PD* 3 ser. xcv 94, 23 Nov 1847.
232 *PD* 3 ser. ci 463–4, 23 Aug 1848.
233 *R and S* 364.
234 Broughton diary 24 Apr 1847.
235 RP 6C, Morpeth to JR 2 May 1847: and Stanley to JR 2 May 1847.
236 CP, 7 Carlisle ser. ii bk 55, JR to Morpeth 3 May 1847.
237 *Life*, I 452–3.
238 Broughton diary 17 May 1847.
239 Clar. P C523, JR to Clarendon 30 Dec 1846.
240 RP 7B, Labouchere to JR Apr 1848.
241 RP 6B, Ashley to JR 2 Mar 1847.
242 *PD* 3 ser. xci 141, 17 Mar 1847.
243 *PD* 3 ser. lxxxix 340, 22 Jan 1847.
244 RA C54, 5 and 6, JR to the Queen copy 14 Oct 1847: and the Queen to JR copy 14 Oct 1847.
245 RP 5B, draft [Jul 1846].
246 *PD* 3 ser. xciii 749, 18 Jun 1847: and xciii 1111, 1 Jul 1847.
247 Broughton diary 23 Jun and 7 Jul 1847.
248 RP 6D, Lansdowne to JR Jun 1847.
249 RP 6B, Wood memo 21 Mar 1847.
250 *PD* 3 ser. xci 1217–18, 22 Apr 1847.
251 *PD* 3 ser. xci 957–8, 19 Apr 1847.
252 *PD* 3 ser. xci 966, 19 Apr 1847.
253 *PD* 3 ser. xci 959, 19 Apr 1847.
254 *PD* 3 ser. xci 977, 19 Apr 1847.
255 *PD* 3 ser. xciv 526, 19 Jul 1847.
256 RP 5E, Ellice to JR 10 Nov 1846.
257 *PD* 3 ser. xci 1209, 22 Apr 1847.
258 *PD* 3 ser. xci 851, 15 Apr 1847.
259 *PD* 3 ser. xcii 283, 30 Apr 1847.
260 *PD* 3 ser. xciv 586–7, 20 Jul 1847.
261 *PD* 3 ser. xciv 583, 20 Jul 1847.

CHAPTER XIII

1 Broughton diary 17 Jun 1847.
2 Broughton diary 16 Jul 1847.

3 Broughton diary 22 Jul 1847.
4 C. S. Parker, *Sir Robert Peel*, III 481.
5 C. S. Parker, *Sir James Graham* (1907) II 61.
6 RP 6E, Le Marcahnt to JR n.d.
7 RP 6D, Le Marchant to JR Jul 1847.
8 Clar. P Irish box 43, JR to Clarendon 22 Jul 1847.
9 RA C45, 18, JR to the Queen 5 Aug 1847.
10 RP 6E, Wood to JR 1 Aug 1847.
11 O. Chadwick, *The Victorian Church*, I 236–7.
12 RA C45, 16, JR to the Queen 1 Aug 1847.
13 N. Gash, *Reaction and Reconstruction* 192 n 1.
14 RA C45, 20, Prince Albert memo: and C45, 22 JR memo 7 Aug 1847.
15 RP 6E, Bedford to JR 6 Aug [1847].
16 Dreyer, thesis 82.
17 RA C45, 18, 25 and 26, JR to the Queen 5, 16 and 21 Aug 1847.
18 RA A20, 60, JR to the Queen 13 Jun 1849.
19 Clar. P Irish box 43, JR to Clarendon 16 Aug 1847.
20 RA C45, 28.
21 RA C45, 27, JR memo.
22 *PD* 3 ser. XCVII 1205, 3 Apr 1848.
23 Clar. P Irish box 43, JR to Clarendon 9 Aug 1847.
24 RP 6B, JR to Bessborough 26 Feb 1847.
25 Clar. P Irish box 43, JR to Clarendon 9 Aug 1847.
26 RP 6E, Fortescue to JR 5 Aug 1847.
27 RP 6E, Fitzwilliam to JR 27 Aug 1847.
28 RP 6E, C. R. Fox to JR Aug 1847.
29 RP 6E, Bedford to JR n.d.
30 RP 6E, Wood to JR 15 Aug 1847.
31 RP 6E, G. C. Lewis to JR 16 Aug 1847.
32 RP 6F, Bedford to JR 3 Sep [1847].
33 RP 6E, Wood to JR 14 Aug 1847.
34 RP 7E, JR to Wood 6 Jan 1849.
35 RP 6E, Fitzwilliam to JR 20 Aug 1847.
36 RP 5A, Loyd to JR 25 Jun 1846: and RP 6E, Wood to JR 20 Aug 1847.
37 RP 6E, Fitzwilliam to JR 27 Aug 1847.
38 Clapham, *Economic History of Modern Britain* (1950) II 527.
39 RP 6D, J. MacGregor to JR 17 Jul 1847.
40 RA C54, 34, Anson memo 3 Nov 1847. The bank cannot be identified for certain.
41 RA C54, 18, Prince Albert memo 24 Oct 1847.
42 Broughton diary 21 and 22 Oct 1847.
43 MP, JR to Minto 10 Nov 1847.
44 RA C54, 21, JR to the Queen 24 Oct 1847.
45 RA C54, 12, JR to the Queen 22 Oct 1847.
46 RA C54, 18, Prince Albert memo 24 Oct 1847.
47 RA C54, 13, JR to the Queen 23 Oct 1847.
48 RA C54, 14, Prince Albert to JR copy 23 Oct 1847.
49 RA C54, 18, Prince Albert memo 24 Oct 1847.

50 RA C54, 30, JR to Prince Albert 28 Oct 1847.
51 RA C54, 23, JR to Prince Albert 25 Oct 1847.
52 RP 6F, Wood to JR 28 Oct 1847.
53 Broughton diary 4 Nov 1847.
54 Broughton diary 5 Nov 1847.
55 RP 6B, JR to Bessborough 28 Feb 1847.
56 RP 6B, Bessborough to JR 20 Feb 1847.
57 RP 6C, Wood to JR 11 Apr 1847.
58 Clar. P Irish box 43, JR to Clarendon 17 Jul 1847.
59 RP 6D, JR memo Jul 1847.
60 Clar. P Irish box 43, JR to Clarendon 10 Sep and 2 Oct 1847.
61 Clar. P Irish box 43, JR to Clarendon 9 Jul 1847.
62 RP 6D, JR memo Jul 1847.
63 Clar. P Irish box 43, JR to Clarendon 18 Sep 1847.
64 RP 6D, JR memo Jul 1847.
65 Clar. P Irish box 43, JR to Clarendon 9 Jul 1847.
66 Clar. P Irish box 43, JR to Clarendon 22 Aug 1847.
67 RP 6E, Clarendon to JR 28 Aug 1847.
68 RP 6F, Clarendon to JR 23 Oct 1847.
69 RP 6F, Clarendon to JR 30 Oct 1847.
70 RP 6G, Clarendon to JR 10 Nov 1847.
71 RP 6H, Clarendon to JR 27 Nov 1847.
72 RP 6G, JR to Clarendon copy 10 Nov 1847.
73 Clar. P Irish box 26, JR to Clarendon 13 Jan 1850.
74 RP 7B, Wood to JR 9 Apr 1848.
75 *PD* 3 ser. xcv 86, 23 Nov 1847.
76 GP, JR to Grey 15 Oct 1846.
77 RP 6D, JR memo Jul 1847.
78 Clar. P Irish box 26, JR to Clarendon 7 May 1849.
79 RP 7E, Clarendon to JR 6 Feb 1849.
80 Morpeth diary 7 Apr 1848.
81 RP 5F, JR to Bessborough 1 Dec 1846.
82 RP 5G, Bessborough to JR 30 Dec 1846.
83 RP 5B, Palmerston to JR 30 Jul 1846.
84 RP 5B, Ponsonby to JR 29 Mar 1847.
85 MP, JR to Minto 2 Nov 1847.
86 Clar. P Irish box 43, JR to Clarendon 5 Oct 1847.
87 MP, JR to Minto 2 Nov 1847.
88 MP, JR to Minto 22 Sep 1847.
89 MP, JR to Minto 26 Sep 1847.
90 MP, JR to Minto 27 Oct 1847.
91 RP 6G, Clarendon to JR 18 Nov [1847].
92 Broughton diary 19 Nov 1847.
93 RP 6G, Clarendon to JR 17 Nov 1847.
94 MP, Palmerston to Minto 3 Dec 1845 [1847].
95 RP 6G, Clarendon to JR 10 and 12 Nov 1847.
96 RP 6G, JR to Lansdowne copy 28 Nov 1847.
97 RP 6G, JR to Clarendon copy 10 Nov 1847.

98 RP 6G, JR to Clarendon copy 15 Nov 1847.
99 Clar. P Irish box 43, JR to Clarendon 14 Nov 1847.
100 RP 6G, Clarendon to JR, 15, 17, 18 and 19 Nov 1847.
101 Broughton diary 17 Nov 1847.
102 MP, Palmerston to JR 19 Nov 1847.
103 Broughton diary 17 and 19 Nov 1847.
104 RP 6G JR to Clarendon copy 15 Nov 1847.
105 RP 6G, JR to Clarendon copy 10 Nov 1847.
106 RP 6G, Clarendon to JR 17 Nov 1847.
107 Clar. P Irish box 43, JR to Clarendon 10 Nov 1847.
108 RP 6F, Clarendon to JR 18 Oct 1847.
109 Clar. P Irish box 43, JR to Clarendon 10 Oct 1847.
110 Clar. P Irish box 43, JR to Clarendon 15 Oct 1847.
111 Broughton diary 15 Oct 1847.
112 Clar. P Irish box 43, JR to Clarendon 21 Oct 1847.
113 RP 6F, Clarendon to JR 18 Oct 1847.
114 RP 6G, JR to Clarendon copy 10 Nov 1847.
115 Clar. P Irish box 43, JR to Clarendon 15 Oct 1847.
116 RP 6G, JR to Lansdowne 28 Nov 1847.
117 See RP 6H, G. Grey to JR 26 Dec 1847.
118 RP 6F, Clarendon to JR 23 Oct 1847.
119 Clar. P Irish box 43, JR to Clarendon 13 Dec 1847.
120 RA F9, 90, Stockmar to Newcastle copy 28 Jan 1852.
121 RA A19, 25, JR to the Queen 9 Nov 1846.
122 RA A19, 73, JR to the Queen 24 Apr 1847.
123 MPNRA, JR to Melbourne 11 Aug 1837.
124 RP 5E, Lansdowne to JR 9 Nov 1846.
125 RP 6C, Hampden to JR 13 May 1847.
126 RP 6E, archbishop of Canterbury to JR 9 Aug 1847.
127 RP 6E, Morpeth to JR 24 Aug 1847: and G. Grey to JR 19 Aug 1847.
128 LP, JR to Lansdowne 8 Nov 1847.
129 LP, JR to Lansdowne 10 Nov 1847.
130 LP, JR to Lansdowne 11 Nov 1847.
131 RP 6G, archbishop of Canterbury to JR 26 Nov 1847.
132 Broughton diary 10 Jan 1848.
133 RP 6G, JR to archbishop of Canterbury copy 27 Nov 1847.
134 Morpeth diary 14 Dec 1847.
135 Life, 1 479.
136 RA C55, 3 and 15, Sam. Wilberforce to Anson 16 and 27 Nov 1847.
137 RA C55, 67, Prince Albert memo.
138 RA C55, 42, Prince Albert memo.
139 RP 6H, Bedford to JR n.d.
140 RP 6H, Palmerston to JR 23 Dec 1847.
141 Life, 1 480 n.
142 RP 6H, Bedford to JR 14 Dec [1847].
143 Clar. P Irish box 43, JR to Clarendon 11 Feb 1848.
144 RP 7A, Bedford to JR 12 Feb 1848: and bishop of Durham to JR 15 Feb 1848.

145 O. Chadwick, *The Victorian Church*, I 239 n I.
146 RP 6H, bishop of Durham to JR 8 Dec [1847].
147 Clar. P Irish box 43, JR to Clarendon 17 Feb 1848.
148 RA C55, 86, JR to the Queen 16 Feb 1848.
149 *PD* 3 ser. xcv 308–9, 29 Nov 1847.
150 *PD* 3 ser. xcv 732, 6 Dec 1847.
151 *PD* 3 ser. xcv 312, 29 Nov 1847.
152 RP 7A, G. Grey to JR 21 Jan 1848.
153 RP 7A, Lansdowne to JR 14 and 27 Jan 1848.
154 Broughton diary 1 Feb 1848.
155 RP 6G, Clarendon to JR 17 Nov 1847.
156 *PD* 3 ser. c 514–15, 17 Jul 1848.
157 *The Times* 13 Mar 1869, letter from Lord Romilly.
158 W. L. Burn, 'Free Trade in land, an aspect of the Irish Question', *Transactions of the Royal Historical Society* (1949) 61–74.
159 RP 7C, Normanby to JR 20 Jul 1848.
160 Broughton diary 19 Nov 1847.
161 RP 7A, Palmerston to JR 10 Feb 1848.
162 Morpeth diary 18 Feb 1848.
163 RP 7A, Bedford to JR 22 Feb 1848.
164 RA A19, 170, JR to the Queen 25 Feb 1848.
165 Broughton diary 28 Feb 1848.
166 RP 7B, Greville to Bedford 14 Mar 1848.
167 RP 7B, Tufnell to JR 15 Mar 1848.
168 Clar. P Irish box 12, G. Grey to Clarendon 14 Mar 1848.
169 Broughton diary 18 Mar 1848.
170 *PD* 3 ser. c 313, 10 Jul 1848.
171 Clar. P Irish box 43, JR to Clarendon 24 Jun 1848.
172 RA C57, 4, JR to the Queen 22 Jun 1848.
173 RP 7C, Bedford to JR 3 Jul 1848.
174 Clar. P Irish box 43, JR to Clarendon 1 Jul 1848.
175 Morpeth diary 23 Jun 1848.
176 RP 7B, G. Grey to JR 7 Mar [1848].
177 RA C56, 28, JR to Prince Albert 11 Apr 1848.
178 RP 7B, Trevelyan memo 4 Apr 1848.
179 RP 7B, Wellington to JR copy 6 Apr 1848.
180 Morpeth diary 9 Apr 1848.
181 Clar. P Irish box 43, JR to Clarendon 17 Apr 1848.
182 RP 7B, G. Grey to JR 9 Apr 1848.
183 RA C56, 14, JR to Prince Albert 9 Apr 1848.
184 Broughton diary 8 April 1848.
185 *RLGP* 36–7.
186 Broughton diary 10 Apr 1848.
187 RA C56, 19, JR to the Queen 10 Apr 1848.
188 Broughton diary 10 Apr 1848.
189 Morpeth diary 16 Jun 1848.
190 RA C8, 11, the Queen to JR 12 Apr 1848.
191 Morpeth diary 10 Apr 1848.

192 RA C56, 28, JR to Prince Albert 11 Apr 1848.
193 RA C8, 18, the Queen to JR 31 May 1848: and C16, 47, Prince Albert to JR 10 Apr 1848.
194 RA C56, 47.
195 Broughton diary 1 Jun 1848.
196 RA J69, 8, JR to the Queen 15 Apr 1848.
197 RP 7B, Labouchere to JR 21 Apr 1848.
198 RP 7C, C. Connellan to JR 8 Aug 1848.
199 RP 7D, Wood to JR 6 Sep 1848.
200 RP 7B, JR memo 30 Mar 1848.
201 Dreyer, thesis 124.
202 Broughton diary 25 Mar 1848.
203 RP 7B, Palmerston memo 31 Mar 1848.
204 Broughton diary 25 Mar, 1 Apr 1848.
205 RA D17, 55, JR to Prince Albert 7 Apr 1848.
206 Clar. P Irish box 43, JR to Clarendon 28 Apr 1848.
207 Clar. P Irish box 43, JR to Clarendon 18 May 1848.
208 Broughton diary 19 May and 14 Jul 1848.
209 Broughton diary 18, 20 and 21 Jul 1848.
210 Broughton diary 31 Jul 1848.
211 Broughton diary 7 and 14 Aug 1848.
212 Lady JR, *Memoir* 99.
213 Clar. P Irish box 43, JR to Clarendon 2 Dec 1847.
214 Clar. P Irish box 43, JR to Clarendon 19 Mar, 3 Apr and 27 Jul 1848.
215 *PD* 3 ser. xcv 1234–49, 16 Dec 1847.
216 RP 8B, Ashley to JR 7 Nov 1849.
217 *PD* 3 ser. ci 705, 30 Aug 1848.
218 Morpeth diary 13 Dec 1847 and 18 Feb 1848.
219 Clar. P Irish box 43, JR to Clarendon 3 Mar 1848.
220 Morpeth diary 9 Mar 1848.
221 Clar. P Irish box 43, JR to Clarendon 10 Apr 1848.
222 MP, JR to Minto 30 Jan 1847 [1848].
223 Howick diary 15 Aug 1848.
224 RP 7C, Dunfermline to Labouchere 28 May 1848.
225 RP 7C, Normanby to JR 20 Jul 1848: and RP 4A, Normanby to JR 3 Apr 1848.
226 Clar. P Irish box 43, JR to Clarendon 4 Aug 1848.
227 RP 5D, JR to Bessborough 4 Oct 1846.
228 Clar. P Irish box 43, JR to Clarendon 21 Oct 1847.
229 Clar. P Irish box 43, JR to Clarendon 12 Dec 1847.
230 Clar. P Irish box 43, JR to Clarendon 15 Aug 1848.
231 Clar. P Irish box 26, JR to Clarendon 13 Feb 1849.
232 Clar. P Irish box 26, JR to Clarendon 24 Feb 1849.
233 Clar. P Irish box 43, JR to Clarendon 23 Mar 1848.
234 Clar. P Irish box 43, JR to Clarendon 8 Aug 1848.
235 Clar. P Irish box 43, JR to Clarendon 18 Sep 1848.
236 Clar. P Irish box 43, JR to Clarendon 12 Oct 1848.
237 RA D18, 56, JR to the Queen 2 Sep 1848.

238 RP 7D, Wood to JR 6 Sep 1848.
239 Clar. P Irish box 43, JR memo 8 Sep 1848.
240 Clar. P Irish box 43, JR to Clarendon 8 Aug 1848.
241 RP 7C, Normanby to JR 20 Jul 1848.
242 RP 7D, Redington to JR 7 Sep 1848.
243 RA D18, 62, JR to Redington copy 9 Sep 1848.
244 RA D18, 84, Prince Albert memo 30 Oct 1848.
245 Clar. P Irish box 43, JR to Clarendon 8 Aug 1848.
246 RP 7D, JR to Redington 6 Sep 1848.
247 RA D18, 57, JR to G. Grey copy 3 Sep 1848.
248 RA D18, 60, Redington to JR copy 7 Sep 1848.
249 RA D18, 62, JR to Redington copy 9 Sep 1848.
250 *Ibid.*
251 RA D18, 60, Redington to JR copy 7 Sep 1848.
252 RA D18, 81, Redington to JR copy 9 Sep 1848.
253 Broughton diary 24 Oct 1848.
254 RA D18, 84, Prince Albert memo 30 Oct 1848.
255 RA D19, 5, Mr Temple to Palmerston 5 Dec 1848.
256 Broughton diary 5 Dec 1848.
257 LP, JR to Lansdowne 17 Nov 1848.
258 Clar. P Irish box 26, JR to Clarendon 28 Feb 1849.
259 RA D18, 90, JR to the Queen 6 Dec 1848.
260 RP 7A, Argyll to JR 24 Jan 1848.
261 *LC* I 185, JR to Lansdowne 4 Jan 1848 [1849].
262 PP, JR to Palmerston 4 Jan 1849.
263 RP 7E, JR to Wood 6 Jan 1849.
264 Morpeth diary 9 Jan 1849.
265 C. S. Parker, *Sir James Graham*, II 74.
266 Clar. P Irish box 26, JR to Clarendon 13 Jan 1849.
267 Morpeth diary 13 Jan 1849.
268 Morpeth diary 9 Jan 1849.
269 Clar. P Irish box 26, JR to Clarendon 11 Jan 1849.
270 RP 7E, Baring to Grey 17 Jan 1849.
271 RP 7D, Clanricarde to JR 1 Sep 1848.
272 Clar. P Irish box 43, JR to Clarendon 25 Nov 1848.
273 Clar. P Irish box 26, JR to Clarendon 14 Jan 1849.
274 Clar. P Irish box 43, JR to Clarendon 30 Dec 1848.
275 RP 7D, Wood to JR 18 Dec 1848.
276 RP 7D, Wood to JR 16 Dec 1848.
277 Clar. P Irish box 26, JR to Clarendon 17 Jan 1849.
278 Clar. P Irish box 26, JR to Clarendon 24 Feb 1849.
279 RP 7D, Clarendon to JR 17 Dec 1848.
280 Clar. P Irish box 26, JR to Clarendon 17 Jan 1849.
281 Clar. P Irish box 43, JR to Clarendon 19 and 21 Dec 1848.
282 Broughton diary 27 Jan 1849: and RP 9K list n.d.
283 RP 7E, Lansdowne to JR Feb 1849.
284 Clar. P Irish box 26, JR to Clarendon 5 Feb 1849.
285 Clar. P Irish box 26, JR to Clarendon 8 Feb 1849.

286 Morpeth diary 8 Feb 1849.
287 Clar. P Irish box 26, JR to Clarendon 29 Jan 1849.
288 Clar. P Irish box 26, JR to Clarendon 11 Feb 1849.
289 Broughton diary 10 Feb 1849.
290 Clar. P Irish box 26, JR to Clarendon 11 Feb 1849.
291 RA D19, 27, JR to the Queen 6 Mar 1849.
292 Morpeth diary 2 Apr 1849.
293 RA D19, 39, extract from *The Globe*.
294 RA D19, 37, JR to the Queen 19 Apr 1849.
295 RA D19.
296 C. S. Parker, *Sir Robert Peel*, III 516.
297 RP 7F, Redington to Clarendon 1 Apr 1849.
298 Morpeth diary 2 and 3 Apr 1849.
299 RP 7F, Lansdowne to JR n.d.
300 *R and S* 195.
301 Clar. P Irish box 43, JR memo 8 Sep 1848.
302 RP 7F, Redington to Clarendon 1 Apr 1849: Romilly to JR 7 Apr 1849:
    and Ellice to JR 9 and 11 Apr 1849.
303 W. L. Burn, 'Free Trade in land; an aspect of the Irish Question',
    Transactions of the Royal Historical Society (1949) 70–1.
304 RP 7D, Labouchere to JR 13 Nov 1848.
305 RA F20, 1, JR memo 10 May 1849.
306 RA C57, 13, JR to the Queen 27 Mar 1849.
307 Broughton diary 31 Mar 1849.
308 RP 7F, Palmerston to JR 14 Apr 1849.
309 RA C57, 16, Prince Albert to Wellington copy 3 Apr 1849.
310 RA C57, 21, Peel to Prince Albert 11 Apr 1849.
311 RA C57, 18, JR to Prince Albert 4 Apr 1849.
312 RP 7F, JR to Palmerston copy 16 Apr 1849.
313 RA C57, 31, JR to the Queen 5 May 1849.
314 RA C57, 32 Wood to Anson n.d.: and C57, 34 and 35, Wood to Anson
    and JR to the Queen 8 May 1849.
315 Morpeth diary 26 Jul 1849.
316 PP, JR to Palmerston 26 Aug 1843.
317 RA D15, 52, the Queen to JR 3 Aug 1846.
318 RA C45, 26, JR to the Queen 21 Aug 1847.
319 Clar. P Irish box 43, JR to Clarendon 10 Apr 1848.
320 RA D19, 46 and 47, Prince Albert to JR 6 Jun 1849 and JR to Prince
    Albert 6 Jun 1849.
321 RP 8A, Palmerston to JR 5 Aug 1849.
322 RP 8A, Clarendon to JR 9 Aug 1849.
323 RP 8A, Clarendon to JR 16 Aug 1849.
324 RP 7C, Trevelyan to JR 21 Aug 1848.
325 RP 7F, Dalhousie to JR 2 Mar 1849.
326 Broughton diary 14 Jan 1847.
327 Broughton diary 1 Apr 1848.
328 Morpeth diary 5 Dec 1849.

CHAPTER XIV

1 Broughton diary 28 Jan 1851.
2 RP 4C, JR to Parkes copy 9 Sep 1841.
3 EP E38, Parkes to Ellice 16 Sep 1841.
4 RP 7B, Bannerman to JR 26 Apr 1848: Macaulay to JR 23 Apr 1848:
   and Normanby to JR 29 Apr [1848].
5 Clar. P Irish box 43, JR to Clarendon 24 Apr 1848.
6 *PD* 3 ser. XCIX 915–33, 20 Jun 1848.
7 RP 7F, JR memo 19 Jun 1849: compare the account in Olive Anderson,
   'The Wensleydale peerage case and the position of the House of
   Lords in the mid-nineteenth century', *English Historical Review* (1967).
8 RA F20, 1, JR memo 10 May 1849.
9 RP 9D II, Grey to JR 9 Jul 1851.
10 Clar. P Irish box 26, JR to Clarendon n.d.
11 RP 6F, JR to Westminster copy 9 Sep 1847.
12 Broughton diary 3 Apr 1849.
13 RA F20, 3, JR memo copy 19 Jun 1849.
14 RA F20, 4, Prince Albert to JR copy 20 Jun 1849.
15 RP 6D, Cottenham to JR 16 Jul 1849.
16 A. C. Benson and Viscount Esher, ed., *The Letters of Queen Victoria* (1908)
   II 237: and DP box 133 bundle 6, Bedford memo on reform.
17 RP 14A, Bedford to JR 5 Aug 1860.
18 LP, JR to Lansdowne 19 Sep 1849.
19 Morpeth diary 9 Oct 1849.
20 PP, JR to Palmerston 24 Oct 1849.
21 RP 8B, JR to G. C. Lewis 13 Nov 1849.
22 GP, JR to Grey 13 Oct and 20 Nov 1849.
23 RP 8B, Palmerston to JR 23 Oct 1849.
24 MP, JR to Minto 11 Jan 1850.
25 BM Add. Ms 40602 fos 305–6, Chas Arbuthnot to Peel 5 Dec 1849.
26 DP box 133 bundle 6, Bedford memo on reform.
27 RP 8C, JR to R. A. Slaney 31 Dec 1849.
28 RP 8A, Wood to JR 1 Sep 1849.
29 RP 8B, Inglis to JR 6 Oct 1849.
30 RP 8C, Baring to JR 4 Jan 1850.
31 RP 8B, J. W. Green to Lord R. Grosvenor 12 Oct 1849.
32 RP 9F, Thos Keightley to JR 16 Sep 1851.
33 Clar. P Irish box 26, JR to Clarendon 26 Sep 1849.
34 Clar. P Irish box 26, JR to Clarendon 28 Dec 1849.
35 Clar. P Irish box 26, JR to Clarendon 8 Nov 1849.
36 Clar. P Irish box 26, JR to Clarendon 17 Dec 1849.
37 Clar. P Irish box 26, JR to Clarendon 18 Nov 1849.
38 Clar. P Irish box 26, JR to Clarendon 7 Jan 1850.
39 W. P. Morrell, *British Colonial Policy in the age of Peel and Russell*, ch. XVIII.
40 RP 8C, Elgin to JR 10 Dec 1849.
41 GP, JR to Grey 27 Jan 1847.
42 RA J7, 59, JR to the Queen 3 Feb 1849.

43 Job, thesis, 418.
44 *PD* 3 ser. cvi 996–1002, 26 Jun 1849.
45 Morpeth diary 7 Nov 1849.
46 RP 8A, Grey to JR 22 Sep 1849.
47 GP, JR to Grey 22 Sep 1849.
48 GP, JR to Grey 19 Dec 1849.
49 GP, JR to Grey 29 Dec 1849.
50 Morpeth diary 6 Feb 1850.
51 Morpeth diary 8 Feb 1850.
52 *PD* 3 ser. cviii 535–67, 8 Feb 1850.
53 Clar. P Irish box 26, JR to Clarendon 21 Mar 1850.
54 RP 8E, Ellice to JR 15 Jun [1850].
55 *PD* 3 ser. cxiii 535, 30 Jul 1850.
56 RA A20, 146, JR to the Queen 23 Mar 1850.
57 Morpeth diary 16 Mar 1850.
58 Broughton diary 16 Mar 1850.
59 Morpeth diary 19 Mar 1850.
60 RP 8D, Denison to JR 18 [Mar 1850].
61 Broughton diary 19 Mar 1850.
62 Morpeth diary 19 Mar 1850.
63 RP 5D, Palmerston to JR 6 Oct 1846.
64 RP 5F, Palmeston to JR 8 Dec 1846.
65 RP 5B, Normanby to JR 23 Aug 1846.
66 RP 5C, Wood to JR 18 Sep 1846.
67 Clar. P Irish box 44, JR to Clarendon 23 Dec 1851.
68 E.g. RA A79, 25, Prince Albert memo 3 Mar 1850.
69 RA A79, 42, Prince Albert memo 8 Aug 1850.
70 EP E47, Bedford to Ellice 25 Dec 1845: RP 4E, Fox Maule to JR 22 Dec 1845.
71 Job, thesis, 411.
72 RA A80, 101, Col Grey memo 8 Jan 1852.
73 RP 5C, Wood to JR 18 Sep 1846.
74 RP 7D, JR to Palmerston copy 1 Oct 1848.
75 RP 7E, JR to Palmerston copy 20 Jan 1849.
76 PP, JR to Palmerston 7 Aug 1849.
77 PP, JR to Palmerston 6 Jan 1849.
78 Brian Connell, *Regina* v. *Palmerston* (1962) 97.
79 RA J7, 26, Prince Albert memo 24 Jan 1849.
80 RP 8C, JR to Palmerston copy 12 Jan 1850.
81 RP 8C, Palmerston to JR 26 Jan 1850.
82 Morpeth diary 2 Feb 1850.
83 RP 8C, JR to Palmerston copy 18 Feb 1850.
84 PP, JR to Palmerston 25 Feb 1850.
85 Benson and Esher, ed., *Letters of Queen Victoria* (1908) ii 235–37.
86 RA A79, 25, Prince Albert memo 3 Mar 1850, not printed in the *Letters*.
87 Morpeth diary 25 Mar 1850.
88 Broughton diary 16 May 1850.
89 Morpeth diary 16 May 1850.

90 Broughton diary 27 May 1850: and Morpeth diary 1 Jun 1850.
91 RA A79, 28, Prince Albert memo 20 May 1850.
92 RP 8D, JR to Palmerston copy 22 May 1850.
93 Morpeth diary 18 Jun 1850.
94 Broughton diary 18 Jun 1850.
95 Morpeth diary 18 Jun 1850.
96 Morpeth diary 20 Jun 1850.
97 Broughton diary 22 Jun 1850.
98 *PD* 3 ser. cxii 106, 20 Jun 1850.
99 RP 8E, Clarendon to JR 1 Jul 1850.
100 RA J96, 39, JR to the Queen 27 Jun 1850.
101 EP E38, Parkes to Ellice 26 Dec 1851.
102 Clar. P Irish box 26, JR to Clarendon 15 Jun 1850.
103 H. C. F. Bell, *Lord Palmerston* (1936) ii 28.
104 RA A79, 31, Prince Albert to JR 9 Jul 1850.
105 PP, JR to Palmerston 22 May 1850.
106 RA A79, 34, Prince Albert memo 11 Jul 1850.
107 RA A79, 31, Prince Albert to JR 9 Jul 1850.
108 RA A79, 38, JR to the Queen 26 Jul 1850.
109 Benson and Esher *Letters of Queen Victoria*, ii 260.
110 Benson and Esher *Letters of Queen Victoria*, ii 264.
111 Benson and Esher *Letters of Queen Victoria*, ii 260.
112 Broughton diary 15 Aug 1850.
113 Morpeth diary 6 Nov 1850.
114 See Appendix.
115 RP 8F, Minto to JR 23 Oct 1850: Wiseman to JR 3 Nov 1850: Minto
      to JR 21 Nov 1850: Abbate Hamilton to Minto extracts 4 Dec 1850:
      RP 8G, Abbate Hamilton to Minto copy 28 Dec 1850: and RP 9B,
      Dr Ullathorne to JR 10 Feb 1851.
116 Clar. P Irish box 26, JR to Clarendon 1 and 7 Oct 1850.
117 Clar. P Irish box 26, JR to Clarendon 13 Nov 1850.
118 Clar. P Irish box 26, JR to Clarendon 1 Oct 1850.
119 RP 7D, Ribblesdale to JR, Rome, 24 Dec 1848.
120 Clar. P Irish box 26, JR to Clarendon 27 Oct 1850.
121 RA A20, 92, JR to the Queen 11 Sep 1849.
122 RP 8G, Wriothesley Russell to JR n.d.
123 Morpeth diary 15 Mar 1850.
124 Clar. P Irish box 26, JR to Clarendon 30 Sep and 13 Oct 1850.
125 BP, JR to Brougham 9 Oct 1850.
126 RP 8F, G. C. Lewis to JR 7 Nov 1850.
127 PP, JR to Palmerston 2 Nov 1850.
128 RP 8F, Lord Edward Howard to JR 2 Nov 1850.
129 C. S. Parker, *Sir James Graham*, ii 114.
130 Clar. P Irish box 43, JR to Clarendon 28 Oct 1847.
131 *PD* 3 ser. cii 444–5, 8 Feb 1849.
132 EP E38, Parkes to Ellice 19 Nov 1855.
133 CP 7 Carlisle ser. ii bk 61, Clarendon to Carlisle 23 Nov 1850.
134 RP 9B ii, Somerville to JR 4 Mar 1851.

135 Broughton diary 6 Nov 1850.
136 Morpeth diary 6 Nov 1850.
137 Broughton diary 6 Nov 1850.
138 Morpeth diary 6 Nov 1850.
139 Morpeth diary 3 and 13 Dec 1850.
140 Broughton diary 11 Dec 1850.
141 Broughton diary 13 Dec 1850.
142 Morpeth diary 13 Dec 1850.
143 Morpeth diary 20 Jan 1851.
144 Clar. P Irish box 26, JR to Clarendon 27 Nov 1850.
145 Clar. P Irish box 26, JR to Clarendon 13 Nov 1850.
146 *Ibid.*
147 MP, Lady JR to Lotty 10 Dec 1850.
148 PP, JR to Palmerston 9 Dec 1850.
149 RP 9A, Chadwick to JR 29 Jan 1851.
150 RP 9A, Sam. Wilberforce to JR 4 Jan 1851.
151 RP 8F, Geo. Sinclair to JR 14 Nov 1850.
152 RP 8F, Bishop of London to JR 7 Dec 1850.
153 Morpeth diary 20 Jan 1851: and Clar. P Irish box 44, JR to Clarendon
    31 Jan 1851.
154 Clar. P Irish box 44, JR to Clarendon 23 and 29 Jan 1851.
155 Morpeth diary 12 Nov 1850.
156 Broughton diary 12 Nov 1850.
157 Morpeth diary 12 Nov 1850.
158 Broughton diary 12 Nov 1850.
159 Morpeth diary 17 Jan 1851.
160 Broughton diary 17 Jan 1851.
161 Morpeth diary 17 Jan 1851.
162 Broughton diary 17 Jan 1851.
163 RA F20, 28, JR to the Queen 24 Jan 1851.
164 Broughton diary 28 Jan 1851.
165 Morpeth diary 28 Jan 1851.
166 RP 9B, Lushington to JR 6 Feb 1851.
167 Clar. P Irish box 26, JR to Clarendon 28 Dec 1850.
168 RP 8F, R. A. Slaney, *Suggestions* (Oct 1850).
169 Morpeth diary 4 Feb 1851.
170 *PD* 3 ser. cxiv 187–211, 7 Feb 1851.
171 Broughton diary 7 Feb 1851: and Morpeth diary 7 Feb 1851.
172 RP 9B ii, Hayter to JR 1 Mar 1851.
173 Broughton diary 20 Feb 1851.
174 Morpeth diary 21 Feb 1851.
175 Broughton diary 21 Feb 1851.
176 Morpeth diary 22 Feb 1851.
177 Broughton diary 18 Mar 1851.
178 RP 9B, JR memos 22 Feb 1851.
179 RP 9B, Ashley to JR 22 Feb 1851.
180 RP 9B, JR memo 24 Feb 1851.
181 Morpeth diary 26 Feb 1851.

182 RP 9B, Lansdowne to JR n.d.
183 RP 9B, Graham to JR 25 Feb 1851: and Aberdeen to JR 25 Feb 1851.
184 RA C46, 37, JR to the Queen 24 Feb 1851.
185 RP 9B II, Baring to JR 5 Mar 1851.
186 RA C46, 120, JR to the Queen 4 Mar 1851.
187 RA C46, 76, JR to the Queen 27 Feb 1851.
188 Clar. P Irish box 44, JR to Clarendon 28 Feb 1851.
189 Broughton, *Recollections*, VI 275.
190 Morpeth diary 3 Mar 1851.
191 RP 9B II, Baring to JR 2 Mar 1851.
192 See GP, JR to Grey 28 Feb 1851.
193 Morpeth diary 27 Feb 1851.
194 Broughton diary 4 Mar 1851.
195 RA C46, 120, JR to the Queen 4 Mar 1851.
196 EP E43, Ellice to Parkes 15 Sep 1851.
197 Broughton diary 2 Mar 1851.
198 Broughton diary 18 Mar 1851.
199 RP 9B II, G. C. Lewis to JR 4 Mar [1851].
200 MP, Minto to JR copy 19 Apr 1851.
201 RA C46, 127, JR to the Queen 4 Mar 1851.
202 Broughton diary 5 Mar 1851.
203 Clar. P Irish box 44, JR to Clarendon 7 Mar 1851.
204 DP box 130 bundle 12, JR to Stanley 21 Mar 1851.
205 RP 9B II, Stanley to JR 21 Mar 1851.
206 *Annual Register* (1851) 64.
207 PP, JR to Palmerston 27 Mar 1851.
208 RP 9G I, Campbell to JR 14 Oct 1851.
209 Clar. P Irish box 44, JR to Clarendon 26 Aug 1851.
210 Clar. P Irish box 44, JR to Clarendon 13 May 1851.
211 Clar. P Irish box 44, JR to Clarendon 30 Aug 1851.
212 RP 16A, JR to Mr Longman copy 10 Feb 1866.
213 Morpeth diary 18 Jan 1851.
214 Morpeth diary 7 Aug 1851.
215 Broughton diary 8 Aug 1851.
216 Morpeth diary 7 Aug 1851.
217 RP 9E, JR memo 12 Aug 1851.
218 RP 9E, Prince Albert to JR 17 Aug 1851.
219 RA F9, 7, JR to Prince Albert 18 Aug 1851.
220 EP E43, Ellice to Parkes 15 Sep 1851.
221 PP, JR to Palmerston 20 Aug 1851.
222 RP 9E, Lansdowne to JR 19 Aug [1851]: and Palmerston to JR 21 Aug 1851
223 C. S. Parker, *Sir James Graham*, II 132–5.
224 RP 9G I, Minto to JR 5 Oct 1851.
225 RP 9F, Wood to JR 28 Sep 1851.
226 RA F24, 138, JR to Prince Albert 2 May 1851.
227 RP 9G I, Minto to JR 5 Oct 1851.

228 MP, Minto to JR copy 19 Dec 1851.
229 RP 9G I, Wood to JR 5 Oct 1851.
230 RP 9G II, Vernon Smith to Bedford 20 Oct 1851.
231 RP 9G II, F. Peel to JR 21 Oct 1851.
232 RP 9G II, Minto to JR 23 Oct 1851.
233 RP 9G I, Palgrave to JR 3 Oct 1851.
234 RP 9G I, president of poor law board to JR 11 Oct 1851.
235 Morpeth diary 14 Oct 1851.
236 Broughton diary 14 Oct 1851.
237 Morpeth diary 14 Oct 1851.
238 Broughton diary 14 Oct 1851.
239 Morpeth diary 15 Oct 1851.
240 Broughton diary 16 Oct 1851.
241 Morpeth diary 17 and 20 Oct 1851.
242 EP E43, Ellice to Parkes 10 Nov 1851.
243 PP, JR to Palmerston 22 Oct 1851.
244 PP, JR to Palmerston 29 Oct 1851.
245 PP, JR to Palmerston 30 Oct 1851.
246 RP 9G II, Palmerston to JR 30 Oct 1851.
247 RP 9G II, Palmerston to JR 6 p.m. 30 Oct 1851.
248 RP 9J I, the Queen to JR 31 Oct 1851.
249 MP, Lady JR to Minto 31 Oct 1851.
250 GP, JR to Grey 31 Oct 1851: and MP, JR to Minto 31 Oct 1851.
251 RP 9H, JR to Palmerston copy 1 Nov 1851.
252 Broughton diary 3 Nov 1851.
253 RP 9H, the Queen to JR copy 21 Nov 1851.
254 RP 9H, Palmerston to JR 28 Nov 1851.
255 RP 9H, JR to Palmerston copy 29 Nov 1851.
256 LP, JR to Lansdowne 20 Nov 1851.
257 Broughton diary 2 Dec 1851.
258 Morpeth diary 4 Dec 1851.
259 Morpeth diary 5 and 6 Dec 1851.
260 RA F9, 40, JR to the Queen 6 Dec 1851.
261 RP 9J I, Palmerston to JR 10 Dec 1851.
262 RP 9J I, Normanby to JR 15 Dec 1851.
263 PP, JR to Palmerston 14 Dec 1851.
264 MP, JR to Minto 16 Dec 1851.
265 PP, JR to Palmerston 16 Dec 1851.
266 RP 9J II, Palmerston to JR 16 Dec 1851.
267 PP, JR to Palmerston 17 Dec 1851.
268 MP, JR to Minto 19 Dec 1851.
269 RP 9J II, Palmerston to JR 18 Dec 1851.
270 H. C. F. Bell, *Lord Palmerston*, II 44.
271 EP E38, Parkes to Ellice 26 Dec 1851.
272 RP 9J II, Lansdowne to JR 19 Dec [1851], Wood to JR 20 Dec 1851.
273 RP 9J II, Lansdowne to JR n.d.
274 MP, JR to Minto 23 Dec 1851.
275 RP 9J II, Clarendon to JR 22 Dec 1851.

276 EP E38, Parkes to Ellice 26 Dec 1851.
277 RP 9J II, Landsowne to JR 23 Dec [1851].
278 RP 9J II, Clarendon to JR 22 Dec 1851.
279 *Ibid.*
280 RP 9J I, Wood to JR 15 Dec 1851.
281 RP 9J II, Clarendon to JR 24 Dec 1851.
282 RP 9J II, G. Grey to JR 25 Dec 1851.
283 RP 9J II, Minto to JR 25–6 Dec 1851.
284 MP, Lady JR to Lotty 6 Jan 1852.
285 Broughton, *Recollections*, VI 292–3.
286 CP 7 Carlisle ser. II bk 62, Labouchere to Carlisle 12 [Jan 1852].
287 RA F9, 44, Prince Albert memo 11 Jan 1852.
288 RP 10A II, JR to Newcastle copy n.d.: and Newcastle to JR 17 Jan 1852.
289 RP 10A II, JR memo 14 Jan 1852.
290 RP 10A I, Minto to JR 3 Jan 1852.
291 CP 7 Carlisle ser. II bk 62, Granville to Carlisle 15 Jan 1852.
292 CP 7 Carlisle ser. II bk 62, Labouchere to Carlisle 12 [Jan 1852].
293 MP, JR to Minto 1 Jan 1852.
294 Maxwell, *Clarendon*, I 331–2.
295 Broughton, *Recollections*, VI 293–4.
296 Broughton diary 15 Jan to 1 Feb 1852.
297 CP 7 Carlisle ser. II bk 62, Labouchere to Carlisle 12 [Jan 1852].
298 Broughton diary 15 Jan 1852.
299 CP 7 Carlisle ser. II bk 62, Granville to Carlisle 15 Jan 1852.
300 LP, JR to Lansdowne 16 Jan 1852.
301 LP, JR to Lansdowne 8 Dec 1851.
302 Broughton diary 25 Jan 1852.
303 RP 9J I, Normanby to JR 15 Dec 1851.
304 PP, JR to Palmerston 22 Dec 1851.
305 MP, JR to Minto 26 Dec 1851.
306 PP, Lady Palmerston to Lady Grey draft 28 Dec 1851.
307 MP, JR to Minto 1 Jan 1852.
308 RP 10A II, Clarendon to JR 22 Jan 1852.
309 Clar. P Irish box 44, JR to Clarendon 2 Feb 1852.
310 CP 7 Carlisle ser. II bk 62, Granville to Carlisle 15 Jan 1852.
311 PP, JR to Palmerston 30 Jan 1852.
312 Broughton, *Recollections*, VI 292.
313 Morpeth diary 9 Feb 1852.
314 Morpeth diary 19 Feb 1852.
315 Broughton diary 21 Feb 1852.
316 Morpeth diary 21 Feb 1852.

CHAPTER XV

1 RP 10A II, Clarendon to JR 18 Jan 1852.
2 Job, thesis, 427.
3 RP 12G, Ellice n.d.

4 RP 10E, Bedford to JR 9 Sep 1852.
5 E.g. DP box 130 bundle 12, JR to Stanley 8 Aug 1839: and GP, JR to Grey 31 Oct 1847.
6 E.g. RP 5C, Wood to JR 28 Sep 1846: and RP 7B, Grey to JR 9 Mar 1848.
7 E.g. RP 13B, JR to G. C. Lewis 3 Sep 1856.
8 RP 5C.
9 Clar. P Irish box 43, JR to Clarendon 6 Nov 1847.
10 RP 5C, Wood to JR 29 Sep 1846.
11 RP 6H, Wood to JR 27 Dec 1847.
12 RP 8E, Lansdowne to JR 25 Jul 1850.
13 RP 8G, Lansdowne to JR 24 Dec [1850].
14 RP 5A, Erroll to JR 28 Jan 1846.
15 RP 12A, Lansdowne to JR 2 Jan 1855.
16 RP 7E, Brunnow to JR n.d.
17 RP 5C, JR to Bessborough 25 Sep 1846: Clar. P Irish box 26, JR to Clarendon 2 Nov 1849: PP, JR to Palmerston 28 Mar 1848: and RP 10D, Aberdeen to JR 13 Aug 1852.
18 RP 5F, Hobhouse to JR 1 Dec 1846.
19 RP 13C, Wood to JR 5 May 1857.
20 RP 10A i, Minto to JR 7 Jan 1852.
21 See RA F9, 103, Col. Grey memo 2 Feb 1852.
22 Broughton diary 14 Jan 1852.
23 PP, JR to Palmerston 4 Mar 1848.
24 RA A20, 65, JR to the Queen 23 Jun 1849.
25 RA F9, 44, Prince Albert memo 11 Jan 1852.
26 Broughton diary 8 Apr 1848.
27 RP 7C, note dated 10 Jun 1848.
28 RP 9H, Wing and Du Cane to JR 4 Nov 1851.
29 Morpeth diary 25 Oct 1847.
30 RP 7B, note dated 19 Apr 1848.
31 MP, Lady JR to Lotty 14 Nov 1851.
32 Morpeth diary 20 Oct 1851.
33 Morpeth diary 9 June 1846.
34 MP, Minto to Lady Minto 18 May 1846.
35 MP, Johnny to Aunt Mary 31 Jul 1848.
36 MP, Lady JR to Lotty 6 Jan 1852.
37 Morpeth diary 4 Feb 1849.
38 Morpeth diary 14 and 28 Feb 1849.
39 RP 9G ii, Vernon Smith to Bedford 20 Oct 1851.
40 EP E39, Parkes to Ellice 6 and 11 Jan 1856.
41 RP 9E, J. Bean [?] to JR 9 Aug 1851: and RP 9J ii, Sam. Colt to JR 18 Dec 1851.
42 RP 9G ii, H. G. Ward to JR 20 Oct 1851.
43 Morpeth diary 27 Feb 1852.
44 PP, JR to Palmerston 4 Mar 1852 and copy of Palmerston's reply.
45 *Life*, ii 150 n 2.
46 RP 10C, Theresa Lewis to JR 19 Jul 1852.

47 Hayter's estimate was 309–31, Parkes' was 318–36: and RP 10C, Wood to JR 27 Jul 1852.
48 *Life*, II 154–5.
49 RP 10D, Aberdeen to JR 8 Aug 1852: and RP 10E, 16 Sep 1852.
50 *Life*, II 157.
51 *Life*, II 156 n.
52 BM Add. Ms 43066 fos 99–104, JR to Aberdeen 13 Aug 1852.
53 RP 10C, Parkes to JR n.d.
54 RP 10E, G. C. Lewis to JR 1 Oct [1852].
55 C. S. Parker, *Sir James Graham*, II 161.
56 C. S. Parker, *Sir James Graham*, II 169–70.
57 EP E43, Ellice to Parkes 31 Jul 1852.
58 Stanmore, *The Earl of Aberdeen* (1893) 210.
59 RA F10, 37, extract from the Queen's journal 16 Oct 1853.
60 MP, JR to Minto 3 Oct 1852.
61 MP, Bedford to Minto 5 Sep 1852.
62 EP E47, Bedford to Ellice 26 Aug 1852.
63 *Life*, II 152.
64 C. S. Parker, *Sir James Graham*, II 168.
65 RP 10D, Clarendon to JR 31 Aug 1852.
66 RP 10C, Minto to JR 28 Jul 1852.
67 Maxwell, *Clarendon*, I 346.
68 H. C. F. Bell, *Lord Palmerston*, II 73.
69 EP E47, Bedford to Ellice 26 Aug 1852.
70 RP 10E, Bedford to JR 19 Sep 1852.
71 RP 10E, Wood to JR 18 Sep 1852.
72 MP, JR to Minto 3 Oct 1852.
73 *Life*, II 158–9.
74 RP 10E, Baring to JR 22 Oct 1852.
75 RP 10E, Lansdowne to JR 11 Oct [1852].
76 Maxwell, *Clarendon*, I 348–9.
77 EP E43, Ellice to Parkes 1 Nov 1852.
78 RP 10F, Graham to JR 1 Nov 1852.
79 EP E43, Ellice to Parkes 1 Nov 1852.
80 RP 10F, JR to Ellice copy 2 Nov 1852.
81 J. B. Conacher, *The Aberdeen Coalition* (Cambridge, 1968) 9.
82 *Life*, II 160.
83 RP 118A, Lady de Clifford to Doddy 16 Dec 1888.
84 MP, Lady JR to Minto 25 Dec 1852.
85 RP 118A, Lady de Clifford to Doddy 16 Dec 1888.
86 MP, Lady JR to Minto 25 Dec 1852.
87 J. B. Conacher, *The Aberdeen Coalition* 10.
88 J. B. Conacher, *The Aberdeen Coalition* 12–13.
89 C. S. Parker, *Sir James Graham*, II 194.
90 MP, Lady JR to Lotty 27–8 Dec 1852.
91 MP, Lady JR to Lady Minto 7 Jan 1853.
92 *LC* I xxxix.
93 J. B. Conacher, *The Aberdeen Coalition* 15–16.

94 RP 10F, Bedford to JR 19 Dec 1852.

95 RP 118A, S. J. Reid to Lady JR 3 Jul 1895.

96 RP 118A, Lady JR to Doddy 15 Jul 1895.

97 Maxwell, *Clarendon*, II 21 : and RP 11F, Wood to JR 7 Dec 1854.

98 MP, Lady JR to Minto 25 Dec 1852.

99 MP, Lady JR to Harriet 28 Jan 1853.

100 Maxwell, *Clarendon*, I 363.

101 RP 10F, Palmerston to JR 24 Dec 1852.

102 MP, Lady JR to Minto 25 Dec 1852.

103 MP, Lady JR to Lotty 27 Dec 1852.

104 *The Panmure Papers*, I 36.

105 BM Add. Ms 43066 fos 142–3, Aberdeen to JR copy 23 Dec 1852.

106 BM Add. Ms 43066 fos 136–7, JR to Aberdeen 23 Dec 1852.

107 BM Add. Ms 43066 fos 144–5, JR to Aberdeen 24 Dec 1852.

108 CP 7 Carlisle ser. II bk 64, Wood to Carlisle 29 Dec 1852.

109 C. S. Parker, *Sir James Graham*, II 198.

110 CP 7 Carlisle ser. II bk 64, Granville to Carlisle 25 Dec 1852.

111 MP, Lady JR to Lady Minto 5 Jan 1853.

112 RP 10G, Panmure to JR 1 Jan 1853.

113 MP, Lady JR to Minto 25 Dec 1852.

114 MP, Lady JR to Lady Minto 8 Mar 1853.

115 J. B. Conacher, *The Aberdeen Coalition* 23 n 3.

116 MP, Lady JR to Nina 2 Jan 1853.

117 MP, Lady JR to Minto 25 Dec 1852.

118 Maxwell, *Clarendon*, I 355.

119 MP, Lady JR to Harriet 16 Jan 1853.

120 RP 10G, JR to Sir Henry Wynne copy 25 Jan 1853 : and Wynne to JR 31 Jan 1853.

121 RP 10H, Hertslet to JR 3 Feb 1853.

122 *Life*, II 166.

123 Maxwell, *Clarendon*, I 361.

124 *Life*, II 167–8.

125 RA C28, 102, JR to the Queen 13 Feb 1853.

126 Maxwell, *Clarendon*, II 10.

127 MP, Lady JR to Lady Minto 8 Mar 1853.

128 J. B. Conacher, *The Aberdeen Coalition* ch. 3–5.

129 BM Add. Ms 44291 fos 46–7, JR to Gladstone 19 Apr 1853.

130 RA C47, 7, JR to the Queen 19 Apr 1853.

131 *Life*, II 171–4 : and J. B. Conacher, *The Aberdeen Coalition* 107–10.

132 MP, Lady JR to Harriet 5 Nov 1853.

133 *Life*, II 181.

134 *Life*, II 184.

135 *Life*, II 184–5.

136 EP E38, Parkes to Ellice 16 Nov 1853.

137 *Life*, II 163 n.

138 J. B. Conacher, *The Aberdeen Coalition* 127.

139 J. B. Conacher, *The Aberdeen Coalition* 173.

140 *Life*, II 186–8.

141 *Life*, II 190-1.
142 MP, Minto to JR copy 27 Oct 1853.
143 MP, Lady JR to Lotty 2 Nov 1853.
144 RA C55, 67, Prince Albert memo.
145 RA M53, 134, JR to Prince Albert 21 Jul 1849.
146 RA F10, 37, extract from the Queen's journal 16 Oct 1853.
147 MP, Lady JR to Nina 2 Jan 1853.
148 J. B. Conacher, *The Aberdeen Coalition* 126.
149 MP, Lady JR to Lotty 28 Oct 1853.
150 RA F11, 17, Prince Albert memo 16 Dec 1853.
151 Names in H. C. F. Bell, *Lord Palmerston*, II 94.
152 RP 11B, Palmerston to JR 14 Nov 1853.
153 RA F10, 41, JR to the Queen 22 Nov 1853.
154 MP, JR to Minto 7 Dec 1853.
155 RP 11B, Graham to JR 11 Dec 1853.
156 RA F11, 2, the Queen to Aberdeen 7 Dec 1853.
157 H. C. F. Bell, *Lord Palmerston*, II 98-9.
158 RA F11, 36, Prince Albert memo 25 Dec 1853.
159 EP E38, Parkes to Ellice 26 Dec 1853.
160 EP E43, Ellice to Parkes 23 Dec 1853.
161 EP E41, Ellice to Parkes 18 Dec 1853.
162 *Life*, II 198.
163 BM Add. Ms 43067 fos 230-1, JR to Aberdeen 21 Dec 1853.
164 BM Add. Ms 43067 fos 187-90 and 198-9, JR to Aberdeen 14 Nov and
    2 Dec 1853: and RP 11B Aberdeen to JR 4 Dec 1853.
165 RA F11, 17, Prince Albert memo 16 Dec 1853.
166 EP E38, Parkes to Ellice 19 Dec 1853.
167 RP 11B, Wood to JR 25 Dec 1853.
168 RP 11B, Aberdeen to JR 31 Dec 1853.
169 RA F11, 43, Aberdeen to the Queen 3 Jan 1854.
170 RP 11C, Palmerston to JR 22 Jan 1854.
171 RP 11C, Palmerston to JR 29 Jan 1854.
172 *Life*, II 204, Lord Jocelyn.
173 RA F11, 60, Palmerston to JR copy 12 Feb 1854.
174 RA F11, 61, Aberdeen to Palmerston copy 12 Feb 1854.
175 MP, Lady JR to Lotty 15 Feb 1854.
176 RA F11, 71, Prince Albert memo 24 Feb 1854.
177 RA F11, 97, Prince Albert memo 5 Apr [1854].
178 BM Add. Ms 43067 fos 278-80 and 286-8, JR to Aberdeen 25 and 28
    Feb 1854.
179 RP 11C, Aberdeen to JR 26 and 28 Feb 1854.
180 BM Add. Ms 43067 fos 290-1 and 298, Aberdeen to JR 28 Feb and
    3 Mar 1854.
181 BM Add. Ms 43067 fos 296-7, JR to Aberdeen 3 Mar 1854.
182 MP, Lady JR to Harriet 27 Mar 1854.
183 RA F11 97, Prince Albert memo 5 Apr 1854.
184 RA F11, 98, Prince Albert memo 7 Apr 1854.
185 RA Y99, 14, the Queen to the King of the Belgians 11 Apr 1854.

186 RA F11, 106, Prince Albert memo 10 Apr 1854.
187 RA F11, 111, Prince Albert memo 11 Apr 1854.
188 RP 11C, Herbert to JR 11 Apr 1854.
189 RA F11, 106, Prince Albert memo 10 Apr 1854.
190 *Life*, 11 190.
191 RA F11, 104, Aberdeen to Prince Albert 10 Apr 1854.
192 BM Add. Ms 43068 fos 28–36, JR memo 24 Apr 1854.
193 BM Add. Ms 43068 fos 53–5, JR to Aberdeen 5 May 1854.
194 *Ibid.*
195 Maxwell, *Clarendon*, 11 44.
196 BM Add. Ms 43068 fos 62–3, JR to Aberdeen 29 May 1854.
197 RP 11D, Aberdeen to JR 30 May 1854.
198 BM Add. Ms 43068 fos 68–73, JR to Aberdeen 31 May 1854.
199 BM Add. Ms 43068 fos 76–8, JR to Aberdeen 5 Jun 1854.
200 RA Y99, 23, the Queen to the King of the Belgians 13 Jun 1854.
201 RP 11D, Aberdeen to JR 7 Jun 1854.
202 J. B. Conacher, *The Aberdeen Coalition* 408.
203 J. M. Prest, Gladstone and Russell, *Transactions of the Royal Historical Society*, 5th ser. vol. 16 (1966) 45–7.
204 BM Add. Ms 44291 fos 202–5, JR to Gladstone 27 Jul 1854.
205 RP 11D, JR memo 19 May 1854.
206 BM Add. Ms 43068 fos 173–4, Aberdeen to JR 9 Nov [1854].
207 RA G17, 89, Prince Albert memo 7 Oct 1854.
208 RP 11F, Minto to JR 15 Dec 1854.
209 RP 11F, Minto to JR 16 Nov 1854.
210 BM Add. Ms 43068 fos 179–84, JR to Aberdeen 17 Nov 1854.
211 RA A84, 15, Prince Albert memo 4 Dec 1854.
212 RP 11F, JR to Aberdeen copy 18 Nov 1854.
213 RA A84, 10, Prince Albert memo 27 Nov 1854.
214 RP 11F, Aberdeen to JR 18 and 21 Nov 1854.
215 BM Add. Ms 43068 fos 194 and 196, JR to Aberdeen 23 Nov 1854.
216 BM Add. Ms 43068 fos 198–205, JR to Aberdeen 28 Nov 1854.
217 RP 11F, Aberdeen to JR 30 Nov 1854.
218 MP, JR to Minto 5 Dec 1854.
219 RP 11F, Palmerston to JR 3 Dec 1854.
220 MP, Lady JR to Minto 2 Jan 1855.
221 *LC* I l.
222 Maxwell, *Clarendon*, 11 53–4.
223 RA A84, 20, Prince Albert memo 9 Dec 1854.
224 RP 11F, Aberdeen to JR 9 Nov and 2 Dec 1854.
225 Maxwell, *Clarendon*, 11 54.
226 RA A84, 23, Prince Albert memo 13 Dec 1854.
227 RA A84, 20 Prince Albert memo 9 Dec 1854.
228 RA A84, 24, Aberdeen to the Queen 16 Dec 1854.
229 RA A84, 23, Prince Albert memo 13 Dec 1854.
230 *LC* I l.
231 RA A84, 20, Prince Albert memo 9 Dec 1854.

232 RP 11F, C. Wood to JR 11 Dec 1854.

233 RA A84, 23, Prince Albert memo 13 Dec 1854.

234 RP 12A, Lansdowne to JR 2 Jan 1855.

235 RA A84, 24, Aberdeen to the Queen 16 Dec 1854.

236 MP, Lady JR to Minto 2 Jan 1855.

237 *Life*, II 233–5.

238 BM Add. Ms 43068 fos 257–8, JR to Aberdeen 3 Jan 1855.

239 *Life*, II 236.

240 MP, JR to Minto 22 Jan 1855.

241 *Life*, II 237–8.

242 RA A84, 30, Prince Albert memo 25 Jan 1855.

243 Maxwell, *Clarendon*, II 60.

244 *LC* II 182: and BM Add. Ms 49531 fos 102–7 and 108–11, Wood to JR copy, and JR to Wood 11 Feb 1855.

245 RA Y100, 6, the Queen to the King of the Belgians 6 Feb 1855.

246 Lady JR, *Memoir*, 148–9.

247 RA G23, 66, Prince Albert memo 2 Feb 1855.

248 PP, endorsed on JR to Palmerston 3 Feb 1855.

249 *The Times* 23 Oct 1865.

250 RP 12A, Clarendon to JR 18 Jan 1855.

251 Maxwell, *Clarendon*, II 63.

252 *Life*, II 243.

253 *LC* II 189.

254 *Life*, II 242.

255 V. J. Puryear, *England, Russia and the Straits Question* (Berkeley, 1931) 372–4: and Maxwell, *Clarendon*, II 77.

256 EP E49, JR to Ellice 19 Feb 1855.

257 RP 12B, Clarendon to JR 21 Feb 1855.

258 PP, JR to Palmerston 23 Feb [1855].

259 MP, Lady JR to Minto 16 Apr 1855.

260 RP 12B, Palmerston to JR 26 Feb 1855.

261 RP 12A, Wm. Deering to JR 6 Feb 1855: and RP 12C, J. A. Smith to JR 2 Mar 1855.

262 MP, Lady JR to Minto 20 Mar 1855.

263 Puryear, *England, Russia and the Straits Question* 375–8.

264 H. C. F. Bell, *Lord Palmerston*, II 128.

265 Puryear, *England, Russia and the Straits Question* 381–7.

266 *Life*, II 257.

267 MP, Lady JR to Minto 1 Apr 1855.

268 Puryear, *England, Russia and the Straits Question* 401–2.

269 H. C. F. Bell, *Lord Palmerston*, II 129–30.

270 Puryear, *England, Russia and the Straits Question* 388.

271 *Life*, II 262–3.

272 *PD* 3 ser. cxxxviii 1075–91, 24 May 1855.

273 RP 13F, JR to unknown copy 7 Apr [1858].

274 Maxwell, *Clarendon*, II 86.

275 *Life*, II 267.

276 EP E39, Parkes to Ellice 21 Aug 1856.

277 *PD* 3 ser. CXXXIX 1930–8, 7 Aug 1855.
278 RP 12F, Bedford to JR 23 Aug 1855.

CHAPTER XVI

1 EP E38, Parkes to Ellice 20 Aug 1855.
2 *Life*, II 276.
3 EP E38, Parkes to Ellice 17 Oct 1855.
4 EP E39, Parkes to Ellice 21 Aug 1856.
5 *Life*, II 276.
6 *Life*, II 273–5.
7 MP, Lady JR to Mary 3 Jun 1856.
8 MP, JR to Minto 18 Feb 1856.
9 RP 12F, JR to Clarendon extract Aug 1855.
10 EP E39, Parkes to Ellice 10 Jan 1856.
11 *Ibid.*
12 RP 12G, Parkes to dean of Bristol 27 Dec 1855.
13 RP 13A, Ellice to Parkes 7 Jan 1856.
14 RP 12G, W. W. Clarke to dean of Bristol 6 Dec [1855].
15 EP E39, Parkes to Ellice 6 Jan 1856.
16 RP 12F, Bedford to JR 27 Sep [1855].
17 EP E39, Parkes to Ellice 11 Jan 1856.
18 RP 13A, Ellice to dean of Bristol 20 Jan 1856.
19 EP E39, Parkes to Ellice 10 Jan 1856.
20 *PD* 3 ser. CXL 1955–80, 6 Mar 1856.
21 MP, JR to Minto 30 Jul 1856.
22 EP E39, Parkes to Ellice 21 Aug 1856.
23 *Life*, II 277.
24 *Life*, II 278.
25 RP 13B, Minto to dean of Bristol 24 Nov 1856.
26 RP 13C, letter to JR 2 Feb 1857.
27 RP 12G, Bedford to JR 3 Dec [1855].
28 RP 12G, Greville to Bedford 6 Nov [1855].
29 RP 12C, Le Marchant to JR 10 Mar: and Hatherton to Bedford 13 Mar 1855.
30 RP 13A, Ellice to Parkes 7 Jan 1856: and Ellice to dean of Bristol 20 Jan 1856.
31 EP E39, Parkes to Ellice 28 Oct 1856.
32 RP 12G, W. W. Clarke to Parkes 6 Dec 1856 [?1855].
33 MP, Minto memo 27 Dec 1856.
34 *Life*, II 286.
35 H. C. F. Bell, *Lord Palmerston*, II 168.
36 RP 13E, W. W. Clarke to dean of Bristol n.d.
37 RP 13C, J. A. Smith to JR 5 Apr 1857.
38 *Life*, II 290–1.
39 EP E49, JR to Ellice 7 Apr 1857.
40 RP 13C, JR to dean of Bristol 4 Apr 1857.
41 EP E49, JR to Ellice 7 Apr 1857.

42 RP 13D, JR to dean of Bristol 16 Sep 1857.

43 RP 13D, JR to dean of Bristol 7 Dec 1857.

44 Maxwell, *Clarendon*, II 140.

45 BP, JR to Brougham 2 Sep 1857.

46 RP 13D, Bedford to JR 20 Oct 1857.

47 EP E39, Parkes to Ellice 28 Nov 1857.

48 RP 13D, Baring to JR 18 Nov 1857.

49 RP 13E, JR to dean of Bristol 8 Jan 1858.

50 *Ibid.*

51 RP 13 D, JR to Vernon Smith 4 Dec 1857.

52 C. S. Parker, *Sir James Graham*, II ch. XIV.

53 RP 13D, Wood to JR 16 Nov 1857.

54 *Life*, II 295.

55 *LC* II 226.

56 EP E49, note by Ellice jnr. 23 Apr 1858.

57 RP 13F, JR to unknown copy 7 Apr [1858].

58 RP 13E, JR to dean of Bristol 9 Mar [1858].

59 RP 13F, Geo. Byng to JR n.d.

60 RP 13F, JR to G. C. Lewis 9 Apr 1858.

61 RP 13E, Aberdeen to JR 30 Mar 1858.

62 *Life*, II 297–8.

63 Greville, *Memoirs*, VII 359, 16 Apr 1858.

64 EP E49, Ellice jnr. memo 13 May 1858: and H. C. F. Bell, *Lord Palmerston*, II 192.

65 *Life*, II 300.

66 C. S. Parker, *Sir James Graham*, II 360.

67 BM Add. Ms 43068, JR to Aberdeen 24 Sep 1858.

68 RP 13G, JR to dean of Bristol 21 Jan 1859.

69 Maxwell, *Clarendon*, II 164.

70 Maxwell, *Clarendon*, II 165.

71 RP 13G, Graham to JR 21 Jan 1859.

72 RP 13G, JR to dean of Bristol 5 Jan 1859.

73 RP 13G, JR to G. C. Lewis 18 Jan 1859.

74 EP E39, Parkes to Ellice 29 Jan 1859.

75 Maxwell, *Clarendon*, II 175.

76 C. S. Parker, *Sir James Graham*, II 365.

77 RP 13G, Argyll to JR 8 Mar 1859.

78 RP 13G, Herbert to JR 9 Mar 1859.

79 *PD* 3 ser. CLIII 405, 21 Mar 1859.

80 EP E39, Ellice jnr. memo 30 Mar 1859.

81 RA Y104, 8, the Queen to the King of the Belgians 1 Mar 1859.

82 RA T2, 52, the Queen to the Prince of Wales 1 Apr 1859.

83 RP 13G, JR to dean of Bristol 12 Apr 1859.

84 RP 13G, JR to dean of Bristol 13 May 1859.

85 RP 13G, Herbert to JR 17 May 1859.

86 PP, JR to Palmerston 18 May 1859.

87 H. C. F. Bell, *Lord Palmerston*, II 212.

88 RP 13G, Palmerston to Granville copy 29 May 1859.

89 H. C. F. Bell, *Lord Palmerston*, II 214.

90 *Life*, II 308.

91 RA Y104, 21, the Queen to the King of the Belgians 14 Jun 1859.

92 PP, JR to Palmerston 16 Jun 1859.

93 BM Add. Ms 44165 fos 203–6, Granville to Gladstone 11 Nov 1868.

94 A. L. Kennedy, ed., *My dear Duchess* (1956) 85.

95 A. L. Kennedy, ed., *My dear Duchess* 70.

96 EP E39, Parkes to Ellice 5 Oct 1860.

97 RP 14A, JR to the Queen copy 12 Jan 1860.

98 *Life*, II 326.

99 RP 13G, the Queen to JR copy 23 Aug 1859.

100 RP 14C, Palmerston to JR 25 Apr 1862.

101 *Ibid.*

102 RP 14B, Palmerston to JR 23 Apr 1861.

103 RP 15D, Palmerston to JR 15 Feb 1865.

104 RP 14D, Palmerston to JR 6 Nov 1862.

105 A. Cecil, *British foreign secretaries 1807–1916* (1927) 208.

106 RA A27, 120, Prince Albert memo 31 Dec 1859.

107 J. Morley, *Gladstone* (1905) I 671.

108 A. L. Kennedy, ed., *My dear Duchess*, 62.

109 A. L. Kennedy, ed., *My dear Duchess*, 64.

110 A. Cecil, *British foreign secretaries*, 209.

111 RP 13H, Phipps to JR 16 Jul 1859.

112 RA Y104, 36, the Queen to the King of the Belgians 18 Oct 1859.

113 *Life*, II 311–14.

114 PP, JR to Palmerston 5 Nov 1859.

115 E.g. BM Add. Ms 48581 fos 42–3, Palmerston to JR 11 Oct 1859 on the feasibility of French gunboats closing the Straits of Gibraltar.

116 PP, JR to Palmerston 5 Nov 1859.

117 BM Add. Ms 44291 fos 296–7, JR to Gladstone 8 Jan 1860.

118 A. L. Dunham, *The Anglo-French treaty of commerce of 1860 and the progress of the industrial revolution in France* (Ann Arbor, 1930) is the best account of these negotiations.

119 RP 13G, JR to Palmerston copy 16 Jun 1859.

120 RA F13, 17, Palmerston to the Queen 24 Nov 1859: and RP 13H, JR to G. C. Lewis 12 and 14 Sep 1859.

121 *Life*, II 333.

122 A. L. Kennedy, ed., *My dear Duchess* 97–8.

123 J. Morley, *Gladstone*, I 656.

124 J. Morley, *Gladstone*, I 664.

125 RA F13, 28, Prince Albert memo 27 Feb 1860.

126 A. L. Kennedy, ed., *My dear Duchess* 98.

127 RP 14A, Brand to JR 30 May 1860.

128 BM Add. Ms 48581 fos 147–9, Palmerston to JR 1 Jun 1860.

129 *AP* I 204–5.

130 RP 14A, Bedford to JR 15 and 20 Jun 1860.

131 RP 14A, Bedford to JR 2 and 5 Jul 1860.

132 W. E. Williams, *The rise of Gladstone to the leadership of the Liberal Party* (Cambridge, 1934) 42.

133 BM Add. Ms 44291 fos 326–7, JR to Gladstone 2 Jul 1860.

134 G. M. Trevelyan, *Life of John Bright* (1913) 290–1.

135 Maxwell, *Clarendon*, II 208.

136 Fitzmaurice, *Earl Granville* (1905) I 355.

137 A. L. Kennedy, ed., *My dear Duchess* 100.

138 G. M. Trevelyan, *Garibaldi and the making of Italy* (1927) 104–8: and Lady JR, *Memoir* 186–7.

139 *Life*, II 326–7.

140 *Life*, II 325.

141 *Life*, II 328.

142 EP E39, Parkes to Ellice 5 Nov 1860.

143 A. L. Kennedy, ed., *My dear Duchess* 137.

144 *LC* II 269.

145 *Life*, II 331.

146 G. M. Trevelyan, *Life of John Bright* 293.

147 A. L. Kennedy, ed., *My dear Duchess* 141.

148 *AP* I 208.

149 Maxwell, *Clarendon*, II 228.

150 RA A29, 41, Palmerston to the Queen 3 May 1861.

151 *Life*, II 336.

152 *Life*, II 337.

153 RP 14D, Palmerston to JR 28 Oct 1862.

154 *Life*, II 402.

155 *AP* I 426.

156 *Life*, II 338.

157 B. Connell, *Regina v. Palmerston* 311.

158 B. Connell, *Regina v. Palmerston* 310.

159 *Life*, II 346–7.

160 *Life*, II 352–5.

161 *Life*, II 359 n.

162 *Life*, II 357–67.

163 *Life*, II 348–50.

164 *PD* 3 ser. CLXVI 12–19, 25 Mar 1862.

165 D. Southgate, *The most English Minister* (1966) 503–5.

166 W. E. Mosse, *The European Powers and the German Question 1848–71* (Cambridge, 1958) 141–2.

167 RP 14B, Palmerston to JR 27 Oct 1861.

168 RP 14G, Palmerston to JR 29 Dec 1863.

169 RP 15A, JR to the Queen copy 15 Jan 1864.

170 W. E. Mosse, *The European Powers and the German Question*, ch. 6 and 7: and 'Queen Victoria and her Ministers in the Schleswig-Holstein Crisis 1863–4', *English Historical Review* (1963).

171 W. E. Mosse, *The European Powers and the German Question*, 208.

172 *PD* 3 ser. CLXXVI 1083, 8 Jul 1864.

173 *AP* I 376.

174 Abbott and Campbell, *Letters* 58.

175 *Life*, II 145: and S. J. Reid, *Lord John Russell* 354.
176 *AP* I 433–5 and 475.
177 S. J. Reid, *Lord John Russell* 335.
178 *AP* I 218.
179 RP 15G, JR to Willy 10 Nov 1865.
180 *AP* I 198.
181 Abbott and Campbell, *Letters* 58.
182 BM Add. Ms 44534 fos 273–4 Gladstone to JR copy 26 Sep 1864.
183 *AP* I 439.
184 From *Punch*, quoted in *AP* I 446.
185 *The Times* 3 Feb 1865.
186 *AP* I 360.

CHAPTER XVII

1 A. L. Kennedy, ed., *My dear Duchess* 236.
2 F. B. Smith, *The Making of the Second Reform Bill* (Cambridge, 1966) 50–4.
3 *The Times* 20 Oct 1865.
4 *Life*, II 407–8.
5 RA Y114, 37, the Queen to the King of the Belgians 28 Oct 1865.
6 BM Add. Ms 44292 fos 190–1, JR to Gladstone 20 Oct 1865.
7 *Life*, II 407–8.
8 BM Add. Ms 44162 fos 258–9, G. Grey to Gladstone 24 Oct 1865.
9 BM Add. Ms 44292 fos 196–7, JR to Gladstone 23 Oct 1865.
10 BM Add. Ms 44294 fos 257–8, JR to Gladstone 11 Jun 1873.
11 BM Add. Ms 44292 fos 201–6, JR to Gladstone 24 Oct 1865.
12 J. M. Prest, 'Gladstone and Russell', *Transactions of the Royal Historical Society*, 5th ser. vol. 16 (1966) 54.
13 RP 15F, W. V. Harcourt to JR n.d.
14 BM Add. Ms 44239 fos 374–9, G. W. Lyttleton to Gladstone 31 Oct 1865.
15 *Life*, II 407.
16 F. B. Smith, *The Making of the Second Reform Bill* 55.
17 M. Cowling, *1867, Disraeli, Gladstone and Revolution* (Cambridge, 1967) 82.
18 BM Add. Ms 44292 fos 212–14, JR to Gladstone 29 Oct [1865].
19 Gladstone *PD* 3 ser. CLXXXII 22, 12 Mar 1866: and RA F14, 58, Derby to the Queen 30 May 1866.
20 *The Times* 2 Nov 1865.
21 BM Add. Ms 44292 fos 221–3, JR to Gladstone 11 Nov [1865].
22 BM Add. Ms 44292 fos 198–9, Gladstone to JR copy 23 Oct 1865.
23 *The Times* 31 Oct 1865.
24 BM Add. Ms 44292 fos 201–6, JR to Gladstone 24 Oct 1865.
25 BM Add. Ms 44292 fos 207–8, Gladstone to JR copy 24 Oct 1865.
26 M. Cowling, *1867, Disraeli, Gladstone and Revolution* 84.
27 BM Add. Ms 44292 fo 211, Gladstone to JR copy 27 Oct 1865.
28 *The Times* 23 Oct 1865.

29 RP 15G, Lady JR notes 14–26 Nov 1865.

30 RP 15G, Gladstone to JR 20 Nov 1865.

31 BM Add. Ms 44292 fo 211, Gladstone to JR copy 27 Oct 1865.

32 RP 15G, Lady JR notes 14–26 Nov 1865.

33 J. Morley, *Gladstone*, 1 788.

34 RP 15G, Lady JR notes 14–26 Nov 1865.

35 F. B. Smith, *The Making of the Second Reform Bill* 58–9.

36 RP 15G, Lady JR notes 14–26 Nov 1865.

37 Maxwell, *Clarendon*, II 304.

38 F. B. Smith, *The Making of the Second Reform Bill* 56.

39 RP 15G, Lady JR notes 14–26 Nov 1865.

40 BM Add. Ms 44292 fo 231, Gladstone to JR copy 6 Dec 1865.

41 RP 15G, Lady JR notes 14–26 Nov 1865.

42 BM Add. Ms 44292 fos 242–3, JR to Gladstone 7 Dec 1865.

43 *Ibid.*

44 BM Add. Ms 44292 fo 253, Gladstone to JR 11 Dec 1865.

45 BM Add. Ms 44292 fos 226–7, JR to Gladstone 17 Nov 1865.

46 RP 15H, JR to G. Grey copy 10 Dec 1865.

47 BM Add. Ms 44292 fos 270–1, JR to Gladstone 27 Dec 1865.

48 RP 15H, C. P. Villiers to JR 23 Dec 1865.

49 Gladstone *PD* 3 ser. CLXXXII 36, 12 Mar 1866.

50 Maxwell, *Clarendon*, II 305.

51 BM Add. Ms 44293 fos 1–2, JR to Gladstone 1 Jan 1866.

52 RP 15H, Gladstone to JR 27 Dec 1865.

53 RP 16A, Gladstone to JR 1 Jan 1866.

54 M. Cowling, *1867, Disraeli, Gladstone and Revolution* 93.

55 RP 16A, Clarendon to JR 4 Jan 1866.

56 RP 15H, Brand to JR 26 Dec 1865.

57 RP 15H, G. Grey to JR 31 Dec 1865.

58 RP 16A, Gladstone to JR 1 Feb 1866.

59 F. B. Smith, *The Making of the Second Reform Bill* 64.

60 RP 16A, JR to Goschen copy 11 Jan 1866.

61 Maxwell, *Clarendon*, II 306.

62 Lady JR, *Memoir*, 202.

63 Maxwell, *Clarendon*, II 305.

64 Andrew Lang, *Sir Stafford Northcote*, 2nd edn (Edinburgh 1891) 144.

65 BM Add. Ms 44293 fos 30–1, JR to Gladstone 25 Jan 1866.

66 RP 16A, Gladstone to JR 25 Jan 1866.

67 F. B. Smith, *The Making of the Second Reform Bill* 65.

68 RP 16A, Lady Palmerston to JR 16 Jan 1866.

69 *AP* I 465.

70 RP 16A, list dated 5 Feb 1866.

71 F. B. Smith, *The Making of the Second Reform Bill* 63.

72 F. B. Smith, *The Making of the Second Reform Bill* 64.

73 *AP* I 471.

74 Andrew Lang, *Sir Stafford Northcote* 149.

75 RP 16B, Gladstone to JR 1 Mar 1866.

76 RP 16B, JR memo 7 Mar 1866.

77 RP 16B, Gladstone to JR 1 Mar 1866.
78 RA F14, 9, Gen. Grey to the Queen 8 Mar 1866.
79 RP 16B, cabinet opinions.
80 RA F14, 6, Granville to the Queen 13 Feb 1866.
81 RA F14, 9, Gen. Grey to the Queen 8 Mar 1866.
82 RP 16B, Lady JR note 24 Mar 1866.
83 *PD* 3 ser. CLXXXII 2116, 26 Apr 1866.
84 *PD* 3 ser. CLXXXII 109, 12 Mar 1866.
85 F. B. Smith, *The Making of the Second Reform Bill* 72.
86 RP 16B, Gladstone to JR 22 Mar 1866.
87 F. B. Smith, *The Making of the Second Reform Bill* 87.
88 BM Add. Ms 44100 fos 100–1, Argyll to Gladstone 29 Mar 1866.
89 *AP* I 481–2.
90 RP 16B, Granville to JR 11 Apr 1866.
91 RA F14, 17, Gen. Grey to the Queen 23 Mar 1866.
92 *AP* I 486.
93 *PD* 3 ser. CLXXXIII 128–9, 27 Apr 1866.
94 RP 16B, Brand to JR 22 Apr 1866.
95 *AP* I 485.
96 F. B. Smith, *The Making of the Second Reform Bill* 90–1.
97 M. Cowling, *1867, Disraeli, Gladstone and Revolution* 88.
98 RA F14, 45, the Queen to JR 29 Apr 1866.
99 *AP* I 483.
100 Clar. P C93 fos 380–1, JR to Clarendon 6 May 1866.
101 RP 16B, Brand to JR 1 Apr 1866.
102 F. B. Smith, *The Making of the Second Reform Bill* 94.
103 *PD* 3 ser. CLXXXIII 504, 7 May 1866.
104 Clar. P C93 fo 393, JR to Clarendon 11 May 1866.
105 Text in *Life*, II 412: see too RP 16B, Gladstone to JR 30 Apr 1866.
106 RP 16C, Jenner to JR 23 May 1866.
107 RA F14, 54, the Queen to Derby 29 May 1866.
108 RA F14, 61, the Queen to JR 31 May 1866.
109 RA F14, 58 and 63, Derby to the Queen 30 May 1866, and JR to the Queen 2 Jun 1866.
110 F. B. Smith, *The Making of the Second Reform Bill* 98–9.
111 RP 16B, Gladstone to JR 14 Apr 1866.
112 *AP* I 512.
113 BM Add. Ms 44293 fo 126, Gladstone to JR 28 May 1866.
114 F. B. Smith, *The Making of the Second Reform Bill* 104.
115 RA F14, 70, Gen. Grey to the Queen 10 Jun 1866.
116 F. B. Smith, *The Making of the Second Reform Bill* 107–8.
117 F. B. Smith, *The Making of the Second Reform Bill* 83.
118 F. B. Smith, *The Making of the Second Reform Bill* 106.
119 F. B. Smith, *The Making of the Second Reform Bill* 110–11.
120 BM Add. Ms 44293 fos 155–7, Gladstone to JR 20 Jun 1866.
121 BM Add. Ms 44755 fo 82, Gladstone memo 19 Jun [1866].
122 RP 16C, Gen. Grey to JR 20 Jun 1866.
123 F. B. Smith, *The Making of the Second Reform Bill* 115–18.

124 RP 16C, Clarendon to JR 25 Jun 1866.
125 RP 16C, JR to Clarendon copy 26 Jun 1866.
126 F. B. Smith, *The Making of the Second Reform Bill* 119.
127 BM Add. Ms 44755 fo 90, Gladstone memo 26 Jun 1866.
128 RA C32, 37.
129 *R and S* 289.
130 *AP* I 462–3.
131 BM Add. Ms 44293 fos 197–8, JR to Gladstone 31 Aug 1866.

CHAPTER XVIII

 1 *The Times* 21 Jun 1866.
 2 RP 16D, Clarendon to JR 14 Aug 1866.
 3 *PD* 3 ser. CLXXXIV 746–7 9 Jul 1866.
 4 BM Add. Ms 44193 fos 226–7, Brand to Gladstone 17 Dec 1866.
 5 BM Add. Ms 44133 fos 93–4, Clarendon to Gladstone 4 Dec 1866.
 6 RP 16D, Gladstone to JR 29 Nov 1866.
 7 BM Add. Ms 44133 fos 93–4, Clarendon to Gladstone 4 Dec 1866.
 8 *R and S* 345.
 9 BM Add. Ms 44293 fos 249–50, JR to Gladstone 28 Mar 1867.
10 GP, JR to Grey 27 Jun 1867.
11 RP 16D, Lady JR to Doddy 19 Feb 1867.
12 BM Add. Ms 44294 fos 153–4, JR to Gladstone 18 Nov 1868.
13 A. Ramm, ed., *The Political Correspondence of Mr Gladstone and Lord Granville 1868–76* (1952) I 22.
14 J. M. Prest, ed., *Jowett's Correspondence on Education with Earl Russell in 1867* – a supplement to the Balliol College Record (1965).
15 BM Add. Ms 44293 fos 331–2, JR to Gladstone 23 Dec 1867.
16 RP 16D, Gladstone to JR 26 Dec 1867.
17 BM Add. Ms 44294 fos 1–2, JR to Gladstone 1 Jan 1868.
18 BM Add. Ms 44294.
19 RA A37, 14, Disraeli to the Queen 24 Apr 1868.
20 BM Add. Ms 44294 fos 137–8, JR to Gladstone 24 Oct 1868.
21 BM Add. Ms 44165 fos 181–8, Granville to Gladstone 8 Oct 1868.
22 BM Add. Ms 44165 fos 203–6, Granville to Gladstone 11 Nov 1868.
23 BM Add. Ms 44294 fos 149–50, Gladstone to JR copy 13 Nov 1868.
24 BM Add. Ms 44165 fos 216–17, Granville to Gladstone 27 Nov 1868.
25 RA C32, 149, the Queen memo 3 Dec 1868.
26 *Life*, II 434–5.
27 BM Add. Ms 44294 fos 170–1, JR to Gladstone 28 Dec 1868.
28 BM Add. Ms 44294 fos 191–2, JR to Gladstone 9 Aug 1869.
29 BM Add. Ms 44294 fos 223–4, JR to Gladstone 2 Jul 1870.
30 Ramm, ed., *Political Correspondence of Gladstone and Granville*, II 327.
31 *R and S* 293–4.
32 Ramm, ed., *Political Correspondence of Gladstone and Granville*, I 62.
33 Ramm, ed., *Political Correspondence of Gladstone and Granville*, I 166.
34 Ramm, ed., *Political Correspondence of Gladstone and Granville*, II 340.
35 Ramm, ed., *Political Correspondence of Gladstone and Granville*, II 365.

36 BM Add. Ms 44538 fos 217–20, Gladstone to JR copy 24 Mar 1870.

37 H. J. Hanham, *Elections and Party Management. Politics in the time of Disraeli and Gladstone* (1959) 203.

38 *Life*, II 437.

39 BM Add. Mss 44537 fos 249–50, and 44538 fos 37–8, Gladstone to JR copies 4 Nov and 16 Dec 1869.

40 BM Add. Ms 44294 fos 219–20, JR to Gladstone 16 Apr 1870.

41 BM Add Ms 44294 fo 261, Gladstone to JR copy 8 Aug 1873.

42 *Life*, II 444–5.

43 *Life*, II 446.

44 BM Add. Ms 44537 fos 233–4, Gladstone to JR copy 27 Oct 1869.

45 B. Russell, *The autobiography of Bertrand Russell* (1967) I 30–1.

46 *Life*, II 451.

47 J. Morley, *Gladstone*, II 190.

48 *Life*, II 452.

49 *Ibid.*

50 S. J. Reid, *Lord John Russell* 367.

51 *Life*, II 452–3.

52 RP 7B.

53 *Life*, II 453.

Index

Abercorn, James Hamilton (1811–1885), 2nd Marquess of (succ. 1818) and 1st Duke of (cr. 1868): Lord Lieut. of Ireland 1866–8 and 1874–6: 299.

Abercromby, James (1776–1858), 1st Baron Dunfermline (cr. 1839): Whig lawyer; entered Commons 1807; Speaker 1835–1839; 68, 87, 89, 123–4, 133, 146, 151; on parliamentary anarchy, 288.

Abercromby, Lady Mary (*née* Elliot) (d. 1874), sister of 2nd Lady JR; wife of 2nd Baron Dunfermline: 198.

Aberdeen, George Hamilton Gordon (1784–1860), 4th Earl of: For. Sec. 1841–6; prime minister Dec 1852–Jan 1855: as For. Sec., 208, 210, 219, 224, 312; JR's conversations with, in 1846, 210, 213; and Navigation Laws, 299; proposed coalition in 1851, 327–8; not offered place in Jan 1852, 340; 347; JR corresponds with, 350–1; appointed prime minister, 353–4; offers JR succession, 354–5; forms cabt, 354–6; and Delane, 356–7; tries to prevent JR leaving For. Office, 357–8; dissociates govt from JR, 358; the Eastern crisis, 358–60; JR embittered by, 360; forms Reform Committee, 361; extrudes Palmerston, 362; offers JR

Home Office, 363; attitude to JR's Reform Bill (1854), 363–5, and to outbreak of war, 364; will not separate War and Colonial Depts, 365; JR seeks to oust, 365–6, and forces cabt reshuffle on, 366–7; Oxford Univ. reforms, 366; Gladstone, Kennedy and, 367; Minto increases JR's hostility to, 367–8; pressed to unite War Depts, 368; blamed by JR for conduct of war, 368, over Kennedy, 369, and for conduct of cabt meetings, 370; defeated, 370–1; JR's behaviour to, i, 139, 376, 414; excluded, 372; slighted, 373; consulted by JR on Derby's India Bill, and Reform (1858), 382.

Acland, Sir Thos Dyke (1787–1871), 10th Bt: High Tory later Conservative; entered Commons 1812: 46, 126.

Adams, Charles Francis (1807–86): U.S. Ambassador to London: 394.

Addington, Henry (1757–1844), *see* Sidmouth, 1st Viscount.

Adullamites: 409, 410, 411–12, 415.

Afghanistan: 165.

Alabama, the: 394–5, 419.

Albert of Saxe-Coburg-Gotha (1819–1861), Prince Consort: JR's mismanagement of allowance, 158; JR to, on hopes of defeating Peel, 189; hopes to see Peel

Printed by offset lithography by Halliday Lithograph Corporation on 55# Warren's University Text. This acid-free paper, noted for its longevity, has been watermarked with the University of South Carolina Press colophon. Binding by Halliday Lithograph Corporation in Scott Graphics' Corinthian Kivar 9.